Blackstone's

Police Operational Handbook:
Practice and Procedure

Blackstone's
Police Operational Handbook: Practice and Procedure

Edited by
Clive Harfield
MSc, LLM, MPhil, PhD
Associate Professor (Criminal Law),
Faculty of Law, University of Wollongong, Australia

OXFORD
UNIVERSITY PRESS

OXFORD

UNIVERSITY PRESS

Great Clarendon Street, Oxford OX2 6DP

Oxford University Press is a department of the University of Oxford.
It furthers the University's objective of excellence in research, scholarship,
and education by publishing worldwide in

Oxford New York

Auckland Cape Town Dar es Salaam Hong Kong Karachi
Kuala Lumpur Madrid Melbourne Mexico City Nairobi
New Delhi Shanghai Taipei Toronto

With offices in

Argentina Austria Brazil Chile Czech Republic France Greece
Guatemala Hungary Italy Japan Poland Portugal Singapore
South Korea Switzerland Thailand Turkey Ukraine Vietnam

Oxford is a registered trade mark of Oxford University Press in the UK and in
certain other countries

Published in the United States
by Oxford University Press Inc., New York

British Library Cataloguing in Publication Data
Data available

Library of Congress Cataloging-in-Publication Data
Blackstone's police operational handbook : practice and procedure/edited by
Clive Harfield.
    p. cm.
    title: Police operational handbook
    Includes bibliographical references and index.
    ISBN 978-0-19-956101-8 (flexicover : alk. paper) 1. Police—England—Hand-
books, manuals, etc. I. Harfield, Clive. II. Title: Police operational handbook.
    HV7921.B53 2009
    363.2'30942—dc22

                                                                2009023586

Typeset by Laserwords Private Limited, Chennai, India
Printed in Italy on acid-free paper by
Legoprint S.p.A.

ISBN 978-0-19-956101-8

1 3 5 7 9 10 8 6 4 2

05731359

For police colleagues past and present, particularly those who joined Hampshire Constabulary, January 1987.

Preface

There were those who said this book could not be written. There were those who said this book should not be written. At times during the editing of it I held both views with equal fervour simultaneously. The objection raised in each argument was the same: the law is the law but police policy and procedure is interpreted differently by each individual police force according to its own circumstances. How, therefore, could there be an adequate companion volume to the Blackstone's *Police Operational Handbook*? There was, nevertheless, wide consensus that there needed to be a companion volume, to assist frontline police officers and staff with using the statutory tools at their disposal, covered in the Operational Handbook. And that is the purpose of this book: to provide a procedural context for policing. Ways of working, drawing upon Codes of Practice and ACPO doctrine, are presented for frontline officers and staff to be applied within the parameters set by individual force policies on any given aspect. This book is to be read as a supplement to organizational policy, not in lieu of it.

It is a tribute to the expertise and dedication of the contributors that I believe they have exceeded the vision for this volume. I am indebted to all of them for their hard work and enthusiasm, and for their forbearance when, just as the writing was beginning and the editor should have been on hand to meet with them, chat through the drafts, offer guidance and support, so I found myself bound for Australia. Not an ideal recipe for editorial team-working. Thank goodness for email! My purpose has been to achieve a degree of consistency in style and approach without detracting from the individual expertise presented in each individual chapter. I hope the contributors feel that I have done them justice in this. The nature of policing is such that there is some overlap between themes but this has been kept to the minimum in order to maximize the benefit of the available word limit.

In their own way just as important as the authors, my parents-in-law have also contributed significantly to this work through their inexhaustible capacity for playing with their grandson, which gave me the time to work on this project over a long, hot Australian summer.

I am grateful, also, for the support of Peter Daniell, Lindsey Davis, and Katie Heath at Oxford University Press who first came to me with the idea and then nurtured and cajoled its progression. Their support and understanding, and that of the production team at Oxford University Press, has been invaluable.

Introduction

This book is intended primarily, but not exclusively, for officers and staff working in neighbourhood and response policing who, for sake of editorial brevity, and certainly with no offence or disrespect intended to other officers and staff working in other aspects of policing often colloquially labelled 'specialist', are termed 'frontline staff' for the purposes of this handbook.

It provides them with an introductory context for their daily work. The framework of this book envisages the procedural functions of policing broken down into four areas. **Evidence** and **Knowledge** are the two key asset tools with which society is policed. **Neighbourhood Policing** and **Protective Services** are the two key paradigms around which twenty-first century policing in England and Wales is currently structured. These elements provide the conceptual framework for this handbook.

Evidence is the cement of the criminal justice system. The integrity of the criminal justice system is founded upon the integrity of evidence, the integrity of the way in which it is gathered, and the integrity with which it is tested at trial. Evidential integrity is the guarantor of fair trial. The first section of this handbook explores various issues concerning evidence-gathering procedure.

Evidence-based strategy and policy is, by the same token, the foundation of effective policing both in terms of criminal investigation and in preserving the Queen's Peace and community safety. To avoid a labelling confusion it is better to think of this in terms of organizational knowledge. If the criminal justice system is dependent on evidence and its integrity, then policing generally is dependent upon the integrity of organizational knowledge. Where does the knowledge with which to police come from? The second section of this handbook introduces the enabling structures and principles that contribute to the establishment of the knowledge necessary for effective policing, its governance, and direction-setting. How is what is to be policed decided upon? What contextual knowledge is required?

The handbook then moves onto the two prevailing paradigms of policing in England and Wales. The historical precedent and strong political preference is for policing locally delivered, locally accountable. The twenty-first century sees this articulated with the relaunching of neighbourhood policing, the new specialization. Neighbourhood policing increasingly involves the wider community alongside the police service, which concept finds expression in neighbourhood policing teams. The third section of the handbook examines the mechanics of neighbourhood policing: the engagement with partner agencies; the use of knowledge to recognize emerging issues and resolve these through problem solving. It is the archetypal proactive policing.

Certain aspects of policing transcend, and challenge structures founded upon, local policing boundaries. Two hundred years of episodic police force amalgamations have been one strategy to address this issue, but the logical endgame of this strategy would be a national police force: for the foreseeable future a notion beyond political acceptability in England and Wales. The paradigm of protective services encompasses those issues that operate both within and beyond local communities; those issues, any one of which may necessitate the request for and provision of mutual aid between forces. Protective services provide the conceptual framework and foundation for such large-scale cooperation by establishing the basis for common understanding amongst the 43 forces. The fourth section of the handbook introduces the various aspects of protective service policing and how these relate to the daily work of frontline neighbourhood policing and response team staff.

Part 1—Evidence Management

Common law has established the legal concept of the best evidence rule (*Omychund v Barker* (1745) 1 Ath 21, 49; 26 ER 15, 33) in which Lord Harwicke held that no evidence was admissible unless it was 'the best that the nature of the case will allow'. Increasingly that has come to include not only original evidence rather than copied, but also the procedural integrity of evidential acquisition and continuity. The structure of this section examines various aspects of how evidence is gathered as part of an investigation, from matters amenable to instant resolution to those involving complex planning and considerable resources.

It starts with instant resolutions: fixed penalty notices, penalty notices for disorder, and cannabis warnings which require the recording of evidence (usually on the notice issued) to be just as meticulous as for a murder investigation. It is not just a traffic ticket: it is the court file, the disposal, and sentence! Scene preservation is vital, particularly in the so-called 'golden hour', and the flow-chart approach adopted for this chapter, using specific examples, will be of particular use to first responders. It is particularly helpful in guiding staff on how best to preserve forensic evidence.

The next three sections of the chapter deal with the management of evidence gathering as prescribed by the Police and Criminal Evidence Act 1984 (PACE), much amended since first coming into force in 1986, not least with a widely expanded portfolio of Codes of Practice. Identification procedures, in particular, are crucial to effective investigation.

The Regulation of Investigatory Powers Act 2000 not only put covert investigation on a statutory basis, in compliance with the principles of the Human Rights Act 1998, but it also brought such methodology in from the cold. Much of it remains the work of specialists, but directed surveillance is a tool made available to any police staff investigating crime. Chapter 6 introduces frontline staff to the framework for covert investigation.

Introduction

In a criminal justice process that privileges oral testimony at trial over other forms of evidence, the role of victims and witnesses is very significant. Chapter 7 highlights the key issues in witness management and interviewing.

Pre-trial disclosure, to minimize the number of issues contested at trial, and the protection of sensitive information are discussed in Chapter 8 before the final stage of evidence management, court procedure, is explained in Chapter 9 using a case study approach.

The contributors to this section are: Matt Ebeling, Sussex Police (Chapter 1); Bob Underwood, Christ Church Canterbury University (Chapter 2); Huw Smart, South Wales Police (Chapters 3 and 4); Nick Yellop, Metropolitan Police Service (Chapter 5); Kevin Smith, Advisor to ACPO (Chapter 7); Paul Hughes, Metropolitan Police (Chapter 8); John Watson, Gwent Police (Chapter 9).

Part 2—Knowledge Management

If evidence is necessary for trials, knowledge is necessary for policing: intelligence-led policing (the mantra that closed the twentieth century) is developing into knowledge-based policing (thus recognizing the increasing level of sophistication necessary to police the twenty-first century information age). To this end there is a variety of knowledge assets from which to draw upon in delivering policing services providing a framework for professionalism and governance (Chapters 10–13), tools for policing and the preservation of life (Chapters 14–16), and contrasting procedures relating to the management of information that can either be shared publicly or which requires protection, even within the police service. In the internet age the presumption is that information will be accessible and those holding it, and particularly withholding it, must be accountable.

Those contributing to this section are Colin Rogers, University of Glamorgan (Chapters 10, 11); Bryn Caless, Kent County Constabulary (Chapters 12, 14, 16); Tony Cook, Greater Manchester Police (Chapter 17).

Part 3—Neighbourhood Policing

Of the two prevailing policing paradigms, the one with which the community will most identify is neighbourhood policing. The socio-political importance of neighbourhood policing is attested by the fact that it is the bedrock upon which current government thinking about policing is built (Home Office, *Building Communities, Beating Crime: a Better Police Service for the 21st Century* Cm 6360 (TSO, London 2004); Home Office, *From the Neighbourhood to the National: Policing our Communities Together* Cm 7448 (TSO, London, 2008)).

This section, authored entirely by Bryn Caless and Barry Spruce, Kent County Constabulary, sets the context for and outlines that paradigm, explains its principles, and considers component parts and practices. Neighbourhood policing is the core tenet of British policing: locally accountable, locally delivered.

Part 4—Protective Services

Those aspects of policing which are beyond the capacity and capability of local policing, and which are outside the neighbourhood model, have been termed (in language consistent with the post-9/11 lexicon) 'protective services'. Protective services, upon which is also based a framework for performance management and inspection, comprise major crimes/homicide; serious organized and cross-border crime; counter-terrorism and extremism, civil contingencies, critical incidents, public order, and strategic roads policing (HMIC, *Closing the Gap: A Review of the Fitness for Purpose of the Current Structure of Policing in England and Wales* (TSO, London, 2005), p 15). Each of these is considered in turn and to the extent necessary to provide frontline staff with an overview and introduction relevant to their likely role in such areas of policing.

To this list has been added a further section on protecting the public and vulnerable persons, an area of work the significance of which has been increasingly recognized, particularly as an area for multi-agency partnership working. As such it is relevant both to neighbourhood policing and to protective services. Its inclusion in Part 4 is a matter of editorial management rather than a political statement.

Those contributing to this section are Tony Cook, Greater Manchester Police (Chapter 27); Stan Gilmour, Thames Valley Police (Chapter 28); Andy Staniforth, Counter-Terrorism Unit (Chapter 29); Brian Dillon, formerly of Lancashire Police (Chapter 30); Allyson MacVean, University of Cumbria (Chapter 31); Adrian Pitt, West Mercia Police (Chapter 32); Mick Doyle, Thames Valley Police (Chapter 33); Laura Richards, Adviser to ACPO, and Allan Aubeelack, Metropolitan Police (Chapter 34).

Chapter sections not otherwise attributed are the responsibility of the editor.

Contents

Contents

List of Abbreviations

ABE	Achieving Best Evidence
ACPC	area child protection committee
ACPO CPI	ACPO Crime Prevention Initiatives Limited
ACPO	Association of Chief Police Officers
ACRO	ACPO Criminal Records Office
AEP	Attenuated Energy Projectiles
ALO	Architectural Liaison Officer
AMHP	Approved Mental Health Professional
ANPR	Automatic Number Plate Recognition
APACS	Assessments of Policing and Community Safety
ASBA	anti-social behaviour agreement
ASBO	anti-social behaviour order
ASW	approved social worker
AVCIS	ACPO Vehicle Crime Intelligence Service
BCU	Basic Command Unit
BME	black and minority ethnic
BTP	British Transport Police
CAD	Communities Against Drugs
CaDO	Community and Diversity Officer
CAIU	Child Abuse Investigation Unit
CBRN	chemical, biological, radiological, or nuclear
CCTV	closed circuit television
CDRP	Crime and Disorder Reduction Partnership
CEO	Chief Executive Officer
CESG	Communications-Electronics Security Group
CHIS	covert human intelligence source
CIA	Community Impact Assessment
CICA	Criminal Injuries Compensation Authority
CJA 2003	Criminal Justice Act 2003
CJPA	Criminal Justice and Police Act 2001

List of Abbreviations

CPIA	Criminal Procedure and Investigations Act 1996
CPR (contextual)	cardio-pulmonary resuscitation
CPR (contextual)	Crime and Policing Representative
CPS	Crown Prosecution Service
CRR	Community Risk Register
CSI	crime scene investigator
CSM	crime scene manager
CSO	community support officers
CSP	Community Safety Partnership
CTC	counter-terrorism checks
DA	domestic abuse
DAT	Drugs Action Team
DETR	Department of the Environment, Transport and the Regions
DfT	Department for Transport
DOA	dead on arrival
DSU	Dedicated Source Unit
DV	developed vetting
DVLA	Driver and Vehicle Licensing Agency
ECHR	European Convention on Human Rights and Fundamental Freedoms 1950
ECM	'Every Child Matters'
EEK	early evidence kit
EFPN	Endorsable Fixed Penalty Notice
EGT	Evidence Gathering Team
EVA	Environmental Visual Audit
FCP	Forward Control Point
FCS	Force Control Strategy
FIB	Force Intelligence Bureau
FIT	Forward Intelligence Team
FLINTS	Forensic Lead Intelligence System
FLO	Family Liaison Officer
FMB	Forward Media Briefing
FPN	Fixed Penalty Notice
FRS	Fire and Rescue Service
GP	general practitioner

GPMS	Government Protective Marking Scheme
GSB	Gold, Silver, and Bronze
GSI	Government Secure Intranet
GSX	Government Secure Extranet
H-2-H	house-to-house
HATO	Highways Agency Traffic Officer
HBV	honour-based violence
HGV	heavy goods vehicle
HMI (CJ)	Her Majesty's Inspectorate (Criminal Justice)
HMIC	Her Majesty's Inspectorate of Constabulary
HOLAB	Home Office Laboratory Form
HOLMES/ HOLMES2	Home Office Large and Major Enquiry System
HRA	Human Rights Act 1998
HSE	Health and Safety Executive
IAG	independent advisory group
ICP	Incident Control Post
IDVA	Independent Domestic Violence Advisers
IED	improvised explosive device
IMPACT	intelligence, management, prioritization, analysis, coordination, and tasking
IO	investigating officer
IPCC	Independent Police Complaints Commission
ISVA	Independent Sexual Violence Advisor
KIN	Key Individual Network
KINEL	Key Individual Network Extended List
LCJB	Local Criminal Justice Board
LCN	Liverpool Community Network
LRF	Local Resilience Forum
LSCB	Local Safeguarding Children Board
MAPP	Multi-agency Public Protection
MAPPA	Multi-agency Public Protection Arrangements
MAPPP	Multi-agency Public Protection Panel
MARAC	Multi-agency Risk Assessment Conference
MLO	Media Liaison Officer
NAFIS	National Automated Fingerprint Identification System

List of Abbreviations

NAG	Neighbourhood Action Group
NAT	Neighbourhood Action Team
NCIS	National Criminal Intelligence Service
NCTT	National Community Tension Team
NIM	National Intelligence Model
NOS	National Occupational Standards
NPIA	National Policing Improvement Agency
NPP	Neighbourhood Policing Programme
NPT	Neighbourhood Policing Team
NRPP	National Reassurance Policing Programme
OCG	Organized Crime Groups
OIC	officer in charge
OPSI	office for public service information
OSC	Office of Surveillance Commissioners
PA 1997	Police Act 1997
PACE	Police and Criminal Evidence Act 1984
PACT	Partners And Communities Together
PAS43	British Standards Institution 2006 Safe Working of Vehicle Breakdown and Recovery Operators
PATP	Pro-active Assessment and Tasking pro forma
PC	police constable
PCC	Press Complaints Commission
PCSO	police community support officer
PDP	Potentially Dangerous Person
PII	public interest immunity
PNC	Police National Computer
PND	Penalty Notice for Disorder
PNICC	Police National Information and Co-ordination Centre
POCA	Proceeds of Crime Act 2002
POLSA	Police Search Advisor
POP	Problem-Oriented Policing
PPAF	Policing Performance Assessment Framework
PPE	personal protective equipment
PPU	Public Protection Unit
PSA	Public Service Agreement

List of Abbreviations

PSD	Professional Standards Department
PSV	public service vehicle
RA	Responsible Authority
RIPA	Regulation of Investigatory Powers Act 2000
RRF	Regional Resilience Forum
RSO	Registered Sexual Offender
RSS	Road Safety Services
RVP	Rendezvous Point
SAGE	Systematic Approach to Gathering Evidence
SARC	Sexual Assault Referral Centre
SBD	Secured by Design
SC	security clearance
SDVC	Specialist Domestic Violence Court
SEG	Special Escort Group
SI	Statutory Instrument
SIO	Senior Investigating Officer
SOCA	Serious Organised Crime Agency
SOXB Crime	Serious Organized and Cross-Border Crime
SNT	Safer Neighbourhood Team
SPI	Statutory Performance Indicator
SPOC	Single Point of Contact
SSAT	Stop and Search Action Team
SSO	serious sexual offence
STC	supervised treatment order
STO	Specially Trained Officer
T&CG	Tasking and Coordinating Groups
TACT	Terrorism Act 2000
TRL	Transport Road Laboratory
TSG	Tactical Support Group
VAA	vulnerable adult abuse
VDRS	Vehicle Defect Rectification Scheme
ViSOR	database designed to hold details of all MAPPA offenders
VOSA	Vehicle Operators Standards Agency
WORM	write once read many
YOT	Youth Offending Team

List of Contributors

General Editor

Dr Clive Harfield is the former Deputy Director of the John Grieve Centre for Policing and Community Safety, London Metropolitan University. He is a serving police officer on a sabbatical and is currently Associate Professor in Criminal Law at the University of Wollongong in New South Wales, Australia. Dr Harfield is the author of two Blackstone's Practical Policing titles *Covert Investigation* and *Intelligence: Investigation, Community, and Partnership*.

Contributors

Allan Aubeelack, London Metropolitan Police
Bryn Caless, Kent Police College
Tony Cook, Greater Manchester Police
Brian Dillon, formerly of Lancashire Police
Mick Doyle, Thames Valley Police
Matt Ebeling, Sussex Police
Stan Gilmour, Thames Valley Police
Clive Harfield, University of Wollongong
Paul Hughes, London Metropolitan Police
Allyson MacVean, University of Cumbria
Adrian Pitt, West Mercia Police
Laura Richards, Consultant Violence Adviser to ACPO
Colin Rogers, University of Glamorgan
Huw Smart, South Wales Police
Kevin Smith, ACPO Adviser
Barry Spruce, Kent Police College
Andrew Staniforth, Counter-Terrorism Unit
Robert Underwood, Kent Police and Canterbury Christ Church University
John Watson, Heddlu Gwent Police
Nick Yellop, London Metropolitan Police

PART ONE
Evidence Management

Chapter 1

Instant Resolutions—Fixed Penalty Notices, Penalty Notices for Disorder, and Cannabis Warnings

1.1 **Introduction**

Increasingly, police officers are being granted the power to deal with matters using methods of instant resolution and disposal. These options include the issuing of Fixed Penalty Notices (FPNs) for road traffic offences; Penalty Notices for Disorder (PNDs) for certain lower level crimes, including criminal damage, some public order offences, and other matters such as drunkenness; Cannabis Warnings and Penalty Notices for 'simple' possession of cannabis.

These methods of disposal are designed as fast track resolutions to save police and court time for lesser offences and allow the police service to focus its time and attention on more serious issues of crime and disorder and those which are capable of having a far greater impact on the community.

It can be seen that the obvious advantages to these instant resolution disposal options are time saving and prioritization of resources and focus. With this comes the responsibility of being investigator, prosecutor, jury, and judge all in one. The burden of this responsibility falls to the individual police officer dealing with the matter at the time.

Matters being dealt with this in this way will, therefore, only go before a court on challenge or appeal. The evidential requirement for FPNs, PNDs, and Cannabis Warnings is just as great as any other evidential requirement, and this needs constantly to be borne in mind by the officer administering the resolution. In these circumstances the penalty notice is also the original record of evidence and so represents 'the best evidence' to be adduced at court if the notice is challenged.

1.1.1 Instant Resolutions as Disposal Options

The resolutions covered in this chapter are options for how an officer can deal with a suspect. Whether these options are appropriate or applicable will depend upon a number of issues, including the necessity of an arrest, as detailed under the necessity criteria in Code G of the Police and Criminal Evidence Act 1984.

This chapter will examine:

- Fixed Penalty Notices (both endorsable and non-endorsable)
- Vehicle Defect Rectification Scheme
- Penalty Notices for Disorder
- Cannabis Warnings and Penalty Notices for possession of cannabis

1.2 **Fixed Penalty Notices**

1.2.1 **Non-Endorsable Offences**

Introduction

A non-endorsable FPN is one which is not accompanied by endorsement of the driver's driving licence with penalty points and is therefore used for less serious road traffic offences, for example parking where prohibited or failing to wear a seatbelt. Non-endorsable FPNs can be issued by a constable to a driver (or user/passenger if applicable) or fixed to an unattended vehicle.

Driver Not Present

Section 62(1) of the Road Traffic Offenders Act 1988 provides the authority for a constable to issue a non-endorsable FPN and fix it to a stationary vehicle.

> Where on any occasion a constable has reason to believe in the case of any stationary vehicle that a fixed penalty offence is being or has on that occasion been committed in respect of it, he may fix a fixed penalty notice in respect of the offence to the vehicle unless the offence appears to him to involve obligatory endorsement.
>
> **Road Traffic Offenders Act 1988, section 62(1)**

The flow chart in Figure 1.1 sets out the procedure for issuing an FPN and fixing it to an unattended vehicle.

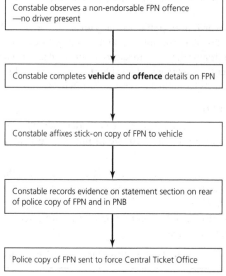

Constable observes a non-endorsable FPN offence
—no driver present

Constable completes **vehicle** and **offence** details on FPN

Constable affixes stick-on copy of FPN to vehicle

Constable records evidence on statement section on rear of police copy of FPN and in PNB

Police copy of FPN sent to force Central Ticket Office

Figure 1.1

Scenario—Issuing an FPN

A constable on foot patrol sees a Large Goods Vehicle parked and unattended on the verge. The constable completes an FPN (BL03—Parking HGV on footpath or verge) and affixes it to the windscreen.

The registered keeper, following the issue of the FPN, has 28 days either to request that the matter be dealt with at court or to pay the penalty at the local magistrates' court. The constable must not accept payment on the spot; the penalty must be paid to the court. If the penalty is paid in full within the 28 days, then no further action is taken. If the penalty is not paid within this period, a fine will be enforced of one and a half times the penalty.

If a court case is requested, the officer must prepare a case file. It is therefore essential that the officer gathers sufficient evidence to support the prosecution at the time of issuing the FPN.

It is worth noting that, in many areas, offences in relation to parking (for example on double yellow lines) have been decriminalized, which means that the local authority is the prosecuting agency and local authority employed parking attendants issue the FPNs for these offences.

Driver Present

Section 54 of the Road Traffic Offenders Act 1988 provides the authority for a constable in uniform to issue a non-endorsable FPN.

This section applies where on any occasion a constable in uniform has reason to believe that a person he finds is committing or has on that occasion committed a fixed penalty offence.

Road Traffic Offenders Act 1988, section 54

Issuing a non-endorsable FPN to the driver is essentially the same as for when the driver is not present except that, instead of affixing the FPN to the vehicle, the FPN is given to the driver. The driver's details need to be established and documented on the FPN.

The flow chart in Figure 1.2 sets out the procedure for issuing a non-endorsable FPN to a driver.

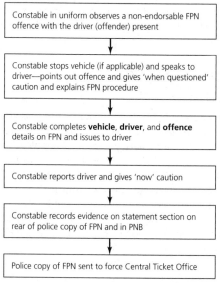

Constable in uniform observes a non-endorsable FPN offence with the driver (offender) present

↓

Constable stops vehicle (if applicable) and speaks to driver—points out offence and gives 'when questioned' caution and explains FPN procedure

↓

Constable completes **vehicle**, **driver**, and **offence** details on FPN and issues to driver

↓

Constable reports driver and gives 'now' caution

↓

Constable records evidence on statement section on rear of police copy of FPN and in PNB

↓

Police copy of FPN sent to force Central Ticket Office

Figure 1.2

Scenario—Issuing an FPN

A constable in uniform on patrol observes a car in slow moving traffic and the driver is not wearing a seatbelt. The constable causes the vehicle to stop and speaks to the driver. The constable points out the offence to the driver, cautions the driver and completes an FPN (BA15—Driver failing to wear seatbelt). The constable issues the FPN to the driver and reports the driver.

The driver has 28 days following the issue of the FPN either to request that the matter be dealt with at court or to pay the penalty at the local magistrates' court. The constable must not accept payment on the spot; the penalty must be paid to the court. If the penalty is not paid within this period, a fine will be enforced of one and a half times the penalty.

If a court case is requested, the officer must prepare a case file. It is therefore essential that the officer gathers sufficient evidence to support the prosecution at the time of issuing the FPN.

1.2.2 Endorsable Offences

Introduction

An endorsable offence is one which, as well as attracting a financial penalty, also requires the driver's licence to be endorsed with penalty points. An example of such an offence is speeding. An FPN issued in relation to an endorsable offence is known as an Endorsable FPN (EFPN).

Twelve penalty points on a driving licence will result in the disqualification of the licence holder. An EFPN can therefore only be issued to a driver whose licence does not have points which when added to the points for the current offence will not reach 12.

As the offence requires endorsement of the licence, an EFPN can only be issued to a driver who surrenders the driving licence (both photocard and paper counterpart) to the constable at the time or later at a police station.

Issuing an EFPN

Section 54 of the Road Traffic Offenders Act 1988 provides the authority for a constable to issue an EFPN for endorsable offences.

> This section applies where on any occasion a constable
> in uniform has reason to believe that a person he finds is
> committing or has on that occasion committed a fixed
> penalty offence.
>
> **Road Traffic Offenders Act 1988, section 54**

If the driving licence is surrendered to the constable at the
roadside, it will be forwarded by the constable to the court
for endorsement. If the licence is not surrendered at the
roadside because the driver did not have it at the time, the
constable will complete the production section of the EFPN
and the driver has seven days to produce the licence at a
police station. At the police station the driver will surren-
der the licence, which will be forwarded to the courts for
endorsement.

An EFPN can only be issued where the penalty points
for the current offence will not, when combined with any
existing penalty points, take the driver up to or over 12,
when disqualification is mandatory.

The flow chart in Figure 1.3 sets out the procedure for
issuing an EFPN to a driver

Scenario—Issuing an EFPN

A constable in uniform on patrol observes a car drive
through a red traffic light. The constable causes the vehicle
to stop and speaks to the driver. The constable points out
the offence to the driver and cautions the driver. The constable requests production of the driving licence, which the
driver surrenders to the constable. The constable notes that
there are no endorsements on the counterpart. The constable offers an EFPN in lieu of court and explains the procedure to the driver, who accepts the EFPN. The constable
completes the EFPN (BF06—Contravening red traffic light),
issues it to the driver, and reports the driver.

1 Evidence Management

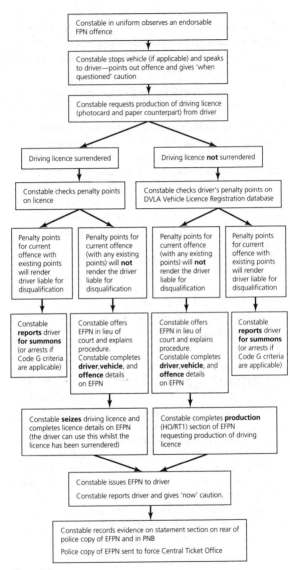

Figure 1.3

Scenario—Issuing an EFPN

A constable in uniform on foot patrol observes a car parked on the zigzag approach to a pelican crossing. The driver returns to the car as the constable approaches. The constable points out the offence to the driver and cautions the driver. The constable requests production of the driving licence. The driver does not have the driving licence. The constable carries out a check of the DVLA driving licence database to confirm that the driver's licence does not already have penalty points which, when combined with the current penalty points, will render the driver liable to disqualification. The constable offers an EFPN in lieu of court and explains the procedure to the driver who accepts the EFPN. The constable completes the EFPN (BF13—Stopping in pelican controlled area) including the request for production of the driving licence, and explains that the driver has seven days to produce the licence when it will need to be surrendered for endorsement. The constable issues the EFPN to the driver and reports the driver.

Following the issue of the EFPN the driver has 28 days either to request that the matter be dealt with at court or to pay the penalty at the local magistrates' court. The constable must not accept payment on the spot; the penalty must be paid to the court. If the penalty is not paid within this period, a fine will be enforced of one and a half times the penalty.

If a court case is requested, the officer must prepare a case file. It is therefore essential that the officer gathers sufficient evidence to support the prosecution at the time of issuing the EFPN.

> In October 2008, the House of Commons Transport Committee published a report on road safety beyond 2010. Part of this report sets out proposals including the introduction of a higher fixed penalty (six points) for drivers who exceed the speed limit by a dangerous and very large margin and also making careless driving a fixed penalty offence.
>
> *Ending the Scandal of*
> *Complacency: Road Safety Beyond 2010*

1.2.3 Conclusion

For the majority of day-to-day road traffic offences, it can be clearly seen that the long standing process of issuing an FPN is the most appropriate and proportionate method of dealing with the offender. It can also clearly be seen that the issuing of an FPN saves officer time, time in a custody centre, and court time.

1.3 **Vehicle Defect Rectification Scheme**

1.3.1 Introduction

The Vehicle Defect Rectification Scheme (VDRS) was introduced as a disposal option to deal with minor vehicle defects. The scheme is purely voluntary and the driver is under no obligation to participate. As well as saving police and court time, the scheme also ensures that the vehicle defects are actually rectified.

Once a driver has agreed to participate in the scheme, the officer will issue a VDRS form to the driver. The driver then has 14 days to have the defect rectified and allow the vehicle to be examined at a Department of Transport approved testing station to confirm that the defect has been rectified.

1.3.2 Issuing a Vehicle Defect Rectification Scheme Form

The flow chart in Figure 1.4 sets out the procedure for issuing a VDRS form to a driver:

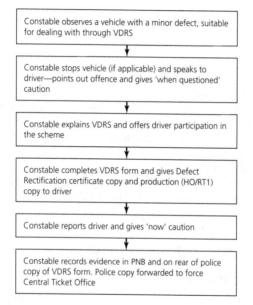

Figure 1.4

> ### Scenario—Issuing a VDRS
>
> A constable on patrol observes a car being driven with no windscreen wipers fitted. The constable causes the car to stop and speaks to the driver. The constable points out the offence to the driver and cautions the driver. The constable explains the Vehicle Defect Rectification Scheme to the driver who volunteers to participate. The constable completes a VDRS form and issues it to the driver. The constable reports the driver.

1.3.3 Conclusion

As stated above, the Vehicle Defect Rectification Scheme, as well as saving police and court time, contributes directly towards making the roads safer by ensuring that minor vehicle defects are rectified rather than merely punished. If the driver fails to comply with the VDRS, the officer will need to prepare a prosecution case file. It is therefore essential that the officer gathers sufficient evidence to support the prosecution at the time of issuing the VDRS form.

1.4 **Penalty Notices for Disorder**

1.4.1 Introduction

Penalty Notices for Disorder (PNDs) were introduced by the Criminal Justice and Police Act 2001 (CJPA) for lower level crime and disorder offences. The system operates in a very similar way to the EFPN system described above.

The Home Office Police Operational Guidance on PNDs states the aims of the scheme to be:

• to offer operational officers a quick and effective alternative means of dealing with low-level, anti-social, and nuisance offending;

- to deliver swift, simple, and effective justice, that carries a deterrent effect;
- to reduce the amount of time that police officers spend completing paperwork and attending court, while simultaneously reducing the burden on the courts;
- to increase the amount of time officers spend on the street to deal with more serious crime.

1.4.2 Issuing a PND

Section 2(1) and (2) of the CJPA provides the authority for a constable in uniform to issue a PND on the spot.

A PND can also be issued at a custody centre or police station, after the matter has been investigated. This means that the PND can be issued following arrest as an alternative to charging the person. Section 2(3) provides the authority for this.

> **Note:** Please see the appendix at the end of this chapter for details of the offences which can be dealt with by means of a PND.

The Home Office guidance for police states that officers may only issue a PND where:

- they have reason to believe[1] a person aged 16[2] or over has committed a penalty offence and they have sufficient evidence to support a successful prosecution;
- the offence is not too serious and is of a nature suitable for being dealt with by a penalty notice;
- the suspect is suitable, compliant (eg does not refuse the PND) and able to understand what is going on (eg is not too intoxicated or does not have a mental disorder);

---

[1] This can be compared to arrest where only suspicion is required.
[2] This was originally 18 and was reduced to 16 by the Anti-Social Behaviour Act 2003, s 87(2).

- a second or subsequent offence, which is known, does not overlap with or is not 'associated' with the penalty notice offence;
- the offence(s) involve(s) no one below the age of 16 (eg as a co-offender);
- sufficient evidence as to the suspect's age, identity and place of residence exists (eg suspect is not homeless or a foreign national who is resident outside the British Isles).

Home Office Police Operation Guidance—Penalty Notices for Disorder

Guidance on other issues is given in relation to the decision as to whether a PND is appropriate. A penalty notice *will not* be appropriate:

- where there has been any injury to any person;
- where there has been a substantial financial or material loss to the private property of an individual;
- where the terms of the Protection from Harassment Act 1997 might apply;
- for any offence related to domestic violence;
- for any offence where there are aggravating factors (hate crime, eg racially motivated or homophobic);
- for any football-related offences;
- where the suspect is already subject to a custodial sentence (including a Home Detention Curfew) or a community penalty other than a fine (including an Anti-Social Behaviour Order);
- if the suspect appears likely to claim the statutory defence to a section 5 Public Order Act 1986 offence.

A penalty notice *may not* be appropriate where the suspect has previous convictions for disorder offences (including a number[3] of PNDs in the recent past or a caution) or is on police or court bail.

PNDs can be issued for retail or commercial theft up to the value of £200 and for criminal damage up to the value

---

[3] Officers should consult force policy and guidelines.

---

of £500. The Home Office guidance recommends that theft of property over the value of £100 and criminal damage with values over £300 should normally be dealt with by other disposal options.

The flow chart in Figure 1.5 sets out the procedure for issuing a PND on the street.

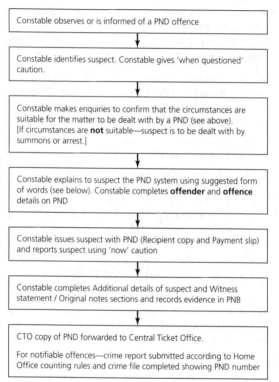

Figure 1.5

Suggested wording by officer issuing PND:

- I have grounds to arrest you for (*offence*).
- However, I intend to deal with this matter by issuing a penalty notice.
- This is an £80 (or £50) fine payable within 21 days.
- You will not have to go to court and you will not receive a criminal conviction.
- It is also not an admission of guilt. You can request a court hearing if you wish.
- If you fail to pay the fine and you do not request a court hearing, the penalty will be enforced by the court.

It is worth remembering that this procedure is an investigation into an offence. Therefore, it will often be appropriate or even necessary to carry out an interview of the suspect according to PACE, which is recorded contemporaneously.

Scenario—Issuing a PND

A constable on patrol in uniform during a summer evening observes a person in a public park, shouting and swearing in a manner which has caused distress to passers by (committing an offence contrary to section 5(1) of the Public Order Act 1986). The constable stops the person and cautions them. The constable makes enquiries to confirm the person's identity and that they are over 16 years of age, and that the circumstances are suitable for the matter to be dealt with by means of a PND. The constable explains the PND system to the person and completes the PND. The constable issues the person with the Recipient copy and Payment slip and reports the person.

Following the issue of a PND, the recipient must, within 21 days, either request that the matter be dealt with at court or pay the penalty at the local magistrates' court. The constable must not accept payment on the spot; the penalty must be paid to the court. If the recipient does not pay or request a court hearing within the 21 days, a fine will be enforced of one and a half times the penalty or court proceedings will be instigated.

If a court case is requested, the officer must prepare a case file. It is therefore essential that the officer gathers sufficient evidence to support the prosecution at the time of issuing the PND.

A PND in relation to a notifiable crime will count as a sanctioned detection for the officer. It will not amount to a criminal conviction for the recipient, although recordable offences will be logged on the Police National Computer as intelligence and to enable checks to establish whether a person has previously been issued with a PND.

> The Theft from Shops (Penalties) Bill 2007–08 is a Private Members' Bill which was introduced to the House of Commons in July 2008. The Bill aims to abolish the practice of issuing PNDs for retail or commercial theft by excluding these offences from the provisions of the CJPA.

1.4.3 Conclusion

It is important to remember that the PND is one of a range of disposal options available. A PND should normally be used after consideration has been taken of the full circumstances and when the PND appears to be the most appropriate and proportionate response.

1.5 Cannabis Warnings and Penalty Notices for Possession of Cannabis

1.5.1 Introduction

In January 2004, when cannabis was reclassified from a Class B drug to a Class C drug, guidelines were introduced in relation to Street Warnings as a disposal option for dealing with offences of possession of cannabis. In January 2006 Street Warnings became known as Cannabis Warnings to avoid confusion. The Cannabis Warning is a disposal option available for 'simple' possession of cannabis, that is to say where the possession is for personal use and not for supply to others.

The Association of Chief Police Officers (ACPO) has provided guidance for the police on the use of the Cannabis Warning scheme. The aims of the scheme are similar to those of the PND scheme and are:

- to give a justifiable and proportionate response...which can be seen to be ethical and non-discriminatory...
- to enable the police service to give greater focus and resources to organizational and community policing priorities...
- to maintain an enforcement and prosecution strategy...

ACPO Guidance on Policing Cannabis—Use of Cannabis warnings (2006)

It is important to remember that the scheme is not intended for offences of supplying or dealing cannabis (Misuse of Drugs Act 1971, section 4(3)) or of possession of cannabis with intent to supply (Misuse of Drugs Act 1971, section 5(3)).

On 26 January 2009 cannabis was reclassified again as a Class B drug. As a result of this, from 28 January 2009 the Cannabis Warning will be the usual disposal option for possession of cannabis on the first occasion only. On the second occasion that a person is found to be in possession of cannabis, the usual option to be employed will be the issuing of a penalty notice.

Possession of cannabis has been brought into the category of PND offences as part of an escalation framework. A person found in possession of cannabis for a third time will usually be arrested.

The Cannabis Warning and Penalty Notice procedure apply to 'simple' possession of:

- cannabis resin
- herbal cannabis
- cannabis oil.

1.5.2 Issuing a Cannabis Warning

A Cannabis Warning can only be issued:

- to a person aged over 18;
- when the drug is intended for the person's own use;
- when the offender admits the offence of possession;
- when the offender is not obstructive;
- when the offence did *not* take place in the vicinity of or would cause a risk of harm to young persons;
- to a person with no previous Cannabis Warnings;
- to a person with no previous PNDs for possession of cannabis;
- to a person with no previous drugs convictions;
- to a person who is not known locally as a persistent offender.

If these conditions are not present, then it will normally be appropriate to arrest the person as the necessity criteria (PACE Code G) will apply. The smoking of cannabis in a public place or in public view is another aggravating factor which must be taken into account when considering arrest or an escalation of response.

> A police officer finding a person aged 18 or over in possession of a substance that they can identify as cannabis and who is satisfied that the drug is intended for that person's own use should not normally need to arrest the person.

ACPO Guidance on policing cannabis, 2006

The person must admit the possession.

The officer must be experienced in handling cannabis in order to be able to recognize it without any doubt before a Cannabis Warning can be given. An officer who is not experienced must ask an officer who is to verify that the item is cannabis.

An officer giving a Cannabis Warning must warn the offender that:

- a record of the investigation will be made at the police station;
- the offence of possession will be recorded against them, for statistical purposes, as a detected crime;
- however, this procedure does not constitute a criminal record against them.

ACPO Guidance on policing cannabis, 2006

A Cannabis Warning is recorded on regional systems and is not recorded on the Police National Computer.

If the cannabis is found during a search of a person arrested for another offence, the Cannabis Warning can be given at a Police Station or Custody Centre.

The flow chart in Figure 1.6 sets out the procedure for issuing a Cannabis Warning on the street.

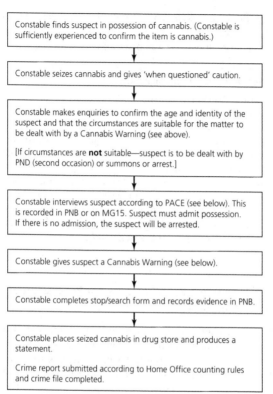

Constable finds suspect in possession of cannabis. (Constable is sufficiently experienced to confirm the item is cannabis.)

Constable seizes cannabis and gives 'when questioned' caution.

Constable makes enquiries to confirm the age and identity of the suspect and that the circumstances are suitable for the matter to be dealt with by a Cannabis Warning (see above).

[If circumstances are **not** suitable—suspect is to be dealt with by PND (second occasion) or summons or arrest.]

Constable interviews suspect according to PACE (see below). This is recorded in PNB or on MG15. Suspect must admit possession. If there is no admission, the suspect will be arrested.

Constable gives suspect a Cannabis Warning (see below).

Constable completes stop/search form and records evidence in PNB.

Constable places seized cannabis in drug store and produces a statement.

Crime report submitted according to Home Office counting rules and crime file completed.

Figure 1.6

The following points are recommended by the ACPO Guidance to be included in the Cannabis Warning to the suspect:

- A record of the investigation will be made at the police station.
- The offence of possession will be recorded, for statistical purposes, as detected.
- This procedure does not constitute a criminal record against the suspect.

In some forces it is also considered to be good practice to ask the suspect to sign a declaration that they agree to the matter being dealt with by way of a Cannabis Warning.

Scenario—Cannabis Warning

During the course of a stop and search, a constable finds a person to be in possession of a small amount of cannabis resin. The constable seizes the cannabis and cautions the person. The constable makes enquiries to confirm the person's identity and that they are over 18 years of age, and that the circumstances are suitable for the matter to be dealt with by means of a Cannabis Warning. The constable carries out a PACE interview, during which the person admits the offence of possession. The constable gives the person a Cannabis Warning. The constable completes a Stop and Search form and gives the person a copy.

1.5.3 Issuing a Penalty Notice for Possession of Cannabis

Prior to 28 January 2009 a person found in possession of cannabis could be given a Cannabis Warning on two occasions. Since then and the reclassification back to a Class B drug, the normal disposal option for a person found in possession of cannabis who has previously received a Cannabis Warning will be the issuing of a Penalty Notice. The sequence of disposal for possession of cannabis is now:

Table 1.1

First occasion	Cannabis Warning
Second occasion	PND
Third and subsequent occasions	Arrest

A person who has received a Cannabis Warning on a previous occasion should not be given a further warning and the intervention by the police officer should be escalated.

If the warning was issued since 26 January 2009 this must be taken into account in deciding upon the level of intervention. If the warning was prior to this date, ACPO guidance allows Forces to decide upon the intervention for repeat offenders taking into account previous Cannabis Warnings as part of the individual's offending history. The same conditions as for the Cannabis Warning must be present for the PND to be used as the most appropriate disposal option for the second incident of possession.

ACPO guidance on the revised intervention framework for dealing with possession of cannabis states that 'an officer may use operational discretion to decide that, although the offender has never received a Cannabis Warning, due to the circumstances they should immediately escalate to the issue of a PND or arrest' (ACPO Guidance on Cannabis Possession for Personal Use, Revised Intervention Framework). Therefore once an offender has received a PND on a previous occasion, the next intervention should be to arrest.

See 1.4.2 for the procedure for issuing a PND.

1.5.4 Conclusion

While cannabis was a Class C drug, the Cannabis Warning was the usual disposal option employed for possession on the first two occasions. Cannabis was reclassified as a Class B drug on 26 January 2009 as this:

> …reflects the fact that skunk, a much stronger version of the drug, now dominates the UK's cannabis market. Skunk has swept other, less potent, forms of cannabis off the market, and now accounts for 81% of cannabis available on our streets, compared to just 30% in 2002.

Home Office

The response to possession on the first occasion now will usually be a Cannabis Warning and a PND on the second. Consideration must always be given to the preconditions and the full circumstances to establish whether the warning or PND is the most appropriate method of dealing with the matter.

1.6 **Summary of Key Points**

1.6.1 **Fixed Penalty Notices**

- FPNs for non-endorsable offences can be affixed to a vehicle or issued to the driver.
- FPNs for endorsable offences can be issued to the driver only if the penalty points for the current offence, when combined with any existing points, will not render the driver liable for disqualification (12 points).

1.6.2 **Vehicle Defect Rectification Scheme**

- Voluntary scheme.
- For minor vehicle defects.

1.6.3 **Penalty Notices for Disorder**

- PNDs are for specified offences only.
- Recipient must be 16 or over.
- Certain conditions must be met and the circumstances must be suitable for a PND to be an appropriate disposal option.

1.6.4 **Cannabis Warnings and Penalty Notices**

- Since 26 January 2009 cannabis is classified as a Class B drug.
- Cannabis Warnings and Penalty Notices only apply to the offence of possession.

- Recipient must be over 18.
- Certain conditions must be met and the circumstances must be suitable for a Cannabis Warning or PND to be an appropriate disposal option.
- First occasion—Cannabis Warning.
- Second occasion—PND.
- Third and subsequent occasion—Arrest.

1.6.5 **General**

- For all of these disposal options to be appropriate, there must be sufficient evidence to support a prosecution.

Further Reading

ACPO—Guidance on Policing Cannabis—Use of Cannabis Warnings <http://www.acpo.police.uk>

ACPO Guidance on Cannabis Possession for Personal Use, Revised Intervention Framework <http://www.acpo.police.uk>

Bryant, R (ed) (2007) *Blackstone's Student Police Officer Handbook*, Oxford University Press, Oxford

Drugs Reclassification, Home Office <http://www.home office.gov.uk/drugs>

Home Office Police Operational Guidance—Penalty Notices for Disorder <http://police.homeoffice.gov.uk>

Offences for which a Penalty Notice for Disorder of £80 can be Issued

Table 1.2

Wasting police time / Giving false report	Criminal Law Act 1967, section 5
Persistently using a public electronic communications network in order to cause annoyance, inconvenience or needless anxiety	Communications Act 2003, section 127(2)
Knowingly giving a false alarm to a person acting on behalf of a fire and rescue service	Fire and Rescue Services Act 2004, section 49
Using words or conduct etc likely to cause harassment, alarm or distress	Public Order Act 1986, section 5
Firing or throwing fireworks	Explosives Act 1875, section 80
Drunk and disorderly in a public place	Criminal Justice Act 1967, section 91
Destroying or damaging property under £500	Criminal Damage Act 1971, section 1
Theft (retail under £200)	Theft Act 1968, section 1
Breach of fireworks curfew (11pm to 7am)	Fireworks Regulations 2004, Regulation 7 under Fireworks Act 2003, section 11
Possession of a category 4 firework	Fireworks Regulations 2004, Regulation 5 under Fireworks Act 2003, section 11
Possession by a person under 18 of an adult firework	Fireworks Regulations 2004, Regulation 4 under Fireworks Act 2003, section 11
Selling or attempting to sell alcohol to a person who is drunk	Licensing Act 2003, section 141
Supplying of alcohol by or on behalf of a club to a person under 18	Licensing Act 2003, section 146(3)

Selling alcohol anywhere to a person under 18	Licensing Act 2003, section 146(1)
Buying or attempting to buy alcohol on behalf of a person under 18	Licensing Act 2003, section 149(3)
Buying or attempting to buy alcohol for consumption on relevant premises by a person under 18	Licensing Act 2003, section 149(4)
Delivery of alcohol to a person under 18 or allowing such delivery	Licensing Act 2003, section 151
Possession of a controlled Class B drug—cannabis / cannabis resin	Misuse of Drugs Act 1971, section 5(2) and Schedule 4

Offences for which a Penalty Notice for Disorder of £50 can be Issued

Table 1.3

Trespassing on a railway	British Transport Commission Act 1949, section 55
Throwing stones at a train	British Transport Commission Act 1949, section 56
Drunk in a highway	Licensing Act 1872, section 12
Consumption of alcohol in a designated public place, contrary to a requirement by a constable not to do so	Criminal Justice and Police Act 2001, section 12
Depositing and leaving litter	Environmental Protection Act 1990, section 87(1) and (5)
Consumption of alcohol by a person under 18 on relevant premises (in a bar)	Licensing Act 2003, section 150(1)
Allowing consumption of alcohol by a person under 18 on relevant premises (in a bar)	Licensing Act 2003, section 150(2)
Buying or attempting to buy alcohol by a person under 18	Licensing Act 2003, section 149(1)

Fixed Penalty Notice

SUSSEX POLICE
FIXED PENALTY NOTICE   **£30**
(NON-ENDORSABLE OFFENCE)
PLEASE READ THE NOTES ON THE REAR OF THIS FORM
IT IS AN OFFENCE TO REMOVE THIS NOTICE WITHOUT AUTHORITY

PART 1   N

On   From   To

At

Town

a vehicle, Registration No.
which you were driving / using / in which you were a passenger / which was
unattended, was seen in circumstances which gave me reasonable cause to
believe that the offence indicated below was being or had been committed.

Offence Code

ISSUED BY:-

Signed

EXPIRY MONTH VEL   2 0

Vehicle Make

Details of Offender interviewed at Scene.   Driver / User / Passenger

M   F   DATE OF BIRTH

SUR NAME

FORE NAMES

HOUSE No.   ADDRESS

POST CODE

ETHNIC CATEGORY   WHITE EUROPEAN   DARK EUROPEAN   AFRO CARIBBEAN   ASIAN   ORIENTAL   ARAB   OTHER

N

Figure 1.7

Extended Fixed Penalty Notice

NO. E/

£60　　　　**SUSSEX POLICE**

| M | | F | | | | | DATE OF BIRTH | | | | | | |

SUR NAME

FORE NAMES

ADDRESS

POST CODE

PNC ID CODE　　　　　　SELF DEFINED ETHNICITY

SEE NOTE	Date										Time			
A	Offence Code													
	Location													
	Town													
	V.R.M											Rec. Speed		

VEHICLE DETAILS		Color	
Make			
Model			

Class/Use		Type		Passenger(s)	Yes ☐	No ☐
Manual	Yes ☐	No ☐		Driver - supervised	Yes ☐	No ☐
Motorway	Yes ☐	No ☐		Rider - qual. passgr.	Yes ☐	No ☐
'L' plates	Yes ☐	No ☐		HGV ☐	PSV ☐	LGV ☐

LEAVE BLANK IF NOT REQUIRED

Tick for Check/Records details　1 ☐　2 ☐　3 ☐　4 ☐　5 ☐　6 ☐　7 ☐　8 ☐　9 ☐　10 ☐

(continued)

1 Evidence Management

B at																	Police Station

C D E   +   PROVISIONAL NOTICE / LICENCE NOT SURRENDERED   +

C E   FULL NOTICE / LICENCE SURRENDERED

Motorist's signature .... (Request only)

Signed .... No: [ ][ ][ ][ ][ ]

Station .... District [ ][ ]

Tick for receipt of Driving Licence/Counterpart   FULL [ ]   PROV. [ ]

Driver Number [ ][ ][ ][ ][ ][ ][ ][ ][ ][ ][ ][ ][ ][ ][ ][ ]

Issue No. [ ][ ][ ]

F   Groups .... Expiry date ....

Signed .... No: [ ][ ][ ][ ][ ]

NO. E/

Date of Full Notice ....

THIS IS THE

CTO COPY

Figure 1.8

Vehicle Defect Notification

Sussex Police - Vehicle Defect Notification

Title:................. Sex: M/F   V

Surname: ....

Forename(s) ....D.O.B.................

Address:..

.... Post Code: ....

Drivers Signature (request only)

PNC ID CODE	☐	SELF DEF CODE	☐	SPECIFY "OTHER"................	
Date: ..../....../20.......		Time: 24 hrs	Location of stop:		

Manual: Yes/No	Motorway: Yes/No		L Plates:	Yes/No
VRM		Passenger(s):		Yes/No
Make		Driver Supervised:		Yes/No
Type/cc		Rider Qual:		Yes/No
Use		Passenger		
Class				

DEFECTS FOUND   (See green form)

1) ....

2) ....

3) ....

4) ....

GROUND FOR INTERVENTION:

....

DOCUMENTS TO BE PRODUCED (See overleaf)									
Check only:	1	2	3	4	5	6	7	8	9	10
Record details:	1	2	3	4	5	6	7	8	9	10

Police station where document(s) to be produced ....

Forward HO/RT2 to: Central Ticket & Summons Unit, Police Station, Ham Road, Shoreham by Sea, West Sussex, BN43 6DB

Issuing Officer Name: ....

Warrant Nos .... Station: T169/3 3/05

Figure 1.9

Penalty Notice for Disorder

SUSSEX POLICE
PENALTY NOTICE
PENALTY AMOUNT £80
IMPORTANT – READ THE NOTES ON THIS BACK OF THIS FORM

PART 1 RECIPIENT COPY **T**

TITLE 　　　　SURNAME

FORENAMES

DATE OF BIRTH (ddmmyyyy)　　ADDRESS

POST CODE

OFFENCE TIME　　OFFENCE DATE
　　24 HRS.　　　**2 0**

AT (LOCATION)

OFFENCE CODE　　DATE OF ISSUE　　**2 0**

YOU (offence particulars) ....

....

CONTRARY TO (Act containing offence)

(continued)

PLACE OF ISSUE: Street ☐   Custody ☐

| I acknowledge receipt of this Penalty Notice |
| Signature |

| ISSUED BY: | Surname | Signature |

Warrant No. ☐☐☐☐☐☐   DIST/DEPT ☐☐☐☐

Rank ☐☐☐

- -

PART 2   **COMPLETE ONE SIDE ONLY**

T ☐

*Sent **Part 2** and payment of £80 to:*
**The Fixed Penalty Office, The Law Courts, Edward Street, Brighton, East Sussex,
BN2 2LG,   Telephone No. 01273 811700.**
I enclose the sum of £80 as payment in respect of the offence mentioned in PART 1 of this notice.

NAME ....
(BLOCK LETTERS)
ADDRESS ....
(BLOCK LETTERS)

....POST CODE ☐☐☐☐☐☐☐

Or, you may phone the Tel. No. above or complete the following section and pay by credit/debit card.
I authorise HMCS to debit my Mastercard, VISA, Switch or Solo account with the sum of £80

Card Holder's Signature ....

Expiry Date ☐☐☐☐   Today's date ☐☐☐☐ **2 0** ☐☐
Credit/Debit Card No.

☐☐☐☐☐☐☐☐☐☐☐☐☐☐☐☐

Issue Number ☐☐   Valid from ☐☐☐☐

Security No. (last 3 digits on signature strip) ☐☐☐

Card Holder's address if different from above ....

PND 3/05

Figure 1.10

Chapter 2
Scene Preservation

2.1 Introduction

When a suspect or victim has been physically involved in a criminal activity, evidence of contact will result. This principle is based upon Edmond Locard's theory (1812) that suggests, 'whenever two objects come into contact, there is always an exchange of material'. To this end it is vital to identify and retrieve evidence left by the suspect at or on the crime scene, as well as evidence of the crime scene left on the suspect. One of the responsibilities of the first officer at a crime scene is to preserve forensic evidence. A crime scene will consist of one or more of the following: the suspect, the victim, and/or the location.

The following section is designed to assist officers in the preservation of crime scenes or potential crime scenes during initial response. The information is progressive and is spread out over several pages. At the start there is an overview of the three sources of forensic evidence to help identify sources, an overview of the process of collection, and some priorities to consider during the whole procedure. In addition, section 2.14 provides generic information for scene preservation at major, critical, and major crime incidents.

Once a source has been identified, a decision must be made as to whether it is an item, person, or location. Section 2.6 is then the starting point for a step-by-step guide to the identification, collection, and preservation of forensic evidence from the source. Simply follow the instructions provided.

2.2 **Sources of Forensic Evidence**

Evidence can be collected and preserved from the following three sources:

Items
- Stolen article abandoned by the suspect?
- Clothes after an assault?
- Implement after a burglary?

People
Victim or suspect
- Sexual assault?
- Assault with injuries?
- Offender after breaking a window?

Locations
- Exit or entry points?
- Tidy/untidy searches?
- Routes to and from an incident?

2.3 **Priorities of Scene Preservation**

The following three areas are priorities which you must consider whilst you are at, or with a crime scene:

Safety
- Self
- Colleagues
- Public
- Identify risks and hazards

Casualties
- Presume casualty to be alive unless decapitated, decomposed, or incinerated
- Administer First Aid
- Seek medical assistance

Forensic Evidence
- Be aware of your environment
- Minimize disruption to potential evidence

2.4 **The Forensic Evidence Process**

For each of the above crime scenes, the following process should be adopted:

2.5 **Identifying Sources of Evidence**

Look at the three boxes below. Decide which source(s) you have identified. Then, turn to the section indicated in the boxes to guide you through how to collect and preserve evidence from each of the sources:

Items	**People**	**Location**
Go to section 2.5.1	Go to section 2.5.2	Go to section 2.5.3

2.5.1 An Item as a Source of Evidence

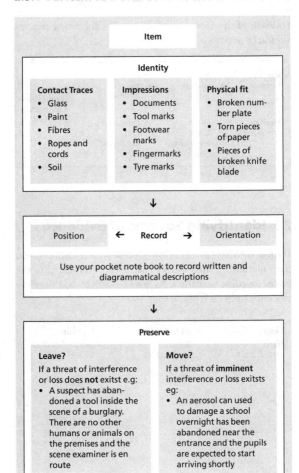

| Item |

Identity

Contact Traces	**Impressions**	**Physical fit**
• Glass	• Documents	• Broken number plate
• Paint	• Tool marks	• Torn pieces of paper
• Fibres	• Footwear marks	• Pieces of broken knife blade
• Ropes and cords	• Fingermarks	
• Soil	• Tyre marks	

↓

Position ← Record → Orientation

Use your pocket note book to record written and diagrammatical descriptions

↓

Preserve

Leave?
If a threat of interference or loss does **not** exitst e.g:
• A suspect has abandoned a tool inside the scene of a burglary. There are no other humans or animals on the premises and the scene examiner is en route

Move?
If a threat of **imminent** interference or loss exitsts eg:
• An aerosol can used to damage a school overnight has been abandoned near the entrance and the pupils are expected to start arriving shortly

Continued overleaf

Continued

Protect?	**Retrieve?**
If a threat of interference from human, animal, or natural elements exists eg:	If a threat of **immediate** interference or loss exists eg:
• A knife has been found covered in blood near to a serious assault. It has just started to rain and so a clean washing up bowl can be placed over it	• An expensive item of jewellery has been dropped outside a store in a busy shopping centre by a suspected shoplifter • Red staining (possibly blood) identified on a surface impossible to protect from rain (CSI with long ETA)

Now go to section 2.6 for Generic Considerations when Collecting and Preserving Evidence from a Source

2.5.2 People as Sources of Evidence

People

Identity		

Contact Traces
• DNA eg
    - Blood
    - Semen
    - Hair
    - Sweat
    - Saliva
• Fibres
	Impressions
	• Finger and palm prints
	• Footwear prints
	• Handwriting
	• Bite marks
		Physical fit
		• Broken, torn, or damaged items being carried

↓

Continued overleaf

1 Evidence Management

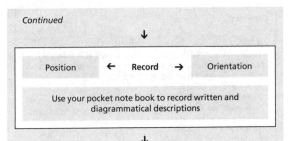

Continued

↓

| Position | ← Record → | Orientation |

Use your pocket note book to record written and diagrammatical descriptions

↓

Preserve

Leave?

If a threat of interference or loss does **not** exist

NB Once potential evidence has been located on an individual this is not usually an option.

Move?

If a threat of **imminent** interference or loss **exists**

NB Once potential evidence has been located on an individual this is not usually an option.

Protect?

If a threat of interference from human, animal, or natural elements **exists**

NB Once potential evidence has been located on an individual this is not usually an option.

Retrieve ?

If a threat of **immediate** interference or loss **exists** eg:

- The recovery of non-intimate samples from mouth, fingernails, hair, and visible, non-intimate areas of skin should be considered as soon as is practicable.

Now go to section 2.6 for Generic Considerations when Collecting and Preserving Evidence from a Source

2.5.3 Locations as Sources of Evidence

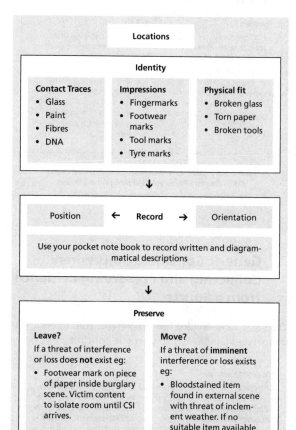

Locations

Identity

Contact Traces	**Impressions**	**Physical fit**
• Glass	• Fingermarks	• Broken glass
• Paint	• Footwear marks	• Torn paper
• Fibres	• Tool marks	• Broken tools
• DNA	• Tyre marks	

↓

Position ← **Record** → Orientation

Use your pocket note book to record written and diagrammatical descriptions

↓

Preserve

Leave?

If a threat of interference or loss does **not** exist eg:

• Footwear mark on piece of paper inside burglary scene. Victim content to isolate room until CSI arrives.

Move?

If a threat of **imminent** interference or loss exists eg:

• Bloodstained item found in external scene with threat of inclement weather. If no suitable item available to protect, then move to covered area.

Continued overleaf

Continued

Protect?

If a threat of interference from human, animal, or natural elements exists eg:

- Bloodstained item found in external scene with threat of inclement weather. Protect with clean, waterproof covering.

Retrieve?

If a threat of **immediate** interference or loss exists eg:

- Bloodstaining on immoveable, external surface, impossible to protect with watertight seal. Recover sample of stain with sterile material.

Now go to section 2.6 for Generic Considerations when Collecting and Preserving Evidence from a Source

2.6 Generic Considerations when Collecting and Preserving Evidence from a Source

Once you have decided how to preserve your forensic evidence consider the following generic principles:

Cross-contamination

The objective of forensic science is to prove the presence of the suspect at one or more of the other two crime scenes (the victim and/or the location). It is vital therefore that post-incident, none of the crime scenes has any further contact with each other. Equally important is that a 'carrier', unconnected with the original incident, does not transport sources of evidence between the crime scenes and contaminate the evidence. Such contamination would impede the ability of the prosecution to prove that the suspect had made contact with the victim and/or location at the time of the incident.

Continued overleaf

Continued

To this end you must ensure the highest level of sterility at all times, for example:

- The same officer must never make contact with the suspect as well as the victim. Instead, different officers at different locations must deal with each victim and each suspect separately.
- The suspect and the victim must never be transported at the same or different times in the same vehicle. Instead, different vehicles must transport each victim and each suspect separately.
- The same officer must never make contact with the suspect having attended the location of the incident or attend the location having made contact with a suspect. Instead, first of all ensure that both of these crimes scenes have been examined for trace evidence.

Integrity

To prove the integrity of an exhibit containing forensic evidence at court, the package must be:

- Sealed by an identifiable person
- Only opened by people who have good reason to gain access to it

Always:

1. Place a signed label across each opening of the package and tape over the label along the full length of the opening making sure the signature is still visible
2. Record the bag number (if it is a police evidence bag) in your pocket note book

Maintain Continuity

To prove the continuity of an exhibit containing forensic evidence at court, each of the people who have taken responsibility for the exhibit must sign a label attached to the package with tape.

On receipt of an exhibit, each person must:

1. Sign and date the next space on the exhibit/continuity label
2. Record the time, day, date, and name of the person
   - from whom the exhibit was received, and
   - to whom the exhibit is passed on

Continued overleaf

Continued

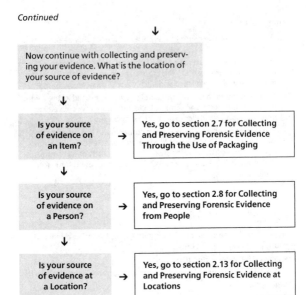

Now continue with collecting and preserving your evidence. What is the location of your source of evidence?

Is your source of evidence on an Item? →	**Yes, go to section 2.7 for Collecting and Preserving Forensic Evidence Through the Use of Packaging**
Is your source of evidence on a Person? →	**Yes, go to section 2.8 for Collecting and Preserving Forensic Evidence from People**
Is your source of evidence at a Location? →	**Yes, go to section 2.13 for Collecting and Preserving Forensic Evidence at Locations**

2.7 Collecting and Preserving Forensic Evidence Through the Use of Packaging

This section describes how to collect and preserve evidence through the use of packaging. Look at the table below and identify the box which contains the article on which your evidence has been left. Then choose the most appropriate packaging for your article.

• Clothing • Footwear • Bedding ↓ **Paper bags** (see section 2.7.1)	• Paper exhibits • Small items for freezing ↓ **Polythene bags** (see section 2.7.2)	• Tools • Bottles • Broken glass ↓ **Rigid containers** (see section 2.7.3)
• Articles believed to be contaminated with ignitable liquids ↓ **Nylon bags** (see section 2.7.4)	• Sharp items • Bladed items ↓ **Plastic screw-threaded tubes** (see section 2.7.5)	• Computers and mobile phones ↓ **Communication and information technology** (see section 2.7.6)

Locate customized versions of some of the above containers which should be available at your police station

Anything that might cause an injury—label with Health Hazard tape

2.7.1 Packaging Articles Using Paper Bags

1. Locate a suitable sized paper bag.
2. Should the evidence be wet, place it in a polythene bag and leave unsealed.
3. Place the article (or wet article in an unsealed polythene bag) into a paper bag.
4. Fold the top of the bag over by approximately 2.5cm twice.
5. Sign a white sticky label with your name, rank, and number, and place half of it on the fold and half on the front of the bag in the middle.

Continued overleaf

Continued

6. Seal the edges of the folds with a length of parcel tape making sure the signed label remains visible. Ensure the ends of the folds are COMPLETELY covered. If a stronger seal is required overlap the original tape with a second length of tape directly below the first. Use Health Hazard tape if required.

7. Enter details into the Special Property Register.

8. Complete pre-printed Criminal Justice Act exhibit label or attach an exhibit label and write all relevant details on external surface of bag including the Special Property number.

9. Inform Crime Scene Investigator that the exhibit has been seized.

2.7.2 Packaging Articles Using Polythene Bags

1. Locate a suitable sized polythene bag.

2. Place the article into the polythene bag.

3. Sign a white sticky label with your name, rank, and number, and place half of it on the front of the bag, fold it over the opening onto the rear of the bag in the middle.

4. Seal the opening of the bag with a length of clear adhesive tape making sure the signed label remains visible.

5. Cut off the ends of the tape approximately 5mm from the sides of the bag.

6. Use Health Hazard tape if required.

7. Enter details into the Special Property Register.

8. Write details such as date, place of seizure, Special Property number onto bag but position the evidence inside so it cannot be damaged by writing on it.

9. Attach exhibit label.

10. Inform Crime Scene Investigator that the exhibit has been seized.

2.7.3 Packaging Articles Using Rigid Containers

1. Locate a suitable sized rigid container.

2. Using cable ties or string, secure the evidence to a piece of cardboard that can fit into an evidence box.

3. Secure the mounted piece of evidence to the base of the rigid container using parcel tape.

Continued overleaf

Continued

4. Sign a white sticky label with your name, rank, and number, and place half of it on the lid of the container and half of it on the side of the container to form a seal.
5. Cover all openings with a length of parcel tape making sure the signed label remains visible.
6. Use Health Hazard tape if required.
7. Enter details into the Special Property Register.
8. Complete pre-printed section on the box or write details of exhibit on the outside of the box including the Special Property number.
9. Attach an exhibit label.
10. Inform Crime Scene Investigator that the exhibit has been seized.

2.7.4 Packaging Articles Using Nylon Bags

1. Locate a suitable sized nylon bag.
2. Place the evidence into the nylon bag.
3. Leave air present with the evidence inside the bag.
4. Twist the neck of the bag.
5. Fold over the twisted neck.
6. Twist the neck of the bag again.
7. Seal the bag with a cable tie.
8. Place sealed bag into a polythene bag and repeat steps 4–7 above with the second bag.
9. Do not write on either bag.
10. Place double-bagged article into a plastic Police Evidence Bag.
11. Use Health Hazard tape if required.
12. Enter details into the Special Property Register.
13. Complete pre-printed section on the bag including the Special Property number.
14. When all evidence has been packaged from the same incident, package and seal an unused nylon bag from the same batch and repeat steps 2–10 with the unused bag. Exhibit is separately labelled as 'Nylon bag control'.
15. Inform Crime Scene Investigator that the exhibit has been seized.

2.7.5 Packaging Articles Using Sharps Tubes

1. Locate a sharps tube.
2. Place the evidence into the inner tube.
3. Screw on outer tube until evidence is held securely.
4. Sign a white sticky label with your name, rank, and number, and place it over the join of the inner and outer tube.
5. Cover the join with clear adhesive tape.
6. Apply Health Hazard tape to the outer tube.
7. Place outer tube and contents into a plastic Police Evidence Bag.
8. Apply Health Hazard tape to the Police Evidence Bag.
9. Enter details into the Special Property Register.
10. Complete pre-printed section on the Police Evidence Bag including the Special Property number.
11. Inform Crime Scene Investigator that the exhibit has been seized.

2.7.6 Securing, Packaging, and Transporting Communication and Information Technology

Switched **OFF** computer equipment	Switched **ON** computer equipment
1. Make sure the computer is off by monitoring activity lights.	1. Do not touch the keyboard or mouse.
2. Allow pending or current jobs on printers to complete.	2. Disconnect the modem.
3. Switch off the power to the computer and other devices at the mains and remove the plug(s) from the socket.	3. Attach signed exhibit labels to each item of equipment in situ.
4. Remove the battery from laptops.	4. Photograph, video, or sketch all the equipment in situ.
5. Do not switch any devices on.	5. Record what is shown on the screen.
6. Attach signed exhibit labels to each item of equipment in situ.	6. Label the cables at each end and attach labels to the corresponding sockets for later reconstruction.

Continued overleaf

Continued

7. Photograph, video, or sketch all the equipment in situ.
8. Label the cables at each end and attach labels to the corresponding sockets for later reconstruction.
9. Record identifying numbers of each piece of equipment.

7. Remove all other connections (not mains) to sockets or devices.
8. If no specialist advisor is present:
   a. Do not close down any programs that are already running
   b. Remove the power supply cable attached to the rear of the computer first not the end plugged into the mains.

Transportation
Protect from magnetic sources (televisions, loud speakers, heated seats and windows).

Hard disks
Place in anti-static bags, tough paper bags, wrap in paper, and place in aerated plastic bags.

Floppy disks/memory sticks/ zip cartridges
Do not fold, bend, or place labels directly on floppies.

Monitors
Place screen down on a car seat and secure.

Main computer unit
Place upright in a car/prevent serious shocks.

Personal digital and electronic organizers
Handle carefully and do not drop on to hard surfaces.

Keyboards/leads/mouse and modems
Place in a plastic bag. Do not place underneath heavier articles.

2.8 Collecting and Preserving Forensic Evidence from People

This section describes how to collect and preserve evidence from the following parts of the body:

- **the mouth** (see section 2.9)
- **fingernails** (see section 2.10)
- **hair** (see section 2.11)
- **skin** (see section 2.12)
- storing and informing crime scene investigator (see section 2.9.4)

2.9 **Preserving Evidence from the Mouth**

Taking samples from the mouth is likely to be most productive in securing forensic evidence, when the person has been:

- carrying material, forcibly or otherwise;
- involved in an incident of biting; or
- concerned in a sexual assault.

This section describes how to collect and preserve evidence from the mouth in the following ways:

- **saliva**
- **mouth swabs and batch control**
- **mouth wash and water control**

2.9.1 **Saliva**

Equipment required for collecting evidence:	Equipment required for personal safety:
• 1 x small, universal plastic container • 1 x police evidence bag	• Mask • Disposable gloves

Method of Retrieval
1. Put on personal safety equipment.
2. Open sealed plastic containers.

Continued overleaf

Continued

3. Request the individual to hold the open container close to their mouth and deposit as much saliva as possible into the container.
4. Replace the lid of the container firmly.
5. Write on the container label:
   1. Your exhibit reference number
   2. The word 'Saliva' and the individual's surname.
6. Place the sealed container into the police evidence bag and seal it.
7. On the bag label write
   • the exhibit reference
   • a description of the contents eg 'Saliva and container' with the individual's surname
   • Special Property number.
8. Store and inform crime scene investigator (see section 2.9.4).

2.9.2 Mouth Swabs and Batch Control

Equipment required for collecting evidence:
• 3 x swab tubes
• 1 x police evidence bag
• Freezer tape

Equipment required for Personal Safety:
• Mask
• Disposable gloves

Method of Retrieval—Upper Gums

1. Put on personal safety equipment.
2. Open one sealed swab tube (container) and remove swab.
3. Request the individual to open his/her mouth.
4. Gently wipe the swab over the upper teeth and gums on both internal and external surfaces.
5. Place the swab back in its original tube and press firmly to form a tight seal.
6. Sign a white sticky label with your name, rank, and number, and place it over the join.
7. Seal the tube with freezer tape.
8. Sign across the join of the freezer tape and tube.

Continued overleaf

1 Evidence Management

Continued

9. Write on the swab tube (container) label:
   - Your exhibit reference number
   - The words 'Swab of **upper** teeth and gums' and the individual's surname.
10. Place the sealed tube (container) into the police evidence bag.

Method of Retrieval—Lower Gums

1. Take the second sealed swab tube (container) and repeat steps 1–8 for the lower gums.
2. Gently wipe the swab over the upper teeth and gums on both internal and external surfaces.
3. Write on the swab tube (container) label:
   - Your exhibit reference number (same as previous number)
   - The words 'Swab of **lower** teeth and gums' and the individual's surname.
4. Place the sealed tube (container) into the police evidence bag.

Batch Control

1. Take the third sealed swab tube (container) but DO NOT break the seal.
2. Write on the swab tube (container) label:
   - Your exhibit reference number (same as previous numbers)
   - The words 'Batch Control swab' and the individual's surname.
3. Place the sealed tube (container) into the police evidence bag and seal it.
4. On the bag label write
   - the exhibit reference
   - a description of the contents, eg 'Two swabs of teeth and gums and batch control swab', including the individual's surname
   - Special Property number.
5. Store and inform crime scene investigator (see section 2.9.4).

2.9.3 Mouth Wash and Water Control

Equipment required for collecting evidence:
- 1 x swab tube
- 10ml sterile water
- 1 x small, universal plastic container
- 1 x police evidence bag
- Freezer tape

Equipment required for Personal Safety:
- Mask
- Disposable gloves

Method of Retrieval—Water Control
1. Put on personal safety equipment.
2. Open one sealed swab tube (container) and remove swab.
3. Open the bottle of sterile water.
4. Apply a single drop of water to the tip of the swab.
5. Place the swab back in its original tube and press firmly to form a tight seal.
6. Sign a white sticky label with your name, rank, and number, and place it over the join, or
7. Seal the tube with freezer tape, and
8. Sign across the join of the freezer tape and tube.
9. Write on the swab tube (container) label:
   - Your exhibit reference number
   - The words 'Water control swab' and the individual's surname.
10. Place the sealed tube (container) into the police evidence bag.

Mouth Wash
1. Ask the individual to use the remainder of the sterile water as a mouthwash to swill around inside his or her mouth.
2. Open sealed plastic container.
3. Request the individual to hold the open container close to their mouth and deposit as much of the swilled water as possible into the container.
4. Replace the lid of the container firmly.
5. Write on the container label:
   - Your exhibit reference number
   - The word 'Mouthwash' and the individual's surname.
6. Place the sealed container into the same police evidence bag as the water control swab.

Continued overleaf

Continued
7. On the bag label write:
   - the exhibit reference
   - a description of the contents, eg 'Mouthwash and container and water control swab' with the individual's surname
   - Special Property reference number.
8. Seal the police evidence bag.
9. Store and inform crime scene investigator (see section 2.9.4).

2.9.4 Storing and Informing Crime Scene Investigator

Exhibits should be frozen as soon as possible. Inform crime scene investigator that the evidence has been collected, exhibited, and stored.

2.10 Collecting and Preserving Evidence from Fingernails

Taking samples from the fingernails is likely to be most productive in securing forensic evidence, when the person has been:

- in physical contact with another person for example during an assault, sexual or otherwise;
- using the hands to damage property or move objects;
- holding articles without protection; or
- near to a situation in which material was torn, sprayed, or otherwise applied.

This section describes how to collect and preserve evidence from fingernails in the following ways:

- **Nail cuttings, right hand** (see section 2.10.1)
- **Nail scrapings, right hand** (see section 2.10.2)
- **Nail cuttings, left hand** (see section 2.10.3)

- **Nail scrapings, left hand** (see section 2.10.4)
- **Batch control samples for nail scrapings and cuttings** (see section 2.10.5)
- **Storing and informing crime scene investigator** (see section 2.10.6)

2.10.1 Nail Cuttings (right hand)

• 1 x nail clippers in sealed pack • 1 x pack of sterile paper • 1 x police evidence bag	Equipment required for Personal Safety: • Mask • Disposable gloves

Method of Retrieval—Right Hand

1. Put on personal safety equipment.
2. Ask the individual to sit on a chair in front of a table.
3. Open one pack of sterile paper.
4. Place the paper on the table top in front of the individual.
5. Request the individual to place his or her right hand on the sheet of paper.
6. Remove the nail clippers from the plastic container.
7. Cut the fingernails of all five digits taking care not to cause injury.
8. Ensure all clippings are retained within the clippers or on the sheet of paper.
9. Place clippers back into container.
10. Replace the lid of the container firmly.
11. Write on the container label:
    - Your exhibit reference number
    - The words 'Right hand nail clippings' and the individual's surname.
12. Place the sealed container into the police evidence bag.
13. On the bag label write:
    - the exhibit reference
    - a description of the contents, eg 'Nail cuttings right hand and clippers and container' with the individual's surname
    - Special Property reference number.

If scrapings from underneath the fingernails are not required or not possible, continue with steps 14 and 15.

Continued overleaf

1 Evidence Management

Continued

If scrapings are required, carry out step 15 and then proceed directly to step 3 of **Nail scrapings**, section 2.10.2 below.

14. Fold up paper taking care to retain any debris and place into the police evidence bag adding 'and paper' to the exhibit description.
15. Seal the police evidence bag.
16. Store and inform crime scene investigator (see section 2.10.6).

2.10.2 Nail Scrapings (right hand)

Equipment required for collecting evidence:

- 2 x fine tip sterile swabs
- 1 x pack of sterile paper
- 1 x bottle of sterile water
- 1 x police evidence bag

Equipment required for Personal Safety:

- Mask
- Disposable gloves

Method of Retrieval—Right Hand

1. Put on personal safety equipment.
2. Request the individual sits on a chair in front of a table.
3. Open one pack of sterile paper.
4. Place the paper on the table top in front of the individual.
5. Request the individual to place his or her right hand on the sheet of paper.
6. Open one sealed swab tube (container) and remove the fine tip swab.
7. Open the bottle of sterile water.
8. Apply a single drop of water to the tip of the swab.
9. Wipe the swab underneath the fingernails of all five digits.
10. Wipe any large pieces of visible debris onto the sterile paper sheet.
11. Place the swab back in its original tube and press firmly to form a tight seal.
12. Sign a white sticky label with your name, rank, and number, and place it over the join, or
13. Seal the tube with freezer tape, and
14. Sign across the join of the freezer tape and tube.

Continued overleaf

Continued

15. Write on the label of the swab tube (container):
    - Your exhibit reference number
    - The words 'Nail scraping right hand—wet' and the individual's surname.
16. Place the sealed tube (container) into the police evidence bag.
17. Repeat steps 1–6 and 9–14.
18. Write on the label of the swab tube (container):
    - Your exhibit reference number
    - The words 'Nail scraping right hand—dry' and the individual's surname.
19. Place the sealed tube (container) into the same police evidence bag.
20. Fold up the sterile paper taking care to retain any debris and place into the police evidence bag.
21. On the bag label write:
    - the exhibit reference
    - a description of the contents, eg 'Wet and dry nail scrapings—right hand and paper' with the individual's surname.
    - Special Property reference number.
22. Seal the police evidence bag.
23. Store and inform crime scene investigator (see section 2.10.6).

For batch control—see **Batch control samples for nail scrapings and cuttings**, section 2.10.5 below).

2.10.3 Nail Cuttings (left hand)

Equipment required for collecting evidence:
- 2 x fine tip sterile swabs
- 1 x pack of sterile paper
- 1 x bottle of sterile water
- 1 x police evidence bag

Equipment required for Personal Safety:
- Mask
- Disposable gloves

Method of Retrieval—Left Hand
1. Repeat steps 1–15 above in method of retrieval for right hand.
2. Store and inform crime scene investigator (see section 2.10.6).

2.10.4 Nail Scrapings (left hand)

Equipment required for collecting evidence:
- 2 x fine tip sterile swabs
- 1 x pack of sterile paper
- 1 x bottle of sterile water
- 1 x police evidence bag

Equipment required for Personal Safety:
- Mask
- Disposable gloves

Method of Retrieval—Left Hand
1. Repeat steps 1–22 above in method of retrieval for right hand.
2. Store and inform crime scene investigator (see section 2.10.6).

2.10.5 Batch Control Samples for Nail Scrapings and Cuttings

Equipment required for collecting evidence:
- 2 x fine tip sterile swabs
- 1 x bottle of sterile water used to collect the previous nail scrapings for right and/or left hands
- 1 x police evidence bag

Equipment required for Personal Safety:
- Mask
- Disposable gloves

Method for Dry Batch Control Sample
1. Take a sealed swab tube (container) but DO NOT break the seal.
2. Write on the swab container label:
   - Your exhibit reference number (same as previous numbers)
   - The words 'Batch Control swab—nails' and the individual's surname.
3. Place the sealed tube (container) into a new police evidence bag then continue.

Continued overleaf

Continued

Method for Wet Batch Control Sample

1. Open a sealed swab tube (container) and remove swab.
2. Open the same bottle of sterile water earlier used on the swab to carry out nail scrapings.
3. Apply a single drop of water to the tip of the swab.
4. Place the swab back in its original tube and press firmly to form a tight seal.
5. Sign a white sticky label with your name rank and number and place it over the join, or
6. Seal the tube with freezer tape, and
7. Sign across the join of the freezer tape and tube.
8. Write on the swab tube (container) label:
   - Your exhibit reference number
   - The words 'Water control swab' and the individual's surname.
9. Place the sealed tube (container) into the same police evidence bag as the dry batch control sample.
10. On the bag label write:
    - the exhibit reference
    - a description of the contents, eg 'Batch and water control swabs for exhibits' (name the exhibit references for the retrieved nail cuttings and scrapings) including the individual's surname
    - Special Property number.
11. Seal the police evidence bag.
12. Store and inform crime scene investigator (see section 2.10.6).

2.10.6 Storing and Informing Crime Scene Investigator

Exhibits should be frozen as soon as possible. Inform crime scene investigator that the evidence has been collected, exhibited, and stored.

2.11 **Collecting Evidence from Hair**

Taking samples from the hair is likely to be most productive in securing forensic evidence when the person has been:

- in physical contact with another person, for example during an assault, sexual or otherwise;
- near to a situation in which material was torn, sprayed, or otherwise applied;
- close to an incident involving bleeding, spitting, or ejaculation;
- in the vicinity of glass being broken; or
- in close proximity to fibrous material contained in clothing, furniture, or flooring.

This section describes how to collect evidence from the hair in the following ways:

- **Visible items** (see section 2.11.1)
- **Matted hair** (see section 2.11.2)
- **Hair combings** (see section 2.11.3)
- **Control sample of hair** (see section 2.11.4)
- **Storing and informing crime scene investigator** (see section 2.11.5)

2.11.1 **Visible Items**

Equipment required for collecting evidence:	Equipment required for Personal Safety:
• Tweezers in sealed container • Police evidence bag	• Mask • Disposable gloves

Method of Retrieval
1. Put on personal safety equipment.
2. Take out tweezers from sealed container.
3. Retrieve the visible extraneous article(s) from the individual's hair using tweezers.

Continued overleaf

Continued

4. Place the tweezers and the extraneous article(s) into a police evidence bag.
5. On the bag label write:
   - the exhibit reference
   - a description of the contents, eg '(extraneous article(s) description) from head hair and tweezers' including the individual's surname
   - Special Property number.
6. Seal the police evidence bag.
7. See **Control sample of hair**, section 2.11.4 below.
8. Store and inform crime scene investigator (see section 2.11.5).

2.11.2 Matted Hair

Equipment required for collecting evidence:
- Scissors in sealed container
- Police evidence bag

Equipment required for Personal Safety:
- Mask
- Disposable gloves

Method of Retrieval

1. Record the location(s) on the individual's head where the hair is matted using diagrams or photography.
2. Put on personal safety equipment.
3. Take out scissors from sealed container.
4. Cut away the matted area(s) of the individual's hair using the scissors.
5. Place the scissors and the matted area(s) of hair into a police evidence bag.
6. On the bag label write:
   - the exhibit reference
   - a description of the contents, eg 'Matted hair and scissors' including the individual's surname
   - Special Property number.
7. Seal the police evidence bag.
8. Store and inform crime scene investigator (see section 2.11.5).
9. See **Control sample of hair**, section 2.11.4 below.

2.11.3 Hair Combings

Equipment required for collecting evidence:
- Comb in sealed pack
- Sterile paper in sealed pack
- Police evidence bag

Equipment required for Personal Safety:
- Mask
- Disposable gloves

Method of Retrieval

1. Record the location(s) on the individual's head where the hair is matted using diagrams or photography.
2. Put on personal safety equipment.
3. Ask the individual to sit on a chair in front of a table.
4. Open one pack of sterile paper.
5. Place the paper on the table top in front of the individual.
6. Request the individual to lower his or her head to a position directly above the sterile sheet of paper.
7. Take out the comb from the sealed pack.
8. Comb through individual's entire head of hair using 20 to 30 strokes.
9. Collect any debris which falls from the individual's hair on the sheet of paper.
10. Place the comb on the paper.
11. Fold up the paper.
12. Place it into a police evidence bag.
13. On the bag label write:
    - the exhibit reference
    - a description of the contents, eg 'Head hair combing and comb and paper' including the individual's surname
    - Special Property number.
14. Seal the police evidence bag.
15. Store and inform crime scene investigator (see section 2.11.5).
16. See **Control sample of hair**, section 2.11.4 below.

2.11.4 Control Sample of Hair

Equipment required for collecting evidence:	Equipment required for Personal Safety:
• Scissors in sealed pack	• Mask
• Police evidence bag	• Disposable gloves

1. Put on personal safety equipment.
2. Take out the scissors from the sealed pack.
3. Cut a sample of the individual's hair as close to the skin as possible.
4. Ensure that all the lengths and colours of hair are represented in the sample.
5. Place the scissors and the samples of cut hair into a police evidence bag.
6. On the bag label write:
   • the exhibit reference
   • a description of the contents, eg 'Control sample of hair and scissors' including the individual's surname
   • Special Property number.
7. Store and inform crime scene investigator (see section 2.11.5).
8. Seal the police evidence bag

2.11.5 Storing and Informing Crime Scene Investigator

If it is likely that DNA evidence is available, exhibits should be frozen as soon as possible. All other exhibits should be stored in a cool and dry place. Inform crime scene investigator that the evidence has been collected, exhibited, and stored.

2.12 **Collecting Evidence on the Skin**

Taking samples from the skin is likely to be most productive in securing forensic evidence, when the person has been:

- in physical contact with another person, for example during an assault, sexual or otherwise, when they may have been bitten;
- near to a situation in which material was torn, sprayed, or otherwise applied; or
- close to an incident involving bleeding, spitting, or ejaculation.

This section describes how to collect evidence from the skin in the following ways:

- **Targetted swabbing**—to retrieve evidence from a stain or bite mark (see section 2.12.1)
- **Batch control swabs for targeted swabbing** (see section 2.12.2)
- **Speculative swabbing**—to retrieve evidence where there are no visible indications of containment such as saliva (see section 2.12.3)
- **Batch control swabs for speculative swabbing** (see section 2.12.4)
- **Storing and informing crime scene investigator** (see section 2.12.5)

2.12.1 **Targetted Swabbing**

Equipment required for collecting evidence:	Equipment required for Personal Safety:
• 2 x sterile swabs • 1 x bottle of sterile water • Freezer tape • Signature seal (small sticky backed label) • 1 x police evidence bag	• Mask • Disposable gloves

Continued overleaf

Continued

Method of Retrieval

1. Put on personal safety equipment.
2. Open one sealed swab tube (container) and remove the swab.
3. If the stain (or if retrieving saliva, the skin surrounding the bite mark) is wet, go to step 6.
4. If the stain (or if retrieving saliva, the skin surrounding the bite mark) is dry, open the bottle of sterile water.
5. Apply a single drop of water to the tip of the swab.
6. Place the tip of the swab onto the area of staining (or if retrieving saliva, the skin surrounding the bite mark) and rotate applying enough pressure on the swab to recover material from the skin.
7. Place the swab back in its original tube and press firmly to form a tight seal.
8. Sign a white sticky label with your name, rank, and number, and place it over the join, or
9. Seal the tube with freezer tape, and
10. Sign across the join of the freezer tape and tube.
11. Write on the label of the swab tube (container):
    - Your exhibit reference number
    - The words 'Swab of (describe the contaminant) stain from (describe the location)' and the individual's surname.
12. If water was applied to the swab add the words 'and water'.
13. Place the sealed tube (container) into the police evidence bag.

Original area of staining remains visible

1. Repeat steps 2–12 using the same exhibit reference as the first swab but numbering it 'swab 2'.

Area control swabs

1. Put on personal safety equipment.
2. Open one sealed swab tube (container) and remove the swab.
3. If the swab was previously used dry go to step 6.
4. If the swab was previously used wet, open the bottle of sterile water.
5. Apply a single drop of water to the tip of the swab.
6. Place the tip of the swab onto an unstained area of skin near to the original stain.
7. If recovering evidence from a bite mark repeat on an area of skin approximately 10cm from the bite mark.
8. Place the swab back in its original tube and press firmly to form a tight seal.

Continued overleaf

1 Evidence Management

Continued

9. Sign a white sticky label with your name, rank, and number, and place it over the join, or
10. Seal the tube with freezer tape, and
11. Sign across the join of the freezer tape and tube.
12. Write on the label of the swab tube (container):
    - Your exhibit reference number (same as the first)
    - The words 'Area control swab' and the individual's surname
    - If water was applied to the swab add the words 'and water'
    - Special Property reference number.
13. Seal the police evidence bag.
14. Place the sealed tube (container) into the same police evidence bag.
15. On the bag label write:
    - the exhibit reference
    - a description of the contents, eg '(Number of swabs) of (describe the contaminant) stain from (describe the location)' with the individual's surname
    - If water was applied to the swab add the words 'and water'.
16. Store and inform crime scene investigator (see section 2.12.5).

2.12.2 Batch Control Swabs for Targeted Swabbing

Equipment required for collecting evidence:
- 2 x sterile swabs
- 1 x bottle of sterile water used to collect the previous contaminates
- 1 x police evidence bag

Equipment required for Personal Safety:
- Mask
- Disposable gloves

Method for Dry Batch Control Sample

1. Take a sealed swab tube (container) but DO NOT break the seal.
2. Write on the swab tube (container) label:
   - Your exhibit reference number (same as previous numbers)
   - The words 'Batch Control swab' and the individual's surname.
3. Place the sealed tube (container) into a new police evidence bag.

Continued overleaf

Continued

4. On the bag label write:
   - the exhibit reference
   - a description of the contents, eg 'Batch control swab for exhibits' (name the exhibit references for the retrieved contaminants) including the individual's surname
   - Special Property number.
5. Seal the police evidence bag.

Method for Wet Batch Control Sample

1. Open a sealed swab tube (container) and remove swab.
2. Open the same bottle of sterile water earlier used on the swab to carry out the previous swabbing.
3. Apply a single drop of water to the tip of the swab.
4. Place the swab back in its original tube and press firmly to form a tight seal.
5. Sign a white sticky label with your name, rank, and number, and place it over the join, or
6. Seal the tube with freezer tape, and
7. Sign across the join of the freezer tape and tube,
8. Write on the swab tube (container) label:
   - Your exhibit reference number (same as the batch control swab above)
   - The words 'Water control swab' and the individual's surname.
9. Place the sealed tube (container) into the same police evidence bag as the dry batch control sample.
10. On the bag label write:
    - the exhibit reference
    - a description of the contents, eg 'Batch and water control swabs for exhibits' (name the exhibit references for the retrieved contaminant swabbing) including the individual's surname
    - Special Property number.
11. Seal the police evidence bag.
12. Store and inform crime scene investigator (see section 2.12.5).

2.12.3 Speculative Swabbing

Equipment required for collecting evidence
- 2 x sterile swab
- 1 x bottle of sterile water
- Freezer tape
- Signature seal (small sticky backed label)
- 1 x police evidence bag

Equipment required for Personal Safety:
- Mask
- Disposable gloves

Method of Retrieval

Split the area to be swabbed into two zones approximately 10 cm x 10 cm each. For example, zone 1 the front of the digits of the individual's right hand (palm side of hand); zone 2, back of the digits of the individual's right hand. Each area will require a wet swab and a dry swab.

Zone 1 (wet)

1. Put on personal safety equipment.
2. Open one sealed swab tube (container) and remove the swab.
3. Open a bottle of sterile water.
4. Apply a single drop of water to the tip of the swab.
5. Using the entire tip of the swab, rub it over half of the identified area.
6. Place the swab back in its original tube and press firmly to form a tight seal.
7. Sign a white sticky label with your name, rank, and number, and place it over the join, or
8. Seal the tube with freezer tape, and
9. Sign across the join of the freezer tape and tube.
10. Write on the label of the swab tube (container):
    - Your exhibit reference number
    - The words 'Swab of (describe the area) and water' and the individual's surname.
11. Place the sealed tube (container) into the police evidence bag.

Continued overleaf

Continued

Zone 2 (wet)
Repeat steps 1–11 above

Zone 1 (dry)
1. Put on personal safety equipment.
2. Open one sealed swab tube (container) and remove the swab.
3. Using the entire tip of the swab, rub it over half of the identified area, for example, the front of the digits of the individual's right hand.
4. Place the swab back in its original tube and press firmly to form a tight seal.
5. Sign a white sticky label with your name, rank, and number, and place it over the join, or
6. Seal the tube with freezer tape, and
7. Sign across the join of the freezer tape and tube.
8. Write on the label of the swab tube (container):
   - Your exhibit reference number
   - The words 'Swab of (describe the area)' and the individual's surname.
9. Place the sealed tube (container) into the police evidence bag.

Zone 2 (dry)
Repeat steps 1–9 above
10. On the bag label write:
    - the exhibit reference
    - a description of the contents, eg 'Two wet and two dry swabs of (describe the area)' including the individual's surname
    - Special Property number.
11. Seal the police evidence bag.
12. Store and inform crime scene investigator (see section 2.12.5).

2.12.4 Batch Control Swabs for Speculative Swabbing

Equipment required for collecting evidence:

- 2 x sterile swabs
- 1 x bottle of sterile water used to collect the original speculative swabs
- 1 x police evidence bag

Equipment required for Personal Safety:

- Mask
- Disposable gloves

Method for Dry Batch Control Sample

1. Take a sealed swab tube (container) but DO NOT break the seal
2. Write on the swab container label:
   - Your exhibit reference number (same as previous numbers)
   - The words 'Batch Control swab' and the individual's surname.
3. Place the sealed tube (container) into a police evidence bag.

Method for Wet Batch Control Sample

1. Open a sealed swab tube (container) and remove swab.
2. Open the same bottle of sterile water earlier used on the swab to carry out the speculative swabbing.
3. Apply a single drop of water to the tip of the swab.
4. Place the swab back in its original tube and press firmly to form a tight seal.
5. Sign a white sticky label with your name, rank, and number, and place it over the join, or
6. Seal the tube with freezer tape, and
7. Sign across the join of the freezer tape and tube.
8. Write on the swab tube (container) label:
   - Your exhibit reference number (same as the batch control swab above)
   - The words 'Water control swab' and the individual's surname.
9. Place the sealed tube (container) into the same police evidence bag as the dry batch control sample.

Continued overleaf

Continued

10. On the bag label write:
    - the exhibit reference
    - a description of the contents, eg 'Batch and water control swabs for exhibits' (name the exhibit references for the retrieved contaminant swabbing) including the individual's surname
    - Special Property number.
11. Seal the police evidence bag.
12. Store and inform crime scene investigator (see section 2.12.5).

2.12.5 Storing and Informing the Crime Scene Investigator

If it is likely that DNA evidence is available, exhibits should be frozen as soon as possible. All other exhibits should be stored in a cool and dry place. Inform crime scene investigator that the evidence has been collected, exhibited, and stored.

2.13 Collecting and Preserving Forensic Evidence at Locations

2.13.1 Contact Traces

Street Robbery eg:
- Non-intimate samples from victim including DNA
- Non-intimate samples from suspect including DNA
- Outer clothing of victim
- Outer clothing of suspect

Vehicle Crime eg:
- Control sample of glass from broken window
- Fibres from driver's seat
- Control sample of fibres from driver's seat
- Outer clothing from suspect

Continued overleaf

1 Evidence Management

Continued

Burglary eg:
- Control glass sample from broken window
- Fibres from edges of broken glass in window
- Non-intimate eg hair samples from suspect
- Outer clothing from suspect

Theft (including shoplifting) eg:
- Control sample from building material damaged by suspects
- Non-intimate eg swab hands of suspect
- Blood on abandoned property with damaged security tag in supermarket
- DNA sample from suspect

Criminal Damage eg:
- Sample of paint from graffiti writing on wall
- Non-intimate eg swab of paint from suspect's hand
- Brick from inside a room with a broken window
- Non-intimate eg wet/dry swabs of suspect's hand

Drugs eg:
- Suspect white powder for analysis
- Non-intimate eg swabs of suspect's hands
- Swabs of interior of suspect's vehicle
- Swabs of drugs equipment at suspect's address

Techniques for preserving contact traces

Street Robbery eg:
- Bloodstained kitchen knife on street/police in attendance/good weather/CSI en route—**Leave in situ.**
- Bloodstained hammer on street/police in attendance/threat of rain/CSI en route—**Protect** with sterile cover.
- Bloodstained baseball bat on street/police in attendance/raining hard/not safe, sterile packaging available/CSI en route—**Move** to protected area.
- Bloodstained pen-knife on street/police in attendance/raining hard/safe, sterile packaging available/CSI en route with long journey time—**Seize** and package.

Burglary eg:
- Offender's torch in lounge identified during report of incident on phone—Police call taker will request victim **leave** in situ for CSI.
- Offender's screwdriver in lounge identified during report of incident on phone/near open window/raining hard/CSI en route—request victim **protect** torch by closing window.

Continued overleaf

Continued

- Offender's knife in lounge/near broken window/raining hard/ police in attendance/CSI en route—**Move** torch to a protected area.
- Offender's jemmy in lounge/near broken window/raining hard/ police in attendance/CSI unable to attend for 24 hrs—**Seize** and package torch.

Theft (including shoplifting) eg:

- Blood on bottle of spirit with damaged security tag in supermarket identified during report of incident on phone—Police call taker will request victim to **leave** blood in situ for police/CSI and **protect** bottle (to avoid contact from staff or members of the public).
- Blood on bottle of spirit with damaged security tag in supermarket/police in attendance/CSI en route—**Move** bottle carefully to a secure area.
- Blood on bottle of spirit with damaged security tag in supermarket/police in attendance/CSI unavailable for 12 hours—**Seize** and package bottle.

Vehicle Crime eg:

- Theft from vehicle on owner's drive/report of incident on phone/ good weather/CSI en route—Police call taker will request the owner to **leave** the vehicle and items on drive for CSI.
- Theft from vehicle on owner's drive/report of incident on phone/threat of rain/CSI en route—Police call taker will request the owner **protects** piece of bloodstained cowling on drive with upturned, clean washing up bowl and await CSI.
- Found stolen vehicle abandoned in field—**Move** to a designated garage with secure examination bays for use of CSI.
- Found stolen vehicle abandoned in field/vehicle recovered/hold-all with tools and documents found nearby—**Seize** and package the holdall and contents.

Criminal Damage eg:

- Broken window at school building/paving slab in classroom/care-taker at scene/CSI en route—Police call taker will request the caretaker to **leave** the slab in situ.
- Broken window at school/caretaker at scene/broken, bloodstained glass outside in playground/CSI en route—police call taker will request the caretaker **protects** the children present and evidence on glass by closing relevant play area.

Continued overleaf

1 Evidence Management

Continued

- Broken window at school/police at scene/broken, bloodstained glass outside in play area/CSI en route with long journey time—**Move** the glass into a secure area for CSI.
- Broken window at school/police at scene/broken, bloodstained glass outside in play area/CSI unable to attend until next day—**Seize** and safely package the glass for CSI to examine at police station.

Drugs eg:

- Suspect arrested at his/her home address on suspicion of dealing in drugs/CSI en route—**Leave** drug equipment/items in situ.
- Suspect arrested at his/her home address on suspicion of dealing in drugs/set of weighing scales found in rear garden/threat of rain/CSI en route—**Protect** the scales with a waterproof, sterile cover.
- Suspect arrested at his/her home address on suspicion of dealing in drugs/small bag of white powder found in toilet bowl/CSI en route—**Move** the bag.
- Suspect arrested at his/her home address on suspicion of dealing in drugs—swab the suspect's hands and **seize** the material collected.

2.13.2 Impressions

Street Robbery eg:

- Footwear mark in mud near incident
- Footwear from suspect
- Fingermarks on items of victims property handled by offender
- Fingerprints from suspect for identification and victim for elimination

Burglary eg:

- Footwear mark on internal windowsill of point of entry window
- Footwear from suspect
- Fingermarks in locations consistent with climbing through window
- Fingerprints from suspect

Vehicle Crime eg:

- Screwdriver marks from driver's door and doorframe
- Screwdriver recovered from suspect
- Fingermarks from internal surface of broken piece of steering column cowling on back seat
- Fingerprints from suspect

Criminal Damage eg:

- Photographs of graffiti
- Handwriting samples from suspect
- Footwear marks in paint near graffiti
- Footwear from suspect

Continued overleaf

Continued
Theft (including shoplifting) eg:

- Tyre marks in mud beneath roof with lead missing
- Tyres from suspect's vehicle
- Jemmy marks on ripped lead on roof
- Jemmy from suspect's coat pocket

Drugs eg:

- Fingermarks on drugs paraphernalia at cannabis cultivation
- Fingerprints from suspects
- Footwear marks on plastic sheeting used to make drug bags at suspected drugs dealer's residence
- Footwear from suspect

Techniques for preserving impressions

Street Robbery eg:
- Footwear mark in mud near incident/police in attendance/good weather/CSI en route—**Leave** in situ.
- Footwear mark in mud near incident/police in attendance/threat of rain/CSI en route—**Protect** with clean waterproof item, eg washing up bowl.

Burglary eg:
- Torn, empty envelope that had contained cash definitely handled by offender in bedroom of house identified during report of incident on phone—Police call taker will request victim to **leave** the envelope in situ for police.
- Torn, empty envelope that had contained cash definitely handled by offender in bedroom of hotel/police in attendance/CSI en route—**Protect** or carefully **move** the envelope to a secure location.
- Torn, empty envelope that had contained cash definitely handled by offender in bedroom of hotel/police in attendance/CSI unable to attend for 12 hours—**Seize** envelope.

Theft (including shoplifting) eg:
- Tyre marks in mud beneath roof with lead missing/police in attendance/CSI en route—**Leave** in situ.
- Tyre marks in mud beneath roof with lead missing/police in attendance/threat of rain/CSI en route—**Protect** with clean waterproof material.
- Suspect's van identified—**Move** the vehicle to a designated garage which contains secure examination bays that CSI can use and **seize** the tyres.

Continued overleaf

1 Evidence Management

Continued

Vehicle Crime eg:

- Theft from vehicle on owner's drive/report of incident on phone/ good weather/CSI en route—Police call taker will request the owner to **leave** the vehicle and items on drive for CSI.
- Theft from vehicle on owner's drive/report of incident on phone/ threat of rain/CSI en route—Police call taker will request the owner **protects** the vehicle by carefully driving it under cover of a carport/garage and await CSI.
- Found stolen vehicle abandoned in field—**Move** to a designated garage with secure examination bays for use of CSI.
- Attempt theft of vehicle on owners drive/police in attendance/CSI unable to attend for 12 hours—**Seize** piece of broken steering column cowling with visible fingermarks in dust on internal surface.

Criminal Damage eg:

- Footwear marks in paint on pavement near graffiti/police in attendance/good weather/CSI en route—**Leave** in situ and await CSI.
- Footwear marks in paint on pavement near graffiti/police in attendance/threat of rain/CSI en route—**Protect** impression with clean waterproof item and await CSI.
- Suspect arrested for criminal damage (graffiti)—**Seize** suspect's footwear.

Drugs eg:

- Visible fingermarks on drugs equipment at the scene of cannabis cultivation in house/police in attendance/CSI en route—**Leave** items and await CSI.
- Visible fingermarks on drugs equipment at the scene of cannabis cultivation in garden/police in attendance/threat of rain/CSI en route—**Protect** items with clean waterproof material and await CSI.
- Visible fingermarks on drugs equipment connected with cannabis cultivation in garden/police in attendance/raining hard/CSI en route—**Move** items to a secure location and await CSI.
- Visible fingermarks on drugs equipment at the scene of cannabis cultivation in garden/police in attendance/raining hard/CSI unable to attend for 12 hours—**Seize** items.

2.13.3 Physical Fits

Street Robbery

- Broken piece of button found at scene.
- Damaged button on suspect's clothing.
- Victims' broken fingernail.
- Piece of broken fingernail on suspect's clothing.

Burglary

- Edge of adhesive tape placed by offender over window.
- Edge of adhesive tape found in suspect's clothing pocket.
- Area of damaged, flaky paint on external window-sill of point of entry.
- Paint flake found on suspect's fleece.

Theft (including shoplifting)

- Edge of damaged lead on roof of church where lead had been stolen.
- Edge of quantity of lead found on back of suspect's lorry.
- Torn hole in tarpaulin side of lorry.
- Piece of tarpaulin found nearby on which finger-marks of offender were developed and identified.

Vehicle Crime

- Broken tip of screwdriver in lock of vehicle.
- Handle of screwdriver with broken tip in suspect's pocket.
- Piece of broken piece of steering column cowling with blood staining found on drive where vehicle had been stolen.
- Broken cowling around steering column of found abandoned vehicle.

Criminal Damage

- Broken knife blade in tyre of lorry.
- Knife with broken blade found in suspect's vehicle.
- Piece of unidentified, planed wood near damaged cars in garage forecourt.
- Damaged, wooden baseball bat recovered from suspect's home address.

Drugs

- Paper wrap containing unknown white powder.
- Torn paper from magazine found in suspect's home address.
- Edge of polythene bag containing unknown white powder.
- Edge of polythene sheeting found in suspect's home address.

Techniques for preserving physical fits

Continued overleaf

1 Evidence Management

Continued

Street Robbery eg:
- Location of violent incident/police in attendance/CSI en route/ good weather/broken piece of button on pavement—**Leave** in situ.
- Location of violent incident/police in attendance/CSI en route/ very windy/broken piece of button on pavement—**Protect** the button with sterile cover or **move** to a more sheltered area.
- Suspect(s) arrested—**Seize** and package all items of outer clothing.

Burglary eg:
- Area of damaged, flaky paint on external windowsill of point of entry/police in attendance/good weather/CSI en route—**Leave** untouched.
- Area of damaged, flaky paint on external windowsill of point of entry/police in attendance/threat of rain/CSI en route—**Protect** with a clean, waterproof material.
- Paint flake found on suspect's fleece—**Seize** the item of clothing.

Theft (including shoplifting) eg:
- Edge of damaged lead on roof of church where lead had been stolen/police in attendance/CSI en route—**Leave** in situ.
- Quantity of lead found on back of suspect's lorry—Arrange for the vehicle and contents to be **moved** and **protected** from further damage by being recovered to a designated garage with secure examination bays for use of CSI.
- Piece of damaged lead found on public road near damaged roof/ CSI with a long journey time—**Seize** and package the piece of lead.

Vehicle Crime eg:
- Theft from vehicle on owner's drive/report of incident on phone includes description of screwdriver tip in door lock/good weather/CSI en route—police call taker will request the owner to **leave** the vehicle on the drive for CSI.
- Theft from vehicle on owner's drive/report of incident on phone includes description of screwdriver tip in door lock/good weather/CSI en route—police call taker will request the car is not used to enable the potential evidence to be **protected**.
- Found stolen vehicle abandoned in field with screwdriver tip in door lock—**Move** to a designated garage with secure examination bays for the use of CSI.
- Handle of screwdriver with broken tip in suspect's pocket—**Seize** the screwdriver.

Continued overleaf

Continued

Criminal Damage eg:
- Broken knife blade in tyre of lorry/police in attendance/CSI en route—**Leave** in situ.
- Broken knife blade in tyre of lorry/police in attendance/lorry needs to be moved for access/CSI en route—**Protect** the knife blade and have vehicle **moved** by lifting and dragging.
- Suspect arrested carrying small knife with a broken blade—**Seize** the knife.

Drugs eg:
- Torn magazine pages found in suspect drug dealer's home address/police in attendance/CSI en route—**Leave** in situ.
- Torn magazine pages found in dustbin at suspect drug dealer's home address/police in attendance/CSI en route—**Protect** or **move** dustbin to ensure it is not emptied by refuse collection.
- Suspect drug dealer arrested—**Seize** all paper drug wraps being carried by suspect.

2.14 **Preserving Forensic Evidence at Major, Critical, and Major Crime Incidents**

During the initial response to a serious incident, it is not always obvious whether death or serious injury is a result of natural causes, an accident, suicide, or crime. If in doubt, the incident should be investigated as if it were the result of a criminal act, until there is overwhelming evidence to prove otherwise. The following section provides additional and generic information for scene preservation at major, critical, and major crime incidents. To begin with, there is an overview of all three situations and examples are provided to help identify the characteristics of each of the incidents.

1 Evidence Management

<table>
<tr><td colspan="2" align="center">Major Incidents</td></tr>
</table>

Major Incidents

Any emergency:
- requiring the implementation of special arrangements by one or more of the emergency services; and
- directly or indirectly involving large numbers of people.

Examples might include the:
- rescue and transportation of large numbers of casualties;
- combined resources of the police, fire, and ambulance services in large numbers;
- mobilization of other emergency services and support services such as the local authority to deal with the threat of death, serious injury, or homelessness to a large number of people;
- handling of large number of enquiries generated by the public and the media.

For initial actions by first officer at the scene of a major incident, see section 2.14.1 below.

Critical Incidents	Major Crime Incidents
Deaths or potentially fatal injuries resulting from incidents on the following transport networks: • Road • Rail • Air	• Suspicious deaths • Unexplained deaths • Murders • Serious assaults • Serious sexual assaults • Fatal fires
For scene preservation see section 2.14.3 below	For scene preservation see section 2.14.3 below

2.14.1 Initial Actions by First Officer at the Scene of Major and Critical Incidents

1. If any of the criteria in the major incidents box above have been satisfied, the control room must be informed that a 'major incident' is being declared.
2. An initial assessment should be conducted using the mnemonic SAD CHALETS (see section 2.14.2 below) and the results given to the control room as soon as possible.

3. At a major incident, the first officer at the scene should not become personally involved in rescue work but initially take charge until relieved by a supervisor and/or manager.
4. Contact with the control room should be maintained at all times.
5. Once the first officer at the scene has been relieved by a supervisor and/or manager, the process of scene preservation should be commenced (see section 2.14.3 below).

2.14.2 Sad Chalets

Mnemonic

S — Survey	=	Look at the scene on approach and on arrival
A — Assess	=	Make an initial assessment of the incident
D — Disseminate	=	Inform control room of the below information . . .
C — Casualties	=	Approximate numbers of dead, injured, and uninjured
H — Hazards	=	Location of present and potential dangers
A — Access	=	Routes to and from the incident for emergency vehicles
L — Location	=	An exact location of the incident using maps or landmarks
E — Emergency	=	A list of services present and ones which are still required
T — Type	=	A description of the incident, eg transport and/or buildings
S — Safety	=	Continually make dynamic risk assessments

2.14.3 Generic Scene Preservation at Major, Critical, and Major Crime Incidents

1.	Conduct an Initial Assessment (if not already completed)	
	• give control room a situation report • adopt an investigative approach to the situation	• observe the scene • make notes • draw diagrams if appropriate/visually record

2.	Make the Scene Safe	
	• ensure the incident does not escalate • check for potential hazards such as electricity and debris	• check for insecure items or material in the immediate area • divert or slow nearby traffic

3.	Preserve Life	
	• check for vital signs of the victim • apply first aid and request medical response if required	• minimize loss of evidence if medical assistance is required, eg make written and visual records

4.	Preserve the Scene	
Identify...		
	• the primary crime scene • routes taken by the victim and suspect	• adjoining and secondary crime scenes • potential locations of evidence
Secure...		
	• the crime scene by restricting entry to authorized personnel only • information by commencing a crime scene log	• the area with a cordon using tape, other officers, or blocking entrances • the exit and entry points by identifying a common approach path

Protect...	
• the scene from further disturbance by humans or animals	• evidence by ensuring protective clothing is worn by those entering the crime scene

5.	Identify Sources of Forensic Evidence
	See section 2.5 above.

Further Reading

'Forensic Guidance' by Kent Police (unpublished)

The ACPO Good Practice Guide for Computer based Electronic Evidence, available at: <http://www.acpo.police. uk/asp/policies/Data/ACPO%20Guidelines%20v18. pdf>

The London Emergency Services Liaison Panel—Major Incident Procedure Manual, available at: <http://www. met. police.uk/leslp/docs/Major_incident_procedure_ manual_ 7th_ed.pdf>

The ACPO Road Death Investigation Manual, available at: <http://www.acpo.police.uk/asp/policies/Data/road_ death_ investigation_manual_18x12x07.pdf>

Chapter 3
Stop and Search

3.1 **Introducing Stop and Search**

A core function of the police service is to prevent and detect crime. A key power given to police officers is the ability to stop and search individuals, or their vehicles, to establish whether they are in possession of weapons, stolen articles, or other items which may be used to commit crimes.

The lawful use of stop and search is regulated by the Police and Criminal Evidence Act 1984 (PACE) and the accompanying Codes of Practice. In addition to using these powers lawfully under PACE, police officers must ensure searches are proportionate and necessary to avoid breaching Article 5 of the European Convention on Human Rights, which seeks to protect a person's right to liberty and security. This means that before conducting a search, officers must either have 'reasonable suspicion' that the person has committed an offence, or consider that the search is 'reasonably necessary' to prevent an offence.

Meanwhile, Article 14 of the European Convention on Human Rights protects people from unlawful discrimination on any ground such as sex, race, colour, language, or religion. Police officers are not entitled to use their stop and search powers solely on the grounds of a person's race or colour.

Under the Race Relations (Amendment) Act 2000, it is unlawful for a public authority to do any act which constitutes discrimination, and the police service (alongside all public authorities) has a duty to eliminate unlawful discrimination, promote equality of opportunity between people of different racial groups, and promote good relations between people of different racial groups.

Historically, the service has a poor record in respect of stop and search. Public enquiry reports such as the Scarman Report and the Stephen Lawrence Inquiry Report identified that the disproportionate use of these powers can damage public confidence and, in particular, lead to tension in black and minority ethnic (BME) communities (see also Stone and Pettigrew, 2000; and the Macpherson Report, 1999). Heavy-handed police operations using these powers have occasionally given rise to confrontation between the community and the police, and even rioting.

When used correctly, stop and search can be an effective crime prevention tool. However, this is a complex area of policing and the service faces a challenge to prevent the erosion of public confidence, thus achieving exactly the opposite of the intended outcome of stop and search: a more peaceful and secure community.

3.2 **Regulating Stop and Search**

Section 95(1) of the Criminal Justice Act 1991 requires the Government to monitor the police service's use of stop and search powers and to produce annual figures in the *Statistics on Race and the Criminal Justice System* (this responsibility was passed from the Home Office to the Ministry of Justice in 2007). Section 95(1) has the dual aim of:

1. improving positive outcomes of searches; and
2. reducing disproportionality in stop and search.

In relation to the first aim, success is measured by the number of positive outcomes from searches—ie those which result in the recovery of property or lead to arrests. Theoretically, if the police use their powers correctly, a high percentage of arrests should result from stop and searches. However, in practice, statistics over a 10-year period show that on average, only 12 per cent of such searches actually achieve a positive outcome.

Dealing with the second aim, searches of black and Asian people have risen steadily over a 10-year period. For example, in 1997/8, 82 per cent of people searched were white European, 11 per cent were black, 5 per cent were Asian, and 2 per cent were classed in 'other non-white' groups. Whereas in 2006/07, 74 per cent of people searched were white European, 15.9 per cent were black, 8.1 per cent were Asian, and 2 per cent were in 'other non-white' groups.

Using Home Office calculations on ethnicity, if stop and searches were conducted in proportion to the population in England and Wales, statistics from the year 2006/07 *should* show that 95 per cent of people searched were white European, 2 per cent were black, 3 per cent were Asian, and 1 per cent were in 'other non-white' groups. The figures appear to show that police officers stop and search 20 per cent more people from minority communities than would seem justifiable. This means that if you are a black person, you are *seven times* more likely to be stopped and searched than a white person living in your community. As an Asian person, you are *twice* as likely to be stopped than a white person.

Neither the police service nor the Home Office has been able to accurately identify why so few searches result in a positive outcome, or why searches of people from minority groups are so disproportionate.

In 2004, the Home Office formed the Stop and Search Action Team (SSAT) to advise the police on how to use stop and search more effectively, in a way that should increase the community's confidence in their use of this power. The SSAT is overseen by an independent community panel which works with the Home Office, the police, Police Authorities, and local communities.

A SSAT *Stop and Search Manual* was produced as a guide in the practice of stop and search to all parties in the police who have a role to play or can impact on the policy and is divided into five distinct areas:

- Policy
- Operation
- Supervision/monitoring
- Community
- Training.

The SSAT *Manual* outlines the responsibilities of Police Authorities and Chief Officers to strategically manage policy making, training, and community liaison. Guidance is also provided for superintendents as to how stop and search policies should be implemented in their command areas.

The *Manual* offers further advice to frontline supervisors on briefing and tasking their staff, to ensure that stop and search is directed towards local problems and priorities in accordance with the National Intelligence Model (NIM). Guidance is also given on supervising poor performance or discriminatory behaviour.

The Home Office anticipates that if all the individuals and departments involved in the process comply with their responsibilities, issues relating to disproportionality and achieving positive outcomes from stop and searches should improve.

3.3 **Stop and Search—Legislative Powers**

The police have numerous powers to stop and search individuals and their vehicles, originating from various Acts of Parliament. For example, under section 47 of the Firearms Act 1968, a person or their vehicle may be searched where there is reasonable suspicion that the person is carrying a firearm. A full list of these powers can be found in ANNEX A, Code A of the PACE Codes of Practice. In this chapter, we will focus on those powers most commonly used by the police.

Regardless of where the power originates from, all stops and searches must be conducted in accordance with guidance laid out in Code A of the PACE Codes of Practice.

3.3.1 Stop and Search Powers Under Section 1 of PACE

This is the power of search most commonly used by police officers. Section 1 of PACE states:

(1) A constable may exercise any power conferred by this section—
    (a) in any place to which at the time when he proposes to exercise the power the public or any section of the public has access, on payment or otherwise, as of right or by virtue of express or implied permission; or
    (b) in any other place to which people have ready access at the time when he proposes to exercise the power but which is not a dwelling.
(2) Subject to subsection (3) to (5) below, a constable—
    (a) may search—
        (i) any person or vehicle;
        (ii) anything which is in or on a vehicle,
        for stolen or prohibited articles or any article to which subsection (8A) below applies or any firework to which subsection (8B) below applies; and
    (b) may detain a person or vehicle for the purpose of such a search.
(3) This section does not give a constable power to search a person or vehicle or anything in or on a vehicle unless he has reasonable grounds for suspecting that he will find stolen or prohibited articles or any article to which subsection (8A) below applies.

Sections 1(1)(a) and (b) restrict the use of stop and searches to places where the public has access. This includes a street or a park, or even a place where the member of the public has had to pay to enter, such as a cinema or a football ground. The term 'as of right or by virtue of express or implied permission' refers to the fact that the person could be in a primarily private place, but one which he/she and other members of the public have been invited into at that time (such as a private art gallery or museum).

Note that section 1(1)(b) prohibits a constable from exercising this power in a dwelling; however, section 1(4) states:

> (4) If a person is in a garden or yard occupied with and used for the purposes of a dwelling or on other land so occupied and used, a constable may not search him in the exercise of the power conferred by this section unless the constable has reasonable grounds for believing—
>   (a) that he does not reside in the dwelling; and
>   (b) that he is not in the place in question with the express or implied permission of a person who resides in the dwelling.

There is a similar power under section 1(5) of PACE to search a vehicle which is on land, or in a garden or yard of a dwelling.

Under section 1(3), a constable must have 'reasonable grounds for suspecting' that he/she will find the article(s) as a result of the search. The PACE Codes of Practice, Code A, paragraphs 2.2 to 2.11 contain comprehensive guidance on this subject and below are some examples of what would and would not amount to reasonable grounds:

Reasonable Grounds

- Information, and/or intelligence relevant to the likelihood of finding an article; eg an officer encounters someone trying to hide something in the street at night.
- Information describing an article being carried, a suspected offender, or a person who has been seen carrying a type of article known to have been stolen recently.
- Reliable information/intelligence that gang members habitually carry weapons or controlled drugs, and wear a distinctive item of clothing or other means of identification to indicate their membership of the gang; the distinctive item of clothing or other means of

identification may provide reasonable grounds to stop
and search a person.

- As a result of questioning a person, the reasonable grounds
  for suspicion necessary to detain that person may be confirmed because of an unsatisfactory explanation.
- A police officer may have reasonable grounds to suspect that a person is in *innocent* possession of a stolen
  or prohibited article or other item for which he or she is
  empowered to search.

Not Reasonable Grounds

- Reasonable suspicion can never be supported on the basis
  of personal factors alone, without reliable supporting
  intelligence or information or some specific behaviour
  by the person concerned.
- A person's race, age, appearance, or the fact that the person is known to have a previous conviction, cannot be
  used alone or in combination with each other as the reason for searching that person.
- Reasonable suspicion cannot be based on generaliza-
  tions or stereotypical images of certain groups or categories of people as more likely to be involved in criminal
  activity.
- If, as a result of questioning before a search, or other circumstances which come to the attention of the officer,
  there cease to be reasonable grounds for suspecting that
  an article is being carried of a kind for which there is a
  power to stop and search, no search may take place.
- There is no power to stop or detain a person in order
  to find grounds for a search. Police officers have many
  encounters with members of the public which do not
  involve detaining people against their will.

Note that under section 1(2)(b), a constable may detain the
person in order to conduct the search—and may use force
if necessary. If the constable finds a stolen or prohibited
article, he or she may seize it (section 1(6)).

3.3.2 Stolen or Prohibited Articles

Section 1(2)(a) of PACE outlines the 'articles' which a constable may seek, when conducting a search. These can be broadly broken down into stolen, or prohibited articles. Stolen articles do not require a specific definition, however, section 1 of PACE does provide a definition of prohibited articles:

> (7) An article is prohibited for the purposes of this Part of this Act if it is—
>   (a) an offensive weapon; or
>   (b) an article—
>   (i) made or adapted for use in the course of or in connection with an offence to which this sub-paragraph applies; or
>   (ii) intended by the person having it with him for such use by him or by some other person.
> (8) The offences to which subsection (7)(b)(1) above applies are—
>   (a) burglary;
>   (b) theft;
>   (c) offences under section 12 of the Theft Act 1968 (taking motor vehicle or other conveyance without authority);
>   (d) fraud (contrary to section 1 of the Fraud Act 2006); and
>   (e) offences under section 1 of the Criminal Damage Act 1971 (destroying or damaging property).

Subsections (7) and (8) divide articles into those which will be used for a crime, for example a stolen credit card to commit a fraud and offensive weapons. An 'offensive weapon' is any article which has been made or adapted for use for causing injury to persons, or which is *intended* by the person having it with him for such use.

There are further powers to conduct searches for prohibited (dangerous) fireworks, under section 1, subsections (8B) and (8C).

3.3.3 **Stop and Search Powers Under Other Legislation**

Section 32 of the Police and Criminal Evidence Act 1984 contains a specific power to search an arrested person for evidence relating to an offence, or if there are reasonable grounds for believing the person may present a danger to himself/herself or others and has something with him or her which may be used to escape from lawful custody.

In this section, we will be focusing on stop and search powers, under other legislation, which are used to prevent and detect offences.

Misuse of Drugs Act 1971

Under section 23(2) of the Misuse of Drugs Act 1971, if a constable has reasonable grounds to suspect that any person is in possession of a controlled drug in contravention of this Act or of any regulations made thereunder, the constable may:

(a) search that person, and detain him for the purpose of searching him;

(b) search any vehicle or vessel in which the constable suspects that the drug may be found, and for that purpose require the person in control of the vehicle or vessel to stop it;

(c) seize and detain, for the purposes of proceedings under this Act, anything found in the course of the search which appears to the constable to be evidence of an offence under this Act.

These powers are relatively straightforward. 'Reasonable grounds to suspect' is similar to 'reasonable suspicion'. Vehicles and vessels will include planes, boats, and hovercraft.

A search under this Act may take place anywhere (in contrast to a stop and search under section 1, which may only take place in a public place). This is necessary because drug searches are often conducted in dwelling houses after the police have entered to execute a search warrant and people inside need to be searched.

Criminal Justice and Public Order Act 1994

Section 60(1) of the Criminal Justice and Public Order Act 1994 states that if a police officer of or above the rank of inspector reasonably believes:

(a) that incidents involving serious violence may take place in any locality in his area, and that it is expedient to give an authorisation under this section to prevent their occurrence, or

(b) that persons are carrying dangerous instruments or offensive weapons in any locality in his police area without good reason,

he may give an authorization that the powers conferred by this section shall be exercisable at any place within that locality for a specified period not exceeding 24 hours.

When a direction has been given under this section, a constable in uniform may stop *any* pedestrian and search them or anything they are carrying for offensive weapons or dangerous instruments. The constable may also stop *any* vehicle and search the vehicle, its driver, and any passenger for similar weapons or instruments.

This power is a step away from the general powers to search under PACE. Although the inspector must reasonably believe that incidents involving serious violence may take place, or that persons are carrying dangerous instruments or offensive weapons, police officers conducting searches are *not* required to form a separate reasonable belief that a person is carrying a weapon and can search any person in the 'locality'.

In practical terms, this power is often used at football matches, to search large crowds on their way to or returning from stadiums. The authorization removes the need for police officers to consider whether the conditions of section 1 of PACE apply to each individual being searched.

Code A, Note for Guidance 10 of the PACE Codes of Practice

The powers under section 60 are separate from and additional to the normal stop and search powers which require reasonable grounds to suspect an individual of carrying an offensive weapon (or other article). Their overall purpose is to prevent serious violence and the widespread carrying of weapons which might lead to persons being seriously injured by disarming potential offenders in circumstances where other powers would not be sufficient. They should not therefore be used to replace or circumvent the normal powers for dealing with routine crime problems.

The reasonable belief on the part of the authorizing officer must have an objective basis, for example: intelligence or relevant information such as a history of antagonism and violence between particular groups; previous incidents of violence at, or connected with, particular events or locations; a significant increase in knife-point robberies in a limited area; or reports that individuals are regularly carrying weapons in a particular locality (see Code A, Note for Guidance 11).

The authorizing inspector must confirm in writing the period during which the authorization is to last, and the geographical area in which searches may be conducted. The period authorized must not be longer than appears reasonably necessary to prevent incidents of serious violence, or to deal with the problem of carrying dangerous instruments or offensive weapons. It may not exceed 24 hours, (see Code A, paragraph 2.13).

If an inspector gives an authorization under this section, he/she must inform an officer of or above the rank of superintendent as soon as practicable. The superintendent *may* extend the period for a further 24 hours if violence or the carrying of dangerous instruments or offensive weapons has occurred, or is suspected to have occurred, and the continued use of the powers is necessary to prevent or deal with such activity. That direction must also be given in writing at the time or as soon as practicable afterwards.

Sporting Events (Control of Alcohol etc.) Act 1985

Police officers are granted additional search powers to deal with alcohol at sporting events. Section 7 of the Sporting Events (Control of Alcohol etc.) Act 1985 states:

(1) A constable may, at any time during the period of a designated sporting event at any designated sports ground, enter any part of the ground for the purpose of enforcing the provisions of this Act.

(2) A constable may search a person he has reasonable grounds to suspect is committing or has committed an offence under this Act, and may arrest such a person.

(3) A constable may stop a public service vehicle (within the meaning of section 1 of this Act) or a motor vehicle to which section 1A of this Act applies and may search such a vehicle or a railway passenger vehicle if he has reasonable grounds to suspect that an offence under that section is being or has been committed in respect of the vehicle.

The Secretary of State may 'designate' either a sporting event or a sports ground. For example, all English Premiership football grounds are 'designated', as are Premiership, European, and International football matches. Matches and grounds in lower divisions are not automatically designated, but their status could be changed if, for example, the team was to play a Premiership team in a cup game. This Act is not restricted to football matches, but is more commonly used in this sport.

The aim is to prevent alcohol consumption in vehicles such as coaches, mini-buses, and trains en route to the ground, as well as prohibiting the possession of alcohol inside the ground, while a match is being played. Any person who is in possession of alcohol, or is drunk at such an event/ground, or whilst attempting to enter the ground, commits an offence. Similarly, an offence is committed where a person is in possession of alcohol whilst in a vehicle to which this Act applies on their way to a designated event/ground.

Under section 7, a constable may search a person or a vehicle they are in if there are reasonable grounds to suspect an offence under this Act is being, or has been committed—and to seize any alcohol found.

Similar powers of search and arrest exist to prevent possession of a firework or flare either at the ground, or while trying to enter the ground.

Terrorism Act 2000

The stop and search powers given to police officers under the Terrorism Act 2000 (TACT) form a critical part of the Prevent and Pursue strands of the Government's CONTEST strategy (Home Office, 2006) to deal with terrorsim.

Schedule 7 to the Act provides police officers, customs officers, and immigration officers working in airports and other ports additional powers to detain and question people to establish links with terrorism. They may also search a person or any vehicle, vessel, or aircraft they are, or were, in for such evidence. However, in this chapter we will be concentrating on police use of stop and search under TACT.

Firstly, you need to understand what the terms 'terrorism' and 'terrorist' mean. Terrorism is the use or threat of action where the threat is designed to influence the Government or an international governmental organization, or to intimidate the public or a section of the public, and the use or threat is made for the purpose of advancing a political, religious, or ideological cause. The action described is one which:

- involves serious violence against a person;
- involves serious damage to property;
- endangers a person's life, other than that of the person committing the action;
- creates a serious risk to the health or safety of the public or a section of the public; or
- is designed seriously to interfere with or seriously to disrupt an electronic system.

1 Evidence Management

Section 40(1) of TACT defines a 'terrorist' as a person who:

(a) has committed an offence under any of sections 11, 12, 15 to 18, 54 and 56 to 63 of TACT, or
(b) is or has been concerned in the commission, preparation or instigation of acts of terrorism.

The offences mentioned above include:

- under sections 11 and 12—a person is a member of, or supports a proscribed (banned) organization (designated by the Secretary of State, such as Islamic or Irish extremist groups);
- under sections 15 to 18—a person is involved in funding terrorist activities, such as possessing, providing, receiving, arranging, concealing, moving, or transferring money or other property, intending it to be used for terrorism;
- under sections 54 and 56 to 63—a person is involved in:

  - providing instruction or training for firearms or explosives, or chemical, biological, or nuclear weapons;
  - receiving instructions or training for firearms or explosives, or chemical, biological, or nuclear weapons;
  - directing, at any level, the activities of an organization concerned in the commission of acts of terrorism;
  - inciting acts of terrorism outside the UK;
  - funding acts of terrorism outside the UK;
  - committing acts of terrorism outside the UK.

Under section 41(1) of TACT, a constable may arrest any person whom he/she reasonably suspects to be a terrorist.

Section 43(1) of TACT outlines the general power to stop and search a person under this legislation:

> A constable may stop and search a person whom he reasonably suspects to be a terrorist to discover whether the person has in his possession anything which may constitute evidence that he is a terrorist.

This broad power to stop and search may be conducted to discover evidence relating to any of the offences listed above. However, as with stop and search under section 1 of PACE, the constable must 'reasonably suspect' that the person is a terrorist, and that evidence of this fact is likely to be found as a result of the search.

There is a separate power under section 43(2) to search a person who has been arrested under section 41(1) to discover whether he/she has in his or her possession anything which may constitute evidence that he/she is a terrorist. A constable may seize and retain anything discovered in the course of a search and which he/she reasonably suspects may constitute evidence that the person is a terrorist, (see section 43(4)).

A search of a person under this section must be carried out by someone of the same sex (section 43(3)).

Section 44 of TACT provides the police with a further power to stop and search people and vehicles, which is similar to section 60(1) of the Criminal Justice and Public Order Act 1994. Authority may be given under section 44 if it is considered *expedient for the prevention of acts of terrorism* and it will:

(1) authorise any constable in uniform to stop a vehicle in an area or at a place specified in the authorisation and to search—

  (a) the vehicle;
  (b) the driver of the vehicle;
  (c) a passenger in the vehicle;
  (d) anything in or on the vehicle or carried by the driver or a passenger.

(2) authorise any constable in uniform to stop a pedestrian in an area or at a place specified in the authorisation and to search—

  (a) the pedestrian;
  (b) anything carried by him.

An 'area' or 'place' will include internal waters adjacent to the area or place where the authorization is to apply and 'driver' will include the driver, captain, pilot, or other person with control of a train, or an aircraft, hovercraft or other vessel, or any member of its crew. A constable has the power to stop vehicles in order to search them under this section (although section 116(2) of TACT rather helpfully states that the constable does not have the power to stop an aircraft which is airborne!).

Authority under section 44 may only be given by a police officer of at least the rank of assistant chief constable (or the equivalent rank of Commander in the Metropolitan Police or City of London Police Force). The authorization may be given orally, but it must be confirmed in writing as soon as is reasonably practicable (section 44(5)).

Unlike an authorization given under the Criminal Justice and Public Order Act 1994 (which has a time limit of 24 hours unless extended), an authorization under *this* section is effective for 28 days. Because of the potential for intrusion of privacy on large numbers of the public, as an additional precaution the authorizing officer must also inform the Secretary of State as soon as is reasonably practicable. If the Secretary of State does not confirm the authorization within 48 hours from the time it was given, it will cease to have effect at the end of that 48-hour period.

This authorization allows a constable to search a vehicle or person for articles which could be used in connection with terrorism and to seize and retain such articles. The constable may, if necessary, use reasonable force to conduct the search (section 114(2)), and offences may be committed if a person fails to stop a vehicle when required to do so, or wilfully obstructs a constable exercising this power.

Similar to the search powers under section 60, a person may simply be searched because he or she is in the place specified in the authorization. It should be noted that the authorizing officer need only 'consider it expedient for the prevention of acts of terrorism' to grant an authorization, whereas under section 60 you will recall that the authorizing officer must 'reasonably believe' there will be incidents of serious violence or people carrying dangerous weapons. 'Expedient' means advantageous, but there is no mention of 'reasonable suspicion' in this section.

Code A, paragraph. 2.25 of the PACE Codes of Practice deals with disproportionality issues relating to searches under TACT, outlining that the selection of persons stopped under section 44 should reflect an objective assessment of the threat posed by the various terrorist groups active in Great Britain; and that the powers must not be used to stop and search for reasons unconnected with terrorism. Paragraph 2.25 states that officers must take particular care not to discriminate against members of minority ethnic groups in the exercise of these powers.

However, paragraph 2.25 does identify that there may be circumstances where it is appropriate for officers to take account of a person's ethnic origin in selecting persons to be stopped, in response to a specific terrorist threat (for example, some international terrorist groups are associated with particular ethnic identities).

The dilemma facing the police is how to identify a 'terrorist' from their physical appearance when the terrorist threat to the UK could come from anywhere. For example, in the London bombing campaign in 2005, terrorists inspired by Islamist extremism were British citizens brought up in British communities, and the people eventually charged in connection with the incidents were of African origin. Also recent terrorist suspects investigated in the UK have come originally from countries as diverse as Libya, Algeria, Jordan, Saudi Arabia, Iraq, and Somalia (see the Government's *Countering International Terrorism: The United Kingdom's Strategy* for further details).

In the publication *Working Together to Protect the Public: The Home Office Strategy 2008–11* it was identified that communities needed to be strengthened in order to deliver the *Prevent* strand of the Government's CONTEST strategy.

> **Working Together to Protect the Public: Home Office Strategy 2008–11**
>
> Perhaps the most important of all these partnerships is between these bodies, led by the Government, and our citizens and communities. Public awareness of the threat, understanding of the measures needed to combat it, and active support and cooperation with the police are critical to the success of the strategy.

Ultimately, the police service needs to find the balance between the use of effective, intelligence-led enforcement methods, such as stop and search, while seeking the support and confidence of the community, on whom they depend for assistance.

3.4 **Conduct of Searches**

> The primary purpose of stop and search powers is to enable officers to allay or confirm suspicions about individuals without exercising their power of arrest. Officers may be required to justify the use or authorisation of such powers, in relation both to individual searches and the overall pattern of their activity in this regard, to their supervisory officers or in court.
>
> **Paragraph 1.4 of Code A**

If there is no legal power of search available, an officer must *not* search a person, even if the person is prepared to submit to a search voluntarily.

Generally, there are three types of search:

- A 'pat down' search—eg checking a person's pockets or a bag they are carrying. In these circumstances, only the outer clothing may be removed;

- A **strip search**—removing more than the outer clothing, eg removing a shirt, trousers, or skirt;
- An **intimate search**—eg searching a person's bodily orifices. (These searches are subject to higher levels of authorization and may only be conducted in either a police station or in a hospital—they are not covered in this chapter).

There are strict guidelines in Code A of the Codes of Practice as to how searches should be conducted, and the extent to which a police officer may search. The guidelines refer to all searches covered in this chapter.

Code A, paragraph 3.1 states that all stops and searches must be carried out with courtesy, consideration, and respect for the person concerned. Searches have a significant impact on public confidence in the police and every reasonable effort must be made to minimize the embarrassment that a person being searched may experience. For some people their clothing and headgear is linked to their religion, such as Muslim women, Sikh men, Sikh or Hindu women, or Rastafarian men or women, and to ask them to remove certain items of headgear may cause dishonour and shame.

The Codes of Practice governing the conduct of a search can be broken down into four areas:

- steps to be taken before a search takes place;
- what the person must be told before a search takes place;
- what items of clothing can or cannot be removed;
- where the search should or should not take place.

3.4.1 Steps to be Taken Before a Search Takes Place

Police officers should attempt to seek the cooperation of the person to be searched in every case, even if the person initially objects to the search. This would include asking the person to hand over any articles voluntarily. However, if necessary, reasonable force may be used to conduct a search or to detain a person or vehicle for the purposes of a search, but only if it has been established that the person is unwilling to cooperate or resists (see paragraph 3.2).

Code A, Note for Guidance 2 concedes that in some circumstances preparatory questioning may be unnecessary, but in general a brief conversation or exchange will be desirable not only as a means of avoiding unsuccessful searches, but to explain the grounds for the stop/search, to gain cooperation, and to reduce any tension there might be surrounding the stop/search.

A search of a person in public should be completed as soon as possible and the length of time for which a person or vehicle may be detained must be reasonable and kept to a minimum (see paragraph 3.3).

3.4.2 What the Person must be Told Before a Search Takes Place

Under paragraph 3.8, before any search of a detained person or attended vehicle takes place, the officer *must* take reasonable steps to give the person to be searched or in charge of the vehicle the following information:

- that they are being detained for the purposes of a search;
- the officer's name (except in terrorism cases, or if the officer reasonably believes that giving his or her name might put him or her in danger—in these cases a warrant or other identification number should be given);
- the name of the police station to which the officer is attached;
- the legal power to conduct the search; and
- a clear explanation of:
  - the purpose of the search, in terms of the article or articles the officer is seeking; and
  - in the case of powers requiring reasonable suspicion, the grounds for that suspicion; or
  - in the case of powers which do not require reasonable suspicion, the nature of the power and any necessary

authorization, and the fact that the authorization has been given.

In summary, the officer must tell the person their name (unless the above exception applies) and where they work; that they are to be searched; the power they are using to conduct the search (eg section 1 of PACE, TACT etc); what they are searching for (eg offensive weapon, stolen goods); what their reasonable suspicion is or alternatively the fact that they do not require reasonable suspicion and an authorization has been given under section 60 or section 44 of TACT.

Before the search takes place the officer must also inform the person (or the owner or person in charge of the vehicle that is to be searched) of his/her entitlement to a copy of the record of the search, (see paragraph 3.10). We will examine the recording of searches in more depth later in this chapter.

If the person does not appear to understand what is being said (eg because they do not understand English or are deaf), the officer must take reasonable steps to bring the above information to his or her attention. If the person is accompanied by someone, then the officer must try to establish whether that person can interpret or otherwise help to give the required information (paragraph 3.11).

3.4.3 What Items of Clothing can or cannot be Removed

There is no power to require a person to remove any clothing in public other than an outer coat, jacket, or gloves, unless the officer is conducting a search under section 44 of TACT (when a person may be required to remove headgear and footwear in public) or under section 60AA of the Criminal Justice and Public Order Act 1994 (which empowers a constable to require a person to remove any item worn to conceal identity). However, although there is no power to require a person to do so, there is nothing to prevent an officer from asking a person voluntarily to remove more than an outer coat, jacket, or gloves in public.

When it comes to ordering the removal of religious headgear, the officer should permit the item to be removed out of public view, for example, in a police van or police station if there is one nearby. Where practicable, the item should be removed in the presence of an officer of the same sex as the person and out of sight of anyone of the opposite sex.

A search in public of a person's clothing which has not been removed must be restricted to superficial examination of outer garments. This does not, however, prevent an officer from placing a hand inside the pockets of the outer clothing, or feeling round the inside of collars, socks, and shoes if this is reasonably necessary in the circumstances to look for an article, or to remove and examine any item reasonably suspected to be the object of the search. For the same reasons, subject to the restrictions on the removal of headgear (referred to above), a person's hair may also be searched in public (paragraph 3.5).

The thoroughness and extent of a search will depend on what is suspected of being carried, and by whom. For example, if it is suspected that an article has been slipped into a person's pocket, then, unless there are other grounds for suspicion or the person has had an opportunity to move the article elsewhere, the search must be confined to that pocket. In the case of a small article which can readily be concealed, such as a drug, and which might be concealed anywhere on the person, a more extensive search may be necessary.

However, if the search is being conducted as a result of an authorization under section 60 or section 44 of TACT, which do not require reasonable grounds for suspicion, officers may make any reasonable search to look for items for which they are empowered to search.

3.4.5 **Where the Search should or should not take Place**

Generally, the search must be carried out at or near the place where the person or vehicle was first detained (see paragraph 3.4). However, in exceptional circumstances,

Note for Guidance 6 states that the person may be taken to a place nearby (eg a police station). If the person is taken somewhere else, the place should be located within a reasonable travelling distance. This power is often used for searches under the Misuse of Drugs Act 1971, where the person may have concealed drugs in their underclothes.

If it is necessary to conduct a more thorough search (eg by requiring a person to take off a T-shirt), this *must* be done out of public view. Such a search may take place in a police vehicle, *unless* the search involves exposing intimate parts of the body, in which case the person should be taken to a nearby police station. If there is no police station within a reasonable distance, the person may be taken to some other nearby location out of public view, but care must be taken to ensure that the location is suitable in that it enables the search to be conducted in private.

Any search involving the removal of more than an outer coat, jacket, gloves, headgear, or footwear may only be made by an officer of the same sex as the person searched and may not be made in the presence of anyone of the opposite sex unless the person being searched specifically requests it.

It should be noted that a search in a street will be regarded as being in public even though it may be empty when it begins.

If an officer is not in uniform, he or she must show their warrant card (but remember that searches under section 60 or section 44 of TACT may only be conducted by a constable in uniform).

3.5 **Recording Information**

In this section, we will examine the requirement for police officers to make records of searches they have conducted on people or vehicles. We will also explore the requirement to submit a record of a 'stop and account', which the Home Office introduced as a result of Recommendation 61 of the Stephen Lawrence Inquiry Report.

3.5.1 Recording Stop and Search

Under paragraph 4.1 of Code A, where a search has been carried out under any of the powers discussed in this chapter, the officer is required to make a record of that search *at the time it was conducted*. If there are exceptional circumstances which would make this wholly impracticable (eg in situations involving public disorder or when the officer's presence is urgently required elsewhere), the officer may make a record of the search at a later time. However, the officer must do this as soon as practicable afterwards.

A copy of the record must be given immediately to the person who has been searched, however, if this is not practicable (because of circumstances described above), the officer should make every reasonable effort to do so. The officer should consider providing the person with details of the station the person may attend for a copy of the record, for example in the form of a simple business card, adding the date of the stop and search. The officer must ask for the person's name, address, and date of birth, but there is no obligation on a person to provide these details and no power to detain the person if they are unwilling to do so (see paragraph 4.2).

Some police forces are trialling hand-held devices, which will electronically store the details of the search and provide the person with a receipt of the record of search, rather than a copy of the search record itself. In these circumstances, the receipt must state how the person can access the full record. The officer must inform the person that the receipt is in place of a full written record, that the full record is available in electronic or in hard copy format. Any person subject to a search may apply for a copy of the search record (if not given at the time) within 12 months of the date of the search.

Under Code A, paragraph 4.3, the following information must *always* be included in the record of a search even if the person does not wish to provide any personal details:

(i) the name of the person searched (or if it is withheld a description of the person);

(ii) a note of the person's self-defined ethnic background;

(iii) the date, time, and place that the person or vehicle was first detained;

(iv) when a vehicle is searched, its registration number;

(v) the date, time, and place the person or vehicle was searched (if different from (iii));

(vi) the purpose of the search;

(vii) the grounds for making it, or if not, the nature of the power and authorization under section 60 or section 44 of TACT;

(viii) its outcome (eg arrest or no further action);

(ix) a note of any injury or damage to property resulting from it;

(x) the identity of the officer making the search (except in terrorism cases, or if the officer reasonably believes that giving his or her name might put him or her in danger; in these cases a warrant or other identification number shall be given).

Note for Guidance 15 states that where a stop and search is conducted by more than one officer, the identity of *all* the officers engaged in the search must be recorded. Also, the record can be made by an officer present who was not the actual searching officer.

A record is required for each person and each vehicle searched. However, if a person is alone in a vehicle and both the person and the vehicle are searched, and the object and grounds of the search are the same, only one record need be completed. If more than one person in a vehicle is searched, separate records for each search of a person must be made. If only a vehicle is searched, the name of the driver and his or her self-defined ethnic background must be recorded, unless the vehicle is unattended (see paragraph 4.5).

If an officer searches an unattended vehicle, or anything in or on it, he or she must leave a notice in it (or on it, if things on it have been searched without opening it) recording the fact that it has been searched. The notice must include the name of the police station to which the officer is attached and state where a copy of the record of the search may be obtained and where any application for compensation should be directed. The vehicle must if practicable be left secure.

3.5.2 **Recording Stop and Account**

The Stephen Lawrence Inquiry Report highlighted the effect of stop and search on police community and race relations. The Report made a number of recommendations, designed to ensure the powers were exercised in a way which would be as effective as possible in reducing crime, but which would also promote trust and confidence in minority ethnic communities.

Recommendation 61, Stephen Lawrence Inquiry Report

That the Home Secretary, in consultation with Police Services, should ensure that a record is made by police officers of all 'stops' and 'stops and searches' made under any legislative provision (not just the Police and Criminal Evidence Act). Non-statutory or so called 'voluntary' stops must also be recorded. The record to include the reason for the stop, the outcome, and the self-defined ethnic identity of the person stopped. A copy of the record shall be given to the person stopped.

This recommendation was accepted and, following a number of pilots, police forces in England and Wales have been recording stops since 2005.

During the course of their duties, police officers frequently have to stop pedestrians or drivers of vehicles to ask them to 'assist with enquiries'. Sometimes a person may be a potential witness to an incident, but on other occasions, he or she may be a potential suspect. In the latter case, a police officer may need to ask the person to 'account' for articles in his or her possession, or for their presence in a particular place. This may either be to eliminate the person from an enquiry, or to determine whether, by their answers, the officer's suspicions have been confirmed. This type of stop would fall within the requirements of Recommendation 61 above.

Police officers *and* police community support officers (PCSOs) are required to make a record of such an encounter, identifying the same details as would be recorded in a stop and search form as described above, eg the time, date, and place of the encounter; the vehicle registration number; the reason why the person was questioned; the person's self-defined ethnic background; and the outcome of the encounter. Paragraph 4.12 also requires that a record of the encounter must be completed at the time and a copy given to the person who has been questioned.

However, in his Review of Policing published in 2008, Sir Ronnie Flanagan identified that the manually recorded system of stop and account which has evolved has led to unnecessary bureaucracy, with each encounter taking an average of seven minutes. Indeed, in the first two years of official recording between 2005/06 and 2006/07, the number of police stops increased by 33.6 per cent from 1.40 to 1.87 million. This compares to 888,700 recorded stop and searches in 2005/06 and 962,900 in 2006/07. The requirement to record stop and account practically trebled operational police officers' workload in respect of stop and search.

Sir Ronnie Flanagan concluded that the stop and account process was not actually fulfilling the need identified by the Stephen Lawrence Inquiry and was possibly leading to suspicion on the part of the members of the public involved because the police were recording details of sometimes ordinary conversations.

Interestingly, when it came to disproportionality, in 2006/07, black people were nearly two and a half times more likely to be stopped to account for themselves than white people. This national ratio is lower for 2006/07 (2.4:1) than for 2005/06 (2.9:1) and is notably lower than the national ratio for stop and search in the same period (7:1).

Asian people were only slightly more likely to be stopped to account for themselves than white people with a rate of 1.1:1 for 2006/07. This is lower than that recorded for 2005/06 when the rate was 1.3:1. Compared with stop and search for the same time period, the disproportionality ratio for Asian people for stop and account was lower. In 2006/07 and 2005/06 the rates for stop and search were 2.2:1 and 2.1:1 respectively compared with 1.1:1 and 1.3:1 for stop and account respectively.

Following extensive consultation (which included speaking to the family of Stephen Lawrence), Sir Ronnie Flanagan recommended in his review that this process should be streamlined to reduce the burden on operational staff.

The Government accepted the recommendation that an officer or PCSO who is involved in a stop and account will still have to record that fact, but will no longer be required to fill out a lengthy form. Instead, the officer or PCSO should provide that individual with a 'receipt' of the encounter in the form of a business card or similar document, and use their radio to record the encounter, including the ethnicity of the person subject to the encounter, to enable disproportionality monitoring.

As a result of these recommendations, Code A is likely to change, but some of the Code is still applicable. The guidance likely to remain is summarized below:

- If there are exceptional circumstances which would make it wholly impracticable for the officer/PCSO to record the stop (eg in situations involving public disorder or when the officer's presence is urgently required elsewhere), a record may be made of the stop as soon as possible, at a later time.
- A separate record need not be completed when an officer has stopped a vehicle and issued the driver with a Penalty Notice for driving offences, or given them a production form to produce their driving documents.

- If a person has been stopped and the recording criteria is not met, but the person nevertheless requests a record, the officer should still provide the individual with a 'receipt' of the encounter in the form of a business card or similar but record the fact that the encounter did not meet the criteria.
- There is no power to require the person questioned to provide personal details. If a person refuses to give their self-defined ethnic background, a record must still be completed, which includes the officer's description of the person's ethnic background.

It would be good to end this chapter with some sensible advice from the PACE Codes of Practice which applies to both stop and search and stop and account:

Code A, Note for Guidance 1

This Code does not affect the ability of an officer to speak to or question a person in the ordinary course of the officer's duties without detaining the person or exercising any element of compulsion. It is not the purpose of the code to prohibit such encounters between the police and the community with the co-operation of the person concerned and neither does it affect the principle that all citizens have a duty to help police officers to prevent crime and discover offenders.

The Note for Guidance further states that the duty to help police officers is a civic rather than a legal one; but when a police officer is trying to discover whether, or by whom, an offence has been committed he or she may question any person from whom useful information might be obtained. A person's unwillingness to reply does not alter this entitlement, but in the absence of a power to arrest, or to detain in order to search, the person is free to leave at will and cannot be compelled to remain with the officer.

Further Reading

Home Office (2006) *Countering International Terrorism: The United Kingdom's Strategy* (CONTEST), Home Office, London

Home Office (2006) *Stop and Search Explained: How police powers work in the community*

Home Office (2008) *The Review of Policing: Sir Ronnie Flanagan 2008*, Home Office, London

Home Office (2008) *Working Together to Protect the Public: The Home Office Strat- egy 2008–11*

Macpherson, W (1999) 'The Stephen Lawrence Inquiry, Report of an Inquiry by Sir William Macpherson' TSO, London

Ministry of Justice Bulletin, *Arrests for Recorded Crime (Notifiable Offences) and the Operation of Certain Police Powers under PACE England and Wales 2006/07*

Ministry of Justice Report, *Statistics on Race and the Criminal Justice System*—1997/8 to 2006/07

Stone, V and Pettigrew, N (2000) *The Views of the Public on Stops and Searches*, Home Office, London

The Scarman Report (1981)

Stephen Lawrence Inquiry Report (1999)

Stop and Search Action Team (SSAT), Home Office, ACPO and APA (2005) *Stop and Search Manual*

Chapter 4

Police Powers of Entry, Search, and Seizure

4.1 Introduction

This chapter examines police powers to enter and search *premises* either to seize evidence of an offence, or to arrest a person. These powers generally fall into two categories:

- search of premises under the authority of a warrant;
- search of premises without the authority of a warrant.

Changes to the Police and Criminal Evidence Act 1984 (PACE) mean that in some cases non-warranted police staff may enter and search premises to seize evidence of an offence and we will examine the circumstances under which this can take place in this chapter.

Any search of a premises, whether under a warrant or not, must be conducted in accordance with Code B of the PACE Codes of Practice. If it is necessary to search a *person* during a premises search, police officers must comply with Code A of the Codes of Practice (see Chapter 3 Stop and Search for the full provisions of Code A).

Finally, when searching premises, whether under the authority of a warrant or not, police officers must take into consideration the European Convention on Human Rights. Article 8 of the Convention states:

1. Everyone has the right to respect for his private and family life, his home and his correspondence.
2. There shall be no interference by a public authority with the exercise of this right except such as is in accordance with the law and is necessary in a democratic society in the interests of national security, public safety or the economic well being of the country, for the prevention of disorder or crime, for the protection of health or morals, or for the protection of the rights and freedoms of others.

Therefore, an unlawful search of a person's premises has the potential to amount to a breach of a person's human rights.

4.2 **Search of Premises under the Authority of a Warrant**

There are three general types of warrant that may be applied for:

- a **'specific premises warrant'**: a warrant to enter one premises on one occasion;
- an **'all premises warrant'**: a warrant to enter more than one premises (eg where it is suspected that there is evidence of an offence, or a person who is wanted, at more than one location);
- a **'multiple entry warrant'**: a warrant that allows a constable to enter a premises (or more than one premises) on more than one occasion (eg where it is suspected that the police are likely to find a significant amount of evidence which may take more than one visit to recover).

The flexibility to apply for different types of warrants was introduced by the Serious Organised Crime and Police Act 2005. Previously, the police were restricted to applying for a single warrant for each premises, and they could only enter the premises on one occasion.

Under section 23 of PACE, 'premises' will include any place, and in particular:

- any vehicle, vessel, aircraft, or hovercraft;
- any offshore installation;
- any renewable energy installation;
- any tent or moveable structure.

4.2.1 Grounds for Applying for a Search Warrant

The police derive their powers to search premises under warrants from several Acts of Parliament. The grounds (or reasons) for applying for a warrant vary. Table 4.1 shows some examples of when the police may apply warrants and the relevant Act authorizing the issue of a warrant:

The police often rely on information from third parties for their grounds to justify applying for a search warrant. Code B, paragraph 3.1 of the PACE Codes of Practice states:

> When information appears to justify an application, the officer must take reasonable steps to check the information is accurate, recent and not provided maliciously or irresponsibly.

An application may not be made on the basis of information from an anonymous source unless the police have sought corroboration from elsewhere. For example, the police should look for at least two pieces of reliable information before applying for a warrant. If the police use information from a registered informant in their application, there is no requirement to disclose that person's identity.

Whatever grounds the police believe they have, an application for a warrant must follow the set procedures as described in section 15 and section 16 of PACE, which are described below.

Table 4.1

Information	Grounds	Act of parliament
The police receive information that a wanted person they have been looking for is hiding in a house.	To search for, and arrest, a person who is wanted for a criminal offence.	Police and Criminal Evidence Act 1984, section 17(1)
The police receive information that a lock-up garage is storing stolen vehicles.	To search for, and seize, evidence (eg stolen vehicles) which is likely to be of substantial value to the investigation of the offence.	Police and Criminal Evidence Act 1984, section 8(1)
The police have traced an internet site to an office where it is believed a person is storing child pornography on a computer.	To search for, and seize, evidence (eg a computer) which is likely to be of substantial value to the investigation of the offence.	Police and Criminal Evidence Act 1984, section 8(1)
The police have been keeping observations on a house which is suspected to be a location where drug dealing is taking place.	To search for, and seize, any controlled drugs and/or documents relating to drug dealing.	Misuse of Drugs Act 1971, section 23(3)
The police have received information that a person is in a warehouse in possession of chemical equipment which may be used to manufacture a home-made bomb.	To enter premises to arrest a person who is or has been concerned in the commission, preparation, or instigation of acts of terrorism.	Terrorism Act 2000, section 42(1)

4.2.2 Applying for the Search Warrant

In order to conduct a search under the authority of a warrant, a constable must make an application to a justice of the peace (a magistrate) or a judge. Before he or she makes this application, a constable must seek the written authority of an officer of at least the rank of inspector (see Code B, paragraph 3.4). In urgent cases, if an inspector is not 'readily available', the senior officer on duty may authorize the application. (An application under the Terrorism Act 2000 must be made to a judge and must be supported by a signed written authority from an officer of superintendent rank or above.)

Applications must be made in person, which will involve the officer attending court with the written authority, which must outline the grounds for the request. However, a warrant may also be applied for out of hours, when the court is not sitting, which will involve the constable visiting an on-call justice of the peace. The constable will be required to take an oath before applying for the warrant and must be prepared to answer any question that the justice of the peace or judge hearing the application asks of him or her.

Under section 15(2) of PACE, where a constable applies for any such warrant, it shall be his or her duty:

  (a) to state—

     (i)   the ground on which he makes the application;
     (ii) the enactment under which the warrant would be issued; and
     (iii) if the application is for a warrant authorising entry and search on more than one occasion, the ground on which he applies for such a warrant, and whether he seeks a warrant authorising an unlimited number of entries, or (if not) the maximum number of entries desired;

  (b) to specify the matters set out in subsection (2A) below; and

  (c) to identify, so far as is practicable, the articles or persons to be sought.

Under section 15(2A), if the application relates to more than one premises, the officer must specify each premises which it is intended to enter and search and why it is necessary to do so. However, occasionally, the police may be aware that the person has access to more than one premises, but are only certain of one address. Their intention may be to search that address for evidence of an offence and hope to discover information linking the person to other addresses. Provided it was not reasonably practicable to specify all the premises when the application was made, an all premises warrant may be issued in such circumstances.

> **Note:** All premises and multiple entry warrants may only be applied for where it is intended to enter and *search* a premises under section 8 of PACE, as opposed to warrants to enter and *arrest* people under section 17(1) or section 42(1) of the Terrorism Act 2000.

The application must identify the person who is in occupation or control of any of the premises where the search is to take place (if it is reasonably practicable to specify the person(s) at that time). Under Code B, paragraph 3.3, the officer must also make reasonable enquiries to:

(i) establish if:

- anything is known about the likely occupier of the premises and the nature of the premises themselves;
- the premises have been searched previously and how recently;

(ii) obtain any other relevant information.

The application must outline the grounds for the search, what the police intend searching for, and, when the purpose of the proposed search is to find evidence of an alleged offence, an indication of how the evidence relates to the investigation. It may not always be possible to specify these points exactly (for example, the police may have reliable information that the person regularly keeps drugs at the premises, but the type and quantity are uncertain). Code B, paragraph 3.2 states that the officer must ascertain as *specifically as possible* the nature of the articles concerned and their location.

If the officer making the application does not comply with PACE and the Codes of Practice, any entry and search made under a warrant will be unlawful and any evidence seized as a result of the warrant may be excluded from a subsequent court case. If an application for a warrant is refused, no further application can be made unless the police find additional grounds (see Code B, paragraph 3.8).

4.2.3 When an Application for a Search Warrant has been Successful

If the application is successful the person granting it will sign the warrant and two copies must be made of it. If the application is for more than one premises, a separate copy will be required for each premises.

The warrant will specify whether authorization is given for entry on one occasion or for multiple entries. If authorization is given for multiple entries, the warrant must also specify whether the number of entries authorized is unlimited, or limited to a specified maximum.

The warrant must also specify:

- the name of the person making the application;
- the date on which it is issued;
- the enactment under which it is issued;
- each set of premises to be searched, or (in the case of an all premises warrant) the person who is in occupation or control of premises to be searched, together with any premises under his occupation or control which can be specified and which are to be searched,

and will identify, if practicable, the articles or persons to be sought.

4.2.4 Executing the Search Warrant

When officers enter a premises and search it under the authority of a warrant, the warrant is said to have been 'executed'. When executing a search warrant, the provisions of section 16 of PACE apply. Section 16 covers:

- the people authorized to enter and search;
- the timing of the search;
- how the search must be conducted;
- seizure and retention of property;
- action after searches.

We will deal with each of these areas separately below.

The People Authorized to Enter and Search

Under section 16(1) of PACE, a warrant to enter and search premises may be executed by any constable, which could be a different constable to the one who made the warrant application.

Schedule 4 to the Police Reform Act 2002 created an additional power, authorizing Investigating Officers (civilian investigators) to enter and search a premises under the authority of a warrant. Under section 16(2A) of PACE, Investigating Officers have the same powers as the constable in respect of:

(a) the execution of the warrant; and
(b) the seizure of anything to which the warrant relates.

However, an Investigating Officer may only enter a premises under a warrant when he or she is in the company, and under the supervision, of a constable (see section 16(2B)).

Code B, Note for Guidance 3C advises that a search warrant may authorize persons other than police officers or Investigating Officers to accompany the constable who executes the warrant. This includes, for example, any suitably qualified or skilled person or an expert in a particular field whose presence is needed to help accurately identify the material sought or to advise where certain evidence is most likely to be found and how it should be dealt with. It does not give them any right to force entry, but it gives them the right to be on the premises during the search and to search for or seize property without the occupier's permission.

The Timing of the Search

Section 16(3) of PACE states that the warrant must be executed within three months from the date of its issue. Any entry to premises outside this time limit will not be under the authority of a warrant and may be unlawful. As a safeguard, warrants not executed within the required time limit must be returned to the court (see section 16(10)(b)). The time limit for the execution of a warrant was extended by the Serious Organised Crime and Police Act 2005. Previously the police were required to execute a warrant within one month of the issue date.

Section 16(4) states:

> Entry and search under a warrant must be at a reasonable hour unless it appears to the constable executing it that the purpose of a search may be frustrated on an entry at a reasonable hour.

Code B, paragraph 6.4 builds on this requirement by also stating that the officer in charge of the search shall first try to communicate with the occupier, or any other person entitled to grant access to the premises, explain the authority under which entry is sought and ask the occupier to allow entry, unless:

- the premises to be searched are unoccupied;
- the occupier and any other person entitled to grant access are absent.

In reality, search warrants are rarely executed 'at a reasonable hour' because it is not difficult to justify executing them when the occupant of the premises is least prepared. Most warrants are executed early in the morning unless intelligence suggests officers are likely to find what they are looking for at a different time of the day.

Sometimes, the execution of warrants by the police can have an adverse effect on community relations. In such cases, Code B, paragraphs 3 to 5, state that the officer in charge must liaise with the local community liaison officer to assess the impact. However, if the case is urgent, the community liaison officer must be advised as soon as practicable after the search.

How the Search must be Conducted

Code B, paragraph 6.14 states that an officer must be appointed as the officer in charge of a search. They are responsible for making sure the search is conducted with discretion and in a manner that causes the least possible disruption to any business or other activities carried out on the premises.

The officer in charge of the search is also responsible for determining how many people are reasonably required for the search, and for ensuring that all those involved in a search are fully briefed about any powers to be exercised and the extent and limits within which it should be conducted (see Code B, Notes for Guidance 6B and 6C).

On entering the premises and before the search begins, the same officer is required to:

- identify him or herself, show their warrant card (if not in uniform) and state the purpose of and grounds for the search; and
- identify and introduce any person accompanying the officer on the search (such persons should carry identification for production on request) and briefly describe that person's role in the process.

Reasonable and proportionate force may be used to execute a warrant, which could include the use of force whilst entering the premises, or the reasonable use of force on the occupants who may try to frustrate the search itself. It may be that while using force, the officer may not be able to comply with the above; however, the officers must identify themselves when it is practicable to do so.

Under paragraph 6.7, unless it is impracticable to do so, the occupier must be provided with a copy of a Notice in a standard format:

- specifying if the search is made under warrant;
- summarizing the extent of the powers of search and seizure conferred by PACE;
- explaining the rights of the occupier, and the owner of the property seized;

- explaining compensation may be payable in appropriate cases for damages caused entering and searching premises, and giving the address to send a compensation application;
- stating that the Codes of Practice are available at any police station.

If the occupier is present, copies of the Notice and warrant shall, if practicable, be given to them before the search begins, unless the officer in charge of the search reasonably believes this would frustrate the object of the search or endanger officers or other people. If the occupier is not present, copies of the Notice and warrant shall be left in a prominent place on the premises or appropriate part of the premises and endorsed, with the name of the officer in charge of the search, the date and time of the search. The warrant shall be endorsed to show this has been done.

While the search is being conducted, the officer should allow the occupier, or if he/she wishes, a friend, neighbour, or other person to witness the search, unless the officer in charge of the search has reasonable grounds for believing the presence of the person asked for would seriously hinder the investigation or endanger officers or other people. A search need not be unreasonably delayed for this purpose.

Under section 16(8) of PACE, the police must restrict their search under a warrant to the extent required for the purpose for which the warrant was issued. In practical terms, this means, for example, that if the warrant was authorized to allow police to search the bedroom of a house for stolen property, the police are not allowed to go on a 'fishing expedition' in the rest of the house unless there are reasonable grounds to suspect the stolen property may be found elsewhere. Searches must also be conducted with due consideration for the property and privacy of the occupier and with no more disturbance than necessary.

The search must not continue once all the things specified in that warrant have been found or if the officer in charge of the search is satisfied whatever is being sought is not on the premises. *However*, this does not prevent a further search of the same premises if additional grounds come to light supporting a further application for a search warrant or exercise or further exercise of another power, for example, when, as a result of new information, it is believed articles previously not found or additional articles are on the premises.

We discussed above the concepts of 'all premises warrants' (warrants to enter more than one premises) and 'multiple entry warrants' (warrants to enter premises (or more than one premises) on more than one occasion)). Section 16 of PACE treats the execution of these warrants in slightly different ways.

If the warrant is an all premises warrant, premises which are *not* specified in it may be entered and searched without a constable having to return to a magistrate to extend the terms of the warrant to include the additional premises. In such a case, a police officer of at least the rank of inspector may authorize, in writing, for the additional premises to be entered (see section 16(3A)).

However, section 16(3B) is slightly more restrictive in respect of multiple entry warrants. Where an officer wishes to return to search premises on a further occasion, even if this was authorized in the original application, a police officer of at least the rank of inspector must authorize that entry to those premises in writing.

Seizure and Retention of Property

Under Code B, paragraph 7.1, an officer who is searching any person or premises under any statutory power or with the consent of the occupier may seize anything:

(a) covered by a warrant;

(b) the officer has reasonable grounds for believing is evidence of an offence or has been obtained in consequence of the commission of an offence but only if seizure is necessary to prevent the items being concealed, lost, disposed of, altered, damaged, destroyed, or tampered with;

(c) covered by the powers in the Criminal Justice and Police Act 2001, Part 2 allowing an officer to seize property from persons or premises and retain it for sifting or examination elsewhere.

This could extend to seizing the whole premises (see Code B, Note for Guidance 7B), when it is physically possible to seize and retain the premises in their totality and practical considerations make seizure desirable. For example, police may remove premises such as tents, vehicles, or caravans to a police station for the purpose of preserving evidence.

Code B, paragraph 7.2 states that officers conducting the search may *not* seize articles which are subject to legal privilege. Such articles are defined under section 10(1) of PACE as communications between a professional legal adviser and a client giving of legal advice.

There is a requirement under (b) above for the officer to consider whether it is necessary to seize an item, or whether it may be retained by the occupier of the premises. An officer may decide it is not appropriate to seize property because of an explanation from the person holding it but may nevertheless have reasonable grounds for believing it was obtained in consequence of an offence. In these circumstances, the officer should identify the property to the holder, inform the holder of their suspicions, and explain the holder may be liable to civil or criminal proceedings if they dispose of, alter, or destroy the property. This will be a risk assessment for the officer conducting the search.

In complex cases, searches can take a considerable amount of time, with the police having to scan through numerous pieces of evidence. The introduction of section 50 of the Criminal Justice and Police Act 2001 provided a solution to this problem. Under this section, the police have the power to seize material where it is not reasonably practicable to sort through it at the scene of the search and take it to another location to sift through it.

1 Evidence Management

Anything seized may only be retained for as long as is necessary. It may be retained, among other purposes:

- for use as evidence at a trial for an offence;
- to facilitate the use in any investigation;
- for forensic examination or other investigation in connection with an offence;
- in order to establish its lawful owner when there are reasonable grounds for believing it has been stolen or obtained by the commission of an offence.

Paragraph 7.15 states that property shall not be retained if a copy or image would be sufficient (unless it is believed that the property has been stolen or obtained by the commission of an offence).

Action after Searches

If premises have been entered by force, before leaving the officer in charge of the search must make sure they are secure by either arranging for the occupier or their agent to be present. If this is not possible, the officer must make separate arrangements for the premises to be secured.

Whether compensation is appropriate depends on the circumstances in each case. Compensation for damage caused when effecting entry is unlikely to be appropriate if the search was lawful, and the force used can be shown to be reasonable, proportionate, and necessary to effect entry. If the wrong premises are searched by mistake there is a strong possibility that the police will have to pay compensation.

Code C, paragraph 8.1 states that following a search, the officer in charge must make sure a record is made of the full details of the search. The record must include:

- the date, time, and duration of the search;
- the authority used for the search;
- all officers/authorized persons who conducted the search (including who was in charge);

- the names of any people on the premises if they are known;
- any grounds for refusing the occupier's request to have someone present during the search;
- a list of any articles seized or the location of a list and, if not covered by a warrant, the grounds for their seizure;
- whether force was used, and the reason (and details of any damage caused during the search, and the circumstances);
- if applicable, the reason it was not practicable to give the occupier a copy of the Notice of Powers and Rights;
- when the occupier was not present, the place where copies of the Notice of Powers and Rights and search warrant were left on the premises.

When the warrant has been executed, the officer in charge of the search must endorse it stating whether the articles or persons sought were found and whether any articles were seized (including articles that were not stated in the warrant application). If the warrant was an all premises warrant, the endorsement is required in respect of each premises searched (see paragraph 8.2).

In section 4.2.3 above, when an application for a search warrant has been successful, we identified that two copies of the warrant must be made available. As outlined above, one of the copies should be given to the occupier of the property. The second copy may be retained by the police to be kept with the record of search. The *original* warrant must be returned (after it has been endorsed) to the court that issued it.

4.3 Search of Premises Without the Authority of a Warrant

In the first part of this chapter, we have studied the police powers to search premises under the authority of a warrant. We will now examine the powers to search premises when a warrant is not required. These powers can be divided generally into two areas:

- search of premises after a person has been arrested;
- search of premises to arrest a person.

4.3.1 Search of Premises after a Person has been Arrested

Police powers to search premises after a person has been arrested can be found in two separate sections of PACE:

- **Section 18 of PACE**—when a person has been arrested and it is necessary to search a premises occupied or controlled by that person;
- **Section 32 of PACE**—when a person has been arrested and it is necessary to search a premises in which the person was when arrested, or immediately before being arrested.

We will examine these powers separately, but firstly, there are some common terms that need to be explained:

Definitions

Items subject to legal privilege—Code B, paragraph 7.2 states that officers conducting the search may *not* seize articles which are subject to legal privilege. Such articles are defined under section 10(1) of PACE as communications between a professional legal adviser and a client giving of legal advice. See section 4.2.4 above.

Indictable offence—an offence which may be heard in the crown court.

Premises—Under section 23 of PACE, 'premises' will include any place, and in particular: a vehicle, vessel, aircraft, or hovercraft; any offshore installation; any renewable energy installation; any tent or moveable structure. See section 4.2 above.

It should be noted that searches covered in this section must be conducted in accordance with Code B of the PACE Codes of Practice.

Search of Premises under Section 18 of PACE

Section 18(1) of the Police and Criminal Evidence Act 1984 states:

> Subject to the following provisions of this section, a constable may enter and search any premises occupied or controlled by a person who is under arrest for an indictable offence, if he has reasonable grounds for suspecting that there is on the premises evidence, other than items subject to legal privilege, that relates—
>
> (a) to that offence; or
> (b) to some other indictable offence which is connected with or similar to that offence.

When a person has been arrested for an indictable offence, the power under section 18(1) provides a constable with the authority to enter and search a premises for evidence relating to that particular offence, or other, similar offences.

Before conducting such a search, the police must be certain that the premises they intend searching is, in fact, 'occupied or controlled' by the arrested person. A person could occupy or control more than one premises, for example, their home, their work place, or their car. This fact alone would not give the police the authority to search all premises occupied or controlled by the arrested person and the officer would require *reasonable grounds for suspecting* that there was evidence on each of those premises.

Similar to searches conducted under the authority of a warrant, a constable may seize and retain anything covered by subsection (1) above, and the extent of the search itself must be that which is reasonably required for the purpose of discovering such evidence.

Section 18(4) of PACE states that a search under this section may not be conducted unless it has been authorized by an officer of the rank of inspector or above. The authorising officer must make a record in writing:

- of the grounds for the search; and
- of the nature of the evidence that was sought.

If the person was in police detention at the time the record is to be made, the officer shall make the record as part of his or her custody record.

The majority of searches under section 18(1) take place when a person has been arrested and has been taken to a police station, where an inspector may make the authorization. However, under section 18(5), a constable may conduct a search:

(a) before the person is taken to a police station; and
(b) without obtaining an authorization under subsection (4),

if the presence of the person at a place (other than a police station) is necessary for the effective investigation of the offence. This power may be used, for example, in the following circumstances:

Scenario—Search of Premises

The police were called to a shoplifting incident yesterday, but the person responsible escaped before they arrived. The person's image was captured on CCTV and the police officer attending recognized him. Today, the person has been arrested for the offence by the same officer. As the person was being taken to the police station, the officer overheard him talking on a mobile phone, telling someone to 'get rid of the evidence'. The officer suspected that the person was talking to his brother at home, and decided that an immediate search of the suspect's home was necessary.

Are the elements of section 18(5) satisfied? The person has been arrested for an indictable offence, the officer would certainly want to search his home address for stolen property, and now has grounds to believe that the person's presence at his house (and not the police station) is necessary for the effective investigation of the offence. The constable is entitled to conduct a search on the way to the police station in these circumstances.

Section 18(6) states that if a constable conducts a search in the above circumstances, he or she must inform an officer of the rank of inspector or above that the search has been made as soon as practicable after it was made.

Search of Premises under Section 32 of PACE

The powers to search under section 32 of PACE are divided into two parts:

(a) search of a *person* after arrest;
(b) search of a *premises* after arrest.

We will be concentrating on searches under (b) above in this section.

Under section 32(2)(b) of PACE, a constable has the power:

> to enter and search any premises in which he was when arrested immediately before he was arrested for evidence relating to the offence for which he has been arrested.

Although it is not mentioned above, Code B, paragraph 4.2 states that a search under section 32 may only be conducted when the person has been arrested for an *indictable* offence, which is similar to the power under section 18(1).

If the person was arrested in a multi-occupancy dwelling (such as a bedsit or flat), or was there immediately before his/her arrest, the police are entitled, under section 32(7) of PACE, to search any parts of the premises which the occupier uses in common with other occupiers of the dwelling.

As with other searches we have studied in this chapter, the constable conducting the search under section 32(2)(b) may only do to the extent that is reasonably required for the purpose of discovering any such thing or any such evidence. The constable must have reasonable grounds for believing that there is evidence relating to the offence on the premises.

The term 'immediately' is not defined under the Act and it will be left for the courts to decide what was immediate. In one case, *Hewitson v Chief Constable of Dorset Police* [2003] EWHC 3296, the court held that it was not 'immediate' where a person had been in a premises over two hours before his arrest. The court has also held that the police should not use section 32 as a substitute for section

Table 4.2

Example	Search under PACE, section 18	Search under PACE, section 32
The premises that may be searched	Any premises occupied or controlled by the person	Any premises the person was in at the time, or immediately before their arrest
When the search may be conducted	Either immediately after arrest or any other time afterwards	Immediately after arrest
What the police may search for	Evidence of the offence for which the person was arrested, or some other indictable offence which is connected with or similar to that offence	Evidence of the offence for which the person was arrested
Who the search may be authorized by	Inspector or above	Any officer

18, when officers returned to premises to search it a considerable time after the arrest (see *R* v *Badham* [1987] Crim LR 202).

Clearly, the powers conveyed by section 32(2)(b) are similar to those under section 18(1) above, but there are differences. Table 4.2 examines these differences:

It should be noted that under Code B, paragraphs 8 and 9, the police are required to record details of any searches conducted under section 18 and section 32, in the same manner as a search conducted under a warrant issued by the court (the details of which are outlined fully in section 4.2.4 above).

4.3.2 Search of Premises to Arrest a Person

The Police and Criminal Evidence Act 1984 contains wide powers of entry, contained in section 17, where a person has not been arrested for an offence. In section 4.2.1 above, we saw that the police may apply for a warrant to enter premises to arrest a person under section 17(1)(a) of PACE. We will now examine other powers of entry under this section, which may be utilized without the requirement to obtain a warrant. It should be noted that an entry and search under this section is governed by the provisions of Code B of the PACE Codes of Practice.

Under section 17(1)(b) of PACE, a constable may enter and search any premises for the purpose of arresting a person for an indictable offence. Before entering premises under this section, the constable must have reasonable grounds for believing that the person whom he/she is seeking is on the premises—eg there is a reasonable expectation of finding the person on the premises (see section 17(2)(a)). Also, as with other powers of entry under PACE, a constable may only search to the extent that is reasonably required for the purpose for which the power of entry is exercised. For example, if a constable enters premises to arrest a person, without other reasonable grounds, there would be no power to commence a search of the premises for stolen property.

Under section 17(1)(c), a constable may also enter and search any premises for the purpose of arresting a person for an offence under:

(i)   section 1 (prohibition of uniforms in connection with political objectives) of the Public Order Act 1936;

(ii)   any enactment contained in sections 6 to 8 or 10 of the Criminal Law Act 1977 (offences relating to entering and remaining on property);

(iii)   section 4 of the Public Order Act 1986 (fear or provocation of violence);

(iiia)   section 4 (driving etc when under influence of drink or drugs) or 163 (failure to stop when required to do so by constable in uniform) of the Road Traffic Act 1988;

(iiib)   section 27 of the Transport and Works Act 1992 (which relates to offences involving workers on transport systems being over the prescribed drink limit);

(iv)   section 76 of the Criminal Justice and Public Order Act 1994 (failure to comply with interim possession order);

(v)   any of sections 4, 5, 6(1) and (2), 7 and 8(1) and (2) of the Animal Welfare Act 2006 (offences relating to the prevention of harm to animals);

While the power under section 17(1)(b) above allows for entry for more serious (indictable) offences, it is also recognized there are occasions when the police require a power to enter premises to arrest people for less serious offences. For example, if there were no power to enter premises to deal with a person for drink driving (as in section 17(1)(c)(iiia) above) drivers could simply avoid prosecution by making it home and locking themselves in their house.

The most commonly used powers under this section are entry to deal with drink drivers and entry to deal with offences under the Public Order Act 1986 (under section 17(1)(c)(iii)).

A constable entering premises under section 17(1)(c) above will be doing so mainly to make an arrest. There are further, similar, powers under section 17(1)(ca) (arrest in pursuance of section 32(1A) of the Children and Young Persons Act 1969, any child or young person who has been remanded or committed to local authority accommodation under section 23(1) of that Act) and section 17(1)(caa) (arrest of a person for an offence to which section 61 of the Animal Health Act 1981 applies—provisions relating to the control of rabies). Again, these powers are infrequently used by the police.

There are further powers of entry under section 17(1), which allow the police to enter premises for other reasons, where the person is *not* suspected of committing an offence:

(cb)   of recapturing any person who is, or is deemed for any purpose to be, unlawfully at large while liable to be detained—

(i)   in a prison, remand centre, young offender institution or secure training centre, or

(ii) in pursuance of section 92 of the Powers of Criminal Courts (Sentencing) Act 2000 (dealing with children and young persons guilty of grave crimes), in any other place;

(d) of recapturing any person whatever who is unlawfully at large and whom he is pursuing; or

(e) of saving life or limb or preventing serious damage to property.

These powers are frequently used by the police, particularly when pursuing or capturing a person unlawfully at large and when entering premises to save life or limb.

Alongside the above powers is another frequently-used power, under section 17(6), to enter premises to deal with or prevent a breach of the peace. Under this power, a constable may enter premises when they have a genuine and reasonable belief that a breach of the peace is happening or is about to happen in the immediate future (*McLeod* v *Commissioner of Police for the Metropolis* [1994] 4 All ER 553).

Under section 17(2)(b), if the police are entering premises which consists of a multi-occupancy dwelling, the powers to enter and search are limited to:

• those parts of the premises which the occupier uses in common with other occupiers of the dwelling, or
• any dwelling which the constable has reasonable grounds for believing that the person whom he/she is seeking may be.

Reasonable Force

In utilizing powers under section 17, a constable has the power to use reasonable force where necessary in order to enter premises. As with other powers under this Act, the officer should attempt to communicate with the occupier first to explain what he or she is doing, unless it is impracticable to do so.

4.4 **Search of Premises with the Consent of the Occupier**

So far in this chapter, we have examined powers of entry, which relate mostly to incidents where the police enter and search premises without the consent of the owner. Code B, paragraphs 5.1 to 5.4 of the PACE Codes of Practice give specific guidance in relation to searches where the owner actually consents.

Under paragraph 5.1, where it is intended to search premises with the consent of the occupier, the constable should seek to obtain that consent in writing and provide the person with a Notice of Powers and Rights before the search. The officer must also make any necessary enquiries to be satisfied the person is in a position to give such consent (eg by confirming that they are, in fact, the occupier).

Further, if the search is to take place in a lodging house or similar accommodation, every reasonable effort should be made to obtain the consent of the tenant, lodger, or occupier. A search should not be made solely on the basis of the landlord's consent unless the tenant, lodger, or occupier is unavailable and the matter is urgent (see Note for Guidance 5A).

If a police officer is searching with the owner's consent, it is likely that there is no authority to conduct a search under one of the powers granted by PACE. In the spirit of cooperation, therefore, paragraph 5.2 states that before seeking consent, the officer in charge of the search shall state the purpose of the proposed search and its extent. This information must be as specific as possible, particularly regarding the articles or persons being sought and the parts of the premises to be searched. The person must be clearly informed that they are not obliged to consent and anything seized may be produced in evidence. If at the time the person is not suspected of an offence, the officer must tell them when stating the purpose of the search.

Paragraph 5.3 is clear that the police should not seek to obtain consent from the occupier by placing them under duress; it would not be true consent. Also, if the occupier withdraws consent before the search is completed, then in the absence of any other power to remain on the premises, the police cannot continue the search. If the police find evidence on the premises after consent has been withdrawn (or if it was obtained unfairly), such evidence is likely to be inadmissible.

Finally, we should examine circumstances where the police need to enter premises to search for evidence, where the occupier is *not* suspected or connected to an offence in any way.

Scenario—Search of Premises with Consent of Occupier

The police have arrested a person suspected of murder. Witnesses have said that this person hid a weapon in a garden in a particular street, but the police cannot be certain where the weapon is. In order to solve the crime, the next day, the police need to search every garden in the street. The police do not suspect that any of the residents in the street were involved in the crime. Clearly the police need to recover the murder weapon, but under what authority could they do so?

From what we have seen in this chapter, the police would have no authority to search any premises under section 18 or section 32 of PACE—the suspect does not occupy or control them and was not arrested there. In these circumstances, the police are likely to seek the occupier's permission to search their premises and would have to comply with the provisions of the Codes of Practice.

If permission is refused, the police could of course apply for an all premises warrant to enter more than one premises. However, they will first seek to search the premises with the consent of the occupier. Of course, if the search is conducted with the consent of the occupier, the provisions of Code B will apply in respect of how the search is conducted.

Chapter 5

Identification Procedures

This chapter deals with the identification procedures available to police governed by Code D (and associated annexes) of the Police and Criminal Evidence Act 1984 (PACE). It will also cover aspects of identification from the ever-growing use of closed circuit television (CCTV) and provide practical advice for the identification of suspects.

The chapter is NOT intended as a substitute for the Code and the reader should always refer to the codes for full details.

5.1 Categories of Identification

Code D divides the methods of identification into two categories:

- Where the identity of the suspect is known.
- Where the identity of the suspect is not known.

In cases where the identity of the suspect is known a further division is made in circumstances where the suspect is available and when not available.

Code D Paragraph 3.4

A suspect being known means there is sufficient information to justify the arrest of a particular person involved in an offence.

A suspect being available means that they are immediately available or will be within a reasonably short period of time and will be willing to take an effective part in at least one of the following which is practicable to arrange.

- Video identification
- Identification parade
- Group Identification.
- A further method of Confrontation is available under the codes where the suspect is known but unavailable (ie will not cooperate) but is of limited use and value.

These are all methods of visual identification and are therefore the most common method of witnesses identifying suspects. In order to prevent cases of mistaken identity and fully test the ability of a witness to identify a person the guidelines of *R v Turnbull and Camelo* [1976] 63 Cr App R 132 should be applied in conjunction with the provisions of code D embodied in the mnemonic ADVOKATE.

Mnemonic

A = Amount of time under observation.

D = Distance between witness and suspect or incident.

V = Visibility at all times and in what light including time of day, time of year, and type of street lighting.

O = Observation impeded or obstructed in any way such as passing traffic, other people, or objects such as street furniture or trees.

K = Known or seen before, how often, and in what circumstances.

A = Any special reason for remembering the offender or incident. Was there something specific that made it memorable?

T = Time lapse between observation and subsequent identification to police.

E = Error or material discrepancy between description given to police and the actual appearance.

It is therefore essential in every case where a witness describes the suspect to include all of the above points in a written statement!

Code D requires that a first description provided of a person suspected of a crime must be recorded. This must be disclosed to the defence in the pre-trial procedure.

5.2 **Identification where there is a Known Suspect**

Where the suspect is known there are four possible methods of identification of Code D (3.4–3.23). These are:

- video identification;
- identification parade;
- group identification; and
- confrontation.

The majority of these procedures are now conducted by video using the Viper system, which has in excess of 25,000 images on its database. In effect, the remaining three methods are now very rarely used.

5.3 **How is Identification Defined?**

- To test the ability of the witness to pick out from a group, if he is present, a person whom the witness has said that he has seen on a specified occasion.
- To prevent cases of mistaken identity.

Checklist—Identification Procedure

An Identification Procedure MUST BE HELD whenever:

- A witness has identified a suspect or purported to have identified a suspect prior to any formal procedures being held.
  OR
- There is a witness available who expresses an ability to identify a suspect or there is a reasonable chance they will be able to identify the suspect.
  AND
- The suspect disputes being the person the witness says he or she has seen.

An Identification Procedure is NOT required:

- when it is not practicable;
- when it would serve no useful purpose in proving or disproving the suspect committed the offence—eg when it is not disputed that the suspect is already well known to the witness who claims to have seen them commit the crime;
- if the witness could only describe clothing or would not be able to recognize the suspect again.

A procedure may also be held if the officer in charge of the investigation considers it would be useful.

The vast majority of police forces now have dedicated staff to organize and manage identification procedures. If it is decided to hold a procedure it should be held as soon as practicable. This is in the interest of fairness to both suspects and witnesses. This will also give witnesses the best opportunity of recognizing the suspect(s).

5.4 **Arranging the ID Procedure**

The responsibility for arranging and conducting the identification procedure falls to an independent officer known as the '**Identification Officer**', currently an inspector, although likely to change allowing designated police staff to perform this role. Other officers or support staff can make arrangements for, and conduct any of the identification procedures. The identification officer must be able to supervise effectively, intervene, or give advice.

Any officer who is involved in the investigation should avoid (to the extent possible) contact with witnesses before the showing. This is in order to preserve fairness and prevent allegations the witness was in any way influenced by police in their identification of the suspect. It is good practice for any officer who necessarily has contact with the witness (for instance in transporting them to a viewing) to explain the fact that they are unable to discuss the case other than explaining the procedure in generic terms and the reasons for this and record this fact in a pocket book. A subsequent statement may then be produced noting the witness's understanding and any reply. This may negate allegations by the defence, especially in cases where the defence seek to attack police procedure.

Prior to an identification procedure paragraph 3.17 Code D details matters that must be explained to the suspect and subsequently recorded in a written notice and handed to the suspect. The suspect should be asked to sign a second copy and indicate if they are willing to cooperate and take part in the identification procedure. The format of the records varies from force to force but all must include the following:

- The purpose of the identification procedures.
- That they are entitled to free legal advice.
- The procedures for holding it, including the right to have a solicitor or friend present.
- That they do not have to consent to or cooperate in the identification procedures.
- That if they do not consent to and cooperate in the identification procedures, their refusal may be given in evidence in any subsequent trial and police may proceed covertly without their consent or make other arrangements to test

whether a witness can identify them (they become known but not available, ie uncooperative).

- If appropriate special arrangements for juveniles, mentally disordered, or mentally vulnerable people.
- That if they significantly alter their appearance between being offered an identification procedure and any attempt to hold a procedure, this may be given in evidence and other forms of identification may be considered.
- A moving image or photograph may be taken of them when they attend any identification procedure.
- Whether, before their identity became known, the witness was shown photographs, a computerized or artist's composite likeness, or similar image by the police.
- That if they change their appearance before an identification parade, it may not be practicable to arrange one on the day or subsequently and, because of the change of appearance, the identification officer may consider alternative methods of identification.
- That they or their solicitor will be provided with details of the description of the suspect first given by any witnesses who are to attend the procedure.

5.4.1 Composition of a Video Identification Procedure

The video identification procedure is the preferred identification method. In this method a witness is shown moving images of a known suspect together with similar images of others who resemble the suspect. Moving images will be used unless:

- the suspect is known but not available (para 3.21 Refers), ie covert filming; or
- in accordance with paragraph 2A of Annexe A of the Code, the identification officer does not consider that replication of a physical feature can be achieved or that it is not possible to conceal the location of the feature on the image of the suspect.

The identification officer may then decide to make use of a video identification but using still images.

Paragraph 2A refers to unusual physical feature such as a scar, tattoo, or unusual hairstyle. It could be extended to include a birthmark or severe skin disorder as well. In the vast majority of cases technology can be used to conceal the mark or scar or indeed replicate it on other images. If the witness describes the unusual mark or feature then, if practicable, the mark or feature should be replicated. However, it may be the case that a video of still images will be used.

The set of images must include the suspect and eight other people who as far as possible resemble the suspect in:

- age;
- general appearance;
- position in life (ie do not line up a bank manager and eight street drinkers!).

Only one suspect shall appear in any set unless there are two suspects of similar appearance, then they may be shown together with 12 other people.

Generally the procedure will take place at an identification suite where all aspects of the procedure are videoed and a set format is used in line with the Codes to preserve fairness and obtain the best possible evidence. This is best practice regardless of whether or not the suspect's solicitor is present.

Once a suitable image has been obtained at the video 'capture' stage, assuming your suspect is cooperating, he or she and or his or her legal representative, friend, or appropriate adult must be given a reasonable opportunity to see the complete set of images before they are shown to any witness. If the suspect has a reasonable objection to the set of images, he or she shall be asked to state what they are and this shall be recorded. If practicable, steps should be taken to remove grounds for the objection. If it is not practicable the suspect or his/her legal representative shall be told the reason and this shall be recorded.

The suspect or his/her solicitor must be served with details of the first description or descriptions if more than one witness. In practice this should be completed when initial agreement to take part in the procedure has taken place and forms served. The suspect or his/her solicitor must also be allowed to view any material released to the media by police for the purpose of recognizing the suspect. However, it must be practicable to do so and not unreasonably delay the investigation.

The suspect's solicitor, if practicable, shall be given reasonable notification of the time and place of the video identification so he or she can attend on behalf of the suspect. If no solicitor is instructed this information is given to the suspect. The suspect may not be present when images are shown to witnesses. In the absence of the suspect's legal representative the viewing itself shall be recorded on video (this is often done now regardless as best practice and to preserve fairness).

5.4.2 Conducting the Procedure

In conducting the procedure the Identification Officer is responsible for the appropriate arrangements to make sure witnesses do not:

- communicate with each other about the case;
- see any images they are about to be shown;
- see or be reminded of any photograph or description of the suspect's identity;
- overhear a witness who has already viewed the material;
- discuss the composition of images or be told if a previous witness has made an identification.

In viewing the images the following procedure should be followed.

- Only one witness at a time.

- They shall be told the person they saw on a specified occasion may or may not appear in the images they are shown.
- If they cannot make a positive identification they should say so.
- They shall be advised that at any point they may ask for a particular set of images to be frozen for them to study.
- They should not be asked to make any decision as to whether the person they saw is on the set of images until they have viewed the whole set at least twice.
- Once they have viewed the set of images at least twice and have indicated they do not wish to see the images or any part of them again, the witness shall be asked if the person they saw on a specified earlier occasion has been shown and to identify the number of the image. The witness shall be shown that image to confirm identification.
- Where a witness has made a previous identification by being shown photographs, a computerized image, or artist's impression the witness must not have been reminded of any description of the suspect.
- After the procedure the witness will be asked if they have seen any broadcast, published film, photograph, or any description of the suspects relating to the offence and their reply shall be recorded.
- All material used must be retained and securely stored and movement of the material accounted for. No one involved in the investigation shall be permitted to view the material prior to it being shown to witnesses.
- A record shall be made of all those participating in, or seeing, the set of images whose names are known to police. A record of the conduct of the video identification must be made. This shall include anything said by the witness about any identification, conduct of the procedure, and any reasons why it was not possible to comply with any of the provisions of Code D.

Practical Considerations

Where a suspect consents to take part in an identification procedure, so is known and available, and has been bailed in order that identification procedures may take place, an officer with knowledge of the case should attend the identification suite or station to ensure the suspect has not sent a friend or other person to take part in the video procedure. This has been known to happen where a relative or similar looking friend has taken the place of the suspect. The officer attending the video capture may also then facilitate the service of forms, give options for dates of viewing, and act as a conduit of information between the ID suite and the case.

The provision of first descriptions to the identification officer in advance is vital to ensure that in creating a video or other procedure the Codes are not breached. The Codes require the first description given by each witness regarding each suspect to be served before the procedure; ie two suspects, two witnesses require a total of four first descriptions.

Identification procedures for persons under 17 require the consent of a parent or guardian, and consent should be signed on the respective forms. Witnesses under 17 require a parent or guardian to attend, and if a parent or guardian is a witness as well, the juvenile must have a separate parent, guardian, or appropriate adult who is independent.

If the witness required an interpreter when a statement was taken they will need one for the identification procedure. They may be able to speak some English but they must be able to understand the procedure. Identification evidence should not be lost for the sake of the victim or witness not fully understanding what is being said. The officer in the case or a colleague will need to be present at the end of the procedure for a short statement to be taken.

If the victim or witness says: 'When I was in there I did not identify anyone but now thinking about it, it was number *' it should be remembered that it is an unnerving experience for people who may be frightened or traumatized by the crime and experience of having to undergo the procedure.

In these circumstances inform the Identification Officer, and if a legal representative is present consider recalling the victim or witness back in to repeat the showing. The Crown Prosecution Service (CPS) should be informed of the circumstances which may be the subject of legal argument later.

The suspect will be 'captured' in a 15-second video clip and put into a moving image of a parade with eight others of similar appearance. At this point the suspect has a chance to view the composition of the video and make any objections as to the content. The video clip will as far as possible show the suspect and other people in the same position, or carrying out the same sequence of movements. They shall show the suspect and other people under identical conditions, unless the identification officer reasonably believes:

- because of the suspect's failure or refusal to cooperate or other reasons it is not practical for the conditions to be identical; and
- any difference in the conditions would not direct a witness's attention to any individual image.

5.5 **Identification where the Suspect is not Known and Available**

One of the most common situations where this occurs is where a street robbery has been committed and police attend the scene and take the victim and sometimes witnesses on a 'drive around or tour of the locality'. This is good practice to make an early arrest and is encouraged as a method to detect crime, provided the Codes are complied with.

It is also known as 'street or scene identification' when it is often good evidence if it produces the arrest of the suspects. It is NOT a replacement for an identification procedure. It can often be the cause of debate between police officers and the CPS over the necessity of holding a procedure when the suspect has been identified on the street in what police argue is group identification. It is not!

The following should be followed.

- Where practicable, a record shall be made of any description of the suspect given by the witness prior to any identification.
- Where possible keep witnesses separate.
- Care must be taken not to direct the witness's attention to a specific person, but if necessary the witness may be asked to look in a certain direction or at a certain group.
- Once there is sufficient information to justify an arrest of the suspect, a formal procedure must be adopted.
- The officer or police staff accompanying the witness must make a record in their pocket book as soon as practicable and in as much detail as possible.

5.5.1 The Showing of Photographs

Another method to trace suspects where they are not known or available is the showing of photographs, often known as witness albums. It is good practice, where street robberies have occurred and a tour of the neighbourhood has proved fruitless, and there are no other leads available, to show the witness a series of photographs, in cases of street robbery normally composed of known and local robbers. This can be replicated for other crimes such as artifice or distraction burglary. In showing photographs the following must be complied with.

- A sergeant or above shall be responsible for supervising and directing the showing of the photographs. Another officer can do the actual showing.
- The supervising officer to confirm the first description of the suspect by the witness has been recorded before they are shown photographs.

- One witness to view at a time, in as much privacy as possible and without being allowed to communicate with any other witness in the case.
- Witness to view not less than 12 photographs at a time, which as far as possible are all of a similar type.
- The witness shall be told the person they saw may or may not be amongst them. If they cannot make a positive identification they must say so. Also that they must view at least 12 photographs before making a decision. They must not be prompted or guided in any way but left to make any decision without help.
- If a positive identification is made from the photographs, unless the person identified is eliminated from enquiries or is not available, other witnesses shall not be shown photographs. The witnesses shall be asked to attend an identification procedure, unless identification is not an issue.
- If a witness makes a selection, but is unable to confirm identification, they will be asked how sure they are that the photograph they have indicated is the person they saw on the specified earlier occasion.
- If a computerized or artist's composite or other likeness has led to the suspect being known and available to undergo an identification procedure, that likeness shall not be shown to any other witness.
- When a witness attends an identification procedure and has previously been shown photographs or a computerized or artist's impression or similar likeness, the officer in charge of the investigation shall make the Identification Officer aware that this is the case. The suspect and his/her solicitor must be informed before the identification procedure takes place.
- No photographs shall be destroyed, whether or not identification is made, as they may be required for production at court. The photographs shall be numbered and a separate photograph taken of the frame or part of the album from which the witness made the identification.

It is often the case that witness albums are produced on a laptop for viewing. This has many advantages over still photograph albums, not least with the number of pictures and ease of update. A record must be kept of the composition of the pages made and viewed. If identification is made, a print out of the page of the albums would satisfy the last requirement.

5.6 **Circumstances where the Suspect is Known and not Available**

There are a number of options open to the investigating and Identification Officer here and they will be dependent on several factors. If the suspect does not consent to any identification procedure or has withdrawn earlier consent, or has radically altered his or her appearance in a bid to thwart the identification process, the Identification Officer may follow identification procedures using covert filming, or make use of any suitable moving or still images. This includes circumstances where the suspect is wanted and has fled abroad. It may be weeks, months, or years before the suspect can be arrested and extradited. There are numerous jurisdictions with which the UK has no extradition agreements. It will only strengthen the prosecution case if a positive identification can be made from suitable moving or still images.

If the suspect has previous convictions there is a good chance he or she will have a suitable up-to-date custody image available, or has recently attended a police station and the custody CCTV is available. It is therefore worth remembering when you take a custody image that you:

- take a good picture, ie in focus, not leaning forward or to one side, or pulling a face;
- without a hat;
- no sunglasses;

- ensure they look into the camera;
- eyes should be open, not closed or squinting;
- no pens or cigarettes behind the ear;
- no disposable clothing such as white disposable suits or wrapped in a cell blanket.

All of the above tips will give the Identification Officer more of a chance to utilize the custody images.

If the suspect has no suitable custody image other alternatives may be a driving licence photograph, or passport photograph. Another option if none of these are available would be to obtain a section 8 PACE search warrant to search premises if circumstances merited this action.

5.7 **Closed Circuit Television Systems**

Considering the vast amount of CCTV available and circumstances where it is viewed and identifications made, there is remarkably limited commentary within the Code.

Attorney-General's reference 2/2002 states where a suspect is filmed committing an offence, it is admissible to give evidence of identification by way of recognition from a witness not present at the scene but who knew the defendant and who, having seen the film, identified the suspect as being the defendant.

In the majority of cases this will apply to police officers; it is therefore good practice that the officer who made the recognition identification on CCTV is not involved in the arrest and subsequent dealings with the suspect if identification is in dispute. This will enable them to take part in any identification procedure if necessary.

Further to this *R v Smith and others* [2008] EWCA 1342 states:

> Where a police officer views a CCTV recording or image it is recognised there is a real difference in comparison to an ordinary witness viewing the same to identify someone seen

committing an offence. Code D provides safeguards that are equally important where a police officer has been asked to attempt to identify someone from a CCTV recording.

Regardless of whether Code D applies a record must be kept of the following:

- any initial reactions to seeing the CCTV images.
- where a police officer fails to recognize anyone on the initial viewing but does so at a later date.
- where a police officer fails to recognize anyone at all.
- anything that an officer may say with regard to any doubt.
- any words of doubt that an officer may use, and
- where there is recognition, any factors relating to the image that caused that recognition to occur.

The record must be available to assist in measuring the reliability of the claim that a police officer recognises a particular individual and it is important that any initial reactions are made available for examination as required.

To conclude this section of visual identification, part of the summary of a stated case is appropriate for the reader to consider. In *R v Forbes* 2000 TLR 19.12.2000:

Code D is intended to be an intensely practical document, giving police officers clear instructions on the approach that they should follow in specified circumstances. It is not old-fashioned literalism but sound interpretation to read the code as meaning what it says.

5.8 **Fingerprints, Photographs, Body Samples, and Impressions**

5.8.1 **Fingerprints**

The National Automated Fingerprint Identification System (NAFIS) should confirm the identity of the person in custody relatively quickly. Section 61 of PACE as amended by the Criminal Justice Act 2003 empowers the taking of finger and palm prints of persons coming into police custody who may be wanted on other matters. It will prevent them from giving false particulars and evading arrest. It also means violent or vulnerable people may be identified and dealt with as necessary.

Pre-conviction

Section 61 of PACE states as follows:

- A person's fingerprints may only be taken in connection with the investigation of an offence with their consent. If at a police station this must be written consent.
- The fingerprints of any person aged 10 or over may be taken without consent if they are (i) detained at a police station having been arrested for a recordable offence; also that they have not previously had their fingerprints taken unless those fingerprints are not of satisfactory quality to allow searching, ie an incomplete set or poor set was taken; (ii) a person detained at a police station who has been charged with a recordable offence or informed they will be reported for summons, and they have not had their fingerprints taken in the course of the investigation or the prints taken are unsatisfactory as above.
- A person's fingerprints may also be taken without consent if he has been convicted of a recordable offence, been cautioned for a recordable offence or warned or reprimanded by virtue of section 65 of the Crime and Disorder Act 1998.
- The fingerprints of a person who has answered his bail at a police station or court may be taken without consent if the court or an officer of at least the rank of Inspector authorises them to be taken. This is to prove or disprove identification of the person concerned.
- Where a person has been charged or informed he will be reported for summons, or has been arrested for a recordable offence. Their fingerprints may be checked against other fingerprints held by or on behalf of any one or more

relevant law enforcement authorities, which are held in connection with or as a result of the investigation of an offence. This is known as a speculative search to see if the suspect is involved in other crimes.

- Before the fingerprints are taken the person must be informed of the reason they are being taken and that they may be the subject of a speculative search.

Post-conviction, Caution, or Reprimand

A person's fingerprints can be taken without consent if convicted of a recordable offence, cautioned for a recordable offence, or was warned or reprimanded and any previous fingerprints were either incomplete or of insufficient quality to allow for comparison. A requirement may be made within one month of the date of conviction, caution warning, or reprimand to attend a police station within a given seven-day period. If the person fails to comply they may be arrested.

5.8.2 Photographs

Detainees at Police Stations

Section 54A(1) of PACE allows a person detained at a police station to be searched or examined or both to establish:

- whether they have any marks, features, or injuries, which would tend to identify them as a person involved in the commission of an offence and to photograph any identifying marks;
- their identity.

A person detained at a police station under a stop and search power is not a detainee for these purposes.

The search or examination to find marks or features may be carried out without consent if authorized by an officer of at least the rank of inspector if consent has been withheld or is not practicable to obtain.

A search or examination to establish identity again may be carried out without consent if authorized by an officer of at least inspector rank if the detained person has refused to identify themselves or the authorizing officer has reasonable grounds for suspecting the person is not who they claim to be.

A person may only be searched, examined, and photographed by a police officer of the same sex.

Photographs taken may be disclosed only for the purposes of the prevention or detection of crime, the investigation of offences or conduct of prosecutions by or on behalf of, police or other law enforcement and prosecuting authorities inside and outside the UK.

The authority to search must be recorded with a separate authority for each purpose to which it applies.

If the person is unwilling to cooperate sufficiently to allow the search or examination to take place, or a suitable photograph to be taken, an officer may use reasonable force to:

- search or examine with out consent;
- photograph identifying marks without consent.

The thoroughness of the search or examination must be no more than the officer deems necessary to achieve the required purpose.

Photographing Detainees at Police Stations and Other Persons elsewhere than at a Police Station

Under section 64A any person may be photographed, with or without their consent, if they have been:

- detained at a police station;
- arrested by a constable for an offence;
- taken into custody after being arrested for an offence by a person other than a constable;
- made subject to a requirement to wait with a community support officer under para2 (3) or 3(a) of the police reform Act 2002;

- given certain fixed penalty notices as per section 64A (1b) through to (e).

The officer taking the photograph may require the removal of any item or substance worn on or over all or part of the face or head. If they fail to comply with the requirement, the officer may remove the item or substance. Consent is not required and reasonable force may be used if necessary. Additionally the photograph may be taken covertly. The photograph taken may be retained and disclosed for the prevention and detection of crime, or investigation of offences or conduct of prosecutions, by or on behalf of, police or other law enforcement or prosecuting authorities inside or outside the UK.

The person photographed must be informed of the:

- purpose of the photograph;
- grounds on which authority given;
- purpose to which the photograph may be used, disclosed, or retained.

This information must be given prior to the photograph being taken. The requirements also apply to any search or examination.

Exceptions are where (i) a photograph is taken covertly, and (ii) is taken without consent by making a still image of a custody CCTV system installed anywhere within a police station. In the second set of circumstances he must be informed as soon as practicable after the photograph has been obtained.

A person who attends a police station voluntarily and is not in police detention, who is suspected of involvement in an offence may be photographed, but no force may be used to take the picture. Photographs or any other images must be destroyed unless they are charged, prosecuted, cautioned, given a warning or reprimand, or informed they will be prosecuted. They may also give what is known as 'informed consent', that is a full explanation of the purposes the photograph may be put to.

5.8.3 **Impressions of Footwear**

Sections 61(a) and 63(a) of PACE state that an impression of footwear may be taken with written consent if a person is at a police station. It may be taken without consent by a constable if:

- the person is detained at a police station having been arrested for a recordable offence, or has been charged or informed that he will be reported for a recordable offence; and
- he has not had an impression of footwear taken previously or the impression was of insufficient quality for comparison or analysis;

the person must be informed prior to the impression being taken that it may be subject to a speculative search. In the same way as with fingerprints it must be recorded, he must also be informed of the reasons why the impressions have been taken if taken without consent.

5.8.4 **Samples**

In sections 62,63,63A, and 65 of PACE samples are defined as either **Intimate** or **Non-Intimate**.

Intimate Samples

- Dental impression.
- A sample of blood, urine, pubic hair, semen, or any other tissue or fluid.
- A swab taken from any body orifice other than the mouth.

The intimate sample can only be taken from a person in police detention where:

- written consent from the person has been given; and
- an officer of at least the rank of inspector has given authority.

1 Evidence Management

An intimate sample may be taken from someone not in police detention if during the course of the investigation two or more non-intimate samples have been taken for the same means of analysis (often DNA testing), and the two or more samples have proved insufficient. Again then written consent of the person is required along with the authority of an inspector or above.

In each case the authorizing officer must have reasonable grounds for believing the person has been involved in a recordable offence and that the sample will tend to prove or disprove his involvement in the offence.

The suspect must be informed of the facts that the authority has been given and of the grounds for its being given. He must also be informed of the offence in question and the fact that the sample may be the subject of a speculative search, all of which must be recorded in the custody record.

All intimate samples, apart from a sample of urine, must be taken by a registered medical practitioner or health care professional, or, in the case of a dental impression, a registered dentist. Should consent not be given without good cause, adverse inferences may be drawn by the court in any subsequent proceedings.

Non-intimate Samples

A non-intimate sample (section 63) means:

- a sample from under a nail;
- a swab taken from the mouth or other non-intimate part of the body;
- an impression of skin;
- saliva;
- a sample of hair but not pubic hair. The hair sample may be plucked or cut and should be no larger than necessary. The suspect should be allowed choice from which part of the body it is taken from.

A non-intimate sample may be taken without consent when in police detention where:

- the person is in police detention and has been arrested for a recordable offence and has not had the same type of sample taken from the same part of the body during the course of the investigation; or any sample previously taken was insufficient;
- a person has been charged, informed he will be reported for a recordable offence, and no sample has previously been taken or was insufficient;
- a person has been convicted of a recordable offence since 10 April 1995, or is a person to whom section 1 of the Criminal Evidence Amendment Act applies (where certain sexual and violent offenders had previously not had samples taken this allowed DNA swabs to be obtained and the results placed on the DNA database);
- a person has been detained following acquittal on the grounds of insanity or unfitness to plead.

Non-intimate Samples in Police Detention and Elsewhere

A non-intimate sample may also be taken from a person who is being held in custody on the authority of a court without consent; where an officer of at least the rank of inspector has reasonable grounds that the person has been involved in a recordable offence, and that the sample will prove or disprove his involvement in the offence. The sample can be taken at any hospital or other place in which he is detained (sections 63(3a) (3b).

The suspect must be informed of the grounds for which the sample is being taken, that it has been authorized, the nature of the offence, and that it will be subject of a speculative search. A record must be made which, if at a police station, will be the custody record.

Section 63A provides a power to require a person to attend a police station in order to provide samples where:

- a person has been charged with a recordable offence or informed that they will be reported;
- a person has been convicted of a recordable offence, and that either no sample has been taken during the course of the investigation or the sample has been taken but is unsuitable for the same means of analysis or is insufficient;
- a constable may require the person to attend a police station within one month of the date of conviction or date of reporting; or
- within one month of the officer being informed that the sample was unsuitable or insufficient.

The person shall be given a period of seven days to attend the police station and may be given a specified time of day or between specified times of day. Should the person fail to attend he may be arrested.

5.9 **Conclusion**

This chapter is not intended as a replacement for Code D, and the latest version of the full codes should always be referred to for full details and suggested wordings.

Further Reading

Listed below are some relevant stated cases and guidance available at time of writing. The list is by no means exhaustive and subject to the dynamics of criminal law.

Attorney Generals reference 2 of 2002. The Times Law Reports 17/10/02—Gives four occasions when identification from video can be used.

R v Campbell [1996] Crim LR 500.—Identification evidence admissibility from accidental meeting.

R v Caldwell and Dixon (1993) Crim LR 862—Procedure for identification from security camera film.

R v Clare and Peach (1995) 159 JP 412—Police officer was expert witness after repeatedly viewing video.

R v Johnson [1996] Crim LR 504—Refers to the use of film or video for identification purposes.

R v Loveridge, Loveridge and Lee [2001] EWCA Crim 1034—The use of covert video for facial mapping.

R v Smith and others [2008] EWCA 1342

R v Turnbull and Camelo [1976] 63 Cr App R 132—Guidelines on identification evidence. Worth reading to better understand 'ADVOKATE'.

Note: All cases are readable in full on the Police National Legal Database, together with others outlining other aspects of identification procedures.

Chapter 6

Covert Investigation

The volume having dealt so far with various aspects of *overt investigation* and evidence gathering—investigation of which the subject is aware at the time police powers are executed or else is made aware as soon as practicable afterwards in the case of search warrants executed at unoccupied premises—this chapter moves on to the second generic form of investigation, *covert investigation*: investigations of which the subject is not aware nor of which they are made aware until such time as evidence there from is adduced at trial. There is a third generic type, *coercive investigation*, but such powers are invested in non-police agencies such as the Crown Prosecution Service (CPS), the Serious Fraud Office, and HM Revenue and Customs, and as such fall outside the scope of this volume. All three types are founded upon specific legislation.

Subject to appropriate lawful authorization, covert investigation is used to obtain information required as evidence. These methods can also be used to obtain information that will be used for intelligence purposes to identify future evidential opportunities and so facilitate long-term investigations.

Overt investigation acquires evidence that implicates the suspect. Covert investigation acquires evidence of the suspect implicating themselves. It is often incontrovertible. Consequently at trial the defence has little option other than to call into question the integrity of evidence covertly obtained by seeking to raise doubts about the procedural propriety of its acquisition. Getting covert investigation procedure right negates this line of attack.

6.1 **Statutory Basis for Covert Investigation**

The necessity of all investigative methods having a statutory foundation is derived from Article 8(1) of the European Convention on Human Rights and Fundamental Freedoms 1950 (ECHR): the right to respect for private and family life. There must be no interference with this right except as provided for by law (see Chapter 13). Essentially, police officers can only use powers granted to them by Parliament.

In the case of general overt investigation, the principal source of legal authority comes from the Police and Criminal Evidence Act 1984 (PACE), supplemented by numerous other Acts in the subsequent 25 years which make provision for specific investigations (notably counter-terrorism legislation, for example).

In the case of covert investigation, the principal legislation falls in two parts that can be simply summarized:

- Police Act 1997, Part III (PA 1997): empowers authorities to interfere with private property in circumstances that would otherwise constitute a tort or trespass; (usually in order to facilitate actions under the RIPA)
- Regulation of Investigatory Powers Act 2000 (RIPA): empowers investigators to use specific methods in order to acquire evidence without the investigation subject being made aware of the investigation through utilization of such tactics.

The basic covert investigation methods available under RIPA are:

- the interception of communications;
- directed surveillance;
- intrusive surveillance; and
- covert human intelligence sources.

The availability of these methods is dependent upon different crime thresholds. The more intrusive the method, the more serious the crime under investigation has to be before that method can be used.

6.2 **Requirement for Authorization**

All covert investigation methods must be authorized before they are used. The level of authorization required is commensurate with the level of intrusion and the degree of interference with the ECHR right. In 1994, when giving evidence to the Home Affairs Select Committee in Parliament, in calling for laws to empower police to use covert investigation, various senior police officers suggested that authority for such actions should be by independent judicial warrant, similar to search warrants, for instance.

The model eventually approved by Parliament was a regime mostly based on self-authorization by the organization seeking to use the power. Self-authorization is not uncontroversial. It has clear operational advantages for investigation and enforcement agencies, but it lacks the rigour of independent oversight provided by judicial warrant. It exposes investigators to allegations of abuse of power.

Table 6.1 gives a very broad overview of authorization levels for covert investigation. A detailed prescription of persons and ranks with power to authorize different covert

**Table 6.1 General overview of authority levels
for covert investigation methods**

Method	Authority level
Interception of communication	Home Secretary
Intrusive surveillance	Chief Officer of Police, subject to prior approval of the Chief Surveillance Commissioner
Covert Human Intelligence Source	Superintendent
Directed surveillance	Superintendent

investigation methods will be found in the various Statutory Instruments (SIs) issued as secondary legislation supplementing RIPA. The relevant SIs for authority levels in relation to directed surveillance, covert human intelligence sources (CHIS), and access to communications data are:

- SI 2003/3171
- SI 2003/3172
- SI 2005/1083
- SI 2005/1084
- SI 2006/594
- SI 2006/1874
- SI 2006/1878

Note: The authorizing officers empowered by these statutory instruments are tabulated for ease of reference in Harfield C and Harfield K, *Covert Investigation* (Oxford, Oxford University Press, 2008, 2nd edition) Appendix C, stating the law as it was in July 2008. They have to be read in conjunction with each other as the later instruments amend in part (but do not entirely replace) the earlier instruments. The full Statutory Instrument texts are available online at <http://www.opsi.gov.uk/stat> (accessed 29 January 2009).

Authority levels for interception of communications and intrusive surveillance are specified in the main text of RIPA.

6.3 **Management of Covert Investigation**

Covert investigation is regulated in order to meet three criteria:

- the rights of the suspect must not be breached except where there is statutory provision to do so;
- the rights of other citizens not suspected of criminal involvement must be protected; and

- the integrity of the investigator(s) must be demonstrated (or, if necessary, its absence exposed).

The underlying principles are that any infringement of human rights must be based on the principles of lawfulness, necessity, and proportionality. These principles have given rise to a set of tests applied in Strasbourg case law to assess the lawful application of covert investigation powers.

(1) Does the investigative act fall within the scope of Article 8?
(2) If yes, has the Article 8 right been interfered with by a Public Authority?
(3) If it has, was this interference in accordance with the law?
(4) If it was lawful, was the interference pursuant to a legitimate aim as identified in Article 8(2)?
(5) Even if it was both lawful and pursuant to a legitimate aim, was it still necessary, and no more than necessary (ie proportionate) in a democratic society?

A similar set of questions provides the test for proportionality.

KEY POINTS—PROPORTIONALITY

(1) Have relevant and sufficient reasons based on reliable information been put forward for conducting the proposed covert investigation in that particular way? *Jersild v Denmark* (1995) 19 EHRR 1.
(2) Could the same evidence or intelligence be gained by a less intrusive method? *Campbell v UK* (1993) 15 EHRR 137.
(3) Is the decision-making process by which the application is made and the authorization given demonstrably fair? *W v UK* (1988) 10 EHRR 29; *McMichael v UK* (1995) 20 EHRR 205; *Buckley v UK* (1997) 23 EHRR 101.

---

(4) What safeguards have been put in place to prevent abuse of the technique? *Klass v Germany* (1979–80) 2 EHRR 214. See paragraph 59 in which it is argued safeguards represent the compromise between defending democratic society and individual rights.

(5) Does the proposed infringement in fact destroy the 'very essence' of the ECHR right engaged?
(Based on Starmer K, *European Human Rights Law* (London, Legal Action Group, 1998) 171, 175–176)

Three possible adverse consequences await investigators who utilize covert investigation methods improperly:

- a stay of proceedings (for instance in circumstances where investigators have entrapped the accused);
- exclusion of evidence improperly obtained (at the discretion of the trial judge);
- formal complaint against police.

Investigators contemplating the use of a covert investigation method may find the following checklist of key issues a useful aide-mémoire.

Checklist—Key Issues When Considering Whether to Deploy Covert Investigation Technique

- What evidence or intelligence is being sought?
- How is it relevant to the operation under consideration?
- What is the least intrusive means of securing such evidence or information?
- Are there sufficient resources (appropriately skilled staff, equipment, and funding) to do the job properly?
- What are the risks to the organization of such tactics?
- What are the risks to the organization's staff of such tactics?
- What are the risks to the public or specific third parties when such tactics are deployed?

- What are the risks to the subject of the investigation?
- Will such methods breach Article 8(1)?
- Is there justification for doing so provided by Article 8(2)?
- How is the legality test met?
- How is the legitimacy test met?
- How is the necessity test met?
- How is the proportionality test met?
- Are the arguments justifying the application to use covert investigation based on reliable information/intelligence, or has the applicant adopted a 'tick-the-box' approach to completing the application without giving full consideration to the facts of the case and the issues arising?
- Have the arguments justifying the granting of authorization to use covert investigation been fully articulated, or has the authorizing officer merely paid lip service to the pro forma authorization template via which authority is granted?
- How are the methods by which the evidence/intelligence will be obtained to be protected at trial?

6.4 **Definition of Surveillance**

Surveillance is defined at section 48(2) of RIPA and includes:

(a) monitoring, observing, or listening to persons, their movements, their conversations, or their other activities or communications;

(b) recording anything monitored, observed, or listened to in the course of surveillance; and

(c) surveillance by or with the assistance of a surveillance device.

A two-part hierarchy of surveillance is prescribed by law because:

- not all public authorities empowered to conduct directed surveillance may also conduct intrusive surveillance, and

- the circumstances in which intrusive surveillance may be conducted are more restricted than those in which directed surveillance may take place.

6.5 **Directed Surveillance**

Directed surveillance engages the lowest level of intrusion within the framework of covert methodology. It is lawful only if it is authorized for one of the purposes prescribed in RIPA.

The threshold for directed surveillance is crime (for intrusive surveillance it is *serious* crime). Hence frontline staff, particularly those in Neighbourhood Policing Teams, may well find themselves engaged in operations or investigations involving the use of directed surveillance.

Such surveillance can be authorized for the purpose of *preventing or detecting crime* or of *preventing disorder*. This means establishing by whom, for what purpose, by what means, and generally in what circumstances any criminal offence was committed. It may also be conducted in order to apprehend the suspected offender (RIPA, sections 28(3), 81(2), and 81(5)).

Directed surveillance is permitted for other purposes as well (RIPA, section 28(3)):

- in the interests of national security;
- in the interests of the economic well-being of the UK;
- in the interests of public safety;
- for the purpose of protecting public health;
- for the purpose of assessing or collecting certain fiscal levies.

It should be noted, however, that outside the police service these additional statutory purposes are restricted to specific agencies and are not generally available. SOCA, for instance, may conduct surveillance for preventing or detecting crime and/or disorder, but not for any of the other specified purposes. The Statutory Instruments referred to above prescribe which agencies can utilize directed surveillance for which purposes. When planning joint surveillance operations with partner agencies it is important to ensure that the authorizing agency has the appropriate surveillance powers for the actions proposed.

Directed surveillance may not be used:

- inside any premises at the time being used as a residence, no matter how temporary, including hotel accommodation, tents, caravans, a prison cell, or even railway arches;
- in any vehicle which is primarily used as a private vehicle either by the owner or the person having the right to use it (taxis are specifically excluded from this definition, RIPA, section 48(7)(a));
- outside such premises or vehicles if conducted by remote technical means (for instance a long-range microphone) which enables events and conversations inside residential premises and private vehicles to be monitored from outside, producing a surveillance product of the same quality as would be obtained by devices or persons inside such premises or vehicles.

In these three circumstances such surveillance is defined as intrusive (see section 6.11 below).

Note: For further information see the Covert Surveillance Code of Practice, available on line at <http://security.homeoffice.gov.uk/ripa/publication-search/ripa-cop/covert-cop?view=Binary> (accessed 30 January 2009).

6.6 **When Authorization is Required**

Surveillance will require a directed surveillance authority if:

- it comprises covert observation or monitoring by whatever means;
- it is for the purpose of a specific investigation or specific operation (any crime or any other offence);
- it will or is likely to obtain private information about *any* person, not just the subject of the operation (this is the key element that engages Article 8 ECHR).

BUT

- this does not include observations conducted in an immediate response to spontaneous events.

Private information is defined (RIPA, section 26(10); *Covert Surveillance Code of Practice* paragraph 4.3) as being:

> any information relating to a person's private or family life or personal relationships with others.

Case law has firmly established the principle that physical presence in a public place does not erode or negate an individual's right to respect for their private life. Therefore the location of an individual does not alter the nature of the information that is being obtained. The information is private even though the location may be public. It is not only the rights of the investigation subject that have to be respected. There will be collateral intrusion into the privacy of third parties present in the surveillance arena and so investigators and authorizing officers must be able to demonstrate why it is proportionate and necessary to violate their Article 8 rights and what measures will be used to minimize collateral intrusion and its consequences.

Regarding the use of town centre CCTV systems the *Covert Surveillance Code of Practice* (paragraph 1.4) provides that a directed surveillance authority is not required unless the CCTV system is being used for a pre-planned operation.

6.7 **Covert Human Intelligence Sources (CHIS)**

The label CHIS covers a number of different functional identities:

- undercover operative;
- test purchase operative;
- informer.

The first two require police staff to be trained to nationally accredited standards. The management of such skilled persons is through specialist units or through Force Intelligence Bureaux.

Informants are members of the public who volunteer information to the police, reporting an incident they have witnessed or encountered for example. Informants may well be called as witnesses in court.

Informers are individuals tasked by police and other agencies to acquire specific information, often as part of an intelligence operation. Informers, who will generally be asked to acquire information from criminal associates, are very rarely called upon to testify and their identities are protected because, as will be seen, they are providing information covertly, and exposure or compromise of this function may render the informer vulnerable to retribution from those against whom they have provided information.

Part of the protection mechanisms put in place for informers by police organizations, which owe all CHIS a duty of care, follows on from the management regime prescribed by section 29 of RIPA for the use of a CHIS. A *Handler* will manage the CHIS on a daily basis and a *Controller* will oversee the use made of a CHIS. At organizational HQ level there will be an *Authorizing Officer* of senior rank who has the statutory obligation to maintain records about the use of CHIS which will be subject to independent scrutiny by the Office of the Surveillance Commissioners.

Nationally-accredited training exists for the roles above and Association of Chief Police Officers (ACPO) guidance recommends that informers only be managed by staff appropriately trained and assigned to *Dedicated Source Units* (DSU).

It follows that frontline staff may have little to do with informers other than to advise DSU staff of suitable potential informers who volunteer their services to police or in circumstances when DSU staff have been tasked with filling an intelligence gap and need actively to recruit an informer.

It is unlawful to manage a CHIS outside the regulatory regime set out in RIPA. What, then, is that regime? A CHIS is defined (RIPA, section 26(8)) as:

- a person who
- establishes or maintains
- a personal or other relationship with another person
- for the covert purpose of facilitating anything that:

  (a) covertly uses such a relationship to obtain information, or
  (b) to provide access to any information or to another person, or
  (c) covertly discloses information obtained by the use of such a relationship or as a consequence of the existence of such a relationship.

A relationship is used covertly if, and only if, it is conducted in a manner calculated to ensure that the person is unaware of its purpose.

It is the actions of the individual on behalf of the police, in the manner described, which constitutes status as a source that requires authorization. Merely providing information to police that is already within the individual's possession does not necessitate authorization.

The following are sequential tests derived from the statutory definition at section 26(8) of RIPA.

(1) Does the potential source establish or maintain a relationship (personal or otherwise)?

(2) Is the relationship conducted in a manner calculated to ensure that one party is unaware of its real purpose? (See RIPA, section 28(9) for a definition of covert purpose.)

If the answer to these preliminary tests is *yes*, three further tests are applied:

(3) Is the purpose of the relationship to facilitate the obtaining of information?

(4) Is the purpose of the relationship to facilitate access to information?

(5) Is the purpose of the relationship to facilitate the disclosure of information obtained during (or as a consequence of) the relationship without the knowledge of one of the parties?

If the answer to any one of these three tests is *yes*, then taken in conjunction with tests (1) and (2), the source is a CHIS whose conduct must be properly authorized and managed.

CHIS authorization is necessary in all circumstances where the CHIS uses and exploits a personal relationship to acquire information from another person that the other person would regard as being private information. The issue is not who the CHIS is or what he or she produces, but the new relationships that are established or the existing relationships that are maintained, and the covert use that is made of these relationships.

The Office of Surveillance Commissioners has noted with disapproval terminology used in some organizations that seems to indicate the organizations concerned are trying to use informers so as to fall outside the RIPA provisions: of particular concern in this regard is the use of so-called confidential sources, confidential contacts, and tasked witnesses. All individuals fitting the definition and meeting the tests above must be managed and authorized as CHIS.

6.8 **When CHIS Authorization is Required**

A person giving authorization for *use* or *conduct* of a source must believe that the authorization is necessary because:

(a) the authorized use or conduct is proportionate to what it seeks to achieve; AND
(b) satisfactory arrangements (eg trained staff; secure information recording systems) exist for the management of the source.

An authorization will be considered appropriate if it is necessary:

(a) in the interests of national security;
(b) for the prevention or detection of crime or for the prevention of disorder;
(c) in the interests of the economic well-being of the country;
(d) in the interests of public safety;
(e) for the protection of public health;
(f) for the purpose of assessing or collecting any tax, due, or levy or other imposition, contribution; or charge payable to a government department; or
(g) for any other purpose prescribed in an order made by the Secretary of State.

Once again, most of the organizations empowered to deploy CHIS are limited in their statutory purposes to the prevention and detection of crime and/or disorder.

Three general types of conduct may be authorized for a CHIS (RIPA, section 29(4); Code paragraph 4.6).

- Any such activities involving conduct by a CHIS or the use of a CHIS as are specified in the authorization. This gives considerable latitude to authorizing officers and is very flexible. By the same token, if a particular conduct is not mentioned on the authority, it will not be authorized. This reaffirms the importance of precision when drafting applications and authorizations.

- Conduct by or in relation to a specified subject to whose actions the CHIS authorization relates.
- Conduct carried out for the purposes of or in connection with a specific investigation or operation, as described in the authorization.

In terms of participation, either by an informer or by an undercover operative, RIPA is silent, leaving much room for interpretation.

6.9. **Risks Involved in CHIS Utilization**

Although information supplied by a CHIS can be very useful to investigators, the use of informers is not unproblematic. Potential dangers include the following.

- Simply tasking an informer may expose and so compromise the purpose of a police operation (creating an opportunity for the informer to play double agent).
- The informer has their own agenda and to that end supplies misinformation.
- The informer acquires more information from the police than they do from the informer.
- Police instigate crimes that would not otherwise have been committed (entrapment; acting as an *agent provocateur*).
- The relationship between informer and handler becomes corrupt.

6.10 **Further Information Concerning CHIS**

To ensure that the rewards of using a CHIS outweigh the risks involved, RIPA and its associated Codes of Practice should be strictly adhered to. The complexity of CHIS utilization requires more consideration than space here allows.

Frontline staff are encouraged to further their knowledge using the following sources:

- *Covert Human Intelligence Source Code of Practice,* available online at <http://security.homeoffice.gov.uk/ripa/publication-search/ripa-cop/human-cop?view=Binary> (accessed 30 January 2009)
- Billingsley R (ed) *Covert Human Intelligence Sources: The Unlovely Face of Police Work* (Hook, Waterside Press, 2009)
- Harfield C and Harfield K, *Covert Investigation* (Oxford, Oxford University Press, 2008, 2nd edition) chapter 9

6.11 **Intrusive Surveillance**

Intrusive surveillance, by definition more intrusive than directed surveillance, operates at a higher threshold and may only be used for the investigation of serious crime.

Serious crime is defined as (RIPA, section 81(2)(b), RIPA, section 81(3) following PA 1997, section 93(4)):

> (a) An offence for which, on first conviction, a person aged twenty-one years or over with no previous convictions might receive three years imprisonment,
>
> or
>
> (b) The conduct

- involves the use of violence;
- results in substantial financial gain; or
- is engaged in by a large number of persons for a common purpose.

Intrusive surveillance is defined as (RIPA, section 26(3)):

- covert surveillance (see 6.4 above);
- carried out on any residential premises or in any private vehicle,

and which involves:

- the presence of an individual on the premises or in the vehicle; or
- the use of a surveillance device (ie audio or visual probe).

Before any investigative action pursuant to the authority can be carried out, the authorizing officer (Chief Officer of Police) must notify the Office of Surveillance Commissioners (OSC) in writing (RIPA, secton 35). To make the authorization effective, prior approval is required from the OSC and written notice of the OSC approval has to be given to the person who granted the authorization (RIPA, section 36(2)).

Surveillance cannot commence until the authorizing officer has received written approval from the OSC.

Intrusive surveillance is resource intensive and requires particular skills and equipment. Frontline staff encountering circumstances in their work in which they believe intrusive surveillance is required must consult senior managers.

6.12 **Interception of Communications**

The interception of communications is generally unlawful and the product cannot be used in evidence.

There are exceptions to this general prohibition and in such circumstances the contents of the communication can be used in evidence. The exceptions relevant to policing are:

- interception for business purposes (eg the monitoring of commercial telephone calls for training purposes or to prevent fraud and corruption);
- two-party consent (where sender and recipient each consent to police using the communication content);
- one-party consent (where either the sender or the recipient consent AND a directed surveillance authority is in place: used in kidnap and undercover operations);

- where an existing statutory power (eg search warrant or production order) is available to access stored communications.

Interception can also take place under the authority of the Home Secretary's warrant to investigate serious crime. In such circumstances the product cannot be used in evidence nor can the fact of the interception be mentioned in court. Force intelligence bureaux can advise on whether it is appropriate to apply for such a warrant.

6.13 **Conclusion**

There are more aspects to covert investigation than can be covered even in basic terms in the space available here. This chapter has provided an introductory overview focusing on the statutory framework. For obvious reasons a significant amount of information about covert investigation is not in the public domain and so cannot be published. Staff inexperienced in or unfamiliar with covert investigation who are contemplating utilizing such information-gathering methodology are urged to seek advice from the appropriate specialists in their organization. These will include:

- force intelligence bureaux;
- force surveillance units (who will be trained and equipped for mobile surveillance);
- force technical support units (who provide and put in place any equipment needed to facilitate surveillance).

The management of covert investigation does not stop when the desired evidence has been acquired. Sensitive sources, tactics, and techniques must not only be protected during the covert investigation, but the information acquired must be managed in a way that continues to protect sources, tactics, and techniques from exposure and compromise. It may be necessary to make a Public Interest Immunity application at court to protect some information from being disclosed at trial.

The 'principle of need' to know applies (see Chapter 18). Casual conversation about a case using covert investigation with colleagues who are not involved in that investigation undermines the strategic argument that covert methods must be protected. If it is okay casually to disclose sensitive information chatting over a cup of tea, why must that information be protected at court?

Investigators should be aware that, in certain circumstances, case law has now established that a court may order the disclosure of surveillance authorities and supporting documents upon which such authorities are based. This has been in direct consequence of police misuse of surveillance (see Ormerod D and Waterman A, 'Abusing a stay for Grant?' [2005] *Covert Policing Review*, 5–14).

The consequences of getting it wrong in covert investigation can cause adverse consequences extending well beyond the immediate investigation.

It is appropriate to close with an aide memoire (the mnemonic PLAN), reinforcing the human rights principles upon which lawful covert investigation is based. It is a useful starting point before seeking advice for the appropriate experts.

Mnemonic

P = **Proportionality**

Why is it proportionate to obtain the intended product of this surveillance in the manner proposed?

L = **Legitimacy**

What is the legitimate purpose of the proposed action: the prevention of disorder or crime; the interests of national security; the interests of public safety; the interests of the economic wellbeing of the country; the protection of health or morals; the protection of the rights and freedoms of others?

A = **Authority to Undertake Proposed Action**

What is the lawful foundation and authority for the proposed action? From whom must authorization be sought?

N = **Necessity of Proposed Action**

Why is the proposed action necessary?

Further Reading

Primary Sources

The following Codes of Practice are available for download from <http://security.homeoffice.gov.uk/ripa/publication-search/ripa-cop/> (as at 30 January 2009):

- Covert Surveillance Code of Practice;
- CHIS Code of Practice;
- Interception of Communications Code of Practice.

The Annual Reports of the Chief Surveillance Commissioner are presented to the Prime Minister and to Scottish Ministers. They are available on the OSC website at <http://www.surveillancecommissioners.gov.uk>.

Secondary Sources

Ashworth A, *Human Rights, Serious Crime and Criminal Procedure* (Sweet & Maxwell, London, 2002), particularly chapters 2 and 3

Harfield C and Harfield K, *Covert Investigation* (Oxford, Oxford University Press, 2nd edition, 2008)

The academic and practitioner journal *Covert Policing Review* contains papers of detailed commentary on specific issues and cases.

Chapter 7

Victims and Witnesses

7.1 Introduction

> Witnesses play a vital role in helping the police to solve crimes and deliver justice. The criminal justice system cannot work without them.[1]

Any comment that suggests that the contribution of witnesses to the criminal justice system is so important that it cannot function without them might seem on first inspection to be a statement of the obvious. While it seems self-evident that the position of witnesses in the system is vitally important, the rather inconvenient truth is that they are sometimes taken for granted. It is, therefore, no coincidence that successive governments have sought to improve the lot of witnesses in our justice system by enhancing the service that they can expect to receive (see, for example, the *Code of Practice for Victims of Crime*, Office for Criminal Justice Reform, 2005). This chapter sets out to consider how the contribution of witness testimony to the investigative and trial processes might be maximized in view of the various legal and procedural developments that have taken place over recent years.

7.2 Who are Witnesses?

The term 'witness' is defined in section 63 of the Youth Justice and Criminal Evidence Act 1999 and section 52 of

---

[1] CJS Online (2008).

the Domestic Violence, Crime and Victims Act 2004. In essence these definitions define a witness as someone, other than a defendant, who might be called to give evidence in criminal or anti-social behaviour proceedings.

While this definition might seem relatively straightforward, it is important to consider what it includes and what it does not include. The definition is clearly not limited to the testimony of someone who was at the crime scene at the time of the offence. It would, for example, include people who are able to provide evidence of an incriminating statement, such as a threat or a confession, or circumstantial evidence such as might relate to the ownership, control, possession, or disposal of material used in the commission of an offence. That having been said, it is important to note that the definition of 'witness' is firmly routed in the idea that the person might be called to give evidence. This effectively excludes, for example, people who are only able to provide background material, such as members of the family of a homicide victim from whom general antecedents are routinely sought.

7.3 **Witness Classification**

The classification of witnesses into one or more of the groups described below is important because it has consequences for the investigation in terms of how the interview is recorded and it may have consequences for the trial process as one of the factors that a court must consider when determining how the witness may give their evidence. Witnesses fall into one or more of the following categories:

- vulnerable;
- intimidated;
- significant;
- Criminal Justice Act 2003, section 137;
- other.

7.4 **Vulnerable and Intimidated Witnesses**

7.4.1 **Vulnerable Witnesses**

'Vulnerable' witnesses are defined by section 16 of the Youth Justice and Criminal Evidence Act, 1999, as:

1. all child witnesses (under 17); and
2. any witness whose quality of evidence is likely to be diminished because they:
   (a) are suffering from a mental disorder (as defined by the Mental Health Act 1983); or
   (b) have a significant impairment of intelligence and social functioning; or
   (c) have a physical disability or are suffering from a physical disorder.

The court must take account of the views of the witness in determining whether a witness falls into this category (section 16(4)). In addition to this, when determining whether the quality of the witness's evidence is likely to be diminished in these circumstances, the court has to consider the likely completeness, coherence, and accuracy of that evidence (section 16(5)).

Section 21 of the Act goes on to effectively create the sub-category of child witnesses 'in need of special protection' with reference to those who are witnesses in cases of 'sexual' or 'violent' offences.

In the case of offences committed on after 1 May 2004, 'sexual offence' means any offence contrary to:

- Part 1 of the Sexual Offences Act 2003; or
- the Protection of Children Act 1978 (as amended by section 45 of the Sexual Offences Act 2003).

Note: Child Witnesses—While the legislation defined child witnesses as under 17 at the time of writing, clause 81 of the Coroners and Justice Bill (2009) included a proposal to increase the age limit to 18 for the sake of consistency with child care legislation.

1 Evidence Management

In the case of offences committed before 1 May 2004, 'sexual offence' means any offence contrary to:

- the Sexual Offences Act 1956;
- the Indecency with Children Act 1960;
- the Sexual Offences Act 1967;
- section 54 of the Criminal Law Act 1977; or
- the Protection of Children Act 1978.

'Violent offence' means:

- any offence of kidnapping, false imprisonment, or an offence under sections 1 or 2 of the Child Abduction Act 1984.
- any offence under section 1 of the Children and Young Persons Act 1933; or
- any other offence involving:
  - assault on;
  - injury to; or
  - a threat of injury to a person.

This sub-category of child witnesses 'in need of special protection' is important because there is a stronger presumption in law that they will give their evidence-in-chief by means of a pre-recorded video and that they will be cross-examined via live television link. The effect of this is that investigative interviews with child witnesses 'in need of special protection' should be video-recorded unless they do not consent or there are other insurmountable difficulties (Office for Criminal Justice Reform, *Achieving Best Evidence in Criminal Proceedings: Interviewing Victims and Witnesses, and Using Special Measures*, 2007, paragraph 2.77).

> **Note**—Primary Rule Presumption
> The presumption that child witnesses will give their evidence-in-chief by means of a pre-recorded video and will be cross-examined via live television link (sometimes referred to as the 'primary rule') was the subject of a proposed amendment in clause 83 of the Coroners and Justice Bill (2009) at the time of

writing. If the proposed amendment features in the final legislation, its effect will be to substantially reduce the strength of the
presupposition that child witnesses in need of special protection
should give their evidence-in-chief by pre-recorded video and be
cross-examined by live TV link.

7.4.2 Intimidated Witnesses

'Intimidated' witnesses are defined by section 17 of the
Act as those whose quality of testimony is likely to be
diminished by reason of fear or distress.

In determining whether a witness falls into this category,
the court should take account of:

- the nature and alleged circumstances of the offence;
- the age of the witness;
- where relevant:
  - the social and cultural background and ethnic origins
    of the witness,
  - the domestic and employment circumstances of the
    witness,
  - any religious beliefs or political opinions of the
    witness;
- any behaviour towards the witness by:
  - the accused,
  - members of the accused person's family or associates,
  - any other person who is likely to be either an accused
    person or a witness in the proceedings.

Complainants in cases of sexual assault are defined as
falling into this category per se by section 17(4) of the
Youth Justice and Criminal Evidence Act 1999.[2] *Vulnerable
Witnesses: A Police Service Guide* (Association of Chief Police
Officers and Home Office, 2001) suggests that victims of

---

[2] At the time of writing, clause 84 of the Coroners and Justice Bill (2009)
included a proposed amendment to the Youth Justice and Criminal
Evidence Act 1999 that would give complainants to sexual offences
greater access to video-recorded evidence-in-chief.

domestic violence, racially motivated crime, and repeat victimization, and elderly and frail witnesses also fall into this category.[3]

7.5 **Special Measures**

Subject to availability, as defined in the phased implementation timetable, the 'special measures' are:

- the use of screens (section 23);
- the use of live TV link (section 24);
- giving evidence in private (section 25);
- the removal of wigs and gowns (section 26);
- the use of video-recorded interviews as evidence-in-chief (section 27);
- the use of video-recorded cross-examination (section 28);
- communication through intermediaries (section 29); and
- the use of special communication aids (section 30).

7.5.1 **Screens**

Screens or curtains (depending on the layout of the court) are positioned around the witness box so as to prevent the defendant from seeing the witness and the witness from seeing the defendant. The witness will still be able to see and be seen by the judge or magistrate, and at least one legal representative of the prosecution and defence (and the jury if the case is heard at the Crown Court). This special measure is available for all vulnerable and intimidated witnesses in all criminal courts in England and Wales.

---

[3] At the time of writing, clause 82 of the Coroners and Justice Bill (2009) included a proposed amendment that would have the effect of automatically including witnesses to certain offences involving weapons in s 17 of the Youth Justice and Criminal Evidence Act definition of 'intimidated' witnesses.

7.5.2 Live TV Link

The witness gives live evidence from a room outside the courtroom (usually, though not always, in the court building). The witness's testimony is relayed live into the courtroom via TV link. This measure is intended to reduce the stress experienced by witnesses while they give evidence by taking them out of the intimidating auditorium of the courtroom and out of the presence of the accused, although it should be noted that the accused will be able to see the witness on the television screen unless additional provisions are made to preserve the anonymity of the witness. This special measure is available for all vulnerable and intimidated witnesses in all criminal courts in England and Wales.

7.5.3 Giving Evidence in Private

Members of the public are excluded from the court while the witness is giving evidence. Only one nominated member of the media is allowed to be present. This measure is intended to be used in sexual offence cases and some cases of intimidation. It is intended to reduce the embarrassment and/or sense of intimidation likely to be experienced while witnesses give sensitive evidence. This special measure is available for all vulnerable and intimidated witnesses in all criminal courts in England and Wales.

7.5.4 The Removal of Wigs and Gowns

The judge and lawyers remove their wigs and gowns with the intention of creating a less formal environment in the court leading to a reduction in the anxiety experienced by the witness. This measure is only of use where the witness does not prefer the formality of the situation to be enhanced by wigs and gowns. Some witnesses might express the view that they want 'their day in a *proper* court'. This special measure is available for all vulnerable and intimidated witnesses in all criminal courts in England and Wales.

7.5.5 The Use of Video-Recorded Interviews as Evidence-in-Chief

The video interview with the police is played as the witness's evidence-in-chief with the intention of reducing the stress experienced by the witness as a result of reducing the number of times on which they have to repeat their account. It is important to remember that the witness must be available to attend court to give evidence (section 27(4) of the Youth Justice and Criminal Evidence Act 1999), although cross-examination often takes place via live TV link in these circumstances. Video-recorded interviews are served on the defence as part of the prosecution case where they are to be played as evidence-in-chief (the visual image can only be pixilated and the voice recording can only be modulated where an application is made under the witness anonymity legislation).[4]

> **Note**: A video-recorded interview can only be played in court where the witness is not available for cross-examination in the wholly exceptional circumstances set out in the hearsay provisions described in section 116 of the Criminal Justice Act 2003.

The appeal court judgment in the case of *R v Rochester*[5] overturned previous views concerning the phased implementation of this special measure. It has been available to all vulnerable and intimidated witness in all the criminal courts in England and Wales since 24 July 2002.

7.5.6 The Use of Video-Recorded Cross-Examination

Cross-examination is video-recorded prior to the trial and played at the trial. This special measure was originally

---

[4] The Criminal Evidence (Witness Anonymity) Act 2008 at the time of writing.

[5] [2008] EWCA Crim 678.

intended to reduce the stress experienced by witnesses as a result of cross-examination having been completed before the trial. It has, however, run into some practical difficulties that include the continuing duty of disclosure by the prosecution to the defence. This special measure had not been implemented at the time of writing as a result of these practical difficulties.

KEY POINTS

The prosecution have a continuing duty of disclosure to the defence by virtue of the Criminal Procedure and Investigations Act 1996 (as amended by section 37 of the Criminal Justice Act 2003). The effect of this is that the witness might still be called to court if fresh information comes to light after video-recorded cross-examination.

7.5.7 Communication Through Intermediaries

The function of an intermediary is to assist 'vulnerable' witnesses (as defined by section 16 of the Youth Justice and Criminal Evidence Act) to communicate by *explaining* questions put to and answers given by them. This special measure is for witnesses who would benefit from the assistance of a specialist, such as a speech and language therapist, a clinical psychologist, a mental health professional, or a special needs education professional, to help them to communicate in a police witness interview and/or while giving evidence during legal proceedings. The register of intermediaries can be accessed by contacting the Office for Criminal Justice Reform.[6] This special measure is available for all vulnerable witnesses in all criminal courts in England and Wales.

---

[6] Interdepartmental body that is located within the Home Office but also has responsibility to the Ministry of Justice and the office of the Attorney General.

7.5.8 The Use of Special Communication Aids

This special measure is intended to help 'vulnerable' witnesses who need to use a 'device' to communicate when giving evidence. This includes computers and voice synthesizers, and might also include symbol boards and books. This special measure is available for all vulnerable witnesses in all criminal courts in England and Wales.

7.5.9 Eligibility for Special Measures

When a witness is considered to fall into either the 'vulnerable' or 'intimidated' category they are deemed to be 'eligible' for 'special measures'. However, whether or not they are actually given access to such measures by the court depends on two considerations:

- whether the 'special measure' in question has been implemented; and
- with the exception of live TV link and video-recorded evidence-in-chief in respect of child witnesses 'in need of special protection', whether the 'special measure' in question is likely to maximize the quality of their evidence (section 19(2)).

In determining whether the quality of the witness's evidence is likely to be maximized, courts are obliged to take account of the circumstances of the case, including the witness's views and the likelihood that the use of the 'special measure' might inhibit the testing of the evidence by any party (section 19(3)). It follows that investigators should ensure that the informed views of 'vulnerable' or 'intimidated' witnesses are sought in relation to those 'special measures' that are currently available to them. Explaining special measures to victims is a police responsibility under the *Code of Practice for Victims of Crime* (paragraph 5.8) (Office for Criminal Justice Reform, 2005). It will also be a responsibility under the *Witness Charter* (Charter Standards 4 and 5) (Office for Criminal Justice Reform, 2007) when it is implemented. Investigators involved in soliciting the views of 'vulnerable' or 'intimidated' witnesses should make it clear to them that the final decision concerning access to 'special measures' is one for the court.

In addition to the availability of the special measure and the likelihood that it will maximize the quality of the witness's evidence, access to video-recorded evidence-in-chief is also contingent on whether playing the video or any part of it is contrary to the interests of justice (section 27(2)).

7.6 **Witness Anonymity and Witness Protection**

In extreme cases of intimidation where it is thought that the best way of protecting the witness or their family or friends from harm or preventing serious damage to property is to conceal their identity from a suspected offender an application can be considered under section 3 of the Criminal Evidence (Witness Anonymity) Act 2008.[7]

Where a suspected offender is already aware of a witness's identity or is likely to deduce their identity because of the nature of their evidence, and the witness or their family is at serious risk of harm, witness protection could be considered, although the life-changing consequences of relocating and adopting a new identity are such that this is only likely to be a consideration in the most serious cases.

7.7 **Significant Witnesses**

Significant witnesses are defined in *Achieving Best Evidence in Criminal Proceedings: Guidance on Interviewing Victims and*

---

[7] This legislation had been incorporated into and extended by the provisions of the Coroners and Justice Bill (2009) at the time of writing.

Witnesses, and Using Special Measures (Office for Criminal Justice Reform, 2007) as people who:

- have or claim to have witnessed, visually or otherwise, an indictable offence, part of such an offence, or events closely connected with it;
- stand in a particular relationship to the victim or have a central position in an investigation into an indictable offence.

Recordings of interviews with significant witnesses cannot be played as evidence-in-chief; they serve rather to demonstrate the integrity of the interview process and to provide a more accurate account of what was actually said than notes alone.

What is said by the witness on the recording is converted into evidence either by means of a transcript that is exhibited by the interviewing officer after the witness has made a brief statement adopting the interview or by the witness signing a full section 9 Criminal Justice Act 1967 statement that is prepared after the video has been reviewed.

Achieving Best Evidence also mentions section 137 of the Criminal Justice Act 2003 (CJA 2003) in conjunction with significant witnesses. Under section 137 CJA 2003 witnesses may be regarded as a discrete category of significant witness in that they are defined as people who have or claim to have witnessed, visually or otherwise, an indictable or prescribed triable either-way offence, part of such an offence, or events closely connected with it and whose recollection is likely to be significantly better at the time of the interview than at the time of giving evidence. In determining whether the witness's recollection is likely to have been better at the time of the interview than it is when the trial takes place, the court must take account of the amount of time between the interview and the alleged event. While there is no guidance on the length of this interval, it seems likely that it will be limited to a relatively short period of time, possibly a few days. Section 137 of the CJA 2003 has not, however, been implemented at the time of writing, nor is there an implementation timetable available.

7.8 **Initial Contact with Witnesses**

When encountering a potential witness to an offence for the first time there is a tension between needing to ask them some questions to find out what they know while trying to minimize the scope for future challenges suggesting that the witness's memory was corrupted in some way by the initial contact.

The 'rules' set out in *Achieving Best Evidence* take account of this tension in that they acknowledge the need for some questioning to take place in order to determine the initial action that is to be taken by the police while seeking to limit questions to those necessary for early decision making. These rules may be summarized as follows:

- Listen, do not interrupt unsolicited accounts.
- Try to ask open and specific closed questions, try to avoid less productive types of question (eg leading questions).
- Only ask what is necessary to determine initial action (this depends on the circumstances).
- Make a written record of what was said, who was present, and the witness's demeanour as soon as possible.

7.9 **Interviewing Witnesses**

7.9.1 **Consent**

Witness interviews should take place with the informed consent of the interviewee. 'Informed consent' in this context refers to understanding the purpose of the interview (eg to be played as evidence-in-chief or, in the case of a written statement, to help the prosecution lawyer guide the witness through live evidence-in-chief). Informed consent is not only a moral imperative it is also a procedural requirement that arises from the *Code of Practice for Victims of Crime* and the *Witness Charter*.

Where the witness is under 17 the interviewer will need to consider the guidelines specified by Lord Fraser in the case involving Victoria Gillick in 1985.[8] The effect of the Fraser guidelines is that a child can consent in their own right if they are capable of understanding the implications of what they are being asked to consent to. If a child can understand the implications of being interviewed as a witness and, where the interview is to be video-recorded, the use to which the recording is to be put, they can consent in their own right. If a child cannot understand these implications the consent of a parent or guardian is required. It is important to note that *Achieving Best Evidence* deals with the issue of informing a child's parents/guardians separately to consent: other than in wholly exceptional circumstances parents/guardians should be informed even where the child has the capacity to consent.

The Mental Capacity Act 2005 applies where the witness is over 16 and there is some doubt as to whether they have the mental capacity to understand the implications of what they are being asked to consent to (for example, where a witness has a severe learning disability). The Act puts an obligation on service providers such as the police to try their utmost to communicate with people for whom capacity may be an issue. The effect of this is that the language used to communicate the information on which a decision is to be based may need to be modified. Where it is determined that a witness still lacks the capacity to make an informed decision, the police are required to act in the person's 'best interests'. Acting in a person's 'best interests' means consulting every available person who is involved in the witness's life about what the witness would want if they had the capacity to make a decision.

7.9.2 Planning and Preparation

Planning and preparation should never be regarded as an expensive luxury that can be dispensed with when interviewers are busy. Planning is essential to the effective conduct of an interview (eg paragraph 3.55 of *Achieving Best*

---

[8] *Gillick v West Norfolk and Wisbech AHA* [1985] 3 All ER 402.

Evidence). It consists of looking at the witness's background and finding something out about the investigation and then using that information to inform the interview plan.

The Witness

The information about the witness that should be established for the purposes of planning the interview includes:

- age;
- gender;
- sexuality (if relevant to the offence and likely to have an impact on the interview, eg in terms of interviewer selection);
- culture, ethnicity, religion, and first language;
- preferred name/mode of address;
- domestic circumstances (including whether currently in a 'safe' environment);
- the implications of any physical, learning, or mental disorder or disability for the interview process;
- the implications of any medication taken for the interview process;
- current emotional state (including trauma, distress, shock, depression, fears of intimidation/recrimination, and recent significant stressful events experienced);
- likely impact of recalling of traumatic events on the behaviour of the witness;
- current or previous contact with public services (including previous contact with police, social services, or health professionals);
- relationship to the alleged offender.

The Offence

Ideally, interviewers should only have minimal offence information because of the potential that such knowledge has to contaminate the interview. Such minimal offence information includes:

- the nature of the alleged offence;
- the time, frequency, and location of the alleged offence;

- how the alleged offence came to the notice of police;
- the nature of any threats or intimidation alleged to have been used by the suspect or their associates.

It is accepted that in many cases interviewers will know far more than this minimal knowledge as a result of their involvement in the investigation. In these instances, it is essential that interviewers do their best to guard against their knowledge of the case contaminating the interview.

Information Important to The Investigation

Information important to the investigation can be thought of as falling into two categories:

- matters of general investigative practice;
- case-specific material.

Matters of general investigative practice include:

- points to prove the offence;
- case law (eg, *R v Turnbull* [1977] QB 224 in the case of eye-witnesses);
- good investigative practice (eg, 'have you told anyone else about this?').

As is suggested in the name, case-specific material very much depends on the particular circumstances of the case. It could include:

- the antecedents of the victim;
- the background to a relationship;
- a history of the alleged abuse experienced by a victim;
- the victim's usual routine;
- the ownership, control or use of property such as vehicles, mobile telephones, and computers;
- access to weapons;
- access to a crime scene;
- access to material that could be used to conceal or cleanse a crime scene;
- significant omissions or inconsistencies between the witness's account and other material.

Matters of general investigative practice are invariably of evidential value; case-specific material sometimes has little or no evidential value. Where the case-specific material has no evidential value its principal function is to aid the investigative process by contributing to the investigator's understanding of the alleged offence and by generating lines of enquiry.

Interviewers should know a great deal about matters of general investigative practice when they prepare for interview. The amount of case-specific material that they have access to prior to the interview usually depends on how much they know about the alleged offence. The interview plan will need to take account of situations in which interviewers have no knowledge of some or all of the case-specific material. In these circumstances the case-specific material might be handled either by being 'drip-fed' to the interviewers at a suitable point in the interview by someone monitoring the process, or, where the case is complex, by the interview taking place in two parts separated by a break during which the interviewers can be briefed on the case-specific material.

Use of Planning Information

The planning information should then be used to determine the following:

- the objectives of the interview;
- the most appropriate structure for the interview;
- the techniques to be used during the interview;
- the method of recording the interview;
- any props and exhibits that should be available to the interviewers;
- the people to be present during the interview:
  - interviewers (if two who will lead?)
  - camera operator
  - interview monitor?
  - witness supporter?
  - interpreter?
  - intermediaries;

- the timing of the interview;
- the likely duration and pace of the interview;
- whether more than one interview session is likely to be needed.

Objectives

The objectives for any interview should be clear, topic-based, and specific. General objectives such as 'to find out what the witness knows about the offence' are of little use in determining the ground to be covered during the interview. Topic-based objectives focus on specific issues such as the witness's movements between particular times, the witness's account of the alleged offence, the witness's knowledge of the suspected offender, etc.

Interview Structure

The most appropriate structure for the interview will usually be the four-phased structure described in *Achieving Best Evidence* (see section 7.9.4 below). There are, however, occasions on which the phased approach is unlikely to be of any use. Typically these occasions include:

- those in which the witness is believed to be a victim of crime but has not disclosed anything, as may be the case where other material such as video recordings or other witness accounts indicate that they have been subjected to an abusive act;
- those in which the witness has a very limited communication ability (particularly where they can only indicate 'yes' or 'no' in response to a question).

In these circumstances a decision will need to be made on an alternative structure for the interview. For example, the Systematic Approach to Gathering Evidence (SAGE) advocated in Roberts and Glasgow (1993) may be appropriate in some cases where a young or learning disabled witness is believed to be a victim who has not disclosed anything, while a series of carefully framed forced-choice questions are likely to be appropriate if the witness can only give 'yes' 'no' responses to the interviewer's questions.

Interview Techniques

The techniques to be used during the interview could include:

- the cognitive interview (see chapter 4B of *Achieving Best Evidence*) where the witness is either an eye or an ear witness to an event and is willing and able to focus their concentration to the extent needed to mentally reinstate the context;
- conversation management (see Association of Chief Police Officers, *Practical Guide to Investigative Interviewing*, 2004) where the witness is unable or unwilling to focus their concentration or where their account does not deal with a specific incident (for example, where background material is to be covered in the interview).

Method of Recording

When interviews with vulnerable and intimidated witnesses are recorded with a view to playing them as evidence-in-chief the recording must be on video because section 27 of the Youth Justice and Criminal Evidence Act only provides for the playing of a video-recording (no provision is made for audio-recordings). It is important, however, to remember that it is the informed views of the witness that determines whether a video is actually made. Where a witness does not want the interview to be video-recorded consideration can be given to making an audio-recording if the witness is also 'significant'. If the witness does not want the interview to be audio-recorded or they are not considered 'significant' a record of the interview should be made in the form of handwritten notes.

Interviews with significant witnesses should usually be recorded on video since this medium is likely to provide the most comprehensive record of the interview. If the witness does not want the interview to be video-recorded consideration should be given to making an audio-record of it. If the witness does not want the interview to be audio-recorded, handwritten notes should suffice (paragraphs 4.53 to 4.54 of *Achieving Best Evidence*).

1 Evidence Management

Location

Video-recorded interviews should ideally take place in purpose-built interview suites because they are designed to keep background noise and visual distractions down to a minimum. Portable video-recording equipment should only be used where it is not practical to access a purpose built suite.

Props and Exhibits

Props and exhibits might include:

- pens and paper;
- body diagrams;
- property;
- photographs.

It can be helpful to have pens and paper in the interview room, but body diagrams, property, and photographs have the potential to distract and, possibly, lead a witness. For this reason they should be kept out of sight, possibly in the room with the camera operator, and only brought out when they are needed in the interview. If the witness writes or draws on any paper in the interview it should be treated as an exhibit.

People Present

A camera operator should always be present when the interview is video-recorded. In addition to this, the circumstances of the witness and the case may merit the presence of the following:

- a second interviewer and/or interview monitor;
- a witness supporter;
- an interpreter;
- an intermediary.

Where a second interviewer is to be present there should be a clear agreement as to who will lead the interview and an understanding of how and when the second interviewer will have an opportunity to contribute towards the interview (for example, by being explicitly invited to do so after the lead interviewer has finished probing each topic).

A supporter may be present with the agreement of the witness to provide them with emotional support during the interview. Witness supporters cannot be other witnesses in the case. *Achieving Best Evidence* generally discourages the use of parents or carers as supporters because they can be an additional source of stress for the witness (paragraph 2.104). Witness supporters are not appropriate adults; it has not been necessary to use appropriate adults in interviews with witnesses since paragraph 11.15 of Code C of the Police and Criminal Evidence Act 1984 was revised on 1 April 2003.

Interpreters and intermediaries should be properly briefed and involved at an appropriate point in the interview planning process. Intermediaries need to assess the witness before the interview to ensure that they have the skills needed to facilitate the dialogue with the witness and establish the most appropriate methods of communication during the interview.

Timing, Duration, and Pace; Number of Interview Sessions

The timing of the interview should take account of factors such as the witness's routine and the effects of any medication they are using (for example, if the witness has been prescribed a slow-release drug that makes them drowsy in the afternoon the best time for the interview is likely to be the morning).

Similarly, the duration and pace of the interview must be influenced by what is known about the witness (for example, the age or medical condition of the witness might be such as to limit any interview to under an hour).

In complex cases or cases in which the witness cannot be interviewed for more than a short period of time, it may be appropriate for the interview to take place over a number of sessions. These sessions can take place over more than one day if necessary.

7.9.3 **Preparation of the Witness for Interview**

Witnesses should always be prepared for an interview. In some cases preparation can take place briefly just before the interview; in other cases preparation might need to take place over a number of sessions several days before the interview. Interview preparation should include:

- an explanation of the role of the interviewer(s);
- an explanation of the purpose of the interview without discussing the details of the offence being investigated;
- the ground rules for the interview (for example, not making any assumptions about the interviewer's knowledge of what was witnessed);
- an outline of the structure of the interview without discussing the details of the offence being investigated.

7.9.4 **The Interview**

Interviews that make use of the phased structure described in *Achieving Best Evidence* proceed through four phases:

- rapport
- free narrative
- questioning
- closure.

It is not within the scope of this chapter to describe each of these phases in detail but they can be summarized with reference to Figure 7.1.

Rapport

The rapport phase consists of three elements:

i. Administration—The administration at the beginning of the interview includes:
- covering personal introductions;
- stating the date, time, and place;
- explaining the reason for the interview without mentioning the offence;

Witness Interview Outline

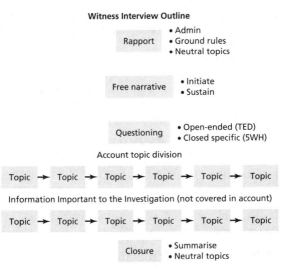

Figure 7.1

- pointing out the positions of the cameras and microphones.
ii. Ground rules—Ground rules include:
  - explaining to the witness that they should try to mention everything, without editing anything out, even partial or apparently trivial detail;
  - telling the witness that they should say what happened in their own way and in their own time;
  - explaining to the witness that they should say if they do not understand the questions that they are asked;
  - explaining to the witness that they should say if questions are asked that they do not know the answer to;
  - telling the witness that they should say so if the interviewer seems to have misunderstood something that they told them;
  - exploring the witness's understanding of truth and lies if they are under 17 or have a learning disability.

iii. Neutral topics—A discussion focusing on neutral topics such as the witness's hobbies and pastimes is intended to serve two purposes:
  • to create a relaxed atmosphere, as far as possible, given the circumstances;
  • to give the witness the opportunity to practice the unusual conversational rules that apply to an investigative interview, where necessary.

In some instances the discussion of neutral topics can be very brief, in other instances it may take some time.

Free Narrative

The free narrative phase consists of two elements

i. Initiation
ii. Sustaining.

In many instances free narrative is initiated by means of an open-ended prompt such as 'tell me what happened last night?' It is then sustained by means of active listening techniques and open-ended prompts such as echo questions.

Questioning

The questioning phase consists of:

i. systematically probing the witness's account after dividing it into manageable topics;
ii. systematically probing topics of information important to the investigation that have not already been covered in the witness's account.

In each instance the topics should be probed using open-ended then specific-closed questions. Whether any given question is open-ended or specific-closed depends largely on context but, in general terms, open-ended questions are typically those beginning with 'tell me ...', 'explain to me ...', or 'describe to me ...' (sometimes referred to as TED questions), whereas specific-closed questions often begin with 'who', 'what', 'where', 'when', 'why', or 'how' (sometimes referred to a 5WH questions).

Closure

The closure phase consists of:

- brief communication between interviewers and between the interviewers and interview monitor to ensure that no more questions need to be asked;
- summarizing what the witness has said;
- answering any questions from the witness;
- asking witness to contact the investigation team if they remember anything else about the incident;
- returning to neutral topics if necessary;
- reporting the end-time of the interview for the purposes of the video/audio recording.

7.10 **Conclusion**

This chapter has considered how the contribution of witness testimony to the investigative and trial processes can be maximized. To this end it has considered witness categorization, the special measures under the Youth Justice and Criminal Evidence Act 1999, initial contact with witnesses, and the planning and conduct of witness interviews.

An understanding of the importance of witnesses to the investigative process forces us to carefully consider the matters referred to in this chapter. If we ignore them we run the risk of taking the cooperation of witnesses for granted. Such a position is likely to lead to our system of justice being undermined as witnesses increasingly opt out of participating in it.

Further Reading

Association of Chief Police Officers (2004) *Practical Guide to Investigative Interviewing*, Wyboston, Centrex

Association of Chief Police Officers and Home Office (2001) *Vulnerable Witnesses: A Police Service Guide*, London, Home Office

Office for Criminal Justice Reform (2005) *Code of Practice for Victims of Crime*, London, Office for Criminal Justice Reform

—— (2007) *Achieving Best Evidence in Criminal Proceedings: Guidance on Interviewing Victims and Witnesses, and Using Special Measures*, London, Office for Criminal Justice Reform

—— (2007) *Witness Charter*, London, Office for Criminal Justice Reform

Roberts H and Glasgow, D (1993) *SAGE: A Systematic Approach to Gathering Evidence*, Children Division of Criminological and Legal Psychology Occasional Papers No 22, Leicester, British Psychological Society

The Criminal Justice System advice document, *Achieving Best Evidence in Criminal Proceedings: Guidance on Interviewing Victims and Witnesses, and Using Special Measures*, is available at <http://www.cps.gov.uk/publications/docs/achieving_best_evidence_final.pdf>

Chapter 8

Disclosure and Public Interest Immunity

8.1 Introduction

Disclosure has lately become of significant importance in criminal trials, especially at the most serious end of the spectrum, where defendants have been acquitted of murder both at trial and on appeal as a result of failures in disclosure by the police and the prosecution. Yet disclosure remains an area that many police officers and other investigators do not properly understand and which a lot of prosecution lawyers—Crown Prosecution Service (CPS) and counsel—avoid if they possibly can.

The last 20 years has seen the development of a 'process' by which disclosure must be dealt with, initially through the development of case law, but since 1996 by the implementation of the Criminal Procedure and Investigations Act 1996 (CPIA). This process amounts to a set of legally binding rules that governs how investigators and prosecutors must fulfil their responsibilities for disclosure. Any breaches of those rules may well allow the defence to argue an abuse of process, which—if successful—could prove fatal to the case.

This chapter aims to introduce those involved at the front line of law enforcement to 'disclosure', including explaining what exactly it is and what it deals with, why it is such an important area, what potential problems it causes, and how the system of dealing with disclosure material is supposed to work, in particular how it is an issue for everyone involved in the investigation of crime, even those seemingly engaged on the periphery of an enquiry.

8.2 **Disclosure of Unused Material**

The word disclosure has become a shorthand term for the unused material generated during a criminal investigation and how it has been dealt with, particularly whether it has been dealt with properly, which means in accordance with the legally binding rules, or what might be called the disclosure regime. To start to understand disclosure it is important to clearly understand what is meant by used and unused material. To do this it is necessary to start with the trial.

8.2.1 **Used and Unused Evidence**

In any criminal case the prosecution lawyers, having assessed the evidence that they have been provided with by the investigators, use as much of that evidence as they think they will need at the trial to prove the guilt of the defendant. Evidence here means either witness statements or exhibits; documents, or items of property that are legally admissible in court.

They will not always need to use all the evidence that they are provided with. Some evidence although being legally admissible may not help to prove a case against a particular individual. For example; a statement from a witness who saw a robbery being committed, but cannot describe the suspect, would be needed if the defence case was that there was no robbery in the first place. If, however, the defence accepted that the victim was robbed, but argued that it was not the defendant who committed that robbery, then the statement would not help. Equally neither would a piece of property, such as a ladies purse, that was found during the search of a defendant's home address but which has not proved to belong to the victim.

8.2.2 **Other Unused Material**

As well as finding evidence, a criminal investigation also generates other material that is not evidence itself, such as a police officer's notebook, a suspect's custody record, or an initial crime report. This material is not evidence as such, but amounts to records of how the investigation was carried out and how evidence was found—what could be called the non-evidential investigative material. This is the 'other' unused material and which taken together with the all evidence—used and unused—should provide a complete audit trail of how that investigation was carried out and what it uncovered.

The 'unused material' in a case, then, is a combination of the non-evidential investigative 'other' material and any evidence that is not used by the prosecution.

8.2.3 Unused Material at Trial

It is reasonable to ask how the unused material can be of any interest at the trial if it is not part of the prosecution case. Experience has shown, however, that in some cases unused material has the capacity to have a substantial and occasionally decisive impact on a trial. For example what a witness said when they made a 999 call reporting an incident may be different to what they said in their witness statement and the evidence that they give at court. The witness's account is inconsistent; there are differences between what they said at the time of reporting a crime and what they said later when they made a statement. The content of the 999 call needs to be made available to the court in order for the reliability of the witness to be tested.

A fingerprint or DNA sample may be found on stolen property that cannot be identified but does not belong to the defendant. If the defence are arguing that it was not the defendant who took the stolen property, it may be that the unidentified fingerprint or DNA sample belongs to the true thief.

Miscarriages of justice have occurred because such material has not been made available to the court, preventing the evidence being properly tested. Article 6 of the European Convention on Human Rights deals with the right to a fair trial, and it is now clear that a fundamental part of a fair trial is the proper application of the statutory disclosure regime.

> **Foreword to Disclosure Manual by Attorney General**
>
> Disclosure is one of the most important issues in the criminal justice system ... the application of proper and fair disclosure is a vital component of a fair criminal justice system.

8.2.4 'Fair' Disclosure

There has been a great deal of disagreement about what it means for a disclosure regime to be 'fair', and before 1996 case law had developed dealing with this issue. The defence became entitled to see progressively more and more of the non-evidential investigative material, until it reached the stage where the defence had access to everything relevant to the case unless a judge accepted a prosecution application that a particular piece of material was sensitive and should not be disclosed. The term 'disclosed' here means a copy is supplied to the defence.

It is certainly fair that the courts are made aware of the type of material mentioned above: material which throws doubt on whether a witness is accurate or being truthful, or material which suggests someone else was responsible. A fair disclosure regime must make this sort of unused material available to the defence.

However, plainly there is a great deal of investigative material which is sensitive, such as the location of observation points, the identity of informants, intelligence, or confidential investigative techniques—commonly called police methodology. It is no less fair that such material needs to be protected, and only disclosed if absolutely necessary.

Finally, fairness also involves making sure that a trial is focused on the issues in the case and does not become sidetracked. The case should be decided primarily on the evidence and not diverted into arguments about disclosure material that does not go to resolving an issue.

In order for the disclosure regime to be fair and in accordance with Article 6, it must therefore deal appropriately with some conflicting interests. It must be fair to the defendant, but it must also be fair to the public—through the police and the administration of justice.

8.2.5 The Law

Disclosure Legislation

- The Criminal Procedure and Investigations Act 1996 (CPIA), as amended by the Criminal Justice Act 2003, Part V.
- The Codes of Practice issued under section 23 of the CPIA.
- The Attorney General's Guidelines on Disclosure 2005.
- Protocol on Disclosure in the Crown Court.

The CPIA sets out how disclosure must be dealt with and provides some instructions about the proper conduct of a criminal investigation. Part II of the CPIA introduced a 'Codes of Practice' for investigators and the Attorney General has compiled guidelines to assist with its interpretation. A 'Disclosure Manual' has been written explaining how investigators and prosecutors must fulfil their duties, and a Protocol has now been produced addressing disclosure in the Crown Court, aimed at ensuring compliance with the regime throughout the Criminal Justice System. It is anticipated that a similar protocol will shortly be produced aimed at the magistrates' court.

The purpose of the Act has been to create a fair method of dealing with unused material that fulfils the disparate needs of the various parties within the criminal justice system. The judges need a system that remains focused on the issues in the trial; the defence need access to unused material that supports their case—or goes against the prosecution case— and the police and prosecutors need a system that properly and appropriately protects sensitive material.

8.3 **The CPIA Regime**

The disclosure regime applies to a *criminal investigation* and may be seen as a series of seemingly straightforward steps:

- investigators carry out all *reasonable lines of enquiry*;
- *material* generated by the investigation is *recorded* and *retained*;
- material *relevant* to that investigation is identified;
- any *sensitive* material is highlighted;
- the CPS are provided with *schedules* of all relevant material;
- any material which *might undermine the prosecution case or assist the defence* is identified;
- if such material is non-sensitive—the defence are provided with copies or access;
- if such material is sensitive—the prosecution may apply for *public interest immunity (PII)*, in order that it is not supplied to the defence.

The key terms are highlighted and need further explanation; however, as can be seen the concerns of each of the parties—as expressed above—is fully addressed.

This regime makes it plain that the defence are entitled to all the unused material which might undermine any part of the prosecution evidence, or which might assist their own case. It focuses the court on just that material, which is capable of having some impact on the trial, rather than the bulk of unused material which is of no concern because it does not affect any evidence in the case. This should ensure that a trial remains focused only on the evidence and anything which might affect it. Finally, sensitive investigative material is protected because if it does not undermine the prosecution case or assist the defence it does not fall to be disclosed, and even if it does it may still be protected by the judge ruling that it should not be disclosed in the greater public interest. This is applying Public Interest Immunity (PII).

This flowchart deals with the regime diagrammatically where the parties are the police and the CPS. It is important to note that informing the CPS of the existence of all the unused material is called *revealing* or *revelation* and not *disclosure*: unused material is revealed to the CPS but *disclosed* to the defence; they are very different processes.

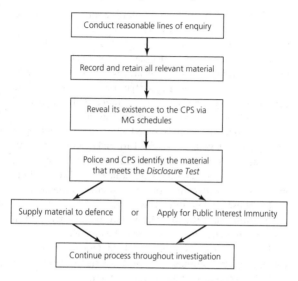

Identifying any material that undermines the prosecution case or assists the defence is called *applying the test for disclosure*, and so such material is deemed to *meet the disclosure test*. It is whether such material is sensitive or not that dictates when a ruling of PII is sought from the judge.

Finally, it must be stressed that this is an ongoing process and a development in the case—for example the service of a defence case statement—should generate a review.

8.3.1 Three Key Decisions

The disclosure regime requires the disclosure officer dealing with the unused material to make three vitally important decisions about the material that has been gathered:

- Is it relevant?
- Is it sensitive?
- Does it fall to be disclosed?

The first decision involves thinking about what unused material should be brought to the attention of the CPS and to assist, the test for relevance is laid out within the Act. This is important because if a piece of material is not at the outset identified as being relevant, it will never feature in any documentation relating to that trial. The court and the defence will be unaware of its existence. This has been a major problem in disclosure cases in the past.

The second decision is based upon a test developed through case law. It is designed to make sure that sensitive material is properly protected whilst at the same time ensuring that the defendant has a fair trial. Failures here may leave sensitive material inadequately protected, or lead to abuse arguments by the defence.

The third test is the most important because its application dictates what unused material the defence have access to. Failure to properly supply to the defence material that undermines the prosecution case or assists the defence has been the predominant disclosure problem.

These three key decisions come together, building on each other to ensure proper compliance with the regime. Each will be addressed individually in this chapter.

8.3.2 When Does it Apply?

This chapter deals with the disclosure regime applicable in an investigation which commenced after 4 April 2005, when the CPIA was amended by Part V of the Criminal Law Act 2003.

The obligations in relation to unused material and its disclosure are determined by the date the investigation begins, and the disclosure officer must make this clear to the prosecutor. This is very important because if an investigation started before that date different rules exist for how the unused material must be dealt with. The advice of the prosecutor must be sought in any case where an investigation began before April 2005.

8.4 **A Criminal Investigation**

Disclosure is a term that has existed in civil law for some time; however, the CPIA expressly applies to criminal investigations conducted in England and Wales by police officers. However there is an expectation that all those involved in mounting criminal investigations, whether police or not, will comply with its provisions.

A criminal investigation is defined as:

- an investigation conducted with a view to it being ascertained whether a person should be charged with an offence;
- an investigation conducted with a view to it being ascertained whether a person charged with an offence is guilty of it;
- an investigation into a crime that has been committed;
- an investigation to ascertain whether a crime has been committed;
- an investigation begun in the belief that a crime may be committed.

Clearly this definition will cover all reactive investigations—where a particular crime is reported—and all proactive investigations—where an individual is targeted in the belief that they are committing offences or about to commit an offence, or a specific location where it is believed a crime may be about to be committed.

A reactive investigation will always begin when the crime first came to police notice, although note that this may not be when the crime was actually committed. This date will never change for the purposes of the disclosure regime that applies. This is regardless of whether a case is unsolved in the first instance and is the subject of a new investigation some years later, as in the cold case reinvestigation of murders and sexual offences.

8.5 **Roles and Responsibilities**

The Codes identify specified roles and associated responsibilities within the disclosure regime. These are:

- the officer in charge of the investigation (OIC);
- the disclosure officer(s);
- an investigator.

These three roles may be performed by one individual, and in most investigations this will be the case; however, there are different functions associated with each role.

8.5.1 **The Officer in Charge**

The OIC is responsible for ensuring that those involved in the investigation carry out their duties in accordance with the Codes and the Act. This includes particular responsibility for making sure that all *reasonable lines of enquiry* are carried out during the investigation. The OIC must ensure that there are proper procedures in place for recording and retaining material, and that all relevant material is made available to the disclosure officer. There is the provision for exceptional circumstances where the OIC may take responsibility for revealing the existence of highly sensitive material directly to the prosecutor without informing the disclosure officer.

8.5.2 **The Disclosure Officer**

The disclosure officer must inspect, view, or listen to all relevant material that has been retained by the investigator(s) and which does not form part of the prosecution case. The disclosure officer must create schedules of that material and supply them to the prosecutor, certifying that all relevant material has been so revealed. The disclosure officer must identify any material that meets the test for disclosure—that is it might undermine the case for the prosecution or it might assist the case for the defence—and provide copies of such material to the prosecutor. The disclosure officer must enable the prosecutor to inspect any other unused material collected if he or she so wishes. The disclosure officer is also responsible for providing the defence with copies of material or allowing the defence to inspect material at the request of the prosecutor.

Finally, it is imperative that the disclosure officer ensures that the process is kept under constant review. This requirement—a continuous duty—is very important to the new regime because the distinction between primary and secondary disclosure has been eliminated. There is no distinct reconsideration of the unused material as there was with secondary disclosure; it must be an ongoing process. This will be especially important where there are developments in the case, such as a defence statement being supplied. This change will be dealt with later in the chapter when the disclosure test is examined in more detail.

8.5.3 Secondary Disclosure Officers

In some more complex cases there may be a need to have more than one disclosure officer, although there should always be a 'lead' disclosure officer. In cases where there is source unit material involving a Covert Human Intelligence Source (CHIS) it may be that the lead disclosure officer is not allowed to have access to the background material. A *secondary* disclosure officer would need to be appointed from within the source unit to deal with such material and liaise with the CPS reviewing lawyer directly. In other cases a secondary disclosure officer could be appointed to deal with particular material such as the CCTV or the contents of computers.

8.5.4 Investigators

An investigator may be a police officer or a police support employee or some other person involved in a criminal investigation. They each have a duty to ensure that any relevant material discovered or created during the investigation is recorded and retained, and they must inform the disclosure officer of its existence and its whereabouts. This is a vital responsibility and every investigator must think about disclosure from the outset. Information or material that is lost or not dealt with in accordance with the regime will allow the defence to argue for an abuse of process, and it is not material itself which becomes important but the failures of the prosecution team—including the most junior investigator on the periphery of an investigation—that will be exposed. Such faults are capable of derailing a trial just as much as any problems with the actual evidence.

8.6 **Reasonable Lines of Enquiry**

> **Codes of Practice, 3.5**
>
> In conducting an investigation, the investigator should pursue all reasonable lines of enquiry, whether these point towards or away from the suspect. What is reasonable in each case will depend on the particular circumstances

This is a very important provision and goes to the heart of the rationale behind the CPIA. The fundamental principle is that the police, or any other investigators, are tasked with mounting an objective investigation into the circumstances of a crime, and that investigation will uncover all sorts of relevant evidence and information. The term *fact-finders* has been used to describe this role.

The evidential product of the investigation is then made available to prosecutors in order for a decision to be made to charge someone. The prosecution will then select from the evidence it will use to prove the case—as has been seen. In the interests of fairness the defence too must be allowed to assess the evidential product for material that will help their case. There is no difference in this principle between the evidence and the unused material.

An investigator is neither a prosecutor nor a defender but a fact-finder, whose discoveries should be equally available to both sides.

This principle would be undermined if an investigator single-mindedly pursued a particular suspect and simply disregarded any evidence or information that suggested he or she was not responsible. For example if an informant named someone as being the person who committed a street robbery it would be unreasonable not to bother to look for CCTV evidence or search for eye witnesses.

Clearly the breadth of an investigation will depend on the seriousness of the crime and the resources available. So what would be reasonable in a case of terrorism would be different from what would be reasonable in a case of shop-lifting. Investigators need to be able to justify the reason-ableness of both the enquiries they carried out and those they did not. This is important for anybody involved in an investigation, no matter how small their role, for their actions need to be reasonable, open, and objective.

8.7 **Material**

Material is defined within the Codes of Practice as:

Material of any kind, including information and objects, which is obtained in the course of a criminal investigation and which may be relevant to the investigation.

It is a common misconception to think only about docu-ments but the definition is much wider. In practice it may be difficult to think of anything either found or created during a criminal investigation which is not material as defined by the Codes. Material would certainly include documentation, but also objects, such as exhibits seized or found but not used in the case, and information. The CPIA makes it explicit that any information must be recorded, and, if relevant to a particular investigation, scheduled and revealed to the prosecutor.

Discussion commonly arises over the interpretation of the term *relevant*. This too is defined and will be addressed later.

8.8 **Record and Retain**

The requirement to conduct impartial and broadly directed investigations would be clearly undone if there were no duty to record and retain material, allowing the possibility of discarding that which did not support the prosecution case.

All those engaged in criminal investigations are required to record and retain any material generated which might be relevant. But since it is difficult to fully appreciate what might turn out to be relevant or not, at the early stages of an investigation it is safest to record and retain everything either generated during the investigation or discovered by it. The officer in charge of an investigation must ensure that this material is recorded in a durable and retrievable form.

Negative information may be important, especially if it is not consistent with other information or material discovered. The following are examples of negative information which might prove significant:

- a CCTV camera that did not record the crime/location/ suspect in a manner which is consistent with the prosecution case (the fact that a CCTV camera did not function or have videotape loaded will not usually be considered relevant negative information);

- where a number of people present at a particular location at the particular time that an offence is alleged to have taken place state they saw nothing unusual;
- where a fingermark from a crime scene cannot be identified as belonging to a known suspect;
- any other failure to match a crime scene sample with one taken from the accused.

Also material which might not normally be recorded, such as conversations with forensic experts, must be recorded and retained.

Disclosure frequently leads to a critical examination of how an investigation has been conducted, and this becomes as much an issue at trial as the evidential product. How was a witness's account obtained, or how were exhibits handled prior to being sent for forensic examination? Poor record keeping has not helped investigators to counter criticism, and since material includes information given orally, if there is anything that is not recorded in any way, it will need to be reduced into a suitable form, for example in writing, on videotape, or on computer disk.

The Codes list particular types of material which will certainly be relevant:

- crime reports (including crime report forms, relevant parts of incident report books or police officers' notebooks);
- custody records;
- records which are derived from tapes of telephone messages (eg 999 calls) containing descriptions of an alleged offence or offender;
- final versions of witness statements (and draft versions where their content differs from the final versions), including any exhibits mentioned (unless they have been returned to their owner on the understanding that they will be produced in court if necessary);
- interview records (written records or audio or video tapes of interviews with actual or potential witnesses or suspects);

- communications between the police and experts such as forensic scientists, reports of work carried out by experts, and schedules of scientific material prepared by the expert for the investigator, for the purposes of criminal proceedings;
- any material casting doubt on the reliability of a witness;
- any material casting doubt on the reliability of a confession.

This list is not exhaustive and much material that does not fit these categories will nonetheless be relevant to the investigation.

8.9 **The Test for Relevancy**

The test for relevancy is the first of the three key decisions that a disclosure officer is required to make. In practice this may be the first step in the disclosure process. Material will have been recorded and retained, but the disclosure officer must now identify that material and apply the test of relevance. A disclosure officer must know this definition and understand how to apply it. Errors made here may be crucial to the disclosure process because something which is not thought to be relevant will not be entered on schedules and so the prosecutor will not know of its existence. If it is not scheduled then it will not be reconsidered if the case develops or if a defence statement is supplied and so it will not be subject to continuous review as the Act indicates it should.

The Relevancy Test—Code of Practice 2.1

Material may be relevant if it appears to have some bearing on:

- any offence under investigation;
- any person being investigated; or
- the surrounding circumstances,

unless it is incapable of having any impact on the case.

In major investigations the gathering of relevant material is generally done for the disclosure officer by the enquiry officers bringing material into the incident room, where it will be stored and recorded on a computerized database. At the conclusion of the investigation all of this material taken together will amount to a full record of that enquiry: how it was organized; what resources it had available; what lines of enquiry were carried out and what, if anything, they yielded; what information was received from the public; how witnesses were identified; how they were dealt with; how they came to provide evidence and so on. It ought to allow a complete reconstruction of the investigation and its evidential product. In such an enquiry the task of deciding on what is relevant is to some extent already done, the database has produced a list of relevant material. There is a simple assumption that if it was not relevant the investigator would not have brought it into the incident room in the first place.

Most cases, however, do not enjoy that luxury, and if you are both the investigator and the disclosure officer the responsibility for identifying relevant material is yours alone. It is helpful to start with the evidence that has been generated and to work backwards, attempting to create an audit trail from how the offence first came to notice and asking oneself about each piece of evidence: how did this come to light?

8.9.1 Understanding—'Incapable of Having any Impact'

It is common to hear arguments about the meaning of 'incapable of having any impact' when discussing whether some piece of material is relevant or not. It is often argued that the decisions are too subjective. It tends to be the case, however, that much of this subjectivity has its basis in an incomplete understanding of what the test means and what it is intended to achieve.

If we assume that a piece of material satisfies the first part of the test—that it has a bearing on the investigation, the person being investigated, or the surrounding circumstances—we now have to think about whether it is, nonetheless, incapable of having any impact. It is very important that the right question is asked, but too often the question is inverted and this leads to a wrong interpretation.

It is tempting to think about this part of the test by asking yourself: 'yes, OK, it has a bearing, but how could it have any impact?' But this is a different question and leads to thinking that the only way material could have an impact on the case is if it is required to be disclosed to the defence, and since the only material the defence are entitled to see is material which might undermine the prosecution case or assist the defence, then the only material capable of having any impact is material which falls to be disclosed.

The consequence of this misreading of the test is that we turn the relevancy test into the disclosure test. Because we ask the wrong question—*how could this have any impact?*—we end up thinking about what should be disclosed and not the much lower threshold of what is relevant. The test does not say that material is only relevant if it *is* capable of having any impact.

There is a wealth of advice throughout the Disclosure Manual and the Attorney General's Guidelines that warns against too strict an interpretation of this test. The safest position is that any material that has been collected and has *some bearing* is best considered as being relevant and should only be disregarded if the disclosure officer is convinced that it cannot have any impact.

8.10 **Third Party Material**

A third party is anyone or any organization that has no responsibilities under the CPIA to record and retain material. Generally investigative organizations such as any police force, HM Revenue and Customs, or the Immigration Service have duties under the Act and are therefore not third parties, even though they are not the organization conducting a specific investigation.

The danger with disclosure and third parties is that because they do not have the duty to make and keep records, relevant material may be lost if the disclosure officer does not act promptly to inform the third party of the need to retain material and to make arrangements to obtain access to it.

Common examples of third parties encountered in criminal investigations include:

- owners of CCTV material;
- social services departments;
- forensic experts;
- police surgeons;
- GPs and hospital authorities.

Usually third parties feature in an enquiry because it is believed that they will have evidence and not just unused material, but in addition to the evidence that you will wish to use there may be other relevant material. Third party material may be highly relevant to a case. CCTV that shows your defendant near to the scene of the offence will be good evidence; however, other CCTV that does not show your defendant may prove to be just as significant at a trial depending upon the defence case. Failure to secure CCTV may lead to allegations by the defence that reasonable lines of enquiry were not undertaken that might have exonerated the defendant; while in cases of domestic abuse local social services are very likely to be in possession of material relevant to any prosecution.

Any third party involved in a case who may be in possession of material relevant to the case should be informed of the investigation and alerted to the need to retain material. The disclosure officer should also inform the prosecutor and together they should consider the need to obtain access to the material, if necessary through a witness summons or court order.

In a recent case involving a third party from abroad—*R v Alibhai* [2004] EWCA Crim 681—the Court of Appeal held that before taking steps to obtain such material the prosecutor should be of the opinion that the material satisfied the disclosure test. This now means that a disclosure officer need only obtain third party material if he or she believes, in consultation with the CPS, that it might undermine the prosecution case or assist the defence.

8.11 **The Test for Sensitivity**

The second key question for the disclosure officer is whether the material is sensitive or not. This involves effectively dividing the unused material into two groups, the default group being non-sensitive.

Sensitive material is any material which it is not in the public interest to disclose, and the test for sensitivity comes from a House of Lords ruling in the case(s) *R v C & R v H* [2004] UKHL 3.

The disclosure officer must be able to show that disclosure of this material would give rise to *a real risk of serious prejudice to an important public interest.*

Each item needs to be considered and justified on its own merits, and only where it can be done in accordance with this test can the material be treated as sensitive. The key to interpreting this test is to begin by identifying the particular public interest that relates to a piece of material. For example, the ability of law enforcement agencies to fight crime by the use of covert human intelligence sources, undercover operations, covert surveillance, etc.

It is clearly in the public interest that the techniques and methods employed in surveillance and undercover work are not made public knowledge. Equally the use of informants or CHIS, in particular their identity, needs to be protected. This public interest would therefore cover any covert methodology and associated material, such as Surveillance Management records.

Suppose there is material which details the location and occupants of a surveillance observation point in a private house. What would be the effect on the public interest if details of the location of an observation point were to be disclosed? How would it affect the future ability to obtain observation points if the occupants knew that their details would be provided to the defendant in any future trial? Clearly disclosure would have a strong adverse effect on the ability to obtain observation points in the future.

What the test for sensitivity seeks to do is protect material which would jeopardize these important public interests. The disclosure officer then needs only to show that disclosure of this particular piece of material would give rise to a real risk of serious prejudice to that public interest.

There are a number of such *public interests* some of which are laid out in the Disclosure Manual, including:

- the ability of the security and intelligence agencies to protect the safety of the UK;
- the willingness of citizens, agencies, commercial institutions, communications service providers, etc to give information to the authorities in circumstances where there may be some legitimate expectation of confidentiality (eg Crimestoppers material);
- the public confidence that proper measures will be taken to protect witnesses from intimidation, harassment, and being suborned;
- the protection of secret methods of detecting and fighting crime;
- the freedom of investigators and prosecutors to exchange views frankly about casework.

This list is not exhaustive but identifying an appropriate public interest is the first step in showing sensitivity.

Each item must be considered on its own merits in the context of the particular case, and although the Codes list examples, there can be no categories of material that will always be sensitive.

8.12 **Scheduling Unused Material**

Once the material has been sorted into sensitive and non-sensitive material the disclosure officer has to create schedules of the material to provide to the prosecutor; this is revelation. The non-sensitive schedule is an MG6C, and the sensitive schedule is an MG6D. The defence are given a copy of the MG6C by the prosecutor, so the disclosure officer must be careful to properly identify and schedule the sensitive material.

8.12.1 **The MG6C—Non-Sensitive Schedule**

The prosecutor does not wish to examine all of the unused material itself, but it is ultimately the prosecutor's responsibility to ensure that disclosure is dealt with properly. Accordingly the level of detail in the descriptions of the material scheduled on the MG6C needs to fully describe the material and its contents such that the prosecutor does not need to see the original in order to be able to make an informed decision about whether the material falls to be disclosed or not. They must be clear, detailed, and accurate. This has been a key problem in the past, resulting in prosecutors lacking confidence in the disclosure officer's decision-making.

8.12.2 **The MG6D—Sensitive Schedule**

The MG6D is not supplied to the defence. This schedule requires the disclosure officer to both describe the item and complete the *reason for sensitivity*, justifying its proper inclusion on the sensitive schedule.

The prosecutor will need to able to make a proper assessment of the material, and the description should be such as to allow the prosecutor to make an informed decision as to whether he or she should view the material itself.

The reason for sensitivity will relate to the identified public interest as described above. Failure to justify sensitivity in accordance with the test has been identified by a number of reviews of the process as a problematic area. Prosecutors may well instruct disclosure officers to move material from the MG6D to the MG6C if the reason for sensitivity is not adequate.

The disclosure officer must provide the prosecutor with all of the prepared schedules and is required to certify to the prosecutor that:

> To the best of my knowledge and belief, all relevant material which has been retained and made available to me has been inspected, viewed or listened to and revealed to the prosecutor in accordance with the Criminal Procedure and Investigations Act 1996 as amended, the Code of Practice and the Attorney General's Guidelines.

8.13 **The Test for Disclosure**

Although the defence will be provided by the prosecutor with a copy of the MG6C this does not count as disclosure of its contents. Having completed the schedules the disclosure officer's next task—and probably the most significant in the whole disclosure process—is to assess all of the material, on both schedules, for anything which falls to be disclosed to the defence.

Although the final decision as to what to disclose to the defence rests with the prosecutor, it is the disclosure officer who will identify such material in the first instance. Failure to disclose to the defence material to which they are entitled lies at the heart of all of the stated cases which lead to the CPIA, and has remained a problem during the time the disclosure regime has been subject to fairly regular judicial review.

The disclosure test was amended in 2005 by the Criminal Justice Act 2003, when primary disclosure, which dealt with material undermining the prosecution case, was conjoined with secondary disclosure, dealing with material assisting the defence, creating the *single disclosure test* which we now use.

> **The Disclosure Test 2005, section 3 of the CPIA 1996, as amended**
> Any prosecution material, which might reasonably be considered capable of:
> undermining the case for the prosecution against the accused or of assisting the case for the accused.

Applying this test is not easy, especially if there is a single person who is the officer in charge, the disclosure officer, and the sole investigator. What the test effectively asks is that a critical approach is taken to the case and the unused material. Only by bringing a defence attitude to the assessment of the material will the desired result be achieved. This really is a matter of attitude and knowledge; knowing the guidance available and approaching the task with an unbiased attitude will ensure a thorough, objective, and fair job.

What amounts to material which might satisfy the disclosure test will always involve considering the following:

- the nature and strength of the case against the accused;
- the essential elements of the offence alleged;
- the evidence upon which the prosecution relies;
- any explanation offered by the accused, whether in formal interview or otherwise;
- what material or information has already been disclosed.

The unused material needs to be examined with these factors in the background, because they will dictate what amounts to the prosecution case, and it is—at least in part—material which contradicts, contrasts with, or even simply does not support that case, which needs to be identified and disclosed to the defence.

8.13.1 Examples of Disclosable Material

The Attorney General's Guidelines indicate some examples of material which would fall to be disclosed because it undermines the prosecution case or assists the defence:

- any material casting doubt upon the accuracy of any prosecution evidence;
- any material which may point to another person, whether charged or not, having involvement in the commission of the offence;
- any material which may cast doubt upon the reliability of a confession;
- any material which might go to the credibility of a prosecution witness;
- any material that might support a defence that is either raised by the defence or apparent from the prosecution papers.

If these examples are seen in the context of the test, it is clear that anything that casts doubt on prosecution evidence, or the reliability of a confession, or goes to the credibility of a prosecution witness, can be seen as undermining the case against the accused. Equally anything that indicates that another person was involved or responsible would assist the defence.

The final example is very important. Material falls to be disclosed not only if it assists the defence that has been raised, but much further: to assess the unused material for anything which would support *any* defence. Again this requires a careful defence-minded assessment of the case, as well as a good knowledge of the appropriate defences to the offence charged. For example, suppose someone has been charged with an assault in a pub and the defence is one of alibi—he was not there. If there is information from someone who does not wish to make a statement suggesting that the victim started the argument, this would be material which might suggest self-defence and so would fall to be disclosed.

The disclosure officer must have the ability to look at the unused material from a critical defence perspective with a commitment to transparency in the investigation and sure knowledge of the case. But engaging in this process will produce tangible gains for the enquiry; problems will be identified sooner and there may be the opportunity to mitigate damage and new fruitful lines of enquiry might be identified.

8.13.2 The MG6E

The disclosure officer is required to identify material that meets this test on a form MG6E, explaining why that conclusion has been reached. Copies of this material must be supplied to the prosecutor who will make the final decision on disclosure. The MG6E will not contain records of any new material. All entries must relate to material already described on either an MG6C or an MG6D. The MG6E is not supplied to the defence, even though copies of the material referred will be (unless subject to PII as sensitive).

Where the disclosure officer (or deputy disclosure officer) believes there is no material that satisfies the disclosure test, the officer should endorse the MG6E in the following terms:

> I have reviewed all the relevant material which has been retained and made available to me and there is nothing to the best of my knowledge and belief that might reasonably be considered capable of undermining the prosecution case against the accused or assisting the case for the accused.

8.14 **Public Interest Immunity**

Where material meets the disclosure test and so falls to be disclosed but is also sensitive, it may be protected by the court. The prosecutor is able to make an application to the trial judge for immunity from disclosure on the grounds that the material is too sensitive to be supplied to the defence and that it is in the public interest not to do so. Making this application is called a PII Hearing.

PII is a principle of law which enables the courts to reconcile conflicts which sometimes arises between two public interests. It does not mean that material cannot, or must never, be disclosed, but that special care must be taken to decide where the balance lies between the two competing public interests before any question of disclosure is decided. In criminal cases, deciding where the balance lies is now a matter for the trial judge.

PII in the context of disclosure will address the conflict between two specific public interests: the right to a fair trial, which as we have seen involves full disclosure of material that might undermine the prosecution case or assist the defence; and the specific public interest that relates to the sensitive material at issue such as the ability of law enforcement agencies to fight crime by the use of covert human intelligence sources, undercover operations, covert surveillance, etc.

Let us say that it is the defence case that the CHIS acted as an agent provocateur in the commission of the offence and they argue that the identity of the CHIS, his history of supplying information, and the rewards that he has received are all matters that would assist their case. In this instance it would be for the judge to balance these two conflicting public interests. It may be that the judge would grant full PII to the material relating to the CHIS. It may be that the judge would decide to allow anonymity, but would allow the defence to know how much he had been paid. Or it may be that the judge would order full disclosure. All options are open to the judge's ruling, and in practice the court will often look to the prosecution and the defence to reach a solution which would protect both public interests equally. In the latter case the prosecution would not be able to accept the judge's ruling and so would probably offer no evidence in order to protect the source.

8.14.1 Is a PII Application Needed?

Clearly there will never be a need for a PII application in relation to non-sensitive material because it can be disclosed if it meets the test. PII will only be an issue if it is sensitive material that falls to be disclosed because it is only sensitive material that it is in the public interest to protect. It is very important to realize however that just because there is sensitive information in a case it does not mean that a PII application is automatically needed.

Considering PII is a three stage process:

- Stage 1—Is there a legal duty to disclose the material?
- Stage 2—Does PII arise?
- Stage 3—Where does the overall balance of the public interest lie?

Stage 1 addresses whether there is a statutory duty to disclose. All this means is does the material meet the test for disclosure—is it material which might undermine the prosecution case or assist the defence? If the answer is no, then there is no duty to disclose and therefore no matter how sensitive the material there is not a public interest conflict because the right to a fair trial does not require it to be disclosed unless it meets the disclosure test.

Stage 2 focuses on whether the material itself is sensitive, that is there is a public interest to protect. Again if the answer is no then the material is probably non-sensitive and there is no conflict, so the material can be disclosed.

Stage 3 looks at the balancing act which will ultimately be a matter for the court. Although there is a requirement for the parties to endeavour to find a compromise that satisfies both.

8.14.2 Types of Application

A PII application will be a matter for the prosecutor and depending on the degree of sensitivity that applies to the material there are three types of application that may be made:

- TYPE 1: In this case the prosecutor must inform the defence that an application is to be made and what the category of material the application relates to. The defence must have the opportunity to address the court and the application is made in the presence of the defence (an *inter partes* application).

- TYPE 2: Here the prosecutor must give notice to the defence that an application is to be made but without informing the defence of the category of material because to do so would effectively disclose what is being protected. The defence may address the court on procedure, but the application is made in the absence of the defence (an *ex parte* on notice application).
- TYPE 3: This is an exceptional process whereby the prosecutor makes a secret application without informing the defence at all (an *ex parte* without notice application).

It is important that the prosecutor makes the most appropriate application type. Type 3 applications should be rare and require high authority levels within the CPS. Most applications tend to be a mixture of a type 1 and type 2, where the defence are informed of the category of material and then address the court, but are absent for the actual application.

8.15 **Defence Disclosure**

A major intention of the CPIA was to forge a regime that focused the court on the issues in the case. To that purpose the act imposed a requirement on the defence to disclose information to the prosecutor and the court after having received the prosecution disclosure—that is a copy of the MG6C together with copies of any material that met the test for disclosure but had not been subject to a successful PII application.

A defence statement is fundamental to the management of the case at trial because without it the issues are not properly made out. Further, the defence statement may generate further reasonable lines of enquiry and additional disclosure. A defence statement is obligatory in Crown Court cases under section 5, and voluntary in the magistrates' court under section 6.

The requirements of the defence statement were strengthened by the Criminal Law Act 2003, and under the amended CPIA a defence case statement should state the following:

- set out the nature of the defence, including any particular defences on which the accused intends to rely;
- indicate the matters of fact on which the accused takes issue with the prosecution;
- set out, in the case of each such matter, why the accused takes issue with the prosecution;
- indicate any point of law (including any point as to the admissibility of evidence or an abuse of process) which the accused wishes to take, and any authority on which he or she intends to rely for that purpose.

Also in a case where the defence is one of alibi, the defence case statement should include details of the alibi witnesses and any other information which would assist the police to trace them.

8.15.1 Actions on Receipt of a Defence Statement

The defence statement should be sent to the prosecutor and then forwarded to the disclosure officer. It is likely that the statement will refer to material on the MG6C schedule asking for copies. However, unless the statement demonstrates how it undermines the prosecution case, or assists the defence case, they are not entitled to that material. Demands for access to material which is not referable to an issue raised in the defence case statement should be resisted.

The disclosure officer must examine the statement for any further lines of enquiry that need to be carried out and it is likely that the prosecutor will ask that this be done. The disclosure officer should also re-examine the unused material in the light of the defence statement and identify any further material that satisfies the disclosure test. The disclosure officer must then submit a further MG6E which either deals with further disclosable material or certifies that there is no more.

8.15.2 Inadequate Defence Statements

Any defence case statement, no matter how inadequate it is regarding the requirements laid out in the CPIA, must be considered by both the CPS reviewing lawyer and the disclosure officer. The defence will be informed by the CPS whether or not their case statement has generated any further disclosable material. Inadequate defence case statements will also be returned to the defence by the CPS.

Unfortunately there is widespread non-compliance with defence disclosure for two simple reasons. First it commits the defence to a particular line of defence and it is often preferable to avoid this at an early stage, and second the sanction for non-compliance—adverse comment to the jury—is inadequate. If the defence commit themselves early and without access to all the unused material the risk to the defence is that the prosecution may have something among the unused material with which to disprove or undermine that defence, and secondly that it allows the police/prosecution time to fully investigate that defence to the same purpose. It is often tactically preferable, therefore, either to provide a very vague defence case statement or provide none at all.

8.15.3 Defence Applications for Disclosure

The defence are entitled under section 8 to apply to a court for further disclosure and such applications are commonly based on the MG6C with which they will have been supplied. Such an application should not be made until the defence have provided a defence statement; however, in practice judges have often allowed applications where there has been no defence statement and, worse, ordered disclosure of material which does not meet the test for disclosure.

This is a problem which can only be resolved by the judiciary itself when they recognize that departing from the CPIA regime in this way absolves the defence from properly engaging in the process. This should be remedied by the introduction of the Protocol for disclosure and tighter case management by the judiciary in the Crown Court.

8.16 **Conclusion**

Hopefully this chapter will have cleared at least some of the mystery that seems to surround disclosure among investigators. Fundamentally disclosure is about transparency; about laying open the whole process by which a criminal investigation is conducted to examination. It is not simply about what evidence has been produced but as much about how that evidence came about or was discovered. The process by which the investigation was conducted is now as important as the evidence it produces.

The three tests, relevancy, sensitivity, and disclosure, need to be understood and applied objectively. The CPIA regime is good news for investigators if it is rigorously applied, but that requires a commitment from all those involved in a criminal investigation no matter how apparently insignificant their role.

Chapter 9

Court Procedure

9.1 **Introduction**

This chapter considers court procedure, covering how cases get to court, the court procedure itself, giving evidence in court, witnesses, exhibits, and digital or electronically held evidence. The chapter is based on a realistic incident, dealing with the specific witnesses and the actual evidence obtained. Although the case study deals with a Crown Court trial the elements of this chapter apply equally to magistrates' courts.

9.2 **Case Study**

Scenario—Accused charged with rape and possession of indecent images

Cheryl is 14 years of age and was constantly reported as missing from home by her mother. One night Cheryl discloses to her mother, Angela, that the reason she runs away is that she is being sexually abused by her mother's common law partner (who is not Cheryl's biological father). The matter is reported to the police and Sergeant Corcoran attends initially to deal with the matter. A case conference is held and Grace Mukula from social services and Inspector Dew from the police public protection unit are assigned to the case. Cheryl undergoes a medical examination by Dr Evans and she is assisted by Constable Porter who secures

---

the swabs taken by the doctor. The common law partner, Dave, is arrested, and as part of the investigation a number of documents are found relating to child grooming, and seized by Constable Meek. The hard drive from his computer is also seized and examined by Constable Watkins from the cyber-crime unit. A number of pornographic images of children are found on the hard drive. Dave is interviewed and charged with several offences of rape, contrary to the Sexual Offences Act 2003, section 1 and possession of indecent photographs contrary to the Protection of Children Act 1978, section 1.

9.3 **The Court System**

We will start by examining the court system.

There are two tiers of 'trial courts': magistrates' court and Crown Court.

9.3.1 **Magistrates' Court**

The magistrates' court tries less serious offence and is presided over by justices of the peace, addressed as 'Your Worship'. The great majority of justices are unpaid lay men or women; a minority are called District Judges (Magistrates' Courts) also addressed as 'Your Worship', who are salaried. They have to be barristers or solicitors of at least seven years' standing.

A magistrates' court is exercised by a court consisting of at least two lay justices sitting in open court. However, District Judges almost invariably sit alone. The law on justices and magistrates' courts is contained principally in:

- the Courts Act 2003 (appointment, removal, etc of justices and organization of magistrates' courts);
- the Magistrates Court Act 1980 (jurisdiction and powers of the courts); and

- the Criminal Procedure Rules (detailed practice and procedure).

9.3.2 Crown Court

The Crown Court was created by the Courts Act 1971. The legislation governing the Crown Court is contained mainly in the Supreme Court Act 1981 (indeed the Crown Court is part of the Supreme Court). Its practice and procedure are laid out by the CrimPR, made by the Criminal Procedure Rules Committee under the Courts Act 2003, section 69.

The Supreme Court Act 1981, section 8 states:

> (1) The jurisdiction of the Crown Court shall be exercisable by—
>   (a) any judge of the High Court; or
>   (b) any circuit judge or recorder; or
>   (c) subject to and in accordance with the provisions of sections 74 and 75(2), a judge of the High Court, circuit judge or recorder sitting with not more than four justices of the peace, and any such persons when exercising the jurisdiction of the Crown Court shall be judges of the Crown Court.

There are therefore three primary types of Crown Court judges:

- High Court judges—about 20 High Court judges may, at any one time, be asked by the Lord Chancellor to sit in the Crown Court; they are addressed as 'My Lord' or 'My Lady';
- circuit judges—circuit judges are appointed to serve in the Crown Court and county courts and to carry out the court's judicial functions; they are addressed as 'Your Honour';
- recorders—recorders are appointed to act as part-time judges of the Crown Court and to carry out the court's judicial functions; they are addressed as 'Your Honour'.

KEY POINT

Note that any circuit judge sitting at the Central Criminal Court and any senior circuit judge who is the honorary recorder of the city in which he or she sits should be addressed as 'My Lord' or 'My Lady' and not 'Your Honour'.

9.4 **First Court Appearance**

Initially Dave will appear at the magistrates' court, either on bail or on remand. In the magistrates' court there will be a pre-trial hearing. This will either be an:

- Early First Hearing—where a guilty plea is anticipated, or
- Early Administrative Hearing—where a not guilty plea is expected.

At this hearing a mode of trial hearing will also take place. This will look at the actual offences Dave has committed and how he may be tried. These offences are:

- summary only—can be tried only in the magistrates' court;
- either way offences—can be tried in either magistrates' court or Crown Court;
- indictable offences—can only be tried in the Crown Court.

Dave is charged with an indictable only offence (rape) and an either way offence (possession of indecent photographs). As Dave is charged with an indictable offence, the magistrates will determine if, based on the facts, they are justified in sending the defendant to the Crown Court under section 51 of the Crime and Disorder Act 1997. This decision is taken at the first hearing where the magistrates will also deal with the defendant's remand status.

9.4.1 The Commencement of the Case

Dave has been remitted to Crown Court to stand trial. The focus now will be on how Dave pleads. He has two fairly self-explanatory choices: guilty or not guilty.

If Dave pleads guilty, that plea must be entered personally (*R v Ellis* (1973) 57 Cr App R 571); the prosecution will then adduce the accused's antecedents and criminal record. Rarely there will be times where the defendant, although pleading guilty, will dispute some of the facts of the prosecution case. In this case the court will hold a 'Newton hearing' (after *R v Newton* (1982) 77 Cr App R 13) in which the prosecution calls evidence in support of the Crown's case.

If Dave pleads not guilty the criminal law presumes that each individual is innocent until proven guilty. The level of proof that is required is that the evidence presented should establish the person's guilt 'beyond reasonable doubt'.

In criminal cases, the courts make decisions on an adversarial rather than an inquisitorial basis. This means that the prosecution and defence test the credibility and reliability of the evidence their opponent presents to the court.

Where the prosecution fails to meet the burden of proof to any element of the offence, the accused is entitled to be acquitted. The defence may submit that the evidence does not disclose a case to answer in respect of any or all the counts on the indictment. If the submission succeeds on all counts, the judge directs the jury to acquit the accused.

After making an initial plea Dave is entitled to change his mind. If he wanted to change his plea from not guilty to guilty he may do so as long as this occurs before the jury return their verdict. The judge then directs the jury to return a formal verdict of guilty (*R v Heyes* [1951] 1 KB 29). Similarly, Dave may be allowed to change his plea from guilty to not guilty and the judge may allow this at any stage before sentence is passed (*R v Plummer* [1902] 2 KB 339).

Dave pleads not guilty and a Crown Court trial will proceed.

9.5 **The Evidence for the Prosecution**

This will be provided by witness evidence, forensic evidence, and exhibits.

9.5.1 **Witnesses**

In the case study the following may well be witnesses and could be called to court to give evidence:

- Cheryl
- Angela
- Sergeant Corcoran
- Dr Evans
- Constable Porter
- Constable Watkins
- Constable Meek
- Inspector Dew
- Grace Mukula

In looking at witnesses, it is crucial to consider two related questions:

- Whether a witness is competent.
- Whether a witness may be compelled or made to provide testimony.

The general rule in English law is that 'All people are competent and all competent witnesses are compellable'.

The exceptions to the general rule of competence and compellability are set in various statutes and these exceptions can be listed as follows:

- the accused;
- spouses and civil partners;
- children;
- those of defective intelligence;
- other special groups.

Generally a person charged in criminal proceedings is not competent to give evidence in the proceedings for the prosecution (either alone or as a co-defendant). However, a person charged in criminal proceedings will be competent to give evidence for the prosecution at such time if they plead guilty, are convicted, or receive a promise from the Crown Prosecution Service (CPS) not to prosecute.

A wife, husband, or civil partner (other than when the wife, husband, or civil partner are jointly charged) is competent to give evidence on behalf of the prosecution against their spouse or partner. However they are only compellable to give evidence on behalf of the prosecution against their spouse or partner (unless jointly charged) in certain circumstances as defined by section 80 of the Police and Criminal Evidence Act 1984 as amended by Schedule 4 to the Youth Justice and Criminal Evidence Act 1999.

These circumstances are:

- the offence charged involves an assault on, or injury or a threat of injury to, the wife, husband, or civil partner of the accused; or
- the offence charged involves an assault on, or injury or a threat of injury to, a person who at the material time is under the age of 16; or
- the offence charged is a sexual offence alleged to have been committed in respect of a person who was at the material time under 16; or
- in the case of attempting or conspiring to commit, or of aiding, abetting, counselling, procuring, inciting,

encouraging, or assisting commission of any of the above offences.

The Civil Partnership Act 2004 made the above exemptions applicable to 'civil partners' as well as wives and husbands.

> **KEY POINT**
>
> Cohabitees, however, are not afforded the same concessions as a wife, husband, or civil partner in giving evidence against each other (that of being competent but not compellable).

Note that issues of compellability only relate to witnesses for the prosecution; there is no restriction where the witness is for the defence.

The Youth Justice and Criminal Evidence Act 1999, section 55 deals with the position of children to act as witnesses in criminal proceedings, and we must consider this as our main witness is a child.

The statutory provisions require that no witness under the age of 14 is to be sworn (see section 9.8.2 below). This means that witnesses are to be sworn if they are 14 or over but only if they understand the solemnity of a criminal trial and that by taking the oath they are responsible for telling the truth.

The 1999 Act provides that a person of any age who is competent to give evidence, but by virtue of section 55(2) is not permitted to be sworn, may give unsworn evidence (section 56(1) and (2)).

As Cheryl is 14 she will be a sworn witness.

9.5.2 **Forensic Evidence**

The forensic evidence is:

- swabs/samples taken during medical examination;
- the hard drive and the images contained on it.

9.6 **Evidence for Court**

Both witness testimony and actual physical evidence must be properly secured in the first instance in order that it may be admissible at any future court trial. The principle that should be applied is 'the best evidence rule'.

This rule of evidence covers the best evidence that the nature of the case will allow. The rule was set out in 1745 and generally required that only the people having immediate personal knowledge of a fact in issue could give evidence as to that fact. With the social and technological changes since the rule was introduced this rule is all but defunct. However, for the purpose of evidence gathering, the general principle to produce evidence from the best practicable source should still be applied.

Evidence can be proved in the following ways:

- original (primary) evidence;
- real evidence;
- secondary evidence;
- documentary evidence.

9.6.1 **Original Evidence**

This is where a witness gives evidence to the court directly from the witness box. The evidence is presented to the court as evidence of the truth of what he/she states. Here the witness is giving direct testimony about a fact of which he/she has personal knowledge and therefore can be challenged on the truth of that fact in cross-examination.

9.6.2 **Real Evidence**

Real evidence typically takes the form of an object for inspection by the court, ie a knife used in an assault. This evidence is to prove either that the object in question exists, or to enable the court to draw an inference from its own observation as to the object's value and physical condition (an example would be the pornographic photographs seized from Dave's computer; the court then determines whether it is 'obscene'). Defence counsel will work on the premise that if you can't prove it existed, it didn't.

Whatever real evidence is presented to the court must be exhibited and accompanied by written testimony and identified by a witness. This testimony should include an explanation of the connection between the exhibit and the case, in other words the relevance of the object to the offence charged.

There is no rule of law that the actual object must be produced before oral evidence may be given about it. For example, it is not necessary for the police to produce the actual swabs taken by the doctor (see *Castle v Cross* [1984] 1 WLR 1372). However, the weight of the oral evidence may be adversely affected if the actual samples couldn't be produced if requested by the defence (see *Armory v Delamirie* (1722) 1 Str 505).

KEY POINT

The court has the responsibility to preserve and retain exhibits until the conclusion of the trial. It is usual for the court to entrust the exhibits to the police or CPS and this places a duty on them to:

- take all proper care to preserve the exhibits safe from loss or danger;
- cooperate with the defence in order to allow them reasonable access to the exhibits for the purpose of inspection and examination; and
- produce the exhibits at the trial (*R v Lambeth Metropolitan Stipendiary Magistrate, ex p McComb* [1983] QB 551).

9.6.3 Secondary Evidence

Secondary evidence, as the name suggests, is not as good as original (primary evidence); it is evidence of a lesser kind, eg a copy of a document or a copy of such a copy. Such evidence can be admissible, by way of exemption in various ways, including where the production of a public document would be illegal or inconvenient, where the original document has been lost, or where a document is subject to legal privilege.

9.6.4 **Documentary Evidence**

Documentary evidence consists of documents produced for inspection by the court, either as items of real evidence or as hearsay or original evidence. Document would include maps, plans, graphs, drawings, photographs, discs, tapes, video tapes and films, including CCTV recordings, and tapes from police control rooms. The contents of a document may be admissible as evidence of their truth or for some other purpose. Documents produced to the court are usually accompanied by some testimony and identified by a witness (see real evidence above).

9.7 **Preparing Evidence for Court**

It is of the utmost importance that evidence is properly obtained and that it is recorded, handled, and, where necessary, exhibited appropriately for it to be admissible at court. A trial is about the jury (or justice) deciding guilt based on all the known facts about a case. This can not be accomplished if some evidence is never heard through being excluded as being improperly obtained; this is inexcusable and a great burden is placed upon the police in this duty.

9.7.1 **Witnesses**

The role of witnesses in the criminal justice system is vital. Without witnesses many criminals would never be convicted. Courts can be intimidating places and witnesses can sometimes feel as if it is they who are on trial. Anyone who acts as a witness should bear in mind the vital role they play in the administration of justice.

In the case study all witnesses who are called to give evidence will be required to give original evidence from the witness box. Prior to giving evidence witnesses can be helped; however, there are restrictions to what help can be offered.

Many witnesses feel worried about going to court, regardless of whether or not they were the victim of the crime. Victim Support runs the Witness Service in every criminal court in England and Wales to give information and support to witnesses, victims, and their families and friends when they go to court.

The Witness Service helps:

- witnesses who are called to give evidence, including defence witnesses;
- victims of crime and their families and friends attending court for any reason;
- children as well as adults.

Witness Service staff and volunteers can give you:

- someone to talk to in confidence;
- a chance to see the court beforehand and learn about court procedures;
- a quiet place to wait;
- someone to go with you into the court room when giving evidence;
- practical help (for example with expense forms);
- easier access to people who can answer specific questions about the case (the Witness Service cannot discuss evidence or offer legal advice);
- a chance to talk over the case when it has ended and to get more help or information.

Like the rest of Victim Support, the Witness Service is free and independent of the police or courts. The leaflet 'going to court' is available from the Victim Support website at <http://www.victimsupport.org.uk>.

Witness familiarization is one thing, witness coaching is entirely another. In *Momodou (Practice Note)* [2005] 1 WLR 3442, the Court of Appeal made clear that, while familiarization of witnesses with the court and procedure is legitimate, it must be carefully regulated. Judge LJ stated (at [61] and [62]):

> There is a dramatic distinction between witness training or coaching, and witness familiarization. Training or coaching for witnesses in criminal proceedings (whether for prosecution or defence) is not permitted. ...So we repeat, witness training for criminal trials is prohibited.

9.7.2 Real Evidence and Exhibits

In our case study the real evidence would be:

- the documents seized;
- the hard drive from the computer;
- images obtained from the hard drive;
- any swab/sample obtained by the doctor from Cheryl.

We need to go right back to how the objects came to light, consider how they should be seized, how they should be exhibited, how they should be retained, how they can be produced in court. It is essential that these processes are completed properly to ensure admissibility in court.

The Documents Seized

If you remember, these documents relate to child grooming. In fact they are typed sheets outlining how a child can be 'groomed' by paedophiles and giving practical advice on how to ensure the child keeps the assaults 'secret'. Constable Meek should have noted where exactly the documents were found, 'third drawer down of filing cabinet in bedroom of ...' , rather than 'drawer in filing cabinet'. It should then have been placed in an exhibit bag and sealed and signed by the officer, and becomes the officer's exhibit. This is noted using, in this case, the officer's initials and the numerical order in which it was found.

KEY POINT

The first document found would be KM1, the next KM2 and so on.

It should also have been shown to the exhibits officer; it is usual in searches of this magnitude for an officer to be deputed to be the exhibits officer. He or she will maintain a search record which will include:

- what rooms have been searched;
- who was present in those rooms;
- what was in each room searched; and
- a record of anything seized;
- the time the item was seized.

This search record will be timed and dated and kept (as an exhibit itself) as a contemporaneous log of events. In this way complaints of impropriety can be refuted.

If the bag the documents are contained in is opened, it must be resealed after use in a separate exhibits bag; the officer doing this must certify that the original seal was broken and that the documents were resealed; a full pocket notebook entry is required. Any interference with an exhibit prior to trial must have a clear audit trail showing that the documents produced in court were the originals found in the filing cabinet. Don't forget the defence motto—if you can't prove it, it didn't exist.

The Hard Drive Taken from the Computer

Electronic evidence is valuable evidence and it should be treated in the same manner as traditional forensic evidence—with respect and care. The methods of recovering electronic evidence, whilst maintaining evidential continuity and integrity may seem complex and costly, but experience has shown that, if dealt with correctly, it will produce evidence that is both compelling and cost effective.

The Association of Chief Police Officers (ACPO) have produced a guide for computer-based electronic evidence, which a comprehensive document dealing with many different types of digital evidence.

Four principles are involved:

Principle 1: No action taken by law enforcement agencies or their agents should change data held on a computer or storage media which may subsequently be relied upon in court.

Principle 2: In circumstances where a person finds it necessary to access original data held on a computer or on storage media, that person must be competent to do so and be able to give evidence explaining the relevance and the implications of their actions.

Principle 3: An audit trail or other record of all processes applied to computer-based electronic evidence should be created and preserved. An independent third party should be able to examine those processes and achieve the same result.

Principle 4: The person in charge of the investigation (the case officer) has overall responsibility for ensuring that the law and these principles are adhered to.

KEY POINTS

These principles are explained:

Computer-based electronic evidence is subject to the same rules and laws that apply to documentary evidence.

The doctrine of documentary evidence may be explained thus: the onus is on the prosecution to show to the court that the evidence produced is no more and no less now than when it was first taken into the possession of police.

Operating systems and other programs frequently alter and add to the contents of electronic storage. This may happen automatically without the user necessarily being aware that the data has been changed.

In order to comply with the principles of computer-based electronic evidence, wherever practicable, an image should be made of the entire target device. Partial or selective file copying may be considered as an alternative in certain circumstances, eg when the amount of data to be imaged makes this impracticable. However, investigators should be careful to ensure that all relevant evidence is captured if this approach is adopted.

In a minority of cases, it may not be possible to obtain an image using a recognized imaging device. In these circumstances, it may become necessary for the original machine to be accessed to recover the evidence. With this in mind, it is essential that a witness, who is competent to give evidence to a court of law, makes any such access.

It is essential to display objectivity in a court, as well as the continuity and integrity of evidence. It is also necessary to demonstrate how evidence has been recovered, showing each process through which the evidence was obtained. Evidence should be preserved to such an extent that a third party is able to repeat the same process and arrive at the same result as that presented to a court.

The flowchart in Figure 9.1 outlines best practice for the seizure of electronic evidence.

KEY POINTS

Note that the advice recommends photographing the equipment in situ; digital images can easily be altered without detection, the integrity and authenticity of the images need to be managed as a priority. The following advice should be followed on all occasions with digital image taking and storing.

- A written audit trail must be made and updated from the moment that images are captured and throughout the evidential process so as to maintain continuity and integrity.
- Where reusable memory cards have been used to make the initial recording, the images will be transferred to WORM (write once read many) media for storage at the earliest possible opportunity, and the disk finalized to prevent further recording. This process must be carried out without using manipulation software.
- Once a master WORM has been produced, the camera memory or flash memory card must be formatted to erase all data.

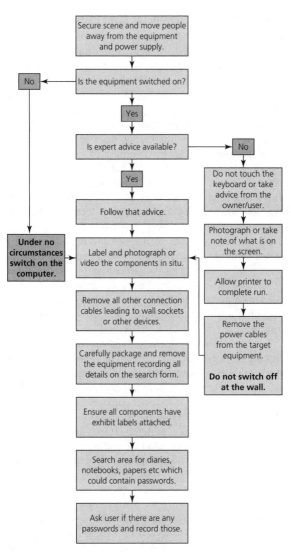

Figure 9.1

The Images Obtained from the Hard Drive

This is a very specialist area and will be performed by someone qualified to do so, in our case Constable Watkins. What is important, though, is the storage and access to those images. Section 1(1)(a) of the Protection of Children Act 1978 prohibits the 'taking or making' of an indecent photograph or pseudo-photograph of a child.

'Making' includes the situation where a person downloads an image from the internet, or otherwise creates an electronic copy of a file containing such a photograph or pseudo-photograph. Section 46 of the Sexual Offences Act 2003 amends the Protection of Children Act 1978, and provides a defence to a charge of 'making'. The defence is available where a person 'making' an indecent photograph or pseudo-photograph can prove that it was necessary to do so for the purposes of the prevention, detection, or investigation of crime, or for the purposes of criminal proceedings. This reverse burden defence is intended to allow people instructed to act for the defence or prosecution who need to be able to identify and act on the receipt of an indecent photograph or pseudo-photograph, to deal with such images.

The Memorandum of Understanding between the CPS and ACPO is the result of the enactment of section 46 of the Sexual Offences Act 2003. The Memorandum of Understanding is intended to provide guidance to those who have a legitimate need to handle indecent photographs of children by setting out how the defence provided in section 46 of the Sexual Offences Act 2003 may be applied. The Memorandum provides guidance to the police service, the CPS, and others involved in the internet industry, in order to create the right balance between protecting children and the effective investigation and prosecution of offences. After charge, the defence solicitor/counsel will always be permitted access to view the images at reasonable hours at either the office of the case officer or the examiner.

The defence have a duty to defend their client, and law enforcement has a duty to ensure that they do not unnecessarily create more paedophile images or compromise sensitive confidential material. It will not always be the case that the defence need full access to a forensic computer image. Likewise it may not be always appropriate for law enforcement to deny access to a forensic computer image.

Any Swab/Sample Obtained by the Doctor from Cheryl

This is again a very important task, ensuring the integrity of the samples obtained. This examination usually takes place either at a hospital or increasingly in accommodation supplied by the police for such examinations. In this particular examination the watch word must be cross-contamination.

The victim will have to be taken to the examination suite; this must be done by an officer/person who has absolutely no contact with either the defendant or the scene of the incident. The transport used must never have contained the defendant or have visited the scene.

KEY POINT

In this case study the 'scene' is inside the house and therefore the transport could park outside, although the driver must not enter the house under any circumstances.

The doctor, and any other person present at the examination suite must also have had absolutely no contact with the defendant or have visited the scene.

Each individual swab or sample (ie under fingernail scraping) must:

- indicate what it is;
- indicate where it was taken from.

It should then be sealed and exhibited; remember it is the doctor's exhibit, not the officer assisting.

All the exhibits should then be noted on the HOLAB (Home Office Laboratory Form) and stored in accordance with relevant guidelines. The officer should note exactly the movements from when they are taken, where they are deposited at the station, to whom they were handed in the forensic submissions office. The forensic submissions office will then be responsible for an audit trail of the samples submission to the lab. In this way we can ensure the samples examined by the scientists have a clear audit trail straight back to Cheryl, and there can be no allegations of cross-contamination. Note that the scientist who examined the samples will have to be added to our witness list.

KEY POINT

So far we have covered in some depth how exhibits and witnesses are prepared for court. This is vital and it is important to recognize that 'court procedure' starts long before the actual proceedings in the court itself. Without recognizing this importance, a witness, what they saw, an exhibit, or a piece of digital evidence may never actually make an appearance in court. Keep in mind that court procedure commences the moment you become involved in an investigation; this will include actually witnessing an incident yourself, eg a fight outside a night club.

9.8 **What Happens in Court**

We move on now to what happens in court during a trial. However, we haven't quite finished what needs to happen before the actual day of the trial. It is worth mentioning again that someone has to be responsible for ensuring all exhibits that will be used are actually taken to court. It is also possible that some witnesses will have special requirements, and these will also have to be arranged pre-trial.

9.8.1 **Special Requirements**

Witnesses who have special requirements—for example those who need an interpreter or who have a disability— should contact the Witness Service prior to the trial. The

Witness Service will make any necessary arrangements to ensure that witnesses are as comfortable as possible.

Special Measures

There are a number of special measures for vulnerable or intimidated witnesses contained in the Youth Justice and Criminal Evidence Act 1999 these are designed to help young, disabled, vulnerable, or intimidated witnesses to give evidence in criminal proceedings.

There are three categories of witness eligible for assistance and it is for the court to determine whether a witness falls into one of these categories:

- a witness who is under the age of 17 at the time of the hearing (section 16(1));
- a witness who suffers from a mental or physical disorder or otherwise has a significant impairment of intelligence (section 16(2));
- a witness whose evidence is likely to be affected on grounds of fear or distress about testifying (section 17(1)).

Both the prosecution and defence may make an application to the court for a special measure direction. The court itself may make such a direction of its own volition (section 19).

As the victim in our case study is a 'child witness' (ie under the age of 17) there are other special provisions. A child witness will be deemed to be 'in need of special protection' if the offence to which the proceedings relate is a proscribed sexual offence or one of kidnapping, assault, etc. These measures are:

- screening from the accused while giving evidence—the witness may be prevented from seeing the accused by means of a screen or other arrangement;
- evidence by live television link—the witness will be able to give evidence in another room through its link;
- evidence given in private—the court may exclude certain people from the courtroom while the child gives evidence. However, this does not include the accused,

legal representatives from the case, or any interpreter required for the case;
- removal of wigs and gowns—the court may order the removal of wigs or gowns while the child gives evidence;
- video-recorded evidence-in-chief—the court may allow a video recording of a previous interview with the witness to be admitted as evidence;
- video-recorded cross-examination or re-examination—where video-recorded evidence is allowed, the courts may also permit the cross-examination of the witness, and any re-examination to be video recorded;
- examination of witness through intermediary—the courts can allow the examination of the witness to be conducted through an interpreter;
- aids of communication—if the child suffers from any disability or disorder, an appropriate device to assist communication will be provided for the child to give evidence.

So Cheryl will be entitled to have her evidence-in-chief video recorded and played in court without her being present at all. However, more likely is that she will appear via a live link from a room somewhere else in the court building. In this way it can reduce the trauma of giving evidence from the witness box in open court.

9.8.2 **The Day of the Trial**

Witnesses should sign in for their case as soon as they arrive at court. Notices will tell visitors to the court where they need to go. If in any doubt, ask a receptionist, usher, or security guard who will be able to point you in the right direction. You should find the 'court list' which will indicate which court you are in and who the presiding judge is. You should then locate where in the building the actual court is, there will be seating areas outside the court itself. Witnesses should also make themselves familiar with where the actual witness box (the place where they will stand to give evidence is); this is one less thing to worry about as you enter court when called to give evidence. Police officers are professional witnesses; look professional by walking straight to the witness box rather than having to be directed towards it. Witnesses will be called in order, as determined by prosecuting counsel. All witnesses must remain outside the court until called in to give evidence.

Refreshing Memory

Witnesses should be able to have a look at their witness statements before they give evidence. A trial will often take place a long time after the statement was given and memories may have faded in the meantime. The Criminal Justice Act 2003 provides for the use of documents and transcripts by witnesses to refresh their memory.

Section 139 of the 2003 Act states:

(1) A person giving oral evidence in criminal proceedings about any matter may, at any stage in the course of doing so, refresh his memory of it from a document made or verified by him at an earlier time if—

   (a) he states in his oral evidence that the document records his recollection of the matter at that earlier time, and

   (b) his recollection of the matter is likely to have been significantly better at that time than it is at the time of his oral evidence.

(2) Where—

   (a) a person giving oral evidence in criminal proceedings about any matter has previously given an oral account, of which a sound recording was made, and he states in that evidence that the account represented his recollection of the matter at that time,

   (b) his recollection of the matter is likely to have been significantly better at the time of the previous account than it is at the time of his oral evidence, and

   (c) a transcript has been made of the sound recording,

he may, at any stage in the course of giving his evidence, refresh his memory of the matter from that transcript.

The fact that the witness refreshed their memory from a document or transcript before going into the witness box does not affect the presumption contained within section 139 above.

KEY POINT

Although witnesses may refresh their memory prior to giving evidence, they must not under any circumstances discuss amongst themselves what their evidence will be. This includes police officers. After giving evidence witnesses must not discuss the case at all with other witnesses who have yet to give evidence.

The Jury is Empanelled

Before the trial can commence the jury must be empanelled and potential jurors are called into court. When 12 potential jurors are seated, advocates may challenge the choice of any individual as a juror. The jury will be asked to stand and will be sworn in. The judge will nominate a juror as foreman and that person will be shown to his or her seat.

The Trial Process

Prior to the trial actually commencing, and after the jury is sworn, there may well be a 'trial within a trial', more properly called a *voir dire*. Where there is evidence to which the defence want to object but it is vital to the prosecution case, so that the case cannot sensibly be opened without reference to it, the question of admissibility is to be determined at the *voir dire*. The judge will decide on its admissibility.

The prosecution has brought the case to court and must prove its case. The court will hear about the prosecution case first. The prosecution will outline in a speech the case against the accused and what it intends to prove. The prosecution will then call witnesses to give evidence.

When this evidence has been given, the defence may put its case; as the burden is on the prosecution to prove the case, the defence need not present any evidence. They can make a submission that there is no case to answer in relation to any or all of the counts and the jury will be sent out during this submission.

> **KEY POINT**
>
> There are two counts in our case study. If the submission succeeds on all counts, the judge directs the jury to acquit the accused. If the submission succeeds on only one of the counts, no verdict is taken on those counts and the jury will be directed to acquit the accused and they should therefore concern themselves only with the other on which there is a case. If the submission fails on all counts, the trial proceeds.

If the defence intend to call evidence as to the facts of the case other than or in addition to the evidence of the accused they may make an opening speech. The accused should be the first witness called by the defence.

When all the evidence has been given, the prosecution and defence advocates may make closing speeches. They will talk directly to the jury about the case. The judge will sum up the facts of the trial, tell the jury about the law which applies to the case, and instruct them as to their duties as a juror. The function of the jury is to determine the guilt or innocence of the accused.

Being Sworn in as a Witness

All witnesses must be sworn, that is to say take the oath or make an affirmation that the evidence they give will be the truth. The manner in which the oath is administered is provided by section 1 of the Oaths Act 1978. This requires the witness to hold the New Testament (Old Testament in the case of a Jew) in his uplifted hand and repeat, after the person administering the oath, the words 'I swear by Almighty God that . . . ', followed by the oath prescribed by law.

Alternatively, other religious followers may take an oath upon a holy book appropriate to that belief. For example, Hindus are sworn on the Vedas, and Muslims are sworn on the Koran.

An affirmation may be made by a witness who objects to being sworn or where his/her request for an alternative form of oath is not reasonably practicable and would delay or inconvenience the proceedings. The witness repeats after the person administering the affirmation, the words 'I [name] do solemnly, sincerely and truly declare and affirm', followed by the words of the oath prescribed by law.

KEY POINT

There are two exceptions to witnesses being sworn:

- children may give unsworn evidence (section 55 of the Youth Justice and Criminal Evidence Act 1999);
- witnesses merely producing a document need not be sworn (*Perry v Gibson* (1834) 1 A & 48).

Any witness who refuses to take an oath or make an affirmation in any court could face imprisonment.

Examination-in-Chief

The witness will be called by either the prosecution or defence and they will examine the witness by asking questions with a view to providing evidence which is favourable to that party's case. This is known as 'examination-in-chief'.

Most witnesses are examined in chief; however, sometimes the prosecution will not question a witness but will allow the witness to be cross-examined by the defence. One police officer can give the evidence-in-chief but other officers involved may be required for cross-examination by the defence.

The witness may be led through their evidence, but may not be asked leading questions, ie those which suggest the desired answer. Of course, as usual, there are exceptions to this rule; however, this is a highly technical legal area and beyond the scope of this manual.

KEY POINT

Any witnesses may find the following tips helpful when giving evidence under oath, even police officers:

- Listen carefully to all questions.
- Make sure you understand the question before answering; only answer the question that has actually been asked.
- If you do not understand a question, cannot remember, or do not know the answer you are entitled to say so.
- Although counsel will be asking the questions witnesses should address their answers to the judge (although research suggests juries find witnesses who do not look at them unreliable).
- Speak slowly and clearly.
- Keep calm and do not argue with counsel.

Cross-Examination and Re-Examination

When a witness has finished giving his evidence, counsel for the other side is entitled to cross-examine that witness. Under Article 6(3)(d) of the European Convention on Human Rights everyone charged with a criminal offence shall be entitled:

> to examine or have examined witnesses against him and to obtain the attendance and examination of witnesses on his behalf under the same conditions as witnesses against him . . .

This examination is usually focused on either undermining their evidence or supporting that of the party's own witnesses.

KEY POINT

Barristers often use the mantra 'never ask a question unless you already know the answer'; after all they would not want to ask a question that elicited evidence against their client that had not already been given!

1 Evidence Management

Unlike examination-in-chief you can, and mostly likely will, be asked leading questions. Cross-examination, like any other form of questioning, is subject to the rules of evidence, and barristers have, and must comply with, a code of conduct. If counsel goes beyond this then the judge or other counsel may step in to 'protect' that witness.

Where a party decides not to cross-examine an opponent's witness, this is held to be an acceptance of the witness's evidence-in-chief.

Although there are rules that counsel must comply with in court in how they treat a witness, there are some statutory protections for certain witnesses. The Youth Justice and Criminal Evidence Act 1999 specifically prohibits defendants from personally cross-examining complainants and particular witnesses in certain circumstances

KEY POINT

Where an accused is prohibited from cross-examining the complainant or a witness, he/she must appoint a legal representative to conduct the cross-examination on his/her behalf. If the accused refuses or fails to appoint a legal representative, the court must consider appointing one on his/her behalf in order to test the witness's evidence.

This Act also creates a structure in relation to questioning witnesses about their previous sexual behaviour, where the defendant is charged with a sexual offence. The defence has to apply to the court if it wishes to introduce evidence or ask questions about the complainant's previous sexual behaviour. Generally a witness should not be asked about their past sexual behaviour unless it is relevant to an issue in the case or is necessary to rebut prosecution evidence. It will also be allowed if it is an issue of consent and relates to sexual behaviour alleged to have taken place at or about the same time as the event which is the subject matter of the charge (section 41(3)). No evidence or question will be regarded as relating to a relevant issue where it is designed to impugn the credibility of the complainant as a witness (section 41(4)). Once a witness has been cross-examined the party calling that witness is entitled to re-examine. The questions put to the witness at this time may only relate to those matters upon which there was a cross-examination. No leading questions are allowed within the re-examination of a witness. After the witness has been re-examined it is open to the judge to ask questions to clear up uncertainties, to fill gaps, or to answer queries which might be lurking in the jury's mind. It is not appropriate for the judge to cross-examine the witness (*R v Wiggan* (1999) The Times, 22 March).

The advice set out above about answering questions is equally applicable when being cross-examined. A witness should not allow themselves to be bullied or badgered into going away from what they know to be true.

KEY POINT

Police officers in particular should avoid getting into conflict with defending counsel; they are in court to do a job, they are doing their job as professionally as they can. As part of their job is to undermine prosecution evidence then any unprofessionalism on the officer's part means they have achieved their aim. It may also mean that they are better at their job than the police officer is. It should be seen by the police officer as a battle of professionalism not a battle of wits; I know who my money is on in the latter case.

Further Evidence

Normally the prosecution must call the whole of their evidence before closing their case (*R v Francis* [1991] 1 All ER 225).

However, there are three well-established exceptions:

- evidence in rebuttal of defence evidence (evidence which becomes relevant in circumstances which the prosecution could not have foreseen at the time when they presented their case);

- evidence not called by reason of oversight; or
- evidence not previously available.

The End of the Trial

After closing speeches and the judge's summing up, the jury are sent out to consider their verdict. This can take minutes, hours, or even days. When they have made a decision the foreman will read out the verdict. If it is not guilty on all counts the accused is free to leave; if it is guilty on some or all of the counts then sentencing falls to the judge.

PART TWO
Knowledge Management

Chapter 10

Police Authorities

10.1 **Introduction**

This chapter will consider the role of the police authority and its influence upon policing the local community, its use of knowledge management in assisting local policing, its role in terms of performance management including a consideration of the new Assessments of Policing and Community Safety (APACS) and the future of Police Authorities in terms of governance and accountability.

The Police Act 1964 (Home Office, 1964) introduced the so called 'tri-partite' system which divided responsibility for policing between three main parties, namely the Home Office, Chief Constables, and police authorities. The idea was to balance the national position in terms of accountability with the local perspective so that all levels of policing were 'controlled' and accountable. The Chief Constable, however, was protected to some extent, in that the chief officer had independence over the operational control of the police force for which he/she was responsible. It was believed that this provided some protection from interference by elected representatives in controlling policy for the police. However, the tri-partite system has not been beyond criticism. Reiner (2000) stated that under the tri-partite system, police authorities 'paid the piper', but never named the tune, indicating that although police authorities provided resources for the police, they had little or no say in how crime and disorder was tackled within the communities the police authority represented.

10.2 **The Current Position**

A police authority is an independent body made up of local people. The police authority's job is to make sure that the community has an efficient and effective local police force. There is a police authority for each local police force—43 in total in England and Wales—plus an additional one for British Transport Police. In Northern Ireland the police authority is called the Policing Board but it has a similar role to police authorities in England and Wales.

All police authorities are members of the Association of Police Authorities.

Most police authorities have 17 members namely:

- 9 local councillors appointed by the local council;
- 5 independent members selected following local advertisements;
- 3 magistrates from the local area.

The Metropolitan Police Authority has 23 members because of London's size.

The main job of the police authority is to set the strategic direction for the force and holds the Chief Constable to account on behalf of the local community. Delivering policing services is the job of the Chief Constable.

In short the police authority:

- holds the police budget and decides how much council tax should be raised for policing;
- appoints (and dismisses) the chief constable and senior police officers;
- consults widely with local people to find out what they want from their local police;
- sets local policing priorities based on the concerns of local people as well as targets for achievement;
- monitors everything the police do and how well they perform against the targets set by the authority;
- publishes a three-year plan and an annual plan which tells local people what they can expect from their police service and reports back at the end of the year;

- makes sure local people get the best value from their local police force;
- oversees complaints against the police and disciplines senior officers.

10.3 **The Function of Police Authorities**

The main function of a police authority, therefore, is to make sure that the local police are accountable for what they do within the community—that is the people who live or work in the area—and that they have a say in how they are policed.

It is the police authority that controls the size of the budget and which is ultimately responsible for maintaining an efficient and effective police force. The police authority consists of 17 local councillors, magistrates, and independent members, and it is mainly through these members that the police service is accountable to the population at large. The responsibilities of the Chief Constable and police authority are shown in Table 10.1.

Table 10.1 Responsibilities of the Chief Constable and the Police Authority

Chief Constable	Police Authority
In overall command of the force and holds ultimate responsibility for operational matters.	Holds ultimate responsibility for the efficiency and effectiveness of the force.
Drafts local plans for Basic Command Units (BCUs).	Sets overall budget and approves any additional expenditure.
Responsible for achieving local force goals.	Drafts local plans and goals for local forces. Drafts three-year force strategy in accordance with National Police Plan.
Has control of expenditure within an agreed budget.	Consults with local population.

Source: Copied and adapted with permission from the APA website at http://www.apa.police.uk/APA/About+Police+Authorities/National+Map/

Figure 10.1 illustrates the geographic location of the police authorities in England and Wales.

10.4 **Local Policing Plans**

The Police Act 1996, amended by the Police and Justice Act 2006, requires police authorities to produce a local three-year rolling policing plan to be issued annually. Police authorities are required before the beginning of the financial year to determine objectives for the policing of the authority's area and include them in the local policing plan.

The policing plan objectives should be consistent with the strategic priorities determined by the Home Secretary.

This guidance continues to use the terminology 'local policing plan' to refer to the new three-year rolling policing plan refreshed and issued annually. The local policing plan contains objectives relating to both the 'national priorities' set by the Home Secretary in the National Community Safety Plan (Home Office, 2007), and further 'local priorities' set by the police authority (developed in consultation with the community, policing partners, and the local force).

The police authority can set local targets against both national and local priorities. The police authority also assesses the force's performance against the policing plan and makes their findings available to local communities. At a national level, the performance of forces will be assessed using the APACS framework. APACS has been designed around a framework of domains and at present the actual domain structure is subject to consultation, and is discussed fully later in this chapter. The domains provide the framework for a set of performance indicators that are agreed nationally, the Statutory Performance Indicators (SPIs).

National priorities are set by the Secretary of State and are detailed in the National Community Safety Plan. However, each authority will have its own unique issues (ie local priorities). When determining the local priorities for the policing plan, authorities should seek input from:

- *Community consultation.* In keeping with the principles of continuous improvement, authorities should ensure that local communities, including hard-to-reach groups, are consulted and their feedback incorporated in the Local Policing Plan. This may involve surveys, workshops, focus groups, or feedback from the website.
- *Partner consultation.* Local police priorities should align with the work of interagency working groups and partners seeking to improve community safety and reduce crime. These include Crime and Disorder Reduction Partnerships, Community Safety Partnerships, Criminal Justice Boards, and Local Strategic Partnerships.

- *Neighbourhood priorities.* Priorities adopted by Neighbourhood Teams across the force/authority area should be consulted to establish if they can be reflected in and supported by force-wide priorities.
- *Force Control Strategy.* The Force Control Strategy (FCS) is an output of the National Intelligence Model, which forces use to ensure that activities are intelligence-led. The FCS will identify important, intelligence-based priorities.
- *Risk Registers.* The force's and authority's risk registers and processes may identify necessary change and therefore be indicative of potential local priorities.
- *Continuous improvement.* Key priorities may also include a focus on internal business processes, systems, and enabling functions to ensure a force is effective, efficient, economic, and delivers the required quality of service. For example, based on the expert view of authority members and staff, efficiency, cost reduction, or service improvements may be identified as priorities.

The priorities identified through the consultation and internal process may overlap with the strategic policing priorities identified in the National Community Safety Plan. However, each authority should aim to identify at least one priority that is not a national priority.

10.5 **The Policing Plan Regulations 2008**

The policing plan regulations which came into being in March 2008 (Home Office, 2008) provided guidance for the production of a policing plan. In producing a policing plan a police authority should consider:

(a) any performance targets established by the police authority, whether in compliance with a direction under section 38 of the Police Act of 1996;

(b) any matters relating to the efficiency and effectiveness of the police force:
   (i) arising out of any inspection of the police force by Her Majesty's Inspectors of Constabulary, or
   (ii) raised with the police authority by the Secretary of State;

(c) any direction given to the police authority by the Secretary of State under section 40 of the Police Act 1996 (power to give directions in relation to a police force) or any information given to the police authority of the grounds on which such a direction might be given;

(d) the strategies for the plan period formulated by the relevant responsible authorities under section 6 (formulation and implementation of crime and disorder reduction strategies) of the Crime and Disorder Act 1998 (Home Office, 1998).

10.6 **The Contents of Policing Plans**

In addition to the above the policing plan of a police authority should clearly set out:

(a) any strategic priorities determined by the Secretary of State under section 37A (strategic priorities for police authorities) of the 1996 Act that relate to the plan period;

(b) any performance targets established by the police authority, whether in compliance with a direction under section 38 of the 1996 Act or otherwise, that relate to the plan period and how it is proposed to meet those targets;

(c) a statement of the financial resources the police authority expects to be available for the plan period and the proposed allocation of those resources;

(d) any planned increases in efficiency and productivity of the police force during the plan period and how it is proposed such increases will be achieved;

(e) any matters relating to the efficiency and effectiveness of the police force;

(f) any direction given by the Secretary of State under section 40 of the 1996 Act or any information given to the police authority of the grounds on which such a direction might be given and how the police authority intends to address such matters;

(g) any planned improvements in the ability of the police force to deliver protective services during the plan period and how it is proposed such improvements will be achieved;

(h) details of any cooperation between the police force and other police forces that is taking place at the time the plan is issued, and is proposed for the plan period.

10.7 **Publication of Policing Plans**

A police authority should arrange for every policing plan issued by it to be published in an appropriate manner by 30 June of the financial year before the beginning of which it was issued, and shall send a copy of the plan to the Secretary of State.

10.8 **The Assessments of Policing and Community Safety (APACS)**

An important aim of APACS is to reflect performance in respect of locally-selected priorities set alongside assessments based on Home Office statutory performance indicators. This is a complex business; individual police authorities and forces rightly set different priorities, objectives, indicators, and targets, so comparison 'between' forces for these local policing plan priorities has limited value. In addition, it has been necessary to establish a common terminology for discussing and populating APACS with locally selected indicators.

APACS will introduce one national performance framework for policing, crime, and drugs. It reflects the performance of the police service working alone or in partnership, and has links to the Communities and Local Government National Indicator Set, the new local performance framework, and Local Area Agreements.

10.9 Knowledge and Performance Management

Strong and effective performance management arrangements have been central to the reduction of crime and improvements in the performance of the police and partners on a wide range of crime and community safety issues.

As well as driving higher levels of service delivery nationally, performance management has helped to reduce the gaps between the strongest and weakest performances across England and Wales, through a combined approach of scrutiny and support. A strong performance management culture has now become firmly embedded in the way that the police and its partners plan and deliver services to reduce crime and ensure safer communities. This is not without criticisms as it may appear that the use of statistics and the managerialist approach is thought, perhaps, to have undermined 'traditional' policing methods in some quarters.

However, the Home Office and its partners are committed to refining the approach to managing the performance of the police, working alone or in partnership with others, on crime and community safety to ensure continued improvements. The Home Office and its partners therefore agreed to develop and introduce a new performance framework which will:

- simplify national and local performance arrangements;
- align the performance management of crime, drugs, and policing by combining existing performance assessment arrangements for these areas in the Home Office;
- join up with the wider performance management frameworks of community safety partners; and
- broaden the scope of performance management to take account of important community safety work which has not been included in previous performance frameworks.

A public statement of support was released by all the partners in February 2007 which was committed to the introduction of the APACS framework to replace and rationalize the existing assessment systems and harmonize with the principal frameworks of our community safety partners.

APACS has replaced a number of assessment systems that were in use for crime and community safety. Principally, the Policing Performance Assessment Framework (PPAF), which was developed by the Home Office and HM Inspectorate of Constabulary, with support from the Association of Police Authorities and the Association of Chief Police Officers. PPAF was introduced in 2004 and brought together a number of police performance indicators and qualitative judgements that the Home Office and HMIC had previously published separately, with the aim of covering the full range of policing activity and giving the public a rounded view of how their local force was doing across the board. This process brought significant improvements, providing greater transparency to the public, and underpinned work to improve police performance.

The new simplified framework reduces the number of measures by which the police and others are judged in terms of their success on crime and community safety and reduces the data demands of central government. The framework covers policing and community safety issues in a balanced way which focuses better on the most serious crimes and criminals. It harmonizes with other related frameworks and contains indicators and targets which are shared between partners.

APACS was introduced from April 2008 and the first assessments will be published in 2009, reporting on the financial year 2008–09.

Table 10.2 illustrates the new APACS strategic aims and the perceived benefits.

Table 10.2

Strategic Aim	Benefits
Simplify existing frameworks used by the Home Office and align clearly with external frameworks. (Eg for criminal justice, local authorities/Local Area Agreements (LAAs, health and transport).	• Less bureaucracy: fewer frameworks. • Better joint delivery via shared priorities, measures and targets. • Simpler, clearer and consistent messages about performance.
Integrate assessment with policy, delivery, and support functions plus associated regimes related to good practice, inspection, and audit.	• Improved performance and reduced performance variation among peers. • Improved knowledge of 'what works'. • Risk-based regulation and support.
Promote a balanced regime of accountability, building on the roles—including any collaborative arrangements—of partners locally, regionally, and nationally.	• Clear roles and responsibilities. • Basis of freedoms and flexibilities plus graduated framework of support. • Sensitive to different arrangements (eg in England and in Wales).
Cover crime, drugs, and policing issues comprehensively but in a way which reflects relative seriousness and which minimizes data demands on partners.	• Less bureaucracy: fewer measures. • Balanced and proportionate coverage. • Address current imbalances/gaps in performance assessment (eg anti-social behaviour and protective services).

Strategic Aim	Benefits
Make best use of available data and professional judgements in producing analysis and assessments which:	• Maximize the value of quantitative and qualitative approaches. Performance data used to inform risk-based audit and inspection.
• reflect relevant Public Service Agreements (PSAs) and other strategic priorities, objectives, and targets as well as performance against priorities for improvement selected locally;	• Clear and consistent expectations. Balance of national requirements and local needs.
	• Scope for innovation in delivery. Option of using other data as proxies where outcome measures are not desirable or feasible.
• use data focused on results (outcomes) but with the capability to use data on inputs, processes, or outputs; and	• Earlier identification of success/problems thereby facilitating delivery, management, and support.
• monitor implementation of key operational strategies such as neighbourhood policing, alcohol misuse, and drug enforcement.	
Communicate data and assessments in a timely manner and in a way which:	• Practitioner-facing data and analysis with public-facing assessments.
• promotes visibility, accountability, and responsiveness of service providers;	• Increased local transparency and accountability.
• supports day-to-day management and which demonstrates service delivery to citizens, communities, and opinion-formers; and	• Increased data scrutiny to identify and resolve problems.
	• Robust, timely data and comparative analysis plus regular assessments, supported by data and commentary.
• shows whether services are effective, equitable, and provide value-for-money and whether they are perceived as such.	• Balanced understanding of performance across a range of key perspectives.

10.10 **Police Authorities, Accountability, and the Future**

Reducing crime and disorder is still a high priority for the public, and this has influenced government thinking regarding the subject. Police authorities play a major role in helping to achieve this priority through their part in the accountability and consultation process, producing policing plans that help in the transfer of knowledge to formulating policing objectives. There have been numerous initiatives and much legislation in the past decade or so aimed at addressing the issues of crime and disorder reduction. There has been considerable investment in expanding police powers and increasing police staff numbers, but research has shown that only half of the public believe their local police are doing a good or excellent job (Kershaw et al, 2007).

Further, the majority of the community served by the police feel they have no influence over them so consequently have little say in police matters. Importantly, those people who have had contact with their local police are less likely to believe they are doing a good job, including individuals who class themselves as victims and witnesses (Kershaw et al, 2007). Police accountability, therefore, has become a topic of great political interest and has stimulated debate and a number of important papers for discussion, including documents by the Local Government Association (LGA, 2008) and the Institute for Public Policy Research (IPPR, 2008), and the influential Home Office White Paper concerning the transfer of power to the community (Home Office, 2008b).

All of these documents clearly indicate the way in which accountability for the delivery of local services within communities, including the police service, are about to undergo a radical overhaul.

However, the seminal document that illustrates the possible changes in accountability and local policing and ultimately will affect the present tripartite arrangement is the Government's Green Paper entitled 'From the Neighbourhood to the National: Policing Our Communities Together' (Home Office, 2008).

The document covers an extensive amount of policy discussion, including neighbourhood teams, leadership, and improving communication between the police and communities. Consequently, strengthening local accountability is a prime feature of this document. In particular the following issues were identified:

- There is at present no direct public participation in the selection of police authority members.
- There appear to be concerns in some police authorities over the selection of some councillors to sit on police authorities.
- If a body of citizens is dissatisfied with the service they receive from the police, they have little means to rectify this.

It is anticipated that the Government will seek to address these issues by the following means:

- Legislation will be introduced to reform police authorities in an attempt to make them more democratic and more effective in responding to the needs of the local community.
- The majority of police authority members will no longer be formed from local councillors. Instead, people will vote directly for individuals known as Crime and Policing Representatives (CPRs) to represent their current responsibilities, particularly ensuring that police forces are working together to address regional and national issues.

10.11 **Conclusions**

The current arrangement for accountability and governance of policing in England and Wales is under review. At present the tripartite arrangement as introduced with the Police Act 1964, subject to some variations, still stands, but changes are about to be implemented which will alter the makeup and roles of the different members of the tripartite agreement. Clearly, there is a strong emphasis upon more local accountability, with perhaps a stronger 'political' influence, which in turn will mean a greater need for closer contact with the public. This in turn means that there will be more emphasis upon local 'hot spotting' and a closing of the gap between what the police believe the community wants and what the community actually needs, which will, it is believed, result in a more efficient and effective delivery of local services to the public. These changes involve the introduction of a different set of management tools such as APACS, and implicit within these changes is the understanding that local success for the police and communities rests upon the creation of knowledge, information, and intelligence formulated in local policing plans to tackle problems identified by community representatives working in partnership with the police.

Further Reading

Home Office (1964) The Police Act, London, HMSO

—— (1996) The Police Act, London, HMSO

—— (1998) The Crime and Disorder Act, London, HMSO

—— (2006) The Police and Justice Act, London, HMSO

—— (2007) *Cutting Crime—A New Partnership 2008–2011*, London, HMSO

—— (2008a) *From the Neighbourhood to the National: Policing our Communities Together*, London, HMSO

—— (2008b) *Communities in Control—Real People, Real Power*, London, HMSO

—— (2008c) *Policing Plan Regulations*, London, Home Office

Institute for Public Policy Research (2008) *A New Beat: Options for More Accountable Policing*, London, IPPR

Kershaw C, Micholas, S, and Walker, W (2007) *Crime in England and Wales 2006/2007*, London, Home Office

Local Government Association (2008) *Answering to You: Policing in the 21st Century*, London, LGA

Reiner, R (2000) *The Politics of the Police* (3rd edition), Oxford, Oxford University Press

Websites

<http://www.apa.police.uk/apa> The Association of Police Authorities

<http://www.homeoffice.gov.uk/police/> The Police page on the Home Office website

<http://www.ippr.org/> The Institute for Public Policy Research

<http://www.lga.gov.uk/lga/core/page.do?pageId=1> Local Government Association

<http://police.homeoffice.gov.uk/police-reform/policegp/> The Government's policing Green Paper

<http://www.inspectorates.homeoffice.gov.uk/hmic/> Her Majesty's Inspectorate of Constabulary website

Chapter 11

Association of Chief Police Officers (ACPO) Values

11.1 **Introduction**

This chapter will consider the organization known as the Association of Chief Police Officers or ACPO for short. It will examine the historical background to the introduction of the Association, its aims and objectives, and its role in policing today's diverse and complex society. It will also consider its role in producing doctrines and a statement of common purpose for policing which are symptomatic of the philosophy of supporting professionalism within police practice. The equivalent association in Scotland (ACPO(S)) is not considered here as the Scottish criminal jurisdiction falls outside the scope of this volume.

11.2 **Historical Context**

ACPO was formed in 1948 by combining the separate chief officer groups representing county and borough police forces that existed up until that point. This amalgamation, however, was forced upon Chief Constables by the Oaksey Report of 1948–1949 (Home Office, 1949) which examined police conditions of service.

ACPO was and is still an informal body, with its functions unspecified by any legal definition or even by any legal recognition. However, as Reiner (1992) points out, its role as a policy-developing body has expanded out of all recognition since its formation and it has close links with the Home Office. Indeed, research by Reiner (1992) suggests that the Chief Officers who make up ACPO regard the Home Office as being one of the most influential bodies on their decision-making progress as opposed to police authorities within the tripartite system (discussed in Chapter 10).

ACPO is not a staff association as commonly understood (the separately constituted Chief Police Officers' Association fulfils that function). ACPO's work is on behalf of the Service, rather than its own members. It is to all intents and purposes, therefore, an independent, professionally-led, strategic body. ACPO states that it operates in the public interest and, in working with Government and the Association of Police Authorities, it leads and coordinates the direction and development of the police service in England, Wales, and Northern Ireland. In times of national need, disasters, and other major threats, ACPO coordinates the strategic policing response on behalf of all chief officers.

The Association has the status of a private company limited by guarantee. As such, it conforms to the requirements of company law and its affairs are governed by a Board of Directors. It is funded by a combination of a Home Office grant, contributions from each of the 43 police authorities of England and Wales and the Police Board of Northern Ireland, membership subscriptions, and by the proceeds of its annual exhibition. ACPO's members are police officers who hold the rank of Chief Constable, Deputy Chief Constable, or Assistant Chief Constable, or their equivalents, in the 44 forces of England, Wales, and Northern Ireland, national police agencies and certain other forces in the UK, the Isle of Man, and the Channel Islands, and certain senior non-police staff. There are presently 280 members of ACPO.

11.3 **Aims and Objectives of ACPO**

Like every organization ACPO has its aims and objectives which help to define it and also to direct its work. By studying these we can gain an insight into the drivers for much of ACPO's work. The aims of ACPO are:

- to provide strong and visible leadership to the police service of England, Wales, and Northern Ireland, inspiring confidence in staff, partners, and the diverse communities that the police serve;
- to ensure, with partners, that the development of doctrine for the service is conducted in a professional and coordinated manner, supporting the continuous improvement of policing for the benefit of the communities that the police serve;
- to be recognized as a principal voice of the service by those seeking a professional view on all policing matters, including the Government, the media, and the agencies with whom the police deal, both nationally and globally;
- to coordinate the strategic policing response, in times of national need, on behalf of all chief officers;
- to support and encourage its members in achieving and continuously developing the highest professional knowledge and standards of performance;
- to provide appropriate member services to its members;
- to continue to develop their business activities to ensure that the ACPO brand name is recognized globally as a mark of excellence in policing.

In achieving these aims, ACPO state they try to be an inclusive organization, acting in an ethical and professional manner, respecting and embracing the diversity of all its members, their partners, and those they serve, and being demonstrably committed to equality and human rights. Clearly ACPO have a large role in supporting the supply of information and intelligence to the police service across the country. In particular, one of the main functions of ACPO appears to be that of turning the police service into a more professionally recognized and functioning organization.

11.4 **Supporting National Policing**

ACPO also oversees and works in partnership with a number of national policing units, agencies, and projects. These include:

- ACPO Criminal Records Office (ACRO). ACRO was introduced in May 2006 after approval by ACPO. The aim of ACRO is to provide operational support to several Chief Officer Portfolios dealing with matters relating to criminal records and associated biometric data, including DNA and fingerprint information. The prime focus of their work is to produce operational benefits and ensure maximum public protection from dangerous offenders. It was set up in response to a perceived gap in the police service's ability to manage criminal records and in particular improve links to biometric data. ACRO provides guidance and management on access to these criminal records and strives to introduce a more effective operational use of this information.
- ACPO Vehicle Crime Intelligence Service (AVCIS). Under the guidance of the ACPO portfolio lead for vehicle crime matters, AVCIS was officially launched in December 2006. Its overarching aim is to develop and promulgate a full range of enhanced capabilities, which will enable the police service and partners to incapacitate offenders who use vehicles in the course of their unlawful activities across the full spectrum of criminal activity. The reality is that 'traditional' vehicle crime, such as theft of or from vehicles is no longer regarded as a policing priority by most forces. However, the use of vehicles in acquisitive crimes, such as burglary, supporting serious and organized

crime, and potential links to terrorist offences cannot be overlooked. For that reason the main thrust of AVCIS is to gather intelligence to tackle 'vehicle enabled crime'. AVCIS works with partner agencies and all stakeholders within the trade and associated businesses to provide the most effective response. As such, AVCIS represents UK policing in respect of vehicle enabled crime matters, and incorporates a number of specialist functions including TruckPol, the national freight crime intelligence service, and the Vehicle Fraud Unit who investigate organized finance fraud. These units provide strategic overviews on the nature and extent of the particular problem to the Home Office to assist in policy formulation.

- National Community Tension Team (NCTT). The NCTT is a team that represents the police service in some of the most contentious areas of policing.

11.4.1 Tension monitoring

Information is received from a wide range of sources about tension issues that might have an impact in the UK. This in turn is disseminated via an intelligence bulletin that is circulated to all police forces and a range of other stakeholders including government departments.

Community impact assessments are also produced for some of the most contentious policing operations including very often counter-terrorist operations.

NCTT has developed a sophisticated tension monitoring process and also devised a community impact assessment process. These processes are now widely used throughout the police service in the UK. It also developed the community intelligence part of the National Intelligence Model.

11.4.2 Prevent

NCTT leads for the police service on the 'Prevent' strand of the Government's national counter-terrorist strategy CONTEST. The government definition of Prevent is 'to reduce the number of individuals attracted to Islamist extremism or become terrorists'. The NCTT definition is broader to ensure that all police forces, partner agencies, and the community as a whole 'supports and contributes to countering terrorism'.

11.5 **Modernizing ACPO**

In an effort to keep itself aligned with the demands of an increasingly complex society, ACPO became a non-profit company in accordance with the Companies Act 1985 (Home Office, 1985). This procedure had formally empowered ACPO to deal with the financial aspects of running a company in a professional manner, as well as embodying the principles of ethically running an organization. Further, during 1999, ACPO Crime Prevention Initiatives Limited was formed, which is a not for profit company to manage Secured by Design and similar crime prevention initiatives at a national level. This company is entirely owned by ACPO with Chief Police Officers on the Board of Directors. The company is funded through partnership with companies whose products meet technical standards identified by ACPO Crime Prevention Initiatives. In return, the licensed company is able to utilize the Secured by Design logo and, on those products which meet the technical standard, the title 'Police Preferred Specification' in accordance with the terms of the licence agreement.

One of the Government's key objectives for the planning of new housing is to secure quality, sustainable places where people choose to live. To achieve this, a greater emphasis was needed to be placed on the design and on the need to encourage higher standards. Designing for community safety is a central part of this, and the 'secured by design' programme, as illustrated in the following key point box, is indicative of this approach.

KEY POINT—SECURED BY DESIGN

'Secured by Design' (SBD) is a police initiative which seeks to encourage the building industry to adopt crime prevention measures in development design to assist in reducing the opportunity for crime and the fear of crime, creating a safer and more secure environment.

Secured By Design is managed by ACPO Crime Prevention Initiatives Limited (ACPO CPI) a 'not for profit' company wholly owned by ACPO. It has the backing of the Home Office Crime Reduction Unit and the scheme has been drawn up in consultation with the Department of the Environment, Transport and the Regions (DETR).

ACPO CPI also licenses companies to use the Secured By Design logo on those of their products which meet the attack test standards drawn up by bodies such as the British Standards Institute.

As well as ACPO modernizing its functions to include crime prevention activities, it also engages, in conjunction with the National Policing Improvement Agency (NPIA), in the production of documents and information which are seen as supporting policing at the front line. These are known as doctrines and guidance advice documents.

11.6 **The Drive for Professionalism**

There has long been a desire for the police service in this country to be regarded as a true profession. However, a neat business or sociological definition of a profession is hard to apply to the police service, especially in its current format. That said, it is possible to move the police service towards a type of professional status, which includes the use of a large body of professional knowledge alongside an ethical use of this knowledge in the delivery of police services to its customers. Perhaps one of the major steps to the introduction of an ethical approach to policing can be seen in the Police

Statement of Common Purposes and Values, introduced by ACPO in 1990. For the first time, there was a commitment to professional and ethical values which could be applied in the way the police operate. The full statement is shown below:

The Statement of Common Purpose and Values

The purpose of the police service is to uphold the law fairly and firmly to prevent crime, to pursue and bring to justice those who break the law and keep the queen's peace, to protect, help and reassure the community, and to be seen to do all this with integrity, common sense and sound judgement. We must be compassionate, courteous and patient, acting without fear or favour or prejudice to the rights of others. We need to be professional, calm and restrained in the face of violence and apply only that force which is necessary to accomplish our lawful duty. We must strive to reduce the fears of the public and, so far as we can, to reflect their priorities in the action we take. We must respond to well founded criticism with a willingness to change.

Despite some criticism that the police service can never become a true profession because it has no code of ethics (but see Chapter 12.3 below: Standards of Professional Behaviour), ACPO has adopted the Nolan Principles as its code of ethics and statement of values. These principles are:

- Holders of public office should take decisions solely in terms of the public interest. They should not do so in order to gain financial or other material benefits for themselves, their family, or their friends.
- Holders of public office should not place themselves under any financial or other obligation to outside individuals or organizations that might influence them in the performance of their official duties.
- In carrying out public business, including making public appointments, awarding contracts, or recommending individuals for rewards and benefits, holders of public office should make choices on merit.

- Holders of public office are accountable for their decisions and actions to the public and must submit themselves to whatever scrutiny is appropriate to their office.
- Holders of public office should be as open as possible about all the decisions and actions that they take. They should give reasons for their decisions and restrict information only when the wider public interest clearly demands.
- Holders of public office have a duty to declare any private interests relating to their public duties and to take steps to resolve any conflicts arising in a way that protects the public interest.
- Holders of public office should promote and support these principles by leadership and example.

The adoption of the Nolan Principles illustrates how ACPO is attempting to steer not only itself but the police service as a whole towards being an ethical and accountable organization.

11.6.1 **Doctrines**

One of the more recent functions of ACPO has been the introduction of doctrines or documents concerning guidance and practice advice which are issued to each Chief Constable with the recommendation that he or she should adopt the doctrine and implement it as appropriate for his or her force. ACPO maintains a register of current doctrines and their website allows access to many of these 'best practice' documents. Further, working in conjunction with the NPIA, ACPO produces guidance documents for assisting police forces across the country in many aspects of their work. The principle purpose of a doctrine is to provide a framework of guidance for policing activities and underpin police training and operational planning.

Examples of doctrines and advice documents include Practice Advice on Tasking and Co-ordination (ACPO Centrex, 2006), Practice Advice on Critical Incident Management (ACPO NPIA, 2007), and Guidance on Investigating Domestic Abuse (ACPO NPIA, 2008).

What all of these documents attempt to achieve is to disseminate not only best practice from around the country, but also to introduce new and sometimes controversial ideas for police services to apply within their areas. They also attempt to introduce a common methodology in dealing with many incidents such as investigations, which brings into being the idea of reasoned decision-making based upon scientific knowledge. In short, these documents illustrate another function of ACPO, that of attempting to professionalize the police service into an organization which draws upon a recognized body of knowledge (doctrines, practice advice, etc) which underpins delivery of policing services in an ethical manner to its customers (those people receiving the services of the police).

11.7 **Conclusion**

The role of ACPO has changed considerably since its creation in 1948. It is now an important consultation group which represents Chief Officers, and the collective influence of these officers has grown. ACPO is seen to increasingly project a 'single voice' (Wall, 1998: 316), and as a body exerts great influence on policy-making which affects policing. This also reflects the increasingly complex social and policing environment that has seen the need for specialist ACPO committees that provide advice, doctrines, and support for the continuation of professionalism within the police service.

Further Reading

ACPO Centrex (2006) *Practice Advice on Tasking and Co-ordination*, ACPO Centrex, London

ACPO NPIA (2007) *Practice Advice on Critical Incident Management,* ACPO NPIA, London

—— (2008) *Guidance on Investigating Domestic Abuse*, ACPO NPIA, London

Home Office (1949) *The Oaksey Report*, London, HMSO

—— (1985) *The Companies Act,* London, HMSO

Lord Nolan's Principles of Public Life: <http://www.archive. official-documents.co.uk/document/parliament/ nolan/localgov.htm>.

Neyroud, P (2003) 'Policing and Ethics' in Newburn, T (ed), *Handbook of Policing* (1st edition), Cullompton, Willan, 578–602

Reiner, R (1992) *Chief Constables*, Oxford, Oxford University Press

The Association of Chief Police Officers website: <http:// www.acpo.police.uk/default.asp>

The National Policing Improvement Agency: <http://www. npia.police.uk/en/index.htm>

The Secured By Design website: <http://www.securedby design.com>

Wall, D (1998) *The Chief Constables of England and Wales: The Socio-Legal History of a Criminal Elite*, Aldershot, Dartmouth

Chapter 12

Standards of Professional Behaviour

12.1 **Introduction**

Many organizations have standards of professional behaviour, or a guide to ethical (correct, right, or proper) behaviour, and the police service is no exception. Indeed, some commentators have argued (Neyroud 2003) that it is more important for the police to have a code of conduct than many other organizations. Why should this be? There are significant opportunities for individuals to engage in crime and corruption within the police service. A professional code of conduct is part of the internal protections against such eventualities. Additionally and importantly, the police are there to protect the weak and the vulnerable, and to help those who are unable to help themselves. It follows that, for the public to have confidence in the police, there must be safeguards: demanding standards of behaviour for the police higher than the norm.

That is why most police forces have a **Professional Standards Department** (PSD), which investigates complaints against individual officers, and which internally investigates officers suspected of wrong-doing. Some police forces may have a unit with a similar function to PSD but with a different name (for example, 'Complaints and Discipline').

PSDs in many forces also investigate complaints against police staff members. External to the police service the national **Independent Police Complaints Commission** (IPCC) investigates serious police actions where there may have been a lapse from professional standards; typically, the IPCC investigates fatal shootings by the police and may review major police investigations.

Other bodies which oversee the police and who may scrutinize the ethics of their activities include **Police Authorities** (one for each police force, see chapter 2.1) and the national **Policing Standards Unit** which is part of the Home Office. The **National Police Improvement Agency** (NPIA) has a generic role in raising police skills, standards, and competences.

Definition

We can define ethical or 'right' behaviour as:

- the ways in which individuals morally govern their actions;
- the way in which organizations distinguish between acceptable and unacceptable behaviour by employees;
- the way in which society governs or controls the actions of its members for the good of all.

Alternatively, we might express these three levels of 'right' behaviour graphically— see Figure 12.1.

Individual standards of behaviour may vary very much from one person to another. One person may have a belief or faith system which another does not; one community, identified and united by its shared standards may feel threatened by another community which has an entirely different set of values. One society, even, may have beliefs and behaviours which another society may find unacceptable. In 2001, in an attempt to identify morally-correct behaviour which could cross national and some cultural

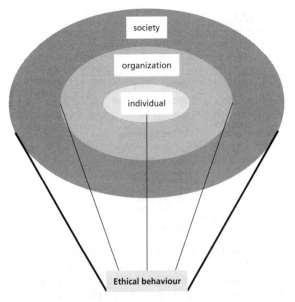

Figure 12.1

boundaries, the European Union published a Code of Police
Ethics, which noted three essential principles:

- **police officers help to safeguard the rule of law**
- **the police depend upon the citizen for support**
- **public confidence is tightly linked to how the police
  treat the public and the issue of human rights**

These principles have been expanded in such areas as the
behavioural competences (Skills for Justice, 2003) against
which all police officers and most police staff members
deployed operationally, are assessed. The behavioural competences are shown in Table 12.1.

Table 12.1

Behavioural area	Behaviour	Minimum standard (patrol constable example)
Achieving results	Problem-solving	C
	Personal responsibility	B
	Resilience	A
Working with others	Respect for diversity	A
	Team-working	C
	Community focus	C
	Effective communication	B

[adapted from Skills for Justice 2003]

Of course, these include many other kinds of preferred or desired behaviours than just the personally ethical, and the Skills for Justice requirements for individual competences are extensive. However, given the emphasis in the European Code (2001) on the importance of ethical interaction between police and the public, it is notable here that a patrol constable, for example, will be assessed as either competent or not competent in his or her dealings with both the community and with colleagues. The 'positive indicators' used to assess competence are firmly based in 'right' behaviour, whilst those 'negative indicators' which are used to identify that competence has not been attained, are largely failures to produce 'right' behaviour.

12.2 **Additional and Developing Codes**

In March 2007, the then Home Secretary, John Reid, wrote to all police forces in England and Wales outlining the values which he asserted should characterize an ethical police service and which the Government expected of the service. These were:

- Fairness and impartiality
- Integrity
- Freedom from corruption
- Respect for liberty
- Freedom from racism
- Equal service to all communities
- Commitment to protection and well-being of all individuals

12.3 **The Standards of Professional Behaviour**

The following Standards of Professional Behaviour for police officers were defined in the Schedule to the Police (Conduct) Regulations, Statutory Instrument 2008/2864, which came into force on 1st December 2008. See also Home Office Circular 26/2008 at http://www.homeoffice .gov.uk/about-us/publications/home-office-circulars/ circulars-2008/ (accessed 16 June 2009).

Honesty and Integrity: Police officers are honest, act with integrity and do not compromise or abuse their position.

Authority, Respect and Courtesy: Police officers act with self-control and tolerance, treating members of the public and colleagues with respect and courtesy. Police officers and staff do not abuse their powers or authority and respect the rights of all individuals.

Equality and Diversity: Police officers act with fairness and impartiality. They do not discriminate unlawfully or unfairly.

Use of Force: Police officers only use force to the extent that it is necessary, proportionate and reasonable to obtain a legitimate objective.

Orders and instructions: Police officers only give and carry out lawful orders and instructions. Police officers abide by police regulations, force policies and lawful orders.

Duties and Responsibilities: Police officers are diligent in the exercise of their duties and responsibilities.

Confidentiality: Police officers treat information with respect and access or disclose it only in the proper course of police duties.

Fitness for Duty: Police officers when on duty or presenting themselves for duty are fit to carry out their responsibilities.

Discreditable Conduct: Police officers behave in a manner which does not discredit the police service or undermines or is likely to undermine public confidence in the police, whether on or off duty.

Police officers report any action taken against them for a criminal offence, conditions imposed on them by a court or the receipt of any penalty notice.

Challenging and Reporting Improper Conduct: Police officers report challenge, or take action against the conduct of colleagues which has fallen below the Standards of Professional Behaviour.

12.3.1 Legislative and Statutory Origins

It is evident that the Standards owe something to the principles in the **Council of Europe Code on Police Ethics** (2001), to the provisions in the **Human Rights Act of 1998** (itself derived from the European Convention on Human Rights) and to the revised **Police (Conduct) Regulations 2004** (Schedule 1, SI No. 645). There was an extensive period of consultation during 2006 before the new Standards were published in 2008.

The Standards reflect *'the expectations that the police service and the public have of how police officers should behave'*. They are not intended to describe every situation *'but rather to set a framework which everyone can easily understand'* (Home Office letter, 2006, see further reading). In many ways, the

Standards build on what gone before but now have new emphases to reflect the Government's 'respect agenda', and are simpler, more all-embracing and more direct than previous codes of practice. The flavour of the Standards of Professional Behaviour reflects many of the principles (and language) of earlier codes, whilst extending the spectrum of preferred behaviour.

12.4 **Guidance and Commentary**

There follows more detailed consideration of the Standards. The Explanatory Notes accompanying Statutory Instrument 2008/2864 make explicit that breach of these Standards 'constitutes misconduct and a breach . . . so serious that dismissal would be justified constitutes gross misconduct.'

12.4.1 **Honesty and Integrity**

Police officers are required to be honest and to act with integrity at all times so as not to compromise their position, colleagues or organization. Perjury is a criminal offence; falsifying documents gross misconduct. Significant issues surround acceptance of gifts. Recipients should 'always consider carefully the motivation of the person offering a gift or gratuity', which is sensible advice, because there is always the possibility that the offer is a bribe or inducement. Authorization may be required to accept any gift. The sensible thing would be to declare the gift and, if it is expensive, ensure that there is an open auction with proceeds going to a recognized police charity or benevolent fund. It is still the case that the recipient of a gift in a public office must declare it or dispose of it ethically. Access to premises other than for duty purposes or obtaining an advantage of some kind by using a warrant card is prohhibited. In some forces, officers in uniform may travel free on public transport (with advantages to both), but generally the warrant card should be used for identification or to demonstrate police authority, not as a 'catch-all' travel card.

12.4.2 Authority, Respect and Courtesy

Police officers must act with self-control and tolerance, treating all others with respect and courtesy. The public has every right to expect that police powers are used professionally, impartially and with integrity, irrespective of who is being dealt with. In other words, the same *'imperturbable impartiality'* should be used by police officers whether dealing with a duke or a dustman, a fellow officer or a paedophile. Additionally, some people who come into contact with the police may be vulnerable, and officers have an absolute requirement to support and protect them. This is especially important when vulnerable witnesses, such as victims of domestic violence, feel very frightened or inhibited – often after years of abuse – about making an allegation against an abuser.

On a lower, but more widespread and familiar level, police officers should use respectful language, appropriate to their dealings with the public and with their own colleagues. There is no toleration whatever of racist, abusive, chauvinist, demeaning, contemptuous or belittling language in the police service and those who flout this rule face dismissal and/or criminal charges.

12.4.3 Equality and Diversity

Officers must act fairly and impartially and may not discriminate against anyone on the grounds of sex, race, skin colour, language, religion, belief, political or other opinion, national or social origin, disability, sexual orientation, property or birth. The murder of black teenager Stephen Lawrence in 1993 and the subsequent Inquiry by Sir William Macpherson which found the Metropolitan Police guilty of 'institutionalized racism' in 1999, were the catalysts for change in all police forces, to rid the service of stereotyping, prejudice and unwarranted assumption. Achieving this principle will require continuous effort on the part of all officers and staff.

12.4.4 Use of Force

Force must be used proportionately; non-physical means to obtain compliance should be tried before physical force is used. This can be something of an ideal prescription, since someone 'fighting drunk' is not usually amenable to verbal reasoning, but for the most part, verbal persuasion is preferable to controlled violence. However, the test here is, as it is with other aspects of the of Standards of Professional Behaviour, whether decisions taken in the heat of the moment will stand up to cold scrutiny in court. Section 3 of the Criminal Law Act of 1967 makes it clear that force may only be used when it is *reasonable in the circumstances*, but 'reasonable' has never been defined in law, and each separate occasion will be assessed on its merits and may well be tested in the courts.

Article 2 of the European Convention on Human Rights (incorporated as law in the Human Rights Act 1998) provides a stricter test than whether the use of *lethal* force was 'reasonable'. The ECHR says that the use of such force must be *absolutely necessary to protect the lives of others* and/or the life of the armed police officer. Police use of force resulting in death will be subject to particular scrutiny as was seen with the fatal shooting of Jean-Charles de Menezes on a London Tube train in July 2005, in the mistaken belief that he was one of the terrorists involved in the bombings which had shocked London two weeks earlier. Belief that de Menezes was a terrorist was described as 'insufficient' justification by lawyers to the Menezes family, when challenging the Metropolitan Police. A Coronial jury returned an 'open verdict'.

Additional caveats in this Principle are about the use of torture, inhuman or degrading treatment or punishment (themselves outlawed under Article 3 of the ECHR). PACE and its Codes of Practice regulate appropriate conduct towards detained and arrested persons.

12.4.5 Orders and Instructions

Only orders and instructions that are lawful may be given. These must be obeyed. An order or instruction that is unlawful will either be a criminal act or misconduct that must be reported. Given the emphasis on individual responsibility in the police service, no officer of rank may order a subordinate to arrest or use (fatal) force against someone. These are individual judgments that may have to be justified in a court of law, or to an IPCC investigation or both. Abiding by police regulations, force policies and lawful orders may impose constraints of officers' private lives.

12.4.6 Duties and Responsibilities

Has an officer or staff member behaved diligently in performing an action or in not doing an action? Police officers have discretion to act or not, whether or not to pursue a line of enquiry, or to follow up a matter or to charge someone with an offence. This may also involve a judgment about priorities, so that an officer may leave one task to undertake another, if s/he judges it appropriate to do so. The tests for this can be scrutiny of conduct in a court (such as a decision not to arrest a man accused of violence against his partner), in a complaints investigation (such as whether reasonable force was used to detain a struggling suspect) or in a complaint from the public about an officer's 'excessive zeal' in pursuing an enquiry. An officer's conduct is open to challenge and the individual must always be aware that such conduct may have to be defended at a later date, and that the individual alone is responsible for what is done or not done. This principle also extends to accurate record-keeping.

12.4.7 **Confidentiality**

Police officers must treat information with respect and access or disclose it only in the proper course of police duties. Policing involves sharing information with other agencies and information that is shared with the police by other agencies similarly must be respected.

Definition—'need to know' principle

'A security principle which states that the dissemination of classified information should be no wider than is required for the efficient conduct of business, and should be restricted to those who have authorized access. A balance must be struck between making information as widely available as necessary to maximize potential benefits, and restricting availability to protect the security of sources, techniques and information. The development of systems helps to support the integrity and effectiveness of the intelligence environment.' (para 2.2)

ACPO, *Guidance on the National Intelligence Model*. (NCPE Centrex, Wyboston, 2005).

'Need to know' is a sound maxim delivering operational effectiveness: it is not a question of trust. Secrecy should never be used arbitrarily or for no good purpose, but some kinds of knowledge should not be available to all and sundry (such as how eavesdropping devices work or which criminals are currently under surveillance). This includes not passing information to family and friends, to private investigators or to the media, without specific authorization. Looking up a car owner's details on the PNC to oblige a friend is a breach of the obligation to confidentiality (as would divulging the details of a sensitive police operation to anyone not involved).

KEY POINT

Need to Know in a nutshell:

1) Who 'needs to know' the information in the format in which it currently exists?
2) Is it possible to sanitize the presentation of the information in its entirety or in part in order to share the intelligence without compromising sources, techniques, or other information?

12.4.8 Fitness for Duty

Officers should not drink alcohol prior to or on duty. Using a prohibited substance for non-medical purposes or intentionally misusing prescription drugs are disciplinary offences, and may also be criminal. If officers admit to alcoholism or drugs misuse problems, support mechanisms are available, but *the use of illegal drugs cannot be condoned*. In all other respects, officers should be fit to undertake their duties, and that includes refraining from hazardous activities in which there is a deliberate risk to life. If absent from duty on account of sickness, officers should abstain from activities likely to delay their return to work. An officer who is unexpectedly called to duty may, without detriment, disclose that s/he has consumed alcohol.

Most forces have occupational health departments which engage in active '*absence management*' and which promote healthy life styles. Such departments may help with any other health-related issue or refer officers for specialist help and advice. Persistent unfitness for duty because of alcohol, or any other form of substance abuse, is a ground for dismissal.

12.4.9 Discreditable Conduct

Bringing the police service into discredit, or acting in such a way as to damage public confidence in the police, is to be

---

avoided, on or off duty. Examples from an officer's private life which may entail 'discreditable conduct' include receiving an Anti-Social Behaviour Order (ASBO), a restraining order from a court or being bound-over to keep the peace. Police officers must be seen to be as subject to the law as anyone else.

Part of 'professional standards' is demonstrating a positive image of the police service, which will include less tangible but no less visible factors such as smartness and punctuality.

Officers must accept some restrictions on their life off-duty, which has to be balanced against their right to respect for their private life. Examples of prohibited conduct include misuse of a warrant card, engaging in inappropriate businesses or using employment by the police as a means of obtaining preferential treatment of an unfair kind (that is, to the disadvantage of others), such as demanding discounts.

Officers have a duty to disclose action taken against them for a criminal offence, and conditions imposed upon them by a court or the receipt of a penalty notice.

12.4.10 Challenging and Reporting Improper Conduct

It is expected that officers will challenge breaches of these standards when encountered and where appropriate, report such actions. Malicious reports or those made in 'bad faith' will not be acceptable. Persistent improper conduct should, of necessity, be reported to a superior officer or to the Professional Standards Department.

12.5 **Summary**

Behavioural standards statements are common in most organizations, and, like adherence to the Standards in

Public Life, must be and must be seen to be complied with. This is especially true of the police service. The public has every right to expect that police officers and staff behave proportionately, acceptably, fairly, and impartially. The Standards of Professional Behaviour set out clearly what standards of behaviour, attitude, tolerance and restraint are expected of every officer. Professionalism is an important part of being a police officer or member of staff and in gaining public trust. In many cases, deviation from the Standards may entail dismissal from the force or disciplinary action. The Standards are grounded in practical common sense: a police force stands or falls by the ethical behaviour of the individual officer.

Further Reading

Bryant, R (ed) (2008), *Blackstone's Student Police Officer Handbook* (3rd edition), Oxford University Press, Oxford, especially section 5.4 on 'Ethics and Policing'

European Union (2001), *Code of Police Ethics*, available at<http://www.coe.int/t/e/legal_affairs/legal_cooperation/police_and_internal_security/conferences/2002>, accessed 29 April 2009

Macpherson, Sir W (1999), *An Inquiry into the murder of Stephen Lawrence*, Cm 4262-I, TSO, Crown copyright and available at <http://www.archive.official-documents.co.uk/document/cm42/4262/4262.htm>, accessed 8 July 2008

Neyroud, P and Buckley, A (2001), *Policing, Ethics and Human Rights*, Willan Publishing, Devon

—— (2003), 'Policing and Ethics' in Newburn, T (ed), *Handbook of Policing*, Willan Publishing, Devon

Nolan, Lord (1995), *First Report of the Committee on Standards in Public Life*, Cm 2850-1, TSO, Crown Copyright; the first five Committee Reports are available at <http://libwww.essex.ac.uk/Archives/Nolan_Committee.htm>, accessed 25 June 2008

Police Code of Professional Standards, Home Office letter of 27 February 2006, Police Leadership and Powers Unit, available at <http://www.Code@homeoffice.gsi.gov.uk>, accessed 24 June 2008

Police Competences, Skills for Justice, 2003, available at <http://www.skillsforjustice.com/websitefiles/NOS_POLICE>

Police Regulations: (2004), Police (Conduct) Regulations, SI 645, available at <http://www.opsi.gov.uk/si/si2004/20040645.htm>, accessed 25 June 2008, and from TSO, Crown Copyright

Chapter 13

Human Rights

The relationship between policing and human rights is often viewed as being one of tension if not antagonistic. The paradigm of human rights can properly be viewed as an enabling structure within policing. It is part of the organizational knowledge upon which policing is based. Policing serves to protect human rights and to sustain a community within which human rights are respected.

13.1 **What are Human Rights?**

Perspectives on human rights are determined by geopolitical circumstance. From the position that governments exist to provide safety and security for their citizens, and that a failure to do so is harmful to human rights, it follows that in some parts of the world, access to the basic provisions necessary for human survival is the predominant human rights issue; elsewhere the degree of and access to democracy is the main issue (also conceptualized as civil and political rights); education and the ability to improve one's economic well-being are considered rights issues; whilst in the UK, relatively well-provisioned and with stable democratic functions in place, the historical perspective is of protecting citizens from abuse of State power or from the failure of the State to promote security and safety through, for instance, the protection and promotion of diversity. Thus human rights can be viewed along the continuum from addressing basic biological needs to protecting cultural quality of life.

Within this context British policing can be seen to have two responsibilities:

- to contribute towards achieving and preserving community safety; and
- a duty not to harm that safety through abuse of police powers.

13.2 **The Statutory Foundation of Human Rights in the UK**

The statutory basis for human rights protection in the UK is derived from international law. In the aftermath of World War II three international human rights instruments were negotiated and opened for signature and ratification (websites accessed on 30 January 2009):

- The Charter of the United Nations 1945 <http://www.un.org/aboutun/charter/>;
- The UN Universal Declaration of Human Rights 1948 <http://www.un.org/events/humanrights/udhr60/declaration.shtml>; and
- The Council of Europe Convention for the Protection of Human Rights and Fundamental Freedoms 1950 (ECHR) <http://conventions.coe.int/treaty/EN/Treaties/html/005.htm>.

The UK is a signatory to all three, and in 1998, through the Human Rights Act 1998 (HRA 1998), ratified and gave domestic effect to the protections defined in the ECHR, thus creating the statutory framework for rights protection in the UK.

The ECHR is enforceable through the Council of Europe Court for Human Rights at Strasbourg. Citizen allegations that their rights have been breached by their government are initially brought before the Commission for Human

Rights and only go before the Court if the Commission can- not first achieve a negotiated remedy.

The UK signed the ECHR in 1950, first allowed UK citi- zens to take matters to the Strasbourg Court in 1966, and, with the enacting of the HRA, has now set in place the mechanisms to ensure that British courts are obliged, when determining matters before them where Convention rights are in question, to decide all cases in a manner compatible with the ECHR, to interpret existing and future legislation in conformity with the ECHR, and to take ECHR case law from the Court at Strasbourg into account when passing judgment. The HRA does not enable primary legislation to be overridden by application of the Convention, but enables courts to make a declaration of incompatibility to be referred to government if primary legislation cannot be applied so as to be compatible.

13.3 **What it Means for Police and Partners**

Section 6(1) of the HRA stipulates that 'it is unlawful for a public authority to act in a way which is incompatible with a Convention right'. This does not just apply to the police service but to all public authorities including the courts, local councils, the fire and rescue service, government departments, and other public sector partner agencies with whom the police work. Equally, it applies to persons con- tracted by a public body to act on its behalf when they are so acting.

The HRA is now the foundation for court procedures, pro- cedural rules, and the rules of evidence. In terms of police functions, whereas historically a negative concept of lib- erty applied—authorities could do anything that was not unlawful—now authorities can act only using powers pro- vided for by statute.

The entering into force of the HRA was delayed until 2000 so as to enable the Regulation of Investigatory Powers Act 2000 to pass through Parliament, which placed on a statutory basis a number of covert investigation methods not previously unlawful but also not previously provided for in statute, and therefore vulnerable at the time to challenge within the framework of the ECHR.

Those convention rights given effect in the UK by section 1 of the HRA 1998, and which are of particular relevance to policing, are reproduced below in the appendix to this chapter.

Space here does not permit an extensive consideration of each of the Convention rights. Table 13.1 identifies the key areas in which policing engages with the Convention rights. This chapter then goes onto examine in more detail issues arising from Article 8.

Table 13.1 Convention rights and policing

ECHR Article	Area of policing engaged
Article 2. Right to life *Does Article 2(2) apply?* *Has Article 2(2) been complied with?*	Use of force. Death resulting from police use of force will not be breach of this article if the use of force was **absolutely necessary** for the purposes of defending any person from unlawful violence; for a lawful arrest or to prevent the escape of a person lawfully detained; or for the purpose of quelling a riot or insurrection. The test of absolute necessity is a far higher test than the Criminal Justice Act 1967 test of reasonable force in self-defence; it is also higher than the test of necessity in Convention Article 8(2).
Article 3. Prohibition of torture *Do any implied restrictions apply?*	Detention, custody, and questioning. This article prohibits not only torture but also inhuman or degrading treatment. In the counter-terrorism arena the UK has been found in breach of this article because of the use of certain coercive interrogation techniques, now banned: *Ireland v UK* (1979–80) 2 EHRR 25.

ECHR Article	Area of policing engaged
	Arousing feelings of fear, anguish, and humiliating inferiority would constitute degrading treatment. Depending upon its severity, physical or mental suffering would constitute inhuman treatment or torture.
	Frontline staff complying with PACE and its Code of Practice C are unlikely to be in breach of this article.
Article 5. Right to liberty and security *Is detention lawful?* *Has domestic procedural law been complied with?* *Is detention permitted under Article 5(1)(a)–(f)?* *Have reasons for detention been given?* *Have the pre-trial rights in Article 5(3) been complied with?* *Does the UK derogation in respect of terrorist suspects apply?*	The right to liberty is linked with procedural rights for detainees (security). Exercise of police powers that involve detention (stop and search) or arrest (to investigate further a reasonable suspicion of an offence) must be in accordance with the law and with procedures prescribed by law (ie how the decision to detain or arrest came to be made). Any detention or arrest that is unlawful under English law will automatically breach Article 5. Whilst arrest clearly engages Article 5, detention (as a deprivation of liberty) is more ambiguous. Detention authorized by statute for the purpose of preventing or detecting crime, and therefore with the same objective as arrest, will also engage Article 5. Stopping a person simply to speak to them may not engage Article 5.
	Article 5(1)(c) prescribes the grounds for arrest.
	Reasonable suspicion 'presupposes the existence of facts or information that would satisfy an objective observer that the person concerned may have committed the offence in question'; *Fox, Campbell & Hartley v UK* (1991) 13 EHRR 157.

(Continued)

ECHR Article	Area of policing engaged
Article 6. Right to fair trial *Have fair trial requirements of Article 6(1) been met?* *Are there any relevant limitations to the Article 6 requirements?* *Has the presumption of innocence been respected?* *Have the minimum guarantees of Article 6(3) been complied with?*	The right to a fair trial begins before a trial in court starts. The right has been held to include the pre-trial investigation and disclosure. All police investigation powers must be used according to law and not outside the statutory framework. The use of unlawfully obtained evidence, whilst not absolutely prohibited by the Convention, is likely to give rise to challenges. The Police and Criminal Evidence Act 1984 (PACE), section 78 gives courts the discretion to exclude such evidence in the interests of a fair trial.
Article 7. No punishment without law *Has there been retrospective application of a criminal law?*	New offences. New offences enacted cannot be applied retrospectively.
Article 8. Right to respect for private and family life *Can the reason for any restriction of this right be found in Article 8(2)?* *If so, is it in accordance with law?* *If so, is it necessary in a democratic society?*	Investigations. Police cannot breach the right to respect for private and family life unless there is a lawful power to do so AND it is necessary for the prevention of disorder and crime AND the use of the police power is proportionate to the objective sought. The notion of 'private life' is very broad. **Covert investigation** methods, in particular, engage Article 8. Police investigation should not be arbitrary or exploratory: it must be focused on specific suspected offences. Likewise, **search and seizure** engage Article 8 and must be justified under Article 8(2).

Questions in column 1 drawn from Starmer (1999: 86–7).

To this necessarily simple overview must be added more detailed consideration of the principles of legality, necessity, and proportionality.

13.4 **Human Rights Principles**

The use of police powers most regularly engages with Article 8, which is a qualified right. The Convention right may be breached in certain prescribed circumstances.

Any court asked to determine a breach of Article 8 will ask itself a series of questions derived from Strasbourg case law.

(1) **Does the investigative act fall within the scope of Article 8?** If the proposed policing activity is intended or is likely to gather information about the private life of an individual (whether or not that individual is the subject of the investigation), or interferes in any other way with an individual's private life, then such activity will fall within the scope of Article 8. The use of police investigative powers will fall within the scope of the article.

(2) **If yes, has the Article 8 right been interfered with by a public authority?** As seen above, all public authorities must act in ways compatible with the Convention. The police service and its partner agencies are public bodies.

(3) **If it has, was this interference in accordance with the law?** The ECHR makes reference to 'in accordance with the law', 'prescribed by law', and 'lawful'. Starmer identifies three criteria as a test to ensure compliance with the principle of legality thus established (Starmer, 1999: 166):

  (1) domestic law must identify the legal basis for any restriction on an ECHR right;

(2) persons likely to be affected by such a restriction must be able to access the relevant domestic law; and

(3) the relevant domestic law must be clear and comprehensible so that anyone should be reasonably able to identify or foresee whether or not their behaviour is breaking or might break the law.

The principle of legality is considered to be satisfied by the following categories of law:

- statute law;
- delegated legislation such as Codes of Practice;
- common (or case) law;
- European Community law.

Investigative and preventative actions employed by frontline staff must be in accordance with powers provided for by law: for example, the Police and Criminal Evidence Act 1984 (PACE); the Police Act 1997; the Regulation of Investigatory Powers Act 2000 (RIPA); the various terrorism laws.

(4) **If it was lawful, was the interference pursuant to a legitimate aim as identified in Article 8(2)?** If the action passes the legality test above, the court will then determine whether the breach was for a legitimate purpose.

The legitimate purposes are outlined in Article 8(2) (see appendix at end of chapter). Of relevance to police is the purpose of preventing disorder or crime.

Other legitimate purposes are:

- in the interests of national security;
- in the interests of public safety;
- in the interests of the economic well-being of the country;
- for the protection of health or morals; and
- for the protection of the rights and freedoms of others.

Laws granting particular powers will define the legitimate purpose for which they can be used. In the absence of clear direction the extent to which the police and partner agencies can avail themselves of legitimate purposes other than the prevention of disorder or crime would seem to be constrained by the policy implemented in RIPA (see Chapter 6 above), which mirrors the language of the Convention in this regard. For example, some agencies can use covert investigation for all of the legitimate purposes above, whilst some can use their powers only for one of the other legitimate purposes.

(5) **Even if it was both lawful and pursuant to a legitimate aim, was it still necessary, and no more than necessary (ie proportionate), in a democratic society?** The test of necessity incorporates the concept of proportionality.

Sedley LJ in *B v SSHD* [2000] 2 CMLR 1086:

> a measure which interferes with a human right must not only be authorised by law but must correspond to a pressing social need and go no further than is strictly necessary in a pluralistic society to achieve its permitted purpose; or, more shortly, must be appropriate and necessary to its legitimate aim.

Proportionality is often presented as a balancing act but it is one in which it is easy to confuse what properly should be balanced. Taylor succinctly draws the crucial distinction: 'a balancing exercise takes place that requires a consideration of whether the interference with the right is greater than is necessary to achieve the aim. . . . this is not an exercise in balancing the right against the interference, but instead *balances the nature and extent of the interference against the reasons for interfering*' (emphasis added, 2006: 26). In terms of practical application: 'an assessment of the proportionality of the resources deployed in an operation cannot be properly undertaken without knowing the nature of the offences being investigated, the evidence required to prove them and the likely dividend to society in preventing and detecting the offence or likely outcomes' (McKay, 2006: 49).

The nature of the offence may offer partial justification for the deployment of certain methods, but it is not the *seriousness* of the offence nor the *extent of the harm* derived from the offence that must be balanced. Rather it is the *use* of enforcement powers against the *value* of the evidential product or other outcome derived therefrom (Ormerod, 2006: 77–78).

13.5 **Victims' Rights**

There is inherent public interest in the prosecution of crime and in having an effective criminal justice system. The power of the State is brought to bear against individuals suspected of or charged with criminal offences. The notion of rights considered so far in this chapter is that premised upon the protection of the accused from abuse of the State power brought against him or her.

Victims also have rights. The 'right' not to become a victim of another individual's criminality is essentially the business of the criminal law, not human rights law. But victims are protected by human rights law in instances where exercise of the rights of the accused may infringe on the human rights of the victim. For example, cross-examination of a rape victim by the defendant could be a humiliating or even mentally harmful episode, in which case the court could find itself in breach of Article 3. Special measures for vulnerable witnesses (see Chapter 7) seek to balance the protection of victims and the right to a fair trial for the accused.

In recent years there has been a political impetus to reform the criminal justice system so as to give more emphasis to the needs and rights of victims and witnesses. To that end, on 1 April 2006, a Code of Practice for Victims of Crime was published. It can be accessed via <http://www.homeoffice. gov.uk/crime-victims/victims/Victims-rights/> (accessed 3 February 2009).

KEY POINT—MAIN REQUIREMENTS OF THE CODE

- a right to information about the crime within specified time scales, including the right to be notified of any arrests and court cases;
- a dedicated family liaison police officer to be assigned to bereaved relatives;
- clear information from the Criminal Injuries Compensation Authority (CICA) on eligibility for compensation;
- all victims to be told about Victim Support and either referred on to them or offered their service;
- an enhanced service for vulnerable or intimidated victims;
- the flexibility for victims to opt in or out of services to ensure they receive the level of service they want.

The Code applies to the following agencies:

- all police forces for police areas in England and Wales, the British Transport Police, and the Ministry of Defence Police;
- Crown Prosecution Service;
- Her Majesty's Court Service;
- joint police/Crown Prosecution Service Witness Care Units;
- Parole Board;
- Prison Service;
- local probation boards;
- Youth Offending Teams;
- Criminal Injuries Compensation Authority;
- Criminal Injuries Compensation Appeals Panel;
- Criminal Cases Review Commission.

Victims are entitled to free confidential advice and support from the charity Victim Support (<http://www.victimsupport.org.uk/> accessed 3 February 2009). Victims have the Article 8 right to respect for their private and family life and must be consulted before their details are passed to the media in any publicizing of the offence or appeal for information. The Sexual Offences (Amendment) Act 1992 makes it an offence to publish name, photograph, or other details of a victim of sexual assault or rape.

13.6 **Conclusion**

Although sometimes portrayed as a threat and inhibitor to effective policing, human rights are more appropriately viewed as the foundation of good policing. Policing that demonstrably is delivered in accordance with human rights principles will enjoy community support. High levels of community support for the police service will deliver practical enhancements for policing: for example, a greater willingness to come forward as witnesses or more effective engagement with neighbourhood policing teams in terms of crime and disorder prevention. The relationship is symbiotic: a sound basis in human rights will deliver effective policing which will, in turn, protect and promote human rights for the whole community.

Further Reading

Amos, M (2006), *Human Rights Law*, Oxford, Hart Publishing

Arnheim, M (2004), *The Handbook of Human Rights Law*, London, Kogan Page

Ashworth, A (2002), *Human Rights, Serious Crime and Criminal Procedure*, London, Sweet & Maxwell

Kennedy, H (2004), *Just Law: The Changing Face of Justice and Why it Matters to Us All*, London, Vintage

McKay, S (2006) 'Approaching the Regulation of Investigatory Powers Act 2000' *Covert Policing Review*, 46–53

Neyroud, P (2003), 'Policing and Ethics' in T Newburn (ed), *Handbook of Policing*, Cullompton, Willan: 578–602

Ormerod, D (2006) 'Recent developments on entrapment' *Covert Policing Review*, 65–86

Starmer, K (1999) *European Human Rights Law*, Legal Action Group, London, 1999

Taylor, N (2006) 'Covert policing and proportionality' *Covert Policing Review*, 22–33

Wadham, J et al (2007), *Blackstones' Guide to the Human Rights Act 1998*, Oxford University Press, Oxford

The Convention Rights given Effect in the UK by Section 1 of the Human Rights Act 1998 that have Particular Relevance for Policing

Article 2

Right to life

1. Everyone's right to life shall be protected by law. No one shall be deprived of his life intentionally save in the execution of a sentence of a court following his conviction of a crime for which this penalty is provided by law.
2. Deprivation of life shall not be regarded as inflicted in contravention of this article when it results from the use of force which is no more than absolutely necessary:
   a. in defence of any person from unlawful violence;
   b. in order to effect a lawful arrest or to prevent the escape of a person lawfully detained;
   c. in action lawfully taken for the purpose of quelling a riot or insurrection.

Article 3

Prohibition of torture

No one shall be subjected to torture or to inhuman or degrading treatment or punishment.

Article 4

Prohibition of slavery and forced labour

1. [...]

Article 5

Right to liberty and security

1. Everyone has the right to liberty and security of person. No one shall be deprived of his liberty save in the following cases and in accordance with a procedure prescribed by law:
   a. the lawful detention of a person after conviction by a competent court;
   b. the lawful arrest or detention of a person for non-compliance with the lawful order of a court or in order to secure the fulfilment of any obligation prescribed by law;
   c. the lawful arrest or detention of a person effected for the purpose of bringing him before the competent legal authority on reasonable suspicion of having committed an offence or when it is reasonably considered necessary to prevent his committing an offence or fleeing after having done so;
   d. the detention of a minor by lawful order for the purpose of educational supervision or his lawful detention for the purpose of bringing him before the competent legal authority;
   e. the lawful detention of persons for the prevention of the spreading of infectious diseases, of persons of unsound mind, alcoholics or drug addicts or vagrants;
   f. the lawful arrest or detention of a person to prevent his effecting an unauthorised entry into the country or of a person against whom action is being taken with a view to deportation or extradition.

2. Everyone who is arrested shall be informed promptly, in a language which he understands, of the reasons for his arrest and of any charge against him.
3. Everyone arrested or detained in accordance with the provisions of paragraph 1.c of this article shall be brought promptly before a judge or other officer authorised by law to exercise judicial power and shall be entitled to trial within a reasonable time or to release pending trial. Release may be conditioned by guarantees to appear for trial.
4. Everyone who is deprived of his liberty by arrest or detention shall be entitled to take proceedings by which the lawfulness of his detention shall be decided speedily by a court and his release ordered if the detention is not lawful.
5. Everyone who has been the victim of arrest or detention in contravention of the provisions of this article shall have an enforceable right to compensation.

Article 6

Right to a fair trial

1. In the determination of his civil rights and obligations or of any criminal charge against him, everyone is entitled to a fair and public hearing within a reasonable time by an independent and impartial tribunal established by law. Judgment shall be pronounced publicly but the press and public may be excluded from all or part of the trial in the interests of morals, public order or national security in a democratic society, where the interests of juveniles or the protection of the private life of the parties so require, or to the extent strictly necessary in the opinion of the court in special circumstances where publicity would prejudice the interests of justice.
2. Everyone charged with a criminal offence shall be presumed innocent until proved guilty according to law.

3. Everyone charged with a criminal offence has the following minimum rights:

   a. to be informed promptly, in a language which he understands and in detail, of the nature and cause of the accusation against him;

   b. to have adequate time and facilities for the preparation of his defence;

   c. to defend himself in person or through legal assistance of his own choosing or, if he has not sufficient means to pay for legal assistance, to be given it free when the interests of justice so require;

   d. to examine or have examined witnesses against him and to obtain the attendance and examination of witnesses on his behalf under the same conditions as witnesses against him;

   e. to have the free assistance of an interpreter if he cannot understand or speak the language used in court.

Article 7

No punishment without law

1. No one shall be held guilty of any criminal offence on account of any act or omission which did not constitute a criminal offence under national or international law at the time when it was committed. Nor shall a heavier penalty be imposed than the one that was applicable at the time the criminal offence was committed.

2. This article shall not prejudice the trial and punishment of any person for any act or omission which, at the time when it was committed, was criminal according to the general principles of law recognised by civilised nations.

Article 8

Right to respect for private and family life

1. Everyone has the right to respect for his private and family life, his home and his correspondence.
2. There shall be no interference by a public authority with the exercise of this right except such as is in accordance with the law and is necessary in a democratic society in the interests of national security, public safety or the economic well-being of the country, for the prevention of disorder or crime, for the protection of health or morals, or for the protection of the rights and freedoms of others.

Article 9

Freedom of thought, conscience and religion

[…]

Article 10

Freedom of expression

[…]

Article 11

Freedom of assembly and association

[…]

Article 12

Right to marry

[…]

Article 13

Right to an effective remedy

[Not enacted by section 1 of the HRA because the HRA is itself regarded as effective remedy]

Article 14

Prohibition of discrimination

The enjoyment of the rights and freedoms set forth in this Convention shall be secured without discrimination on any ground such as sex, race, colour, language, religion, political or other opinion, national or social origin, association with a national minority, property, birth or other status.

Article 15

Derogation in time of emergency

[Not enacted by section 1 of the HRA]

Article 16

Restrictions on political activity of aliens

Nothing in Articles 10, 11 and 14 shall be regarded as preventing the High Contracting Parties from imposing restrictions on the political activity of aliens.

Article 17

Prohibition of abuse of rights

[Not enacted by section 1 of the HRA]

Article 18

Limitation on use of restrictions on rights

The restrictions permitted under this Convention to the said rights and freedoms shall not be applied for any purpose other than those for which they have been prescribed.

Together with the following articles from the First and Sixth Protocols to the ECHR.

...

FIRST PROTOCOL

Article 1

Protection of property

Every natural or legal person is entitled to the peaceful enjoyment of his possessions. No one shall be deprived of his possessions except in the public interest and subject to the conditions provided for by law and by the general principles of international law.

The preceding provisions shall not, however, in any way impair the right of a State to enforce such laws as it deems necessary to control the use of property in accordance with the general interest or to secure the payment of taxes or other contributions or penalties.

Article 2

Right to education

No person shall be denied the right to education. In the exercise of any functions which it assumes in relation to education and to teaching, the State shall respect the right of parents to ensure such education and teaching in conformity with their own religious and philosophical convictions.

Article 3

Right to free elections

The High Contracting Parties undertake to hold free elections at reasonable intervals by secret ballot, under conditions which will ensure the free expression of the opinion of the people in the choice of the legislature.

...

SIXTH PROTOCOL

Article 1

Abolition of the death penalty

The death penalty shall be abolished. No-one shall be condemned to such penalty or executed.

Article 2

Death penalty in time of war

A State may make provision in its law for the death penalty in respect of acts committed in time of war or of imminent threat of war; such penalty shall be applied only in the instances laid down in the law and in accordance with its provisions. The State shall communicate to the Secretary General of the Council of Europe the relevant provisions of that law.

As read with Articles 16 and 18 of the Convention.

Chapter 14

Knowledge Management

14.1 Introduction

The effectiveness of policing can be judged by the capability of a police agency to harness and utilize the skills of its staff. A key function in this regard is knowledge creation and management, within which functions lies the contributory function of intelligence. Frontline staff will develop skills of information acquisition that will inform the intelligence function. This chapter introduces frontline staff to the key ideas and activities relevant to their role in information gathering, intelligence processing, and knowledge creation; all of which serve to *identify*, *analyse*, and *manage* threats.

Vincent H (1881) *Police Code and General Manual of the Criminal Law*, 202

'Police work is impossible without information, and every good officer will do his best to obtain reliable intelligence, taking care at the same time not to be led away on false issues. Information must not be treasured up, until opportunity offers for action by the officer who obtains it, but should be promptly communicated to a superior, and those who are in a position to act upon it. Not only is this the proper course of action to take, in the public interest, but it will be certainly recognised, both by authorities and comrades, promoting esteem and confidence, which will bring their own reward.'

Assistant Commissioner Howard Vincent established the new Criminal Investigation Department of the Metropolitan Police and later also created the Special Branch.

---

2 Knowledge Management

Vincent's instructions to frontline officers regarding intelligence-led policing are as relevant 130 years later as they were in 1881. What has changed since 1881 is organizational capacity and capability for acquiring information, analysing it, and thus creating the organizational knowledge that drives both strategic policy-making and the daily investigation of crime and disorder undertaken by police first responders. Frontline staff are the eyes and ears of the service. The 'local knowledge' that they acquire is the key tool of their trade, to be contributed as information to the force and Basic Command Unit (BCU) intelligence departments, for the benefit of the organization, partner agencies as required, and public safety.

The Association of Chief Police Officers (ACPO) *Guidance on the National Intelligence Model* (2005a: 196) defines intelligence as 'information that has been subject to a defined evaluation and risk assessment process in order to assist with police decision making'. John Grieve, former Deputy Assistant Commissioner, Metropolitan Police and one of the architects of the modern era of intelligence-led policing, has described it as 'information designed for action . . . making sense of ambiguities or contradiction and recognising the relative importance of different elements'.

> **Note:** See Grieve J, 'Developments in UK criminal intelligence' in J Ratcliffe (ed), *Strategic Thinking in Criminal Intelligence* (The Federation Press, Sydney, 2004), 25–36 (quotes from 25; 35).

Sir David Phillips, former Chief Constable of Kent and another commentator on intelligent approaches to criminal investigation, makes the point that criminals, like any humans, are essentially creatures of habit, and therefore are rendered vulnerable through recognition and knowledge of their habits (modus operandi, areas frequented, criminal associations).

Equally, criminals live and operate in local communities and it is through active engagement with local communities that frontline police staff will learn most about local criminals and the environment in which they commit crime.

But intelligence, both as concept and practice, is not unproblematic:

KEY POINT

'Intelligence merely provides techniques for improving the basis of knowledge. As with other techniques, it can be a dangerous tool if its limitations are not recognised by those who seek to use it.'

Review of Intelligence on Weapons of Mass Destruction, House of Commons Paper 898, 2004, p 14.

Very rarely do police acquire a full intelligence picture (who, what, when, where, how, and why) before a crime or disorder occurs. Information is a tool to aid investigation and neighbourhood policing; information analysed to add value and so develop it into knowledge is only as good as the accuracy of the raw material acquired by frontline staff and the skill of the intelligence department analysts.

The relatively recent statutory provision for covert investigation techniques has, coincidentally, added to some of the confusion about intelligence. An erroneous view has emerged that intelligence is only that information which authorities have acquired by covert means (through surveillance, intercepted communications, informers). This is a misleadingly narrow conception, perhaps unduly influenced by media representations of the work of intelligence agencies and espionage. Information is information howsoever obtained. The manner of its acquisition does not alter that. The way in which information once acquired is managed and processed determines whether or not it is developed through intelligent analysis into useable knowledge. If 'intelligence' is conceived of as only information obtained covertly, then investigators will overlook alternative and additional sources of information in contributing to the intelligence function. Such an approach can also tempt investigators to structure their work only around covert acquisition which is problematic because any given investigation may not meet the statutory threshold set for a given covert technique and, since covert investigation is highly skilled and resource-intensive, staff relying upon it will be in competition with colleagues for use of scarce resources. For further discussion of covert investigation see Chapter 6 above.

Frontline staff provide the vast majority of raw material for analysis in the intelligence department leading to the creation of organizational knowledge which police forces and partner agencies use to execute their functions and manage their organizations. They acquire this information simply through public and partner agency contact in the course of their daily duties.

Frontline staff, for instance those serving with Neighbourhood Policing Teams (see Chapter 21 below), need to develop a broad understanding of the context in which they gather information from and about their communities. The information they gather initially will be *tacit knowledge*, local knowledge about their immediate working area, which they carry around in their heads. Converting this tacit knowledge, which will be shared only episodically through casual conversation with colleagues, into *explicit knowledge* retained on organizational systems and so available to the organization as a whole, is the key to successful knowledge management and intelligence-led policing.

14.2 Thinking about 'Intelligence'

Ratcliffe illustrates the three generic uses of the word 'intelligence' within the police service. Frontline staff need to recognize the different possible contexts within which the word 'intelligence' is used.

Table 14.1

Intelligence as . . .	Defining characteristics
. . . **Structure**	The existence of an intelligence unit or department as an individual entity within an organizational framework, equipped with people, skills, methods, and organizational structure.
. . . **Process**	A continuous cycle of tasking, information collecting, analysis, evaluation, dissemination leading to intervention action or the identification of an intelligence gap requiring further tasking.
. . . **Product**	The output of the intelligence process, the processed information, such as a Subject Profile or a Tactical Assessment, intended to inform decision-makers.

Ratcliffe J, *Intelligence-led Policing*, Australian Institute of Criminology: Trends and Issues, Paper 248, (2003)

These three conceptual areas are now considered in turn.

14.3 **Intelligence as Structure**

Police forces, typically, have a Force Intelligence Bureau (FIB) situated as a HQ function, supported by local intelligence units located within Basic/Operational/Borough Command Units (BCUs). Each organization will have one or more computer-based system for storing information: systems which may or may not be compatible, a factor influencing the ease and practice of inputting and analysing new information. (Intelligence unit staff will often have the responsibility for inputting a given piece of information onto as many systems as required: frontline staff generally only input the information to the intelligence department.) Some systems are shared between forces, for instance FLINTS, the Forensic Lead Intelligence System developed by West Midlands Police.

FIB will manage intelligence of force-wide, regional, and national application and will have structures in place for sharing such intelligence with partner agencies.

At a national level a number of systems exist to store and access information of relevance to policing. HOLMES and HOLMES2, the Home Office Large and Major Enquiry System, have been developed following the Yorkshire Ripper serial murders, the better to manage information gathered during large-scale investigations. Each force has access to these systems, which are used on an individual investigation basis. The Police National Computer (PNC) contains information about convicted and wanted persons and itself is linked into the Europe-wide Schengen Information System, accessed via Europol.

The Government has introduced the IMPACT programme (intelligence, management, prioritization, analysis, coordination, and tasking) in order to enhance police computerized intelligence capabilities across the country. As HOLMES was a response to problems incurred in the Yorkshire Ripper case, so IMPACT is a response to problems of intelligence sharing identified following the Soham murders.

> **Note:** For further information see, Bichard M, *The Bichard Inquiry Report*, HC 653 (London, The Stationery Office, 2004). Available online at <http://www.bichardinquiry.org.uk>

Frontline staff must understand how they can contribute to and access their own force systems, and how access to information and intelligence held by partner agencies can be obtained. It is the individual responsibility of each staff member to ensure they have such knowledge and skills and so contribute effectively in sharing information they have acquired through working for the organization, thus enabling it to be developed through intelligent analysis into workable knowledge.

14.4 **Intelligence as Process**

Frontline staff should be aware of two basic concepts regarding the processing of intelligence; the intelligence cycle, and the National Intelligence Model (NIM).

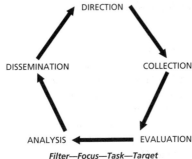

Filter—Focus—Task—Target

There are a number of representations of this cycle. This figure represents an amalgam of such representations. Cross-reference this simple schematic with ACPO (2005) *Guidance on the National Intelligence Model*, p.14 for the relationship between the cycle and the NIM.

Figure 14.1 The Intelligence Cycle

The intelligence process is often described as a cycle, as seen in Figure 14.1. The **Direction** phase is the decision-making process in which raw material information that needs to be collected is identified. A number of different drivers influence such decision-making:

- The Force Control Strategy, derived from the strategic tasking and coordination group, identifies the priorities for intervention across the force. These priorities are implemented at BCU level with direction about specific interventions being given from the tactical tasking and coordination group.
- The BCU Control Strategy, taking into account force priorities and those determined by the local Crime and Disorder Reduction Partnership (or Community Safety Partnership in Wales).

The direction phase having identified the intelligence requirement, the next phase is the **Collection** of raw material information relevant to the identified intelligence gap. Besides dedicated intelligence unit staff, frontline staff and

Police Community Support Officers (PCSOs) will contribute to the collection phase by being tasked to gather the required information.

The reliability and operational or strategic value of information thus gathered is then *evaluated* before being *analysed*. Analysis informs investigative and operational hypothesis, inferences, and decisions. It also contributes to strategic and policy decision-making regarding the identification, assessment, and management of emerging threats. The intelligence is presented in a form prescribed by the National Intelligence Model (see below) or in such format as is required within other agencies.

Dissemination of the product then takes place informing one or more of three *intervention options*:

- further collection to address new intelligence gaps identified during evaluation and analysis;
- preventative action; or
- direct enforcement action.

An alternative view of the information processing functions is the 'Filter—Focus—Task—Target' model.

In this description *filtering* distinguishes from the overall picture of crime and disorder those issues on which it is feasible to take action. Priorities upon which to *focus* can then be identified. Selected priorities then dictate specific information-gathering or intelligence-processing *tasks* in order to develop intervention options for individual *targets* (people, organizations, problems).

Building on the concept of the intelligence cycle, the **National Intelligence Model (NIM)** is a business process designed to facilitate the prioritization of tasks based on current intelligence and the consequent allocation of resources. The NIM was devised by the National Criminal Intelligence Service (NCIS) following the HMIC thematic report, *Policing with Intelligence* (1997), and as of 1 April 2004 all police forces in England and Wales should be

NIM-compliant in their tasking and coordination of investigation, preventative, and community safety activity.

The business process is envisaged as shown in Figure 14.2.

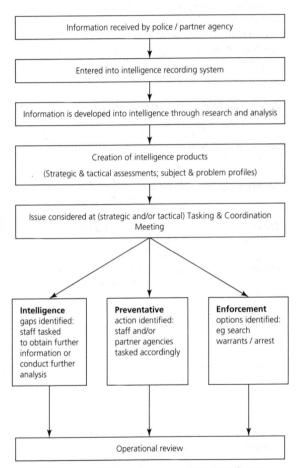

Figure 14.2 See the ACPO Guidance on the National Intelligence Model (ACPO/NCPE, 2005), for further information.

14.4.1 NIM Products

- **Analytical products, tools, and techniques** (eg results analysis, demographic analysis).
- **Intelligence products** (eg strategic and tactical assessments; subject and problem profiles).
- **Knowledge products** (eg data-sharing protocols).
- **System products** (eg appropriate information technology support).

14.4.2 The Nine NIM Analytical Tools and Techniques

Table 14.2 The NIM analytical tools and techniques

Tool	Purpose
Results analysis	To evaluate effectiveness of law enforcement activities, in particular of intelligence, prevention, and enforcement operations undertaken.
Crime pattern analysis	To identify the nature and scale of emerging and current crime trends and patterns, linked crimes or incidents, and hotspots of activity.
Market profiles	To analyse the criminal market around a given commodity or service in a specified geographical area.
Criminal business profiles	To detail how criminal operations/business and techniques work at a micro (individual) or macro (thematic) level in the same way that legitimate businesses may be explained.
Network analysis	To understand the nature and significance of the links between people who form criminal networks, or organizations that interrelate, together with the strengths and weaknesses of criminal groups or organizations.
Target profile analysis	To provide sufficient detailed analysis to initiate a target operation or support an ongoing operation against an individual or networked group of individuals by identifying options for intervention or disruption.

Tool	Purpose
Demographic/ social trends analysis	To examine the nature of demographic changes and their impact on criminality, as well as the analysis of social factors that might underlie changes or trends in crime or offending behaviour.
	To describe statistically the constitution of the population of a given area and the associated economic/social/environmental indicators with reference to law enforcement requirements.
Risk analysis	To support assessment of the scale of risk posed by individual offenders, organizations, or crime types to potential victims, the public generally, the law enforcement agencies, or the criminal justice system.
Operational intelligence assessment	To ensure that on-going investigations remain focused and are not side-tracked by new and unanticipated intelligence that may require a separate operational response.

14.4.3 The Four NIM Intelligence Products

Table 14.3 Intelligence products, their purpose, and anticipated outcomes

Product	Purpose	Outcome
Strategic Assessment (reviewed every six months)	1. Identifies at organizational and partnership level the apparent and emerging medium to long-term issues likely to influence intervention priorities and resource allocation. 2. Informs the business of the Strategic Tasking & Coordination Group.	• Informed decisions at command level about intervention priorities, articulated in the 'Control Strategy'. • Revised intelligence requirement. • Policing and partnership engagement and collaboration that is responsive to local community needs.

Product	Purpose	Outcome
		(NB: performance targets prescribed by central government may not reflect local community needs but will have to be incorporated in the Control Strategy)
Tactical Assessment (reviewed every fortnight)	1. Identifies short-term issues requiring prevention/ enforcement intervention or intelligence development, linked to Control Strategy priorities. 2. Monitors progress of ongoing interventions. 3. Identifies new and emerging issues that fall outside the Control Strategy but which may have to be considered in forthcoming strategic assessments.	• Informed decisions at service delivery level about local problem-solving and specific prevention, intelligence, or enforcement interventions. • Revised intelligence requirement. • Policing and partnership engagement and collaboration that is responsive to local community needs. (NB: performance targets centrally allocated may not reflect local community needs but will influence local intervention resource allocation)
Subject Profile (previously labelled Target Profiles)	1. Analysis of an individual or community to identify vulnerabilities that will increase risk of victimization. 2. Analysis of an individual or network to identify opportunities that will facilitate problem-solving and authority intervention.	• Informed decisions about the proportionality of a proposed intervention. • Informed decisions about intervention priorities and partnership opportunities. • Bespoke interventions, responsive to victim or community needs.

Product	Purpose	Outcome
	3. Identification of relevant risks to be managed.	• Informed decisions about operation/ investigation management.
	4. Identification of partner agency involvement.	• Revised intelligence requirement.
	5. Identification of intelligence gaps.	
Problem Profile	1. Analysis of individual problems or an identified series of problems to understand scope and context.	• Greater understanding of individual and community needs.
	2. Identification of intervention and prevention opportunities.	• Enhanced problem-solving capability.
	3. Identification of relevant risks to be managed.	• Informed decisions about the proportionality of a proposed intervention.
	4. Identification of partner agency involvement.	• Informed decisions about intervention priorities and partnership opportunities.
	5. Identification of intelligence gaps.	• Bespoke interventions, responsive to partner agency, victim, or community needs.
		• Informed decisions about intervention management.
		• Revised intelligence requirement.

14.4.4 Knowledge Products

NIM-based intelligence processes are supported by guidance and procedure documented in **knowledge products**. This accumulated doctrine facilitates the acquisition, analysis, and application of intelligence. A business process model, the NIM is itself a knowledge product. Knowledge products include:

- intelligence training;
- statutory investigation powers;
- case law;
- procedural manuals, standards, doctrine, and guidance documents;
- the Data Protection Act and associated guidelines;
- intelligence-sharing protocols.

Alongside practitioner doctrine and learning in knowledge products, are the enabling facilities: systems established to record and process information and intelligence. These include:

- databases (crime recording, intelligence, PNC, Sirene/SIS, custody records);
- information acquisition systems such as NAFIS, ANPR, CCTV;
- DNA;
- surveillance products;
- secure accommodation within which intelligence staff can operate ensuring the proper handling of sensitive material.

Completing the lexicon of the NIM is the three-level hierarchy of criminality based on a similar hierarchy first conceptualized in a 1987 ACPO report on drugs policing. The primary purpose of this hierarchy is to facilitate the allocation of intervention responsibility at either BCU, force, or national agency level. Criminality, of course, does not divide itself into so neat a hierarchy, but intervention responsibility has to be made to fit policing infrastructure as best possible. The hierarchy is presented in Table 14.4.

Table 14.4 The NIM three-level hierarchy of criminality

Level 1	Crime and disorder contained within police force areas, amenable to local intervention and resolution with the key unit of service delivery being the BCU rather than the force. Scope for partnership intervention within the context of Crime and Disorder Reduction Partnerships (CDRPs).
Level 2	Criminality and disorder that transcends BCU and/or force boundaries, requiring additional resources and partnership collaboration in order to effect an intervention and resolution. (A common misperception is that Level 2 refers only to criminality that transcends force boundaries and not BCU boundaries as well. It could also include criminality that a BCU lacks the capacity and capability to address.)
Level 3	Serious and organized crime at a national or international scale. The basic intervention options (intelligence, prevention, enforcement) remain the same as for Levels 1 and 2 but given that organized crime is an economic activity operating at global market levels, the additional intervention option of disruption (possibly through use of civil or fiscal laws rather than criminal laws) is also considered politically acceptable. Heavy reliance on resource-intensive covert investigation demanding capability and capacity beyond the resources of most local police forces, hence the creation of first the National Crime Squad and subsequently the Serious Organised Crime Agency.

14.4.5 Intelligence Gaps

The NIM is a business process that can generate intelligence requirements. It does not, of itself, fulfil those requirements. Intelligence gaps will be identified through the NIM processes but the information needed for analysis and evaluation still needs to be obtained. Staff will be tasked to acquire the information. These tasks will be delegated either to specialist intelligence department staff or to frontline staff. It is through acquiring information to fill intelligence gaps that frontline staff most regularly engage with the NIM process. Recalling Vincent's maxim above, staff should not wait only to be asked for information as a result of an intelligence collection tasking, but should also submit relevant information they encounter during the routine course of their duties (eg stop-checks) because such information, once analysed, can initiate any one of the intervention options (intelligence, prevention, enforcement) at the fortnightly tasking and coordinating meetings or the six-monthly strategic coordination meetings. There is a danger of unintended consequence in promulgating the NIM as the bedrock of proactive policing; that by implementing a system requiring staff to respond to intelligence tasking they will actually became less proactive in seeking out intelligence outside the tasking regime. Let there be no misunderstanding: the most important tool for frontline officers in neighbourhood policing teams or response teams or detective teams is local knowledge.

As a post-script to the 'intelligence as process' discussion, Ratcliffe has examined the ways in which analysis and evaluation, the core business of any intelligence department, can promote effective policing. To illustrate this succinctly he has devised the 3i model (see Table 14.5). This provides the strategic context for the application of business models such as the NIM.

Table 14.5 Ratcliffe's 3i model and its relationship to the NIM

Interpret	Analysts and intelligence staff must have the capacity and capability to interpret the wider criminal environment, both as a means of maximizing the options for intervention and as a benchmark for results analysis and evaluation.
	The NIM analytical tools and techniques are the foundation for this, but depend upon intelligence units having adequate levels of trained staff in dedicated roles.
Influence	Intelligence staff must have the capacity and capability of influencing those making decisions about intervention and use of resources.
	The NIM has the communication framework through which influence could be exerted. But this element is also dependent upon the willingness of the decision-makers to listen to the intelligence staff as well as the force performance manager.

Impact	Decision-makers must have the enthusiasm and skills to be able to have a positive impact on the whole criminal environment.
	This is the element that in particular is supposed to focus attention on outcomes. There is a danger, however, that 'outcome' may be defined in any given situation as nothing more sophisticated than performance targets.

14.5 **Intelligence as Product**

Intelligence products, as conceived within the NIM, have already been considered above. Within the three different understandings of intelligence around which this chapter is structured, intelligence products are viewed from a more strategic perspective within intelligence theories.

To understand the breadth of the intelligence concept and the contribution intelligence products can make, it can be helpful to think in terms of different types of intelligence. Table 14.6 illustrates four generic types of intelligence (product) used in the police service and identified as such by academics studying intelligence processes in the police service. Such a representation helps dispel a common misconception that intelligence is only information that has been obtained covertly.

Table 14.6 Four types of intelligence, based on Innes and Sheptycki (2004: 10): the order is alphabetical rather than hierarchical

Crime intelligence	'Insight in relation to particular types of crime, crime hot spots, or crime series.'
Criminal intelligence	'Data that provides some understanding about the identity and activities of a particular nominated individual or group of individuals.'

Community intelligence	'Information provided by ordinary members of the public . . . tends to refer to the local problems they view as significant.'
Contextual intelligence	'Concerned with the meso-and macro-structures of social organization . . . predicting how changes at this level shape the environment for policing.'

Frontline staff should bear in mind that all the above types of information are crucial to effective policing (both the preservation of the Queen's peace and the investigation of crime). They should therefore be alert to any information that contributes to any of these areas. The re-launch of intelligence-led policing in the late 1990s threw the intelligence spotlight onto the activities of high-volume criminals, arguably at the expense of other types of intelligence, because it was argued that a minority of prolific offenders commit the majority of crime. Where success is defined as convictions (including offences taken into consideration rather than tried at court) then focusing on suspected high-volume criminals could provide the desired detections. But detection and conviction is not the only purpose of modern policing where community safety achieved through partnership working is now considered as important as detecting offenders.

Some commentators have argued that covert operations against criminals are, essentially, the only really effective source of intelligence (Phillips et al, 2007: 444) yet the narrowness of such an approach is revealed in the investigation of terrorism. In the 1970s and 1980s infiltration and the use of informers were very effective means of gathering intelligence about Irish-related terrorism because of the way that terrorism was structured and operated. No such similar structures exist to be infiltrated in the al-Qaida inspired terrorism now being attempted by disaffected individuals. Consequently security service and Special Branch intelligence efforts are increasingly expanded to include community intelligence about radicalization as a means of identifying potential terrorists. If the only tool in the box is a hammer, then all problems will be treated as if they were nails: which will not always be appropriate.

The intelligent use of intelligence products to deliver knowledge-based policing requires an open mind about all possible solutions and avenues of approach, and therefore about all the potential intelligence products that may be available.

14.6 **Sources of Information**

ACPO (2001), *Investigation of Volume Crime*, NCPE Centrex, Wyboston: 9

'. . . the evidence and intelligence gathering trail commences with the initial contact between the person reporting an offence and the police.'

Drawing upon theories of commercial intelligence, generic sources of information that can contribute to the intelligence process may be identified as follows:

Table 14.7

External Secondary Sources	**External Primary Sources**
eg partner agencies, other police forces, external databases such as DVLA records	eg victims, witnesses, community members, CHIS
Internal Secondary Sources	**Internal Primary Sources**
eg databases, staff knowledge	eg NPTs, response team members, PCSOs, staff engaged on surveillance

When planning an investigation or applying problem-solving methodology to a community issue, frontline staff should give consideration, using the framework in

Table 14.7, as to where information of use to their present purpose might be obtained.

Information known privately to individuals can be volunteered to the police or partner agencies either unilaterally by the individual who knows the information or in response to questions posed by the authorities. Frontline staff who take the trouble to foster good relations with their local communities will find that information is volunteered more regularly or is easier to obtain when actively sought.

Information sources can also be categorized as open and closed.

14.6.1 Open Information

Open information is information from sources to which the public have access: public directories, the internet, newspapers, publicly-accessible records such as birth, marriage, and death registrations, electoral rolls. This list is illustrative, not exhaustive.

14.6.2 Closed Information

Closed information is not generally accessible to members of the public: for example, the PNC, agency intelligence databases, bank records, phone company billing records, police investigations. Typically, closed sources will require some source of authority before they can be accessed: for example, a Data Protection Act notice; a Production Order; a Search Warrant depending upon the source. Where a generic statutory authority exists for sharing information between partner agencies, such a regime will generally be supported by information-sharing protocols negotiated between the partners. FIB and BCU intelligence staff will be in a position to offer advice to frontline staff about how such information can be accessed. Telephone billing data, for instance, can only be accessed through the formal Single Point of Contact (SPOC) who will generally be located within the FIB.

Accessing closed information requires understanding of the procedures to be complied with in order to achieve access. Requests should be specific, as 'fishing trips' will be prohibited. There may be a cost implication in such access.

Obtaining information covertly about an individual may utilize either open or closed information. Open sources can be examined without the subject of the investigation having to be notified and so alerted. It should be noted, however, that some searches (particularly computer-based searches) will leave 'footprints' that could identify both the fact of the search and the identity of the searcher. Advice from specialist staff (eg the computer crime unit) should be sought.

Closed information, as seen above, will generally require some form of coercive authority, some of which have supplementary non-disclosure restrictions prohibiting the holder of the information from alerting the subject of the investigation that an enquiry has been made. Gathering evidence about an individual's activities through the various methods of covert surveillance that are available will require different levels of statutory authority depending upon the seriousness of the crimes the subject is suspected to be committing. See Chapter 6 on covert investigation.

14.7 **Information is Evidence**

The distinction between intelligence and evidence has been long debated (although Vincent does not seem to draw the distinction). In the 1990s conventional wisdom dictated that the National Criminal Intelligence Service (NCIS) (and its forerunner, the National Drugs Intelligence Unit) should be entirely separate from any investigative agency: that there should be a sterile corridor between intelligence and evidential functions. Consequentially, whilst the NCIS was expected to enhance and develop intelligence passed to it by contributing agencies, as a matter of strategic policy it was specifically denied the operational capability and capacity to undertake anything other than static surveillance. Mobile surveillance capability, the Home Office argued to the Home Affairs Committee in 1994, would generate evidence rather than intelligence. Static observation would generate only intelligence. The distinction, of course, is artificial and false. A perspective challenging the Home Office position might perceive it to be a means of running an intelligence agency on the cheap. Practitioners also argued for the distinction, and the questioning perspective on that might perceive that position as a desire to sustain separate agencies. Since the creation of the Serious Organised Crime Agency (SOCA), that conventional wisdom has been consigned to history.

All information leading to intelligence is *always* evidence. Whether or not investigators and prosecutors would always want to use intelligence as evidence is an entirely different debate.

Protection of intelligence sources or techniques dictates that intelligence can be used to generate more conventional evidential opportunities. Telephone intercept product is very important in the investigation of serious organized crime. But it is also unlawful to use it in evidence or even to hint in a trial that such a product has ever existed. Hence telephone interception is used to identify opportunities for more conventional surveillance which will enable police witnesses to testify at trial what they saw, heard, and did in relation to the accused. Likewise, authorities have always sought to protect the identity of informers from exposure at trial because of the danger of retribution being exacted against the informers by the accused or their associates. Information from informers, which must always be corroborated, will generally be used to identify conventional evidential opportunities rather than be used in evidence itself, although the latter course of action is not unknown.

It should also be noted that deliberate misinformation passed to the police by hostile informers or through organized crime group agents who have infiltrated a police organization (either directly or through corrupting an employee), whilst not evidence of what it purports to be, is nevertheless evidence of attempts to disrupt police investigations with a view possibly to perverting the course of justice.

Specialist intelligence acquisition methods (surveillance, managing informers) are the preserve of appropriately trained and skilled staff who will know from operational planning the likelihood of the product to be acquired being used in evidence and will plan its acquisition accordingly. For frontline staff the relevance is that frontline staff routinely acquiring information suitable for input into the intelligence process should always manage that acquisition in a manner that makes the information suitable for evidential use at a later stage.

All information gathered for intelligence purposes must be treated as potential evidence.

Faced with incontrovertible proof, an accused has little option other than to attack the process by which the information was acquired and brought into evidence. Getting the process right is not about feeding a mindless bureaucratic machine, but is about doing the job professionally to ensure evidential integrity.

14.8 **Protecting Information**

The acquisition of information for intelligence processing into usable knowledge requires a high degree of professionalism and integrity at all phases of the process. Structures and systems exist for this purpose. The rationale is not to keep information so secret it cannot be used, but to ensure that it can be used by the appropriate staff in such a way that its use does not generate more harm than good, which usually means protecting the identity of the source of information.

This starts with frontline staff describing the information they are inputting in terms of key characteristics using the 5 x 5 x 5 evaluation system which attempts, to the extent possible at the time of submission, to answer the following key questions:

- What is the provenance of the information? Where does it originate?
- How does the source providing the information come to be in possession of the information (eg directly or indirectly)?
- Has that source provided reliable information in the past?
- If the source provides information in relation to only some of the questions above, why does the source not know the remaining pieces?
- Can any of the above information be corroborated by a second source?
- And if a second source does have the same information, did the second source acquire it independently or did they acquire it via the first source? The former circumstance, of course, corroborates the information, the latter circumstance does not.
- Is there any likelihood that the information, even if it can be corroborated, is being planted in order to confuse and mislead the investigators (and the power of deception will of course be reinforced if misleading information can be corroborated)?

The answers to these questions help to determine the sensitivity of the information and the degree of risk attached to any compromise and so identifies what measures above and beyond the minimum standards of security and integrity might need to be applied. What should its classification under the *Government Protective Marking Scheme* (GPMS) be for instance? See Chapter 18 for a discussion of how the GPMS applies within the police service. The scheme views information as an asset, the compromise of which could cause defined harms. The degree of harm determines the level of protected access assigned.

Having been submitted by frontline staff the information is an organizational asset that needs to be protected because its misuse may generate harm to individuals outside or within the organization or to the organization itself. At a more general level, the lack of an effective criminal justice system harms society as a whole.

The checklist below highlights a series of threats to a professional intelligence environment existing within an organization.

Checklist: Threats to a professional intelligence environment

- Lack of robust ethical standards explicitly set and constantly promoted
- Lack of training in intelligence skills
- Lack of security awareness and policies, including physical security and restricted access to intelligence department offices
- Lack of regular auditing
- Lack of effective management and supervision
- Tolerance of improper procedure
- Tolerance of unauthorized disclosure
- Tolerance of improper relationships with sources or with persons seeking access to intelligence (including colleagues)
- Organizational culture that views procedure as an impediment to performance and something to get round or overcome
- Organizational culture that does not support or encourage the challenging of inappropriate behaviour
- Organizational culture that fails to observe the proper 'need to know' principle (this can work both ways—a department that fails to disseminate anything useful in assertion of this principle is as unprofessional as a department that leaks)

Within this environment, the management and handling of informers (Covert Human Intelligence Sources—CHIS) in particular has been made more professional through the introduction of accredited national training and the creation of Dedicated Source Units, as well as through statutory regulation that has, since 2000, reinforced pre-existing case law.

In determining with whom information should be shared whilst taking into account the need to protect, if required, the source of that information, two key questions apply:

- Who 'needs to know' the information in the format in which it currently exists?
- Is it possible to sanitize the presentation of the information in its entirety or in part in order to share the intelligence without compromising sources, techniques, or other information?

At court, if necessary and if no more conventional means have been achieved with which to adduce a piece of information as evidence, protection of the source's identity or the technique used to acquire the information can be achieved through applying for a Public Interest Immunity order from the court, but this will be the exception rather than the rule. Frontline staff should seek guidance from senior detectives and the Crown Prosecution Service concerning such measures.

All of which discussion indicates that information, intelligence, and knowledge management require constant attention and professionalism within both the police service and its partner agencies. It is an ever-present, ongoing concern. Frontline staff may engage rather more with the input end of the process than with other phases, and may never engage with some of the specialist aspects of information acquisition, but it is important that they understand the overall picture and the context within which they will be supplying information. This chapter has been a brief introduction to that overall picture. The bibliography that follows will further the introduction presented here.

Further Reading

Official sources

ACPO (2001) *Investigation of Volume Crime*, Wyboston, NCPE Centrex

—— (2004) *NIM Regional Tasking and Co-ordination—Protocol/Procedures/Policy and Performance Framework*, Wy-boston, NCPE

—— (2005a) *Guidance on the National Intelligence Model*, Wyboston, NCPE

—— (2005b) *Practice Advice on Core Investigative Doctrine*, Wyboston, NCPE

—— (2005c) *Code of Practice on the National Intelligence Model*, Wyboston, NCPE

—— (2006a) *Guidance on the Management of Police Information*, Wyboston, NCPE

—— (2006b) *Guidance on the National Briefing Model*, Wyboston, NCPE

Bichard, M (2004) *The Bichard Inquiry Report*, London, TSO

Butler, Lord (2004) *Review of Intelligence on Weapons of Mass Destruction*, HC 898, London, TSO

HMIC (1997) *Policing with Intelligence: Criminal Intelligence—A Thematic Inspection on Good Practice*, London, HMSO

HMI Probation (2006) *An Independent Review of a Serious Further Offence case: Anthony Rice*, London, HMIP

Home Office (2005) *Practical Lessons for Involving the Community in Crime and Disorder Problem Solving*, London, TSO

Secondary sources

Bowers, A (2008) 'Knowledge management and the National Intelligence Model: fads or fundamentals, complementing or contradicting? What are the opportunities for transferable learning?' in C Harfield, A MacVean, J Grieve, and D Phillips (eds), *The Handbook of Intelligent Policing: Consilience, Crime Control, and Community Safety*, Oxford, Oxford University Press: 271–87

Brodeur, J-P and Dupont, B (2006) 'Knowledge workers or "Knowledge" workers?' *Policing & Society* 16(1): 7–26

Cope, N (2004) 'Intelligence-led policing or police-led intelligence?' *British Journal of Criminology* 44, 188–203(2004)

Dean, G and Gottschalk, P (2007) *Knowledge Management in Policing and Law Enforcement*, Oxford, Oxford University Press

Ericson, R and Haggerty, K (1997) *Policing the Risk Society*, Oxford, Oxford University Press

Gill, P (2000) *Rounding Up the Usual Suspects? Developments in Contemporary Law Enforcement Intelligence*, Aldershot, Ashgate

Grieve, J (2004) 'Developments in UK criminal intelligence' in J Ratcliffe (ed) *Strategic Thinking in Criminal Intelligence*, Sydney, The Federation Press: 25–36

Harfield, C and Harfield, K (2008) *Intelligence: Investigation, Community, and Partnership*, Oxford, Oxford University Press

—— MacVean, A, Grieve, J, Philips, D, (eds) (2008) *The Hand-book of Intelligent Policing*, Oxford, Oxford University Press

——and Kleiven, M (2008) 'Intelligence, knowledge, and the reconfiguration of policing' in C Harfield, A MacVean, J Grieve, and D Phillips, *The Handbook of Intelligent Policing: Consilience, Crime Control, and Community Safety*, Oxford, Oxford University Press: 239–54

Heaton, R (2000) 'The prospects for intelligence-led policing: some historical and quantitative considerations' *Policing and Society* 9, 337–55

Innes, M, Fielding, N, and Cope, N (2005) 'The appliance of science? The Theory and Practice of Crime Intelligence Analysis' *British Journal of Criminology* 45, 39–57

—— and Sheptycki, J (2004) 'From detection to disruption: intelligence and the changing logic of police crime control in the UK' *International Criminal Justice Review* 14, 1–24

Kleiven, M (2007) 'Where's the intelligence in the National Intelligence Model?' *International Journal of Police Science and Management* 9(3): 257–73

Maguire, M (2000) 'Policing by risks and targets: some dimensions and implications of intelligence-led crime control' *Policing and Society* 9, 315–36

—— and John, T (2006) 'Intelligence-led policing, managerialism and community engagement: competing priorities and the role of the National Intelligence Model in the UK' *Policing and Society* 16, 67–85

Phillips, D, Caless, B, and Bryant, R (2007) 'Intelligence and its application to contemporary policing' *Policing: A Journal of Policy and Practice* 1(4): 438–46

Ratcliffe, J (2002), 'Intelligence-led policing and the problems of turning rhetoric into practice' *Policing and Society* 12, 53–66

—— (2008), *Intelligence-led Policing*, Willan, Cullompton

Sheptycki, J (2004), 'Organizational pathologies in police intelligence systems: some contributions to the lexicon of intelligence-led policing' *European Journal of Criminology* 1, 307–332

Tilley, N (2003), 'Community policing, problem-oriented policing and intelligence-led policing' in T Newburn (ed) *Handbook of Policing*, Willan, Cullompton): 311–39

Chapter 15

Planning and Risk Management to Achieve Harm Reduction

15.1 **Introduction**

Planning, risk management, and knowledge management are intrinsically linked in achieving an outcome of harm reduction. Planning for harm reduction operates at a number of levels, to any of which information from frontline staff may contribute. It is important that frontline staff have an understanding of the various planning processes and how such processes might be applied and how frontline staff are directly involved. As primary information-gatherers for the force, frontline staff need to be able to recognize when their first response is likely to acquire information that will trigger planning and risk assessment elsewhere in the organization. Not all the processes and available tools are appropriate in all circumstances. A comprehensive approach to this subject requires a book in its own right. This chapter offers a general introductory overview to place planning processes in context for frontline staff.

Planning involves the marshalling of available knowledge in order to identify appropriate courses of action. Risk management is itself a form of knowledge creation as well as a process in which available knowledge about the operational environment is regularly assessed. Both functions lend themselves to structured models that aid thinking. The structured models have inherent rationales and must therefore be used appropriately, otherwise the effort invested will be wasted or diversionary. Part of the rationale of each model or tool is that they help identify the nature and amount of information needed in order to proceed with effective planning and intervention.

The common purpose in all planning and risk assessment is to deliver a desired outcome through identified responsibilities and actions. Planning for outputs alone will not necessarily deliver outcomes.

Such models are tools that can be applied across the spectrum of policing function from strategy-setting for forces, Basic Command Units (BCUs), neighbourhood policing teams (NPTs), or partnership-working to the tactical management of individual operations, investigations, and other interventions. This chapter is structured around a sequential approach, starting with the strategic planning level in which long-term objectives are identified and the path to their achievement mapped out, and then drilling down into the sorts of processes applied when given circumstances that arise need to be responded to. Planning has both proactive and reactive aspects, and the tools outlined below can service both needs depending upon the circumstances. The sequence followed in this chapter is:

- a strategic approach to harm management;
- understanding the environment;
- risk assessment;
- impact/probability assessment;
- risk management;
- planning;
- human rights;
- multi-agency options for prevention;
- documenting decisions.

The associated function of problem-solving, which has its own suite of tools, is discussed in detail within the context of neighbourhood policing in Chapter 25 below.

15.2 **Duty: the Defining Context for Planning**

The police have a number of recognized duties and all planning, assessment, and knowledge-management functions should be pursuant to those duties.

Overarching the delivery of neighbourhood policing is the Policing Pledge: an example of a policing pledge is accessible online at <http://police.homeoffice.gov.uk/publications/police-reform/Policing_Pledge.pdf> (accessed 11 February 2009).

At the general level police have a duty established through common and statute law to:

- protect life;
- preserve the Queen's Peace;
- prevent and detect crime;
- protect property.

(The general duty to prevent and detect crime does not extend to a specific duty of care to protect individuals from harm caused by criminals: *Hill v Chief Constable of West Yorkshire* [1989] AC 53, re-affirmed (Lord Bingham dissenting) in *Smith v Chief Constable of Sussex Police* [2008] UKHL 50.)

At the specific level and depending on the test of circumstance discussed below, the police also have a duty of care towards:

- the public;
- police officers and staff;
- the organization;
- the source of sensitive information (if applicable);
- the offender.

The existence of *a duty of care* is established through a three-point test:

1. Damage/harm must have been done.
2. There must be proximity in the relationship between the person alleging damage/harm and the party alleged to be negligent.

3. It must be reasonable, in the circumstances, for a duty of care to exist.

This test was established in *Caparo Industries PLC v Dickman & Others* (1990) 1 All ER 568, and among the case law examples of how a duty of care applies to police is the case of *Donnelly v CC of Lincolnshire & Others,* [2001] All ER (D), in which the *Caparo* test was applied. A covert human intelligence source (CHIS) claimed his anonymity had been assured by Lincolnshire Police who subsequently revealed his identity during suspect interviews. The CHIS suffered damage/harm (his life was imperiled); his relationship to Lincolnshire Police was proximate (he was an informer providing information covertly to the police); and it was reasonable in these particular circumstances for the informer to expect a duty of care from police. These and other cases are considered at length in R Billingsley, 'Duty of care for informers', *The Police Journal* 78, 2005, 209–221.

Swinney and another v Chief Constable of Northumbria [1996] 3 All ER 449 affirmed that there was a general duty of care to take reasonable steps to avoid public disclosure of information provided by a CHIS. Documented information provided by an informer was stolen from an unattended police car. The person about whom the information had been provided subsequently subjected the informer and her family to threats and arson attacks, having been told who had provided information to the police. Such a duty of care is likely to arise from all sensitive information held by police.

These over-arching duties define the context within which planning and risk assessment takes place. This over-arching context is given further definition through application of the National Intelligence Model (NIM) tasking and coordination process.

Where feasible and reasonable, police have a duty to act which has been further defined in the concept of positive obligation. Within the UK context that was defined by the Strasbourg court in the case of *Osman*.

Definition: Positive obligation

A positive obligation was held to exist where 'the authorities knew or ought to have known at the time of the existence of a real and immediate risk to the life of an identified individual or individuals from the criminal acts of a third party and that they failed to take measures within the scope of their powers which, judged reasonably, might have been expected to avoid that risk.'

Osman v UK (1998) 29 EHRR 245, note 19 at para 116
Reaffirmed in *Van Colle v Chief Constable of Hertfordshire Police* [2008] UKHL 50

Thus defined, the concept of positive obligation can be extended to matters beyond those engaging Article 2 of the European Convention on Human Rights (ECHR). Where a duty or positive obligation exists, plans informed by risk assessment must be made for action or contingency.

15.3 **Harm Management**

In fulfilment of the duties above, policing has traditionally been thought of in terms of basic functions: crime/disorder prevention and investigation leading to enforcement. Planning can be ordered accordingly, but in such cases will only be directed at individual outputs and actions. An alternative way of structuring thinking about policing, and so the way in which planning and risk assessment can be approached, is to think in terms of the aspired outcome: harm reduction. This is a particularly useful approach in partnership working where different agencies have different functions with different outputs that nevertheless can contribute to a common outcome.

Harm reduction can be presented as a linear process:

IDENTIFY - ASSESS - MANAGE

in which current and emerging social harms or organizational issues are identified; analysis is undertaken to identify potential solutions; and the solutions are then implemented and managed.

15.4 Understanding the Policing Environment

Long-term planning and risk identification can be more effective if the prevailing policing environment is better understood. At both the strategic and operational level, there exist two planning tools to assist in marshalling the knowledge that will lead to enhanced understanding: STEEPLES and SWOT analysis. Environmental scanning can help to prevent teams and organizations from becoming too inward-looking. It can be helpful in identifying new and emerging issues.

STEEPLES is a development of the model that formerly went by the mnemonic PESTLE (or PESTEL). The mnemonic identifies categories of issues that may have an impact upon achieving an objective and which therefore should be considered in the planning stage of any operation or policy. It is useful to think of these categories in terms of current status and foreseeable changes.

Mnemonic	
S—social	= What demographic and community cultural factors (likely to affect the work of the NPT/BCU/force/partnership) need to be taken into consideration? Do NPT staff need to be bilingual to service properly the needs of their community? If so, in which languages must they be proficient?

T—technical	=	What new challenges or opportunities are presented by ongoing technological developments? Does a new CCTV system, for instance, really reduce the need for physical patrol? Does the development of mobile communication technology enable crimes to be committed in new ways?
E—environmental (aka ecological)	=	What changes in the *physical* environment need to be taken into consideration? For instance, what will be the impact of a new housing estate on NPT demands and resources? How might the building of new youth facilities be harnessed to reduce anti-social behaviour attributed to bored teenagers?
E—economic	=	How will the prevailing and changing economic climate affect current working practices and priorities? What will be the effect on local communities of workplace closures? What policing demands will that generate?
P—political	=	What are the current priorities set by central and/or local government and how might they change? Will political events overseas affect the local (immigrant) communities?
L—legal	=	What offences and investigative powers currently exist? What new laws are proposed and when will they come into force? How will staff and partners be made ready for the changes? What are the implications of new case law?
E—ethical	=	Is the proposed action consistent with human rights and professional standards? What possible threats of corruption and compromise need to be guarded against?
S—safety	=	What duties of care exist? What health and safety precautions have to be made? What harms to the community are evident and how might they be prevented? Can partner agencies assist?

This scanning process is one that should be kept under regular review. Although more likely to be used at the organizational strategic level, in the neighbourhood policing arena, for instance, NPTs could use this regularly to re-assess emerging issues. It is a process that could usefully be undertaken both internally amongst the team members or at BCU level, as well as externally with partner agencies.

The policing environment can also be scanned using SWOT analysis. Table 15.1 gives some example questions: the list below is not exhaustive.

Table 15.1

	Internal	External
Positives	**Strengths**	**Opportunities**
	What skills, powers, techniques, and equipment are available and appropriate?	What gaps can be filled? Can a useful and productive partnership be formed to achieve the objective? What will be learnt that can be put to future use?
	What information is held by the organization or a partner that can be used in tackling the present issue?	What changes identified in the STEEPLES analysis can be used to police advantage?
Negatives	**Weaknesses**	**Threats**
	What organizational/staff inhibitors will prevent the successful outcome of the intended action/policy?	Will other demands for police services create conflicting priorities that could inhibit the planned intervention/policy?
	What skills/resources needs must be addressed before intervention or policy can be implemented?	What obstacles are faced?
	What can be improved?	What will be learnt that can be put to future use? What challenges identified in the STEEPLES analysis must be addressed if they are not to become threats?

The SWOT analysis need not be confined to a police perspective. It may be especially useful in a partnership context. It can also be undertaken from the perspective of the criminal, in order to identify tactical options and possible avenues of *prevention*; *enforcement* or other intervention; and information-gathering opportunities for *intelligence* analysis.

15.5 **Risk Identification Through Threat Assessment**

Policing is about preventing or dealing with the eventuality of risk manifestation. As such the identification and management of risk is a key function at all levels of the organization from strategic planning to individual intervention planning.

> **Definition**
>
> *Risk* can be defined as the likelihood of an adverse harm occurring. This is not to be confused with a *threat*, which is the source of that harm. *Vulnerability* is the measurement of probability against impact (the probability of a given outcome occurring may be very low but the adverse impact may be very significant). A *risk assessment* is the means by which identified risks can be balanced against the benefits. If the risks cannot be appropriately managed, should the benefits sought still be pursued?

The emergence and manifestation of risks is dynamic. Consequently risk management must be a dynamic process, constantly reviewed. In some operations it will be so dynamic that the commanding officer will have undertaken several revised risk assessments during the course of any given phase of the operation, possibly within a very short space of time and with little or no opportunity to record the rationale at the time, in which case documenting the variation as soon as practicable after the event must suffice. But where frontline staff and their supervisors have time to consider potential threats and attendant risk, time spent in careful planning will maximize the benefits of the intended intervention or policy.

Particularly where policing engages Article 8 rights, risk assessment provides a structure for planning that can deliver the following benefits:

- professional, credible risk management/reduction processes;
- reviews of working assumptions, taking into account changing risk circumstances;
- a process for real-time decision-making amenable to subsequent review (either in an operational debrief or a subsequent public enquiry);
- reduction in the number of perverse decisions;
- reduction in corporate/personal liability.

It is important not to confuse risk management with risk aversion. Since nothing is ever risk-free, a strategy of risk aversion merely leads to nothing being done. Risk management, based on considered assessment, enhances professional policing (an inherently risky activity) by ensuring that possible collateral and consequential damage arising from policing is minimized.

A generic model for risk assessment, not dissimilar from the STEEPLES policing environment scanning model discussed above, has been developed within the police service: PPPLEM or 3PsLEM. It is structured around six categories of threat. Planners anticipate on the best available information the likelihood of a given identified threat causing an adverse impact, document it accordingly, and develop a plan for managing the identified risk. The model is set out in Table 15.2.

15.5.1 The PPPLEM Model for Risk Assessment

To facilitate consideration of all relevant human rights and duties of care, it can be helpful to think of the PPPLEM model as a matrix in which risk management is structured around different risk arena: risks to the organization (including as an organization, as a partnership, or as an organization within a partnership); risks to staff; risks to the subject of any police/partnership intervention; and risks to third parties. By identifying each of the risk categories to ascertain whether they are relevant in any of the risk arenas, an appropriate management plan can be devised. See Table 15.3.

Table 15.2 The PPPLEM model for risk assessment

P—Police and community risks	Alternatively, public and organizational risks. In general terms: what are the risks to the organization within the community of engaging in this operation? Is there any general risk to/from the community at large? Adverse publicity? Public disorder possible? What are the risks to the organization from the investigation subject/staff/public at large? What are the risks to the community from the organization engaging in this operation? What are the risks to the community from the investigation subject? What are the risks to the community from the organization staff? What are the risks of not doing anything?
P—Physical risks	What are the physical risks to staff/subject/third parties? Organization premises or premises borrowed for the purpose?
P—Psychological risks	What are the psychological risks to staff/subject/third parties?
L—Legal risks	What are the legal risks to the organization? Its staff? The subject? Third parties?
E—Economic risks	What are the economic risks to the organization? Its staff? The subject? Third parties? The community? Cost of operation? Possible litigation claims?
M—Moral risks	What are the moral risks to the organization? Its staff? The subject? Third parties? Can the operation be justified morally/ethically as well as legally? Is there a danger that the very essence of the ECHR will be breached as well as any qualified rights in question? What are the risks of not doing anything?

Table 15.3 The PPPLEM matrix

PPPLEM matrix	Police/ community	Physical	Psychological	Legal	Economic	Moral
Organization / Partnership						
Staff						
Subject						
Third parties						

Effective risk assessment and management is dependent upon using the best available information: information that is as accurate and as complete as possible. The process of investigation will always provide additional material for risk management. Once an intervention is underway, whatever the outcome, information will be generated that confirms anticipated risks were present and appropriately managed, or that further risk-management actions are required, or else indicates that anticipated risks were not manifest. This is important information for the ongoing risk management of the current intervention and for future risk assessments.

The extent to which frontline staff become involved in the specialist risk assessments that follow will vary according to circumstance and local force procedure. It is important for staff to be aware that there are specialist risk assessments and where they fit into the organizational planning and intervention processes. With these specialist areas police forces will have their own procedures mapped out and frontline staff must familiarize themselves with their own organizational policy.

This section now looks at three specialist areas of risk assessment but other relevant associated areas include health and safety (see Chapter 16 below), community tension assessment, and critical incident response (see Chapters 23 and 31 below).

15.5.2 National Criminal Intelligence Service Risk Management Process

Information and intelligence generate their own risks as has been seen in Chapter 14.8 above with discussion of the Government Protective Marking Scheme and the professional intelligence environment. The National Criminal Intelligence Service (NCIS), operating as an independent non-departmental public body between 1998 and 2006, devised a seven-step intelligence risk management process which remains relevant and is adaptable to all levels of policing. In summary this process can be structured around a sequence of questions:

1. Is information acquired or held by the police/partnership sensitive and/or classified?
2. If yes, what special handling conditions and requirements pertain?
3. What consequential ethical, operational, and personal risks arise from the acquisition, retention, and management of this information?
4. Does the purpose for which this information is to be used or disseminated generate any additional risks?
5. Does retention/dissemination necessitate special management requirements?
6. How are the identified risks to be managed? What established protocols must be observed?
7. Continuous review: in light of the above what changes, if any, need to be made to the assessment criteria and information management plan?

15.5.3 Risk Assessment Models for Domestic Abuse

Intelligence risk assessment is not the only specialist area of risk assessment used by the police service. Various forces and partnerships are developing and elaborating risk assessment models for *domestic abuse* with particular reference to the prevention of domestic violence-related murder.

One such model is SPECIAL CASS developed by Thames Valley Police. Frontline staff, such as those deployed in NPTs, are well-placed to identify early signal behaviours of or acquire relevant information about instances of domestic abuse, and as such need to be alert to the sort of information that can usefully be passed to domestic abuse teams to trigger planning for specialist intervention. The relevant stress factors are:

Mnemonic

S = Separation or child contact dispute

P = Pregnancy or recent birth

E = Escalation and severity of violence

C = Child abuse

I = Isolation

A = Attempts or threats of suicide or homicide

L = Legal obligations

C = Controlling behaviour

A = Afraid of subject

S = Sexual assault

S = Substance misuse

The above represent risk criteria that can assist in identifying the need for and structuring domestic abuse intervention. Risk assessment for domestic abuse is a procedure for which most if not all police organizations and partner agencies will have a policy and procedure. The relationship of risk assessment to the overall force approach to domestic abuse in Thames Valley Police, for sake of example, is set out online at <http://www.thamesvalley.police.uk/3440_dv_leaflet_web.pdf> (accessed 11 February 2009). Recognition by first responders of any of the symptoms identified above will, through organizational reporting procedures, trigger a specialist risk assessment. Thus even though frontline staff may not themselves be involved in the risk assessment and planning, they can nevertheless play a vital role in identifying when specialist risk assessment and intervention planning is required.

The theme of protecting vulnerable people is considered in greater detail in Chapter 34.

15.5.4 PLAICE Model for Risk assessment

One further specialized form of risk assessment has been developed in relation to the use of *covert investigation* methods. In many forces, the PPPLEM model already discussed will form the basis of risk assessments made in support of applications for authority to conduct covert investigation. Much software developed for making such applications uses this generic model. But the Metropolitan Police Service has developed a model specifically designed for covert operations.

Structured around the mnemonic PLAICE, it is summarized below. Once again, it presents certain risk criteria that are helpful in structuring the thinking of those responsible for assessing risks and devising or reviewing risk management plans. Using the PPPLEM approach for covert investigation is not wrong: the designers of the PLAICE model argue, however, that, unlike the generic PPPLEM model, PLAICE is specifically tailored to covert investigation needs.

Mnemonic

P = Physical risks

L = Legal risks

A = Risks to organizational assets

I = Information and information technology risks

C = Risk of compromise to staff, tactics, and techniques

E = Environmental risks

Note: For further information and reading see R Billingsley, 'Risk management: is there a model for covert policing? *Covert Policing Review* (2006) 98–109.

15.6 **Impact /Probability Assessment**

Following identification of risks through threat assessments, the next stage of the risk management process is to consider vulnerability, in order to prioritize risk management options and actions.

Table 15.4 Impact/probability matrix

High impact	*Contingency plan*	**Action required**	**Action required**
Medium impact		**Action required**	**Action required**
Low impact			
	Low probability	Medium probability	High probability

Greatest vulnerability, and therefore risk, will be inherent where the probability and impact are both high or where one is high and the other medium. In such circumstances action to mitigate or manage the risk is required (darker areas in Table 15.4). Where the occurrence of harm would have a high impact but the probability of that harm occurring is in fact low, then a contingency plan may be a suitable risk management response, thus avoiding the need to expend dedicated resources in anticipation, whilst ensuring an appropriate response can be quickly mustered as required.

Risks that are both low in impact and low in probability need to be identified in the planning process but need not concern managers and supervisors too greatly.

15.7 **Risk Management Options**

Once the vulnerability factor has been identified, risk management and reduction prioritization can be undertaken.

In slightly different ways two models identify the strategic options for risk management.

The first is the RARA model which identifies four strategic options that can be adopted in relation to any given risk: *Remove* it, *Avoid* it, *Reduce* it, *Accept* it—hence RARA. Ideally interventions and policies should be planned so as to remove all risks, but this is rarely achievable. Adopting different methods to achieve the same objective can avoid a risk. If the risk cannot be removed or avoided, then there may be measures that can be put in place to reduce the risk. Finally, police or partners may be willing to accept risks that have a low vulnerability factor.

As an alternative to RARA there is the TTTT model: *Terminate, Treat, Transfer,* or *Tolerate*. The terminology is different and the order in which the strategic options are presented is slightly different, but in essence this model is the same as the RARA model, certainly in terms of the types of options it identifies for risk management. Frontline staff may encounter either model depending upon the preference of their own organization or its partner agencies.

As with the PPPLEM and PLAICE models, using the RARA or the TTTT models to identify and devise an appropriate risk management strategy and control measures illustrates and records the thought processes of the decision-takers based on available information at the time. Given that available information may change in quantity or quality (if a piece of information is corroborated or its accuracy comes into question), there is a need regularly to review risk assessments and management.

15.8 **Planning Frameworks**

Information, intelligence, understanding through environmental scanning and risk assessment each contribute to the available knowledge upon which plans are based.

Other contributory sources are statute and case law, professional expertise, good practice guidance, and organizational memory. In using this information, two frameworks are available to help devise how to achieve a desired objective or outcome.

The first might be termed the *identification of need*—be that need for information, or a need for operational resources (and the consequential need to identify the costs involved)—which can be sub-divided into the basic interrogative objectives that underpin all police enquiries:

- Who?
- What?
- Where?
- When?
- How?
- Why?

Chapter 27 discusses how these fundamental questions form the foundation of an investigation planning and management matrix (see Figure 27.1). They can equally apply to the planning of neighbourhood policing and partnership working and also to strategic and policy planning.

The second planning framework is known as the **Seven S**s, which considers the different factors that need to be taken into consideration when planning.

- Strategy
- Structure
- Systems
- Staff
- Skills
- Style
- Shared values

These are the foundational elements for making things happen. Structuring a plan around these themes is the first step in working towards achieving control and solutions within an unstable environment. It is helpful to understand what these terms mean for other agencies in any given partnership. This framework could also be used as an alternative template for risk assessment.

Other tools relevant to planning frameworks specifically relate to problem-solving, a primary function for NPTs, are identified by the mnemonic SARA and the acronym PAT. As indicated at the start of this chapter, this next logical sequence in the planning process is dealt with specifically within the context of neighbourhood policing in Chapter 25 below.

15.9 **Human Rights**

Fundamental to efficient and effective policing is the protection of human rights. Accordingly, such protection needs to be an intrinsic part of the planning process at the strategic, operational, and tactical levels of policing. Human rights having been addressed at length in Chapter 13 above, there is no need to dwell in detail here. It suffices to remind the reader that human rights can be modelled in two basic ways. Whose rights and how are they to be protected?

Whose rights?

- Victim
- Offender
- Police officer/staff member
- Third party members of the public

All of the above could have a claim of action against the police or a partner agency if an avoidable unauthorized violation of a protected right occurs.

The ECHR, key articles of which have been given domestic effect in the UK under the Human Rights Act (see Chapter 13 above), provides the starting point in how to protect rights by defining which rights have to be protected absolutely and for which rights protection may be qualified in achieving the balance between the rights of an individual and the rights of other individuals.

The principles by which unlawful infringements of such qualified human rights can be avoided by the authorities can be modelled in the planning process, and the following provides a framework for documenting decisions in which human rights issues are engaged:

P—PROPORTIONALITY	Why is it proportionate to use the proposed tactics to obtain the intended product? Is the outcome of the specific action proportionate to the methods used?
L—LEGITIMACY	What is the legitimate purpose of the proposed action: the prevention of disorder or crime; the interests of national security; the interests of public safety; the interests of the economic well-being of the country; the protection of health or morals; the protection of the rights and freedoms of others?
A—AUTHORIZATION	What is the lawful foundation and authority for the proposed action? From whom must authorization be sought?
N—NECESSITY	Why is the proposed action necessary?

Planning with this framework in mind, and using this framework in documenting planning and operational decisions, will help to minimize unlawful violations of human rights. An amended form of this mnemonic is PLAN BI, in which the BI stands for 'Best Information' available; a reminder that planners and decision-makers must equip themselves with up to date, accurate information in order to inform their deliberations and decisions.

It is important to remember that section 6(1) of the HRA is structured so as to include not only public authorities but private individuals or organizations sub-contracted to act on behalf of a public authority in providing that authority's functions.

15.10 **Multi-Agency Options for Harm Reduction**

The ten principles of crime reduction provide a starting point for multi-agency intervention to achieve harm reduction.

> **Note:** To understand how the ten principles interact with problem-solving tools see the Home Office website at <http://www.crimereduction.homeoffice.gov.uk/learningzone/passport_to_cr.htm> (accessed 11 February 2009).

The ten principles are summarized as:

1. Target hardening (physical security at buildings for instance).
2. Target removal (for example, inbuilt car stereos rather than units easily removed from the dashboard).
3. Remove the means to commit crime (enhanced card security such as 'chip-and-pin' for bank cards and accessing social security payments).
4. Reducing the pay-off/profit for the criminal.
5. Controlling access to vulnerable sites.
6. Surveillance (private and/or public).
7. Environmental design (urban areas designed so as to maximize public safety and reduce opportunities for crime).
8. Rule setting (defining acceptable behaviour/unacceptable behaviour, for example, through legislation).
9. Increase offender vulnerability to enforcement sanction (eg enhanced professionalism of policing; consideration of regulatory (ie non-police) enforcement as a disruption technique).

10. Deflecting individuals from offending to non-offend-
    ing behaviours or environments.

It will be seen from the above list that not all options
involve the police as lead agency. Nevertheless police can
contribute to partnership planning to achieve such ends by
sharing experience and evidence of issues encountered by
neighbourhood policing teams, response teams, and other
frontline staff. Equally, when problem-solving within the
neighbourhood policing context, consideration of these
wider issues may identify possible opportunities outside the
police service for achieving the desired outcome, in which
case a partnership approach would be appropriate and
should be explored at the earliest planning opportunity.

15.11 **Documenting Decisions**

Documenting decision-making is an important on-going
process in planning. When more than one possible option
was available, on what basis was the final decision made?

Such documentation evidences thought processes and
contributes to both individual learning and organizational
memory as well as contributing to accountability processes.
Derived from the discipline of investigation management,
the following decision log mnemonic provides a framework for documenting decision and planning rationale. It
can be used in conjunction with the human rights PLAN
(BI) framework.

Mnemonic

S = Situation presented

A = Aims of operation (objectives)

F = Factors for consideration (apply STEEPLES)

C = Choices facing decision-maker/planner (apply SWOT)

O = Options selected

R = Risk assessment

M = Monitoring

15.11 **Conclusion**

The starting point for any given planning and risk assessment process will vary according to circumstance. Strategic planning for forces, BCUs, and NPTs will follow an annual business cycle defined in force policy and procedure. Project planning will follow the identified need for project work. Proactive intervention and prevention planning will be triggered through the NIM tasking and coordination processes or through the diary of community events (forces may have a dedicated events-planning team). Investigation planning will be triggered by the discovery of crime. Problem-solving will be initiated by problem identification within the community. Spontaneous events will activate contingency plans. Specialist planning and risk assessment will be initiated by recognition and appropriate reporting of signal behaviours.

Common to all these scenarios is the recognition that police (and partner agencies) need to do something in order to achieve a desired outcome, and that appropriate actions to achieve the desired outcome will only be identified through adequate and accurate information. Using tools such as those identified above and others which forces may have prescribed within local procedure will assist planners in identifying the correct set of choices.

This chapter has presented an introductory overview to planning for harm reduction. It is not intended to be definitive or exhaustive—available space in a work of this nature prohibits such an aspiration. For frontline staff unfamiliar or inexperienced in planning interventions it provides a starting point. Increasingly NPTs, BCU response teams, and other frontline staff find themselves working with partner agencies who will have their own approaches to issues in which the various partners can contribute to a solution. The planning tools above can be used to plan for working with partners as well as for working in partnership to achieve a common outcome. The knowledge and expertise of partner agencies will become part of the shared organizational memory that informs future planning. There is an extensive literature on strategic and operational planning, too vast to summarize here, but basing interventions on good practice guidance and doctrine published by ACPO and the NPIA will be a good starting point.

Further Reading

<http://www.acpo.police.uk/policies.asp>
<http://www.npia.police.uk/en/6534.htm>
From these websites (accessed 16 February 2009), guidance and policy that is not restrictively marked can be accessed and downloaded. Guidance that is protectively marked will be available only to those authorized to access it through force information systems.

Chapter 16

Health and Safety and First Aid

16.1 **Introduction**

This chapter is in two parts: Part 1 examines the importance of Health and Safety legislation in policing. Part 2 examines first aid training and what police officers need to know when confronted with casualties.

16.2 **Part 1: Health and Safety**

16.2.1 Health and Safety Legislation

Until 1 July 1998, most police officers, as 'Crown servants' or 'office holders of appointments under the Crown', were not protected by the main legislative provisions of the Health and Safety Act 1974, because they were not 'employees'. This led to anomalous situations in some police forces where officers could enter a hazardous crime scene, for example, but 'civilian' crime scene investigators (CSIs) could do so, if at all, only after making a formal risk assessment. The Police (Health and Safety) Act 1997 brought police officers (and 'office holders') into line with the 1974 legislation:

> **Police (Health and Safety) Act 1997, Chapter 42, section 1:**
>
> 1. Application of Part I of Health and Safety at Work etc Act 1974 to police
>   After section 51 of the [1974 c 37] Health and Safety at Work etc Act 1974 there is inserted—
>   '51A   Application of Part to police
>   (1) for the purposes of this Part, a person who, otherwise than under a contract of employment, holds the office of constable or an appointment as a police cadet shall be treated as an employee of the relevant officer [...]'

A 'relevant officer' in this case means a Chief Constable or equivalent (who is deemed to be the employer only for the purposes of the Act). The Act of 1997 means that any activity engaged in by a police officer must entail awareness of health and safety considerations and an assessment of consequent risk.

The Health and Safety Executive (HSE) brought prosecutions in 2003 against two former Commissioners of the Metropolitan Police, Lord Condon and Lord Stevens. In the first case a police officer, pursuing a suspect in 1999, had fallen through an unsafe roof and had been killed, whilst another officer in a separate, similar incident in 2001, had been injured. The HSE alleged that each Commissioner, respectively, as the 'relevant officer', had an obligation to ensure that officers in their employ were protected, and that the Metropolitan Police had clearly failed to protect its officers while they were carrying out their duties.

The HSE lawyers argued that 'It is plainly right—or at least reasonable—for the HSE to have regarded the Metropolitan Police as it would regard any other large employer, taking into account the nature of the undertaking'. This led the trial judge, Mr Justice Crane, to observe that the HSE prosecution—estimated to have cost £3 million—showed a 'fundamental lack of understanding of the unique nature of policing'.[1] The prosecution failed and the matter did not go to retrial. There may be unique features in policing which are not as amenable to health and safety 'at work' as they may be in other occupations, but any chief officer who breaches the legislation is vulnerable to prosecution.

There is no need to examine risk assessment in detail here as it has already been examined in Chapter 15. When front-line staff are confronted with an immediate health and safety or first aid situation it is important that they respond in a professional manner. Two mnemonics assist structured thinking in this regard.

One way of assessing *what needs to be done* in a crisis is through the mnemonic SPRAIN.

Mnemonic	
S—Situation	= What am I dealing with? What is going on?
P—Plan	= What am I going to do? How will I do it?
R—Risks	= What might get me or someone else injured or put in danger?
A—Alternatives	= Are there other ways to do this?
IN—INcrease safety	= How do I reduce the risks and yet do what I must, to make the situation safer for all involved?

Caless et al (2007: 445) have devised a further mnemonic, BEWARE, which helps to raise awareness of the specific hazards in any situation:

Mnemonic	
B	= Biological (or chemical) dangers
E	= Exposure to fire
W	= Weather conditions
A	= Assault or Asphyxiation
R	= Radiological contamination
E	= Effort and physical exertion

---

[1] Reported verbatim by the BBC on Friday 27 June 2003, available from <http://news.bbc.co.uk/1/hi/england/london/3024948.stm>, accessed 25 July 2008.

Linking BEWARE with SPRAIN enables effective dynamic risk assessments to be made by frontline staff in response to spontaneous incidents in which life is imperilled. Assessment of an officer's competence in risk assessment is through the Skills for Justice National Occupational Standards (in the case of a patrol officer it is Unit 4G2: *Ensure that your own actions reduce risks to health and safety*).

The HSE points with some pride to efforts since 2002 which have reduced sickness absence in the police service by some 25 per cent, especially absence arising from musculoskeletal disorders, stress, violence, and workplace hazards, though HSE acknowledges that more work is needed on the health and safety aspects to reduce absence through injury. Its guidance to the police service has been published as a strategy (*The Strategy for Healthy Police, 2006–2010*, HSE, TSO and available at <http://www.hse.gov.uk/services/police> (accessed on 25 July 2008).

16.2.2 Health and Safety Policies

Police forces will have health and safety policies identifying how each individual organization complies with the legislation. Frontline staff should be aware of their own force policies on health and safety.

16.2.3 Summary

Health and Safety legislation and force policies are vulnerable to adverse, ill-informed comment and cynicism. Almost any group of patrol officers will produce examples (many of them certainly of the 'urban myth' variety) in which Health and Safety has been invoked to be *risk-averse* and to prevent a seemingly commonsense action. When they themselves have only had a few seconds to make a judgment in a crisis, officers can also resent the 'you should have' critical attitude of those who later pick over such decision-making with the luxury of hindsight. And yet this is no different from the cold objectivity of a court of law analysing an officer's actions or decisions in the heat of the moment, and there will always be those who may pass judgments on actions which they themselves have never been called upon to make, such as the Independent Police Complaints Commission (IPCC) investigations of fatal shootings.

16.3 **Part 2: First Aid**

The first and unchangeable priority for a police officer at any incident anywhere will always be *the preservation of life*. Recognizing the importance of this principle, police officers may at common law enter any building or site and render any necessary aid or help to ensure that lives are saved.

> **Note:** IMPORTANT this Handbook is **not** a first aid manual, and cannot contribute specifically to the learning of first aid,[2] but it is possible to outline what a police officer's duty is to anyone injured:
>
> * **Assess the injury**
> * **Give appropriate first aid (including resuscitation)**
> * **Call for assistance, and ensure 'second aid' assessment**
> * **Prevent further danger**

Police forces' training modules will vary in terms of health and safety training and first aid awareness. There are National Police Improvement Agency (NPIA)-sponsored training programmes, ranging from those for general patrol duties, through first aid for custody officers, to specialist training in trauma injuries for firearms officers, which forces can

---

[2] See eg Red Cross or St John Ambulance manuals of first aid, police, or NPIA force notes and policies and training DVDs on aspects of first aid. **No responsibility is accepted, expressly or by implication, for any shortcoming, error or misjudgment in the administering of first aid by anyone who has used only these pages for reference and who has not sought to acquire testable competences.**

adopt together with recommended providers (see Further Reading below).

One of the strongest recommendations which emerged from the 1999 Macpherson Inquiry into the death of Stephen Lawrence (see Further Reading) was that first aid training for police officers should be mandatory. This was because the aid rendered to the dying teenager was inadequate in the circumstances. Certainly, police officers often find that they are first on the scene of an injury, and a positive intervention on the part of a police officer in rendering first aid may mean the difference between a casualty's survival or death. This is especially so when paramedics are delayed from reaching the scene.

Frontline staff have an individual responsibility to learn, practise, and refresh their knowledge of first aid at frequent intervals, preferably in properly supervised group sessions. Following an approved course leading to a qualification—such as those recommended and outlined by the NPIA—is a certain way of obtaining competence.

The National Occupational Standards (NOS) require assessment of officers' competence in first aid as follows:

Unit 4G4: Administer First Aid:

4G4.1: Respond to the needs of casualties with minor injuries

4G4.2: Respond to the needs of casualties with major injuries

4G4.3: Respond to the needs of unconscious casualties

4G4.4: Perform cardio-pulmonary resuscitation (CPR)

(adapted from Skills for Justice, developed by the British Red Cross in consultation with the St John Ambulance Service, 2002)

16.3.1 **First Aid Priorities**

Police officers can save lives by maintaining a casualty's vital needs for an open airway, breathing, and sustaining circulation. This is known as the '**ABC Rule**':

Mnemonic

A = is for an open **AIRWAY**

B = is for adequate **BREATHING**

C = is for **CIRCULATION**

Some versions of this mnemonic are structured DR ABCD: Danger—Responsiveness—Airway—Breathing—Circulation—Defibrillation. The first duty of frontline staff encountering a medical casualty is to assess whether they and the casualty are in continuing danger: if so, can the danger be removed, or can the casualty safely be removed from the danger without causing further injury? Secondly, in assessing the casualty, is there any response when talking to the casualty, or squeezing the casualty's hand or ear lobe? The ABC elements are as above, and the final element prompts first responders to apply defibrillation IF the necessary equipment is available AND there are persons trained in its use AND it is appropriate given the casualty's circumstances.

Thus there are three emergency situations where an injured person is especially at risk because of something which inhibits or interferes with vital needs:

- lack of breathing or heartbeat;
- severe bleeding;
- unconsciousness which affects the airways and breathing.

Dealing with any or all of these three emergencies takes priority at the scene of an accident and police officers *must* be able to deal with them. **The techniques involved must be learned through instruction, simulation, and practice** in an approved programme to cover Emergency Life Support as follows.

16.3.2 Airways

The airways must be opened, or kept open, to allow air to the injured person's lungs. If a casualty is unconscious, the airway may be blocked, for example by the tongue lolling back, or by dislodged false teeth, vomit, food, or impaired reflexes. The priority is to establish a clear airway by removing the blockage: The prone and injured person's chin needs to be lifted forwards, so that the jaw will pull the tongue forward. A finger in the mouth will establish if there is a further blockage which can be cleared. Wherever possible, the casualty should be on his or her back, or, if legs are trapped, the casualty's head turned to one side. Some conditions, such as suspected spinal injuries, may mean that specialist help is required, but the choice between life or death does not admit of degrees of seriousness, and so an officer's first duty is to ensure that life is maintained, even if that does not mitigate injury to the casualty.

16.3.3 Breathing

If the injured person has stopped breathing, the priority is to restore the function, and this usually means **artificial ventilation**, also known as '*the kiss of life*'. The first aider blows air from his or her own lungs into the lungs of the casualty, covering the latter's mouth and pinching his/her nose closed. As the first aider's mouth is withdrawn, the casualty will breathe out as the lungs empty under pressure, which may be enough to stimulate re-breathing unaided. If not, the ventilation continues until the casualty's own breathing resumes or specialized help arrives to take over. Artificial ventilation is best performed if the casualty is supine (on his or her back), but may be done with the casualty in any position, provided there is access to the mouth. If there are very serious facial injuries or if the casualty is pinned face down, then ventilation by mouth may not be possible. This may also be the case if the casualty has taken a corrosive substance, such as an acid, into the mouth.

There is no point in ventilating if the casualty's heart has stopped beating, and it is important to check periodically during ventilation that there is a pulse. If there is not, **external chest compression**, by pressing rhythmically for a specified time on the lower half of the casualty's chest, may stimulate the heart to beat again. Some police officers are trained to use a *defibrillator* (an electrical apparatus to restart the heart by pulsing), which is carried in some patrol cars, but officers should not expect to have access to any external means of getting a heart beat. Artificial ventilation must precede and accompany external chest compression. Compression must cease as soon as a pulse is detected, but, as noted above, ventilation may have to continue for some time.

16.3.4 Circulation

The only reliable way to establish if there is a pulse and therefore circulation of the blood is by checking the **carotid pulse**. This can be felt in a casualty's neck under the jaw and beside the voice box. There is a slight hollow between the muscle in the neck and the voice box. The wave of pressure, which a heart beat sends, is felt here (wrist pulses are unreliable). Checks should be made every three minutes: a carotid pulse will only be felt if the casualty's heart is beating.

Bleeding, especially if serious and heavy, is a danger to life if left unchecked. It is the second part of the circulation check. To stop bleeding without interfering with the rest of circulation, a first aider will apply **direct pressure** on the wound. This process flattens blood vessels in the area and slows down the flow of blood, so that clotting can take place. Direct pressure has to be maintained for anything from five to fifteen minutes. Raising the injured part, if possible, will also slow blood flow. As soon as possible, or as soon as available, the wound should be covered with a piece of clean (preferably sterile) material. If bleeding continues, more covering should be applied. The original covering should not be removed lest clots are disturbed, whereupon bleeding may intensify.

It is not appropriate in a very brief description of this kind to discuss the various **indirect** ways to apply pressure to wounds (these involve identifying compression points to inhibit arterial bleeding), but any reputable first aid course will identify the *brachial* and *femoral pressure points* (arm and groin respectively) and provide instruction in location and use of the pressure points to control severe bleeding.

16.3.5 The Recovery Position

All other things being equal (no spinal injury, no major skull trauma—consider the circumstances in which harm came to be caused to the casualty), an unconscious casualty who is breathing and whose heart is beating should be placed in the recovery position. This ensures continued open access to airways and ensures that the casualty cannot choke on, for example, residual vomit or food.

Basically, the casualty has to be moved so that the head is to one side, one knee is raised to support the lower body and one arm is raised and the other lowered to support the upper body (this would be practised extensively in a reputable first aid programme). If the injured person cannot be safely moved into this position, perhaps because of limb fractures, then a recovery position may be modified by using a rolled blanket or heavy coat to support the chest positions and lower body. *The really important factor is to ensure that the airways remain unobstructed.*

16.3.6 Summary of Action at an Emergency

First aid instructors usually summarize the role of someone applying first aid as follows:

Approach

This should be as quick as possible but also calm and controlled. If access is difficult, thought must be given to making it easier (propping doors open, opening windows, for example). If there is smoke, the possibility of touching or getting a shock from electrical wiring, noxious air (such as from a sewer), or a danger of falling materials, then officers need to think about their safety before proceeding (see Part 1 of this chapter).

Assess

Any continuing or potential danger to casualties (water, power lines, traffic, unsafe structures) should be assessed as quickly as possible, and some provision made to deal with any dangers. The needs of casualties should then be assessed, and help given to those whose need is greatest (see Priorities below).

Ensure safety

It is vital that officers ensure their own safety and that of others at the scene, otherwise casualties will multiply. This is especially the case at road traffic collisions or where there are physical hazards.

Help from others

Officers should have no scruples about getting others, including bystanders, to help. Where it is safe to do so, help can be employed to make a structure safer, to control hazards such as water or moving traffic. Officers should be prepared to find people dazed and disorientated and not necessarily thinking calmly, especially at the scene of an explosion or widespread disaster like a train crash.

Priorities

The priorities are simple:

- The most badly-injured need aid first.
- The *ABC Rule* applies.
- Place the injured in recovery position. Then other, lesser, casualties can be treated.
- Officers should continue to check periodically that unconscious casualties are still breathing and have a heart beat.

16.4 **Conclusions**

Health and safety awareness and first aid are part of a police officer's 'toolbox'. Knowing the potential hazards in any course of action may well persuade an officer to a safer alternative. Where there is no option, the assessment of what is practicable and even counter-intuitive, to what is instinctive but possibly rash and ill-considered, may mean the difference between a successful and an unsuccessful outcome. The process whereby an officer arrives at a risk assessment of a situation is what ensures his or her calmness and control in the face of the disorder and panic on every side.

Knowing what is important in rendering first aid, and fulfilling the police officer's first duty to preserve life is also risk assessment of a different but related kind. People will look to a police officer for a lead in a crisis, so the proper prioritization of casualties and the logical delivery of ABC to those in need of it marks out the professionalism of the police officer and may help to bring order to chaos. And, whilst acknowledging that neither health and safety, nor first aid is likely to head the 'most popular topic' stakes, nonetheless many officers have cause to be thankful that their decisions in a fraught moment were rooted in solid, unspectacular risk assessment, most especially when those decisions are challenged in a court of law.

Further Reading

BBC, Friday 27 June 2003, reports on *HSE Prosecution of the Commissioner, The Metropolitan Police Force*, available at <http://news.bbc.co.uk/1/hi/england/london/3024948.stm>, accessed 25 July 2008

Caless, B (ed), Bryant, R, Morgan, D, Spruce, B, and Underwood, R (2007) *Blackstone's PCSO Handbook*, Oxford, Oxford University Press

Police (Health and Safety) Act 1997, Office of Public Service Information (opsi), Crown Copyright, TSO, also available at <http://www.opsi.gov.uk/Acts/acts1997/ukpga_19970042_en_1>, accessed 25 and 28 July 2008

Macpherson, Sir W, (1999) *The Stephen Lawrence Inquiry: Report of an Inquiry by Sir William Macpherson of Cluny*, Cm 4262, Crown Copyright, TSO, Chapter 10, 'First Aid', available at <http://www.archive.official-documents.co.uk/document/cm42/4262/sli-10.htm>, accessed 28 July 2008

NPIA, (2008) *First Aid Training*, course details available at <http://www.npia.police.uk/en/5000.htm>, accessed 25 July 2008; including 'First Aid Skills for Policing' (FASP), Module 1: *Emergency Life Support*, 633; Module 5: *First Aid Skills for Specialists*, 637, etc

St John Ambulance (2003, revised from 1987) *First Aid Manual*, (the authorized manual of the St John Ambulance, St Andrew's Ambulance Association and the British Red Cross Society), Dorling Kindersley Ltd

Chapter 17

Media

17.1 **Introduction**

Increasing demand for news about serious crime and major or critical events has had a profound affect on police media relations. The police carry an exceptional duty in the public sector for the protection of life and property, and must remain highly accountable. Obtaining and releasing information about police efficiency and effectiveness through media coverage in news outlets is an effective method of public scrutiny; therefore the professional management and handling of the media is extremely important. Publicity helps build and shape images and perceptions of the modern police service, whether they are positive or otherwise.

Local, national, and worldwide correspondents amongst a large range of competing outlets cater for the high intensity 24/7 news cycle. The UK alone has experienced a steady increase in local and national radio, cable, and satellite channels. Improvements in digital technology and the development of the World Wide Web as a means of news distribution have increased the access, speed, and capability at which news is demanded and reported. Breaking news is by nature spontaneous and can become global within minutes to any number of outlets, appearing on specific news programmes or in 'ticker tape' style at the bottom of TV screens.

News gatherers can and do rapidly descend on incident scenes and create a media frenzy. So called 'citizen journalists' with lightweight camcorders and mobile phones can also capture instant pictures, some of which do not always portray the police in a favourable light (eg the American officers arresting Rodney King in Los Angeles). Most people, however, have limited contact or experience with real life dramas and rely upon the media for information when they occur.

The murders of Holly Wells and Jessica Chapman in Soham, missing child Madeline McCann in Portugal, or the fraudulent canoeist John Darwin from Hartlepool illustrate the extreme levels of media interest some cases generate. Intense public and press interest places the police in the full glare of the media spotlight, which is either prolonged or resurfaces at regular intervals (eg the moors murders by Brady and Hindley). Mundane occurrences also become newsworthy if they contain interesting features, such as those involving celebrities.

Case Study—'Canoe Man' John Darwin

Extensive media coverage in the case of the missing canoe-ist from Cleveland prompted Darwin to hand himself in at a London police station. The case had become front page news all over the world with one national newspaper publishing a photograph of him and his wife alive and well in Panama. This development, aided by the media, led to Darwin and his wife being arrested, charged, and convicted of offences in connection with fraudulently faking his own death and claiming the life insurance.

The needs of modern major incident management and those of newsrooms can be very compatible. Journalists participate in mutual arrangements to obtain essential information, conduct interviews, and arrange photograph or interview opportunities, and the police usually take full advantage of the free publicity. Working with the media not against them has to be the norm, and without such arrangements it would be more difficult to solve crime, gain public support, and reach out to witnesses and communities.

These mutual working relationships have produced an increase in forces adopting formal media strategies and employing specialists to manage their communications. Consequently the police are far more likely to become engaged in activities that promote and project positive images. For example, it is not uncommon for forces to allow film crews and cameras behind the scenes to film investigations or live operations (eg like 'fly on the wall' type documentaries). These strategies are aimed at corporate identity management, marketing, and policy making to improve police–media relations. They are also intended to project greater efficiency, economy, and effectiveness, maintain public support, and demonstrate openness, transparency, and accountability.

The police service must always strive for professionalism when dealing with the media, and this chapter provides help and guidance for those who may become involved in doing so. The media should always be treated with respect because, used effectively, they can make an important contribution to police operations and investigations. Alternatively, they can unduly interfere with and may sometimes even impede an investigation. The media have the power and the means to relay vital messages and accurate information to tens of thousands or even millions of people. Included in these audiences will be the suspect(s), witnesses, and sources of information, the very people needed to help solve crime and protect neighbourhoods and communities.

17.2 **Who the Media are**

There are a variety of different types of media communication, for example:

- television (eg news bulletins by the BBC, ITV, SKY, etc);
- radio stations (local and national);

- newspapers, magazines, journals, leaflets, and posters;
- World Wide Web news sites (BBC, Sky, Reuters etc);
- local community websites;
- social networking sites (eg 'Flickr', 'Facebook', 'My Space', 'Piczo', 'Photo bucket' etc);
- public meetings, or using local community contact networks.

KEY POINT

The term 'media' (or mass media) refers to the main means of mass communication regarded collectively, especially through newspapers and TV/radio broadcasting.

17.3 How the Media can Support Investigations

The media can assist with:

- keeping the public informed of significant events;
- locating stolen items or those involved in the commission of an offence, eg a vehicle;
- disseminating information quickly to large audiences;
- providing accurate and timely information to the public;
- helping the public understand what the police do and why;
- making appeals for information and witnesses (eg tracing history of a vehicle involved in an offence, locating stolen items etc);
- identifying victims;
- establishing a victim's last movements;
- tracing named suspects;
- putting pressure on offenders to give themselves up, and/or admit offences;

- finding the whereabouts of missing persons;
- increasing public confidence in the police (key national target under the new police reform agenda);
- providing reassurance and/or crime prevention advice;
- developing good relations with the community;
- providing positive publicity for good work and raising the police profile.

17.4 **Avoiding Media Compromise**

If the police aren't proactive in providing accurate and regular updates of information the media will conduct their own enquiries. If they do so they may get up to mischief by reaching incorrect or inaccurate conclusions that are subsequently broadcast or published in the public domain. This can lead to a misrepresentation of facts or false information being circulated that seriously undermines an enquiry or destabilizes police/community relations and confidence. Some examples of this are:

- speculative *links* to other offences/incidents in a region or elsewhere;
- critical comments about the *location* where the incident took place;
- assertions about *motive* or *cause* behind an offence/incident/operation;
- assertions about the details of *offender(s)*;
- assertions about the details and background of *victim(s)*.

This re-emphasizes the importance of managing and working *with* as opposed to *against* the media. If a clear strategy for cooperating, managing, and controlling their activities and information flows is neglected the consequences may wreak havoc on police/public relations. It is not uncommon, for example, for reporters to track down potential witnesses and present their version of events on news bulletins

without a thorough evaluation and some necessary evidential safeguards being put into place. Worse still, reporters
could approach victims or their family and relatives before
the police get a chance to do so, which will have a devastating effect on police/community relations in causing unnecessary alarm, confusion, or distress.

KEY POINT

The media like to make attempts at negative portrayals of or challenges to the integrity or effectiveness of the police operation or
criminal justice system. They may even make links to wider social
trends, causes, or policy issues, eg increases in gun/knife attacks
or sexually motivated crime. The impact of such reporting may
be avoided or minimized by working with media agencies and/or
feeding them positive information to counterbalance the nega-
tivities anticipating in advance any adverse publicity and managing it as part of a comprehensive media strategy. Note: This may
require positive rebuttals from other agencies such as the CPS as
well as the police.

17.5 **Holding Back Information**

As a general rule it is always advisable to be open with
the media wherever possible without compromising an
enquiry. Sometimes, however, it can be tactically advantageous to withhold unique features or information about
the case under investigation. This can be useful for investigative interviewing reasons or for future appeals for
information. Unusual features of the modus operandi
are obvious examples to consider holding back, such as
the specific manner in which a crime was committed,
eg how many bullets were fired, blows struck, what part
of the body was hit, how the scene was left, what items
were stolen, or what type of weapon was used. In such

circumstances it may be worth being open by explaining why certain details are withheld, for example: 'we would not wish to reveal these details as it might prevent us from identifying the offender later on' or, 'for operational reasons we cannot reveal that information at this stage of the enquiry'.

Note: never say, *'no comment'* as it sounds dishonest or untrustworthy.

Withholding certain facts can be an extremely useful tactic in helping to prove the veracity of the offender's guilty knowledge, involvement, or subsequent confession. It can also help eliminate people who wish to falsely admit their responsibility or mislead an enquiry. Other types of information from intelligence or confidential sources (eg from CHIS) can also be more easily eliminated if it does not match with factual information that has not been disclosed.

The security and integrity of the storage of any withheld information may have to be proved to the satisfaction of a court at subsequent proceedings, particularly if the offender or a key witness provides information that has been deliberately withheld (therefore increasing its probative value). It may have to be proved beyond any reasonable doubt there was no possibility that withheld details did not leak out, therefore could only have been known by those close to the incident itself.

There may also be some instances where releasing information would breach a duty of confidentiality or contravene statutory requirements or national guidance (eg not naming rape victims). These should be carefully considered in line with relevant legislation and guidance. In difficult, sensitive, or exceptional cases the matter should be referred to a more senior officer, eg Association of Chief Police Officers (ACPO) rank and/or Senior Investigating Officer (SIO), Divisional Commander, or branch head who will make a strategic policy decision. A strategic 'Gold Group' may need forming comprised of senior officers and community representatives and other agencies to discuss and agree a media and community impact strategy on the release, timing, and format of publicly disclosed information. Such is the importance in some cases, particularly those involving critical incidents, of getting the right message across in the right manner at the right time.

17.6 **Using Holding Statements**

Initial or 'holding statements' are often used after serious incidents or in any other circumstances when it is necessary to make an early press release. This is often at a time when there is insufficient detail known about the matter being dealt with and when the media are hungry for the early release of police information. Initial statements are useful in allowing investigators to 'buy time' to consider what can and cannot be released. For instance, in homicide cases a holding statement is usually confined to the following details:

1. Confirmation the police are dealing with an incident.
2. Details of the location.
3. What it is being treated as (eg murder or suspicious death).
4. If and when there is to be a post mortem.
5. Details of an incident room location and telephone number.
6. Initial appeal for witnesses/information.

Note: Details of a deceased person are never released until after formal identification and the next of kin have been made aware.

17.7 **Managing the Media Following a Major Incident**

Not every encounter with the media occurs at major or serious incident scenes, but this is where things can go badly wrong if not brought quickly under control. An appreciation of the likely risks and complications is very important, particularly for first responders who have to take initial command and control.

The media tend to be notified quite quickly and they are likely to descend on crime or incident scenes very soon after. They may happen to be already there when the incident occurs if connected to an event they are already reporting on or involved in (eg a public event). Competitive and intimidating reporters can present an awkward distraction for responding officers, especially if TV crews, bulky vehicles, and technical equipment block or commandeer valuable space and obstruct access and egress routes. Reporters invariably try to get as close as possible to get the best shots and begin hunting around for witnesses, interviewees, and information. They will invariably try to record all police activities at the scene plus casualties, victims, crime scene evidence, or even fatalities and corpses.

In order to manage such a situation secure cordons must quickly be put in place around scenes to protect them. This must be done as quickly as possible in order to preserve and protect the integrity of a scene and keep the public and media out. This may include the use of high-sided screens to keep certain things out of the line of sight (eg corpses).

> **KEY POINT**
>
> The media have a right to be present at crime scenes provided they are public places but only in areas outside of cordons. As long as they are in a public place while they are taking photographs and filming there is no legal power to ask them to leave or to confiscate camera equipment. However, if there is a problem with the proximity of the media and public to the scene the answer lies in extending or further screening the cordons, not in arresting photographers.

Activities of the media should be managed through an appointed Media Liaison Officer (MLO) (or similar) who should aim to direct the media to an agreed location suitably positioned away from important police activities (ie a media briefing point, see below). This is where and how they are best controlled and kept regularly updated with information to service their appetite and requirement to regularly inform their viewing and listening public. A key rule about where and when not to give interviews or provide information to reporters must be strictly complied with, that is, only to be conducted in a formal, agreed manner and not informally or 'off the record'.

It is usually the role of an incident commander and/or SIO (ie silver commanders) to assume responsibility for making strategic or tactical decisions involving the media. However, sometimes more junior staff get approached and offered the chance of speaking to a reporter or providing impromptu interviews. This should generally be avoided and/or refused unless undertaken with full permission and approval of a senior manager or supervisor **beforehand.**

Two Case Studies—Media management

1. The discovery of the body of a murdered young boy in a park early one morning led to a proliferation of (inter)national and local media reporters and their vehicles and equipment converging on the scene. Large vans with transmitting dishes were soon parked in every available space, potentially disrupting scene examination and security. Reporters were keen to interview people from the local community and potential witnesses, rendering the management of the incident and investigation in danger of compromise. The first response officers, incident commander, on- call SIO, and MLO acted quickly to put secure cordons in place and gather all the media together in a location away from the scene to hold an early media briefing to satisfy their need for information and official interviews. There were some 30 to 40 journalists present at the initial briefing plus supporting technical crews, and live pictures were transmitted. Had swift action not been taken to control and manage the media the police would not have kept control of the incident scene or investigation.

2. Two males entered a public house one Sunday afternoon and opened fire on the customers. There was an exchange of gunfire and the gunmen ran out of the premises but fell to the floor, dying close by in an area overlooked by high rise flats. The media attended quickly and began taking photographs. The first officers in attendance had to use their initiative and improvise by placing loose covers over the upper bodies of the deceased and arrange makeshift secure cordons as photographers were able to take pictures from the high vantage points provided by the flats. This led to publicized pictures of the half-covered bodies on the front page of newspapers, one headline stating underneath a photograph: 'Bloodbath as families watch Manchester United on TV' (source Manchester Evening News).

17.8 Checklist for Media Management—First Responding Officers

1. Get cordons in place as quickly as possible to keep the media and public out of the scene(s).
2. Do not discuss any aspect of the case with representatives of the media. There is limited knowledge at this stage and any disclosure of incorrect information will be magnified by the press and may hinder the investigation.
3. Request attendance of an MLO as quickly as possible and inform reporters they will be officially dealt with in due course by the MLO.
4. Only engage with the media if permission is granted by a senior supervisor involved in the incident—probably of at least inspector rank or equivalent (and ideally after advice taken from an experienced MLO).
5. Remain vigilant for cunning reporters. Any approaches or requests for 'off the record' or 'informal' interviews—apply rule (2) above.

Note: Media gaffes are often caused by the actions of those who say the wrong thing inadvertently at the scene of an incident; or when they are heard talking indiscreetly within earshot of reporters, or photographed in compromising or unprofessional circumstances.

17.9 Media Briefing Points

Despite cordons media crews will still attempt to get into the best vantage points to take shots of the scene and surrounding activities. Media representatives come from a wide variety of agencies, and although the majority may be well-known and trusted, others from less well-known news agencies should be treated with caution. If there is more than one scene this will compound matters further, making the media even more difficult to control. The best option is to arrange a suitable media briefing point for all agencies. This is normally sited where journalists can still see some amount of police activity, provided it does not impact on the investigation, and serves as a place where enquiries can be fielded and formal briefings held. MLOs and/or the incident commander/SIO should consult with the media to negotiate with them if it is felt that any distressing images have been obtained that may be published or broadcast; and their own codes of practice discourage the use of inappropriate images, although the police have no formal powers of censorship.

17.10 **Devising Media Strategies**

Important in any list of investigative strategies should be an effective and comprehensive communication strategy via the media. This is a carefully formulated and recorded policy containing details of what objectives are required and how a carefully considered media strategy will assist. It can be linked to a list of objectives (eg filling information gaps), indicating what media appeals are necessary, how they can be communicated, and when, where, why, and by whom. For example, it may be a tactic to provide media interviews to appeal for witnesses directly from the crime scene by the officer in charge of the case on day two of the enquiry. The reasons would then be recorded as:

(i) the incident is likely to have been witnessed as it occurred at a time when members of the public were likely to be in the vicinity;

(ii) this is the most suitable and effective way of getting an early request out for public assistance;

(iii) images of the scene in the background may jog people's memory;

(iv) an early opportunity for an appeal is to capture testimonies before recollections are forgotten or contaminated;

(v) the officer in the case has the best knowledge and is known within the local community.

Media strategies should be dynamic, flexible, and tailored to individual circumstances as things develop. Applying too prescriptive an approach to the strategy from the outset and not adjusting to changing circumstances will invariably fail. Typical media strategies may include the following objectives:

- To manage media interest effectively and minimize misinformation.
- To prevent interference with scenes, witnesses, victims' relatives, and suspects.
- To provide the public with accurate information about the incident (or offence) and subsequent police response.
- To gain public support by showing the veracity and seriousness of an offence.
- To give due concern to the potential negative portrayal of victims, their relatives, friends, and communities.
- To request cooperation and appeal for public assistance and witnesses.
- To reduce community concerns over the fear of crime.
- To disseminate crime prevention advice.
- To request communities not to take their own action and/or appeals for calm.
- To publicize the professionalism and good work of the police and increase public confidence.

It is usually the role of the incident commander or SIO/IO to work with the MLO to formulate the media strategy. The MLO will usually be invited to take a permanent place on the SIO's management team for the duration of the investigation, including right through to conclusion at court.

17.11 **Role of Media Liaison Officers (MLOs)**

Sometimes also referred to as 'press officers', MLOs (usually part of corporate communications units) have a coordination and liaison role. This is not only for media and communications activities, but also marketing and sponsorship to promote and manage the image of the force. MLOs work at both strategic and tactical levels, communicating with external agencies and providing support to operational staff. This occurs both 'backstage' in facilitating preparation and 'frontstage' in acting as an important buffer and conduit between the media and the police. Police media relations are, by and large, far more professional when managed by MLOs who are an extremely valuable asset for those engaging with the media.

MLOs can assist in formulating media strategies and are adept at finding the right form of words and choosing the most appropriate methods and timing for communicating with the public. Creative ideas are often better discussed and developed jointly and it is the job of the MLO to spot or create media opportunities or use local contacts to improve media involvement. They also monitor the media and gauge their reaction, level of interest, and accuracy of story lines in order to anticipate media interpretations and reporting of incidents and circumstances. This is an early-warning mechanism to give ample opportunity to react and prepare a response. Knowing what has been published in the media should influence communication strategies.

An MLO usually collates all relevant media publications for enquiries and disclosure purposes at court. It is not uncommon for defence teams to make allegations about what has been said in the media, particularly when misquoting facts provided by the police. Preserved extracts then come in useful to fend off allegations.

17.12 **Checklist—Role of the MLO**

> **Checklist**
>
> - Preparation and dissemination of information about incidents
> - Analysis of media reports
> - Liaison and management of journalists and reporters at scenes
> - Logging information given out to journalists
> - Mediating between the police and media over interviews
> - Organizing media facilities/opportunities
> - Monitoring all press coverage to check accuracy and interpretation
> - Assisting in development of media strategies

17.13 **Generating Media and Public Interest**

There is generally some criterion by which news producers and gatekeepers (editors and sub-editors) select events to be presented in the news. Matters that are judged 'newsworthy' include things such as the specific characteristics of an offence or incident, the location, any victim's age, status, and background, vulnerability of victims, involvement of celebrities, linked or series crimes, race/hate crime, or major disasters. Some stories or incidents are major headlines from the very outset, while others are not considered newsworthy at all. Both of these extremes have implications for the police either in engaging with the media or getting them interested in sending out any required messages.

Incidents involving major crime such as murder and rape usually attract a substantial amount of press interest, particularly in the first few days. Thereafter interest tends to diminish, although some particularly newsworthy offences sustain media interest. Not all offences, however, attract the desired level of attention, and in these circumstances the challenge is to gain and maximize media interest and publicity.

The media like to incorporate unusual features or anything that adds value or drama to their stories. For example: CCTV footage; pictures of offenders; artists impressions; details of missing clothing; reconstructions; horrifying injuries; personal appeals from a victim's family or friends; dramatic recorded 999 calls; pictures of police raids or specialist units such as underwater search teams in full action. All these 'extras' make stories more appealing because they are dramatic and interesting. They can therefore be used to tempt media agencies into running an appeal.

Sometimes it pays to be creative. There are many methods of pro-actively putting messages across without the need to provide media interviews. Useful examples of innovative publicity-generating ideas that have been used for witness and information appeals are as follows:

- Full-size billboard posters sponsored by local/national advertising agencies.
- Full-size upright cardboard cut-outs of victims holding messages (eg 'Please help find my killers') placed in popular stores and public areas in order to attract attention and public assistance.
- Use of celebrities and sports personalities to make appeals.
- Use of modern media outlets on internet sites that attract certain audiences, eg young people (such as [[http://www. YouTube.com]], Facebook etc).
- Use of publications to target specific communities, eg gay/lesbian communities or medical journals to help identify unusual physical features, characteristics or operations of patients, victims, or suspects.
- Leaflet drops in specific geographical locations.

17.14 **Importance of Timing—Media Releases**

The timing of media releases is not only of importance to investigative needs but also to avoid causing offence to any victims, family and close friends, and the wider community. It is extremely important that any developments or releases of important information are shared with the victim's family *before* being released to the media to avoid unnecessary or unpleasant surprises.

The release of information via the media must be made at a time that produces maximum benefit for the investigation. It may, for example, be linked into other (eg covert surveillance) investigative tactics. Any release of material such as pictures or CCTV must not compromise witness interviewing strategies by contaminating or influencing recollections. It is worthwhile seeking the advice of the Crown Prosecution Service if in any doubt about the legal implications on identification procedures, for example of photographs or details of possible suspects (note: sometimes parts of images can be pixellated).

To generate maximum publicity it may be advantageous to make appeals that coincide with a significant event, such as the arrest of offenders, execution of search warrants, court appearances, or anniversaries of incidents. These can be useful links to attach appeals to and generate media and public interest.

The wider news agenda must be considered and some form of scanning to see what other newsworthy events or stories are taking place that may compete for media attention. These could be major sporting or political events and anything of a local nature that would occupy the headlines. Print deadlines or publication dates are something else to consider, particularly if it is important to include a popular local media outlet that is not printed daily.

As a general rule:

- The timing of information, messages, and appeals may be crucial to other significant lines of enquiry.
- Chronological events and developments can enhance media attention, eg the arrest of suspects or the finding of crucial CCTV footage.
- The release of information must be *after* the close family, relatives, and friends of any victim(s) involved have been traced and officially informed of the details about the incident (although not possible in every case).
- It is important, as far as possible, to check what other events are taking place that may compete for the same media interest (provided they can be foreseen).

> **Case Study—Badly timed appeal**
>
> A pre-recorded media appeal regarding the case of a hotel arsonist and double murder investigation was scheduled to go out on news bulletins on a particular day. The appeal was regrettably superseded by an unforeseen major terrorist incident that occurred at the same time. Consequently the appeal received very little or no publicity at all. The date was 11 September 2001.

17.15 **Preparing for Media Interviews**

It is advisable to establish what the primary question(s) will be, what area(s) will be covered, how long an interview will last, and any other supplementary questions or issues that need to be covered. It is vital to be clear on what objectives have to be met and what topics should be avoided. In order to anticipate lines of questioning an interviewee should remember that the interviewer, like all good investigators, will make use of the interrogative pronouns commonly referred to as the **5 × WH + H principles** (Who What, Why,

Where, When, and How). For example: Who was responsible? What happened and what do the police know? Why did it happen? Where and when did it happen? How did it happen? etc.

Drafting key words and messages (usually three is sufficient) and keeping them handy on a small piece of paper for ease of reference and last-minute rehearsal is a great tip. It must also be remembered that the media may have their own agenda and try to ambush or embarrass an interviewee with a certain topic or critique and it is worthwhile anticipating this in advance. If it does happen a rule to remember is one of *turning negatives into positives*. So if an interviewer focuses on any negative aspect of a police response or investigation, the interviewee should aim to try and turn it back into a positive. For example, a reporter may say that a crime is one of a series and the police seem to be doing nothing about it. This can be turned into a positive by a response along the lines that the police have done a lot of excellent work (including other agencies if involved) since the first occurrence and a major police operation is underway with targeted high visibility patrols in the locality who are working with local community groups and arranging crime prevention advice etc.

Thinking and preparing carefully about the objectives of an interview is the key to success, together with a rehearsal on putting it across beforehand (which is what the professionals do). Then it can be delivered in a more confident, enthusiastic, and positive style.

17.16 **Using Appropriate Language**

Plain 'everyday' language is always more preferable with a strict avoidance of police jargon, buzz phrases, or acronyms. Frequently repeated internal police terms such as 'intelligence-led policing' or 'sanction detections' are not phrases easily understood by members of the public and sound artificial when used in media interviews. It is better to use clear and understandable terms that the public can relate to and understand; for example, 'females' are women and 'males' are men. The use of everyday language reaches out to listeners and readers and is a lot better than using official terminology, so the key is to resist any temptation to use police clichés. The best way to get people's interest and support is to use language that has meaning for them, such as: 'Can you imagine what it must have been like for a poor lady to have her handbag ripped out of her hand and pushed to the floor while walking home from the shops...?'; or 'What if it was your son, brother or best friend left bleeding to death on the pavement. . .?'

When providing interviews or contributing to media releases and publicity material, there must be strict adherence to what in some forces is termed 'appropriate language'. This is simply to safeguard against offending certain sections of the community and should recognize issues of diversity, such as faith and culture. The use of discriminatory, prejudicial, or exclusive language indicates a lack of professionalism and encourages the exclusion, devaluing, and stereotyping of groups or individuals. Correct terminology is important, together with a strict adherence to force diversity policies (eg knowing what the correct term is for 'gangs' or 'street workers', ie not prostitutes).

17.17 **Who Should Speak to the Media?**

Subject to the safeguards and protocols mentioned earlier, generally speaking all officers or police staff are able to speak with the media, particularly if the subject matter is within their own area of knowledge or expertise. The interviewee should be an appropriate person who can talk on the given subject and provide factual information. If the interview is going to be about a significant or controversial issue then advice should always be sought from an MLO, and in all cases officers and staff below inspector rank or equivalent should secure the agreement of their line manager. Usually the seriousness of the incident will dictate what level of rank or position should be used for fronting-up media interviews or being the strategic lead for communicating as 'one voice' (or 'talking head' as they are sometimes called).

It is sometimes a useful tactic to utilize locally recognizable officers, especially if public reassurance or community issues and tensions are at stake. Use should be made of specific skills or knowledge of relevant staff and those who may have particularly relevant language, faith or cultural skills or background that can provide effective communication for a specific audience.

KEY POINT

1. Anticipate the line of questioning. It can be agreed beforehand what topics a police interviewee is willing to answer. For example, local policing issues that may be at stake such as a build-up of previous similar incidents, concerns about crime prevention, safety issues, or where police cordons or activity post-incident are likely to be disruptive.
2. Draft out key words and **3 x key messages**, keeping them readily accessible on a small piece of paper for ease of reference and last minute rehearsal.

17.18 **Types of Media Interviews**

Whatever the type of media, whether print, radio, TV, or internet etc, interviews generally have the following different levels of engagement:

- **Formal Interviews**. These are pre-arranged with the interviewer and likely to have prepared questions and researched areas to discuss. The interviewee gets a chance to fully prepare. Usually recorded in note form, on tape, or on camera.

- **Pre-recorded Interviews**. These provide an opportunity to pause and re-record comments that haven't come across well or have been said badly (provided the reporter agrees). Sometimes for convenience they are recorded down a telephone line. The main disadvantage is they can be edited and important messages, such as public appeals may be blanked out.

- **Live Interviews**. Far more pressurized as there is only one shot at it and the interviewer can stray from agreed areas and ask awkward questions that are difficult to avoid because the broadcast is 'live' (eg about mistakes or criticisms). This is a favoured method in 'breaking news' headlines on news bulletins. Not for the 'faint hearted' or inexperienced, although there are benefits because messages cannot be edited once they have been made by the interviewee.

- **Press Conferences (or 'media facilities')**. The traditional method of allowing a large number of media representatives to hear the same message all at once to save time. Used for significant announcements that are likely to attract a lot of media interest. Prepared statements can be read out and members of the public such as victims' relatives may appear on them. Question and answer sessions can be added if appropriate at the end.

> ### KEY POINT—INFORMAL INTERVIEWS
>
> These often occur when a reporter gets a police source to agree (often spontaneously and unprompted) to provide an interview, either in person or on a phone. A superficial, casual, or friendly nature and approach may lull the interviewee into becoming 'off guard' and saying something they later regret. Absence of note-taking or recording devices may betray the intent to use the comments, or produce a distorted version. They are also known as 'off the record' interviews and must be treated with extreme caution. It is wiser to treat everything as being 'on the record' as the reporter may be trustworthy but their editor who has final say may not be.

17.19 **Partner Agencies**

The police normally act as the lead agency for crime matters and a coordination point for all statements released by other agencies that may also be involved in the incident and/or investigation. It is good practice to ensure all parties are kept appraised of media statements and are given an opportunity for feedback. Partners should, when appropriate be involved in formulating joint press releases (eg local authority or Crown Prosecution Service). It must firstly be discussed and agreed with the partner agency as to who has primacy in providing the information. Partners could include the following, although not an exhaustive list:

- Local authorities (in particular social services or education Departments)
- Local schools
- Youth clubs
- Community organizations
- Health authorities, mental health trusts, hospitals, etc
- Prison authorities
- UK Border Agency, Home Office, etc

- Probation Service
- Crown Prosecution Service
- Other emergency services, such as ambulance or the fire and rescue service
- Private sector companies, including airports, airlines
- Retail outlets, football clubs, etc
- Other forces, including British Transport Police (BTP).

Good liaison ensures nothing is issued that compromises an agency or an enquiry. In a major investigation this may involve close working arrangements and perhaps even co-location. There may be a requirement for seeking external advice and guidance from bodies such as independent advisory groups (IAGs) regarding specific community issues and formulating the precise wording of media statements or responses. This may be a vital strategic requirement as badly chosen/offending wording can sometimes have a dramatic effect on community and/or victim relations.

17.20 **Legal Issues**

The police must be careful with providing information and anything issued or released must be accurate and should not jeopardize criminal or civil proceedings, compromise investigations, put lives at risk, or impact inappropriately on people's right to privacy (eg ECHR Article 6 right to a fair trial, Article 8 right to a private and family life, and Article 14 prohibition on discrimination).

Any information released to the media must be properly recorded and retained and is potentially disclosable under the CPIA rules (Criminal Procedure & Investigations Act 1996). When taking a case to court the Crown Prosecution Service and in most cases defence teams are allowed access to everything, including what has appeared or been stated in the press. For this reason all media interviews and press cuttings need to be retained and stored ready for court, normally a function of the MLO.

When an investigation goes into post-charge phase, the due legal process comes into force. Historically some cases have encountered particular problems over the press gaining access to, and in one case publishing, pictures of a suspect prior to charge or the commencement of the trial. Media agencies invariably have access to their own legal advisors and forces should be willing to draw this kind of behaviour to the attention of the Press Complaints Commission (PCC).

After criminal proceedings become active the media are bound by the subjudice rule and provisions of the Contempt of Court Act 1981. These prevent them from publishing or broadcasting material that creates a 'substantial risk of serious prejudice' to the impending proceedings.

Case study—Harold Shipman trial

During the trial of the serial killer Dr Harold Shipman one radio station broadcast the news that Shipman had been found guilty before the jury had returned with their verdict. The radio station was held in contempt of court by the trial judge.

17.21 **Training**

The earlier in a career officers and frontline staff get used to talking to the media the easier it becomes, and there is generally a lot of training and support available. The most should be made of any opportunity to get training and practise because it may one day come in very useful. Appearing in the media is an ideal way of not only promoting the force but also promoting a unit's or an individual's image and profile amongst colleagues, supervisors, and the general public.

Checklist—Media handling and interview tips

The Dos...

- Take full advantage of advice from an MLO.
- Be clear about the aims and objectives of an interview.
- Retain control of the interview by refocusing on the issues the interviewee wants to talk about (and get messages in as often as possible).
- Ask what type of questions will be asked beforehand so answers can be prepared.
- Prepare and practice thoroughly—identify and remember 3 x key messages.
- Research any current 'hot topics' in the media. Think outside the box—know what's going on currently and if it could have an impact on your interview.
- Remember the interviewer will use the 5 x WH & H principles—Who? What? When? Where? Why? and How?
- Don't waffle. Answers are probably whittled down into 'sound bites' so make sure they're good ones.
- Stay relaxed, confident, and positive.
- Don't be nervous—treat the interviewer as one individual and ignore how many others may watch or listen.
- Check appearance, hair, tie, etc (if on camera).
- Check what material is displayed in the background and remove inappropriate or confidential material.
- Ignore noise and/or activity taking place off-camera.
- Look at the person interviewing, not the camera (unless directed otherwise).
- Use straightforward, everyday, plain language, *not* police-speak or jargon.
- Try to empathize if dealing with a tragic or sensitive incident or issue (offer condolences when appropriate).
- Be clear about the things that cannot be talked about, such as pending or ongoing court cases (or sensitive issues).
- Steer clear of giving personal views on subjects—know your force's media policy and stick to the party line.
- Ensure the victim's family is informed about the contents of any media release or interview *before* it is released.
- Ensure messages are clear and strong, stating exactly what is wanted from the public (ie do not just appeal for 'general information'—be specific).

- Be creative, consider other means of getting messages directly out to communities, eg leaflets, posters, or the internet.
- Never say 'No comment'—it sounds suspicious. Give reasons why a question cannot be answered, or information released (useful alternatives are 'It is too early to say . . .' or 'That will be looked into as part of the ongoing investigation. . .').
- Avoid comments that imply guilt or innocence—never discuss the evidence.
- Use cognitive prompts wherever possible (eg such as a major sporting event).
- Emphasize the importance of all information, no matter how trivial.
- Remember to state the number of the incident room (write it down!).
- Ensure there is an appropriate answering-machine recorded message and policy for regularly checking the incident room number, if giving out to the public or media.
- Inform the media as soon as possible when a suspect is charged. This helps to prevent the possibility of them inadvertently breaching the Contempt of Court Act and jeopardizing the case. Confirm the name, date of birth, address, full details of charges, and court date.
- Consider giving positive crime prevention advice along with reports of crime and offer public reassurance and help ease the fear of crime.
- Publicize good work, particularly heroics or important court results.
- Use interesting facets of the case to gain extra publicity and interest from the media (eg some useful CCTV footage).
  The Don'ts...
- Give out information concerning the incident to members of the public or media without being authorized by a senior supervisor.
- Wear checked or stripy clothing on camera (they go blurred on camera).
- Have an alcoholic drink beforehand to calm your nerves.
- Fidget or sway on or stare at your feet.

- Stare directly at the camera—look at the interviewer (unless you are doing a 'down-the-lens' where the reporter is at a different venue.
- Drop your guard and make 'off the cuff' remarks, as the microphone could be still switched on.
- Respond to the reporter's questions with just 'Yes' or 'No' answers. Try to avoid starting your responses with 'Yes that's correct, I think . . .'.
- Let the reporter try to put words into your mouth or try to get you to agree to what they are saying. (Instead use phrases such as 'well, that's one point of view but from a force perspective . . .').
- Lower your voice or appear uninterested—always look and sound confident, enthusiastic, and in control.
- Never criticize the criminal justice system or other agencies.

And remember. . .dealing confidently with the media is an ideal way of raising your profile.

17.22 **Conclusion**

The media are a highly influential institution that hold the police to account for their actions and progress in operations and investigations. As a publicly-funded body it is the duty of the police to remain open and transparent with them wherever possible. For most people there is no regular or direct contact with the police or criminal justice system, and heavy reliance is placed on media news reports for access to information. What the public watch, read, or listen to has major implications on perceptions and opinions of the police and other law enforcement agencies, including offenders and victims.

The best way to ensure a clear and positive message is sent out is by pro-actively engaging with media agencies. Most forces employ MLOs who are specialists and should, wherever possible, be consulted for their assistance and advice.

Inaccurate reporting and negative coverage can be avoided by being more professional. Provided the important safeguards and guidelines outlined in the chapter are adhered to there should be no reason to fear the task of engaging with or managing the press and broadcasting agencies.

The police should always take full advantage of opportunities for access to free publicity and support for major investigations in order to reach out and appeal to witnesses and communities. Improving the police image and increasing public confidence and support through good use of the media has been incorporated into routine police procedures and has to be at the forefront of any investigative strategy.

Chapter 18

The Government Protective Marking Scheme

18.1 **Introduction**

The Government Protective Marking Scheme (GPMS) is a system for protecting information that comprises the classification (marking) of documents, the storing of material, and audited handling (including destruction) of classified documents. It has been adopted widely across government and amongst public authorities and is also used by some private sector organizations that regularly work with public sector organizations employing the GPMS.

The Association of Chief Police Officers (ACPO) formally adopted the GPMS for use in the police service in 2001 but its implementation within the service appears to have been inconsistent and unequal.

Other criminal justice sector and security sector organizations use GPMS, and its consistent application across all users is integral to the safe passing of information between partner organizations and a more integrated partnership working. Proper implementation demonstrates to other organizations that any information they share will be appropriately handled. Organizations implementing GPMS undertake to handle information that is passed to them in compliance with the standards set in GPMS. This fundamental confidence underpins partnership working.

For example, the probation service utilizes the GPMS and information shared with probation officers should be shared on the basis that it will be handled according to

GPMS standards. Within Multi-Agency Public Protection Arrangements (MAPPA) collaborations, where universal application of GPMS could facilitate information-sharing, it will be necessary to ensure all parties comply with, or are capable of complying with, GPMS standards.

Most police officers and staff will probably encounter RESTRICTED and CONFIDENTIAL material. Those assigned to certain duties will encounter material with higher classifications.

18.2 **GPMS Criteria Explained**

The classification criteria used within the GPMS are:

- TOP SECRET
- SECRET
- CONFIDENTIAL
- RESTRICTED
- UNCLASSIFIED

These are further defined in terms of harm likely to be caused in the event of improper handling, unauthorized disclosure, loss, theft, or destruction of the information contained within the classified document (see Table 18.1).

In other words: **if this information fell into the wrong hands, what damage would be caused?**

Organizational or personal embarrassment arising from disclosure by inefficiency or administrative error is not a valid reason for classifying a document.

Table 18.1

The Government Protective Marking Scheme, adopted and implemented by ACPO, 16 February 2001
Top Secret   • threaten directly the internal stability of the UK or friendly countries   • lead directly to widespread loss of life

- cause exceptionally grave damage to the effectiveness or security of UK or allied forces or to the continuing effectiveness of extremely valuable security or intelligence operations

- cause exceptionally grave damage to relations with friendly governments

- cause severe long-term damage to the UK economy

Secret
- raise international tension

- seriously damage relations with friendly governments

- threaten life directly or seriously prejudice public order or individual security or liberty

- cause serious damage to the operational effectiveness or security of UK or allied forces or the continuing effectiveness of highly valuable security or intelligence operations

- cause substantial material damage to national finances or economic and commercial interests

Confidential
- materially damage diplomatic relations, that is, cause formal protest or other sanctions

- prejudice individual security or liberty

- cause damage to the operational effectiveness or security of UK or allied forces or the effectiveness of valuable security or intelligence operations

- work substantially against national finances or economic and commercial interests

- substantially undermine the financial viability of major organizations

- impede the investigation or facilitate the commission of serious crime

- seriously impede the development or operation of major government policies

- shut down or otherwise substantially disrupt significant national operations

Restricted
- adversely affect diplomatic relations

- cause substantial distress to individuals

- make it more difficult to maintain the operational effectiveness or security of UK or allied forces

(continued)

- cause financial loss or loss of earning potential to, or facilitate improper gain or advantage for, individuals or companies
- prejudice the investigation or facilitate the commission of crime
- breach proper undertakings to maintain the confidence of information provided by third parties
- impede the effective development or operation of government policies
- breach statutory restrictions on disclosure of information
- disadvantage government in commercial or policy negotiations with others
- undermine the proper management of the public sector and its operations

Unclassified   All other material

It is the responsibility of the document creator to classify the document.

When assigning a classification it is not necessary to try to calculate the likelihood of unauthorized disclosure, merely the consequential harm of such disclosure.

All classifications are determined on the basis of the likely harmful impact of an unauthorized disclosure to a third party (see Table 18.2).

Table 18.2

Example (based on Home Office guidance to probation officers available at <http://www.probation2000.com>, accessed 16 August 2008)

Appropriate classifications when measured against consequences of unauthorized disclosure of a document containing personal details

No one would be affected (subject to there being no breach of Data Protection Act requirements)	**Not Protectively Marked**
Person(s) identifiable from the document may be subject to verbal abuse and become distressed	**RESTRICTED**

Person(s) identifiable from the document would be unable to carry out normal activities and movements	**CONFIDENTIAL**
Person(s) identifiable from the document would be subject to physical harm	**CONFIDENTIAL**
There would be a direct threat to life	**SECRET**
There would be a serious risk to public order	**SECRET**

Recipients of the document are expected to handle it in accordance with the appropriate procedures laid down for each classification standard.

Potential weaknesses of the classification element of the GPMS are the dangers of under- and over-classification. Over-classification is more likely given that individuals are risk-averse and more likely to 'play safe'. But, as the ACPO guidance below illustrates, over-classification creates its own significant problems.

ACPO guidance

ACPO memo (unclassified) to police forces, dated 16 February 2001, paragraph 5 (emphasis added).

'Users should be made aware of the dangers of over-classification, which, in the experience of the armed forces and other Government organizations, quickly becomes endemic unless stringent controls are applied at local level. **Over-classification leads rapidly to a devaluation of the entire protective marking scheme.** It can also result in substantial, but largely unseen costs as a result of greater use of expensive secure channels of communication, a requirement for extra numbers of specially trained and vetted staff, waste of time and resources on unnecessary use of cumbersome document handling procedures, etc.'

18.3 **GPMS and Freedom of Information**

Classification does not automatically exempt documents from duties to disclose under the Freedom of Information Act 2000. Material content should be considered and the relevant statutory exemptions applied only after consultation with the owner of the information and other relevant parties. The length of time that has passed since information was originally classified may be an important factor in considering whether restrictions are still necessary.

For further information see: ACPO *Freedom of Information Manual* (produced on behalf of ACPO by Hampshire Constabulary, 2006).

18.4 **Classification of Collected Material**

Whereas individual documents may attract one level of classification, taken together as a body of information a collection of documents may warrant a higher classification than any of the constituent documents, because the likely harm were all these documents to be subject to unauthorized disclosure exceeds the potential harm arising from just one of the documents being disclosed. So in reviewing whether information and intelligence has been appropriately classified, it will be necessary to consider whether documents taken together warrant a higher level of classification.

For example, documents A, B, C, D, and E have each individually been classified as 'Restricted' in status. Before disseminating all five documents as a collection, the person undertaking or authorizing the dissemination will need to decide whether the collection taken as a whole should be reformulated into one dissemination document with an overall 'Confidential' classification because of the cumulative risk of harm should all the information taken as a whole fall into the 'wrong hands'.

18.5 **Reduced Classification**

Where information that has been previously classified legitimately enters the public domain and is available from open sources, then reclassification or declassification of documents relating to that information must be considered, provided that no harm might arise to the original source of the information as a result of declassifying documents and rendering them liable to wider disclosure and dissemination.

18.6 **Handling Guidelines**

Organizational policies may prescribe enhanced measures, but the the minimum standards necessary in order to comply with GPMS are as laid out in Table 18.3.

Table 18.3

Action	RESTRICTED	CONFIDENTIAL
Marking	Displayed in block capitals at top and bottom of every page.	Displayed in block capitals at top and bottom of every page.
Storage of information	Protected by one barrier (eg locked filing cabinet in a secure building).	Two barriers required (eg locked filing cabinet within a locked room in a secure building.
Disposal of information	Secure waste sacks, in secure location when unattended.	Cross-cut shredder.

(continued)

Action	RESTRICTED	CONFIDENTIAL
Disposal of magnetic media	Cut floppy discs into quarters, dispose with normal waste. CD Roms destroy completely.	Cut floppy discs into quarters, dispose with normal waste. CD Roms destroy completely.
Internal mail within the organization	Sealed envelope with protective marking shown.	Sealed envelope with protective marking shown. (Re-usable transit envelopes may not be used.)
Transmission between different force areas or other agencies	By post or courier, in a sealed envelope, with NO protective markings visible.	By post or courier in two sealed envelopes, both fully addressed. Protective marking on inner envelope only. Outer envelope to show sender's address.
Internal/public telephone networks	May be used.	May be used.
Mobile phones (including text messaging)	Digital phones may be used.	Digital phones may be used if cases of operational urgency. Brief conversations using guarded speech.
WAP phones	Not allowed.	Not allowed.
Pagers	Not allowed.	Not allowed.
Government Secure Extranet (GSX) or Government Secure Intranet (GSI)	May be used.	May be used with Communications-Electronics Security Group (CESG) enhanced encryption.
Internet	Government-approved encryption required.	May not be used.
Fax	Ensure recipient is at receiving machine to take immediate possession.	May not be used.

NB: The Criminal Justice Secure email system has been designed to support transmission of information only up to RESTRICTED level.

Secret and Top Secret information requires separate handling regimes and enhanced security. Seek advice from the organizational security officer.

It will be seen from Table 18.3 that classified documents should not be left unattended on desks (clear desk policy).

18.7 **Access to Classified Material**

Access to certain categories of classified information is restricted to individuals who have undergone *security vetting*. Security vetting is a requirement attached to certain roles and posts within the police service and partner agencies.

There are different levels of security vetting. In ascending order of significance they are:

- counter-terrorism checks (CTC);
- security clearance (SC); and
- developed vetting (DV).

This hierarchical framework determines who may access what. It will also dictate with which members of an organization members of partner agencies are prepared to collaborate.

18.8 **'Need to Know' Principle**

The *'need to know' principle* applies to ensure that, even within the hierarchical vetting framework, access to sensitive information is restricted to those who have a specific need to know. Dissemination should be limited to colleagues (from whichever agency including the information holder's own) which have a legitimate need to know AND have the appropriate clearance to access the information.

Those who 'own' the information usually decide who has a specific 'need to know'. This has the potential flaw that in making such decisions, the decision-makers may not always be aware of whether others have a specific need to know a particular item of information. The 'need to know' principle focuses on the protection of sources, techniques, and information itself. This narrow perception, however, has the potential to sustain an overly restrictive approach.

There are two questions decision-makers have to ask themselves in applying the 'need to know' principle:

- Who 'needs to know' the information in the format in which it currently exists?
- Is it possible to sanitize the presentation of the information in its entirety or in part in order to share the intelligence without compromising sources, techniques, or other information?

These tests will determine the widest possible options in terms of information sharing, which should minimize occasions in which information that could and should have been shared is withheld.

18.9 **Conclusion**

The purpose of the GPMS and its related practices is to reinforce the professionalism of and professional standards within policing. In an age of increasing partnership working the GPMS provides an information security norm that is intended to transcend individual agency and organizational practice and so enhance multi-agency collaboration.

PART THREE
Neighbourhood Policing

Chapter 19

The Context and Importance of Neighbourhood Policing

19.1 **Introduction**

The sense of community, of belonging to a defined geographical location or self-identified social/religious/ethnic group, and the importance of security, order, and well-being within that community, is fundamental to human well-being. Increased population, increased industrialization and urbanization, increased access to travel and communications have all influenced the development of communities, including new intangible communities extant within the virtual world of the internet, members of which may never have met each other. The purpose of policing is to keep the peace within and between communities.

It is sometimes a difficult balance between, on one hand, the careful monitoring of who is doing what in order to prevent crime and anti-social behaviour, and on the other, not interfering with the rights and freedom of the individual to do whatever is not prohibited by law. The police are key players in these local partnerships, making the connections, encouraging communication with all groups and people within those neighbourhood communities, helping with problem-solving, and meeting local needs for social order and good behaviour.

Neighbourhood policing is posited as a return to traditional policing forms and methods after some periods of necessary adjustment to a changing world, including perhaps the rise and rise of the motor vehicle, the increased mobility of the population, and the increase in the expectations of comfort and prosperity which have meant changes in the way that people are policed. Further, modern communities are not static in the old way; populations flux, work patterns develop or mutate, neighbourhoods physically change, and, especially within urban areas of towns and cities, districts can rise or fall in the economic sphere, thus attracting (or repelling) different kinds of communities to settle, however temporarily.

There has also been a seismic shift in police attitudes to such communities. No longer is policing simply something which is 'done to' neighbourhoods and to people. The role of the police officer was never entirely about obtaining compliance with the law; there was always an element of the role of social worker, community supporter, and protector of the vulnerable or weak. However, there has been a very tangible shift indeed in the police priorities for any community. *Now the emphasis is upon reflecting the needs, anxieties, and concerns of that community, and attempting to address them through mutual help and partnerships.*

It is that which we will explore throughout this Neighbourhood Policing section of the Handbook. For the remainder of this short introduction, though, we want to show how 'the mental landscape' of policing has changed to encompass neighbourhoods within the last ten years and what this means to those who work in local partnerships.

19.2 **Public Consultation**

In 2004, the Government produced a pre-legislative White Paper (a consultation document) called *Building Communities, Beating Crime*, which sought views about how policing and other public service providers could work *with* communities, and provide a response to communities' anxieties about crime. For a number of years previously, public consultation had shown (through research studies like the annual (from 1981) British Crime Survey) that, whatever the reported state of crime, the public was anxious and perturbed about many different manifestations of local disorder and anti-social behaviour. In many instances, recorded crime had gone down, but people's perception of lawlessness had increased. The Government concluded that the way forward was to give communities the opportunity to be consulted about how they were policed. The then Home Secretary announced a commitment to create:

> neighbourhood policing teams across the country using the latest real time data and intelligence and backed up by the latest technology.

In 2005, a national *Community Safety Plan* (CSP) was published, which incorporated much of the substance of the opinion-gathering heralded by *Building Communities, Beating Crime*. The CSP gave key priorities and key actions to the police to deliver in partnership with other public services and with the communities, in order to deliver safer neighbourhoods. These can be summarized as:

- making neighbourhoods stronger and safer;
- protecting the public and building confidence in the police and other public services;
- reducing crime and anti-social behaviour;
- improving people's lives so that they are less likely to commit offences, or to re-offend.

At the time of writing the Government is engaged in the latest consultation project seeking to understand community expectations of the police service in a changing world: *From the Neighbourhood to the National: Policing our Communities Together* (Cm 7448, Home Office, London, 2008). The Government envisages an enhanced role for the public in determining the direction of policing and an enhanced community role in tackling crime. The success of such a vision depends on healthy and robust relations between the police and the community.

19.2.1 Distinctions: 'Community' and 'Neighbourhood'

It may be timely to think of the difference between 'neighbourhood' and 'community', which, until this point, have been used almost interchangeably. For the purposes of clarity, we may define **neighbourhood** as *a distinct geographical location* (where people live), *with recognized political or physical boundaries*. A **community**, by contrast, may be much looser, because it can be *a group with shared interests or occupations*, it can be *demographic* (based on age), or derived from *shared beliefs* (church or faith groups); it can even refer to groups of *people with common problems* (like those with some form of impairment, or those brought together by a fear of social disorder). In its *Progress Report on Neighbourhood Policing* (Baggott and Wallace in 2006; see Further Reading), the Home Office noted that:

> A 'neighbourhood' to an inner-city resident is very different from someone living in a rural area. For the former, their neighbourhood could be a few streets or the estate where they live; for the person in the country, it could be their village, or group of villages, or parish. Local communities, police forces, police authorities and partners are deciding what neighbourhoods mean—rather than being told by the Government—but typically, we would expect it to cover one or two local authority wards.

With all these distinctions in mind, it may be simplest to think of 'neighbourhood' as place and 'community' as groups of people with something in common.

19.2.2 Creating Neighbourhood Policing Teams

The Home Office produced a strategic plan called *Confident Communities in a Secure Britain* in 2005 and it was this which committed the Government to new investment to strengthen the role of neighbourhood policing (59–67). Indeed, central government has put some energy into urging both police forces and local government/public service providers to cooperate in neighbourhood policing teams (NPTs), and it made a commitment to have an NPT operating in every community by April 2008. The Government actually missed its target by some distance, but there is an undeniable momentum, backed with some central funding, for the creation of NPTs across England (Wales has a complementary system, backed by the Welsh Assembly). We look in detail at the composition and role of such teams in Chapter 21, but it is worth summarizing here the components of the 'typical' NPT, bearing in mind the likely variations between police forces. NPTs may differ in some respects from what is described below; but, as the Government noted, it is up to local communities, police forces, and partners to decide what they will do at a local level to create an NPT and what characteristics that team will have. The components of the actual team will be decided by available local resources.

A typical NPT would consist of:

- **a police sergeant**: team leader and responsible for tasking individual team members; liaison into the rest of the force and with the local Basic Command Unit (BCU);
- **uniformed police officers**: acting as community leaders and tackling problems (not always crimes) which might at some point require the full range of police officer powers, such as arrest or caution;
- **police community support officers** (PCSOs): uniformed support staff members of the police force, with lesser powers than those of police officers (and, some would argue, less extensive training) but who provide a 'high-visibility, reassuring presence in communities and who provide follow-up to victims of crime' (Baggott and Wallace, 2006). They can have an immediate impact on a neighbourhood in dealing with nuisance behaviour and disorder. The 'police' element in the title comes from PCSOs acting under the authority of the Chief Constable of the police force. Other community support officers, such as rural or neighbourhood wardens (see below), are

employed by local authorities. Some are part-financed by partners, such as schools and local authorities;

- **Special constables** are part-time, unpaid volunteers with full police powers. 'Specials' carry warrant cards and work alongside their 'regular' police colleagues. It may be that in some areas, there are few or no Specials in NPTs;

- **neighbourhood and other warden schemes**: as noted above under PCSOs, neighbourhood wardens, rural wardens and the like, are often designated as community support officers, with uniforms distinct from the police and usually carrying a local authority logo. Wardens can be the first point of contact for local people with local concerns, particularly in matters outside the criminal law such as street lighting and littering;

- **other local authority staff**: these work within communities in roles such as park-keepers, environmental health inspectors, local authority housing officers and so on. They are tuned into neighbourhood needs and problems and can often bring potential problems to the attention of the NPT. They are not usually under the command of the NPT police sergeant but are invited to share common approaches and to feel part of the team tackling local problems.

19.2.3 The Focus is Upon Delivery

Some forces will have internal divisions within these roles (such as supervising PCSOs), but variations in the local composition of teams are to be expected. The essential points are that:

- teams should focus on the delivery of neighbourhood safety and respond to community concerns;
- members of the teams should be familiar faces and known by the communities in the neighbourhood;
- abstraction of the police officers on other duties should be kept to a minimum;

- there should be widespread and continuous consultation with the communities in determining any given NPT response.

That said, the police response to crime cannot be varied or set aside; communities cannot expect that the police will ignore some crimes, such as drugs taking, in favour of dealing with community concerns about, say, car theft and 'joyriding'. Policing a neighbourhood must be imperturbably impartial. But the communities can and do indicate to the NPT what their own priorities are. These are reflected in the **key principles of neighbourhood policing** (which we explore in greater detail in Chapter 20), which include *visible and accessible police*, an *influence* over community safety priorities, *interventions* in joint actions, and the *provision of answers* and responses to community concerns, such as tackling anti-social behaviour.

19.3 **Partnerships**

Wherever possible, neighbourhood policing teams will seek to make common cause with other agencies and public service providers in the locality. Crime and Disorder Reduction Partnerships (CDRPs) were created by the 1998 Crime and Disorder Act (section 6 (c37)); such partnerships were reviewed in the 2004 White Paper, *Building Communities, Beating Crime*. Local Criminal Justice Boards (LCJBs), introduced in April 2003 to improve the delivery of justice, improve the service to witnesses, and increase public confidence in the criminal justice system, are also instrumental in working with NPTs in providing coherent responses to crime reduction, the misuse of drugs, and anti-social behaviour. Both CDRPs and LCJBs tend, though, to operate at a tactical level similar to that of a BCU. Neighbourhood problems of a more parochial nature might not be surfaced, which is why the role of the NPT team leader in liaising with local community leaders, local authority members, and with key opinion formers is so important.

19.3.1 Partnership at Work—a Scenario

Scenario—Disruption at the Museum

The town's museum had been a bit of a quiet backwater until a smart new shopping complex was built directly opposite the museum's entrance. People began to take a half hour 'wander' in the museum, including visiting its coffee shop, as well as shopping in the new mall. Unfortunately, this proximity attracted some anti-social elements as well, who sometimes abused museum stewards, whilst the area behind the museum, which adjoined a public park, became a haunt for drugs-taking and alcohol abuse. Some objects on display in the museum were stolen and the Trustees from the Borough Council were at a loss what they should do.

Contact was made within the museum, informally, with local PCSOs, who patrolled the shopping mall, and PCSOs began to include the museum site and the park beyond in their 'beats'. More formal contact was then made between the museum manager and the sergeant leading the local NPT, which developed the museum's concerns into a full-blown Tasking and Coordinating Group (T&CG) intelligence-requirement and led to specific NPT deployments. Additionally, the local police training college provided conflict-management training for the museum stewards, who felt more confident as a result that they could challenge poor behaviour by visitors. The NPT sergeant also ensured that other local authority teams were involved; the replacement of a gravel path with a tarmac strip, and the removal altogether of a rockery in the park meant that idle stone-throwing ceased. The provision by the Borough Council of CCTV cameras at the rear of the museum's premises, as the result of a CDRP initiative, reduced nuisance behaviour further.

> The museum manager now sits on the local CDRP and has regular liaison with the NPT leader. The museum is not just part of the NPT's informal beat, but an active part of its daily tasking and interaction. The reduction in offences has generated good local publicity and visitor numbers to the museum have increased because families no longer feel threatened by the congregation of drinkers and other rowdy elements.

This scenario shows that coordinated effort, the coming together of parts of the community which may not routinely consult with each other, can produce dividends in terms of local law and order. The role of the NP team leader in actively promoting this is crucial. In our example, the NPT had applied national intelligence model (NIM) principles—see Chapter 14—to the problems, and the involvement of the local BCU's T&CG as well as the CDRP, meant that solutions were swiftly found.

This may not be the end of the local nuisance and offending at the museum of course; conditions would rapidly deteriorate if matters were allowed to slide and patrols, for example, were neglected. This leads us to state an important principle about neighbourhood policing: *it will be credible and desirable only as long as the crime reduction initiatives are sustained*. Reduced vigilance may discredit local efforts and dismay the communities involved. Crime prevention and crime reduction are explored further in Chapter 26.

19.4 **Evaluating Neighbourhood Policing**

Perhaps we need to draw a distinction, in any objective evaluation, between community perceptions of safety and improved quality of life on one hand, and whether or not neighbourhood policing has direct influence on crime attrition and 'brought to justice' outcomes, on the other.

19.4.1 Extended Evaluation

From 2002 to 2005, the Research, Development and Statistics Directorate of the Home Office conducted an evaluation of the National Reassurance Policing Programme (NRPP), which underpins neighbourhood policing, across 16 sites in 8 police forces. The research sought to measure the impact of the NRPP, particularly the public perception of crime, anti-social behaviour, worry about crime, public engagement, satisfaction and confidence in the police and levels of social capacity. The evaluation concluded in 2006 that there was a consistent picture of positive change:

- Reported crime fell by *twice as much* in the pilot areas compared with other sites which did not have neighbourhood policing.
- Public confidence in the police *increased by a third* in the NPT sites, five times that in the sites without NPT.
- Communities noticed *a decrease in anti-social behaviour* in sites with NPT. Sites without NTP saw an increase in perceptions of problems with young people.
- The communities in the pilot sites *reacted favourably* to knowing their NP teams by name.

(adapted from the Home Office: *Neighbourhood Policing Progress Report* 2006, see Further Reading)

Of these indicators, the reduction in reported crime is probably the most important and the factor that most needs to be sustained. There have been subsequent surveys (few on the same scale), as we note in Further Reading, the principal findings of which corroborate initial positive findings concerning the fall in reported crime and improved police/community relations.

19.5 **Conclusions**

At the time of writing the nature and role of policing is under review. However the purpose and infrastructure of policing may change, the need to reflect and respond to community concerns will remain.

Further Reading:

ACPO with Centrex (2006) *Practice Advice on Professionalising the Business of Neighbourhood Policing*, NPIA, available at <http://www.neighbourhoodpolicing.co.uk>, accessed 16 May 2008

Baggott, M and Wallace, M (2006) *Neighbourhood Policing Progress Report*, May, Home Office, Crown copyright

Caless, B (ed), with Bryant, R, Morgan, D, Spruce, B, and Underwood, R (2007) *Blackstone's PCSO Handbook*, Oxford, Oxford University Press

Home Office (2004) White Paper: *Building Communities, Beating Crime*, available at <http://police.homeoffice.gov.uk/publications/police-reform/wp04_complete.pdf>, accessed 29 April 2009

—— (2005–2008) *National Policing Plan*, particularly 3.20–3.27, Crown Copyright

—— (2006) *Neighbourhood Policing Progress Report*, Crown Copywright

—— (2007) *National Community Safety Plan*, Crown Copyright

Mistry, D (2007) *Community Engagement: practical lessons from a pilot project*, Home Office Development and Practice Report No 48, Crown Copyright

PricewaterhouseCoopers (2006) *ACPO Neighbourhood Policing Survey*, ACPO

Quinlan, P and Morris, J (2008) *Neighbourhood Policing: The impact of piloting and early national implementation*, Home Office On-Line Report 01/08, available at <http://www.homeoffice.gov.uk/rds/pdfs08/rdsolr0108app.pdf>, accessed 20 May 2008

Tuffin, R, Morris, J, and Poole, A (2006) *An Evaluation of the impact of the National Reassurance Policing Programme*, Home Office Research Study 296; available at <http://www.compassunit.com/docs/hors296.pdf>, accessed 20 May 2008

Chapter 20

The Ten Principles of Neighbourhood Policing

20.1 **Introduction**

The Association of Chief Police Officers (ACPO) has articulated 'Ten Principles' of neighbourhood policing, consulted upon and developed in 2005–06 (see Further Reading) in order to achieve consistency across England and Wales in professionalizing the 'business' of neighbourhood policing. Defining the Principles by which neighbourhood policing is governed means that inspection and assessment of any neighbourhood policing activity can be made against a national standard within general parameters set by the Principles. Police forces will have individual approaches to neighbourhood policing, and conditions, resources, and problems will vary from neighbourhood to neighbourhood, BCU (Basic Command Unit) to BCU, and from force to force. All police forces are now assessed by Her Majesty's Inspectorate (Criminal Justice) (HMI (CJ)) on the effectiveness of their neighbourhood policing among the other policing services which they deliver.

This engages with the 'reassurance agenda', the desired outcome being that communities feel safer.

The Ten Principles are as follows:

Neighbourhood Policing

(1) is an organisational strategy that allows the police, its partners and the public to work closely together to solve problems of crime and disorder, and improve neighbourhood conditions and feelings of security;

(2) is a mainstream policing activity and integrated with other policing services;

(3) requires evidence-based deployment of neighbourhood teams against identified need;

(4) establishes dedicated, identifiable, accessible, knowledgeable and responsive neighbourhood policing teams which provide all citizens with a named point of access;

(5) reflects local conditions and is flexible, responsive and adaptable;

(6) allows the Police Service to work directly with the local community to identify the problems that are most important to them, thereby giving people direct influence over local policing priorities;

(7) establishes a regime for engaging other agencies and the public in problem-solving mechanisms;

(8) uses the NIM as the basis for deployment;

(9) requires an effective engagement, communication and feedback strategy, and a clear explanation of where accountability lies;

(10) should be subject to rigorous performance management including clear performance monitoring against a local plan and commitments made to neighbourhoods.

Note: For more information see 'Key Principles of Neighbourhood Policing', *Practice Advice on Professionalising the Business of Neighbourhood Policing* (2006) NPIA for ACPO, 10.

20.2 **Discussing the Ten Principles**

20.2.1 **Organizational Strategy**

> **Principle**: Neighbourhood policing is an organizational strategy that allows the police, its partners and the public to work closely together to solve the problems of crime and disorder, and to improve neighbourhood conditions and feelings of security.

The key elements here are 'police, partners and public'. To be effective, neighbourhood policing must be based on collaborative partnerships genuinely engaging with communities to identify what local problems are, and then seeking ways in which the problem can be sorted out. Solutions to crime or disorder problems do not come exclusively from the police, whose primary tool is prosecution. Solutions outside the criminal justice system may be available from partner agencies or within communities themselves.

Factors central to the success of an applied operational strategy include clear leadership and force policing plans implementing neighbourhood policing principles. Partnership is more than a simple 'awareness' process, which may merely involve briefing other agencies; rather, partners must be active and able to contribute and be prepared to engage with the communities in a neighbourhood in the same way that the police are prepared to engage. This collaboration could be at both BCU and at force levels, but the engagement process itself has to have impact.

Strategic engagement will give rise to project plans, clearly setting out what is to be achieved (the 'vision'), ways of assessing progress on the way ('milestones'), when things are to be completed ('end dates'), and clear indications of who is to deliver what ('task ownership' and 'outcomes'). This will entail regular meetings to check progress and drive through the project. The strategic lead (often by default) may be the BCU Commander, but could be the Assistant Chief Constable for local or area policing; or the Chief

Executive Officer (CEO) of the local or borough council, a strategic partner, or a prominent member of the communities locally. Even if they have not taken the lead, police members of the partnership have important roles to play

Part of any strategic planning for neighbourhood policing initiatives should involve estimation of the time which solutions will take to be achieved. People lose heart easily if they think that solutions are beyond them or if success signs take too long to surface. People who feel threatened by open drugs-dealing or visible prostitution on their streets will be reassured if the dealing or accosting is no longer on public display. Almost always this entails a request for visible police presence at those peak times when the activity complained of takes place. The engagement of partners might entail, for example, better street lighting, CCTV, Neighbourhood Watch patrols, measures to make kerb-crawling difficult or more problematic, and a media/publicity campaign.

The key to effective strategy is that all participants buy into its milestones, means, and outcomes. Keeping the strategic plan simple and attainable, with achievable interim targets, is a certain way of sustaining commitment on the part of all involved (see Figure 20.1).

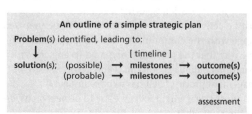

Figure 20.1

20.2.2 **Integrated Policing Activity**

Principle: Neighbourhood policing is a mainstream policing activity, integrated with other policing services.

Experience has shown that a visible policing presence, combined with positive attention to and impact upon the local overt signs of crime and disorder, drives crime down and means that the demands for a police presence diminish over time. This does not mean, of course, that the need for neighbourhood policing teams (NPTs) will disappear, but that a police presence has a deterrent effect for as long as it is visible. Disorder and crime will return to a neighbourhood if it is believed by offenders that the police presence is a mere token, half-hearted, or intermittent. Ironically, a continued presence removes the open need for a presence at all, yet continuing neighbourhood patrolling and engagement reinforces the return of 'law and order' to a community.

Local BCU Tasking and Coordination Groups (T&CG, see Chapter 15) may take a longer-term view of any crime issues in a neighbourhood integrating specific neighbourhood measures with other policing operations (the sex trade and drugs-dealing are local examples common to a number of neighbourhoods, where the T&CG may have other factors to address and bring together in joint initiatives).

Factors critical to integrated policing include ensuring force communication centre staff and response officers are aware of the most vulnerable neighbourhoods and what the strategic planning is for the area, so that responses are considered and proportionate, where possible they mesh with police responses or operations involving NPTs, and taking advice from those who have detailed knowledge of local conditions. Intelligence about crime and disorder locally, gathered from members of the communities among others, will determine appropriate police responses, one aim of which must always be to increase local feelings of security and safety. Measures of success outcomes include public confidence and satisfaction with local police action: again the examples of integrated action against the open sex trade or drugs-dealing illustrate how the public might respond to controlling the open or obvious signs of crime and disorder.

20.2.3 Evidence-Based Deployment

Principle: Neighbourhood policing requires evidence-based deployment of neighbourhood teams against identified need.

The principle of evidence-based deployment is intended to guide the management of scarce resources and aid prioritization in instances where not all needs can be met immediately. It is the purpose of the National Intelligence Model (NIM) business process to aid identification, assessment, prioritization, and management of crime and community security issues. Continuous and detailed assessment of community tensions, victimization (or repeat victimization), and the vulnerability of a community or neighbourhood is required based on community, crime, criminal, and contextual intelligence. This provides the evidence upon which to base deployment of resources. BCUs have a duty in this respect to ensure that teams are deployed in the right numbers, at the right times, to deal with issues which are causing local unease or fear of crime. Engaging with partner agencies will assist in identifying those issues for which alternative solutions, other than police or criminal justice sector intervention, may be appropriate.

20.2.4 Dedicated Teams

Principle: Neighbourhood policing establishes dedicated, identifiable, accessible, knowledgeable and responsive neighbourhood policing teams which provide all citizens with a named point of access.

NPTs should be familiar with the localities they police and have a clear commitment to providing the 'visible guardianship' which creates orderliness and trust. That commitment entails the time to consider problems holistically and to put in place crime prevention and crime reduction initiatives over time, so that longer-term solutions can be found and jointly-owned between the police, the partners, and the public. This may involve a balance between what is needed to 'fix' a problem now and what is needed over a longer period. Members of the public will be reassured and have confidence in decisions taken if they know the people they are dealing with. If the NPT is familiar, consistent, known by name, and knowledgeable about the area and its problems, and the team has been seen to be effective, public trust will be sustained.

Members of the NPT should receive appropriate training for the role, but specific training should also be available to partners, other agencies, and members of the public where this would be appropriate. A specific example might be in ensuring that all participants in problem-solving have training in problem-solving models and methodologies (see Chapter 25). Another might be training for the application for an anti-social behaviour order (ASBO) as such initiatives may not always come from the police.

20.2.5 Locally Dependent

Principle: Neighbourhood policing reflects local conditions and is flexible, responsive and adaptable.

Essentially, there can be no definitive prescription for an NPT because local conditions will vary greatly.

A glance at the deployment of NPTs in Kent illustrates this. The latest (2008) data on deployment in the county[1] is that there are 47 teams in Kent and Medway, consisting of 387 police community support officers (PCSOs) and 190 police officers (including Specials). Six 'task teams' were added in September 2008, consisting of a police sergeant and five police constables in each team, aimed at 'problem areas' and law enforcement. One team, in operation since 2006, was established in North Kent (Dartford), and consists of a PS and 9 PCs with no PCSOs or other members, largely

---

[1] Derived from the public information website <http://www.kentpolice.uk>, accessed December 2008.

because the problems are crime 'hot spots' which need, initially at least, the deployment of police powers and criminal justice interventions. Over time these deployment configurations will change and mutate, as problems are resolved, new problems arise, or the teams attend to other priorities in the neighbourhood. Whilst Kent's deployment of neighbourhood policing teams may be considered indicative, it is not a template for other forces, each of which will have their own priorities and views on the composition of teams.

The key words in this Principle are 'flexible, responsive and adaptable'. Sound judgment and initiative are required, together with reaching out to the 'hard to reach' or 'hard to hear' groups, which are or can be hostile to the police, or frightened of them, in innovative ways, such as arranging 'have a say' days or finding ways to make unthreatening 'house calls'. We can summarize this Principle as an iterative or cyclical process (see Figure 20.2)

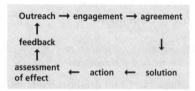

Figure 20.2

The feedback 'loop' to the police and other agencies is a useful measure of how the 'solution' was perceived, and again, the application of this process will depend very much on the identification of local priorities and the determination of responses.

20.2.6 Public Priorities

Principle: Neighbourhood policing allows the Police Service to work directly with the local community to identify the problems that are most important to them, thereby giving people direct influence over local policing priorities.

To 'work directly' with the local communities in identifying problems entails mechanisms enabling local people to air their concerns. A variety of methods can achieve this, and their use will depend very much on local conditions and the relative sophistication of police/community relations. Some consultations can be done through public meetings, though the disadvantage here is often that those who make the most noise or who wield the most local influence are the ones most likely to influence the police, rather than, perhaps, members of the community who struggle to articulate their fears or who are inhibited in public meetings.

'Surgeries' where police officers or PCSOs are available for private consultation at set times may work for people who prefer one-to-one meetings: typical venues include local libraries, schools, or community centres. NPTs may consider installing a public noticeboard where citizens can write about things which concern them, and of course, officers may give their duty email addresses and police-issue mobile phone numbers. 'Key Individual Networks' (KINs) created in this way are effective ways of communicating and should, naturally, include partners as well as public.

Historically, police took decisions about how to deal with crime on the basis that the police were the experts and knew best. This could mean that people's concerns were not addressed because what worried them about minor crime or minor disorder did not reach the police 'threshold'. Policing is no longer something which is 'done to' people, but is 'done with' people. Their fears and concerns should modify the police approach and should determine local law and order priorities. This 'citizen primacy' is not always easy to sustain, or even initiate, with the many pressures on a modern police force, but if neighbourhood policing is to succeed it must be predicated on genuine engagement with the public listening to what they want and responding appropriately. Anything less would be lip-service. Of course, response leads to action, and an important component of this Principle is that police and partners regularly feed back information on progress about issues of concern and that priorities can be reviewed at regular intervals. Experience has suggested that once every three months is the optimum for progress review. 'Crime mapping' now means that local statistics are available on police websites, enabling citizens to make up their own minds about crime control and police effectiveness in their neighbourhoods.

Public expectation will have to be managed if there is not to be an unrealistic expectation of progress or action. Simply 'moving on' or breaking up gatherings of young people whom the elderly community find menacing will not solve any of the deep-seated worries, because the youths may simply gather again once the uniformed presence has moved on, possibly with an added resentment against those residents who complained in the first place. Often, such groups of young people will not have been causing any problems at all, which points up the difficulty of providing reassurance if the mere sight of youngsters 'hanging about' makes the elderly feel unsafe. Additionally, the police and other partners may not necessarily be able to act solely on the say-so of residents; independent evidence may be needed, which takes time to amass. People expecting a 'quick fix' may be disappointed by the occasional ponderousness of evidence-gathering and will have to be briefed about realistic time-frames. Finally, there should be an opportunity for members of the communities to hear what has been happening and what progress has been made, and this is best done at regular meetings and consultations, where feedback could be part of a standing agenda.

20.2.7 Collaborative Problem-Solving

Principle: Neighbourhood policing establishes a regime for engaging other agencies and the public in problem-solving mechanisms.

Problem-solving is considered in detail in Chapter 25. The intention is a shared activity to identify, in detail, what a problem is and how (and when) it occurs. Solutions are proposed from all sides of the collaboration or consultation and discussed in terms of practicability, effectiveness, and cost, among other considerations. What emerges as the best option to deal with the problem is then prioritized and implemented over time, reviewed, and assessed. It is essentially a joint process between police, partners, and the public, with none predominating.

20.2.8 Intelligence-Led Deployment

Principle: Neighbourhood policing uses the NIM as the basis for deployment.

ACPO 2006: 14
Neighbourhood policing should be driven by information that has been rigorously analysed and by the disciplines of multi-agency tasking and coordination at appropriate levels.

For intelligence-based neighbourhood policing to be effective, there must be the systematic accruing of data about the locality, from demography (age profiles) to incident logs, from structured Environmental Visual Audits (EVAs) to source targeting. This will lead to 'problem profiles' in which locations of greatest need will be identified. This process, dove-tailing with the community's expression of its priority concerns, will help the structuring of the joint response to crime and disorder. The NIM (discussed above, Chapter 14) is the process devised for this purpose and is the mechanism through which issues can be appropriately assigned for resolution at policing levels 1, 2, or 3.

20.2.9 Community Engagement and Communication

Principle: Neighbourhood policing requires an effective engagement, communication, and feedback strategy, and a clear explanation of where accountability lies.

'Effective engagement, communication and feedback' all serve to reinforce a community's sense of security and safety. This is almost commonplace with articulate, well-resourced citizens, but may be less true of the 'hard to reach' and 'hard to hear'. Those most in need of being listened to include minority communities who may be disadvantaged (ethnic or language groups), discriminated against (gay and lesbian communities, for example), ignored (the elderly), demonized (the young), or uninvolved (new immigrant communities). These again are merely indicative examples, and there will be particular groups in any force or neighbourhood that are not normally engaged in dialogue with the police, and may include those, like offenders, who are hostile to the police and unwilling to engage with them.

ACPO advice (2006: 14) specifies that 'police and partners have a responsibility to engage' with communities, their concerns, and their identified (and mutually agreed) priorities, which also means that citizens engage with partnerships at the level they choose. This could range from merely receiving information (which is broadly what is entailed in Neighbourhood Watch), reassurance (including visits and contact), helping to provide solutions to local problems, and influencing strategic priorities and decisions, some of which will be taken by Chief Officers in consultation with the Police Authority. This means that the potential for influencing police actions and priorities could enable citizens to impact on the topmost levels in the force. It follows that it is incumbent on the NPT to engage with everyone, not just those artful in the ways of consultation and the machinery of public meetings.

To reinforce the message of safety and security, police and partners have to engage in marketing and sending messages with some expertise and sophistication. People have become used to slick and professional means of communicating, and the police cannot be seen to lag behind or be out of touch with modern communication; hence blogs, websites, internet contacts, and multi-messaging must be exploited by police and partners to get the reassurance message across. This must demonstrate that the police are listening, not that the police are 'spin doctors'. The public distrust 'spin' and will be disillusioned if they think that the police are manipulating the message or the medium. There are more channels now than ever before whereby the police and partners can speak to their communities.

20.2.10 Performance Management

Principle: Neighbourhood policing should be subject to rigorous performance management including clear performance monitoring against a local plan and commitments made to neighbourhoods.

Ranging from a need to demonstrate value for money to demonstration of effective delivery of a service, performance measurement has become embedded within the public service culture. There is a Green Paper proposal, provisionally entitled 'The Policing Pledge',[2] which is an example of commitment to improve performance. Too early to evaluate 'The Policing Pledge', it is indicative of how performance management is embedded in government thinking. In neighbourhood policing terms, local measures will be established and agreed which monitor public priorities,

---

[2] A 'Green Paper' is a government consultation document which gathers opinions, often prior to a White Paper (proposal for statute law), itself preceding an Act of Parliament. Information about this consultation can be found on police websites or at <http://www.homeoffice.gov.uk/documents/policing-pledge?view=Binary >.

what has been put in place to meet the needs, and feedback received from the public on the efficacy of actions.

This also needs data: what commitment has been made; what resources deployed; when, how often, and where; and with what effect on a BCU, NPT, and individual basis. This last brings the performance measurement down to the level of the individual team member whose performance will be assessed in terms of contribution to the agreed neighbourhood policing priorities, thus reinforcing the importance of the team member's function in delivering reassurance and feelings of safety and security to the citizen. This is examined in greater detail in Chapter 23 on Citizen Focus.

Police forces will be assessed regularly in relation to their dedication to neighbourhood policing, partnerships, and relations with the public. Her Majesty's Inspectorate of Constabulary (HMIC) will assess factors which relate directly to neighbourhood policing such as anti-social behaviour (and associated) orders, as well as 'customer satisfaction/accessibility'. Actions of the NPT member at street level thus may have an impact on his or her force overall assessment and credibility with its citizens, with attendant publicity and media comment.

20.3 **Conclusion**

This chapter has considered the Ten Principles underpinning neighbourhood policing, and has noted that they are to do with listening to the various communities that make up the geographical neighbourhood, responding to residents' concerns, and dealing effectively, in concert with others, in resolving local crime and disorder issues. Successful outcomes increase confidence in the police and enhance people's sense of their own security. Solutions have to be credible and sustainable, and officers in NPTs should be there 'for the duration', trying to find workable long-term solutions to sometimes quite intractable social problems, as well as achieving some quick wins on the way.

Further Reading

The standard text for considering the Ten Principles of Neighbourhood Policing is ACPO (2006) *Practice Advice on Professionalising the Business of Neighbourhood Policing*, which is produced for ACPO by the National Centre for Policing Excellence (NCPE) on behalf of the NPIA. It is available at <http://www.npia.police.uk/>, or at <http://www.neighbourhoodpolicing.co.uk> (accessed 15 July 2008 and 6 January 2009 respectively)

Other useful references include:

Central Office of Information (COI) (2006) *Respect Action Plan*, Crown Copyright

Cooper, C, Anscombe, J, Avenell, J, McLean, F, and Morris, J (2006), *A National Evaluation of Community Support Officers*, Home Office Research Study 297, Home Office, Crown Copyright

Ditton, J (2008) 'Fear of Crime' in T Newburn and P Neyroud (eds), *Dictionary of Policing*, Cullompton, Willan: 105–6

Farrell, S (2007) *Experience and Expression in the Fear of Crime*, Economic and Social Research Council (ESRC) publication

Home Office (2005a) *National Policing Plan 2005–2008*, available at <http://police.homeoffice.gov.uk/national-policing-plan/policing-plan-2008.html> (accessed 21 January 2009)

Home Office (2006) *Review of the Partnership Provisions of the Crime and Disorder Act 1998—Report of Findings*, Crown Copyright

Laycock, G (2008) 'Crime Prevention (Situational and Social)' in T Newburn and P Neyroud (eds), *Dictionary of Policing*, opcit above: 59–61

The *National Community Safety Plan 2008–2011* is available at <http://police.homeoffice.gov.uk/national-policing-plan/national-community-safety-0609> (accessed 21 January 2009)

Chapter 21

Neighbourhood Policing Teams

21.1 Introduction

In the previous chapter, we looked at the principles which underlie neighbourhood policing and, when considering the role and function of the Neighbourhood Policing Teams (NPT) themselves, it is important to remember the Principle which establishes:

> dedicated, identifiable, accessible, knowledgeable and responsive neighbourhood policing teams which provide all citizens with a named point of access

since such teams are deployed against identified need and reflect local conditions. In other words, NPTs must be known, consistent, available, and properly engaged in and with the various communities in the 'neighbourhood'. This provides local policing of a kind not seen in England and Wales for more than 40 years, so the concept has been quite a departure for communities and police forces alike.

Surveys suggest that the NPTs are very popular with residents within geographic communities, who are reassured by a visible police presence, whose fear of crime and disorder is thereby lessened, and who point to a diminution in public nuisance, reductions in criminal damage incidents, and greater safety in the neighbourhood as a result of the presence of NPTs. The level of public confidence in the police has risen steadily since the introduction of NPTs, from 47 per cent in 2003–04, to 52 per cent in 2007–08 (British Crime Survey data, see also <http://www.npia .police.uk/en/10211.htm>).

There is some anecdotal evidence of the NPTs being less popular among the police themselves, though there are suggestions that this is changing, particularly with the development of police constables (PCs) as 'NPT managers' (see below). For example, whilst neighbourhood policing is bread-and-butter to police community support officers (PCSOs), reflecting their specific training in engagement with communities, the task seems less congenial to some Special Constables and regular police officers, whose clearly expressed preference is for vehicle-based patrol work as part of a fast-response team.[1]

Other issues, such as the extent of the involvement of volunteers and problem-solving training, will be examined in the context of the NPTs; but it is important at the outset to acknowledge that, whilst patrolling on foot in a neighbourhood is a traditional and time-honoured element in policing, it is new to most current police officers (including police commanders), and some of them find that this takes some getting used to.

21.2 **The Numbers Game**

The aim of establishing dedicated NPTs in every police force in England and Wales, set by the Government in 2005 with an implementation deadline of 31 March 2008, has been achieved. There are, at the end of 2008, some 16,500 PCSOs and 13,000 police constables and sergeants dedicated to neighbourhood policing, representing some 92 per cent of all PCSOs and about 18 per cent of all sworn police officers

---

[1] Information from discussions at the NPIA Neighbourhood Policing Communications Practitioners' Conference, Manchester, November 2007.

(NPIA *Neighbourhood Policing Programme* (NPP) data, referenced above). According to the Government, introducing neighbourhood policing has already cost over £1 billion, an investment which demonstrates NPP's 'flagship' status in a resource-hungry period (Waddington, 2008:17, Home Office, 2008: 1.17).

Even more fundamentally, responding with policing plans and operations which are tailored to a community's concerns is a radical inversion of the standard model of 'compliance' policing, where the police 'know best' and respond according to police principles, rather than to residents' priorities. The change from enforcement to cooperation, and from compliance to consensus has been well noted and analysed by commentators on the police (see McLaughlin, 2007 and Wright, 2002), but is yet to bed down comfortably across all police forces in England and Wales. It may be that some police forces, especially in high density urban areas, feel less able to allow neighbourhood consultation initiatives to determine police priorities, because of more urgent calls on their resources from gun, drug, and gang crime.

21.3 **Dedicated Teams**

The explicit insistence on identifiable NPTs, dedicated to the neighbourhood task, is fundamental to the deployment of NPTs. An inherent danger is the abstraction of officers to meet other, more pressing, needs with consequent disruption of the composition and membership of policing teams. This was a recurrent complaint when communities and residents were first consulted about neighbourhood policing, and it is addressed in the ACPO/NPIA *Practice Advice* (ACPO/NPIA, 2006, paragraph 2.1.5) to ensure that citizens are reassured that they can deal with a consistent member of the NPT whose name is known to them and who is abstracted for other police business only rarely and when there is overriding operational urgency.

A further development has been that the role of the NPTs is as much about crime prevention and crime reduction as it is about investigating and responding to crimes in a locality. As we note below in Chapter 26, crime prevention has never been fashionable or attractive to police officers, despite the evident importance of trying to prevent crimes from happening in the first place. Richard Mayne, one of the first Commissioners of the Metropolitan 'New Police', said in 1829 that the function of the police was:

> The prevention of crime, the protection of life and property and the preservation of public tranquillity [quoted in Wilson et al, 2001: 35]

which could have been a prescription for neighbourhood policing. Peace-keeping in local communities is less headline-grabbing than audacious acts, whether crimes or the capture of criminals.

As a result, despite crime prevention and reduction being fundamentals of policing from the very beginning, police forces these days have to develop new ways to 'sell' the concept of prevention to their own officers as well as to communities. Anyone involved in neighbourhood policing will be expected to support both crime reduction and crime prevention very positively. Within NPTs, there are growing numbers of specialist officers who have been trained in advanced forms of crime reduction (such as in knowledge of architecture-based 'designing crime out' principles, or in the installation of vandal-proof lighting, for example in underpasses), and it is demonstrable that these officers are often among the first to gain the trust of a community because of their visible and repeated attempts to reduce localized crime (Tilley, 2005 for instance). The provision of shed or purse alarms is not glamorous, but it is effective, practical, and specific, as well as opening opportunities for NPTs to engage with some members of the community whom they might otherwise not meet until they were responding to a crime or disorder incident.

Other positive aspects arising from the dedicated team may include *Safer Schools Partnerships* where members of the NPT become known to staff and students alike at neighbourhood schools. Here again are opportunities for crime prevention advice, crime reduction initiatives, local intelligence, and engagement with young people which may be of benefit in the wider community. Routes to and from schools can be monitored for drugs dealing, whilst issues such as bullying, victimization, disorder, vandalism, arson, and criminal damage can be the focus of NPT-inspired 'awareness campaigns'. Indeed some schools now have PCs or PCSOs permanently assigned to the premises, as a potent and symbolic attestation to the inroads that have been made. All of this, of course, is predicated on consistent membership of an NPT with familiar faces who build trust gradually with citizens, some of whom, for a host of reasons, may initially be hostile to the police.

21.4 **Neighbourhood Policing Teams**

The actual size of an NPT will depend on the neighbourhood to be policed. The concept of 'neighbourhood' is almost as elusive as that of 'community', but for the purposes of this discussion, we shall assume that a neighbourhood is a geographical description, even though the ACPO/NPIA *Practice Advice* (2006: 18) notes that:

> People will have their own understanding of their neighbourhood, not necessarily based on the geography of the area but on their personal lifestyle[s], culture and history.

But the police do not deploy operationally according to people's lifestyles, culture, or history. Police deployment is geographical, or at least spatial and temporal, and for the purposes here of describing an NPT, the existence of 'neighbourhoods' in fixed physical locations, containing residences, will be assumed.

What follows describes a 'typical' NPT. There may well be some local variations and some forces will have a greater preponderance of one constituent of NPT than another. Some forces have large numbers of Special constables who can be regularly deployed in neighbourhoods, whilst others rely more on PCSOs. Some will have many volunteer groups to draw from; others may have very few. Some NPTs will have invested heavily in partnerships with wardens and parks officials, in particular through the auspices of the Community Safety Accreditation Scheme; others will not. Some NPTs may be staffed entirely by police constables, in shifts, headed by sergeants; other NPTs may keep sworn officers to a minimum, using only constables as 'beat managers' (see below) of other members and participants. We do not seek to prescribe, merely to identify likely participants in NPTs, all with the common purpose of interacting positively with the communities encountered during deployment. We do the same in Chapter 22 in identifying possible partners in neighbourhood policing.

Those in the NPT, from the police side, are expected to be strongly committed to neighbourhood policing, to have undergone a 'robust selection procedure', to possess any appropriate language skills, and to have been specifically trained for the purpose (ACPO/NPIA, 2006: 18). Consideration about co-location with any partners will have taken place; participants will have clear role descriptions and performance expectations, and, as noted above, will not be abstracted 'for more than a defined percentage of their time' (ACPO/NPIA, ibid). These are very much ideal prescriptions for the membership of NPTs, but increasingly, as the concept takes hold in forces and as it is supported with funding and real commitment from higher ranks in the force, so the training and investment in the NPTs will develop. The current position, in reality, is still some way short of the ACPO/NPIA ideal 'steady state'.

21.5 **Police Sergeant: Team Leader**

Whilst the sergeant is an important factor in the leadership of the NPT (indeed, in any police deployment, it could be argued), his or her role in this instance also includes interaction with the Basic Command Unit (BCU), the Tasking and Coordinating Group, the rest of the force, and liaison with neighbourhood partners. In other words, in addition to leading the NPT, the sergeant is the main linkage between the NPT and other parts of the local police service as well as other agencies, representatives, and community stakeholders, and the range of qualities and skills which this calls for is extensive. The uniformed police sergeant must also manage diverse staff, with a range of needs and abilities, each requiring different modes of learning and development, must deal with shifts, rest days, rosters, leave, sickness absence, and appraisal, as well as commendation, development, discipline, and performance.

In addition, he or she must be responsive to the BCU Commander's local crime-fighting and community policing priorities as well as to those of any police authority representative(s), must ensure consistency with the Force Policing Plan which articulates the overall triennial policing priorities for the county or unitary authority, must deal with partners (and their often contradictory or oppositional agendas, see Chapter 22 below), and must interface with important community leaders, including the inevitable and intractable complainants, as well as dealing with local budgets, funds, and project finance (though all on a small scale).

We can show the variety of what an NP team leader has to do more effectively through a diagram like Figure 21.1.

Figure 21.1 The varied functions of a Neighbourhood Policing team leader (Police Sergeant NPT)

21.6 **Police Officers**

The role of sworn or warranted officers in neighbourhood teams has been subject to much debate in the years since the NPTs were trialled and set up (2005). This arose because much of what worried local residents was not crime, or if it was, then it was (to the police) of a petty and minor order. PCSOs were conceived to deal with this kind of low-level offending and disorder, and the PCSO's initial powers reflected the issues they were expected to deal with (in Schedule 4 of the Police Reform Act 2002). However, it soon became apparent that some PCSOs in some situations needed enhanced powers, and all needed statutory powers (given additional legislative backing in the Police and Justice Act 2006); and that there were also some situations where a warranted police officer was required, in preference to a PCSO, to enforce compliance, arrest offenders, or move people on. Although NPTs have existed since late

2005, there is still debate about whether a warranted police officer is necessary to the team, or whether a combination of local by-laws and PCSO powers are sufficient for most NPT purposes.

It is probable that this debate will become academic in the years to come, since the role of NPT constable has evolved beyond its original concept. Increasingly, constables are taking on, and relishing, the role of local 'beat manager', and increasingly, this entails managing the workload and staff in parts of an NPT and, in some areas, the NPT itself, leaving the police sergeant to oversee a number of NPTs. All police officers have leadership competencies, and training often consists in learning how to take the lead in managing some crisis or event. However, until now constables have seldom 'managed' other people within a police force and, traditionally, the first supervisory rank is that of sergeant— a position often jealously defended by the Police Federation among others.

However, just as there is progression around the role of the sworn officer, and increasing use of non-warranted police staff in many situations where police officers would once have had a monopoly (like crime scene investigation), so there is blurring of the edges between supervisory ranks and 'senior' constables. Provided that those constables who act as 'beat managers' have requisite training in per-formance and people management, there does not seem to be much that is cogent in the objections. Besides, the police officers are *not* supervising, or managing their fellow officers but rather non-warranted staff, in a variety of roles and involving people with different levels of expertise and knowledge, who usually need coordinated management to function competently.

That said, some NPTs do deploy police constables solely for the purpose of policing a neighbourhood and engaging with its residents, operating on an equal basis with other NPT members. Where that happens, as noted above, the police officers' powers are invoked only when coercion is required, or when a particular police operation (such as against drugs-dealing, or against kerb-crawling) is needed. There are intelligence dividends from close involvement with a particular district, but these are not confined to police officers; indeed, there is some evidence to suggest that residents are often happier and less inhibited in talking to PCSOs rather than to warranted officers (Cooper et al, 2006).

21.7 **Special Constables**

The use of Special constables in NPTs is not merely another facet of volunteering (which we look at in more detail below). Using Specials in neighbourhood policing is relatively new and has different emphases and subtleties from using regular officers in the same role. Special constables are volunteers—unpaid—who are trained to the same standards as regular police officers (albeit over a longer period), who attain the same core sets of competences as their full-time counterparts, and who carry warrant cards and have full police powers. They are, to all intents, fully-functioning sworn officers who work for some hours every week (usually a minimum of four, or sixteen hours per month) in addition to other, usually full-time, employment.

Specials some years ago were derisively labelled as 'hobby bobbies' who turned out only to direct traffic and parking at fêtes and fairs, mainly in the countryside. *Those times are long gone.* Today, few forces could function without Specials working alongside regular officers, particularly at weekends. There are now some 16,000 Special police officers throughout England and Wales, and numbers are growing steadily, and they play a complementary role in patrol and uniformed police duties (as, for instance, a Section Special constable). Part of those duties include, in many forces, membership of NPTs, and Specials often bring local knowledge, familiarity with neighbourhoods where they patrol, and a close parochial understanding of communities' tensions and problems.

Whilst regular officers may come to a particular location from anywhere else in the force area, frequently Specials work in locations which they know well and in which they may have grown up (they are sometimes designated, variously, as 'Neighbourhood' or 'Parish' Specials). That local knowledge is a firm base from which to construct partnerships; indeed ACPO/NPIA assert that:

> where special constables have worked alongside neighbourhood policing teams, they have increased the effectiveness of those teams [2006: 3.3.1, 20].

Additionally, whilst significant numbers of Specials use their policing experience and skills as a route to joining the regulars, many others do not and this gives Specials, in the eyes of residents, a consequent continuity, offers familiarity with local conditions and personalities, and reinforces their own 'recognizability' to neighbourhoods. These are prized additions to the NPTs. That Specials possess full police powers is a bonus when compliance is required. Off-duty, Specials continue to acquire intelligence and information of use to NPTs, whilst often 'embedded' in the locality because of their full-time work.

21.8 **Police Community Support Officers**

The public makes virtually no distinction between a sworn police officer and a PCSO, at least superficially, because the uniforms are the same even if the labelling on them is different. Other kinds of community support officers (CSOs) may form part of a neighbourhood policing team, especially those in rural areas (see section 21.9 below), but the PCSO is granted powers by the Chief Constable of the police force in which the PCSO serves, and, as a consequence, is a valuable member of the NPT, bridging, effectively, the gap between volunteer or council 'official', and sworn police officer.

That said, the PCSO is frequently embedded in a community in a way that police officers are not. People approach PCSOs on a basis of familiarity and tell them things which they would not tell a police officer, and the police for their part are learning to trust the PCSOs as 'eyes and ears' within a neighbourhood, picking up and relaying valuable community information. It is important, therefore, to distinguish between the respective roles of police officer (regular or Special) and PCSO. *The Guide to Becoming a Police Community Support Officer* (Home Office, 2006) says this of the PCSO:

> You can't arrest anyone. You've got no handcuffs, no baton. All you've got is you. It's down to your ability to get on with some of the most challenging people in some of the most difficult situations. The way you win cooperation is through good-humoured persuasion.

Caless (2007a: 1.4, 25) goes on to observe:

> It is actually difficult to imagine a more succinct and persuasive description of a PCSO's role than this, nor one in which the range of skills and qualities which a PCSO must have is so clearly and practically illustrated.

ACPO/NPIA declare (2006: 19–20) that PCSOs 'are most effective' when they 'work in a fixed local area, which enables the build-up of trust and familiarity'. That is certainly true for some neighbourhoods, but in others, especially those hostile to the police (or indeed to 'authority' in any form), bridging the gap may be much more problematic, particularly when PCSOs are simultaneously tasked to collect and collate 'evidence for Anti-Social Behaviour Orders'.

This is at the heart of some unease about the PCSO's role; on the one hand PCSOs are to 'embed' themselves within the communities, becoming a trusted and familiar part of the problem-solving for neighbourhoods, whilst at the same time they retain the authority of a police uniform, of patrolling with police officers, and having delegated powers to enforce ASBOs, issue fixed penalties, and be part of the system of authority which enjoins compliance.

One way through this apparent contradiction is the active part which PCSOs can play in bringing parts of the neighbourhood itself into contact. It cannot be assumed that all neighbourhoods are homogeneous and that a general term like 'neighbourhood' will actively and comprehensively describe all the factions, divisions, occupations, groups, associations, communities of identity, and communities of interest which may be contained within a single geographical area.

Parts of one community (eg strong faith groups) may be hostile to other parts (eg against a gay community), whilst the commonest divide of all, in almost any community, is in the tensions between young people and older residents. PSCOs actively seek out and talk to young people, representing their views and needs in partnership meetings and in discussions with other parts of the community. This not only gives young people a 'voice', but also ensures that their needs are given serious consideration at decision-making meetings. Young people are notably 'hard to reach' by conventional police officers and certainly they are 'hard to hear' in community or neighbourhood politics. The PCSO can actively bring young people into meaningful contact with other residents, to the benefit of all.

This doesn't always work, of course. Some young people, especially those in gangs in inner cities, or those who are largely skilless, unemployed, and disaffected, or those for whom crime is already a way of life, may never engage with PCSOs in a positive way. The best efforts of PCSOs to make the views of young people heard may not prevail against a tendency among older people to 'demonize' youth as the cause of all crime and disorder. And, even though PCSOs are sometimes concerned with enforcement of the law and with making young people comply with norms of acceptable behaviour, they are much more about cooperation, consensus, and compromise, which can make them appear to be 'on the side of' young people; an apparent stance which sometimes dismays older residents.

Unlike the authoritative figure of the police officer, however well-known and familiar to the neighbourhood, the PCSO is the member of the NPT who engages at the deepest level and who is willing to talk and to listen about things which may not be crimes or matters of civil disorder. This can be caricatured as 'the police deal with crime, PCSOs deal with trivia' by some (notably the Police Federation), but the response in many communities, notably in countrywide surveys, is to evince more trust in PCSOs and reassurance with their regular appearance, than with police officers, even in the same NPT (Cooper et al, 2006).

PCSOs began patrolling in 2002 and are now a familiar part of many neighbourhoods. Surveys, such as that referenced above, have shown that public reassurance is boosted by the PCSO's patrol function and they are seen as more approachable than police officers. However, it is probably still too early to make a definitive appraisal of the contribution which PCSOs make to the police engagement with neighbourhoods and it may also be too early to distinguish substantively between the roles of a PCSO in a neighbourhood and a police officer; particularly since each is evolving according to the problems their particular neighbourhood faces. Some evidence of wilful misunderstanding, coupled with belittlement, continues to characterize the relationship between some police officers (normally not serving in NPTs) and PCSOs. The Police Federation, representing all police ranks from constable to chief inspector, has never compromised on its unwavering hostility to the PCSO concept (see Caless, 2007b).

21.9 **Other Community Support Officers**

We noted above that PCSOs are designated by the Force Chief Constable in which they serve as having particular powers. Other kinds of Community Support Officers (CSOs) are employed by borough, county, or unitary authority councils. Although CSOs may receive training from the police—especially in calming manoeuvres such as 'dealing with an angry man' or how to observe and report, rules of evidence and so on—they are working primarily to a council or local authority agenda, dealing with council priorities, and may function as the liaison point across a widely scattered rural community (sometimes coordinating Horse Watch and other awareness schemes), or work within small urban communities to spearhead local authority schemes, such as in a community leisure complex. Alternatively, many are integrated into an NPT, serving alongside police and PCSOs, but without the range of powers which the police members have.

The primary functions of CSOs are very similar to those of PCSOs: embedding in the neighbourhood and various communities, becoming a familiar and trusted face, acting as a conduit for people's unease or concerns, and attempting, through problem-solving techniques and coordination of partners, to promote greater law and order locally and establish safe communities. Inevitably, CSOs will pick up 'community intelligence' and will have detailed and in-depth knowledge of groupings, families, personalities, and frictions within their 'beat' and thus may be of considerable value to the police requirement for information. There is an obligation on the police to ensure that CSOs know what local crime and disorder priorities are and what sort of information they are seeking, and this is where the coordinating role of the NPT team leader (sergeant or senior constable 'beat manager') comes into play. It follows that team briefings should be frequent, updated regularly, and made an opportunity for effective two-way communication—both the NPT to the CSO and from the CSO to the rest of team.

21.10 **Other Local Authority Staff**

This may cover a wide range of local authority officials who have well-defined and familiar roles in the community. Parking attendants, for example (the erstwhile 'traffic warden'), may play a part in NPT initiatives to drive down vehicle crime (theft of or theft from a motor vehicle), as well as assisting a neighbourhood in preventing careless or insensitive parking (eg near a school). Park keepers and others employed in the provision and maintenance of local facilities may be attached to NPTs for specific tasks—such as the denial of 'safe' areas to deal drugs or sell sex—or more generally to engage with residents and communities who use the facilities.

Most other local authority officials might engage with the NPTs on a 'needs' basis, whenever the focus for neighbourhood policing is upon areas where such officials are engaged, and this can range from the collection of abandoned or stolen vehicles (many of which are 'torched' by the thieves), through highways departments engaged in road and street maintenance, local housing authorities and housing trusts, local authority departments dealing with gardens, planting schemes, street lighting, and footpaths, graffiti removal teams, officials dealing with illegal 'fly-tipping', local trading standards inspectors, and people working at swimming pools, gyms, and other council-owned leisure facilities. The NPT might have need of such local knowledge and specialist skills from time to time, but such employees are unlikely to be a permanent part of the NPT itself. However, on a more general basis, such officials have responded well to police initiatives to brief on local residents' concerns and on the need for informal Environmental Visual Audits (EVAs) as part of the local authority employees' daily routine.

21.11 **Voluntary Organizations**

There are many voluntary organizations, ACPO/NPIA declared (2006: 20), that can 'play important roles' in 'improving the quality of life in neighbourhoods'. These range from Neighbourhood Watch to charity groups such as Shelter and Citizens' Advice Bureaux, encompassing a spectrum of groups in between, from faith groups working within communities—especially deprived communities— clubs for young people (martial arts, cadet forces, Scouts, Young Farmers, leisure and sports clubs), environmental groups, groups concerned with animal welfare and wild-life—like county-based Wildlife Trusts, local branches of the Royal Society for the Protection of Birds, the RSPCA and the People's Dispensary for Sick Animals—and sports clubs, the Women's Institute, the British Legion, community groups such as pre-school and playgroups, mother and toddler groups, theatre, dance and music societies, 'working men's clubs' (now with women), and pub teams for darts or snooker. Every community has some groups like these and they are an important focus for people's social lives and 'sense of belonging' as well as an opportunity to engage for the NPT.

There is a note of caution to be sounded, however, conspicuously missing from the ACPO/NPIA Practice Advice, and that is that NPTs need to be aware—just like partnerships, as we note in Chapter 22—that voluntary organizations can have their own agendas and preoccupations, which may not always fit easily with the larger social and community picture which NPTs promote. For example, environmental groups may be hostile to any further building schemes in a locality or to increased 'light pollution', however, much more street lighting might improve local safety; whilst private leisure groups may be hostile to rival community-provided facilities, particularly where this may result in commercial disadvantage.

Some charity groups may not always welcome police involvement locally (drugs rehabilitation schemes, for example, or 'halfway housing' for released prisoners), whilst Neighbourhood Watch itself can sometimes be an area of some local difficulty: at its best Neighbourhood Watch is an effective and persistent contributor to community safety, but there have been occasions when individual Neighbourhood Watch schemes, usually dominated by elderly white males, sought to suppress the natural exuberance of young people and in one instance even went so far as to try to prevent public access to a local park which provided harmless but noisy fun for local children. This has sometimes gained one or two Neighbourhood Watch groups the unenviable reputation of being 'killjoys' or, worse, enabling busybodies to spy on their neighbours. Close association with such a degenerated Neighbourhood Watch might be counterproductive for an NPT. Here again, adequate and specific briefing by the NPT will focus what Neighbourhood Watch does, and the likely results will be evident enhancement of local safety and not the promotion of the narrow interests of a local pressure group. This is not to condemn Neighbourhood Watch groups, who generally do a fine job, but over-zealousness can often forfeit good will. Ultimately, of course, unwarranted interference with another's reasonable and lawful liberty is not compatible with neighbourliness.

21.12 **Volunteers**

Individuals, rather than groups and organizations, can undertake helpful and specific actions in support of NPTs. ACPO/NPIA point to recruitment of volunteers to help to administer the NPT, or conducting 'reassurance call-backs' to people who have a problem, or they can organize and lead EVAs. Additionally, if volunteers have the skills, they can help with drafting letters, setting formal meeting agendas, organizing and facilitating such meetings, booking rooms, copying posters or 'flyers', and a host of other activities which free up the personnel in NPTs to concentrate on getting out into the neighbourhood. Some volunteers in community safety roles—such as those organizing the cycling proficiency scheme, or 'walking buses' or crossings patrols—can act as a useful information source for NPTs. There is a process called the Community Safety Accreditation Scheme which formalizes such an arrangement and in some circumstances those taking part can be designated with limited enforcement powers.

21.13 **Conclusion**

We began this chapter by noting (in section 21.4) that there was no template for the composition of an NPT and that local conditions and resources would always determine who was in the NPT. There are many potential sources for teams, from the professional core of police officers (regulars and Specials) and PCSOs, through other community support officers and local authority officials, including partners, to voluntary organizations and individual volunteers. The police will always be at the heart of neighbourhood policing teams, by definition, but this should not exclude looser formations which co-opt individuals with specific skills or which channel the enthusiasm of those who want to help. If flexibility is a defining characteristic of the engagement of NPTs with local communities, then breadth of membership—suited to the occasion—should ensure the NPT's relevance and effectiveness in the eyes of the neighbourhood itself. The primary aim of an NPT in enhancing local perceptions of safety and security, effectively delivered, should produce, in time, localities in which crime cannot flourish.

Whether that will be sustainable seems to us to depend on three things:

- that NPTs deliver solutions mutually arrived at through effective engagement with communities in the neighbourhood;
- that consistent, long-term investment in the notion of NPTs is sustained and enhanced; and
- that NPTs are sufficiently flexible in composition and elastic enough in purpose to evolve alongside changes in perceptions of community safety and what constitutes reassurance.

If these are firmly embedded in local policing, neighbourhood policing will thrive. If not, then NPTs will become another footnote in the history of relations between the police and the policed.

Further Reading

ACPO/NPIA (2006), *Practice Advice on Professionalising the Business of Neighbourhood Policing*, NPIA, Wyboston <http://www.neighbourhoodpolicing.co.uk/doclib/doclib_view.asp?ID=528>, accessed 19 December 2008

Brogden, M and Nijhar, P (2005), *Community Policing: national and international models and approaches*, Willan Publishing, Devon

Caless, B (ed) (2007a), *Blackstone's PCSO Handbook*, Oxford University Press, Oxford, especially Chapters 1: 'Coming In' and 6: 'Community Focus'

—— (2007b) 'Numties in Yellow Jackets', *Policing, A Journal of Policy and Practice*, 1(2), August, Oxford University Press, Oxford

Cooper, C, Anscombe, J, McLean, F, and Morris, J (2006), *A National Evaluation of Community Support Officers*, Home Office Research Study No 297, Crown Copyright

Home Office (2005), *Community Policing: The Neighbourhood Policing Programme*, available at <http://police.home office.gov.uk/community-policing/neighbourhood-policing/>, accessed 29 April 2009

—— (2006), *Guide to becoming a Police Community Support Officer*, ref 275499, Central Office of Information (COI), August, Crown Copyright

—— (2008), *From the neighbourhood to the national: policing our communities together* (Green Paper), Cm 7448, London TSO

McLaughlin, E (2007), *The New Policing*, Sage Publishing, London

Tilley, N (ed), (2005), *Handbook of Crime Prevention and Community Safety*, Willan Publishing, Devon

Waddington, P (2008), 'Local standards in a global world' [on community policing], *Police Review*, 26 September, 16–17, available at <http://www.policereview.com>, accessed 20 October, 2008

Wilson, D, Ashton, J, and Sharp, D (2001), *What Everyone in Britain Should Know About the Police*, Blackstone Press, Oxford

Wright, A (2002), *Policing: an introduction to concepts and practice*, Willan Publishing, Devon

Chapter 22

Crime and Disorder Reduction Partnerships and Community Safety Partnerships

22.1 **Introduction**

This chapter looks in some detail at the nature and composition of partnerships and in particular, the Community Safety Partnership (CSP), which used to be called the Crime and Disorder Reduction Partnership or CDRP. In 2007, the name change was widely welcomed as being rather more user-friendly than the clumsy CDRP and also reflected the Government's new emphasis on community safety in all its aspects. The context for these partnerships and the Government's stress on the need to engage with local communities is the public fear of crime.

This emphasis on partnership coincided with a police acknowledgement that there was a dislocation between its claims that crime was reducing and the public's increasing unease, reflected in the annual British Crime Surveys, about crime and disorder. Put simply, the police were claiming, correctly, that 'all crime' was reducing (not all of it as the result of police action) whilst communities were indicating that the things which bothered them the most, such as petty crime, vandalism, graffiti, incivility, and gang menace, were not being dealt with by the police at all, with the consequence that people's fear of crime, paradoxically, was getting stronger. Some meeting of minds was called for, and the public agreement by the police service that it could no longer be the sole responsible body for maintaining law and order, helped to pave the way for partnerships to develop.

This was not all. The newly elected Labour Government was determined that local authorities would be obligated, by statute, to take responsibility alongside the police for the maintenance of law and order in each authority area.

22.2 **Origins and Legislation**

Section 17 of the Crime and Disorder Act 1998 imposes a duty on a local authority:

> without prejudice to any other obligation imposed on it—[to] exercise its function with due regard to the need to do all it reasonably can to prevent crime and disorder in its area(Crime and Disorder Act 1998, section 17)

This is the primary legislation which places the responsibility to tackle crime and disorder firmly at the door of the local authority. The police are a key component of any crime and disorder partnership, but in reducing crime, local authorities have now to take the lead. Following the enactment of the Crime and Disorder Act 1998, Crime and Disorder Reduction Partnerships (CDRPs) were set up in each local authority area. (One difficulty which the police found was that local authority boundaries did not always coincide with police Basic Command Unit (BCU) boundaries: some juggling and adjustment characterized the early years of the relationship between the police and the local authorities, and in one or two forces, is yet to be fully resolved.)

22.2.1 What did Local (and Unitary) Authorities have to do?

The reduction of crime was expected to be structured within a three-year cycle, in the course of which local (and unitary) authorities would:

- produce an audit of local crime and disorder problems;
- consult locally on the basis of the audit;
- establish priorities on the basis of the local consultation;
- formulate a strategy to deal with the priorities.

Whether local authorities liked it or not, the legislation obligated them to find out what was happening at a local level and to ascertain what residents felt about it. This meant in practice that authorities had to consult the police about 'official' or 'recorded' crime at a BCU level, but also to work with others, such as hospitals, primary care trusts, schools, social services and local public service organizations, councils, and charities, to find out what was happening about incidents which did not come to police attention but which constituted 'disorder'. An example might be hoaxers phoning the local Fire and Rescue Service repeatedly, or children truanting from school, or, as latterly, incidents where injuries were caused by bladed weapons.

The result of all the formal and semi-formal consultation was, or should have been, an audit of crime and disorder on a local basis. In many ways, such an audit is very much like a BCU intelligence 'map' of local crime and incidents, in which hot spots, 'hot' victims, and repeat offending are often highlighted. Indeed, this may be linked to the current capability to make crime mapping data available to the public. The local authority 'intelligence' about crime and disorder needed supplementing by discussion with those most affected, the residents of the estates or streets where incidents were taking place.

It is possible to understand from this occasionally cumbersome 'machinery' of consultation that it would be easy for authorities to pay lip service to residents' fears or uneasiness without actually doing very much (indeed, some authorities merely conducted a consultation exercise which gratified residents initially, but which soon produced disillusion and criticism of councils' inactivity). It was evident that authorities would be held to account for what they did to reduce crime and disorder, which is where the final elements in the formulation of an action plan come into play.

22.2.2 Determining Priorities

Neither the collective authorities, nor the police acting alone, are particularly good at understanding what it is that residents most want—other than the tangible presence of 'law and order'. It follows that consultation must include some way of determining the priority issues to be dealt with locally and in what order. The difficulty here is in the assumption that residents will necessarily speak with one voice, or that they (or their representatives) will always agree on what has to be done. Experience shows this is often not the case; indeed, some residents' associations can be caricatured as 'nimby' (not in my backyard) or protectionist—such as those wanting to exclude gypsy travellers or immigrants—or prone to demonize, like those groups of elderly residents who are frightened of gatherings of youths and want them moved on.

A characteristic of such consultation exercises can sometimes be that those who shout loudest or who wield the most political or media clout (such as having a 'collective' vote, or constituting a powerful local lobby) are those whose views are acted upon. One contributor to a Home Office online discussion about problem-solving in community engagement noted:

> Re too many surveys. We've had the same experience.
>
> When rolling out PACT [Partners And Communities Together] we've found that some areas have never been consulted and others consulted to death by a range of different council departments and agencies. Possibly the most valuable thing about PACT is that we now have a mechanism in place to coordinate any consultation and share the results—we now have proper evaluation mechanisms as well and those areas previously unconsulted [sic] are now being engaged.
>
> Kate, a contributor from Wigan, Lancashire on <http://www.crimereduction.homeoffice.gov.uk/chat012.htm>, accessed 15 September 2008

Nonetheless, it is incumbent on local authorities, and through them, local public service agencies including the police, to listen to all shades of opinion, to take all views into consideration, and to make efforts to reach or listen to those who tend to be under-represented or not heard. An example might be opposition locally to the establishment of a 'halfway house' for released prisoners to be gradually reintegrated into society. Fears about paedophiles, violent offenders, or drug addiction may colour local residents' responses, and there may have to be a considerable exercise of reassurance to pacify local opinion. In all the possible furore involved in such emotive issues, the inhabitants of the 'halfway house' themselves may not be heard at all. It follows, therefore, that consultation has to be comprehensive and it has to embrace the widest possible spectrum of opinion—which may include opinions hostile to the police or views which are anti- or un-social by conventional measurement.

Only then can the local authority proceed with any certainty to draw up a plan which identifies the priorities. This can involve a major exercise in local reassurance, especially as not everything can be done at once, and because there will be resource constraints as well as inhibitors on what is practically achievable.

An example of this might be residents' fears about youths 'joyriding' in the vicinity. This can be worrying to local people, not just because of the noise and the appearance of anarchy which stealing and racing cars through a residential area may suggest, but also because of residents' safety, fear for injury to children, or unpleasant aftermaths such as burned-out cars or collisions which damage other vehicles and property. The overwhelming priority for most residents would be for the activity to stop immediately, but achieving this may not be easy—intensely desired though it may be. Joyriding may occur only when there is no 'official' presence (see the PAT models in Chapter 25.7, where absence of a 'guardian' may facilitate crime), and perpetrators may be hard to detect. Installing counter-measures, such as CCTV, may take time and may use resources which are needed elsewhere equally urgently.

Permanent solutions, such as building 'sleeping policemen' ramps on the road to slow traffic, may take time to put into place, and may be counter-productive to some residents who want easier passage along any such route. There was a case in the Midlands in 2005, where the installation of speed ramps was overturned (physically) by local residents who did not want traffic slowed. Some argued additionally that the ramps merely encouraged the young thrill-seekers in stolen cars to 'bounce' the axles and sumps of the vehicles concerned, for the sheer spectacle which inflicting such damage caused. In other words, putting ramps in, far from solving the problem, may actually have exacerbated it and may indeed have led to unnecessary expense without solving the original disorder problem.

22.3 **Further Initiatives and Community Safety**

The Government did not, or could not, remain satisfied with the provisions in the Crime and Disorder Act 1998, and embarked on a series of initiatives to enhance community safety and the perception of increased security. The principle was that all had a part to play in making communities safer, and in November 2005 a National Community Safety Plan was published which set out the Government's key objectives in this area:

- Making communities stronger and more effective
- Further reducing crime and anti-social behaviour
- Creating safer environments
- Protecting the public and building confidence
- Improving people's lives so that they are less likely to commit offences or re-offend.

Note: For further information see <http://www.crimereduction.homeoffice.gov.uk/communitysafety01.htm?fp>, accessed on 22 September 2008

The plan was put out to consultation and reportedly was well-received, leading the Government to issue, in December 2007, an updated and revised National Community Safety Plan (NCSP) 2008–2011. The full text of this is available as a PDF download from the website address referenced above. The plan claims to be 'a new way of working on community safety' entailing 'much closer collaboration between central government and local agencies'. The emphasis is still on:

local partnerships on a range of matters such as health, children's issues, employment and environmental issues as well as policing, drugs prevention, crime and anti-social behaviour

NCSP 2008–2011; 'the vital role of local partners'

Aside from renewed emphasis on the importance of obtaining local solutions to local problems, the CSP seems only to bring together some of the more scattered elements in problem-solving which were not gathered up in the Crime and Disorder Act 1998. The same emphasis is there upon the primacy of the local authority collaborating with partners, and the same insistence on community consultation, even though the opportunity to define or describe 'a community' was not taken in the 2005 CSP and subsequent versions. The undertaking of a crime audit, and of spearheading attempts to reduce crime and disorder (or 'anti-social behaviour'), remains with the local authority.

22.4 **Undertaking a Crime Audit**

Prioritizing local disorder and crime problems, then, is not a bureaucratic function on its own; it reflects local unease and local fear, embraces what is practical and achievable, and determines—as far as possible—what is done in what order. For example, a local authority might produce this audit of local crime in a given district:

- Mugging: 2 incidents, 3 weeks apart
- Stealing vehicles: 22 incidents across 4 months
- Stealing from vehicles: 18 incidents within 14 weeks
- Graffiti: 33 occasions across 10 weeks
- Criminal damage to gates and lamp-posts: 12 incidents in 1 night
- Criminal damage to property: 8 incidents across 2 months
- Fights and local disturbances among youths: 16 incidents Friday through Saturday, between 2300 and 0400
- Breaking windows: 9 incidents at different locations in a week
- Theft of lawnmowers from garden sheds: 7 over 2 weeks
- Theft of goods and personal property: 21 incidents over 2 weeks
- Theft of goods from shops: 39 incidents over a month

Prioritizing what is to be done is not just a question of dealing with the most numerous offences, or the most serious (arguably, the muggings and local fights), but in establishing occurrences over significant periods. Intelligence analysis, familiar to the police, would be most valuable in an audit of this kind, because it would establish consistency in measurement (or, as the police often put it, 'comparing apples with apples'). Statistical analysis itself is less helpful, because there are too many variables in the way that data are recorded in the example given. Residents would indicate, fairly readily, which of the incidents upset them most (theft and criminal damage, as well as the graffiti outbreak, perhaps), but the police in consultation with the local authority might feel that some incidents are more easily detectable than others (lawnmower thefts have 'seasonality'; shoplifting might well have an evidence trail in CCTV footage and so on).

It is probable that the first set of priorities, taking all constraints and variables into account, might look like this:

1. Deal with fights and disturbances.
2. Erase graffiti, investigate 'tags'.
3. Patrol to inhibit criminal damage (especially alcohol-fuelled as likely cause, route from pub/club).
4. Theft from motor vehicle.
5. Theft of motor vehicle.
6. Theft of goods and personal property.

This would not be fixed in stone: as priorities are dealt with, new ones will emerge, and some will leap-frog others as perceptions change about the effect of different kinds of disorder, in the same way we accept triage at Accident and Emergency departments in NHS hospitals. Additionally, local authorities would want to impose some sort of time line or 'target discipline' on the priorities, noting when interim steps could be achieved, how consultation will monitor the progress or steps towards a solution, and by what point in the year the solution may be said to be under control. Many local authorities and police forces incorporate such targets in their annual, or more commonly, triennial (every three years), planning and published documents. Some local authorities have commissioned 'crime and disorder surveys', akin to the British Crime Survey, but on a parochial scale, to find out how residents feel about the combined agencies' efforts to tackle unease about crime and disorder.

22.5 **Composition of Partnerships**

Having established a strategy, with timed deadlines and targets, a local authority might reasonably look for partners in the scheme to increase the sense of community safety. The police are obvious partners, but who else might be approached to play a role? How willing are partners? What problems might be encountered in getting a group of very different people, representing very different interests, to work together?

We shall look now at possible and likely partners, noting of course that not all community safety partnerships will include everyone noted below, and some PACT (Partners And Communities Together) members will be very local and specific to an area, and this may not always translate to a larger stage or apply in all forces or BCUs. What we examine is a typical, or characteristic, set of partners in a CSP, not a definitive or an exhaustive selection.

22.5.1 **Local Authority Services**

Local authority services include services which the local authority generally controls and finances, such as street cleaning, street lighting, the removal of graffiti, and so on. Where such services may have an impact on local crime and disorder—the obvious example is good and effective street lighting—the local authority is in prime position to deliver. This can often represent some quick and effective 'hits',

provided that a proper assessment of need has been established. This is often provided through an 'Environmental
Visual Audit' (EVA—see section 24.7 below) also known as
a 'structured patch walk', where the local neighbourhood
policing team on its routine patrols notes matters or factors which will blight or threaten the community, such as
damaged street lights, fresh graffiti, abandoned vehicles
(especially those which have been used for joyriding), or
criminal damage. The EVA is often made more effective by
having along a member of the community itself, as well as
a representative of the local authority. This way, irritations
can be dealt with before they become problems, and the
community involved receives continuous reinforcement of
its protection and oversight. The local authority, then, has
two roles in the partnership: it usually runs or chairs the key
meetings and gives direction to the partnership planning,
but also provides many of the services which may remedy
the appearance of disorder.

22.5.2 The Police

The police are central to any of the partnerships, and play
a role in most of the collaborations which ensue. Since
they sit, by right, on Local Criminal Justice Boards, Youth
Offending Teams, and Drug Action Teams, as well as leading some initiatives in crime prevention and reduction (see
Chapter 26), the role of the police is seminal and no local
authority will succeed in reducing crime and disorder without close cooperation with the police. The Neighbourhood
Policing Teams (NPTs), set up to deal with issues of public
confidence and communities' fear of crime, have major
roles to play in encouraging local intelligence on crime and
disorder, as well as engaging with individual residents and
groups in any given neighbourhood.

That said, there are parts of any community which may
be hostile to the police, and this may show itself in open
aggression on one hand or refusal to cooperate on the other,
and may range from alienated young offenders through

the gypsy-traveller community, through immigrant communities (with an imported fear of the police), to gay or minority ethnic communities which have hitherto found the police to be unsympathetic or indifferent to matters such as homophobic or racist crime. The picture is steadily changing, of course, and herculean efforts have been made by many police forces to reach out to such marginalized or 'hard-to-reach' groups (or groups that the police have made little effort to reach), but progress is slow and many of the problems identified by the Stephen Lawrence Inquiry, chaired by Sir William Macpherson in 1999, continue to reverberate throughout the police service and its relations with sections of the public. It will probably always be the case that parts of any community in any neighbourhood will be reserved in dealing with the police, just as there will always be a (white, elderly, retired) segment of the community which is supportive and positive about the police. What this may also reinforce is that the police cannot solve the local instances of crime and disorder alone; they too need partnerships to help to obtain solutions.

22.5.3 Local Education

Many community problems involve young people, skills issues, and employment. One or more representatives from the provision of local education (including teachers, pastoral care workers, education trusts, and so on) can give insights into, and propose educational solutions for, problems associated with youth and local crime and disorder. Among other criminological explanations for the causes of crime, the common factors of low skills levels and unemployment characterize many young offenders.

In an online exchange about the role of partnerships, moderated by the Home Office, an acting sergeant from West Mercia Constabulary described her local efforts to engage with young people, involving consultation teams and CSPs:

> We hold dedicated School PACTS, in local high schools, and also face to face consultations at youth clubs etc. We have been mindful no[t] to just engage one area of the youth, and have looked at using PACT at Final Warning clinics etc. In many of the PACT panels, there is a representative of the youths, so there is always consultation.
>
> Rebecca Handy available at <http://www.crimereduction.homeoffice.gov.uk/chat012.htm>, accessed 15 September 2008

Local business representatives may be able to add to the debate about skills levels by noting what skills are required to obtain work and the nature of local unemployment. For example, low local take-up of places for learning practical trade skills such as carpentry, plumbing, and electrical repair/installation could be revived by the use of local business grants to support the unemployed in a return to learning. Education representatives can bring valuable expertise to bear on how to engage disaffected youth in attending college classes or night school.

22.5.4 Primary Care Trusts

Local general practitioners (GPs) and medical practice nurses are highly valuable members of any CSP. In the first place, such representatives will have first-hand experience of the problems experienced by local communities (treating, for example, the symptoms of domestic abuse, depression, anxiety, and so on), as well as understanding what matters to the communities as a whole (disorder, incivility, rowdy behaviour, anti-social activity in residential areas, etc). Additionally, doctors and nurses are normally well-regarded across the population and their participation may lend considerable credibility to the role of the partnership. That said, doctors tend not to live in the communities they tend, except in rural areas, and may not be available for 'after hours' activities and meetings. So, too, nurses may not wish to engage after the day's work, so the timings of local partnership meetings are crucial to the success of the engagement. Other members of the local medical teams, such as medical social workers (in some hospitals, they are still called 'almoners') and practice managers, can be valuable additions to partnership working.

22.5.5 Local Criminal Justice Boards

At local level, the work of the Criminal Justice agencies is coordinated by 42 Criminal Justice Boards (LCJBs) in England and Wales. They are based on police force areas. Membership typically is made up from one of the chief officers of police (usually the Deputy Chief Constable), the county or city Chief Prosecutor from the Crown Prosecution Service, a representative from HM Courts Service, members of Youth Offending Teams, the Prison Service, and the Probation Service. In other words, those involved are heavily engaged professionally in the criminal justice system. With such weighty membership, LCJBs focus on improving the effectiveness of criminal justice and supporting the delivery of key targets and reform. The targets for LCJBs currently include:

- bringing more offences to justice;
- reducing the number of trials which do not proceed as planned (in both the magistrates' courts and in the Crown Courts);
- increasing the percentage of the public which has confidence in the effectiveness of the criminal justice system;
- increasing the percentage of payment of fines and fixed penalties;
- reducing the number of days from arrest to sentence of 'persistent young offenders';
- improving the timeliness of Crown and magistrates' courts.

It needs to be observed that, given the strategic level representation in LCJBs and the large geographical canvas which they survey (each with an entire police area), it is unlikely that the full LCJB will be represented at every local authority partnership group. The latter scale is simply too small. The best that might be obtained is that a representative attends some meetings of one PACT group. More feasible is that there are channels whereby information of use to LCJBs can be fed from the CSP meetings and that a two-way flow is encouraged. There are police channels as well, of course, and those for the local magistracy, but these tend to be large, diffuse, and complex. Nonetheless, there are successful examples of partnerships involving the LCJB and the community; and it is after all in the interest of the LCJB to demonstrate that its consultation with the public is effective and continuous. Using PACT as a mechanism is one way to demonstrate that.

22.5.6 Youth Offending Teams

Often seen as key elements in any attempts to deal with young offenders, Youth Offending Teams (YOTs) are in every local authority in England and Wales. They are composed typically of representatives from the police, the Probation Service, social services, education, health, drugs and misuse, and the local authority housing department. YOTs are usually managed or chaired by whoever is responsible for coordination of the work of the youth justice services (often informally called a 'Yot Master').

In some ways, the YOT is a miniature PACT, except that those engaged in managing youth offending are invariably professionals and YOTs do not normally include members of local communities, though they may be consulted on specific matters.

The way that YOTs work is that each young offender's needs are assessed (using a national template to ensure consistency) in an attempt to find out what makes the person offend, what risks the person poses to others, and what, if anything, can be done to prevent re-offending. There is no magic formula and assessments are deliberately carried out at an individual level, so that any solution is equally personal. The downside is the workload and the sheer number of offenders, organized on a fairly wide geographic basis. For example, the box below shows the number of YOTs for a sample regional development agency, and it can be quickly seen that the areas defined are pretty much 'county-sized':

West Midlands YOTs:

Birmingham
Coventry
Dudley
Sandwell
Shropshire & Telford/Wrekin
Solihull
Staffordshire
Stoke on Trent
Walsall
Warwickshire
Wolverhampton
Worcestershire and Herefordshire

Any parallels with the LCJBs are apt, and it can be seen that, whilst LCJBs are concerned primarily with the passage of young offenders through the courts, and YOTs are concerned with all forms of juvenile offending, nonetheless there are areas of evident overlap and community of interest.

22.5.7 Drugs Action Teams

Drugs Action Teams (DATs), like YOTs, are focused on highly specific forms of offending, but the DATs are concerned with controlling drugs supply and abuse, as well as the rehabilitation of users, at all levels in society, not just among young people, though it is here of course that the greatest or more open prevalence is to be seen. DATs are normally composed of representatives from the police and the Probation Service, with social services, Primary Care Trusts or the local Health Services, Drugs and Rehabilitation Services, and the local authority housing department, though other groups may be asked to contribute on an informal basis.

DATs also help to organize local versions of national initiatives such as Communities Against Drugs (CAD), by supporting interventions to disrupt local drugs markets (tackling both supply and demand), to counter drug-related crime—especially petty theft to 'feed' a habit—and to address any associated anti-social behaviour, such as nuisance, the use of municipal premises for dealing, the prevalence of used needles in parks, and so on. Community organizations are encouraged to get involved in CAD, since much local crime and disorder may be driven by drugs, from dealers targeting school students to using derelict properties as 'crack houses'.

22.5.8 Multi-Agency Public Protection Arrangements

Multi-Agency Public Protection Arrangements (MAPPA) were first formed in 2001 for the very specific purpose of monitoring, assessing, and managing the most serious sexual and violent offenders, particularly in their return to society after serving prison terms. The MAPPA Responsible Authority brings together the police, the Prison Service, and the Probation Service, who then encourage cooperation from other 'responsible authorities', including social care, health, housing, and education. For example, the police will share information with offender managers, such as the Prison Service, what they may have gathered about an offender's behaviour from surveillance or from intelligence gathering, such as preferred haunts, continuing patterns of offending, triggers to offending, and so on. Offender managers may take steps to inhibit the returning offender's access to such places, whilst at the same time encouraging the offender to realize what situations they must avoid to ensure that they do not offend again. In their turn, local authorities may help to find offenders suitable accommodation where they can be effectively managed away from perceived risks or triggers to re-offending.

It is a highly professional and often technical activity, but the assessments of the risks posed by these socially dangerous people are key to preventing a dreary cycle of 'offence, sentence, offence sentence' which characterized sexual and violent offenders in the past. There are three broad levels of risk where MAPPA offenders are managed:

Level One: normal agency management
Most offenders are managed at this level; in 2004–2005, 71% of MAPPA offenders were managed at this level
Level Two: local inter-risk agency management
Includes offenders assessed as High or Very High risk of harm; normally about 25% of MAPPA offenders are at this level (2004–2005)
Level Three: entailing Multi-Agency Public Protection Panels
Appropriate for those offenders who are assessed to pose the highest risk of causing serious harm, or whose management is so problematic and unpredictable that oversight at a senior level and the commitment of exceptional resources. In 2004–2005, 3% of MAPPA offenders were at this level and the incidence really is small numerically.

Source: <http://noms.justice.gov.uk/protecting-the-public/supervision/mappa>

We do not mean to suggest here that MAPPA is formally part of any PACT arrangement or local authority CSP, but invariably, some of the same people and possibly even the same representatives will be on MAPPA as on YOT, as on LCJB, and on the CSP groups, and equally invariably, the problems which MAPPA were set up to deal with and to manage are sometimes those which generate lurid media coverage and much local unease, including vigilantism, so that communities are engaged with the issues of public protection whether or not there is formal consultation and discussion.

Case Study

For an example of MAPPA collaboration which generated lessons equivalent in significance to those of the Lawrence enquiry, see HM Inspector of Probation, 2006, *An Independent Review of a Serious Further Offence Case: Anthony Rice* (HMIP, London).

Anthony Rice, a convicted murderer released on Life Licence, was able to murder again despite being subject to MAPPA supervision. HMIP reviewed the case and found that despite the fact that all MAPPA participants had seriously and conscientiously executed their responsibilities, yet there were still mistakes, misjudgements, and miscommunications that enabled Rice to kill again.

22.5.9 Other Public Service Organizations

The Fire and Rescue Service for the region or county or city is often engaged with CSPs, partly to help deal with the prevalence of hoax calls and false alarms to the Fire and Rescue Service but also because of the characteristic fire-setting which accompanies (particularly vehicle) crime and local social disorder. Similarly, the Ambulance Trust or Paramedic Services may be useful to a partnership, at least in the initial stages of evidence and information gathering, because of the role of the emergency services in attending incidents and logging events where there have been injuries or accidents.

22.5.10 The Business Community

It is a common fallacy to think of the business community as a single entity with one mind and one voice, when the reality is quite different. It is the businesses which bring prosperity to a district because not only do commercial enterprises provide employment and a degree, consequently of social stability, but they also invest in an area and can be encouraged to sponsor activities or to help support the provision of amenities. Typically, though, business communities are not prevalent on 'problem' housing estates, nor is ethical business likely to be attracted to a neighbourhood where there is widespread disorder and crime.

That said, the owners of individual enterprises are often well-informed about the district and about the residents, and they are often articulate 'movers and shakers' within the communities, who are well able to take on the burden of partnership working with public agencies. There can be a tendency for such groups, especially through aggregate or large business community representatives, to undertake special pleading, such as for the siting of supermarket shop outlets, or for some kind of commercial advantage, about which both the public service agencies and the community of residents need to be alert. At the same time, large employers and branches of national chains will support local initiatives where there is direct retail benefit or 'worthy' advertising.

22.5.11 Voluntary Groups and Charities

Whilst many charities and voluntary groups are about single issues (housing, the elderly, local security), they are firmly rooted among communities and neighbourhoods and can often speak with conviction and passion about local issues. Partnerships need to be aware of the sometimes unseen pitfalls involved in local politics, where single issues (such as experimental testing on animals or live animal exports) can hugely inflame localities; and over-simplification of complex matters, such as offences against children, can lead to vigilantism.

That said, there are many voluntary organizations, ranging from the Women's Institutes to Citizens' Advice Bureaux and from charities like Shelter, Help the Aged, and Mind, which can bring considerable local knowledge, commitment, various forms of expertise, and a focus for community 'spirit' into partnership working; indeed the police are now recognizing the skills that volunteers can bring and are increasingly utilizing them, particularly within NPTs.

22.5.12 **Community Groups**

Self-help groups from within communities are important sources for partnership working, and early engagement with organized structures within target communities is recommended. NPTs, particularly PCSOs, are often well-tapped into such groups, which can range from loose groupings such as 'Mother and Toddler' meetings through to long-standing Residents' Associations (often protectionist and 'nimby', often dominated by white retired people, but always with a powerful voice). Some groups in some communities will be hostile to the police (Myhill, 2006) and some will be antagonistic to any public service agency or mutual social initiative (Foster et al, 2005: 57).

That said, if consultation is to be genuine, if hard-to-reach and hard-to-hear groups really are to be brought into partnership, then the police and other public service agencies, including local authorities, have to be prepared occasionally for some uncomfortable fellow passengers, for criticism and for challenge. Evidence so far suggests that greatest success is achieved when public agencies listen effectively, when mutual benefits are stressed and when problems are seen to be solved effectively (see Chapter 25.7, and Jones and Newburn, 2001).

22.5.13 The Private Security Industry

Those who are paid to patrol shopping malls, maintain order in night clubs or discos, and who front the security presence in 'gated' communities and other parts of private security provision, may be valuable sources for community intelligence. They see and hear a great deal, and have close acquaintance with, among others, the young and with those who have abundant material resources. All localities have one or more private guarding companies, either in protecting commercial properties or in patrolling building sites at night, as well as representative branches from national companies such as Securitas and Group 4.

The police are already well used to exploiting such private security provision for criminal intelligence (not least the obtaining of 'private' CCTV images); and local authorities, since they grant licences and approve deployments in public areas, have considerable influence which can be helpful in establishing partnership arrangements with the private security industry. This should not be made too much of. Some public service agencies have found to their embarrassment that what they thought were informal arrangements with a local security company were exploited to see off rivals and to boost the industry's 'image' at a time when private security had somewhat seedy overtones and fringe criminal associations. It behoves any partnership arrangement to be of mutual benefit to the communities and not to involve something, even as innocent as enthusiastic endorsement, which can be hijacked by the companies themselves for commercial gain.

22.6 Caveats and Concerns about Partnerships

We have explored briefly the range of potential partners which may be available to a local authority in setting up a PACT or CSP. As we noted at the beginning, not all of these will be engaged in partnership working all the time. Some will come and go, some will be permanently on all groups and all committees—like the police—and some will not engage at all. Some will be very local indeed, and of short duration, such as pressure groups to keep open an NHS hospital or to protest against a local by-pass plan. All who become involved will have their own ideas about what a community wants or needs, and all will have a private or in-house agenda which will dominate their thinking.

This has been extensively researched (Gilling, 2005; Myhill, 2006; Rogers, 2006), because partnerships often find it hard to understand each other, and paradoxically, common goals are often hard to achieve and sustain. Colin Rogers puts the problem most succinctly:

> . . . it is the very diverse make-up of many of the agencies that constitute partnerships [which] may be problematic . . . Partnerships, especially within the field of crime control and criminal justice, by their nature, draw together diverse organisations with very different cultures, ideologies and traditions that pursue distinct aims through divergent structures, strategies and practices. Deep structural conflicts exist between the parties that sit down together in partnerships.
>
> *Crime Reduction Partnerships*, Rogers, 2006: 12

The data, though partial and incomplete, suggest that there may be a dislocation of intent when voluntary groups, such as those which support drug addicts or offenders, sit down with the police. So too, those with single issues, such as Neighbourhood Watch, may find that their agendas are markedly at variance to those from youth groups or representatives from 'sink' estates.

It is the role of the local authority Chair of the PACT or CSP which is key here, since the opposed agendas can be reconciled (just) if a common and mutually acceptable target is defined at the outset and if the Chair ensures that a kind of studied neutrality characterizes the carefully controlled discussions about any given issue. In practice, however, local authorities do not always provide people with the requisite tact and diplomatic skills to hold the ring between antagonistic and unwilling partners. Equally, it may be argued that the police practice of rotating its staff regularly, and often within a short space of time, does not always aid partnership building.

It would be wrong to end this examination of partnerships on such a negative note—realistic though it is—because there are plenty of instances where partnerships have worked perfectly successfully, often because of a strong Chair, or because the issues are so pressing and urgent, or a combination of all of these factors. Here is one example from Merseyside, where the Liverpool Community Network (LCN) has engaged with public service agencies to influence local decision-making on the reduction of crime and disorder through networking with over 1,600 voluntary and community groups ('in ten networks of identity, interest and place'). LCN's manager, Jane Groves, noted these areas of common agreement and progress:

> We run a 'cleaner, safer, greener' grants programme for our CDRP linked to the neighbourhood element of the Local Area Agreement—here local voluntary and community groups apply for up to £5,000 to tackle 'crime and grime' issues in their local area. One of these projects, to tackle anti-social behaviour (under age drinking) through the installation of CCTV, has resulted in zero calls to the police. To back up this preventative work, the police and local RSL are supporting extra detached youth work.

Edited version, see <http://www.crimereduction.home office.gov.uk/chat012.htm>, accessed 15 September 2008

Another successful example of partnership working comes from Yorkshire, where in the discussion referenced above, an online observation was made that:

> In East Riding we are developing Neighbourhood Action Teams (NATs). Our latest project is to develop 'Operation Community Challenge' . . . designed to target criminal damage hotspots by working in partnership with our Environmental Services Section, volunteers from the NATs, town councils, police, [and] partners in the community. The operation is on one morning or afternoon where everyone comes together to clean up, remove graffiti, litter pick, [and] mend street furniture, that has been identified from visual audits.
>
> Edited version, see <http://www.crimereduction.home office.gov.uk/chat012.htm>, accessed 15 September 2008

22.7 **Conclusion**

There is still considerable political will for partnership working to liaise with communities and to reduce crime and disorder, and some mileage still to be made from the process. After some ten years, though, it is not unreasonable to expect to see prolific instances of success and high achievement, but research is lacking, as is evidence that all these disparate groups can work together. Colin Rogers' concerns (2006: 12) continue to resonate. It is probably the case that putting PACT and CSP partnerships together is relatively straightforward, but getting to mutual targets without division or recrimination has proven more difficult. As is clear from some of the examples instanced throughout this chapter, this has not stopped partnerships from trying and succeeding, albeit with more modest gains than first hoped for.

Further Reading

Forrest, S, Myhill, A, and Tilley, N (2005), *Practical Lessons for Involving the Community in Crime and Disorder Problem-Solving*, HO Development and Practice Report 43, Home Office, Crown Copyright

Foster, J, Newburn, T, and Sauhami, A (2005), *Assessing the Impact of the Stephen Lawrence Enquiry*, Home Office Research Study 294

Gilling, D (2005), 'Partnership and Crime Prevention' in N Tilley (ed), *Handbook of Crime Prevention and Community Safety*, Willan Publishing, Devon

Home Office (2007), *National Community Safety Plan 2008–2011*, Crown Copyright; available at <http://www.crimereduction.homeoffice.gov.uk/communitysafety01.htm?fp>, accessed 22 September 2008

Jones, T and Newburn, T (2001), *Widening Access: improving police relations with hard to reach groups*, Police Research Series, Paper 138, Home Office, Crown Copyright

Newburn, T and Jones, T (2002), *Consultation by Crime and Disorder Partnerships*, Police Research Series, Paper 148, Home Office, Crown Copyright

Phillips, C, Jacobson, J, Prime, R, Carter, M, and Considine, M (2002), *Crime and Disorder Reduction Partnerships: Round One Progress*, Police Research Series Paper 151, Home Office, Crown Copyright; available at <http://www.homeoffice.gov.uk>, accessed 6 August 2008

Kershaw, C, Nicholas, S, and Walker, A (2008), *Crime in England and Wales 2007–2008*, Home Office, Crown Copyright

Myhill, A (2006), 'Community Engagement in Policing: lessons from the literature', Home Office Report 47, available at <http://www.crimereduction.gov.uk/policing18.htm>, accessed February 2007

Newburn, T and Jones, T (2002), *Consultation by Crime and Disorder Partnerships*, Police Research Series, Paper 148, Home Office, Crown Copyright

Phillips, C, Jacobson, J, Prime, R, Carter, M, and Considine, M (2002), *Crime and Disorder Reduction Partnerships: Round One Progress*, Police Research Series Paper 151, Home Office, Crown Copyright; available at <http://www.homeoffice.gov.uk/rds/prgdfs/prs151.pdf>, accessed 6 August 2008

Rogers, C (2006), *Crime Reduction Partnerships*, Oxford University Press, Oxford

Solomon, R and Flores, F (2003), *Building Trust in Business, Politics, Relationships, and Life*, Oxford University Press, Oxford

Chapter 23

Citizen Focus

23.1 **Introduction**

If there is a current leitmotif for policing, it is that of Citizen Focus. This phrase has become ubiquitous within all 43 forces of England and Wales and has implications for Neighbourhood Policing, as we shall later explore.

> Essentially 'Citizen Focus' Policing seeks to establish (or, strictly, re-establish) the explicit linkage between policing and the numerous, and sometimes disparate, communities that it serves.

Several commentators (Ipsos MORI, 2008; Muir and Lodge, 2008; Carlisle and Loveday, 2007) have argued that the natural corollary of performance-driven police management is that policing becomes divorced from its local environment:

> Recent attempts by the Government to increase control from the centre through target setting and top-down initiatives have had limited success and have made policing even less responsive to local needs and circumstances.
>
> (Muir and Lodge, 2008: 8).

Citizen Focus seeks to bridge this perceptual gap, between what the public wants and what the police can deliver, by ensuring that the police work *with* communities, not just for them. It is therefore not just an internal management issue, nor is it merely a public relations issue; it is fundamentally about organizational culture.

The police need to involve the community in decision-making to increase their accountability and legitimacy. The citizen is no longer a passive observer of policing, but in a 'post-modern' sense has become a true '*consumer*' of the policing product and therefore will not tolerate being ignored, left on the sidelines, and not consulted. Twenty-first century policing must encompass this societal change, and Citizen Focus seeks to do this in a proactive and collaborative way.

However, it is not surprising that for some in the police, brought up in a culture which 'does' law and order to the public, this change is uncomfortable and threatening. It seems to them to erode the 'command' position of the police, to undermine the *requirement to comply* upon which the police have traditionally relied in order to control and enforce. Having to consult and to listen to the views of those without, perhaps, much knowledge of the law or the conventions of policing can be a cultural change of a high order. Undoubtedly, some long-serving officers find this change difficult to accept. There is little evidence, however, that the younger generation of police officers has any problem with the concept of citizens having a say in how they are policed.

23.2 **What is Citizen Focus?**

The rationale for Citizen Focus within policing was based upon what was understood as a gap between the police and the communities in which they worked. A 2003 Home Office Report *Public Perceptions of Police Accountability and Decision-Making* highlighted research amongst members of the public that had identified a distance between the police and the communities they worked in:

> There was a general consensus in the focus groups that the public does not participate in decisions about policing and that they should have an opportunity to state their opinions

The focus groups suggested that the public was, in general poorly informed about policing . . . and wanted more commu-nication, information and involvement

It was not just a policing issue, but was one that had reper-cussions throughout the public sector, in particular in health and education. However, policing, or rather policing as a by-product of crime, has a particular resonance within the British media, and this serves to ensure that any issues around crime also impinge on debates about policing. There is a contemporary media focus upon violent crime and youth crime, particularly on manifestations of anti-social behaviour. This fuels the desire for policing to reflect the concerns of the communities they serve, and Citizen Focus has become the 'popular' policy to bridge this gap.

The Home Office published its definition of Citizen Focus in a 2006 report *Citizen Focus: Good Practice Guide*.

Definition

Citizen-focused policing means reflecting the needs and expectations of individuals and local communities in decision making, service delivery and practice. The objectives of citizen-focused policing are to improve public confidence, to increase satisfaction of service users and to increase public involvement in policing . . . Citizen focus is not a new area of business or a stand-alone project. It should be embedded through everything we do and the way we do it. This applies at all levels of policing

---

It is therefore evident that citizen focus is about concen-trating policing on the qualitative aspects of service deliv-ery, perhaps in recognizing that target-driven performance management has resulted only in those things that need measuring being considered important. The public has grown suspicious of governmental claims that crime fig-ures are in decline, particularly when announced against a media-fuelled backdrop of violent crime events, even though independent surveys such as the biannual British Crime Survey show a trend decrease in reported crime that parallels the decrease in crime reported to the police.

Citizen Focus gives due prominence to a theory that has been utilized within Neighbourhood Policing: that it is not just crime, but also the fear of crime that needs to be tackled. Some people will be influenced by what they hear or read or see about events elsewhere in the country, such as gang crime, or attacks with a knife, and may project those fears on to their own community. By involving residents at a community level, Citizen Focus seeks to combat both crime *and* the fear of crime by understanding that both have an impact on how reassured the public feels.

23.3 **Citizen Focus and Policing**

One of the key measurements utilized within citizen-focused policing is that of satisfaction. This becomes an important issue within policing because '*satisfaction*' can be a subjective matter that can be difficult to measure or to quantify. However, the Home Office in a 2007 report *Citizen Focus: A Practical Guide to Improving Police Follow-Up with Victims and Witnesses* found that the key aspects of satisfaction in public services were:

- delivery
- timeliness
- information
- staff attitudes
- professionalism.

It is therefore a measurement that will vary from police force to police force and from incident to incident, and, as such, has an ephemeral quality that is at odds with much that has been measured, counted, and quantified previously. It is relatively easy to measure the number of burglaries in a district from one year to the next, but *satisfaction* about what the police have done about burglaries, and how safe citizens feel as a consequence, is a much less tangible concept.

In order to open up the discussion, the Home Office, in its 2006 report *Citizen Focus: Good Practice Guide*, identified four areas of satisfaction within citizen-focused policing. This was presented in a diagrammatic fashion, as in Figure 23.1.

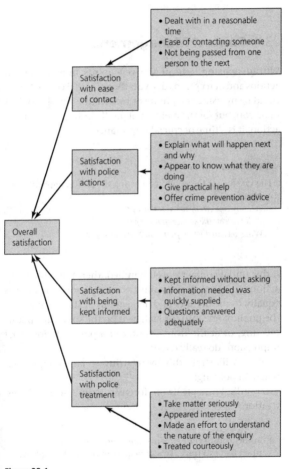

Figure 23.1

This approach identified key areas for each of the four satisfaction levels and this in turn established that citizen focus was not just confined to one aspect of policing. The concept needs to be embedded across all areas of service delivery and cannot be seen as the responsibility of one department.

23.4 **Contact Management**

Within policing, one of the key points from which all actions and perceptions derive is that of initial contact. This could be by using the phone or by meeting a police officer in person, but for the member of public initiating the interaction, it is a time of crucial importance.

Contact Management

The member of the public, contacting the police, implicitly or explicitly asks:

Will my concern be taken seriously?

Will I receive the service that I expect?

Will I get satisfaction from what has occurred?

If this initial contact is well-handled, then the subsequent actions are based on an established foundation. This applies equally to the manner and demeanour of staff with whom the public come into contact, be it on the street, at a public meeting, or at the front counter of a police station. First impressions do really count.

We can illustrate this by referring to an example elsewhere in policing:

Locard's Principle from forensic (crime scene) investigation:

Consider Locard's Principle in crime-scene management—**every contact leaves a trace.** This principle can equally be applied to

Neighbourhood Policing. Such traces, including every contact made within this environment, might involve:

- meeting someone on the street;
- addressing a public meeting;
- dealing with concerns at a local surgery;
- advertising a crime reduction campaign;
- answering the phone;
- attending a crime scene;
- taking a crime report;
- talking to a school's assembly;
- dealing with partnership agencies;
- establishing a Neighbourhood Watch scheme.

(This list is by no means exhaustive but gives a flavour of the breadth of typical actions).

Each of these will leave people with an impression of the police, sometimes favourable, sometimes not. This could be about standards of dress, demeanour, language used, courtesy (or lack of it), informing people of actions taken, making sure people are kept informed and so on. These all go to providing the elusive *satisfaction* with the police, a key measurement used by the HMIC when assessing Neighbourhood Policing. This is clearly not just a neighbourhood policing issue, but is one that cuts across all boundaries within policing and therefore needs to be taken seriously.

The *Citizen Focus: Good Practice Guide* (2006) provides an example from Surrey Police which established a mnemonic for a comprehensive customer service package that established excellence as a benchmark for all.

Mnemonic—LISTEN

Listen to customers and take their concerns seriously.

Inspire confidence and help people to feel secure.

Support with information, including reference numbers and contact details.

Take ownership and deliver on our promises.

Explain what we can and cannot do.

Notify people of progress regularly and the final outcome.

23.5 **Victim and Witness Care**

One of the key areas within which Citizen Focus can be most successfully utilized is that of victim and witness care. This area already has its own *Code of Practice for Victims of Crime* (2006) as well as a *Witness Charter* (2005), but it was recognized that there were further benefits to the police that could accrue from having a Citizen Focus perspective. By utilizing citizen focus techniques, witnesses and victims should be provided with information and reassurance which would help both them and the police. The Home Office (2006) has identified ways in which this good practice would benefit the police and the criminal justice system:

- opportunities for the victim to provide new evidence;
- developing a relationship of trust with the victim;
- increasing the chances of the victim appearing as a witness in court;
- making it more likely that the victim will report crimes in the future;
- making it more likely that the victim will trust and have confidence in the police.

These principles are transferable to all those who have contact with the police and that is one of the long-term aims of the Citizen Focus agenda. The Home Office 2007 report *Citizen Focus: A Practical Guide to Improving Police Follow-Up with Victims and Witnesses* identified six factors that would improve the service offered to victims and witnesses.

- understand the needs of victims and witnesses;
- deliver a personalized service;
- systems and processes;
- leadership;
- training and development;
- performance management (staff and corporate).

The factors specified reassure victims and witnesses that their concerns and what they have to offer to the police investigation of crime are being taken both seriously and professionally, and apply as equally to police staff, supervisors, and management, as to those specifically involved in Neighbourhood Policing.

23.6 **Citizen Focus and Neighbourhood Policing**

While we may agree that citizen-focused policing is now something that informs all aspects of contemporary policing, there is perhaps a recognition that areas of policing where there is a large degree of public–police interface are going to bear the brunt of that citizen focus.

The satisfaction themes developed by the Home Office offer an insight into this because the focus comes upon four areas that will impact most heavily on the kinds of policing that has the most contact with the public. Neighbourhood Policing will therefore need to take into account the ethos of Citizen Focus as it affects all aspects of a policing style that has the citizen at the forefront. To some extent, this may make Neighbourhood Policing a natural bedfellow for Citizen Focus, and many of the principles will find a natural resonance within the activities of Neighbourhood Policing Teams (NPTs). However, with this resonance will come expectation. NPTs will be under pressure to demonstrate their affinity to Citizen Focus and will need to ensure that team members not only 'talk the citizen focus talk', but also 'walk the walk', by putting the concept to practical use in all they do locally.

The Government has spent a lot of time and effort on disseminating the citizen focus message to communities at a time when the latter have also been assailed with information about Neighbourhood Policing. The cumulative effect is that many members of communities are educated in some detail about what to expect from policing, and this expectation now has to be supported with appropriate access.

Citizen Focus has increased the accountability required from local NPTs. They are expected to have public consultation, are expected to publicize their contact details, and are expected to listen and to take specific notice of community concerns. For Neighbourhood Policing practitioners, and particularly for their managers, there will be an explicit expectation that Citizen Focus goes beyond making sure their staff are simply smart, courteous, and punctual. There needs to be a recognition that Citizen Focus is at the core of neighbourhood policing activity.

Table 23.1 highlights areas of activity where NPTs can satisfy Citizen Focus satisfaction performance indicators:

Table 23.1

Citizen Focus Theme	Neighbourhood Policing Activity
Satisfaction with ease of contact	Publication of individual officer contact details
	NPT contact number
	Accessible Community Safety Unit
	Public meetings/surgeries publicized and available at different times and locations
	NPT working in the community
Satisfaction with police actions	Local priorities reflected in NPT activities
	Reassurance through visible foot patrols
	Targeted action against locally identified problems
	Practical assistance offered in crime prevention
	Partnership working in collaborative problem-solving

Satisfaction with being kept informed	Feedback on local priorities provided at public meetings or through newsletters
	Individuals to be apprised of progress
	Problem-solving to reflect the need for feedback
Satisfaction with police treatment	Local problems taken seriously
	Due prominence given to signal crimes
	Local problems understood in a local context
	Courteous treatment of all
	Understanding from police of disparate nature of community—not policing to the perceived majority/or to a vocal and organized minority

One particular area where Neighbourhood Policing and Citizen Focus are in a 'conjoined' relationship is Signal Crimes (see Chapter 24 for an extended explanation of signal crimes and their relevance to Neighbourhood Policing). Essentially, the **signal crimes perspective** counsels the police to listen to the concerns of residents in a community, because the latter's perspective on a particular problem is not only localized within that neighbourhood, it also has profound repercussions on residents' feelings of safety. Therefore, successful utilization of the signal crimes perspective could lead to NPTs identifying and solving those problems that the community care most about. In doing so, the problem-solving initiatives around this local issue could also satisfy all four aspects of the Citizen Focus agenda. There is no need to separate the two.

23.7 **Links to Community Engagement**

As well as linking Citizen Focus with Neighbourhood Policing, it is possible to construct a link between Citizen Focus and community engagement. Like Neighbourhood

3 Neighbourhood Policing

Policing, 'community engagement' is a wide-ranging concept that involves engaging with the community, either at an individual or at a group level, and includes residents in decisions that affect them and/or the areas in which they live. The Home Office has identified three main forms of engagement: information gathering; consultation; and participation—and it is possible to map this across the Citizen Focus aspects as well as the Neighbourhood Policing ones (see Table 23.2).

Table 23.2

Community Engagement Mechanism	Citizen Focus Satisfaction Target	Neighbourhood Policing Activity
Information gathering	Satisfaction with ease of contact	Neighbourhood survey
	Satisfaction with police actions	NPT distribution of contact details
		Officers collating a Key Individual Network contact list
Consultation	Satisfaction with police actions	PACT meetings
	Satisfaction with being kept informed	Community surgeries
	Satisfaction with police treatment	Focus groups
		Street briefings
Participation	Satisfaction with police actions	Problem-solving activity eg EVA
	Satisfaction with police treatment	Community forums
		Diversity forums

This demonstrates an important concept within Neighbourhood Policing: it is not divorced from the context in which it occurs, nor does it take place in isolation from other policing or public sector activity. Neighbourhood Policing exists in symbiosis with Citizen Focus and community engagement, as the diagram in Figure 23.2 makes clear.

Figure 23.2 The components of community engagement

By constructing a strategy that encompasses Citizen Focus and community engagement, Neighbourhood Policing has an opportunity to bridge the 'satisfaction gap' and help in combating the public's fear of crime. There is also an opportunity to take the satisfaction measurements out of a staid managerial environment and place them into an actual neighbourhood context. In other words, performance measurement in a police context may begin to have meaning rather than existence.

23.8 **Community Impact Assessments**

One facet of Neighbourhood Policing that has tangible links to other aspects of policing is found in Community Impact Assessments (CIA). It is concerned, *inter alia*, with the impact that critical incidents can have on a victim, family, or community, and that the traditional approach of the police arriving, dealing with an incident, and then leaving is not good enough. Critical incidents can have a devastating effect on communities and when we consider the complementary aims of Neighbourhood Policing and Citizen Focus, it is apparent that careful consideration of the long-term impacts is required.

The NPIA *Practice Advice on Critical Incident Management* defines a critical incident as:

> any incident where the effectiveness of the police response is likely to have a significant impact on the confidence of the victim, their family and/or the community.

This is a deliberately inclusive definition so that *all* critical incidents are correctly identified and dealt with accordingly. It also signifies the importance of community confidence, and has definite resonances within the Citizen Focus agenda.

As part of any critical incident management procedure, it is advised that a CIA is completed, and this can be after a spontaneous incident or as part of the organization for a forthcoming event. The CIA focuses police attention on ensuring that the needs of the local community are considered at all times and that part of the follow-up to an incident is to restore community confidence. It documents the actual or anticipated impact on a community of a particular incident or threat using the seven C's.

KEY POINT—THE SEVEN CS

Quite often the **catalyst** (which is one aspect of the 'seven C's) requires something, in this case, a reaction resulting in an event. The catalyst indicates that a situation has changed and an individual or group may be in **confrontation** with another. The reaction of the police and the community begins with **causality,** an examination of cause and affect. Analysis will be conducted by the police to examine these three themes, resulting in **Community Impact Assessment (CIA),** enabling the police to understand the process of different groups uniting and then coming into conflict with others. We view this as a form of **crystallization,** a process whereby groups of individuals have formed, defining themselves as having a common purpose. They share the same resonance and can be easily recognized. Within the Police there is one principle individual charged with the responsibility of identifying the consequences of the catalyst. Within Thames Valley Police the function is performed by the Community and Diversity Officer (CaDO). It is their responsibility to **communicate** the potential or actual impact of a **critical incident.**

Bhatti, A, 'The mobiles are out and the hoods are up' in C Harfield et al (eds) *The Handbook of Intelligent Policing* (Oxford University Press, Oxford, 2008: 173).

An effective CIA depends upon accurate and up to date information and intelligence about the threat and the community, which needs to be kept under continuous review. The Association of Chief Police Officers (ACPO)'s National Community Tension Team (NCTT) have identified the key elements of a CIA:

- a record of who has been consulted (eg Independent Advisory Group (IAG), community groups, Gold Groups, community officers/Safer Neighbourhood Teams (SNTs), partner agencies, NCTT), what information they have been given and what advice has been received from them in consequence;
- the presentation of information upon which assessment is based;
- a compliance assessment for legislation relevant to the circumstances;
- an identification of risks to community peace and well-being and/or to community/police/partner agency relations and reputations;
- an identification of response options; and
- an implementation plan.

Taken together CIAs form part of the organizational knowledge informing strategic approaches to partnership and the NIM Control Strategy.

Case Study—CIA

A local animal rights pressure group decided to hold a protest demonstration outside a farm where it is alleged that animals are bred for supply to the local vivisectionist laboratory. The group applied to the police for permission to hold their protest and, as part of its operational response, the police decided that a Community Impact Assessment would gauge the potential effect on the local community. Similar demonstrations had attracted national media coverage and had led to disorder and violence, with a consequent large numbers of arrests.

The police officer in charge of the Community Impact Assessment looked at a number of issues in relation to the local community and utilized all sources at her disposal. The key point was that not just the appropriate police response needed careful assessment, but equally how any demonstration might affect the community. The needs of the community were added to the normal police operational logistical requirements.

Internal sources—what intelligence is available on the groups; is the local NPT able to gauge public reaction through their meeting/engagement structure?

External sources—what is the local media saying about the event? Are there letters from members of the public expressing support or concern? Is there internet activity promoting the demonstration?

Points to consider—is the date significant? Previous history of group; intelligence reports; local media sources; community groups; the pressure group themselves; will a pro-vivisectionist group also be coming?

Utilizing the CIA, the police are able to establish the needs of the community before, during, and after the demonstration.

23.9 **Conclusion**

Citizen Focus provides one of the central tenets of Neighbourhood Policing because it highlights a rationale for such policing, improving the satisfaction and confidence that members of the public have in the police. By focusing on the *service* provided, Citizen Focus ensures that policing is carried out in line with the needs of the community. However, in seeking to measure Citizen Focus, the danger is that police forces will measure only that which is quantitatively measurable and ignore the more challenging *qualitative* issues that will truly make a difference if successfully confronted.

Therefore a survey that looks at 'consumer', or 'customer', satisfaction when accessing the police is achievable, but ensuring a coherent community focus where there are multiple and disparate groups within the community, is much less so. Citizen Focus has indeed focused the minds of the police and the whole public sector, but in seeking to do so, and with the potential to make an exponential difference to the relationship between the police and the policed, there is a danger that it may become merely another adjunct to performance management.

Further Reading

Carlisle, P and Loveday, B (2007) 'Performance Management and the Demise of Leadership', *The International Journal of Leadership in Public Services*, 3(2), July: 18–26

Home Office (2003) *Public Perceptions of Police Accountability and Decision-Making*, available at <http://www.home office.gov.uk/rds/pdfs2/rdsolr3803.pdf>, accessed 2 July 2008

Home Office (2006) *Citizen Focus: Good Practice Guide* available at <http://police.homeoffice.gov.uk/publications/community-policing/citizen-focus-guide/>, accessed 2 July 2008

—— (2007) *Citizen Focus: A Practical Guide to Improving Police Follow-Up with Victims and Witnesses* available at <http://police.homeoffice.gov.uk/publications/police-reform?CF-victimsandwitnesses.pdf>, accessed 2 July 2008

Ipsos MORI (2008) report *Closing the Gaps. Crime and Public Perceptions* available at <http://www.ipsos-mori.co.uk>, accessed 2 July 2008

Muir, R and Lodge, G (2008) *A New Beat: Options for More Accountable Policing*, Institute for Public Policy Research, available at <http://www.ippr.org>, accessed 20 June 2008

NPIA (2007) *Practice Advice on Critical Incident Management*, NPIA Circular to Home Office police forces

Chapter 24

Signal Crimes Perspective: a Practical Tool for Neighbourhood Policing

24.1 **Theory in Neighbourhood Policing**

There are still those within policing who maintain that doing the job is such that theoretical knowledge is of little use. They prefer instead to promote the merits of practicality. The police 'nose', or intuition, or gut feeling, is favoured over any kind of academic, or theoretically-based, approaches, and much is made of common sense. By contrast with this 'Life on Mars' intuitive school of police response, the development of what is currently referred to as Neighbourhood Policing (but which, in recognition of the partnership approach may soon be relabelled Neighbourhood Management (Flanagan, 2008, see Further Reading)), has utilized academic methodologies to develop street level policing techniques. One of the key merits of such an approach is that it has enabled the police to move away from defining problems solely within their own experience. Instead, value and weight is given to the opinions and perceptions of others—particularly those most directly affected by perceptions of lawlessness and disorder.

This in turn has affected the quality and breadth of solutions proffered to particular issues. Neighbourhood Policing has demonstrated that the fears of a community may not be the same as those that the police (and other agencies) have identified. We may be able to point to a number of possibly complementary explanations for this disparity between what the communities perceive on the one hand and what the police and partners perceive on the other:

- a target performance culture that focuses attention only on those areas identified as important by the Home Office;
- a lack of ways for local communities to articulate their concerns to the police;
- a lack of leaders in communities willing to engage with the police;
- an unwillingness on the part of the police to listen to what the communities are saying;
- arrogance in the police mentality that assumes that they, and only they, can truly understand law and order issues.

However, as we have noted above, the introduction of Neighbourhood Policing has attempted to bridge these perceptual gaps, utilizing not just practical methods but also considering and adapting theoretical concepts as well. We shall see below how incisive academic understanding has led to effective Neighbourhood Policing Team (NPT) action in neighbourhoods.

24.2 **Fear of Crime**

One of the key factors that gave rise to Neighbourhood Policing in its current format was the understanding that crime does not affect only the victims of crime. Crime and anti-social behaviour affect whole communities who see the effects, hear the tales from fellow residents, or read about such things as reported, more or less sensationally, in the local media. Crime is therefore filtered through a perceptual lens, and from this can emerge a fear of crime that is not proportionate to the event itself. The fear of crime is a powerful concept because it is a 'quality of life' issue that can affect even an entire neighbourhood. Police responses have traditionally focused on the reduction of crime and reaction to the committing of offences, but these alone do not automatically lead to positive changes in how people regard crime (Christmann et al, 2003). Put simply, whilst crime statistics may be going down, people's fear of crime has actually risen. This has a resonance with the partnership approach that Neighbourhood Policing has adopted, through local arrangements as well as Crime and Disorder Reduction Partnerships (CDRPs), because the fear of crime cannot be separated from environmental factors. The absence or poor quality of street lighting, the often inadequate design of local authority housing estates ('designing crime in'), a lack of communal facilities, dealing only slowly with fly-tipping, the depressing accumulation of evidence of degeneration, such as open drugs abuse, drinking alcohol in public and blatant prostitution, all contribute, separately as well as cumulatively, to a sense of community unease. The fear of crime is not just about policing.

24.3 **Signal Crimes Perspective**

One of the theoretical insights that have informed Neighbourhood Policing is the persuasive concept of the Signal Crimes Perspective. This was developed in 2002 by a research team led by Dr Martin Innes at the University of Surrey, working in conjunction with Surrey Police (see Further Reading). The outcome of this research was the identification that certain crimes and forms of anti-social behaviour (itself a term that carries negative 'baggage') have a disproportionate impact upon how people feel about their communities and the risks of living within them. People interpret these local crimes and offences as warning signals and use them to decide about the security of an area. What Innes' team's research demonstrated was that these warning signals do not just apply to the major crimes but apply equally to 'lower-level' incidents.

3 Neighbourhood Policing

This has far-reaching significance for policing because it shows that the public does not always share perceptions about the gradation of types of criminal behaviour that the Home Office does. If someone living in a low crime area perceives litter to be a huge problem then that is as important to that person as the fear of violence felt by someone else living in an area where assaults are frequent. One problem is not necessarily 'worse' than the other; rather, each poses a threat to law and order and therefore both require policing interventions. It is the *signal* of criminality or disorder which is important to the person on the receiving end, who feels that his or her safety is threatened.

Innes and his team identified a series of possible signal crimes/disorders:

- litter
- graffiti
- vandalism
- congregation of young people (seen as threatening)
- signs of drugs usage
- aggressive begging
- abandoned vehicles
- misuse of alcohol
- nuisance noise.

This list, of course, is not definitive and more items may be added and some taken away, since communities' fears will vary from one to another. Indeed, some whole *neighbourhoods* could be said to be a signal crime as they may exhibit a 'no-go' menace that frightens people away.[1] Neighbourhood Policing is not about a tick-box mentality; rather it promotes at its core a localism that stresses the

---

[1] A United Nations Report in 2008 on Britain's punitive youth justice system (Aynsley-Green et al, 2008), criticized the use of Anti-Social Behaviour Orders (ASBOs) 'to break up groups of law-abiding young people who are simply 'hanging around'. The UN characterized this approach as 'the vilification of teenagers as yobs', but it is as much to do with the perception of groups of youths as threatening as with anything criminal or anti-social that such groups actually do. We look at this further in Chapter 25.

need to listen to communities so that their concerns are effectively understood and acted upon. The signal crimes perspective provides an effective means of listening to communities and understanding how they feel about issues in their neighbourhoods. The police should no longer assume that they alone know what the problem is and what should be done about it.

Innes identified that a signal crime/disorder is composed of three distinct yet related parts.

- The **expression**—the incident or crime/act of disorder that gives rise for concern for the person seeing it, or just as pertinently, hearing about it.
- The **content**—how the person seeing it or hearing about it makes sense of what has occurred, especially how it makes them feel about their security or being at risk.
- The **effect**—what effect does the incident have? Does it change behaviour or how the person feels about things?

Example

The signal crimes perspective:

> When I go to the play park with my young children, I often see that the equipment is covered in offensive graffiti (the **expression**). It makes me feel embarrassed because my children want to know what these words mean (the **content**). I now don't take my children to the play park (the **effect**).

24.4 'Broken Windows' Theory

The Signal Crimes Perspective approach has been unhelpfully linked to the 'Broken Windows' work of George Kelling and James Wilson in the United States (see Further Reading). This theory argues that it is the responsibility of the authorities to deal with the smaller problems when they occur, such as broken windows in public housing, because without such intervention, the problems will get worse and more serious crimes may emerge. This was the rationale for attempts at 'zero tolerance' policing that were in vogue five to ten years ago. In the 'broken windows' theory, the police are responsible, at least in part, for social order, actions in support of which are *done to* the community. However, it is now believed that 'broken windows' treated the symptoms rather than the disease. By contrast, Signal Crimes Perspective, whilst not a panacea for all social disorder, does provide a greater emphasis on listening to, and therefore understanding, the communities involved. It emphasizes the crucial link between partnership and collaboration that Neighbourhood Policing seeks to embody.

24.5 Control Signals

As well as proposing the existence of signal crimes, the work of Innes identified the need for a *control signal* to counteract the negative influence of the crimes and disorders that disproportionately affect the security of communities. Essentially, signal crimes theory is about *the need for action and the communication of that action*. It understands that acts of crime and anti-social behaviour have a symbolic message, as well as an actual one, for those people who witness it or subsequently hear about it.

To return to our play park analogy in the example above, the parents who do not want their children to see the offensive graffiti change their behaviour. Those who hear about it and who also have small children may also be influenced to avoid that area. Those who read about 'the graffiti boycott' in the local paper are provided with evidence that the neighbourhood is going downhill, and perhaps may not visit local shops, so that prosperity dwindles. The potential effect goes a long way beyond the mere writing of graffiti; it affects people's perceptions of risk and security. What is needed in this instance is an appropriate response from the authorities responsible for the play park—a control signal that will reassure people that action has been taken (and that further transgressions will not be tolerated). If the signal crime affects people's perceptions of security, so can the authorities' positive response to the signal crime. If nothing is done, then the control signal sent to that community is that the authorities do not care and therefore the fear of crime increases. The Signal Crimes Perspective shows that there is a causal relationship between public perception and authority action or inaction. The control signal can be a powerful tool of reassurance when used correctly.

Example

Control signals: the play park example continued:

The offensive graffiti must be removed from the children's play equipment. **Signs** could be erected to warn potential offenders of the consequences of committing further acts of vandalism. **Lighting** could be improved to ensure that **police patrols** or **community warden activity** can see clearly what is occurring. **Educational programmes** could be utilized within schools to ensure that children are aware of the effects of vandalism. **More youth services** could be provided to ensure that the efforts of young people are channelled into areas that are more constructive. Above all, these efforts could be reported in the **media** to ensure that people in the community are aware of the efforts that are being made, especially if any transgressors are caught.

The control signal is not one event in this example, but for others it may be. The key point is that a control signal is attempted and that this message is communicated to the neighbourhood because it shows that the NPT is listening.

24.6 **Signal Crimes and Neighbourhood Policing**

Neighbourhood Policing is about providing communities with:

- Access
- Influence
- Intervention
- Answers.

An evaluation of the National Reassurance Policing Project (ACPO, 2006) suggested that the Signal Crimes Perspective is an important success factor in the 'reassurance agenda'. It provides **access** for the community through public meetings and identification of public priorities so that the correct signal crimes are identified. It gives communities **influence** over the way things are dealt with and through correctly managed signal controls seeks to provide **intervention** and long-term **answers** to these issues. In essence, Neighbourhood Policing can be likened to the attempt to provide a series of control signals in the campaign against crime and anti-social behaviour. It also makes explicit the need for partnership involvement. The control signals used in the play park example are not solely the responsibility of the police, of course; without a proper partnership approach the control signal would fail. We can model this process quite simply:

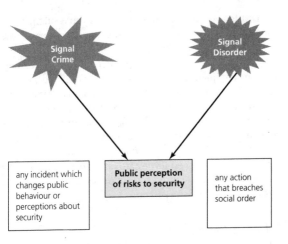

any incident which changes public behaviour or perceptions about security

Public perception of risks to security

any action that breaches social order

24.7 **Environmental Visual Audits**

One of the tools that can be utilized within Neighbourhood Policing that captures the potency of the Signal Crimes Perspective is the Environmental Visual Audit (EVA). This approach is sometimes referred to as a '*structured patch walk*' and is designed to identify the signal crimes that exist in a given area. It is simply a method of capturing those community concerns that have created a fear of crime and which affect the quality of life for residents. It is obviously difficult to provide a definitive list of items that will feature on EVAs, because these will vary from neighbourhood to neighbourhood and from community to community. However, such a list might feature those fixed environmental issues that can be seen daily and which continually remind people that there are problems in their community. The EVA seeks to identify these factors and therefore it would be best accomplished with the help of the residents themselves. Some forces have supplied cameras to individuals with which to capture the signal crimes that blight their communities. Certainly, joining together to undertake an EVA would show partnership in action, rather than being a paper exercise. An invitation to partnership agencies to help with the completion of an EVA would not only increase the chances of successfully identifying the signal crimes, but would also start the process of problem solving by highlighting what steps need to be taken. A further outcome of an EVA is that its completion, particularly when publicized, acts as reassurance to the community. People know what signal crimes are, even if they are unaware of the theoretical concept, and therefore any action seen in dealing with these issues will reassure them.

24.7.1 EVA Scenario

Scenario—Community Concerns

A community of residents on a new housing estate have identified several concerns about anti-social behaviour in the area. These concerns have been articulated at a public meeting held by the police to discuss the issues and three issues in particular were highlighted:

- Litter
- Graffiti
- Vandalism in the play park

Police intelligence about these three concerns is scarce. As part of the problem-solving approach, the police organize an Environmental Visual Audit to provide a systematic logging of the problems, as well as to collate intelligence. Community residents are invited to take part in the EVA and, since they live with the problems all the time, they will be able to highlight the issues that most concern them. The police also invite representatives from the various partnership agencies who will be required to help solve these problems, such as representatives from the local authority,

---

community wardens, housing association staff, park keepers and so on. A day is fixed for the EVA and is publicized in the local paper and via a leaflet drop to residents on the estate so that people are aware of actions that are being taken.

The EVA is conducted on the day advertised and the police attend as part of a high visibility reassurance approach, intended to alleviate the fear of crime. Residents are supplied with cameras to take pictures of the problems that they have identified. These pictures can then be utilized in a presentation to the wider partnership agencies so that they are also aware of the issues that face the residents of this estate. They will also be used in a 'before and after' approach to monitor the success of any initiatives undertaken. A further public meeting is scheduled for three months' time so that residents can be given feedback on how the initiatives have progressed. This meeting will include representatives of the partnership agencies who can then report on their part of the problems.

This partnership approach has recognized that no one agency has sole responsibility for any of the three problems identified by the community. The communities themselves have been involved throughout because their lives have been blighted by the issues. Effective channels of consultation have been opened with the community and feedback is being given so that residents are being kept informed (fulfilling the government requirements for a 'citizen focus' objective). Those willing to volunteer may be trained to conduct subsequent EVAs so that the situation on the estate can be monitored and police resources can be utilized for problem-solving. The communities feel reassured by the process as they are being listened to and their concerns are being dealt with. If any further problems arise, there is now a mechanism that can channel community concerns into a partnership for problem-solving.

24.8 **Conclusion**

The Signal Crimes Perspective provides a useful resource for Neighbourhood Policing since it encompasses many of the themes that define this sphere of policing:

- citizen focus
- community engagement
- community consultation
- public priorities
- partnership
- problem-solving.

It brings all these strands together so that communities are kept in the forefront of policing action and it provides the police with a rationale for action, even with seemingly low-level or 'non-crime' issues. Whilst further research may be required to assess how effective the Signal Crimes Approach is for solving the long-term problems of 'disorder' and the fear of crime; its key components are likely to remain relevant to the practitioner of neighbourhood management.

Further Reading

ACPO (2006), *Practice Advice on Professionalising the Business of Neighbourhood Policing*, available at <http://www.neighbourhoodpolicing.co.uk>, accessed 8 June 2008

Aynsley-Green, A, Towler, K, Marshall, K, and Lewsley, P (2008), *United Nations Report on Britain's Youth Justice System*, reported as Bennett, R 'Law creates underclass of child criminals' in *The Times*, 9 June, available at <http://www.timesonline.co.uk/news>, accessed 9 June 2008

Christmann, K, Rogerson, M, and Walters, D (2003), 'New Deal for Communities: the National Evaluation', Research Paper 14, *Fear of Crime and Insecurity in New Deal Communities Partnerships*, Sheffield Hallam University

Flanagan, Sir Ronnie (2008), *The Review of Policing. Final Report*, available at <http://www.homeoffice.gov.uk/about-us/news/flanagan-report>, accessed 8 June 2008

Innes M, Fielding, N, and Langan, S (2002), *Signal Crimes and Control Signs: Towards an Evidence-Based Conceptual Framework for Reassurance Policing, A report for Surrey Police*, University of Surrey

Kelling, GL and Wilson, JQ (1982), *The police & neighbourhood safety*, available at <http://www.theatlantic.com/doc/198203/broken-windows>, accessed 8 June 2008

Chapter 25

Problem-Solving

25.1 Introduction

Many of the problems which Neighbourhood Policing Teams (NPTs) face will not be crimes. We noted in both 21.1 and 24.2 some of the differences between actual crime and people's fear of crime, and how the perception of lawlessness can lead people to suppose that risks are greater and dangers more present than may be the statistical reality. The same factors apply to people's perceptions of problems in a neighbourhood. We looked at signal crimes and signal disorder in detail in Chapter 24, but precisely the same negative factors of neglect, public service indifference, lack of cohesiveness in the community, lack of a shared resolve, lack of partners to help, and a lack of police interest may combine to make people think that local problems are insuperable. Littering and graffiti are cases in point; and, although these offences can be punished with fixed penalties and fines, the police may seem indifferent to such offences whilst they pursue what they see as 'real' crimes (of violence, serious, and organized crime etc). To the community, accumulated litter, grime, used needles, poor street lighting, and broken windows are aspects of the same perception: the neighbourhood is neglected, it is degenerating and no one cares.

It took the police generally a considerable time to understand that, say, a decline in the burglary of commercial premises did not increase feelings of security in communities. Indeed, communities were faced daily with evidence of other kinds of lawlessness, such as criminal damage, vandalism, prostitution, and drugs and alcohol abuse. The community, for its part, found it difficult to persuade the police and other public service providers of its cumulative fears and anxieties.

This, then, is the context against which we want to look at problem-solving. The NPT needs to understand that what may appear trivial to the police (excessively noisy parties, groups of young people 'hanging about', minor incivility, and petty vandalism) may be real and abiding concerns for the community where such things take place. The community in its turn needs to understand that the police cannot always take punitive action if no 'recordable offences' have been committed. In other words, instead of mutual and continuing misunderstanding, there needs to be a meeting of minds and a willingness to share responses to problems, always noting that there will inevitably be parts of the community which are hostile to or prejudiced against, the police.

The aim behind any NPT problem-solving strategy is that the community helps itself to solve the particular problem, because only in that way can the community take ownership of the outcome. The choices otherwise are either that the solution is 'done' to the community (which entails some sort of external imposed action and so the responsibility for success or otherwise lies elsewhere), or that the community takes the law into its own hands in a form of vigilantism, or nothing is done at all, in which case the community sees no end to its difficulties and there is no meeting of minds between the police and the public. None of these negative outcomes is desirable. **Problem-solving in partnership** is the essence of neighbourhood policing and it is in understanding how this may be achieved that we should begin.

25.2 **Problem-Solving Methods**

Before we look at what actually may be done to resolve community problems, we must explore the very considerable body of experience, commentary, and theory which surrounds problem-solving, particularly in the policing context.

25.2.1 **Goldstein and POP**

It is generally agreed that the first commentator to draw genuine attention to the nature of neglect in neighbourhoods as contributing to perceptions of crime and danger, was Herman Goldstein. An American academic who had spent many years observing and analysing US (city) police responses to crime, Goldstein published a seminal essay in 1979 (see Further Reading) which discussed what was necessary to bring police and community together to solve problems. What came to be called '**Problem-Oriented Policing**' or **POP**, arose from Goldstein's perception that the police should be concerned with order, safety, security, and with a neighbourhood's well-being, even to taking action on matters of social concern, rather than merely enforcing the law.

He saw four distinct stages in problem-solving at the police 'beat' level. The first involved *defining and researching* what the problem was. Sometimes gathering even the most basic data can be difficult; an example is someone who plays music very loudly late at night to neighbours' detriment. Before any action can be taken, facts and figures are needed to convince the authorities (including noise abatement or environmental control officers of the local authority as well as, or even instead of, the police) that there is a problem. The frequency of the 'noise pollution', the times when it happens, the response of the perpetrator when confronted by distressed neighbours with requests to turn down the volume, the loudness itself (measured in decibels), and the number of people affected, must all be recorded and presented, if anything tangible is to be done.

The second stage is *exploring alternatives*. Goldstein found that, often, the resolution of a problem might not entail arrest or coercion by the police; sometimes a discussion with a uniformed officer was enough; at other times, a formal caution might be preferred. There were instances, too, where the police acted as a conduit for complaints to be resolved elsewhere, an example of which is found in dealing with vagrancy. Unlicensed begging is an offence, being homeless is not. In the old days, police officers did not bother to make a distinction and homeless people were often arrested and charged with begging or with various forms of nuisance, including being drunk and disorderly, simply to get them off the streets or away from causing a nuisance. An officer now is much more likely to refer a 'vagrant' to social services or to a charity like Shelter, than to charge the person with an offence. Other alternatives to charge can include *crime-prevention* (including making people aware of their vulnerability, see Chapter 26); sometimes remedies as simple as shed alarms or good stout locks can deter criminals. These are solutions to problems which can be suggested by officers and provide an opportunity to do something positive, but as a general rule it is better to let the suggestion come from the person in the community than to attempt to impose a solution from outside.

'Exploring alternatives' offers a choice to the community, alongside which we would include NPT briefs to town planners and architects for 'designing out' crime in any new builds or refurbishment of local authority housing and public amenities. This entails, for example, ensuring that public areas are well lit and not amenable to undetected loitering or lurking; that households are well secured; that glazing is adequate; that shrubberies and trees are well tended and that criminals do not therefore have opportunities to exploit the architecture and landscaping for their own ends.

The third stage in problem-solving concerns *reliable information*. Members of the community may not know what their rights are in any given set of circumstances, whom they should contact, or what contacts they need to make. The NPT can play a positive role in facilitating contact with partners, as in the case of the tenant locked out of his flat by his landlady without explanation. The tenant's rights can be explained and contact made with, for example, the Citizens' Advice Bureau or local housing association. The NPT could intervene with the landlady to ascertain the reason for the 'lockout' (faults could be on both sides, of course). Here is another example where reliable information is key:

Scenario—Noises Off

Jan kept hearing strange scrabbling sounds in the alley at the side of her ground floor flat during the hours of darkness. At first she dismissed the sounds as coming from cats or other animals such as foxes, but gradually she realized that the sounds happened at a particular time in the late evening for two or three nights a week and she sometimes heard hoarse whisperings which suggested that the noises were being made by humans.

She kept a log of incidences and mentioned the problem to her NPT which, having consulted with the BCU Crime Team, was able to arrange for a covert IR camera to be installed temporarily in a nearby flat, overlooking the alley. Jan was surprised to be visited by the NPT after a couple of weeks to thank her, because the scrabblings and whispers she had heard were actually from drugs-dealing, going on away from public view. Two people had been arrested and a quantity of drugs had been seized. The noises have ceased and Jan's life has returned to normal.

This is an example of an ordinary citizen reporting something odd and a crime being found at the end of a chain of events, which the NPT in concert with the local Crime Team was able to resolve quickly. Reliable information, knowing whom to contact, and acting decisively were the principal factors. Even had the perpetrators not been caught, police interest in the site would have displaced the illegal activity quickly. As it was, prompt concerted action produced a good result, not simply a displacement.

The fourth and final stage involves *developing community help through partners*. We have drawn attention throughout on the need to engage with partners, and this can be done at any stage in the 'self-help' process, but there should always be a deliberate phase of consultation built in to any problem-solving process (Goldstein's 'stage' model is one among many, see below). Once the problem has been researched and defined, the alternatives considered, and reliable information obtained, it is logical to seek assistance from specialists and experts. Suppose that a community was concerned about the activities of a person with some form of mental impairment. There is always a danger of *vigilantism* (a community taking the law into its own hands) or of *victimization* of such an individual, who may not understand that his or her actions are causing concern. This is especially the case when the apparent offender needs proper care and assessment.

Case Study—Who is this man? What does he want with our children?

A recent case in the South-West concerned a male with mental impairment who had taken to hanging around the gates of the local primary school, where he was observed talking to the children at break times. Not unnaturally, there were fears that the man was a paedophile intent on grooming children, and a local group of mothers decided that he should be warned off in no uncertain terms. In fact the man was badly beaten, and by the time the police arrived, he needed hospital treatment. It emerged that the man meant no harm at all, but because of his impairment, he actually

---

found it easier to talk to young children than to adults, who often frightened and confused him. Here was an instance of a community jumping to the wrong conclusions. Had the man's impairment been dealt with more sympathetically, the assault on him might not have taken place. In the event, though, it would have been nearly impossible to convince the anxious parents that their children were not under threat and the only remedy would have been to remove an entirely innocent person from his harmless activity, to ensure that beatings (or worse) did not recur.

Similar problems may arise if calls are heeded for the addresses and identities of convicted paedophiles in a neighbourhood to be made publicly available. Vigilantism or violent forms of retribution are likely to be the result.

Goldstein was describing a *process* and the necessary steps to be taken to ensure that the problem is as amenable to resolution as possible. Subsequently, a number of problem-solving models have been developed to help NPTs and partners. We shall look at two of the most popular, SARA and PAT, but please note that these models are suggestions only. They may not reflect what your NPT or Crime and Disorder Reduction Partnership (CDRP) or Community Consultation Group does. What follows is not a prescription, but a description.

25.2.2 The SARA Model

Scanning: identifying the problem and defining its nature or limits

Analysis: interrogating the problem and finding out root causes, characteristics, timings and so on

Response: determining what is to be done to address and solve the problem

Assessment: how effective was the response? What else needs to be done?

Figure 25.1 The SARA model of problem solution

3 Neighbourhood Policing

The **SARA** model, as may be evident, emerged from modifications to Goldstein's original process for problem-solving in POP, and SARA is in widespread use in many police forces. Let's look at each step in the model.

Scanning is essentially the same process as defining and scoping the problem: unless we can identify what the problem is, where it begins and ends, and what it means to the community, it will remain elusive. We might even end up trying to resolve a different matter altogether. What is important in this initial attempt to agree the nature of the problem is that the community is encouraged to own it. Into this activity would fall the seasonality of a problem (dark nights, light nights, warmth, cold, and so on) and which aspects exacerbate the situation (such as youths 'hanging about'), the recurrence ('hot spots', 'hot victims', repeat offending, etc) and any actions for members of the partnership, such as the creation of somewhere for youths to congregate safely.

Analysis may proceed *sequentially*, that is, once the problem has been defined and described, or it may proceed *concurrently*, that is, at the same time as Scanning. Inevitably there will be some overlap between the stages. The key driver in analysis is to understand what the problem is, what causes it, who is involved with it, and what more needs to be done. If we go back to our example of the mentally impaired man, it is clear with hindsight that not enough time was spent in analysing *why* he loitered near the primary school gates and *who* he was and *where* he came from. The military have a mantra that '*time spent in reconnaissance is never wasted*', and this is equally true of the analysis phase of problem-solving. The clearer the definition of the problem and the more positive our attempts to understand it, the nearer we shall get to the best solution.

Response is more proactive than the stage identified by Goldstein as 'obtaining reliable information' (indeed, that process has been subsumed from Goldstein's POP into SARA's *Analysis*). What is required at this stage is the formulation of a plan to deal with the problem and putting it into action. If the matter of concern is bored kids throwing stones at the windows of a museum (the example we used in Chapter 19), then part of the solution should be the removal of the opportunity to throw stones. In the museum example, the gravel paths were covered with tarmac and a rockery was dismantled. Without missiles conveniently to hand, the vandalism sputtered to a halt. Inherent dangers in response include mistaking the symptoms for the cause. One example may clarify what this means.

Case Study: Treating the symptoms, not the disease

The youths on a housing estate near Manchester congregated after school and at weekends on a low wall beside a butcher's shop and their presence intimidated shoppers both to the butcher and to other shops in the vicinity. Some littering and graffiti were seen and a broken window was blamed on the children. The community members took this matter up with the NPT and wanted the youths moved away (saying it didn't matter where). Members of the NPT spoke directly to the youths and found that they met by the low wall because there was nowhere else for them to gather; they were bored and some of the jibes and remarks by passers-by made them resentful and angry. They claimed that they were blamed for everything that went wrong, including the broken window which had actually occurred because a resident had angrily banged it shut.

The NPT approached the owner of a field adjacent to the row of shops, who agreed that, for a lease fee, part of it could be set aside for the youths as a 'sanctuary' away from disapproving adults. The local council and businesses were approached for funding and a skateboard park was built in the short space of two months. The youths now have somewhere of their own to go, over which they have some ownership. The community, freed of the real or perceived intimidation of the youths congregating near the butcher's shop, has agreed to build an assault course in another part

---

of the field, and the local council has purchased the field outright. There are plans to make the remaining area of the field into a MUGA (a Multi-Use Games Area) for the whole community.

The community was too apt to blame the youths for what was seen as a problem, mistaking the presence of the young people as both threatening and as having caused things like the broken window. The youths became the symptom of the community's unease, yet the former's having nowhere to go was actually the underlying cause. Until the NPT tried it, no one had thought of asking the young people what *they* wanted and needed. *The youths had themselves become the signal crime.* There is a danger that groups like this can be demonized unless they are engaged and encouraged to become part of the solution. There is a fine sustained polemic in David Dixon's (1999) 'Beyond Zero Tolerance'. Noting that '*"community" means as much of society as possible*' (p 494), Dixon berates those who create 'a politics of exclusion which operates through dichotomies' such as:

> 'decent folk' versus 'drunks and derelicts' … a 'stable neighborhood of families' versus one populated by 'unattached adults'; … 'good citizens' versus 'the homeless' …'citizens trying to protect their own territory' threatened by 'predators'.

Dixon (1999: 494–495)

This is a point worth making, and Dixon makes it well. We may be in danger of making 'community' mean something like 'those who think like us' or even describe it as a gathering of 'the right-minded', with all the exclusionary dangers and demonization which that entails. Communities have bad and good, neutral and angry, law-abiding and lawless. It makes at least as much sense to try to engage with the lawless as it does with the law-abiding.

What had been a problem with youths and a low wall was transformed by a bit of lateral thinking into a solution, but the point we have made throughout this section is that initiatives of this kind *must be sustained*; time and effort must be put into the solution so that the problem does not resurface. To this end, the NPT in meetings with the community regularly reviews the use of the field and the maintenance of equipment in it.

The final element in SARA is **Assessment**. No project, solution, or remedy can be considered effective until some sort of evaluation has been made of its effectiveness. In our example, the youths no longer sat on the wall beside the butcher's, so that would be one element to show the solution's effectiveness. The youths now had somewhere of their own to go, which is another part of the solution. The community members now felt less concerned and intimidated, so that is a further element in the equation. When all these factors are assessed, the solution may be said to have worked. It is often good practice to empower someone within the community to make the assessment, with partner help if needed, so that ownership of the solution can remain with the community itself. Time spent on assessment and evaluation is well worth the effort. It avoids the frequent police activity of going straight to another project without having properly evaluated what has been achieved and learned; and also ensures that future problem-solving will benefit from experience.

25.2.3 **SARA Model Disadvantages**

The SARA model is not without its critics. Many, including eminent authorities like Professor Nick Tilley (2003), have pointed out that the process of finding solutions is actually much messier than shown by the neat model. Things are not as cut and dried as the process steps might suggest. Factors overlap, repeat themselves, and some can remain undeveloped while others move to completion. Commentators have noted that simple attempts to define the problem need not necessarily lead to clarity (our example of the youths on the low wall above is a case in point), and that scoping the problem can become an activity in its own right, with too much talking and not enough focused action. It has been suggested, too, that the SARA model is a bit glib and that police officers actually do not go steadily through the four stages to arrive at solutions, but cut across some stages when experience tells them that people want specific guidance, not a learning curve.

These drawbacks and disadvantages should not obscure the fact that SARA is alive and well and functioning in many forces, and it is standard practice in many Basic Command Units (BCUs) for the neighbourhood teams to use SARA or something very like it in diagnosing community concerns. NPTs are likely to encounter it; if not, the chances are that the problem analysis triangle is being used instead.

25.2.4 The PAT Model

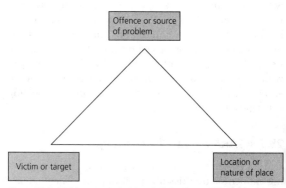

Figure 25.2 Problem Analysis Triangle (PAT, also called the 'crime triangle')

PAT is a different kind of model from **SARA**. Instead of showing processes or stages which have to be worked through, the PAT model indicates three components of a problem: in crime terms this might be **offence**, **victim**, and **crime scene**; in non-crime terms it might be **problem**, **target**, and

place. The simplest way to explain this problem analysis triangle, which may be referred to as the 'crime triangle' in some police literature, is to populate it with a couple of examples. The first is a crime example (Figure 25.3).

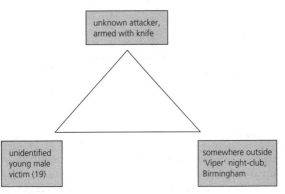

unknown attacker, armed with knife

unidentified young male victim (19)

somewhere outside 'Viper' night-club, Birmingham

Figure 25.3

The essential problem here is one of identification. There is no doubt that a crime has been committed, a young male has been stabbed outside a notoriously unruly night-club on the outskirts of Birmingham. The problem for the police is *who did it?* The ancillary problems are: *who is the victim* and *where did it happen?* Were any of these three to be resolved, the problem diminishes, even if it doesn't disappear. In reality, there would have been witnesses to the incident; the young victim could be identified from possessions, by his own admission, or by friends and associates; the crime scene should be evident; others will give testimony and so on. The model proposes what the parts of the problem are, and clears away much of the inevitable confusion which accompanies such dramatic events.

Now, a non-crime[1] conundrum (Figure 25.4).

---

[1] Strictly it is criminal damage, but the police often tend to treat graffiti as nuisance or anti-social behaviour unless it is extremely persistent or racist or obscene.

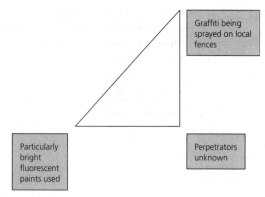

Figure 25.4

In Figure 25.4 we have deliberately changed the shape of the triangle to reinforce the fact that the model is simply indicative; there is no fixed shape except the essence of a triangle (three interdependent angles, as the name suggests). Here the problems to be resolved are: *who is committing these offences* and *what can be done to deflect or catch the offender(s)?* There are fruitful lines of enquiry, such as checking with local stockists of fluorescent paints, forensic recovery from any abandoned spray cans, and investigation of the graffiti itself for the 'tag' or identifier, used by the sprayer. The members of the community can be involved in trying to establish the offender's identity, whilst partners can be engaged in tracing sources of the paint and ensuring the prompt removal of the graffiti. Temporary CCTV cameras could be installed. Again, the removal of any one difficulty in the triangle makes the whole easier to resolve. A piece of lateral thinking in this instance might also be to persuade the local authority to establish a 'graffiti wall' where sprayers may create harmlessly (many of these already exist throughout the country). A more refined form of the PAT is PAT 2 (Figure 25.5).

Figure 25.5 The PAT 2 model

It can be seen from this that the triangle overlaying the standard PAT diagram shows the control measures or ownership that can be utilized to deal with offending. Each 'control' element links with the corresponding PAT element; so there is **management** of the place where crime can occur, there is a **guardian** of the target or victim (official or not), and there is a mechanism to **handle** the offender. (The handler in this model is not to be confused with the role statutorily defined in section 29(5)(a) of the Regulation of Investigatory Powers Act 2000 and the accompanying Covert Human Intelligence Source Code of Practice at 4.26, also generally referred to as a handler.)

Control measures of this simple kind can be effective and reassuring to members of a community besieged by crime, provided that they are prompt, sustained, and embedded controls rather than window-dressing.

The **Problem Analysis Triangle** (PAT) itself is akin to what is elsewhere called *'routine activities theory'* (a theory of 'environmental criminology' developed by Lawrence Cohen and Marcus Felson, see Further Reading and our discussion in Chapter 26.5) in which crimes can be understood in terms of the *co-presence* of *likely offenders* and *suitable targets*, and an *absence* of effective *deflectors or guardians* (the police or strong community disapproval). It is what is described sometimes as 'crimes waiting to happen'. An example might be drunken males who steal a high performance car—they *might* quietly subside in a corner and be sick, but it is far more likely that they will embark on a testosterone- and alcohol-fuelled rampage, being chased by the police and/or colliding with some innocent passerby. The prime factors of likely offenders, suitable targets, and no inhibitors until the police are involved, is a heady mix. There are numerous other examples, such as the threat of violence at night clubs or raves, where possessive (and alcohol-fuelled, again) males may jealously compete over women, or the meeting of rival inner-city gangs on disputed territory, or an electricity failure leading to darkened, unprotected shopping streets which are then subject to looting and burglary. No matter how attractive a target is, an offence will seldom occur unless the guardian or deflector element is not there. A likely offender must also be present. In other words, *the crime or offence will not happen unless there is a crime/offence opportunity, there is someone to do it, and there is no-one to prevent it.* We look at other theories about crime in Chapter 26.5, when we discuss crime reduction.

The removal or diminution of any one of the elements of the PAT 1 or PAT 2 Triangles will normally be sufficient to defuse or displace the potential problem. In neighbourhood policing terms, this probably entails concerted action between partners and community through a number of 'action options'. The options available might mean that all three 'legs' of the problem are tackled simultaneously, but it is more likely that matters will proceed consecutively, with a further set of options brought into play if earlier ones fail or take too long to address the problem (such as the length of time and the bureaucratic hoops involved in creating a play park or recreation area for young people). In an area which is prone to crime because it is ill-lit, the likelihood is that the provision of adequate or enhanced street lighting will displace the offending. If that doesn't work, then more proactive measures such as targeted patrolling or the installation of passive CCTV may be options to be pursued.

25.2.5 **PAT Model Disadvantages**

The same disadvantages attend the PAT model as attend the SARA model: too much neatness, an over-simplifying of complex social issues, and the often subtle ways in which models can become semi-automatic mantras rather than stimuli to think. No NPT should place too much reliance on a process model (even the National Intelligence Model (NIM)) when doing so may inhibit an imaginative, swift, or inexpensive solution to a community or neighbourhood problem. Even the Home Office, avid espouser of both models, counsels that:

> although SARA [and PAT] can be used as a guiding process for problem solving, it would be wise not to see [them] as the answer to everything as [they] can be limited in [their] effectiveness if ... employed in too mechanistic a fashion.

> <http://www.crimereduction.homeoffice.gov.uk/learning-zone/sara.htm> (pp 4–5, accessed 26 May 2008)

Refinements have since been developed which claim improvements in the basic modelling, such as **PROCTOR** (**PRO**blem, Cause, Tactic or Treatment, Output, and Result; a clumsy structure which did not move things on), **Conjunction of Criminal Opportunity** (CCO) which merely elaborates routine activity theory, and the **5Is**, which tried systematically to overcome SARA's limitations by focusing on Intelligence, Intervention, Implementation, Involvement, and Impact. The modelling process seems to have become a bit wordy and over-wrought, as though modelling alone was the magic bullet for problem-solving. It seems that NPTs would be better advised to use the models to focus attention on the nature of the problem, rather than as some sort of template for action. Listening to the community may already have the seeds of a solution which merely requires coordinating to be effective. The NPT role in bringing partners together may be all that is needed to surface the solution to an apparently intractable problem.

25.3 **Training and Education**

Many people find dealing with officialdom difficult. This may be because they feel powerless to challenge authority, because they find it hard to articulate what they feel, or because they are shy and not given to displays of outward assertiveness. So, too, people without strong formal educational qualifications can be inhibited by those who have them; indeed some 12 per cent of the adult population is illiterate and many more will find formal letter-writing a skill too far. Often, frustrated or inarticulate people may resort either to violence or its threat (as any school teacher will testify in dealing with frustrated parents), or they will just mutter complainingly and never take the problem any further.

NPTs can do something to break this mental or emotional log-jam. Having identified that an issue may be that people don't have the basic skills to solve problems, NPTs can facilitate the same people to obtain skills. Suppose the community wants to write to its MP; are there people who know how to write formal letters? Or suppose the community wants to start a media campaign, are there people who know how to draw up a strategy, deal with journalists, radio and television reporters, and sustain interest in the community's problem? If there are not, then partnerships can help, but so can local evening study courses, online advice and guidance, the Citizens' Advice Bureau, local schools and teachers, adult education, the Learning and Skills Council, and many other bodies. It should not be the role of an NPT to educate members of a community and the will for this self-help has to come from the community. All the team can do is facilitate; not take on and solve the problem or seek to impose skills—especially on people who may have strong fear factors about 'going back to school'. Far more appealing might be the use of the local library's access to the Web, where templates and guidance in writing formally can be easily accessed. NPTs should encourage community members engaged in such activity to seek a more experienced eye to look over the text of letters or press releases before they are sent.

Information about such facilities can be developed through NPT 'surgeries', in public meetings, or in 'talking walls' in community centres. The leading figures in the community can be pressed into service to support the acquisition of skills, for example where older members of the community find IT problematic. One community we studied in north-west England actually enlisted the help of local teenagers to help its 'silver surfers' understand basic IT. Whilst the young people were amazed that anyone could function at all without texting and mobile phones, let alone a computer, some of the elderly people found that their rusty but usable typing skills served them well on keyboards, and that once embarked, say, on a Google search, the process was enjoyable rather than frightening. Some young men, whose IT skills were actually pretty minimal, found that they could learn alongside the elderly community residents without being teased or derided. As a result, members of the community who seldom met on level ground, actually found themselves working together, and much previous demonizing was discarded as a result. Of course, no solution will ever be ideal, nor will literacy/IT skills on their own solve a community's social and interaction problems. But they will help, and there can be, as we have noted in our example, unexpected spin-offs of benefit to all.

25.4 **Getting People Together: PACT**

The joining of partners with communities in attempts to solve the community's problems has been given the happy acronym **PACT**—Partners And Communities Together. Not all police forces will have PACT or call it that, but the principles of engaging with the community's problems are broadly the same, whatever name is given to the process. It is important to find somewhere that people can meet safely and without competing with other activities (so a pub is not usually a good idea for a venue). Sites which have proved successful include:

- school halls, local college's meeting rooms;
- church and other faiths' halls and meeting rooms;
- village or community centres;
- local theatres;
- British Legion centres;
- Working Men's Club committee rooms;
- sports centres, hotels;
- mobile police stations (especially helpful in scattered rural communities);
- local primary care trusts (including GPs' surgeries).

There may be many other good sites. Prime considerations include *safety* (the building should be in good repair, dry, warm, and well-lit) and *ease of access*—so arranging a meeting at the top of a hill may exclude the elderly who may find the climb too tiring; making a meeting venue accessible only by car may exclude those without transport and the young. *Timings* are also important; meeting during the working day excludes those who work or learn; meeting later in the evening may exclude the vulnerable who do not venture out after dark. So, too, meetings should avoid obvious clashes such as school leaving times or the start times for adult evening classes, for example.

The great value of public meetings is that they can introduce partner members to members of the community and vice versa; this may bring alive the notion we looked at earlier of mutual aid to resolve problems. The aim always is to obtain the widest spectrum and largest buy-in from as many parts of the community as possible. One of the inherent problems in Neighbourhood Policing is ensuring that those who attend genuinely do represent all strands and opinions in the community: too often, the members of the community who do attend are characterized as white, retired, middle class, and therefore not representative of the whole community.

Professor Waddington, a prolific commentator on the police, quotes another academic, Sharon Bolton, in defining this exclusivity as having:

> flourished among stable, affluent communities with low mobility, where residents have time to get to know their neighbours, have the resources to obtain physical crime prevention measures ... and to purchase insurance.

Professor Waddington himself points up the contrast with deprived inner-city housing estates where neighbourhoods lack:

> the material, social and personal resources necessary to organize and energize their neighbours to address issues of mutual concern. They [are] not embedded in stable neighbourhood networks and [have] no experience of organizing or managing other people.

Waddington (2007)

'Inclusivity', not exclusivity, is what NPTs should be aiming at, even if that makes for sometimes uncomfortable meetings, in which groups may trade insults and in which there may be antipathy between individual members. The key is to ensure the firm but neutral chairing of such meetings, allowing groups to have their say but not to dominate or monopolize proceedings. Indeed, the disadvantages of having public meetings (as opposed to small groups with NPTs) may include hijacked agendas, the use of the public forum to make speeches, and the 'talking shop'; known to all who have sat through interminable meetings which led nowhere. Some people believe that meetings are an end in themselves and that to hold a meeting is to make progress. *This is not true, and is absolutely counter to real movement.* Only a carefully planned agenda, with defined outcomes and assigned actions, will make progress. There have to be rules too: people should speak one at a time, notes should be kept, and the agenda adhered to. Only through a 'meetings discipline' can all sides have a say and actions be agreed. The needs of the audience are paramount; these are not meetings to satisfy police objectives. Those inhibited about speaking can be encouraged to write their thoughts down beforehand, and NPTs will have to try hard over a longish period truly to achieve a representative spectrum attending. Good guidance for the conduct and structure of public meetings with a neighbourhood policing theme may be found at <http://www.communityengagement.police.uk>. Note that this site appears not to have been updated since 2005.

Sometimes, public meetings can be counter-productive or too difficult to organize regularly, so it is important that there are other ways of engaging with the communities in the neighbourhood. These can include:

- **postal surveys** (can be expensive and it is rare to get a higher than 25 per cent response);
- **open days** (need considerable organization if they are not to be simply 'the police on display' days);
- **street briefings** (the equivalent to small group briefings, informal and usually wind-blown; a danger sometimes that they become 'one-way' briefings);
- **focus groups** (useful to include representatives of those who cannot attend public meetings for any reason);
- **house-to-house calls** (expensive of NPT's time; can't guarantee people in or wanting to answer, may not catch all the community);
- **'drop-in' surgeries** (held by the NPT at a set venue and set time; good for voluntary contact, poor for reach and breadth);
- **mobile police station** (effective for smallish groups, but the mobile has to be regularly available, and it should be sensitively used (and parked!)).

(ACPO Advice (2006))

There is, inevitably, a model for the range of community engagement activities derived from work by Sherry Arnstein in 1969, later adapted by David Wilcox in 1995 (see references to both in Further Reading). This is 'Arnstein's Ladder' (see Figure 25.6).

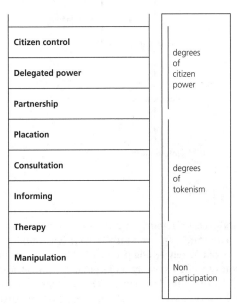

Citizen control	
Delegated power	degrees of citizen power
Partnership	
Placation	
Consultation	degrees of tokenism
Informing	
Therapy	
Manipulation	Non participation

Figure 25.6 'Arnstein's Ladder' (Arnstein, 1969)

Arnstein was trying to map out movement from non-participation at the bottom of the ladder, through various stages (including tokenism, where people, including the police, 'play at' community engagement without really meaning it) to the top which is such full engagement that citizens themselves have control. However, many people found this 8-stage model hard to apply, and David Wilcox simplified it considerably in 1995 (see Figure 25.7).

Figure 25.7

D.Wilcox (1995)

Wilcox's version retains the sense of movement (upwards and downwards) in Arnstein's Ladder; but simplifies the stages from merely telling people what is going on ('Information') through steadily more proactive phases leading up to 'Partnership' and beyond. The last of these stages in Wilcox's version is rather weakly described as '**Supporting**'. Arnstein was surely more accurate when she characterized this completing stage as 'citizen control'? The NPT 'philosophy' now embraces people taking control of their own lives in their own neighbourhoods; where the NPT acts in support of citizen control, not the other way around. The NPT is doing the supporting, not the community.

The value of these models is that they give a sense of direction and a 'ready reckoner' for where particular initiatives are, but, like all neat pictograms, they are not infallible and can't cover every eventuality.

25.5 **Partners**

Who are these partners, aside from the police, whom we have referred to so often? As we have stressed throughout, there is no rigid template for *any* of the activities involved in Neighbourhood Policing. Partners and agencies will vary widely from BCU to BCU and from 'beat' to 'beat'. What we can say is that it is *probable* that most of the partners in NPT may be drawn from:

- **local authorities**, ranging from parish and borough councils through to unitary authorities; they control so much of interest to neighbourhoods, from graffiti removal to refuse collection, parks and recreation, schools and colleges, and from street lighting to local authority housing. No NPT can function properly without close and plentiful partners within local authorities;
- **education**, because many problems involving communities concern young people and raise skills issues and learning;
- **local Criminal Justice Boards**, because NPT is 'about' law and order in the community which entails control of crime and criminals;
- **Youth Offending Teams** or YOTs, which deal with criminalized young people and attempt to rehabilitate them before a 'lifestyle' of crime takes hold; the YOT is a major partner if neighbourhood problems seem exclusively derived from its young inhabitants;
- **Crime and Disorder Reduction Partnerships** (CDRPs): many of these already exist in the BCU area (or jointly between BCUs) and are experienced in addressing precisely the problems which the community has surfaced to the NPT. CDRPs usually have a *tactical* approach to problems, based on a larger geographical responsibility than an NPT. Our focus here is operational rather than tactical, but members of the local CDRP will almost certainly be found within those partnerships for the community which NPT helps to organize;

- **Drug Action Teams** (DATs) are also likely to be focused on larger geographical areas than the specific neighbourhood beat of the NPT, but drugs respect no borders and if the problems faced by the community includes drugs-dealing and addiction, then members of the DAT should be involved. Team members are very experienced in dealing with drugs supply, dealing, and addiction, and will be able to advise on effective counters and resolutions (such as disposal of needles, 'clean-up' operations, and the like);

- **Multi-Agency Public Protection Arrangements** (MAPPA): this is a strategic partnership which nonetheless looks closely at neighbourhood issues because MAPPA is a joint-agency approach to the reintegration of violent and sexual offenders when released from prison. Members of MAPPA will not necessarily be part of any neighbourhood or community team, but the NPT should certainly consult MAPPA about releases back into the community of those whose prison terms have been served, and understand how control of them will be exercised;

- **Primary Care Trusts**: GPs and practice nurses, ancillary medical and psychiatric staff, the Ambulance Service and paramedics, as well as district nurses and health visitors, may have a very clear idea of the problems besetting a community. In addition, the presence of the medical profession will lend credibility to the partnership and perhaps reassure members of the community that this is not just about the police and public service agencies;

- **other security and law-enforcement agencies**: this includes agencies such as the Probation Service and the Prison Service where their roles are relevant to community concerns, but MAPPA (see above) also makes use of these public bodies, so it is not always necessary to seek separate bilateral partnerships for the community;

- **Fire and Rescue Service** (FRS): the FRS in any county or city generally enjoys a good relationship with the police and is usually held in high esteem by most of the community. The FRS's importance is in the safety advice which it can give and in the promptness with which it deals with 'torched' vehicles or those who set fires. Hoax calls are always a concern;

- **the business community**: not always prevalent on 'sink' estates or where crime is rife, the business community is nonetheless of great importance to local community and neighbourhood partnerships. Local businesses can be a source of funding or of sponsorship. They may lend prestige to longer-term projects, they may have helpful views and experience of dealing with petty crime. They may be helpful with fundraising ideas. Local businesses create local prosperity and employment, so they constitute a vital part of the balance of law, order, and amenities;

- **voluntary groups**: these vary from local charities like hospices to Citizens' Advice Bureaux, and from national organizations such as Shelter or Mind to groups like the British Legion or the Women's Institute. There may be considerable reserves of expertise in such groups, including understanding media strategies, influencing politicians, lobbying, legal advice, architects and building design, and consumer rights. There are two caveats to remember: members of voluntary groups are busy and committed people; NPTs should not add to voluntary group members' burdens with unnecessary work or duplication, and such people may have a strongly focused view on what needs to be done which may run counter to the NPT's law-and-order emphasis (think of drugs rehabilitation for example). The children's trusts and charities, such as Barnardo's and the National Society for the Prevention of Cruelty to Children (NSPCC), will also come under this general category, though NPTs may engage with children's organizations separately;

- the final category is the **private security industry**, which may or may not figure prominently in the NPT locale. There is no overall organization called 'the private security industry', though there is a national association (the Security Industries' Authority) which attempts—with variable success—to register security companies and to apply industry-wide standards. The neighbourhood is likely to have a few local guarding and patrol companies (often employing between one and ten people) and local branches or depots for national security organizations such as Group4 and Securitas. There are also door stewards for clubs and 'night entertainment' venues, security guards for shopping malls and complexes, and sometimes guards for gated or restricted communities. Where their knowledge, expertise, or assistance is required, it makes sense to involve them in partnerships, but NPTs must be careful not to be seen to approve of or endorse in any official way the actions and roles of private security firms. If NPTs do this, other firms will cry 'foul', while the firms concerned will have little scruple about publicizing 'as approved by' widely and loudly.

The partnership list is wide-ranging and includes some major local players. However, a potential flaw or inherent problem in the bringing together of so many different partners is that *partnerships often find it very hard indeed to understand each other*, particularly each other's priorities. Some partners may demonize the police as either too repressive or too weak; local businesses may have rather blinkered views of local youth or the elderly; whilst some public service agencies persist in believing that they alone know what is best for the neighbourhood and the communities within it. Research by Colin Rogers (2006) has shown that 'deep structural conflicts exist between parties that sit down together in partnerships'. Common goals with common approaches can effectively replace private agendas and power politics.

25.6 **Key Individual Networks**

There is nothing magic about a Key Individual Network (KIN): it is the list with contact details of everyone and anyone who may be able to help with community problems. Normally kept by individual members of an NPT, it should be available to all in the NPT and passed on when an individual officer moves away for any reason. It provides new officers with an instant 'in' and is invaluable in building a picture of the cooperative elements (and sometimes the less cooperative) in the neighbourhood. A KIN begins with the numbers and details (say, occupation) of key community leaders, together with the 'street level' representatives of partnerships. Although the phone, fax, and mobile numbers for the Chief Executive may be helpful in a dire emergency, the KIN's more practical use is for contacts who actually perform roles for the locality. The team should ensure that its KINs include faith leaders, local councillors, and the local and regional media, as well as contacts in building, glazing, plumbing, and allied trades who may be needed quickly to secure a dwelling or repair vandalism. Some forces have adapted the KIN by adding an Extended List (KINEL) to ensure the capture of a wide spectrum of contacts.

25.7 **Profiling Vulnerable Neighbourhoods**

An intelligence-based approach, not yet widely adopted by police forces, helps to identify and focus upon *neighbourhoods that are vulnerable*: that is, they have a high likelihood of continuing crime and disorder problems. In other words, such neighbourhoods have a plethora of long-term problems which will take time and much effort to solve.

Briefly, analysis of data may show that acquisitive and non-acquisitive crime, anti-social behaviour incidents, a concentration of persistent offenders, unemployment and lack of education, repeat victimization, crime 'hot spots' and offending patterns can be profiled in considerable detail. These profiles (see Chapter 14) may highlight perhaps 10 or 15 residences in a single neighbourhood where much of the offending happens, so that police action may be focused upon the vicinity, whilst any further social and demographic profiles may help partners to understand what is happening. This is not the same as anecdote: plenty of experienced officers in the NPT will characterize (or demonize) areas in the neighbourhood which 'has most villains' or 'all the robberies'. Properly collated and analysed data, presented in current detail, will be much more persuasive and is more likely to be accurate. Several police forces, including Kent and Devon and Cornwall, use software called MOSAIC, developed by Experian, to collate the data sets.

25.8 **Putting it all Together**

If there were no problems in a neighbourhood, there would be no need for an NPT. The communities which face daily difficulties of anti-social behaviour, a breakdown of order, petty vandalism, theft, and violence are not at ease and not confident of solutions. The NPT must act as the catalyst which changes the communities' focus by helping them to find solutions, in consultation with and actively assisted by partners from the wider community. We have looked at various ways in which such community problem-solving may be modelled, and we have considered the many potential partners whose help communities can enlist. The persistent fact is that solutions don't just happen, they have to be worked at and tackled directly; and this is where the NPT has such vital bridging and facilitating roles to play. In bringing the public together with partner agencies and groups, NPTs are doing more than mere matchmaking; they are making a genuine difference by giving back to a neighbourhood its right to a peaceable and secure existence. What NPTs must ensure, though, is that all sides are represented and that no single interest group has monopoly or dominance.

Further Reading

For further information on specific models referred to in this chapter see <http://www.crimereduction.homeoffice. gov.uk/> (includes the double PAT model) and <http:// www.crimereduction.homeoffice.gov.uk./learningzone/ sara.htm>, both accessed 26 May 2008

ACPO (2006), *Practice advice on professionalising the business of neighbourhood policing*, issued for ACPO by the National Centre for Policing Excellence, NPIA

Arnstein, S (1969), 'A Ladder of Citizen Participation' in *Journal of the American Planning Association*, July, 35(4): 216–24; reprinted in R Gates and F Stout (eds) (1996), *The City Reader* (2nd edition), Routledge Press

Cohen, L and Felson, M (1979), 'Social Change and crime rate trends: a routine activity approach'; reprinted in Part XI, 'Environmental Criminology', in F Cullen and R Agnew (eds) (2007), *Criminological Theory: Past to Present, essential readings*, Oxford University Press, Oxford

Dixon, D (1999) 'Beyond Zero Tolerance' in T Newburn (ed) (2005) *Policing: Key Readings*, Willan Publishing, Devon: 483–507

Eck, J and Spelman, W (1988), 'Who ya gonna call? The police as problem-busters', *Crime and Delinquency*, 33, January: 31–52

Felson, M and Clarke, R (1998) *Opportunity makes the thief: practical theory for crime prevention*, Police Research Series, Paper 98, Home Office

Goldstein, H (1979), 'Improving policing: a problem-oriented approach', *Crime and Delinquents*, 25, April: 236–58

Rogers, C (2006), *Crime Reduction Partnerships*, Oxford University Press, Oxford

Tilley, N (2003), 'Community Policing, problem-oriented policing and intelligence-led policing', Chapter 13 in T Newburn (ed), *Handbook of Policing*, Willan Publishing, Devon: 311–39

—— (ed) (2005), *Handbook of Crime Prevention and Community Safety*, Willan Publishing, Devon

Waddington, P (2007), 'Time to own up and accept blame', *Police Review*, 25 May, quoting contributions to *Community Engagement, Criminal Justice Matters* No 64, Summer 2006, published by the Centre for Crime and Justice Studies at King's College, London

Wilcox, D (1995), *The Guide to Effective Participation*, Joseph Rowntree Trust, also available from <http://www.partnerships.org.uk/guide/index.htm>, accessed 5 June 2008

Chapter 26

Crime Prevention

26.1 **Introduction**

Two prominent commentators on crime prevention have described it as 'the Cinderella specialism' in policing (Hough and Tilley, 1998). Discussing crime prevention more recently, Simon Byrne and Ken Pease noted that crime reduction:

> has not been accorded a status commensurate with the importance organisationally assigned to it.
> Byrne and Pease (2003: 286)

And they go on to note how odd it is that crime prevention is now seen as a separate function within modern policing, when it was at the very heart of the principles of policing drawn up for the Metropolitan Police in 1829. Byrne and Pease conclude that 'crime prevention has never fully permeated police thinking and practice' (Byrne and Pease, 2003: 287).

We might add in turn that crime prevention is still largely associated in both the police's and the public's minds with 'technical aids to security' rather than being a central premise of policing; and it seems still to be perceived by police officers at large to have marginal value at a time of resource-intensive responses to crime and disorder. The Audit Commission in 1999 found that only one per cent of police officers was engaged in crime prevention (Byrne and Pease, 2003: 291), even though the Association of Chief Police Officers (ACPO), in a paper entitled *Towards 2000* written two years earlier, had asserted that crime prevention was actually *the responsibility of **all** police officers*. However, there are some signs now that this attitude may be changing, not least because of the throughput of police officers in Neighbourhood Policing Teams (NPTs); a sea-change that may be linked with partnership problem-solving (see Chapter 25), and also because a tactical delivery of crime reduction is core to Crime and Disorder Reduction Partnership (CDRP) strategies and neighbourhood renewal.

> ### KEY POINTS—IMPORTANT DISTINCTION: CRIME PREVENTION AND CRIME REDUCTION
>
> Crime reduction is the strategy, crime prevention one of the means to that end. Indeed, 'individual acts of crime *prevention* result, in the aggregate, in crime *reduction*'.
> Byrne and Pease (2003: 287)

The Home Office **Standing Conference on Crime Prevention** in 1991 (facilitated by the 'Morgan Harris Burrows Partnership') resulted in what is now called 'The Morgan Report' (Morgan et al, 1991), which shifted responsibility for crime reduction from being the sole preserve of the police to being a key responsibility for CDRPs. This was made law in the Crime and Disorder Act 1998, where:

> section 17 imposes statutory duty on local authorities to consider the crime consequences of all their decisions

leading to a new state for local authorities and CDRPs of what has been described as 'crime consciousness' (Garland, 2000). The Home Office has made substantial funds available for crime reduction strategies, based on crime prevention initiatives such as the provision of CCTV cameras; and the role of partnership agencies in the delivery of crime reduction has been centralized and given prominence.

That said, some partnerships, such as those involved with 'people processing', like Probation and Social Security, have proved keener to engage with the police in crime reduction than those departments that make physical changes, like Housing, Health and Direct Works, which have tended to engage only reluctantly with the police or communities; though there will obviously be individual exceptions to this across the UK (Byrne and Pease, 2003: 296). This partial engagement has led to a perception that crime reduction may be shaped by the preferences and prejudices of those keenest to be involved, and that therefore this may exclude participation by the communities most concerned. For example, there is no consistency nationally in physical prevention measures, such as 'designing out' crime, which we look at below.

Notwithstanding the reservations of experienced commentators, it is important to note that the onus for crime reduction now lies firmly at the door of local authorities and agencies, rather than only with the police. The police involvement with crime reduction continues to be vital, and it is, or should be, a central tenet of all NPTs to have crime prevention and reduction as key priorities in delivering community reassurance. 'Crime consciousness' is no bad thing in local partnerships, but occasionally the police will have to tread a carefully discreet line between being expert in knowing what crime prevention measures work and yet allowing 'lay' partners the chance to learn by experience.

26.2 **Attrition of Crime**

One of the first lessons which any non-police partners learn is that there is a strikingly diminishing pattern between the commission of criminal acts and the subsequent bringing offenders to justice. This pattern is called the attrition of crime and Hough and Tilley (1998) pointed to it as an indicator within which the usefulness of crime prevention could be defined. Briefly, **crime attrition** describes the process whereby 'committed crime' is progressively whittled down to tiny percentages of caution, conviction, and imprisonment (the *brought to justice* outcomes, used as performance measures of policing by the Home Office). Crime attrition can be shown graphically as in Figure 26.1.

Rates of attrition have not changed much since 1997/98, indeed, in some crime types, they may have worsened. Aside from being indictments of the efficacy of the criminal justice system in England and Wales, these crime attrition data highlight what it means to be a victim of crime, and demonstrate the very low likelihood of the crime being cleared up or 'solved' to the victim's satisfaction (punishment for the offender, restitution of stolen property, etc). This in turn has a direct effect on how the victim views the criminal justice process and the negativity of the experience directly feeds a community's fear of crime. This was highlighted in a 2008 report analysing people's fears about crime and disorder (Casey, 2008), which culminated in 32 recommendations to improve the community's sense of ownership of the fight against crime. It is argued more generally that *crime reduction* can impact on this fear of crime and progressively upon attrition rates, provided that reduction measures are effective and sustained. One further problem which police forces point to, however, is that there

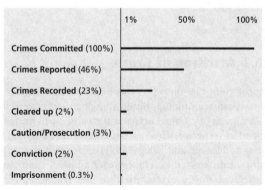

Figure 26.1

are few performance measures for the effective reduction of offending, compared with all those for investigation, charge, and prosecution. This may be another explanation for the traditional and persistent belief that crime prevention is marginal to 'real' police work. Qualitatively, crime reduction is complex to measure: performance figures on their own are not usually able to 'prove a negative'.

26.3 **Partner Problems**

Compounding these difficulties in crime reduction are problems likely to be encountered with partners. We drew attention above to Byrne and Pease's conclusions that, sometimes, membership of CDRPs can be unbalanced by the keenly engaged as against the apathetic. The *potential* for generic partnership problems was also noted in 25.5. However, Hough and Tilley noted that there were specific difficulties in *crime prevention partnerships*, including:

- interagency suspicion and ignorance;
- marginalization of crime prevention issues;
- disruptive turnover of personnel;
- not enough resources to implement action;
- conflicting missions;
- attempts to exploit partnership to pursue other agendas;
- local political imperatives skewing decision making;
- creation of mere 'talking shops';
- lack of expertise and/or experience in crime prevention;
- competing ideological positions;
- key individuals reluctant to adjust to joint working;
- failure to realize that partnerships need more than initial goodwill to sustain momentum.

(adapted from Hough and Tilley, 1998: 14)

In part, of course, these shortcomings are down to failures in communication and the absence of clearly-defined goals or outcomes, but they may also derive from imperfect understanding on the part of all or any of the participants about what crime prevention is. Hough and Tilley then describe the contrary picture; their conclusions can be summarized by saying that successful crime prevention/reduction partnerships need:

- information of high quality from properly-assessed data;
- a vision shared with partners of where all this is going;
- training and education for all participants in crime prevention partnerships;
- the primary purpose to be made clear to all participants;
- areas with specific problems to have specific solutions;
- leadership to be dedicated and effective;
- communication is all-important (both *hi-lo* and *lo-hi*, that is from top to bottom and bottom to top);
- officers in the NPT to have a central facilitating role;
- vigorous local engagement with communities;
- representatives from communities to be given a full voice in the partnership;
- solutions based on consensus.

(adapted from Hough and Tilley, 1998: 14)

It is evident that obtaining genuine 'buy-in' to crime reduction entails educating the partners about crime and crime theories, defining goals carefully, and probably going for some quick hits which will give all involved a sense of purpose.

One area in which hits can be immediate is in structured liaison to 'design out' crime. Some forces have a police officer who is a designated Architectural Liaison Officer (ALO) and whose job mainly consists in working with architects, builders, and planners of local authority-owned buildings, including residential housing, but also community meeting places. ALOs often work alongside other force liaison officers, which means that NPTs have ready access to ranges of specialist advice.

Partnerships between designers, planners, architects, and builders on one hand and the police and community on the other have proved fruitful in physically reducing crime opportunities and working on 'core principles' to design out crime. These principles, in summary, are:

- **an integrated approach** between all concerned and all with a valid input (including advice from reformed offenders);
- **quality of the environment and sense of ownership**, which covers areas such as poorly designed environments, site management, and landscape design;
- **'natural' surveillance**: this simply ensures that footpaths, buildings, ground-floor windows, parking areas, and the like, are open to view and not screened or shrouded by shrubbery or walls. The casual passer-by is the deterrent to the would-be offender, ranging from the graffitist to the sexual assailant;
- **access and footpaths**, including the planning issues around construction and siting, cycleways, and road design;
- **open space provision**, entailing the mutual benefit of open space for a community's recreation, long-term management of the site and ensuring that the amenity can be accessed and enjoyed by all;
- **lighting**, including research on effective public lighting, security lights, motion-sensitive lights, and so on, together with protecting the light courses from vandalism or casual damage and avoiding insensitive siting which leads to light 'spillage' into people's houses.

(adapted from ACPO, *Secured By Design Principles*, 2004)

Sadly, at the time of writing, there is no consistency from one force to another or even from one community to another about the need to 'design out' crime, and instances persist of faulty design, both public and private, affording opportunities to offenders to commit crimes which they might not otherwise have. This leads us to consider now the role of opportunity as a crime factor, and some of the thinking about it.

26.4 **Opportunity as a Key Factor: Theories of Crime**

One primary part in educating partners will involve their understanding of the role that *opportunity* plays in crime, and how all crime prevention will entail in some way the reduction of opportunity. We looked briefly at routine activity theory in Figure 25.4, which is a variant of 'opportunity crime theory', and we want now to look at two other theories to show how they can impact on our understanding of crime opportunity and therefore our understanding of crime reduction.

26.4.1 Crime Pattern Theory

A central component of 'environmental criminology', crime pattern theory considers how people and things involved in crime move about in time and space. There are three main concepts:

nodes:	where people travel **to** and **from**; why they choose these places; what informs their choices; what transport options they select or prefer.
paths:	the routes chosen for travel or movement such as the commuter work flow; pub closing-times' dispersal patterns (how people travel home after drinking); shortcuts to the shops, main road to the sports centre, and so on.
edges:	boundaries of where people live, shop, work, seek entertainment, relax or get fit; edges can help to define racist crimes, for example, since they tend to take place at or beyond boundaries where the attackers are not known.

adapted from Felson and Clarke, 1998: 6–7

In other words, crime pattern theory pays a great deal of attention to the geographical distribution of crime: broadly, 'insiders' commit crimes close to or inside their own communities, whilst 'outsiders' offend at the edges or boundaries of their neighbourhoods. This has clear implications for reducing crime, or preventing it, in a neighbourhood context. Identifying the preponderance of crime types might in turn define some of the reduction and prevention processes which CDRPs adopt locally. Part of the application of this theory depends on the offender following routine practices and acting in a conventional manner, which is not always the case, of course.

26.4.2 Rational Choice Theory

Rational choice theory (sometimes called 'rational choice perspective') is about an offender's decision-making. The theory assumes that *offending is purposeful* (it is intended and is not simply random) and that the offence is in some way intended to *benefit* the offender. This does not mean that all offences are pre-meditated, but that offenders will have aims when they commit crimes, even if those aims are short-sighted or apparently inadequate. For example, it has been known for a long time that young men do not consider the consequences of their actions when they commit some violent assaults. The individual does not need to be alcohol-fuelled, though that can remove any remaining inhibitions to the act of violence. So, a man who attacks another because he 'looked at' the attacker's girlfriend, will not have thought rationally about the possibilities of going to prison because the attack was vicious and resulted in 'grievous bodily harm' or death. In other words, knowing about the potential punishment for an act will not always be an inhibitor to the offender committing that act. The 'aim' or purpose in the example we have used will be to do with 'disrespect' or with potential 'loss of face' forcing one alpha male to defend his 'territory' against another alpha male, who may threaten to take over the girlfriend. Much of the motivation is posturing and bluster, but the violence is real enough and the offending is usually clear cut.

Rational choice theory refers to specific offences, and, in an often complex way, differentiates between forms of offence. For example, Felson and Clarke (1998) showed that within the broad category of 'car crime', there can be very different motivations and means, ranging from stealing a car for 'joyriding', to theft of auto parts, to smuggling luxury cars abroad for resale, to someone who simply steals a vehicle to get home. Rational choice theory tries to see the world from the offender's perspective and tries to ascertain how the offender makes choices: why this house and not that one to burgle? Why this supermarket and not that off-licence to steal bottles of spirits? Why is this shelf of goods considered vulnerable and not that one? (Felson and Clarke, 1998: 7–8).

The *modus operandi* (the characteristic way of doing some act) is the key component to this theory, which is dominated by the offender's need to seize opportunity to commit a crime for his or her benefit. Critics of rational choice theory have commented on how some crimes are instinctual: the offender lashes out without taking thought or making a rational decision. However, for the majority of acquisitive crimes, rather than crimes of violence, rational choice theory does seem to work. *Understanding why offenders make the choices they do* is therefore central to any crime reduction strategy because it will entail denying offenders the opportunity to offend; hence the emphasis on keeping street lights on all night, enhancing lighting in areas where thefts and muggings have happened, and the cutting back of foliage which had previously enabled offenders to lurk undetected.

In the majority of cases, proponents of the theories of crime such as rational choice and crime pattern point to the role of *opportunity*. They conclude, simply enough, that if opportunity is reduced, crime is reduced in proportion. The aim therefore, is:

- to increase perceived *effort* to commit crime (that is, to make it harder for the offender to carry out a crime successfully, such as tagging clothes electronically in shops);
- to increase the perceived *risks* to commit crime (that is, to make the consequences of the offence much less worth the risk of committing the offence, such as enhanced sentences for carrying a knife, or 'going equipped' to steal);
- to reduce the perceived *rewards* from committing crime (that is, to make the result of the crime less attractive as a prospect, such as the ease with which a stolen mobile phone can be rendered useless. A further consequence is to lower the price of objects, like iPods or Blu-ray discs, so that re-sale profit is reduced);
- to *remove excuses* for crime (that is, to take away the opportunity such as those crime reduction activities we discussed above).

(see Felson and Clarke, 1998)

Felson and Clarke are at pains to point out that reducing the opportunities to commit crime does not necessarily *displace* crime, although the effect may be *to change the nature of the crime*. For example, the prevalence of the offence of 'theft of' a motor vehicle might go down, as a result of crime reduction measures, to 'theft from' or merely to criminal damage (supremely irritating to the owner when it happens of course, but usually less permanent deprivation than having the vehicle 'torched' after joyriding).

26.4.3 'Opportunity Makes the Thief'

Felson and Clarke (1998) summarize this approach about the role of opportunity in crime:

- Opportunities play a part in causing all crimes.
- Crime opportunities are highly specific.

- Crime opportunities are concentrated in time and space.
- Crime opportunities depend on everyday movements.
- One crime can often provide opportunities for another.
- Some products are more tempting than others (CRAVED criteria apply, see Clarke, 1999).
- Social and technological changes create new crime opportunities.
- Opportunities for crime can be reduced.
- Reducing opportunities does not displace crime.
- Opportunity decline produces wider declines in crime.

If we understand that reducing the opportunity to commit crime will, through reduction in crime, positively affect people's fear of crime, then it follows that a major plank of any crime reduction strategy will entail preventive measures. We shall look at 16 of these measures now, in the expectation that some or all of these have been adopted and are in use by NPTs and CDRPs across the country.

26.5 **Primary Crime Prevention: Sixteen Techniques**

We noted above that the strategic aim in crime reduction was fourfold (increase perceived *effort*, increase perceived *risks*, reduction in perceived *rewards*, and removal of *excuses* for crime). This strategy can be expanded, or amplified, to include evidence-based techniques of primary crime reduction demonstrated through familiar everyday examples, as the summary in Table 26.1 shows

Table 26.1 Sixteen crime reduction techniques

Situational crime reduction techniques

Crime reduction technique	Examples
Increasing effort:	
1. Target hardening	steering locks; car immobilizers; locks on windows; burglar alarms
2. Access control	entry phones; computer passwords; gate barriers; staffed checkpoints
3. Deflecting offenders	confiscating bottles/cans from groups drinking in public; keeping rival football fans apart
4. Controlling means	photographs on driving licences; the availability of firearms or bladed weapons
Increasing risks:	
5. Entry/exit screening	Merchandise tags in shops; X-ray machines at airport security checks
6. Formal surveillance	CCTV; Automated Number Plate Reader (ANPR)
7. Employee surveillance	door stewards at night clubs; store 'detectives'; 'live-monitored' CCTV
8. 'Natural' surveillance	movement-triggered sensor lights; windows; spy-holes in front doors
Reducing reward:	
9. Target removal	removing satellite navigation equipment when leaving a vehicle; putting objects of value in the boot of a car, out of sight
10. Identify property	vehicle engine chassis number; ultra violet (UV) pens for marking property
11. Remove inducements	clean up graffiti; repair damage; cut back shrubbery; enhance lighting; close doors and windows
12. Rule setting 1	housing tenancy agreements; anti-social behaviour agreements (ASBAs)

Crime reduction technique	Examples
Removing excuses:	
13. Rule setting 2	hotel registration; customs declarations; anti-social behaviour orders (ASBOs)
14. Stimulating conscience	roadside speed displays; drink/drive campaigns
15. Controlling disinhibitors	drinking age laws; parental control of the Internet
16. Facilitating compliance	temporary barriers; bag searches; 'funnelled' queues of people

Adapted from Byrne and Pease, 2003 who summarized Clarke and Homel, 1997

As well as tabulating the many complementary possibilities open to those in NPTs and partnerships who implement crime reduction techniques, Table 26.1 also shows the practical, hard-headed instances which work on the ground and in most circumstances. The essential argument is that *inhibition of opportunity* (through these and other techniques) will in turn *inhibit crime*.

26.7 **Starting with the EVA: an Action Plan for Crime Reduction**

How does crime reduction theory translate into a plan of action at the neighbourhood policing team level? Right from the start we must emphasize that *any plan we outline here is merely indicative*. Individual BCUs (Basic Command Units), or Forces, or Partnerships, or CDRPs will have important local concerns, and one neighbourhood team will have different priorities even from others in the same BCU. In other words, all we can offer here is the typical way of drawing up a crime reduction action plan; it will be for individual teams to fill in the important local detail and add any extras, modifications, or special practices. As a template, though, what follows is tried, tested, and has worked.

The **National Intelligence Model** (NIM), which we looked at in Chapter 14, includes *inputs* from 'government and local community initiatives', and thereby imparts rigour and relevance to local plans for crime reduction and prevention. We also discussed the Environmental Visual Audit (EVA) or 'structured patch walk' in Chapter 24 where the EVA input to the NIM is a starting point for any community-based, intelligence-derived action plan. The EVA helps to identify what is locally a problem and picks up early crime or disorder patterns, which will entail solutions—one of which is reducing the opportunity for crime. As we saw in Chapter 25, *problem identification* is a necessary precursor to considering solutions, a process which helps the local NPT to *prioritize* what can be tackled first. The necessary data, on matters such as hot spots, repeat victimization, and the crime pattern/rational choice information, helps to determine the *geography of crime*. This will lead the BCU's Tasking and Coordinating Group to decide on its operational plan, in consultation with the local CDRP and the communities, following which may come the familiar *four phases of crime reduction*, which reduce the opportunity to commit offences, together with redesigned environments. The process which synchronizes all these actions is then *evaluated* to ensure that the original outcomes have been achieved. It is easier, perhaps, to envisage this process in terms of a model than laboriously to describe it in words—see Figure 26.2.

We can see from the model in Figure 26.2 that the inter-relationship between the parts shows the complexity of an effective 'universal' crime reduction strategy. Far from being the 'Cinderella' of policing, this crime reduction strategy is at the heart and very core of the engagement between the police and the communities, between the NPTs and the CDRPs, between the police and the various partnerships

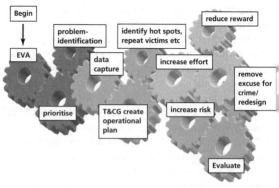

Figure 26.2 The 'gear-mesh model' for a crime reduction action plan

which are cultivated to tackle local problems. It does not matter if local arrangements differ in some respects from what we have shown here. What matters very much is that everywhere communities' fears of crime are directly addressed by what can be done to reduce offending and prevent the opportunities to commit crime.

Further Reading

One of the best texts is a little dated now, but it covers the essentials cogently and well. It is Michael Hough and Nick Tilley's 1998 paper: 'Getting the Grease to the Squeak; research lessons for crime prevention', Police Research Group, Crime Detection and Prevention Series, Paper 85, Home Office, Crown Copyright. Another excellent, and definitive, study is Tilley, N (ed) (2005), *Handbook of Crime Prevention and Community Safety*, Willan Publishing, Devon. Felson and Clarke, 1998, and Byrne and Pease, 2003 (both collaborations referenced below) are each seminal to our understanding of the strategic importance of crime reduction. Practical applications are in the *Secure by Design* work and the *Think Thief* publication on the Home Office website, both referenced below.

Further useful references, for those of you who want to follow up on some of the topics covered in this chapter, include:

ACPO (1996) *Towards 2000*, Association of Chief Police Officers, available at <http://www.acpo.org.uk/>, accessed 28 June 2008

ACPO (2004) *Secured by Design Principles*, ACPO, available at <http://www.securedbydesign.com/pdfs/SBD-principles.pdf>, accessed 27 June 2008

Byrne, S and Pease, K (2003) 'Crime reduction and community safety' in T Newburn (ed), *Handbook of Policing*, Cullompton, Willan, Part III, 'Doing Policing': 286–310

Casey, L (2008) 'Engaging Communities in Fighting Crime', *Cabinet Office Crime and Communities Review*, Crown Copyright; available at <http://www.cabinetoffice.gov.uk>, 120 pages (or /cc_sum for the summary, 32 pages), accessed 27 June 2008

Clarke, C (1999) 'Hot Products: Understanding, Anticipat-ing and Reducing Demand for Stolen Goods', *Police Research Series*, Paper 112, Home Office, Crown Copyright

Clarke, R and Homel, R (1997) 'A revised classification of situational crime prevention techniques', in S Lab, S (eds), *Crime Prevention at a Crossroads*, Nashville, Kentucky, USA, Anderson Publishing

Design Council (2008) *Think Thief: A Designer's Guide to Designing Out Crime*, in collaboration with the Home Office, available at <http://www.crimereduction.homeoffice.gov.uk/business/business32.pdf>, accessed 27 June 2008

Felson, M and Clarke, R (1998) 'Opportunity makes the Thief: Practical Theory for Crime Prevention', *Police Research Series*, Paper 98, Home Office, Crown Copyright

Fielding, N (1995, revised 2002) *Community Policing*, Oxford, Oxford University Press

Garland, D (2000) 'The culture of high crime societies: some preconditions of recent law and order policies', *British Journal of Criminology*, Vol 40: 347–75

Hughes, G and Edwards, A (2002) *Crime Control and Community; the new politics of public safety*, Cullompton, Willan Publishing

Kappeler, V and Gaines, L (1990 and 2005) *Community Policing; a contemporary perspective*, Cincinnati, Ohio, USA, Tin Box Studio Inc

Karman, A (2007), *Crime Victims; an introduction to victimology*, Belmont, California, USA, Thomson Wadsworth

Morgan, J (1991) 'Safer Communities: the local delivery of crime prevention through the partnership approach', ('The Morgan Report'), *The Home Office Standing Conference on Crime Prevention*, August, available at <http://www.mhbuk.com/reports.aspx?sm=c_b>, accessed 17 June 2008, and additional material relating to the Morgan report and the Crime and Disorder Act 1998, is available at <http://www.crimereduction.homeoffice.gov.uk/toolkits/p010301.htm> accessed 17 June 2008

Newburn, T and Jones, T (2002) 'Consultation by Crime and Disorder Partnerships', *Police Research Series*, Paper 148, Home Office, Crown Copyright

Home Office research papers generally can be accessed online by year and title, at <http://www.homeoffice.gov.uk/>, accessed 12 June 2008

Chapter 27

Major Crime and Homicide Response

27.1 **Introduction**

Major crime and homicide investigations demand the very best in police professionalism and dexterity. The police are usually first on the scene and carry an important responsibility for conducting 'fast time' actions. Adopting an effective and thorough approach in the performance of those duties is pivotal and forms the bedrock of a successful investigation. The objective is to lay the foundations of a seamless process from crime scene(s) to court, involving not only the first responders but also all others who no less contribute. This extends to supervisors, senior detectives, silver commanders, experts, and specialists from which a good team effort is also expected.

All activities and actions completed (or not completed) during these initial stages are critical. Any indecisivenss or unprofessionalism will skew the investigation, reduce the likelihood of identifying offenders, and compromise the case at court. The chances of success for an investigation are greatly enhanced by efficiently carrying out key functions and procedures required during the dynamic and spontaneous response phase and adhering to the highest ideals of police tradecraft and competence.

Whether the reported incident involves a suspicious death, high risk missing persons, armed robbery, aggravated burglary, or violent or sexual assault, the principles remain the same. Any potential critical incident, regardless of uncertainty surrounding the circumstances or severity, should be assessed on its own merits and treated respectfully, especially with regard to homicide and terrorism cases.

A good initial assessment is always vitally important because it is fed back to a supervisor and/or a control/communications room, and ultimately determines how the incident is graded, categorized, and the level of response required. Time is critical because the initial response phase falls within a period often referred to as the 'golden hour(s)'.

Initial decision-making and actions vary according to the nature and type of the incident. All homicides, for example, are unique in that each one is shaped by the circumstances in which they occur and in which offenders, witnesses, and communities respond. In some cases responding officers are greeted by calm, rational people who provide detailed accounts of exactly what happened. In contrast, there may be pandemonium with hysterical, traumatized, or alcohol-affected people who are difficult to get any sense from. Language or cultural barriers can add further complications, and there may even be dangerous lurking offenders nearby. In such situations response officers have to remain calm and composed, taking all necessary steps to protect people, begin a preliminary investigation, and identify and preserve evidence.

Dealing with a major crime scene, such as homicide, is the ultimate test and one of the most important roles an officer will be required to perform. It may only happen once or twice (or not at all) during a career. Rarely is the first officer an actual witness to the incident, so they must rely upon all their training, knowledge, and expertise to ascertain what they are dealing with and decisively perform the necessary duties. Aspects that at first seem irrelevant seldom remain so and often gain greater significance; therefore nothing can be ignored or missed.

Therefore this chapter has been designed to help prepare for such occasions, and contains explanations of important processes, guidelines, and reminders, together with checklists that serve as practical guides or aide memories. A precautionary note is that over-reliance on fixed routines can sometimes be detrimental to the essential principle of 'keeping an open mind': so any investigative decision or action must be guided by the circumstances and not mere compliance with checklists.

27.2 **The Important '5 x WH & H' and 'ABC' Principles**

Two extremely important principles that apply to all investigations, serious or otherwise, are known as the '5 x WH & H' and 'ABC'. Making good use of these investigative mantras will allow useful information to be obtained and properly tested. The '5 x WH & H' principle contains a list of interrogative pronouns and stands for:

- Who?
- What?
- Where?
- When?
- Why?
- How?

There are many sources of information that can provide answers to these questions. People who report crimes or incidents, victims, witnesses or people offering information, forensic evidence, passive data (eg CCTV), admissions from offenders, or reliable sources of intelligence are the main providers. This helps to identify important lines of enquiry by highlighting information known and information not known but required (ie knowledge gaps) about the incident under investigation (ie questions for which there is currently no answer). Using this process also prompts the asking of supplementary questions that need addressing methodically as the following example shows.

In an investigation into the suspicious death of a young adult male whose body was found by officers in a dwelling house after a 999 call to the police, the '5 WH & H' model is applied as follows:

- Who is the deceased?
- What has happened immediately prior to his death?
- Where did he die?
- When did he die?
- Why did he die?
- How did he die?

These then produce supplementary questions such as:

- Who found the body?
- Who called the police?
- Who else resides at the address?
- Who are his friends and associates?
- What did the initial caller say and what is their background and relationship to the deceased?
- What other information is available (eg linked incidents or reports such as previous crimes reported at the address)?
- What do the neighbours know?
- What does the scene tell us (eg signs of a disturbance)?
- Where are the deceased's wallet, keys, and other personal belongings?
- What is known about the deceased (eg criminal convictions, sexual orientation, racial background, previous suicide attempts, medical history, subject of previous attacks etc)?
- What possible motive is there for a murder?

- Where does it appear that death occurred (in one room or signs of blood or disturbance elsewhere)?
- When was the first call to the police?
- When was the deceased last seen alive and under what circumstances?
- What is the latest date on newspapers, documents, or letters at the address?
- Why were the police initially called (eg male not seen recently or anonymous tip-off that he was dead)?
- How did it happen (ie post mortem result and scene interpretation about cause and manner of death)?
- How many witnesses or intelligence reports are there?
- How secure was the house when the body was found?

These form the basis of a logical sequence of questions for those making an investigative assessment into what has occurred. The example above could have been a natural death, suicide, or murder.

Note: The safest way to handle this incident after medical attention and/or life is pronounced extinct would be to secure the primary scenes—ie the body, the entire house, and immediate curtilage—and commence enquiries before any hasty conclusions are made about what has occurred or forensic evidence destroyed.

When gathering information, intelligence gaps are always identified because information isn't currently known or available. Therefore those making initial enquiries should always record everything that is known in a legible and durable format, keeping a note of any information gaps that need filling. It is important when handing over or briefing others such as supervisors that not only the known details are provided, but also those that are not known. Good practice is to record all the information gathered in a simple matrix/table format leaving clear gaps against any queries that still need answering (see the Case Study in Figure 27.1).

This helps keep everything organized, easier to remember and understand, and, when giving briefings, keeps everything logical and sequential rather than fragmented or disjointed. Supervisors can also use the '5 WH & H' method as a means of asking questions of responding officers to obtain a systematic briefing, rather than using random or ad hoc questions in an unstructured manner. Additional material can always be captured at the end by requesting further information not already covered.

All source material or information relied upon for providing answers or generating questions to the '5 x WH & H' model should be regularly reviewed as to reliability and relevance. Any material relied upon or assumptions made should be thoroughly and continuously tested, recorded, reviewed, and evaluated. There may be conflicting or contradictory information, and material needs to be interpreted accurately to see if there is any other competing explanation for what is being relied upon. Any hypothesis or suggested explanation that depends upon facts should remain dynamic and under constant review as information may change over time (eg conflicting times over when a deceased was last seen alive). This is where the '**ABC**' rule applies, which means:

A	Assume nothing
B	Believe nothing
C	Challenge (and check) everything*

* Also cited in ACPO, *Practical Advice on Core Investigative Doctrine* ACPO Centrex, 2005

Figure 27.1 Case Study: Information gathered and gaps remaining matrix

QUESTION	WHAT DO WE KNOW?	WHAT ELSE DO WE NEED TO KNOW?	WHERE CAN WE GET IT FROM?
WHO WAS KILLED	41-yr-old lone white female (victim named). Has child from previous relationship but single. Well known in local area, liked and respected. Still resides with parents. Possibly had/having affairs with married men. Always carries two mobile phones. Works at local convenience store.	Detailed victimology. Any previous attacks against this victim? Was she the intended victim? Are other attacks likely to occur? Full details of previous relationships.	Family & friends, work colleagues, local community, intelligence checks. Victim profile and lifestyle analysis. Crime recording checks. Insurance claims checksComparative Case Analysis (SCAS) and Crime Pattern Analysis. Full intelligence checks (incl corporate databases). Risk analysis for further victims.
WHO IS/ARE THE SUSPECT(S)	Victim in stormy relationship with boyfriend—possible suspect? Recently threatened in her place of work by 2 x unknown males.	Is she having any other affairs? Full details of incident and of persons involved.	Identify and declare suspect(s) and TIE categories. Victimology. Subject profile(s). T/I work colleagues. Telecoms data analysis. Intelligence assessment.

QUESTION	WHAT DO WE KNOW?	WHAT ELSE DO WE NEED TO KNOW?	WHERE CAN WE GET IT FROM?
WHO WITNESSED IT	Male walking dog found body at 06.30.	Identify all potential key and significant witnesses.	Media appeals & H2H enqs. Priority T/I actions.
WHAT HAPPENED	Battered and strangled. Found in woods near to home address. Semi-naked, trousers pulled down around ankles. Contents of handbag emptied onto floor.	Was anything stolen from victim? Any defensive marks on the body? Does manner of death give indication as to age/sex/physical capability of offender? Weapon—present/missing. Brought to scene by the offender, victim, or improvised?	Conduct inventory of personal belongings. Re-examine body for further bruises. Check clothing for damage, rips, and tears. Consult National Injuries Database.
WHAT OCCURRED PRIOR TO MURDER	Victim in public house with friends. Then spent time alone with her boyfriend. Walked home alone after leaving boyfriend's flat after argument.	Sequence of events for movements of victim. Establish if any forensic evidence in boyfriend's flat.	Crime scene examination of flat. Telecoms data analysis. T/I/E all persons in vicinity of scene and at public house (time parameters?). Search for CCTV in area. Analysis of witness statements.

QUESTION	WHAT DO WE KNOW?	WHAT ELSE DO WE NEED TO KNOW?	WHERE CAN WE GET IT FROM?
		Did victim have any significant arguments or activities in hours before last known sighting?	
		Did victim meet anyone after leaving boyfriend's flat by prior arrangement or by chance?	
WHAT OTHER SIGNIFICANT EVENTS TOOK PLACE	Raised voices of couple possibly arguing at approx. 01.15 hrs.	If linked to murder incident.	HP action—T/I/TST witness(es). Consider media appeal & conduct H2H enqs. in vicinity.
WHEN DID IT HAPPEN	Bet 12.30 and 06.30 Sat. 20.4.02.	More precise time of death.	Witnesses, back record conversion of alcohol/blood levels, pathologist, entomologist.
			Gastroenterology (stomach contents exam), CCTV, assessment of physical evidence in conjunction with other events—eg weather—victim's clothing on ground and clothing wet after the rain.

QUESTION	WHAT DO WE KNOW?	WHAT ELSE DO WE NEED TO KNOW?	WHERE CAN WE GET IT FROM?
			Is ground under clothing wet yes/no? What time did rain start/end?
WHERE DID IT HAPPEN	(named location)	Was this where it occurred or is it deposition site?	Full scene interpretation.
			Forensic analysis of body plus palynological survey.
		Risk analysis for further attacks.	Crime pattern analysis. Social & demographic information.
		How did victim/ offender get to this location?	Geographical profiling.
WHY DID IT HAPPEN		Establish motive.	Check mobile calls made by victim.
		Victim knew offender? Stranger/ sexual attack? Robbery/ theft? Anger/ jealousy?	Forensic and pathological interpretation of scene. Use of Offender profiler.
HOW DID DEATH OCCUR	Post mortem revealed cause of death as asphyxiation.	Re-examine to see if further bruising/ marks on body are now visible.	HO pathologist.
		Full medical history of victim and antecedents.	Victim's GP and hospital records.

QUESTION	WHAT DO WE KNOW?	WHAT ELSE DO WE NEED TO KNOW?	WHERE CAN WE GET IT FROM?
		Toxicology results for alchohol levels and drug traces.	Forensic Science Service results.
HOW WAS THIS LOCATION CHOSEN?	Was it on or near victim's route home?	Scene interpretation. Has victim been there previously? Is it linked to any suspect or T/I/E?	Victimology. CPA data. Subject profile analysis. Possible media reconstruction. High profile enquiries in location.
HOW DID OFFENDER GET TO & FROM THE SCENE?	Is there an easy escape route?	Was offender on foot? Any vehicle used? Local transport?	Scene examination. Enqs with local taxis and bus companies. CCTV trawl and speed cameras. Intelligence checks on suspect/TIEs. Use of scene 'tracker' expert.

KEY POINTS—THE ABC PRINCIPLE:

1. Nothing should ever be taken for granted. It cannot be assumed things are what they seem or information has been recounted accurately. Looking for corroboration, rechecking, testing, reviewing, and confirming are important requirements. Unfortunately people do get mistaken and get things wrong, or even sometimes elaborate and embellish facts.

2. It is highly appropriate to apply a degree of scepticism to avoid pitfalls and mistakes by over reliance or trust in things that may later be proved inaccurate.

3. Always check the detail, detail, and detail again—this cannot be stressed strongly enough.

27.3 **Using Initiative, Intuition, or Creativity**

In investigations there is always a need for practical skills and shrewdness. Responders and investigators should be alert to spotting or noticing things that appear unusual or out of place, and using their 'sixth sense'. Attending reports of sudden deaths, suicides, or reports of missing persons requires a great deal of tenacity. Things may not always be what they seem.

For example, a person who reports a missing partner but has in fact murdered them will make mistakes and leave plenty of clues. Closer inspection may reveal things that seem or feel 'out of place'. This could include missing or broken items of furniture, ornaments, or furniture imprints in the carpet (perhaps indicating an argument has taken place), signs of recent cleaning, disinfectant, a small bonfire in the garden, or a missing shower curtain (eg to wrap a body in); or even the reportee's nervous demeanour, hesitance, or inability to provide information.

Using initiative, having a 'gut instinct', or applying creative and practical thinking and questioning assumptions should not, however, override responsibilities to perform basic duties correctly.

Case Study—The 'Yorkshire Ripper'

At 10.50 pm on Friday 2 January 1981 Sgt Robert Ring and PC Robert Hydes were on patrol off Melbourne Avenue in Sheffield when they saw a V8 Rover 3500 parked up with male and female occupants on board. His name was Peter William Sutcliffe of 6 Garden Lane, Heaton, Bradford, and she was Olivia Reivers. When Sutcliffe got out of the car, which was bearing false number plates, he went to use the toilet behind a nearby stone porch and an oil storage tank. He was later arrested on suspicion of theft of the car number plates. However, relying on his intuition, the sergeant later went back and searched the area around the storage tank

---

and lying on the ground by the wall he found a ballpein hammer and a knife (weapons he had used to murder previous victims). When later confronted with this evidence Sutcliffe confessed to being the man dubbed the 'Yorkshire Ripper' and having been responsible for murdering 13 women and attempting to murder 7 others, for which he was tried and sentenced to life imprisonment.

27.4 The 'Golden Hour(s)' Principle

The 'golden hour(s)' concept, borrowed from the medical profession, is applied to the first actions at reported serious incidents. The benefits associated with maximizing evidence-gathering opportunities and decision-making are virtually identical to those in medical settings, except there are threats not only to life but also to the potential loss of evidence that may never be recouped. The clock starts ticking immediately the first report is received, either to call management centres, public service desks, enquiry counters, or via reports made directly to police officers and staff.

The golden hour(s) is the period when evidential material is abundant, forensic material is most fresh and easiest to detect (eg blood is still wet), memories are still sharp, and lies and alibis are at their most vulnerable. It is a time when initial observations are most crucial, such as noting vehicle numbers rapidly leaving a scene, stopping and talking to witnesses (from whom there may only be one chance of getting details), and noting people's behaviour, demeanour, etc.

Many homicides and other serious crimes are detected as a direct consequence of very prompt and decisive actions, such as locating and/or spontaneously arresting potential suspects; obtaining witness details; seizing valuable CCTV and ANPR data before it gets destroyed or recorded over;

preserving forensic evidence; seizing vehicles, clothing mobile phones; recording unsolicited comments; checking false identities; or identifying urgent lines of enquiry.

Case Study—Bomb threat/Blackmail

A call was made to a shopping centre from a public call box stating that a bomb would detonate inside the premises that was packed with shoppers unless money was handed over. The call was eventually traced to a call box which was found to be empty when checked. Officers quickly treated the phone booth as a crime scene and put a secure cordon around it. The store was evacuated and a hoax device safely dealt with by bomb disposal experts. The phone box was forensically examined and the offender's DNA found, which led to him being arrested and charged with making a false bomb threat and blackmail. The successful identification and arrest was entirely down to the swift actions taken by the officers who effectively protected the crime scene from which the crucial evidence was recovered.

Those who comply with the golden hour rules and make good use of the first opportunity to note things and take immediate action help solve many crimes.

27.5 **'Golden Hour' Actions**

After saving life the most important task is to identify secure, and protect evidence and crime scenes. In order to do so it is necessary to ensure all areas relating to any scene(s) are cordoned off and a crime scene log(s) commenced. The duty of the first officers attending is to prevent any disturbance and where possible stop all unauthorized persons entering the scene(s). This includes supervisory and senior personnel unless there is an urgent operational need for them to gain entry. In order to do this there must be a rapid and objective assessment based on information known at the time, the location of any victims, the presence of any physical evidence, and/or any useful natural boundaries. This entails a thorough yet careful *initial visual check* of the scene(s) and surroundings.

KEY POINT

During the initial assessment of a scene the brief examination of a body may be unavoidable because, for example, death or the cause of death is not immediately obvious. While checking for any wounds, injuries, or recent trauma on exposed areas of the body, however, *protective gloves* should be worn and the minimum of disruption made wherever possible. Consideration should also be given to any religious practices that do not like a body being touched at all, and guidance sought on how best to manage cultural sensitivities.

In some cases there may be more than one scene that requires identifying and securing quickly. For example, a continuing violent or sexual attack that has occurred in a block of apartments or flats may have *multiple crime scenes* (ie in one of the flats, in an elevator, on a landing, on an interior stairwell, or in an adjacent carpark). Additional staff would be immediately required to assist with containing, cordoning, and protecting all the affected areas to minimize or exclude potential contamination from bona fide residents or visitors—a prime example of 'golden hour' actions for incident responders.

There are other 'fast track' actions that may also need rapid attention in addition to initial scene identification and management, such as searches for further victims, suspects, witnesses, and physical evidence. This may include searches for discarded weapons, vehicles, clothing, or stolen property along escape routes, all of which should be treated as separate scenes once found.

In homicide cases the golden hour(s) is also a time when the victim's family, relatives, and friends are extremely vulnerable and in some circumstances, can very soon attend at or nearby the scene of the incident, which is an extremely upsetting and traumatic experience for them. For example, a cordon may have been placed around an area containing the body of a loved one, who they cannot see or go to so they need to be managed tactfully and supportively. A Family Liaison Officer (FLO) should be appointed, but initially the family of victims need preliminary support with appropriate officers nominated to stay with them at all times until a trained FLO becomes available. This is to provide initial support, information, and advice, and protect them, if needs be, from the media intrusion.

KEY POINTS—THE GOLDEN HOUR(S)

1. Initial responders and supervisors should consider what/where/how and when supporting resources can be put to best use—for instance, covering possible exit routes instead of all patrols going to the scene to check for suspects who may be taking an escape route.
2. Initial searches should be systematic and methodical in order to make a swift identification of useful evidence, suspects, or witnesses, and recorded as to their extent and nature in order to assist fully managed (eg Police Search Advisor (POLSA) or forensic) searches later.
3. Public areas and transport opportunities such as taxis can be checked for offenders or witnesses (including hospitals).
4. Air support is a useful tactic but the use of helicopters hovering directly over crime scenes may attract curious onlookers or disturb forensic evidence, possibly making scenes harder to protect.
5. Specialist resources such as firearms officers may be an important consideration if there is suspected firearms involvement in the incident, or other specialists such as search trained dog units or POLSA teams.
6. Initial support and assistance to the family, relatives, and friends of victims should always be provided.

Below is a list of **10 x 'golden hour' actions** for an initial response at the scene of a homicide/suspicious death;

remembering the importance of remaining visible, not putting anyone at risk, and by considering the overarching priority of safety:

Checklist—First officers attending—Responsibilities

1. Preserve life. Identify and attend to any victims, casualties, or fatalities, and administer first aid or check for signs of life. Summon medical assistance if required. If obviously deceased, cause as little disturbance as possible and ensure life pronounced extinct.

2. Conduct initial visual search and scene assessment using available resources to identify scenes, physical evidence, suspects, witnesses, etc. Make a sketch plan if possible.

3. Secure evidence. Identify and preserve any crime scene(s) and identify entry/exit with only one point of entry, a designated approach route and rendezvous place for other attending resources. Protect perimeter with barrier tape and cordons. Prevent unauthorized access and cross-contamination and commence incident scene log(s).

4. Check for and preserve any physical or obvious forensic evidence, eg CCTV, weapons, discarded clothing, blood distribution, footprints, or other potential exhibits.

5. Record exact time of arrival and all actions taken.

6. Compile a situation report using the 5 x WH & H method (including nature and severity of circumstances), summon assistance, request additional resources (eg fire service, ambulances etc), and supervision as required.

7. Try to establish the victim's identity and next of kin without disturbing evidence (descriptions, identifying marks/tattoos/features/clothing/vehicles can also be used). If family, relatives, and friends present, deal sensitively, giving preliminary support and advice.

8. Identify and arrest any suspect(s) if possible (ideally by person who has not visited the crime scene to reduce risk of cross-contamination).

9. Identify and separate witnesses, record details, and get first accounts.

10. Identify, prioritize, maximize, and exploit any intelligence opportunities and urgent lines of enquiry (eg circulation of vehicles involved or descriptions of suspects etc).

27.6 **Preservation of Life and Protection of Public Safety**

Any initial response to a major crime scene (eg homicide, rape, or terrorism) presents an important first priority to preserve life and safeguard the welfare and safety of any victim(s) and other members of the public. This always takes precedence over gathering evidence or managing forensic issues. In homicide cases if possible signs of life or death are not clearly obvious, first aid and resuscitation techniques should be attempted and medical assistance summoned immediately. There have been significant advances in medical science, and resuscitation techniques and people who have suffered serious trauma can often be kept alive for a longer period of time and make a full recovery provided they receive early medical attention. There are in some instances obvious indications of death, such as decapitation, rigor mortis, decomposition, and lividity marks. However, a suitably qualified medical professional still must pronounce life extinct or certify death, which should be done with the minimum of disturbance to the body.

KEY POINTS

1. If in any doubt whether a person is deceased a presumption should always be that they are alive. People may appear dead even when they have life signs that are very slight and hardly noticeable (eg hypothermia cases).
2. A duty of care and provision of welfare and support extends not only to victims but others at the scene, including traumatized witnesses, onlookers, police personnel, and other agencies (even offenders).

Other useful guidelines are as follows:

- No attempt should be made to search any deceased victims for identification at this early stage as this could destroy vital evidence.

- Where any disturbance of a body has had to take precedence over preservation of evidence in order to try and save a life (paramedics may have had to administer initial treatment) a record should be made of exactly what has been disturbed.
- If items have been moved, a note should be made of the original and final position.
- Officers should be prepared to hand over their footwear and outer clothing to the Crime Scene Investigator to check for evidential material, plus details of all police vehicles that have attended the scene for elimination purposes.
- Any materials used by medical teams should remain in place, at the location and on the person in the case of fatalities.
- Full details of those who have come into contact with the scene and victims should be carefully recorded.

27.7 **Emergency Services**

Other emergency services that attend incidents, such as paramedics or firefighters, require debriefing quickly. Their normal duties will demand that they resume from the crime scene as soon as possible and they must be debriefed, if at all possible, before leaving. At the very least contact details and a brief account of their actions at the scene should be obtained provided that doing so does not impede a victim's medical treatment. Other emergency services have sometimes arrived at an incident prior to police attendance, particularly if dispatched by their own control room. Paramedics make their own records of the circumstances and injuries, and may obtain or hear accounts from victims and/or witnesses while they are in attendance. In some instances, consideration may need to be given to treating them as 'significant witnesses' dependent on what they have seen or heard. Ambulance crews are not trained investigators and must be properly debriefed as to how they gained entry to the scene (indoors or outdoors), where they have been, and what they have moved. They should be asked questions such as: Who was present? What did they see? What did the victim say? What is the likely prognosis on the condition of the victim? (ie the '5 × WH & H' principles).

KEY POINTS

1. As a general rule medical personnel have primacy at a scene until death is confirmed. The preservation of evidence then takes precedence, and if the death is considered suspicious a body should not be transported to hospital or further disturbed and should remain in tact at the scene.

2. Medical staff at scenes tend to disturb and/or contaminate potential evidence. This is mostly unavoidable and should be borne in mind when interpreting the crime scene. There is every possibility the body will have been moved to administer medical aid. Use of emergency resuscitation devices such as defibrillators may even cause slight injuries to the body, which, together with any discarded medical equipment, need to be retained and accounted for. This is important information which needs communicating to the person in charge of the investigation.

27.8 **Reports Made Directly to Patrol Staff**

Sometimes reports are made directly to officers on patrol or at an enquiry counter. Officers and staff are then placed in a position similar to that of a telephone 'call handler' and should adopt the same principles and methods by eliciting factual information (using the '5 x WH & H'), carefully noting the time reported and recording full circumstances. The person making the report should, wherever possible, remain with the officer(s) and not be allowed to disappear.

This allows sufficient time to determine the full extent of what they have seen or heard and if necessary arrange for a fuller interview. If personal details are refused a record should be made of their full description, clothing worn, who they are in the company of, vehicles, etc. This will assist in later trying to establish true identity and conduct a follow-up interview. It must be stressed that these persons could well be involved in the incident or even be an offender. If there are reasonable grounds to suspect involvement, then consideration should be given to having them arrested. It is not uncommon for offenders to speak to officers or make reports at or near the scenes of crime, trying to look helpful, or return to crime scenes to see what is going on, or even offer themselves as witnesses. Sometimes they also court the media (Ian Huntley, responsible for the Soham murders of Holly Wells and Jessica Chapman did so). This is one of the reasons it is vital to record as much accurate detail as possible.

KEY POINTS

Exact words spoken by the person who first reports the incident may prove crucial to the investigation. There must be careful questioning and eliciting of information from the person making the report and accurate recording of all details, either contemporaneously or immediately afterwards. It may be a useful evidential advantage to have them agree and sign the notes afterwards.

27.9 **Crime Scene Preservation**

The forensic science 'principle of exchange' states, 'when two objects meet there is a mutual exchange of material from one to another' (Locard's principle). This has been summarized as the well-known phrase, 'every contact leaves a trace'. The purpose of scene preservation is to enable this evidence to be found uncontaminated.

Examples of trace evidence that can link an offender to a crime scene include blood, hair, DNA, body fluids, fibres, glass, paint, soil, pollen, explosive traces, and firearms discharge residue. The advantage of such physical evidence is that it is not vulnerable to the vagaries of witness testimony.

Immediate steps must be taken to minimize and eliminate the possibility of cross-contamination occurring, as failure to do so can render any potential evidence inadmissible in a prosecution case. The preservation and security of a scene may have to be proved to the satisfaction of a court if vital forensic evidence is found upon which a case hinges. Defence rigorously cross-examine police procedures to identify possible exculpatory reasons for existence of trace evidence on the defendant. The 'integrity of the scene' demands that there must be no interference through contamination or cross-transfer that could have occurred either accidentally or deliberately. 'Continuity', or the evidence audit trail, refers to the continuous record of all movements and processes of an exhibit right up to the time of trial to prove an item has not been corrupted or interfered with at any time or stage in the process.

Crime scenes must be identified and preserved in order to maximize the potential for gathering any material that can be used to implicate or eliminate suspects and corroborate or refute allegations or versions of events. The Criminal Procedure and Investigations Act 1996 requires that any potentially *relevant* material (material meaning evidence, intelligence, information or a combination of all three) must be retained. The first opportunity to gather material is often the last, and it is much better to preserve rather than leave something behind or allow it to get contaminated by taking a chance. This links in the ABC rule, that of *Assume nothing*.

Crime scenes vary considerably in type, ranging from domestic buildings to outdoor scenes and vehicles, although often the most important scenes are in fact the victim and the offenders themselves. Crime scene evidence and characteristics can also provide other useful information that may help solve a crime. For example, the personality traits of the offender or motive may be represented as an *organized* offender, ie one likely to leave behind very little evidence at a crime scene by taking time and consideration to plan and prepare for the execution of their crime. By contrast, a *disorganized* offender will probably leave behind lots of information and evidence, especially if the offence has occurred during a mad frenzy or spontaneous act.

27.10 **What Constitutes a Crime Scene?**

There are various types of crime scene and some are not so obvious. The primary scene is always that which is deemed the most important, ie usually where the offence took place. It is important to be aware of the potential for multiple (or satellite) crime scenes and the need for their protection also (using Locard's principle). For example, a witness to an armed robbery might experience an offender brush past them as they escape from the scene, or the offender may have brushed past a bystander's vehicle. In either case, the witness and the vehicle are also 'scenes' and urgent action is required to preserve the potential cross-transfer evidence linking the offenders to the crime. For ease of reference all potential scenes are always numbered, starting with Scene (1). In this case the actual site of the robbery would be the primary crime scene. Here is a list of some other crime scene examples:

- Location where offence took place—always Scene (1).
- A victim.
- A witness.
- An attack site.
- A body (or body part) (note: a body itself should be treated as a crime scene and an evidence recovery strategy determined with external samples (eg DNA swabs) normally being taken prior to any removal, wherever possible).

- A place where a body has been moved to/recovered from (eg deposition site).
- Anywhere there is trace or physical evidence (tyre marks, footprints, location of a weapon or ammunition, blood distribution, clothing, etc).
- Articles connected to victim(s), witness(es), or offender(s).
- Vehicles or vessels connected to the incident.
- Premises connected to offenders or suspects.
- Access or escape routes to/from primary scene taken by offender(s).
- Bodies removed to hospitals or mortuaries (note: try to prevent hospital staff placing all clothing in one bag to avoid cross-contamination).
- Any location where a crime has been planned.

There are usually a minimum of two crime scenes, for example the location and the offender. These generally increase as more information becomes available. Early recognition of the various different and potential scenes assists in taking the necessary steps to reduce any risk of cross-contamination. Those dealing with an incident must be mindful of who has been connected to which scene. **It is particularly important to ensure an officer who deals with the primary crime scene does not come into contact with a suspect or victim or any other associated scene.**

KEY POINT

A fundamental principle when attending any potential serious incident is that it should always be treated as a crime scene until proven otherwise. Irrespective of the time that may have elapsed since the incident occurred and attendance, failure to protect and preserve a scene at the earliest opportunity can lead to potential evidence being lost.

27.11 **Common Approach Paths (CAP)**

At incident scenes officers may need to summon specialist support quickly to take responsibility for setting and reviewing scene parameters, ensuring sterility, and developing examination and recovery strategies. Initial approach paths need to be determined for use by subsequent resources. A 'common approach path' is used by subsequent attendees in order to minimize confusion and unnecessary contamination of the scene. The path chosen has to be the *least likely route taken by the offender(s) or victims* and one that causes the least damage to potential evidence, eg if the offender is likely to have entered and exited by the front door, the back door should be used, and vice versa. It is important that crime scene investigators/managers and SIOs are informed of the route taken in and out of the scene, The best way to do this is with the aid of a sketch plan, which should be exhibited.

KEY POINT

Parking of police or other emergency vehicles can disrupt evidence in and around the scene and care should be taken when choosing where to leave them. It is questionable whether all police attendees need to park close to the scene when they could be kept at a distance to ensure no tyre marks or blood traces etc are destroyed by police vehicles. A good tactic is to park away from kerbs, for instance, so as to avoid areas where offender's vehicles are likely to have been located.

27.12 **Avoiding Cross-Contamination**

Clear understanding of contamination prevention and following correct procedures is necessary to reduce the chances of contamination. Regardless of individual circumstances, important rules of sterility always apply. Any officer or member of staff who was/has been involved in the arrest of suspects, been to a scene, been involved in a forensic search, had any contact with firearms or explosives or any other scene (such as vehicles, premises, or victims) must declare this information to the incident commander, Senior Investigating Officer (SIO), and/or crime scene investigator/crime scene manager (CSI/CSM). This should be done at the earliest opportunity so any potential cross-transfer of material across different scenes can be avoided.

Carelessness causes enormous complications later on in the investigation and/or during court proceedings if mistakes are made. The possibilities of cross-contamination can be avoided if careful. The simple act of separating prisoners and not getting involved with arrests or house searches if having previously been to an incident scene can make a massive difference to forensic evidence.

A clear audit trail of who has done what, been where, when, and how ('5 x WH & H' again) should be maintained and/or provided. This is a task usually undertaken by a person of supervisory rank. These are specific details of which persons or teams have been used on which tasks and searches and what measures have been put in place to minimize cross-contamination. This will help eliminate any possibility of people and equipment being used at the same scenes when multiple scenes are involved (and invariably there are).

Case Study—Cross-Contamination Defence

A victim had been brutally beaten, raped, and strangled at an outdoor semi-rural location adjoining parkland. The outer cordon required wide boundaries and parameters because of the large number of potential entry and exit routes to/from the attack location. Unauthorized access was prevented by use of uniform staff, dog handlers, and the mounted branch. The offender was later found to have valuable botanical trace evidence on his jeans linking him to the primary crime scene. At a subsequent trial his defence

---

team claimed the officer who had first spoken to the defendant and placed him in a police vehicle had also visited the crime scene beforehand and therefore transferred the damning forensic evidence onto the offender. The police vehicle had also been to the scene and was therefore a further source of cross-contamination. The professionalism of the officers concerned and their accurate record keeping (especially in the police vehicle's log book) were able to refute these claims to the satisfaction of the court. Despite rigorous inquisitorial attacks the defence was rejected by the jury and he was found guilty of the murder.

27.13 **Cordons, Scene Security, and Logs**

Security cordons are vitally important not only for guarding the scene, but also for protecting the public, controlling sightseers and the media, preventing unauthorized interference and access (eg by suspects), facilitating the emergency services, response, and for *preserving evidence and avoiding contamination*. Thus an initial response should involve arranging scene security by putting effective cordons in place. At some point the appointment of a dedicated Cordon Manager may be required. This is normally a duty for a supervisory officer and in Gold, Silver, and Bronze command and control (a 'Bronze Commander' role).

Note: Advice regarding crime scene preservation is available from force Crime Scene Investigation Units by use of on-call systems or immediate telephone or radio advice should the need arise.

Cordon Managers ensure adequate resources and arrangements are in place to safeguard the integrity of and eliminate unauthorized access to crime scenes. This role can be difficult if there is a large area to cordon, particularly if outdoors and in rural settings. The role also involves supervising the completion of logs and ensuring staff are adequately briefed so they know what their role entails and its importance to the investigation.

In the early stages it is difficult to know or determine exact boundaries or parameters for crime scene cordons. If an incident occurs indoors, the task is that much easier because the scene is self-contained. However, with outdoor scenes there can be additional considerations and complications, such as the weather, crowds, traffic, security, media intrusion, helicopters, etc. In such cases cordons should be made as wide as possible, as they can always be brought in later, but it cannot be done the other way around.

There are a number of ways of putting cordons in place, for example using crime scene tape to mark out the perimeter together with sufficient officers (including PCSOs) to ensure the line is not crossed, stationary police vehicles positioned to prevent entry, the use of natural boundaries such as walls, hedges, and fences, using temporary metal barriers and road diversions or road blocks for wider scenes, or making use of the mounted branch or dog handlers to guard perimeters.

There are usually two types of cordons—inner and outer. The inner cordon usually has quite small parameters (eg close to where a body lies or the attack site) and provides a boundary for very detailed forensic examinations to be conducted. It must be very tightly controlled. The outer cordon allows for a larger area to be contained and covers the perimeter of all the peripheral parts of the inner scene. This provides a secure area not only for examination but also preparatory work to be undertaken and the adequate distancing of members of the public and media. This area may also be subject to forensic examination but it is unlikely to be as detailed as the inner cordon.

In major crimes and homicides, policies will be set and recorded to decide who is allowed inside inner and outer cordons. The SIO and/or CSM are usually the ones to decide. Both cordons, however, require a separate scene 'logist' who is armed with the correct documentation (ie forms or booklet) to contemporaneously record details of all those who come in and out of each cordon (so there will usually be at least two logs for each scene). This is so that the integrity of the crime scene(s) and that no contamination has taken place can be proven later to the satisfaction of a court. Security is also of paramount importance. The cordons must be adequately guarded along their entire perimeter to ensure there is no unauthorized access. A rendezvous point should be arranged at a suitable location, and this is where an officer maintaining the scene log should be positioned.

Nominated scene logists should record on the log only details of those who actually enter or leave the crime scene (ie the 'sterile' area). There should be clearly recorded reasons for any person entering the scene on the log. The logs need to be detailed, accurate, and comprehensive. Most forces have pre-printed forms for scene logs, and if for any reason the correct log forms are not immediately available, then a pocket book or other durable note-taking format should be utilized, but the same amount of care must be taken even if it is recorded on plain paper.

The scene log becomes an important exhibit and is an official document subject to the disclosure rules. Minimum details to be included are:

- details of all those entering or leaving (note: names must be spelt accurately);
- times of arrival and departure;
- details of any protective clothing worn;
- purpose of visit;
- signatures of all those entering;
- weather conditions;
- handover details (ie change of logist).

KEY POINTS

1. In suspected terrorism cases cordons should take account of potential secondary devices. A recognized terrorist tactic is to place additional devices at locations the terrorists believe will be used by the emergency services to attend as a rendezvous point.

2. The size of a cordon is important to protect and preserve evidence. A cordon that is too big can be reduced, whereas a cordon that is too small cannot be enlarged. The rule is always to be cautious—'bigger is better'.

3. Precise detail on scene logs is vitally important, including the correct spelling of people's names, otherwise the same person may get created more than once in the investigation database (ie HOLMES—that manages the investigation).

4. Cordon officers should not give out details of the circumstances or investigation without prior permission of a supervisory officer (eg to media reporters).

Checklist—Scene preservation and cordons

- Set both inner and outer cordons. Where a body lies and/or attack site is the inner; the outer is to cover a larger area to preserve peripheral evidence and control access.
- Commence a separate log for each cordon ie both inner and outer.
- Clear the largest area possible—parameters can always be narrowed later.
- To determine boundaries make a quick and objective evaluation based on the location of the incident (or body) and the presence of any physical evidence or eyewitness accounts.
- Make good use of natural boundaries (eg trees, gates, fences, lamp-posts, building lines, etc).
- Establish a common approach path—**least likely used by offenders**.
- Consider possibility of other linked crime scenes (eg abandoned vehicle, attack site).
- Do not examine anything at this stage—stabilize, secure, and protect the area. Use sterile covers but *not* anything that touches the evidential item (eg blanket over a body).

- Recover or protect any physical evidence that is at immediate risk of being lost or destroyed (eg cover any tyre or
footwear impressions if inclement weather).
- Mark out the area clearly (ie with identifiable crime scene
tape).
- Restrict access to unauthorized persons.
- Avoid contact with suspect(s) and those who have been in
any other scene to reduce risk of cross-contamination.
- Try to protect evidential items that may get contaminated,
eg by weather conditions or animals (if outside) but only
when absolutely necessary.
- Record all actions and produce sketch plan if possible.

27.14 Basic Crime Scene Kits

In order to assist those attending crime scenes to be
equipped to preserve the scene and minimize the chance
of contamination, kits should be carried by all operational
staff. As a minimum standard these should contain:

- roll of barrier tape;
- 2 × pairs of disposable overshoes;
- 2 × pairs of disposable gloves;
- major incident scene log forms and clipboard;
- first aid kit;
- aide-mémoire card of checklist actions.

27.15 Health and Safety Considerations

Crime scenes present a range of hazards that require dynamic risk assessments. Examples of these include:

- liquid blood and body fluid samples;
- items stained with blood or other body fluids;
- items infested with parasites;

- drugs and drug paraphernalia, eg syringes;
- hazardous chemicals;
- explosives, explosive devices, etc;
- unsafe buildings;
- firearms and ammunition;
- sharp items;
- difficult terrain or dangerous environment (eg high volt-age electricity, dangerous buildings, traffic conditions etc).

Generic risk assessments may exist for attendance at crime scenes. However, given the above, it is essential wherever possible that appropriate advice is sought and personal protective clothing is worn when required. In addition to protecting the individual this minimizes the possibility of contamination. At a major or serious crime scene standard protection usually consists of a scene suit with hood up, facemask, overshoes, and protective nitrile gloves.

KEY POINTS

1. When dealing with scenes containing bloodstaining or known infectious diseases extra care must be taken to avoid hazards and risk from potential blood-borne infections (eg HIV or hepatitis B). Gloves should always be worn when handling items or persons covered in blood or other body fluids. Dried blood is also a hazard as it can enter the body through mucus membranes. Wearing a disposable mask can reduce the risk of inhaling particles. Footwear or other items of police clothing may also need to be decontaminated to reduce risks of transfer.
2. Firearms must never be handled until they have been rendered safe by a qualified firearms officer or equivalent expert.

Sometimes crime scenes are hazardous places and officers must remain alert to spot any dangers, think quickly, adapt, and take a flexible approach. In extreme cases, staff may have to instinctively abandon crime scenes, pick up weapons, or leave a deceased in place because of the severity of the danger or risks involved. Potential threats to members of the public and/or officers in some circumstances may present no alternative. Some priorities may therefore override the needs of the investigation and it may not always be possible to keep a crime scene sterile.

In some inner-city areas or amongst unruly communities, for example, there may be a distrust of the police, gang feuds and regular firearms usage, or hostile or distressed families and friends of victims, which can pose difficult circumstances to work under. Fortunately these are the exception rather than the rule. In such cases it may be possible to have a small cordoned area (for example immediately around a victim) and extend it when support arrives and crowds are dispersed. Later there may also be alternative ways of recreating crime scenes by use of CCTV, media footage, witness accounts, or photographs, for instance.

Safety of the public and the personnel sent to deal with emergencies and serious crimes is at all times of paramount importance and non-negotiable. If there is a conflict of interest between public safety and the investigation, the former always takes precedence, although it should always be the aim to try to minimize the destruction or loss of evidential material.

Reasons why emergency actions were taken should be recorded and made known to the senior investigator as soon as practicable. Actions that have limited the potential for forensic recovery must be justified at a later stage, and it is wise to record in precise details exactly what and why there was a necessity for not preserving evidence. This demonstrates good standards of integrity and honesty of purpose.

27.16 **Victims Transferred to Hospital**

In some circumstances a victim may not be present at the primary crime scene because they have been conveyed to hospital either by paramedics or by their own means (eg by friends or relatives). Wherever possible an officer should travel with the victim (eg in the rear of the ambulance), making sure there is no interference with any medical treatment being administered. If practicable an officer should remain with the victim once they have arrived at hospital and be ready to listen and receive any comments or facts they may wish to make about the incident, particularly if it forms a dying declaration. Liaison with hospital staff is required about the careful removal of any of the victim's clothing, although local arrangements and agreements may exist to cater for and standardize this process. For instance, any cuts to remove clothing should avoid bullet holes, or tears, or cuts that may have been caused by other weapons. Pre-transfusion blood samples are also necessary for the investigation to perform toxicology tests.

As a general rule casualty treatment rooms and theatres should not be sealed off as crime scenes unless an incident has taken place within them. The same rule applies for ambulances and emergency vehicles, and usually the only items worth seizing are the sheets or blankets used to cover the victim.

If a victim subsequently dies in hospital their body can be moved to side rooms to free up emergency treatment rooms and avoid any disruption to other patients. These decisions will form part of a forensic strategy and should at some point be entered into an SIO's policy file for audit purposes.

27.17 **Victims Pronounced Dead on Arrival at Hospital**

If a victim is pronounced dead on arrival (DOA) at the hospital, an officer must do the following:

- Obtain full details of medical staff involved.
- Confirm precise time that victim was officially pronounced life extinct and who certified death (and collect any accompanying documentation).

- Establish any probable cause of death.
- Check and agree where body will be transferred to and how (eg if being moved from emergency ward or treatment room).
- Declare body a crime scene and commence a scene log.
- Ensure body is protected as a crime scene (keep it sterile).
- Seize any exhibits such as clothing and personal belongings, and anything removed from the victim, eg bullets or sharp instruments.
- Obtain any pre-transfusion blood sample.
- Beware of possible interference and contamination of body by medical staff and/or relatives, friends, and associates.
- Obtain medical notes and any x-rays in readiness for pathological post mortem.
- Relay details of death to supervision and SIO at earliest opportunity.

27.18 **Recording Dying Declarations**

Under common law, on an indictment for either murder or manslaughter, a dying declaration from a victim can be accepted in evidence, provided that the judge is satisfied they were conscious of their dying state at the time it was made. The general principle for a dying declaration to be admitted in evidence is that there must be a settled hopeless expectation of death in that the victim must have abandoned all hope of living. They do not need to be expecting to die immediately, but certainly within a short time. It must be shown that when the declaration was made the victim believed death was impending. Dying declarations are admissible only where the death of that victim is subject of the charge and the cause of death subject of the declaration.

Checklist—Dying Declaration

- Can be taken anywhere
- Can be taken by any person
- Need not be in writing
- The accused need not be present
- The victim need not be on oath, but must be in settled and hopeless expectation of death
- The contents of the declaration must relate to the cause of death.

27.19 **Ambiguous Deaths**

Some circumstances allow for a quick identification of what is likely to have happened because the circumstances are relatively unambiguous. They are more recognizable as murders, and the necessary 'golden hour' tasks can commence immediately (cordons, logs, etc). However, more ambiguous circumstances are not so readily identifiable, and for these there is a danger that golden hour tasks may not be completed with the same degree of urgency or importance. Incidents (particularly critical incidents) that go wrong are characterized by failing to complete precautionary routines.

The key is to follow the logical principles mentioned throughout the chapter by applying the '5 x WH & H' formula. If there are no instant satisfactory answers or conclusions to the interrogative pronouns, the circumstances must be treated as potentially a serious crime. Senior detectives and experts are specifically trained and more qualified to be called upon to assume responsibility for making crucial decisions or as tactical advisors when circumstances are unclear.

Ambiguous cases can be resource intensive and costly because of scene protection and examination and expensive forensic post mortems. But the performance of essential procedures are *still necessary* because once a crime scene is ruined it can never be restored to its original state. There is usually only one chance to find and seize best evidence, and it is the duty of the police to conduct thorough investigations, whatever the outcome. Coroners need a professional investigation to assist in their duty of recording an accurate cause of death.

Therefore initial responding officers if at all unsure when dealing with sudden or unexplained deaths should never take chances and always treat the circumstances with respect. Doing a thorough job is easily defensible—the same cannot be said the other way round. The public, media, and agencies such as the Independent Police Complaints Commission (IPCC) are unlikely to investigate the police for wasting time and resources on a thorough investigation, but they most certainly will if failing to perform golden hour actions, and losing precious evidence compromises a murder investigation.

KEY POINTS

1. Those who may comment about enquiries into sudden or unexplained deaths being over-cautious are being unprofessional. Front line officers are not trained SIOs, CSIs, or medical practitioners, nor are they forensic pathologists or scientists, and should rely upon the expertise of those who have the right training and qualifications to make informed decisions whenever there are any ambiguities.

2. When dealing with deaths that are or have become suspicious or ambiguous, the initial investigation should be halted and any scene(s) closed down and secured. Immediate assistance should be summoned from supervision, senior detectives, and CSIs who can authorize the use of specialists such as forensic pathologists, scientists, or any other experts that may be required.

> **Note:** These rules apply to other types of circumstances that may, for example, involve missing persons. A very high profile media case of an infant having gone missing while on holiday attracted much criticism about the way the matter was dealt with by the police in the initial stages (ie not conducting a thorough search or preserving the scene for forensic evidence).

27.20 **Special Procedure Investigations**

Some cases may require a more in-depth investigation than others and in some forces are known as 'special procedure' enquiries. These require a higher degree of investigation and are always led or supervised by senior personnel. It is worth establishing what policies and procedures have been pre-determined in order to comply with force policy for these types of incidents. The list is not exhaustive but they are likely to include:

- murder or attempted murder;
- manslaughter;
- work-related deaths;
- assaults where injuries are life-threatening;
- death of any person under the age of 18;
- illicit drug-related deaths;
- suicides;
- death resulting from accidents, not being road collisions;
- other serious enquiries, eg rape with significant violence, cash in transit robberies involving violence etc;
- kidnap or blackmail;
- terrorism;
- high risk missing persons.

27.21 **Dealing with Witnesses**

A key investigative strategy is to identify potential witnesses (and victims who may be one and the same) and capture their details and information, particularly if at or near a crime scene. Witnesses are extremely valuable assets and can provide evidential answers to the '5 x WH & H' questions. Steps must be taken to avoid them changing their intentions to assist, disappearing completely, or getting discouraged by others. Testimonies can become contaminated if witnesses talk to or listen to others, watch news reports, or speak directly to the media. Therefore it is best to seek out and speak to them while the incident is still fresh in their minds, which constitutes a golden hour(s) task.

Witnesses come from a wide range of sources and people who are at or around crime scenes are always potential witnesses. The type, location, and time of day of the incident under investigation will largely determine where and how witnesses can be found. Regular visitors to the area such as taxi drivers, shift workers, postal staff, milk deliverers, dog walkers, party goers, or local authority workers should be considered for witness trawls. The incident log created for the initial call(s) may also contain details of potential witnesses who have contacted with details of what they have seen or heard. It is usual to obtain the original tape recording of emergency calls to try and identify callers (listening for noises in the background, etc), particularly if they do so anonymously.

Officers shouldn't be discouraged from seeking and obtaining *initial accounts* from potential witnesses. There are useful guidelines and legislation on how and when certain categories of witnesses should be interviewed (eg on video as vulnerable, intimidated, or significant witnesses). This shouldn't detract from the importance of finding out what people have seen or heard, and without such information they cannot be classified. The information may be required immediately in order to identify high-priority lines of enquiry, such as the description of an offender or identification of a scene. If the material is not secured at this time, some difficulty may be encountered in obtaining it afterwards if they change their minds about cooperating with the police.

Initial accounts can and should be taken from potential witnesses and should be conducted without prompting or correcting and be accurately recorded. The notes should be accompanied by accurate details for identifying the individuals afterwards and re-contacting them; or it may be more appropriate (depending on the veracity of the evidence and circumstances of the case) to make arrangements for the witness to be hastily formally interviewed (ie on video) by trained officers. Sometimes there may be welfare implications, and it could be more suitable to take witnesses to a place of safety such as a police station to take these matters into consideration.

KEY POINT

Details obtained from witnesses relayed to control rooms must contain accurate information. They are input onto incident logging systems and if mistakes are made, particularly with regard to descriptions of offenders, they can seriously undermine a witness's testimony. What is contained on logs is potentially disclosable and can be picked over by defence teams.

Some witnesses need encouragement to provide evidence and their first impression of how they are dealt with may make the difference between agreeing to give evidence or otherwise. Much evidence gets missed from those who are reluctant to 'get involved' or fear reprisals. These types of witness must be dealt with sensitively and given plenty of encouragement and support with professionalism on open display by those who they first come into contact with. This may make the difference between assisting the enquiry or not. There are very effective procedures available to support reluctant witnesses, such as witness protection schemes, and advice can be sought on what can be offered and by whom.

Witnesses may also be crime scenes, particularly if they have come into contact with offenders, for example, where there is a likelihood of cross-transfer of fibres, DNA, fingerprints, or body fluids from offender to witness. Consideration must be given to obtaining advice from a CSI about how to seize any cross-transfer material on their outer clothing, for instance. This may need dealing with tactfully so the cooperation of the witness is not adversely affected.

27.22 **Identifying and Arresting Suspects**

Arresting offenders is always a priority for officers and investigators attending incidents, being mindful that suspects may remain at a scene or return soon afterwards (eg it is a particular fact that arsonists like to stay and watch the emergency service response to their handiwork). Wherever there is an opportunity to be proactive and make an *early arrest* based on available information then generally it should be done. This is because the closer to the time the offence was committed the arrest is made, the more opportunity there is to recover forensic evidence or any other useful items or material. It prevents the offender from concocting an alibi, threatening potential witnesses, destroying evidence, or committing further offences. It is also a good means of providing victim and/or community reassurance, and prevents any potential for 'taking the law into their own hands'.

In order to reduce the risk of cross-contamination, wherever possible the arrest of a suspect should always be made by an officer who has *not* already attended the crime scene. However, there may be a situation when the first officer responding is forced to make an arrest. In such cases the officer should take steps to reduce contamination and fully report the circumstances to the SIO and CSI/CSM.

> **KEY POINTS**
>
> 1. Under no circumstances should a suspect ever be returned to a crime scene.
> 2. Separate vehicles should be used to transport suspects, victims, and witnesses to avoid cross-contamination, and record keeping showing usage details and history of any vehicles used (ie logbooks) should be accurate and up to date to refute any defence allegations.

If an officer makes an early arrest then as a rule they should not interrogate the suspect. This is something that will need a carefully managed strategy under an SIO's direction. If, however, the suspect is talkative and insists on providing a version of events (ie a 'significant statement'), once the caution has been administered their comments should be accurately recorded. The treatment and questioning of a suspect are contained in Code C, paragraphs 11.1, 11.1A, 11.4, and 11.4A of the Police and Criminal Evidence Act 1984 (PACE). The Code ensures that all persons suspected of involvement in a crime are dealt with in a fair and proper manner in accordance with the law. Code 11.4A defines what a 'significant statement' is:

> A **significant statement** is one which appears capable of being used in evidence against the suspect, in particular a direct admission of guilt. A significant silence is a failure or refusal to answer a question or answer satisfactorily when under caution, which might, allowing for the restriction on drawing adverse inferences from silence, give rise to an inference under Part III of the Criminal Justice and Public Order Act 1994.

> **KEY POINTS—SUSPECTS**
>
> 1. What a suspect says and how they behave during and immediately after arrest can prove highly influential evidence. This should be recorded as soon after the event as practicable and the suspect given an opportunity to sign the notes. Not many offenders say nothing when arrested, and comments must be

brought to the attention of the interviewing officers (and SIO) at the earliest opportunity (if different from arresting officers).

2. Prompt action taken at a scene can lead to the identity and/ or location of an offender. The initial police response should incorporate a search for suspects, such as the use of dog officers because dogs can follow human scent. The checking of local hospitals in case the offender(s) is injured is also worth considering. Care should be taken, of course, not to destroy any forensic opportunities in whatever initial actions are taken.

27.23 **Identification of Suspects by Witnesses**

The guidelines used for identifying suspects connected to any criminal investigation and the requirement to keep records are contained under Code D (revised on 1 August 2004), PACE, sections 60(1)(a), 60A(1), and 66(1) Codes of Practice A–G.

They state that a record shall be made of the suspect's description as first given by a potential witness. This record must:

(a) be made and kept in a form which enables details of that description to be accurately produced from it, in a legible form, which can be given to the suspect or the suspect's solicitor in accordance with this Code; and

(b) unless otherwise specified be made before the witness takes part in any identification procedures under paragraphs 3.5–3.10, 3.21, or 3.23;

(c) a copy of the record shall where practicable, be given to the suspect or their solicitor before any procedures under paragraphs 3.5–3.10, 3.21, or 3.23 are carried out.

27.24 **Transporting Suspects**

There are usually force guidelines on how to transport prisoners to custody suites, but in exceptional cases they may have to travel in the rear of 'ordinary' police vehicles instead of prisoner vans. If this must happen it needs managing carefully to avoid any inferences of unsolicited comments and admissions made during the journey. Any comments or admissions about the case are best saved for the formal interview process when the suspect's rights under PACE can be assured and proper legal representation arranged.

Care should be taken when managing these arrangements and, if there is more than one prisoner, separate vehicles/vans should be used to transport them. Separate custody offices should also be used wherever possible to avoid cross-contamination or contact between them. A CSI/CSM may advise that covers are placed on the internal surfaces of vehicles being used to transport detainees and in custody areas to capture any forensic material that may drop off them and eliminate possible secondary transfer.

27.25 **Treating Suspects as Crime Scenes**

Each and every suspect must be treated as a potential crime scene and is a source of vital evidence to prove or disprove their involvement in the offence. The time scales between incident and arrest will of course vary in each case; however, the sooner the arrest and detention, the better in terms of evidence recovery. Crucial forensic material can come from the suspect, therefore it is vital to arrange for the recovery of their clothing, footwear, and other samples as quickly as possible. Apart from obvious fingerprints, DNA, and recovery of clothing and footwear, the suspect can provide a wealth of forensic evidence, from transfer of hair, blood, semen, paint, soil, gunshot residue, glass fragments, fibres, pollen, etc. Sometimes it may be necessary to obtain these samples or seize clothing at the point of arrest rather than wait until arrival at the custody office. Firearms discharge and explosives residue in particular need to be recovered as soon as possible, and, in some cases, the covering of exposed areas such as the suspect's hands is necessary to maximize opportunities. Officers should take advice on all forensic recovery issues and contamination avoidance from a CSM/CSI as soon as possible.

27.26 Intelligence-Led House-to-House Enquiries

Conducting house-to-house (H-2-H) enquiries can be an effective investigative strategy in order to identify witnesses, gather local information and intelligence, or as part of a community reassurance or crime prevention policy. In a high number of cases the victim is known by the offender and often resides within close proximity of the crime scene. It is therefore feasible that a H-2-H enquiry team may uncover and/or interview the offender during the course of their enquiries.

This is a valuable tactic in most major investigations and can be commenced during the 'golden hour(s)' period. Even if no particular parameters for the H-2-H have been determined, it is still a method of quickly requesting general information and capturing an immediate line of enquiry. Accurate records must be made of any premises visited and persons spoken to, including negative responses.

Initially there should be a concentration on premises *within the line of sight* of the primary crime scene or within any other known locations of interest, such as escape routes, or at any linked scenes, eg abandoned vehicles. Any opportunity to capture witnesses and information should not be wasted and H-2-H enquiries commenced as early as possible.

H-2-H interview tactics can be used to try to identify:

- people who may have witnessed the incident under investigation;
- people who may have witnessed related events (eg in the area where a getaway vehicle has been stolen from or abandoned);
- sightings of the victim or offender before or after the event (eg along the likely entry and exit routes of the offender(s));
- sightings or information regarding relevant property (eg clothing or items of significance that may have been discarded);
- sightings of potential witnesses or unidentified persons seen by others or elsewhere (eg where witnesses are captured on CCTV, enquiries can be made by use of H-2-H tactics to try to identify them).

At some stage a formal list of questions will be formulated for a questionnaire that enquiry officers can carry with them as they conduct their H-2-H enquiries. However, during the initial stages enquiry teams can either make a general request for information at each address visited and to each occupant, such as: 'Have they seen anything?' 'Do they know what happened?' 'Have they any information to assist?' or they can make use of intelligence-led questions that have been tailored to fit the individual circumstances. For example:

1. Were you in between (time) and (time) on (date)?
2. Did you hear a disturbance at (address/location)?
3. Do you know anything about (incident) that has taken place at that location?
4. Do you know the occupants at that address?
5. Did you see anyone or anything suspicious at or near this address between these times?
6. Have you any knowledge of (particular details eg black saloon car with a rear spoiler driving around the area)?

7. Have you got any CCTV fitted?
8. Have you any further information that might assist?

KEY POINT

Sightings or information regarding discarded or abandoned property can prove useful. Offenders tend to be less careful when they believe they are away from the crime scene and make mistakes such as changing or discarding clothing, dropping or concealing weapons, hiding stolen property, etc. If a stolen vehicle has been used then later abandoned, H-2-H should be used in both locations to try to identify potential witnesses who may have seen the offenders prior to or after commission of the offence.

27.27 **Operational Debriefing**

The objective of a debriefing session is to identify what action has been taken and by whom, and to capture all possible evidence and information that will assist the investigation. For example, details of potential witnesses, useful observations or comments from bystanders, information and opinions regarding possible suspects, suspicious circumstances that may be linked, any persons or vehicles of interest, and possible intelligence. A debriefing is a meeting aimed at obtaining as much detailed information as possible from those who have dealt with an incident, particularly the initial response. It involves clarifying the chronological breakdown of events as they occurred, the people who did them, outcomes, and learning points. Generally this will occur when the team stands down after a tour of duty at an incident, when recollection is at its strongest and the incident is probably still ongoing. Debriefings should contribute to the formulation of urgent actions, potential lines of enquiry, and the development of useful intelligence. So-called 'hot debriefs', as they are sometimes known, form a

---

major source of vital information to supervisors and lead investigators.

All those who have been involved in the initial response should be required to attend, with no exceptions, and people should be notified *before going off duty*. Those in attendance must have already completed any notes, pocket books, etc *before* attending the debrief in order to avoid allegations of collusion of evidence and to prevent any compromise of integrity. Relevant documents and exhibits must be handed in (copies of notebooks, etc) at the end of the session. Everything should be recorded for the purposes of disclosure rules (Criminal Procedure and Investigations Act 1996 (CPIA)).

27.28 **Retention of Material (CPIA)**

Requirements under the CPIA are highly relevant and place additional legal responsibilities on police who conduct investigations. Section 5.1 of the Codes of Practice under the Act states:

> An investigator must retain material obtained in a criminal investigation which may be relevant to the investigation. This includes not only material coming into the possession of the investigator . . . but also material generated by him/her (such as interview records).

Section 2.1 of the same Codes of Practice provides a definition of 'relevant material':

> Material may be relevant to an investigation if it appears to an investigator, or to the officer in charge of an investigation, or to the disclosure officer, that it has some bearing on any offence under investigation or any person being investigated, or on the surrounding circumstances of the case, unless it is incapable of having any impact on the case.

27.29 **Conclusion**

Checklists of duties for various tasks are never going to be exhaustive, nor are they intended to replace initiative. The final decision about appropriate investigative action and activities must be driven by the circumstances and nature of each individual circumstance, not mere compliance with mnemonics or checklists. They are nonetheless a useful framework for clear and logical thinking.

The early organization of thoughts around initial duties and responsibilities is a good process to apply on a regular basis, and the procedures discussed in this chapter are equally transferable to other areas of policing. Checking and re-checking detail and information, using the interrogative pronouns and applying the investigative tactics, should assist in any performance of investigative duties.

It is always a team effort that kick-starts a major investigation and depends on the dedication, commitment, professionalism, and cooperation of everyone. Time and again those who pay close attention to detail and the quality performance of their duties are pivotal to success. There never will be a substitute for a qualitative and thorough approach to important functions and duties completed within the golden hour(s).

This chapter has outlined key functions and procedures for those involved in the initial response to a serious crime or homicide. It included and explained what important tasks and high standards are expected. It is hoped the information will provide those who face these important responsibilities with a good appreciation and understanding of what is required.

Chapter 28

Serious, Organized, and Cross-Border Crime

28.1 **Introduction**

Organized crime costs the country an estimated £20 billion each year. It is a massive problem but there are still many people who believe that it is committed by 'Mafia'-style crime families, rather than the more mundane truth of the loose networks of criminals who get together to steal, rob, or swindle their way into 'dirty money' and the legitimate and seemingly legitimate people and corporations that assist in the laundering process for this cash. Frontline staff may encounter serious, organized, and cross-border crime in one of several ways, and it is important to be aware that almost any crime could be an indicator of the presence of organized crime.

KEY POINT

Organized crime is different from crime that is organized. If someone burgles a house after dark, using some specialist tools that they brought with them, then this shows some elements of organization. Organized crime goes further than this; it involves more people and tackles more complex problems, eg the transfer and disposal of the proceeds of crime, recruitment and retention of criminal associates, geographic influence, and power over legitimate authorities (local business and government agencies).

There is no statutory definition of organized crime.

28.2 **What is Serious, Organized, and Cross-Border Crime?**

There are three basic elements which assist in the understanding of what Serious, Organized, and Cross-Border Crime (SOXB) crime is. The first element is the requirement for the crime to be 'serious':

28.2.1 **Serious**

There are few definitions of what constitutes serious crime but the most generally used is reproduced below:

> **The Police Act 1997, section 93(4)** states that criminal conduct shall be regarded as serious if, and only if:
>
> a) it involves the use of violence, results in substantial financial gain or is conducted by a large number of persons in pursuit of a common purpose, or
> b) the offence or one of the offences is an offence for which a person who has attained the age of twenty-one and has no previous convictions could reasonably be expected to be sentenced to imprisonment for a term of three years or more.
>
> (It is also defined by the Regulation of Investigatory Powers Act 2000, section 81 which reverses the order of (a) and (b) above)

In its effect this conduct will cause, or has the potential to cause, significant harm to its victims and the wider community. This harm can be characterized by one or more of the following descriptors:

- significant profit for the criminal; and/or
- significant loss to the victim;
- significant impact upon community safety;
- serious violence;
- corruption of public officials (including the police);
- the exercise of control over others.

The second element is the requirement for the crime to be 'organized':

28.2.2 Organized

There is a huge and ever growing body of work that discusses the meaning of 'organized' in a criminal context. There is no need to add to this debate here, it is sufficient to say that with regard to serious crime ,'organized' refers to the complexity of the crime and the size and durability of the criminal group involved in the crimes (for further information please see the Further Reading section at the end of this chapter).

The third element is the requirement for the crime to 'cross a border'.

28.2.3 Cross-Border

This element involves determining the geographic reach of the persons involved in the crime. Are they offending in their own neighbourhood or does their criminality stretch across police or other political or geographic borders?

> ### Scenario
>
> A group (two or more people) decide to travel into the next police area to steal some cars. They do this because they are less well known in the other area and will therefore be less likely to be stopped by the local police.
>
> These are organized criminals, they have thought through how to deal with a particular problem and have come up with a solution that requires cooperation and additional resources to accomplish. Because of this they are more of a threat than they were before.

Note that there is a difference between those who travel to commit crime because it gives them an advantage over law enforcement agencies and those who, when committing a crime, 'accidentally' cross a border. Although both may constitute the 'cross-border' element of SOXB crime, doing something on purpose generally requires more planning, more resources, and more discipline and is therefore likely to be more serious.

KEY QUESTION

Has this group crossed a border on purpose and for an instrumental reason (to avoid capture, etc)? If so they are exhibiting some strong warning signs that indicate they should be treated differently: let supervisors know and seek advice.

In summary, if a crime encompasses all three of the above elements (serious, organized, and cross-border) it will constitute SOXB crime. The Association of Chief Police Officers (ACPO) recognizes groups that commit SOXB crime and refer to them as 'Organized Crime Groups' (OCG). (ACPO have nurtured methods for dealing with OCG that seek to limit their development. These methods are beyond the scope of this chapter.)

These may be mundane incidents but they may also lead to revealing the activities of serious and organized cross-border criminals that may be encountered by frontline staff in local policing.

28.3.3 How can Staff Learn More About and Recognize SOXB Crime?

Accessing the National Intelligence Model's Intelligence

Each force maintains its own up to date intelligence on the threat from crime, including SOXB crime, which is included in their Strategic and Tactical Assessments. ACPO produces an annual National Strategic Assessment and the Serious Organised Crime Agency (SOCA) publishes an annual Threat Assessment of serious organized crime. Together these provide an in-depth assessment of current, emerging, and long-term threats from SOXB crime. These can be accessed through the Force Intelligence Bureau.

Recognizing SOXB Crime in the Neighbourhood

Neighbourhood police officers, together with community support officers, members of the Special Constabulary, partner agencies, and charity and volunteer workers all help local people to improve the quality of life in their communities. Part of their work is to ensure that community information is gathered to assist in the identification of SOXB crime. There are several ways that such crimes can be revealed to the police and these focus areas are (a) Nominations, (b) Radiation, (c) Gravity, and (d) Covert tactics.

(a) Nominations: People may be more than aware that some of their neighbours are active in SOXB crime and may be willing to tell the police, or a community worker, all about it, ie making a 'Nomination'. Neighbourhood officers should be alive to the potential for such confidants to come forward and have a strategy in place to encourage this and to deal with the information that is obtained.

(b) Radiation: The existence of SOXB crime in the neighbourhood can be obvious and may be characterized by the overt signs of criminal lifestyles, eg people living beyond their means (this is where the catch phrase 'Too much bling? Give us a ring!' has successfully been used in police campaigns), an increase in marriages of convenience that can identify illicit migration patterns, changes to houses that could indicate illegal use (eg windows covered up to hide cannabis cultivation), etc. Patrol officers should be active in identifying the above and should pass this information to their local intelligence unit.

(c) Gravity: Another sign of the presence of SOXB crime in a neighbourhood may be the way in which it attracts more obvious crime, eg an increase in street robbery, violent attacks, or the presence of street prostitution may indicate the arrival of a SOXB drug dealer; street traders may indicate the arrival of goods that infringe copyright (eg pirate DVDs or fake designer clothes); and an increase in losses through shoplifting could indicate the arrival of a specialist OCG.

(d) Covert tactics: The police are often involved in covert intelligence gathering, which may be further directed using information from the above focus areas.

However it is done it is clear that, just like counter-terrorism, activity against SOXB crime is very dependent on active participation in neighbourhood policing and in gaining the confidence of law-abiding citizens to assist in providing necessary information.

KEY QUESTION

Do I have the mindset that allows me to make the best use of information that comes into my possession?

28.4 **Investigating and Dealing with SOXB Crime**

28.4.1 The National Intelligence Model and the Three-Level Response to Criminality

The National Intelligence Model (NIM) has developed a three-level response to criminality:

- Level 1: Local issues, crime that can be managed within a Basic Command Unit (BCU).
- Level 2: These are cross-border issues, the actions of organized criminality affecting more than one BCU and potentially across boundaries into neighbouring forces.
- Level 3: This is serious and organized crime operating on a national or international level.

SOXB crime necessarily falls within Level 2 or Level 3. Level 2 or Level 3 crimes can attract greater resource allocations (people, finances, and their prioritization) from forces to investigate their activities.

Level 2 SOXB crimes will generally be dealt with at a force level, perhaps with some assistance from other forces in the region. Level 3 SOXB crimes are generally dealt with by SOCA, especially if they have an international element.

The Serious Organised Crime Agency (SOCA)

SOCA was set up in 2006 and is an Executive Non-Departmental Public Body sponsored by, but operationally independent from, the Home Office.

It is a law enforcement agency with responsibilities focused on reducing the harm to the UK from organized crime (see <http://www.soca.gov.uk>).

In addition SOCA is tasked with providing support to UK law enforcement partners, eg the police and HM Revenue and Customs. It employs about 4,000 staff, and although it has a UK-wide remit there are devolved relationships with Scotland and Northern Ireland that means it has less of an active operational presence there.

SOCA agents are not constables and therefore have different duties in dealing with crime. Constables have a duty to react to crime, SOCA agents do not; they can therefore take a more strategic role in developing a response to organized crime.

Assistance from SOCA can normally be arranged through the Force Intelligence Bureau; they will have SOCA liaison officers available for help and advice.

SOCA is becoming more involved in targeting Level 2 OCG in recognition of the scale of the SOXB crime problem and its potential for causing harm to our communities. The decision on who has primacy over a crime problem takes place in one of the NIM Tasking and Coordination meetings.

28.4.2 Dealing with SOXB Crime Information

Sources of Information

Sources of information about SOXB crime can come from various areas, including the analysis of crime data from the focus areas mentioned at 28.3.3 or from people who wish to provide information about illicit activity (covert human intelligence sources (CHIS)).

Covert Human Intelligence Source (CHIS)

Definition: RIPA, section 26(8)(a)–(c):

A person who establishes or maintains a personal or other relationship with a person for the covert purpose of facilitating the doing of anything that

- covertly uses such a relationship to obtain information or to provide access to information to another person; or
- covertly discloses information obtained by the use of such a relationship, or as a consequence of the existence of such a relationship.

Conduct and use of a CHIS: RIPA, section 26(7)(a)(b):

- *Use*
  Actions inducing, asking or assisting a person to act as a CHIS *ie setting the rules for what a CHIS will do.*

> • *Conduct*
> Establishing or maintaining a personal or other relationship
> with a person for the covert purpose of (or is incidental to)
> obtaining and passing on information *ie setting the rules
> for how they will do it.*

Protecting Sources

People who pass information to the police quite rightly
expect that it will be treated as confidential. SOXB criminal
information is especially sensitive because of the power that
OCGs can wield over people who cross them. It is therefore
vital when receiving information about SOXB criminals
that appropriate steps are taken to protect sources. ACPO
guidance encourages forces to establish Dedicated Source
Units (DSU) staffed by personnel trained in handling and
controlling CHISs to nationally-accredited standards.
Generally individuals volunteering information as CHISs
should be passed on to the DSU.

Police information should never be divulged to sources;
OCGs are known to make attempts to infiltrate police operations against them by offering information in the hope
that they will gain the confidence of their police handler
such that they will be able to glean information that will
assist them.

What to do with Crime Information—the 5 × 5 × 5 Information Report

Treat all information about SOXB criminals as confidential and do not discuss it in an open forum. Information
received from a source should be recorded on the police 5 ×
5 × 5 Information Report and passed in a secure manner to
the Intelligence Department.

It is good practice to separate the source of information
from the execution of operations to deal with it; so if information is received on SOXB crime staff should be prepared
to hand it to someone else to deal with. This doesn't mean
that frontline staff do nothing; it just means that they either

take responsibility for gathering information or for making the arrest, not both. This is to protect sources and ensure the integrity of the investigation and is generally referred to as the 'sterile corridor'.

Status Drift: When does a Public Spirited Neighbour Become a Covert Human Intelligence Source?

A CHIS is someone who begins or maintains a relationship with another person, and whose activities are likely to intrude on that person's private life, with the intention of passing on information to the police regarding that person, without that person's knowledge. Their activities (in breach of another person's right to privacy on behalf of the police) are only lawful if they are authorized under the Regulation of Investigative Powers Act 2000 (RIPA) (see Chapter 6 above).

If, however, as part of regular duties frontline staff speak to someone who provides information about the activities of a local criminal, then this is community information and does not need to be gained under a RIPA authority. If the person providing the information is then asked to find out more information for police or partner agencies the KEY QUESTION is: has this person established or are they maintaining a covert relationship with a person in order to pass information on to the police or partner agencies? If the answer is yes then before they can be tasked to gather any information they must be registered as a CHIS. Seek advice from the force DSU.

Witness Protection

Emergency legislation was passed in 2008 to offer protection to witnesses who fear for their safety by allowing them to give their evidence anonymously. The Criminal Evidence (Witness Anonymity) Act 2008 was brought in to restore the power of judges to grant anonymity to witnesses insofar as it will not prejudice the right to a fair trial.

The Criminal Evidence (Witness Anonymity) Act 2008

- makes provision for any party to criminal proceedings to apply for a 'witness anonymity order', either the prosecution or the defence may apply;
- sets out the conditions which must be satisfied before a court can make a witness anonymity order;
- sets out considerations for the court when deciding whether to make an order;
- sets out a list of the kinds of special measures that the courts may apply in order to protect the identity of an anonymous witness, for example, the use of screens and voice distortion.

Most SOXB crime investigations are intelligence-led and it is therefore essential to the success of the force in combating SOXB crime that every patrol officer plays his or her part in gathering and passing on information.

Accessing or passing confidential information, outside of the proper course of police duties, is usually a criminal offence and will certainly contravene the police standards of professional behaviour. Criminals involved in SOXB crime are notoriously resourceful and can employ a range of tactics to gather intelligence on police operations against them, and on the manoeuvrings of their rivals. These can range from 'befriending' people who can help them without knowing it to bribery and blackmail.

Frontline staff asked to provide police information to anyone outside of their proper duties, or who believe that a colleague is doing so, should report it immediately either to a supervisor or to the professional standards department.

8.4.3 Action Required in the Event Frontline Staff Believe they have Encountered SOXB Crime

Establish the facts, ensure people's safety to the extent that is possible to do so, then pause and consider where in the organization advice and assistance can be sought. Act on

that advice and feed back any information gathered durin
enquiries.

Witnesses may need protection at an early stage an
police must be active in identifying their needs. It is a crimi
nal offence, at common law and under the Criminal Justic
and Public Order Act 1994, to intimidate a witness or any
one helping the police in an investigation.

28.5 **Encountering and Dealing with the Proceeds of SOXB Crime**

28.5.1 **The Proceeds of Crime Act 2002**

Money Laundering

Money laundering means an act which falls within sectio
340(11) of the Proceeds of Crime Act 2002 (POCA). Mone
laundering is the concealment of the benefit from crimina
conduct and is not limited to money alone but encompasse
a range of 'criminal property'. Criminal property is prope
ty that has been gained as a result of or in connection wit
criminal conduct (and the offender knows or suspects tha
it constitutes or represents their benefit from this conduct
this includes cash but can also include other property, suc
as a car, a house, or an interest in land. Criminal conduc
is anything that would constitute an offence in any part c
the UK, or would constitute an offence if it was committe
there (ie it covers criminal conduct abroad if it would be
crime in this country).

Common Money Laundering Offences

Section 327 Concealing, etc. A person commits an offence if
they conceal, disguise, convert, or transfer criminal property or
if they remove criminal property from the UK. This means that
someone who hides a stolen car, or changes its number plate,
may be guilty of money laundering. (Concealing or disguising

---

criminal property includes concealing or disguising its nature, source, location, disposition, movement, ownership or any rights connected with it.)

Section 328 Arrangements. A person commits an offence if they enter into or become concerned in an arrangement which they know or suspect will facilitate (by whatever means) the acquisition, retention, use or control of criminal property by or on behalf of another person. This could be allowing another person to use a third party's bank account to transfer cash.

Section 329 Acquisition, use and possession. A person commits an offence if they acquire, use or have possession of criminal property.

Criminal Lifestyle—POCA, Section 75

The purpose of a 'criminal lifestyle' investigation is to question the ability of a person to account for their assets, and may lead to any assets that they cannot legitimately account for being seized from them, as proceeds of crime. OXB criminals, by definition, live off the proceeds of crime. As such they will generally have a criminal lifestyle; there are three tests in deciding this:

1. Has the suspect been convicted of drug trafficking, money laundering, directing terrorism, people trafficking, arms trafficking, counterfeiting, intellectual property (copyright/patent) offences, pimping, brothel keeping, or blackmail offences—or aiding, abetting, attempting, conspiring, or inciting any of these? OR

2. Has the suspect been charged with an offence or series of offences committed over a period of at least six months where they have obtained £5,000 from that offence or others taken into consideration at the same time? OR

3. Has the suspect been convicted of a combination of offences amounting to 'a course of criminal activity'? This test is more complicated than the other two. The suspect satisfies it if they have:

   (a) been convicted in the current proceedings of four or more offences of any description from which he has benefited, or

      (b) been convicted in the current proceedings of any one such offence and has other convictions for any such offences on at least two separate occasions in the last six years. In addition, the total benefits from the offences and/or any others taken into consideration by the court on the same occasion (or, in the case of (b), occasions) must be not less than £5,000.

Confiscation of Assets

Confiscation orders are available from a court following the conviction of an offender who has benefitted from criminal conduct. The court decides the value of the confiscation order based on the offences for which the defendant has been convicted, and any others taken into consideration in determining the defendant's sentence.

If a court decides that the suspect has a criminal life style then they need to assess their benefit from 'general criminal conduct' (POCA, section 6). This includes not only the specific criminal conduct for which they have been convicted, but also their other criminal conduct at any time, all of which can be proved on the balance of probabilities. The benefit can be calculated over a period of up to six years and can therefore be considerably more than the offence for which they have been charged.

It is therefore important staff plan for dealing with SOXX crime suspects in a way that will expose their criminal life style and the benefit they have made from their general criminal conduct. This plan may include thinking about how to conduct suspect interviews and carrying out searches of suspects' premises.

Interviews

Questions should not be confined to the incident under investigation but should consider the wider money

---

laundering offences and seek out information regarding the suspect's lifestyle. For example:

- How long have they been involved in their current business, what is their salary, how are they paid, ask them to describe their working routine. If self-employed then who does the accounts, who do they bank with, are they registered with any trade body, or for VAT?
- How long have they lived at their current address, who else lives there, who owns the property, how much does it cost, how is it paid for?
- What work have they been doing for the past six years?

Searches

- Contact the force's economic crime unit at the earliest opportunity for advice and guidance.
- Consider a visual recording of the search for later scrutiny.
- Seize items of financial interest and package them separately; these will be of interest to a financial investigator. Look for: bills, bank, and credit details; evidence of employment; money transfers; details of state benefits; holiday information, housing and property information; and receipts that could show expenditure that does not tally with their apparent income.
- Wear gloves when seizing cash and think forensics; don't count it, don't place it on a potentially contaminated surface.

Cash Seizures—POCA, Section 294

All cash seizures are potentially linked to money laundering offences and because of the problems associated with attempting to launder money through legitimate institutions there is a large amount of 'cash only' business associated with SOXB crime.

4 Protective Services

Cash can be 'attended' or 'unattended', ie it is either with someone or not. It can also be found in a 'dispatch', ie a letter, a parcel, or a container, which can also be attended or unattended.

Search Powers—POCA, Section 289

A police or customs officer may only exercise the power to search if the following criteria are fulfilled:

(1) Search of premises:

    (a) The officer must already have lawful authority to be present on the premises either in the exercise of a power of entry conferred by other legislation or by invitation.

    (b) There must be reasonable grounds for suspecting that there is 'cash' on the premises which is either 'recoverable property' or is intended for use in 'unlawful conduct'.

    (c) There must be reasonable grounds for suspecting that the amount of 'cash' is not less than the 'minimum amount' (currently set at £1,000).

(2) Search of a person:

    (a) There must be reasonable grounds for suspecting that a person is carrying cash which is 'recoverable property' or intended for use in 'unlawful conduct'.

    (b) There must be reasonable grounds for suspecting that the amount of 'cash' is not less than the 'minimum amount'.

'Recoverable property' is property obtained through unlawful conduct and includes cash (POCA, section 304).

'Unlawful conduct' is conduct unlawful under the criminal law of the part of the UK in which it occurs, or if it occurs abroad is unlawful in the country in which it occurs and would also be unlawful if it occurred in a part of the UK (POCA, section 241). (See separate Code of Practice for searches under POCA, section 289 at <http://www.crimereduction.homeoffice.gov.uk/crimereduction026a.pdf>)

A constable (or customs officer) who has reasonable grounds for suspecting that any cash (money and coins in any currency, postal orders, cheques, bankers drafts, and bearer bonds/shares) that they suspect to be over £1,000 is either recoverable property or is intended for use in unlawful conduct may seize the cash.

When attended cash is seized, consideration should be given to arresting the suspect for money laundering and serving them with a 'restraint order' (POCA, section 42). Only a Crown Prosecutor, the Director of the Assets Recovery Agency, or an Accredited Financial Investigator may apply for a restraint order, so early advice should be sought from the force's Economic Crime Unit or the Crown Prosecution Service (CPS).

Restraint Orders—POCA, section 42

A restraint order is made by a Crown Court to protect property during a criminal investigation or criminal proceedings where there is reason to believe that the person subject to investigation has benefited from the criminal conduct subject to the investigation. A restraint order may be made at any time after a criminal investigation has been commenced, if there is reasonable cause to believe that the defendant has benefited from their criminal conduct.

The intention of a restraint order is to prohibit a suspect from interfering with property until the court is able to make a confiscation order at the conclusion of the proceedings. The order may make provision for an allowance for general living expenses, or funds to enable the continuation of a trade, business, profession, or occupation.

The Proceeds of Crime Act 2002—Quick Guide to Cash Seizures (POCA, Section 294)

The procedural rules for cash seizure are found in Statutory Instrument 2002 Number 2998 (SI 2998, available to download at <http://www.opsi.gov.uk/si/si2002/20022998.htm>).

Timescales: Cash seized under the Act may not be retained for more than 48 hours, unless by the order of a magistrate. The 48-hour period does not include Saturday, Sunday, Good Friday, Christmas Day, or any Bank Holiday (POCA, section 100).

First Application: The first application to retain seized cash is made on 'Form A' (found in SI 2998 referred to above) and must be sent to the justices' chief executive for the petty sessions area of the court before which the application is to be made.

A copy of the written application and notification of the hearing of the application must also be given to the person from whom the cash was seized (unless the cash was unattended). This should be done at the earliest opportunity. The court will want to know if they have had sufficient time to prepare.

If the cash was in an unattended dispatch then the copy of the application and notice of hearing must be sent to the sender of the dispatch and its intended recipient (unless they cannot be identified). The court will not delay matters until it receives proof of delivery, but police must be able to satisfy the court that the details have been sent.

> **Note:** It is worthwhile calling the court to make an appointment for the hearing before going there with the cash; this will give enough time to notify the suspect (if they are not in custody) and serve the required papers there and then. Plan for this if conducting a lengthy house search and it will save time later.

An order for continued detention is requested on Form B and an application for forfeiture is made on Form G (both found in SI 2998 above).

Further Reading

Armao, F (2003) 'Why is organized crime so successful?' in F Allum and R Siebert (eds) *Organized Crime and the Challenge to Democracy*, Routledge, London

Cornish, D (1994) 'The Procedural Analysis of Offending and its Relevance for Situational Prevention' *Crime Prevention Studies*, Vol 3, Monsey, NY: Criminal Justice Press

Gilmour, S (2008) 'Understanding Organized Crime: A Local Perspective' *Policing,* 2008 2(1): 18–27

Wright, A (2005) *Organised Crime*, Willan, Cullompton

For guidance and the forms required for POCA cash seizures: <http://www.opsi.gov.uk/si/si2002/20022998.htm>

For information on the Serious Organised Crime Agency: <http://www.soca.gov.uk/>

For access to academic research on organized crime: <http://www.organized-crime.de/>

Chapter 29

Counter-Terrorism and Extremism

29.1 Introduction

Protecting the public remains the highest priority of the police service, but the perceived growing risk of terrorism over recent years has resulted in the public's protection being severely threatened. No community is immune from the global reach of international terrorism and the UK is a prime target for extremists who believe they can advance their aims through acts of violence. This threat is considered to be both serious and enduring, being international in scope and involving a variety of individuals, groups, and networks who are driven by extremist beliefs.

The way in which the UK counters terrorism is developing in response to the present threat. This area of policing is no longer the sole responsibility of specialist departments. To counter the threat effectively, all police officers are required to broaden their knowledge and understanding of terrorism and extremism supporting the Government's strategy to counter international terrorism known as the 'CONTEST' strategy (an acronym of **COuN**ter **TE**rrorism **S**Trategy). The key aim of the strategy is:

> to reduce the risk from international terrorism so that people can go about their business freely and with confidence.

The strategy is divided into four key pillars which provide the scope to counter terrorism effectively. The four pillars are commonly known as the four Ps which are Prevent,

Pursue, Protect, and Prepare. Every aspect of policing terror ism and violent extremism is now nationally strategically managed by the Home Office under one of these four key pillars as shown in Table 29.1.

Table 29.1

Prevent	Tackling terrorism and its underlying causes by working together.
Pursue	To reduce the terrorist threat by pursuing terrorists and bringing them to justice.
Protect	To protect the public by 'target hardening' the UK.
Prepare	To prepare for such consequences by improving resilience to cope with any attack.

To respond to terrorist incidents and investigate terrorist and extremist-related matters, a clear understanding of terrorism and extremism as a concept is required. Developing an understanding of terrorism and extremism will ensure that first responders are better prepared to identify, report and manage terrorist-related incidents.

29.2 **Defining Terrorism**

Lord Carlile of Berriew QC, the independent reviewer of terrorism legislation in the UK, presented a report to Parliament in March 2007 which focused upon the legal definition of terrorism. The report identified that a definition of terrorism is of real practical and operational significance, as it triggers many powers as well as contributing to the description of offences. Defining terrorism is also important as saying that the threat from terrorism is 'severe', or that terrorist-related incidents are increasing annually has little meaning unless we are clear what terrorism actually is. Defining terrorism provides focus for those with the esponsibility of making key strategic decisions. It ensures hat law enforcement partners and government agencies ɪnderstand from the outset what it is they are protecting he public from. A clear definition of terrorism is also vital o that the police can distinguish adequately between legit- mate and illegitimate activities related to political policies. he special laws devised to deal with terrorism, which will ɪften be draconian in impact compared to 'normal' laws, hould not affect legitimate political activity, even if they ɪre highly aggressive or unpopular.

The legal definition of terrorism can be found in section of the Terrorism Act 2000 which states:

Definition

'Terrorism' means the use or threat of action where:

(a) it involves serious violence against a person, involves seri- ous damage to property, endangers a person's life (other than that of the person committing the action), creates a serious risk to the health or safety of the public, or a section of the public, or is designed seriously to interfere with or seriously to disrupt an electronic system;

(b) it is designed to influence the Government, or an interna- tional government organization, or to intimidate the public or a section of the public; and

(c) is made for the purpose of advancing a political, religious, racial, or ideological cause.

The legal definition provided by section 1 is broad and is lesigned to capture the diverse range of activities associ- ated with terrorism. It also provides a detailed description ɔf what acts are involved in terrorism, what the acts are lesigned to do, and for what purpose; but does the defi- ɲition really help us to clearly understand what terrorism ɑctually is?

KEY POINTS

First and foremost terrorism is a crime, a crime which has serious consequences and one which needs to be distinguished from other types of crime, but it is a crime nonetheless. Individuals who commit terrorist-related offences are subject to the processes of the Criminal Justice System and those who are otherwise believed to be involved in terrorism are subjected to restrictive executive actions. However, the key features of terrorism that distinguish it from other forms of criminality are its core motivations. Terrorism may be driven, as the legal definition provided in section 1 of the Terrorism Act 2000 states, by:

- politics
- religion
- race
- ideology.

These objectives are unlike other criminal motivations, such as for personal gain or in the pursuit of revenge. Terrorists may be driven by any one or any combination of the four core motivations but the primary motivator is political as the diagram in Figure 29.1 shows. Individuals who are driven by religious or ideological beliefs have to gain some political ground to compel others to conform to their point of view, especially if they are operating within a democratic society.

Acts of terrorism whether motivated by politics, religion, race, or ideology convey a message. This message attempts to persuade its audience or force them to accept their views and beliefs. The victims of terrorism are often distinct from this audience, victims may be passers-by, on a train, or travelling on a plane but a political audience would be a government or the electorate. Terrorism therefore has a three-way relationship between the terrorist, the victim and the audience, which is not usually the case in other types of crime. This relationship also means that a greater degree of control and oversight is required to counter terrorism so innocent and non-combatant victims are protected. Terrorism is a very powerful way in which to promote beliefs and has potentially serious consequences for society. If allowed to grow and flourish terrorism can undermine national security, it can cause instability

---

to a country, and in the most extreme of circumstances can lead to war. These are a very different set of outcomes when compared with other types of crime. This is the very reason why policing terrorism is different to policing other types of crime and why it requires a different approach to prevent it.

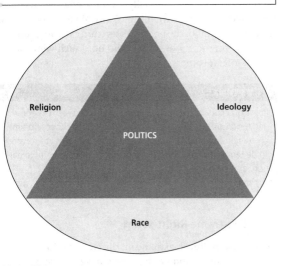

Figure 29.1

29.2.1 **Politics**

Understanding the political motivations of terrorist groups is key to countering their activities. Politics is central in society, it is the way in which governance and authority within society is managed. The Oxford Dictionary defines politics as:

Definition

politics—1 a the art and science of government. **b** public life and affairs as involving authority and government. **2 a** particular set of ideas, principles or commitments in politics. **b** activities concerned with the acquisition or exercise of authority or government. **c** an organizational process or principle affecting authority, status etc.

In a liberal, pluralist, and democratic society, which the police have a duty to defend, a wide range of political views are acceptable and desirable, even views which may offend others, are aggressively pursued, or are highly unpopular. An understanding of the spectrum of politics is important for police officers and especially for those engaged in countering terrorism and extremism. Political views that are at the extreme ends of the political spectrum can cause serious issues within society, as people who hold such views often cannot tolerate others.

KEY POINT

Police officers should continue to distinguish between extremism and terrorism; one does not necessarily lead to another, and simply to hold extremist views is not an offence and is not terrorism. To be terrorism, there must be elements of violence or intimidation, or the planning of it.

29.2.2 Extreme Right-Wing

Right-wing political extremism can take various forms. Some individuals and groups seek strong centralized government and the preservation of their national domestic culture. Others, such as militia in the US, believe in the preservation of personal rights, including strong forms of personal property and privacy and the right to bear arms, with central government becoming weak. Extreme right-wing views are often associated with fascism and racism. They are individuals and groups who advocate severe, stringent, and immoderate measures using violence and intimidation to promote their beliefs and their priority over other cultures and communities.

29.2.3 Extreme Left-Wing

Left-wing political extremists also take various forms. A common theme is to bring about what they perceive as a more equal distribution of power and wealth, whether in a particular locality, in the country as a whole, or on an international scale. Existing instruments of power and wealth, such as governmental structures and international organizations, therefore become targets.

29.2.4 Religion

Religion can be a key component of terrorist motivations. Defining religion and understanding its complexities and potential links to terrorist activity in modern society presents a real challenge for those engaged in preventing terrorism. An awareness of world faiths and cultures is required to counter terrorism and extremism effectively. Religion is a fact of society, having its own historical development which is often set in a specific social and economic climate. Individuals find religion can guide them through life, and is often described as a treasure for those within a faith who find hope, comfort, and blessing. The powerful belief of followers of different faiths needs to be recognized, especially by extremists who twist the truth of religious teachings and scriptures to legitimize the pursuit of their aims. A clear definition of religion can be found in the Oxford Dictionary:

Definition

religion—1 the belief in a superhuman power, in a personal God of gods entitled to obedience and worship. **2** the expression of this in worship. **3** a particular system of faith and worship. **4** life under monastic vows. **5** a thing that one is devoted to.

KEY POINT

Most terrorist action based upon religion could be counted also as political but it is possible that violence wholly within a small religious sect might not be characterized in that way, and so the definition of terrorism has been expanded to include religious motivations.

29.2.5 **Race**

Section 75 of the Counter-Terrorism Act 2008 amended the definition of terrorism. The Act inserted the word 'racial' after 'religious'. During his review of the definition of terrorism, Lord Carlile concluded that he saw no demanding reason for changing its wording, but he did, however, identify that it was not consistent with the United Nations Resolution 1566 from 2004 and the Council of Europe Convention on the Prevention of Terrorism 2003 which states that the purpose of terrorism is to advance a 'political, philosophical, ideological, racial, ethnic, religious or similar cause'. Lord Carlile believed that a move closer to this definition would have advantages for consistency and would cement into law clarity that terrorism includes campaigns of terrorist violence motivated by racism. It is for this reason that recommendation 12 of his review report confirmed that the existing definition should be amended to ensure that it is clear from the statutory language that terrorism motivated by a racial cause be included. A 'racial' cause implies that the terrorist may be 'racist' or 'racially motivated'. Race concerns the division of the human species. A racial act would include hostile or oppressive behaviour towards a person because they belong to a different race. A racial element also suggests that there exists a belief that some races are innately superior to others because of hereditary characteristics.

29.2.6 **Ideology**

An ideology is an organized collection of ideas. Understanding the context of a particular ideology will assist in tackling the justifications offered by terrorists who seek to legitimatize their actions. The Oxford Dictionary defines ideology as:

> **Definition**
>
> **ideology**—**1** the system of ideas at the basis of an economic or political theory. **2** the manner of thinking characteristic of class or individual. **3** visionary speculation. **4** the science of ideas.

The key purpose of an ideology is to offer a change in society which is different from the common or normal perspective. Individuals or organizations that promote their ideology do so believing it will provide a better life in society. There are many types of ideology, but the most prominent are the collection of political ideologies which may contain certain ideas on the best form of government, legal, and economic systems. It is therefore difficult to conceive that there can be ideological terrorism which is not political terrorism. Most terrorist groups want to trigger action of some form and not just to change mind-sets.

29.3 **Terrorism Classification**

There are different types of terrorism and extremism, and it is important to identify which type of terrorism an individual or group belongs to in order to counter it effectively. Terrorism can be classified into five broad categories:

Table 29.2

Political and Religious Terrorism	Political and religious terrorism perceives to act upon orders of a higher or divine authority. They are often the most violent and robust of terrorist organizations as they believe their actions are sanctioned by this higher authority. They believe that their actions are morally justified and that they will be vindicated of any wrong-doing when carrying out orders in pursuit of their objectives.

Ideological Terrorism	Ideological terrorism and extremism seeks to change the social, economic, and political systems of a country. They are violent individuals and groups who can come from either the extreme left-wing or extreme right-wing of the political spectrum. Ideological terrorism objectives are set very high and attempt to achieve a great deal. In order to achieve these objectives it often requires a full social revolution to take place and the term 'social-revolutionary' is often used to describe this grouping.
Nationalist Terrorism	Nationalist terrorism groups claim to be the authentic voice of a national culture. Through acts of violence they attempt to restore their lands back to one single larger country or seek complete independence from it by creating a new separate state. Well known nationalist terrorist organizations include the Irish Republican Army (IRA) and Euskadi Ta Askatasuna (ETA) of Spain.
State-Sponsored Terrorism	State-sponsored terrorism requires a State to support terrorist activities in pursuit of achieving its political objectives. These terrorist activities are sometimes carried out in the State's own territory or conducted in a third or neighbouring country. This tactic is often used to fulfil political agendas as any allegations of State involvement in terrorism can be easily denied or disassociated from political parties when such acts are conducted in other countries.
Single-Issue Terrorism and Extremism	Single-issue terrorism and extremism focuses on a specific policy, practice, or procedure. The key objective is to change, block, or at the very least disrupt or deter one issue from continuing in its present form. Unlike purely ideological terrorism and extremism, single-issue groups do not seek a full-scale political revolution, but they do want real action and changes to be made.

KEY POINT

Identifying the type of terrorism or extremism an individual or group belongs to is an important step in beginning to understand what it is they actually want to achieve. This understanding forms the basis of how we can most effectively employ countermeasures. It provides an insight into what the key characteristics of the individual or group may be, and what tactics may be used to convey their message and promote their beliefs.

29.4 **Terrorism Characteristics**

Terrorism may be the only tactic used by an individual or group to further their particular cause, but it may also be used as part of a much wider strategy which includes non-violent or legitimate components. So, terrorists have been associated with legitimate political movements, such as the relationship between the IRA and Sinn Fein. There are three common characteristics of terrorism wherever it is used throughout the world which are:

- pre-meditated
- indiscriminate
- breach of human rights.

29.4.1 **Pre-Meditated**

To evidence the level of forethought within terrorist organizations we need only to observe the activities of the Al-Qaeda-inspired terrorist cell responsible for the Madrid train bombings in 2004.

Case Study—Madrid, Spain, 2004

On the morning of Thursday 11 March 2004 terrorist cell members placed ten rucksack improvised explosive devices (IEDs) packed with nails on four separate commuter trains in Madrid. Within a space of three minutes all of the devices were detonated on busy carriages during the rush hour at El Pozo Station, Calle Tellez, Atocha Station, and Santa Eugenia Station.

The co-ordinated explosions claimed 191 lives, leaving more than 1,800 injured. The victims came from 17 countries including Spain, France, Bulgaria, and Poland, but they also came from as far as Brazil, Peru, Chile, and Cuba, making this attack truly global in scale, an attack that so far remains Europe's worst terrorist incident this century.

This attack was planned to coincide with the Spanish general elections, occurring three days before voting commenced. The timing of this attack also had greater significance being committed exactly 911 days after the 9/11 terrorist attacks in the United States. Was this just a coincidence of attack planning of the Al-Qaeda-inspired cell? Or part of the powerful delivery of their message?

29.4.2 Indiscriminate

The second common characteristic found in acts of terrorism throughout the world is the indiscriminate nature of attacks. A target-rich environment is offered to those terrorist groups who seek civilian casualties. They can carefully select a target and decide when and how to attack for maximum impact. There are many tactical options available to terrorist groups. Some of the most commonly used tactical options are indiscriminate by their very nature, including vehicle devices and suicide bombings. Even if a terrorist organization selects what it perceives to be a 'legitimate target' such as a military installation or government building, innocent civilians are often killed or injured. The sheer number of potential targets and tactical options therefore provides the terrorists with a high probability of success, and, where desired, with the very minimum of risk.

29.4.3 Human Rights

The third common characteristic to be found in acts of terrorism throughout the world is their disregard for fundamental human rights. Terrorist attacks cross the boundaries set by society. They deliberately breach human rights to maximize fear amongst communities so that we may be forced to make concessions in order to prevent further attacks. The Human Rights Act 1998 now protects citizens from violation by state agents of fundamental rights and freedoms that are contained within the European Convention of Human Rights agreed by the Council of Europe at Rome, on 4 November 1950 (the criminal law serves to protect citizens from violations by other citizens). It is these very rights that terrorist activity can often breach.

This does not, however, justify breaches of rights by the security authorities, including the police. Activities such as torture, illegal detentions, and threats against political activists are counter-productive to the aim of upholding the values of a liberal, pluralist democracy, and they damage confidence in the police, especially amongst the communities from which the terrorists are drawn and which might otherwise help the police.

KEY POINT

Identifying the characteristics of an individual or group provides an insight into the terrorists' determination to achieve their objectives. It is then possible to make informed decisions on the most effective ways to protect the public and counter potential threats.

29.5 **Terrorist Motivations**

Identifying what drives people towards terrorism and identifying the climate which provides such extreme beliefs to grow and flourish, may present an opportunity to tackle terrorism at its source.

29.5.1 Intervention

No one is born with extremist beliefs, such beliefs develop over time. It is this period of development that provides an opportunity to identify where extremist beliefs are emerging. There are many factors that may influence an individual, including parenting, social inclusion or exclusion, education, employment, health, and poverty. It is also important to acknowledge that their treatment at the hands of government agencies, including discriminatory and abusive treatment by the police, can also give rise to extremist behaviour, such as occurred in Northern Ireland. Many of these factors are social issues for the wider government and society to address, but all may contribute in their own way to push individuals towards an extremist perspective. Identifying those who are most vulnerable to accepting and adopting extremist beliefs could lead to the implementation of intervention strategies designed to channel individuals away from extremist activity.

KEY POINT

Individuals can be recruited to support a cause by being systematically exposed to extremist beliefs. The way in which people move towards extremist beliefs is often referred to as 'radicalization'. It is simply a process by which people adopt an interpretation of religious, political, or ideological belief that ultimately leads to them legitimizing the use of violence through acts of terrorism. However, it is not an offence or terrorism to be 'extreme' or 'radical'.

29.5.2 Justification

An important aspect of a terrorist's motivation lies in their belief system'. As terrorists develop extremist beliefs of their particular cause they do so seeking justification for their actions. Individuals who teach, preach, and promote extremist beliefs often provide a single narrative of events. They are able to skilfully convince individuals that their manipulated version of events is true and alternative opinions are false.

KEY POINT

Whatever the motivation, terrorists claim justification for their beliefs and actions. Individuals and groups who claim that a terrorist act is justified means that they pursue a purpose which they believe is 'just' and one that they believe can be given a reasonable explanation.

Many terrorist organizations see their enemy as the stronger body, the more dominant power. Usually, this assessment is true; their ability to access and use force and the apparatus of force is far less than the means possessed by state forces. This position then allows terrorists to justify the use of terrorist tactics against this dominant power. Terrorists justify and legitimize their acts in this way even though the use of force is illegitimate and there are, at least in the UK, democratic and peaceful ways to pursue political agendas. Al-Qaeda has a strong belief in their actions which is promoted to new recruits. It is this belief that over time becomes a duty, a duty that must be fulfilled. This was highlighted in January 2007 when Ayman al-Zawahiri, Al-Qaeda second-in-command and spiritual leader, stated in a recording that:

> It is your duty today to bear arms, Jihad is the obligation of our time

It is important not to underestimate the powerful delivery of some of these messages. They seek to influence individuals who may feel disappointed with their standing in life, individuals who believe that they are not part of a community, who may feel that they have no identity or voice in their society, with no hopes or future life aspirations. It may be difficult to understand why people would be influenced in this way but it is very real, as evidenced by the attacks in London on 7 July 2005.

Case Study—Mohammed Siddique Khan (MSK)

Mohammed Siddique Khan from Leeds, the oldest of the four suicide bombers, provides some justification for his actions whilst recording a 'martyrdom' message prior to the attacks. He stated that:

> Our drive and motivation does not come from tangible commodities this world has to offer—your democratically elected governments continuously perpetuate atrocities against my people all over the world and your support of them makes you directly responsible—we will not stop this fight, we are at war and I am a soldier, now you too will taste the reality of this situation.

29.5.3 Profile

A profile of a terrorist, or a person vulnerable to the process of radicalization would directly assist the police, partner agencies, and communities to identify potential individuals; after all, there are many areas of policing where a profile of a suspect or group of criminals would be developed to assist in the identification of offenders. There is, however, no one single profile that would assist frontline police officers or members of the community to identify a terrorist. This view is supported by the Government's official account of the bombings in London on 7 July 2005 which states that:

> There is not a consistent profile to help identify who may be vulnerable to radicalisation. (HM Government, Intelligence and

Security Committee (2006) *Report into the London Terrorist Attacks on 7 July 2005)*

The Prevent Strategy launched by the Government during 2008 aims to stop people becoming or supporting terrorists and violent extremists. The assessment from the Government is that violent extremism is caused by a combination of interlocking factors which include:

- an **ideology** which justifies terrorism by manipulating theology as well as history and politics;
- **radicalizers and their networks** which promote violent extremism through a variety of places, institutions, and media;
- **individuals who are vulnerable** to the messages of violent extremists;
- **communities** which are sometimes poorly equipped to challenge and resist violent extremism; and
- **grievances**, some genuine and some perceived, and some of course directed very specifically against government.

KEY POINTS

Persons engaging with terrorist activity do so for a variety of reasons. It is often a personal and individual journey as individuals move towards developing extremist beliefs. Terrorists come from a variety of cultural and religious backgrounds, social standing, education, and with a variety of life experience. The real danger in establishing one single generic profile of a terrorist is that whilst seeking positive indicators on a profile it may overlook an individual or group, failing to identify them as a potential threat.

Terrorists want to blend into our communities, they operate beneath the radar not wishing to draw attention to themselves or their activities. To bring them out into the open a thorough understanding of what patterns of behaviour are routine and common are required to be developed so that changes can be identified.

29.6 **Terrorist Organizations**

Schedule 2 of the Terrorism Act 2000 provides a list of terrorist organizations that are outlawed in the UK. The Home Secretary has the power to proscribe organizations that are concerned with terrorism. The list includes terrorist organizations that are proscribed under the 2000 Act, organizations proscribed under powers introduced in the Terrorism Act 2006 as glorifying terrorism, and additional organizations in Northern Ireland which are proscribed under previous temporary and emergency provisions.

> **KEY POINT**
>
> The list of proscribed organizations may change. To keep updated on the current list of outlawed terrorist groups in the UK access the Home Office website following the links at <http://security. homeoffice.gov.uk/legislation/current-legislation/terrorism-act-2000/proscribed-groups>.

29.7 **Terrorist Tactics**

Terrorists and their organizations choose which tactic they wish to deploy. There are many factors which influence this decision which includes the nature of the intended target, the abilities of its operatives, and the hostile environment in which they operate. Whatever the target, there is an abundance of attack options and methods.

Over time terrorist organizations develop a preferred method of operating; often referred to as their 'signature' or 'hallmark', this would be a tactic that they trusted and had refined through operational experience. Terrorist activities throughout the world include the following:

- arson
- assassinations
- bombings
- hijacking

- hoaxes and threats
- hostage-taking
- hostile reconnaissance
- infiltration
- kidnap
- propaganda
- recruitment
- training
- sabotage
- suicide missions.

Terrorist organizations may use these activities alone or as part of a much broader strategy. Tactics such as propaganda, threats, or hoaxes are designed to raise fear and tensions within communities. Criminal activities are also used to support terrorist organizations, particularly for raising funds. Terrorists have also used toxic agents to conduct attacks, though this is extremely rare. The risk of the terrorist use of chemical, biological, radiological, or nuclear weapons is low because of the difficulties of obtaining and deploying such materials and, Al-Qaeda aside, most terrorist groups do not seek innocent mass casualties. Many of the terrorist tactics described above have been used in the UK.

KEY POINTS

It is important for police colleagues to increase their awareness of terrorist tactics so that they can respond effectively to them. We should not fall into the trap of thinking that just because a place has been attacked by a specific tactic that it will not be attacked again in the same way or by an alternative method. Neither should we assume that a tactic which has not been used before is not under development and will not be used in the near future. Transport systems, international aircraft, iconic sites, and state buildings will always be prime targets, alongside other premises forming part of a country's critical infrastructure such as power stations and key utilities. Such vulnerable sites and economic key points are located within every police force area, and patrolling officers must be aware of their location and how to respond in the event of a terrorist incident.

29.7.1 Recruitment

Terrorist organizations seek to spread their political, religious, or ideological motivations to new individuals who are recruited to their cause. One of the most alarming threats that has developed over recent years is the number of UK citizens travelling to Iraq and Afghanistan to join insurgent groups to fight coalition forces. Individuals from our communities are being recruited for this cause.

KEY POINT

Police officers must be aware of the wider implications of these issues. Not all of the recruits who join the insurgents will die during combat in Iraq and Afghanistan; some will survive and may return home to their communities having received military training and combat experience. What will they do when they return to the UK? This is a specific threat which you may not have previously considered, but it provides some evidence of the broad types of activity that may potentially impact upon the threat to the UK from international terrorism.

29.7.2 Training

Over recent years there has been considerable focus upon terrorist training camps. It is important to understand what may constitute such a place. On one level they can relate to camps in the mountain regions of Pakistan or Afghanistan where individuals attend from all over the world. These camps are located in secure locations, they are lightweight, very mobile, and often move around to avoid identification and capture. Given the terrain in which they are located they are also difficult to track by military units. It is estimated that at the time of the 9/11 attacks in 2001 there were over 120 training camps in Afghanistan alone. Individuals attending these camps would typically be trained for between one and six months. At the other end of the scale, terrorist training camps may relate to an outward bound centre or paint-balling facilities located anywhere in the UK.

KEY POINT

So what turns a paint-balling centre into a 'terrorist training camp'? It is the **purpose** for which individuals are at that place at that time that is important. Therefore, terrorist training camps do not need to be clandestine in nature and may be carried out in what is effectively the complete open. Persons attending these types of 'camps' do so in full view of everyone. Outward bound and activity centres are clearly legitimate ventures; however, it is the reason why these people attend which may bring them into conflict with the law.

So why would persons who are intent on radicalizing individuals take them paint-balling or to a white water rafting centre, for example? Counter-terrorism investigations in the UK have revealed that a key purpose is to identify potential individuals, who are often vulnerable young men, who might be susceptible to radicalization by the 'mentor' of the group. There would be no point sending a young Western male out to a mountain-based training camp in Afghanistan if they couldn't cope with the hardship of an outward bound centre in the UK. Many of the young people training in the UK have been brought up in relative comfort, and trekking over hills and sleeping in tents may well be a novelty, but in reality is it something they could regularly adapt to? Many of these young people may wish to return home to their creature comforts of computers, video games, and DVDs. If the UK climate presents a tough challenge for some of them it provides an early indication of whether they could operate in harsher conditions to be found in Afghanistan training camps.

> **KEY POINT**
>
> Police officers working in both urban and rural areas must be aware that terrorist training at the lowest level in the UK is more likely to be involve outdoor activities which tests potential recruits. It may not just relate to physical training as it can involve training via the use of books, manuals, or via the use of the internet. It can also be conducted via 'virtual training camps' through a 'chat room' with individuals who do not know each other, have never met each other, and who are potentially thousands of miles apart.

29.7.3 Hostile Reconnaissance

Hostile reconnaissance involves the gathering of information for use in a terrorist attack. It forms an integral part of the attack-planning process as terrorists seek to obtain a profile of a target. Hostile reconnaissance is a feasibility study to identify what method of attack would be most appropriate and when would be the preferred time of attack to ensure an operation is successfully completed. Identifying hostile reconnaissance is important as it very often provides the first indication that a terrorist cell is planning an attack and is a vital role of patrolling officers in preventing terrorist activity. A number of other disrupted terrorist plots have revealed evidence of hostile reconnaissance having been conducted. The types and methods of obtaining or gathering intelligence during hostile reconnaissance are wide and varied, and may include any of the activities shown in Table 29.3.

29.7.4 Infiltration

Terrorist organizations seek information about their enemies. As part of hostile reconnaissance they will attempt to elicit information about an identified target or test security measures to analyse reaction and responses. Terrorists are aware that an effective method of gathering this informa-

Table 29.3

Suspicious Sightings	Presence at a place which appears unusual or unnatural.
Surveillance	Recording or monitoring of activities which includes the use of cameras, mobile phone cameras, and other vision-enhancing devices.
Security Tests	Attempts to measure security systems, protocols, or responses.
Elicitation	Attempts to gain information in person or by electronic means.
Dry Run	Rehearsal to test attack plans.

tion is to infiltrate the ranks of its target. The security measures the police service puts in place to protect its assets is vital to the success of countering not only terrorism and extremism but all other types of criminal activity. The police, like many other organizations, invest millions of pounds on protective security, including swipe card entry systems, CCTV, biometric identification, and information technology firewalls. All of these layers of protection are necessary to prevent hostile attacks from individuals with ulterior motives who seek information to further their cause.

KEY POINT

Police officers all have an important part to play in adopting and enforcing security measures. People are the most important asset that any organization has, yet they are also the most vulnerable and they pose the greatest risk to security protocols. Every employee of every organization has gigabytes of information stored within their heads; information which, if accessed, could lead to serious compromise. Police colleagues need to understand that they have privileged access to sensitive information which terrorist and extremist groups would only be too willing to exploit.

29.7.5 Chemical, Biological, Radiological, and Nuclear

Whilst suicide terrorism can claim mass casualties, the most dangerous terrorist tactic is the potential use of chemical, biological, radiological, or nuclear agents. The UK has also witnessed some interest in toxic attacks with the intended use of Ricin (but no actual attack or remotely viable attack), and the US has also investigated (without success) the use of anthrax in late 2001. Police officers must pay particular attention to those locations that store chemicals and other materials in their force area, and remain alert to suspicious activity at and around these sites.

KEY POINTS

It is important for police officers to note that the spectacular images you may see of vehicles exploding and devices being detonated accounts for less than 1 per cent of the terrorist attack plan process. These images are the final result of a much wider effort, but they are the images that we often remember. For a terrorist to use the tactics we have discussed requires a number of ways of operating, ways which provide the police with an early indication that attack planning is being developed. Police officers must seize upon these opportunities and identify terrorist activity taking place.

Members of the public, police officers, and partners are required to report information about terrorism. Thousands of people take photos everyday, but what if you see something that appears out of place? Terrorists use surveillance to plan attacks; they take photos and make notes about security measures such as the location of CCTV cameras. Terrorists require effective communications to develop attacks, they often collect and use many anonymous pay-as-you-go phones, as well as swapping SIM cards and handsets. Terrorists live within our communities; they require accommodation for planning attacks, storing equipment and chemicals. They require protective equipment for handling such chemicals such as gloves, masks, and goggles. Terrorists also use multiple identities to conceal their activities and use false documentation to achieve this. They also require meeting rooms, training facilities paid for

---

by funds raised as part of cheque and credit card fraud. Terrorists also need vehicles to assist in the transportation of such equipment or to help them to blend into the community whilst conducting hostile reconnaissance.

If you suspect any of this activity is taking place, think about terrorist tactics, trust your instincts, and report it. In an emergency which may present an immediate threat then the **999** emergency service telephone number should be used by members of the public but the confidential anti-terrorism hotline number, **0800 789321**, which is staffed around the clock by specialist counter-terrorism police officers and staff, provides an additional service and is waiting to receive information. The terrorist threat remains real and there is no room for complacency; the public and the police need to remain alert and be aware of their surroundings.

At all times they should be notified and kept informed of any issue relating to matters of counter-terrorism or extremism. All police colleagues must be aware of their own forces intelligence requirements for countering terrorism and extremism which can be accessed via each force's local policing plan and Chief Constables framework which sets out intelligence, prevention, and enforcement markers. In addition, all police officers must know how to submit terrorism- and extremism- related information to specialist counter-terrorism policing departments within their force.

29.8 **Terrorist Communications**

We live in a technological age that provides the ability to access information anywhere in the world. The media has changed the way in which we now view the world, and the development of the internet and the constant feeds from 24-hour news channels now form part of our everyday lives. While these advances have brought improvements to social, educational, and commercial communications, they are also used by terrorist and extremist groups. Police colleagues are required to develop an awareness and understanding of how communication technology and the media are used by such groups. The extent of their usage is vast, creating a new threat referred to as 'cyber-terrorism'.

Case Study—Cyber Terrorist 007

When police officers raided a flat in West London during October 2005, they arrested a young man, Younes Tsouli. The significance of this arrest was not immediately clear, but investigations soon revealed that the Moroccan-born Tsouli was the world's most wanted cyber-terrorist. Tsouli adopted the user name 'Irhabi 007', Irhabi meaning Terrorist in Arabic, and his activities grew from posting advice on the internet on how to hack into mainframe computer systems to assisting those in planning terrorist attacks.

Tsouli trawled the internet searching for home movies made by US soldiers that would reveal the inside of US military bases. Over time these small pieces of information were collated and passed to those planning attacks. This virtual hostile reconnaissance provided insider data; no longer do terrorists need to conduct physical reconnaissance if information can be pieced together from the internet.

Police investigations revealed that Tsouli had 2.5 million euros worth of fraudulent transactions passing through his accounts used to support and finance terrorist activity. Pleading guilty to charges of incitement to commit acts of terrorism Tsouli received a 16-year custodial sentence to be served at Belmarsh High Security Prison in London. Unsurprisingly he has been denied access to the internet.

Then National Co-ordinator for Terrorist Investigations Peter Clarke stated that Tsouli: 'Provided a link to core Al-Qaeda, to the heart of Al-Qaeda and the wider network that he was linking into through the internet', going on to say that 'What it did show us was the extent to which they could conduct operational planning on the internet. It was the first virtual conspiracy to murder that we had seen.'

29.9 **Tackling Domestic Extremism**

In recent years the UK has seen an increasing protest activity directed at a broad range of 'causes'. It is important for the police service to manage these potential threats that, whilst they may not reach the threshold of terrorist activity or seriously threaten issues of national security, they can cause harm to communities and the economic well-being of the UK. It is important to keep the threat from 'domestic extremists' in perspective. The majority of protests in the UK are perfectly peaceful, lawful, and undertaken in pursuance of the right of assembly and freedom of speech that we all enjoy as part of living in a democratic society. There is, however, a more complex side to extremists who wish to further their cause by committing criminal acts, being involved in incidents of public disorder, and using violence and intimidation. It is these individuals who are of concern to the police service. It must be recognized that some extremists will, under certain circumstances, adopt a 'soft' style of protest, behaving in a perfectly law-abiding manner being part of a legitimate and peaceful protest. Their attendance at such events may, however, have different motives as they progress a more extreme agenda.

29.9.1 **Domestic Extremism Categorization**

There are a broad range of individual causes that individuals can be engaged in. These include anti-globalization, animal experimentation, medical research, the pharmaceutical industry, the food industry, hunting, sports involving animals, the financial industry, environmental issues, and many more that have been the subject of attention and protest. Protests have also been directed at commercial premises, city centres, as well as employees away from their place of work in addition to suppliers of those targeted companies, shareholders, and financial institutions providing funding. The key 'domestic extremist' groups are categorized in Table 29.4.

Table 29.4

Anarchism	Anarchism is the political belief that society should have no government, laws, police, or other authority, but should be a free association of all its members. Anarchism rests on the doctrine that no man has a right to control by force the action of any other man.
Animal Rights	Animal Rights, which is also referred to as animal liberation, is an ideology based upon the very basic interests of animals. There are a wide variety of individual belief structures within this movement, but principally people who support this cause believe that animals should be afforded the same consideration as humans in that they should not suffer harm, that they should not be considered as property, used as food, clothing, or be the subject of experimental research or for entertainment. A widely accepted view amongst animal rights activists is that all animals should be regarded as legal persons and members of the moral community.
Anti-Capitalism	Capitalism is a term used to describe the economic system which promotes private ownership for profit operating within a free market. Those that oppose this system of economics are described as anti-capitalists who seek a fair central economic system based on the principles of safeguarding individual employees' rights.
Anti-Globalization	Globalization is the term used to describe the process or transformation of local or regional issues that rise into a global phenomena. Anti-globalization is the term used to describe those individuals with a political stance that oppose what is often an economic issue concerning the power, influence, and impact of large multi-national corporations and the spread of migration, technology, and investment.

Anti-War

Anti-war protestors should be distinguished from 'peace' movements. Anti-war activists are engaged in more protest activities aiming to put an end to a nation's decision to begin or continue an armed conflict. There are a variety of belief strands within this category of domestic extremism, as some anti-war protestors may believe that both sides of the conflict should discontinue their activities, while others may only support the withdrawal of one side of the conflict which is often the more powerful body widely seen as the aggressor or invader.

Environmentalism

The protection of our planet has become a social movement centred upon the primary concern for the conservation and improvement of the natural environment. An extreme environmentalist is a person who would advocate unlawful activity to sustain the management of resources and stewardship of the natural environment through changes in policy or individuals or group direct action.

Fascism

Fascism is a political ideology that seeks to regenerate the social, economic, and cultural life of a country by basing it on a heightened sense of national belonging or ethnic identity. Fascists reject liberal ideas such as freedom and individual human rights and democracy. Fascism is often associated with right-wing fanaticism, racism, and violence. Nazism, the short name for national socialism, is considered to be a form of fascism focusing upon the belief in the superiority of an Aryan race. The term Neo-Nazism refers to post World War II activities and those who now seek to resurrect those social movements and ideologies in place during that time.

29.9.2 Domestic Extremist Tactics

Extremists groups use a wide variety of tactics. They are creative in their approach to disrupting the activities of businesses and targeting employees. Police officers need to be aware of these tactics when deciding and developing responses. The targeting of protest activity is directed towards 'Primary' and 'Secondary' sites consisting of:

- **day-to-day activities**—protests by local group members at the primary and sometimes secondary sites; and
- **regional and national days of action**—where substantially larger numbers of protesters gather together or in organized groups. They will target both primary and secondary sites. Often the majority of the protesters are not local people and there is more likelihood of more extremist involvement.

'Primary and 'Secondary' sites are defined in Table 29.5.

Table 29.5

Primary	Primary sites consist of the main target premises or organization where the activity of that business is the primary issue against which the protest is directed. It has to be recognized that protesters will sometimes deliberately target another site, which is less prepared for such an eventuality. If a place is identifiable as being connected or associated to a particular organization protesters may regard it as a target.
Secondary	Secondary sites consist of all other sites, which are linked in any way whatsoever to the primary target site. For example, home addresses of directors, shareholders, employees of primary and secondary targets, suppliers or customers of primary and secondary targets, local authorities, solicitors, banks, shops, and public places. The list of potential secondary targets is extensive. It is generally any target that will have a direct impact or assist in the continuing and increasing pressure to bring about the closure of the primary target organization.

Domestic extremism groups have used a wide variety of tactics to progress their cause. Table 29.6 provides examples of some of the tactics that have been used by extremist groups in the UK.

Table 29.6

Mass Demonstrations	Organized and pre-planned mass demonstrations covering a large area, for example city centre May Day protests.
Spontaneous Demonstrations	Spontaneous or pre-planned demonstrations at specific locations, for example outside company addresses.
Home Address Demonstrations	Pre-planned or spontaneous demonstrations at an individual's home address, or immediate neighbourhood.
Bomb Telephone Threats	Bomb or other malicious telephone threats to a third party, company premises, or an individual's home address.
Improvised Explosive Devices	Improvised Explosive Device (IED), for example in shops or upon vehicles at distribution centres.
Hoax Devices	Real or hoax devices left at company premises or an individual's home address.
Intrusions	Intrusions into company premises for 'sit-ins'; obtaining information, for example details of staff or supplying companies; or releasing or stealing animals.
Malicious Mail	Real, hoax, or malicious mail sent to company premises or an individual's home address.
Harassment	Harassment of staff at or away from company premises.
Intimidation	Intimidation of staff at or away from company premises.

Unsolicited Goods	The sending of unsolicited goods to company and individual employee addresses.
Assault	Physical assault on individuals.
Switchboard Jamming	Telephone switchboard jamming campaigns.
Fax Machine Blockades	Fax machine blockade—a continuous piece of black paper is faxed to the machine.
Email Saturation	Email saturation campaigns.
Infiltration	Social engineering and infiltration, for example, organizations unwittingly employing extremists or sympathisers.

29.10 **Terrorism Legal Framework**

The Terrorism Act 2000 drew together many new areas of anti-terrorism legislation and it remains the cornerstone of the new terrorism legal framework currently being built in the UK. Not only did the 2000 Act define what 'terrorism' and 'terrorist' were, it also outlawed terrorist organizations, providing new offences and procedures for port and border controls.

As the threat from international terrorism emerged in the UK following the events of 9/11, new powers were introduced by the Anti-Terrorism Crime and Security Act 2001 to cut off terrorist funding and protect the aviation and nuclear industry. It was, however, the events of 7 July 2005 that required an urgent response from the Government to protect the UK from a real dynamic threat which resulted in Control Orders being established through the introduction of the Prevention of Terrorism Act 2005. The introduction of the Terrorism Act 2006 extended police powers to counter the new threat from international terrorism. With the creation of nine new offences it significantly lowered the threshold for persons to be arrested for terrorism offences.

The new Counter-Terrorism Act 2008 was introduced to the House of Commons on the 24 January 2008 and received royal assent on the 26 November 2008. It amends the definition of terrorism and includes new provisions to strengthen the terrorism legal framework.

Police officers are required to understand complex legislation and operationally apply it appropriately and sensitively. The two key pieces of anti-terrorism legislation and associated powers used by patrolling officers are the powers of arrest and powers of stop and search under the provisions of the Terrorism Act 2000.

29.10.1 Powers of Arrest

A broad power of arrest is provided under section 41 of the Terrorism Act 2000. There is no requirement to fulfil any necessity test, only that officers reasonably suspect that the person is a terrorist. A 'terrorist' is defined as a person who is or has been involved in the commission, preparation, or instigation of acts of terrorism or has committed an offence under the Act which includes, amongst others, those linked to outlawed terrorists groups, terrorist property, weapons training, and inciting terrorism.

KEY POINT

An arrest made under section 41 should not be used indiscriminately; there must be real and reasonable suspicion. It is always advisable that wherever possible officers considering the use of these powers should contact local specialist counter-terrorism units for advice, guidance, and support. Clearly, this will not always be operationally possible to achieve, which is why knowledge of anti-terrorism legislation and confidence in its practical application is required by all police colleagues. In any event, an arrest of a person under section 41 should be communicated to local specialist units as soon as practicable; time is very much of the essence and the sooner counter-terrorism officers can be informed the better.

29.10.2 Stop and Search

Specific stop and search powers are provided under sections 42, 43, and 44 of the Terrorism Act 2000. The Home Office has provided detailed guidance for police officers in relation to the appropriate use of terrorism stop and search powers. It specifically highlights that stop and search activity has raised concerns over the disproportionality of its use among visible ethnic minority groups. This is liable to be accentuated by its use in relation to terrorism, especially when countering the threat from international groups. It is not appropriate to stereotype people of a certain faith or ethnicity as terrorists, but these factors may be significant when taken as part of a combination of other factors. It is known that some terrorists may adopt behaviours and appearances typical of local cultures to avoid identification, but it is not appropriate to use these factors as a preconceived basis for searches. It is important to remember that where profiles of suspects are available, they are subject to change and can become quickly outdated.

> **KEY POINT**
>
> All officers using stop and search powers under terrorism legislation should be aware of the cultural sensitivities surrounding the removal of clothing and especially headgear. A thorough understanding of religious and cultural differences is an essential element of policing communities sensitively but effectively.

29.10.3 Sections 42 and 43 of the Terrorism Act 2000

Sections 42 and 43 of the Terrorism Act 2000 deal with the powers to enter premises under the authority of a justice's warrant and search for a person suspected to be a terrorist (section 42), stop and search a person reasonably suspected to be a terrorist (section (43(1)), and search persons arrested under section 41 (section 43(2)).

A constable may stop and search a person whom he reasonably suspects to be a terrorist to discover whether he has in his possession anything which may constitute evidence that he is a terrorist. Section 114 of the Act states that a constable may use reasonable force for the purpose of exercising a power conferred on him by virtue of this Act and that this power is additional to and does not affect the powers that a constable has at common law or under any other enactment.

Stop and search powers in section 43 and elsewhere in the Act are also subject to section 116(2) of the Terrorism Act 2000 by which a power to stop a person includes the power to stop a vehicle (other than an aircraft which is airborne), and a person commits a summary offence if he/she fails to stop a vehicle when required to do so. A search of a person under this section must be carried out by someone of the same sex, and the powers are exercisable in public and in private provided that in the latter case officers can establish a legal basis for entry.

Under section 43 a police constable may seize and retain anything which he discovers in the course of a search of a person and which he reasonably suspects may constitute evidence that the person is a terrorist, and may be retained for so long as is necessary in all the circumstances. A person who has the powers of a constable in one part of the UK may exercise a power under this section in any part of the UK.

Section 1 of the Police and Criminal Evidence Act 1984 and Code A of the associated Codes of Practice applies to the conduct and recording of searches, paragraph 4.4 of which states that in lieu of their names, officers may give their warrant or other identifying number and duty station on any records required to be made under this code in the case of enquiries linked to the investigation of terrorism.

KEY POINT

Unlike section 44 authorizations, the power applies to constables whether they are in uniform or not, and unlike section 44 the removal of headgear and footwear in public cannot be required. The removal of a jacket, outer coat, or gloves can only be required if the search takes place out of public view and nearby the place where the person was stopped.

This power is exercisable only where there are reasonable grounds to suspect a person of being a terrorist. Once these grounds have been established then a search may be made of the person for anything which may constitute evidence that he/she is a terrorist.

29.10.4 Section 44 of the Terrorism Act 2000

The powers enabling an officer of ACPO rank to authorize constables in uniform to stop and search persons and vehicles, without reasonable grounds, in certain specified geographical areas and for articles which could be used in connection with terrorism, are contained within sections 44 to 47 of the Terrorism Act 2000. The authorization is also subject to ministerial scrutiny, and once confirmed can remain in force for a period of up to 28 days.

The Police and Criminal Evidence Act 1984 Code 'A' (paragraphs 2.19 to 2.26) governs the conduct of statutory stop and search powers under section 44 of the Terrorism Act 2000, and paragraph 4.4 of Code 'A' allows police officers to state their warrant or other identification number and duty station in lieu of their names on any search records in enquiries linked to the investigation of terrorism.

There are two distinct powers within the legislation, firstly, section 44(1) allows a constable in uniform to stop a vehicle in an area or place specified in an authorization and search the vehicle, the driver, the passenger(s), anything in or on the vehicle, and anything being carried by the driver or passenger. Secondly, section 44(2), allows a constable in

---

uniform to stop a pedestrian in an area or place specified in an authorization and search the pedestrian and anything carried by him or her. The purpose of both searches is to discover articles which the constable reasonably suspects is intended to be used in connection with terrorism, and the constable may also seize and retain any such articles.

A person commits an offence if he fails to stop, fails to stop a vehicle, or wilfully obstructs a constable, and may be liable on summary conviction to imprisonment not exceeding six months, a fine not exceeding level 5 on the standard scale, or both. An authorization can be required to stop and search vehicles drivers and passengers, and/or it can also be required to stop and search pedestrians; however, the authorization must indicate whether it is one or the other or both.

These powers are only exercisable when an authorization is in place, and an authorization may only be given if the person giving it considers it expedient for the prevention of acts of terrorism. Such an authorization may only be given by an officer of ACPO rank for the police area that the specified area or place forms the whole or part of. However, the Energy Act 2004 amends these powers to allow authorizations from the British Transport Police, the Ministry of Defence Police, and the Civil Nuclear Constabulary. The Terrorism Act 2006 also extends the geographical scope to include internal waters.

The authorization must clearly describe the area or place where the powers apply and an accompanying map will be useful to the Minster in deciding whether or not to confirm. The authorizing officer will also be required to justify the geographical extent of the stop and search area, and the necessity for deploying these powers in the first place.

An authorization can be given orally but must be confirmed in writing as soon as it is practicable to do so. All authorizations must be confirmed by the Secretary of State within 48 hours of the time of its signing. If the authorization is not confirmed by the Minister it ceases to have effect at the end of that 48-hour period; however, anything done in reliance on the authority during that time will still be lawful. Effectively, Chief Officers can authorize the first 48 hours without seeking the Minister's confirmation, which in practice makes this legislation particularly useful in short-term operational counter-terrorism planning, where the power is only required for a limited period of time or for a one-off event. It is considered reasonable for the Home Office to have received a copy of an authorization within two hours of its authorization in these particular circumstances.

An authorization may last a maximum of 28 days commencing with the day on which the authorization is given. For example, an authorization signed at 09:00 hours on 1 January 2008 must cease to have effect by 23:59 hours on 28 January 2008 and not 09:00 hours on 29 January 2008. Although an authorization cannot commence before the time it is signed, the effect is to bring forward the start time of an authorization to 00:01 hours on day one purely for the purpose of calculating the 28-day period.

KEY POINT

The Home Office states that community consultation is essential when seeking to exercise these powers, excluding exceptional and urgent cases when consultation will have to occur as soon as possible after the authorization has been granted.

In all cases, completed section 44 authorizations must be forwarded to the Metropolitan Police National Joint Unit which is responsible for the coordination and processing of all authorizations through to the Home Office. Draft practice advice issued by the National Policing Improvement Agency suggests that officers could, in future, be issued with memo cards detailing their powers, leaflets to hand out to members of the public explaining the rationale for police action, and posters for display within the search area, so that those subject to stop and search are made better aware of the grounds for and objectives of police activity.

KEY POINT

Lord Carlile of Berriew QC, HM Government's independent reviewer of terrorism legislation, in his annual report on the operation of the Terrorism Act 2000 during 2007, warned that stop and search powers under sections 44 to 47 were to be examined more critically by the Home Office and that those charged with a responsibility for deploying these powers on the ground must be accurately briefed, adequately trained, and know what they are doing and why they are doing it, if the police service is to avoid future criticisms over its misuse of the power.

Chapter 30

Civil Contingencies

Civil Contingencies is an area of protective services policing frontline staff will have to deal with in their service. Their initial response will largely determine the effectiveness of the response. It is therefore important that frontline staff and first responders understand the significance and context of this element of protective service.

30.1 Civil Contingencies Act 2004

In recognition of the increased threats posed by terrorism and climate change the profile of civil contingencies has increased in recent years and now forms part of core policing activity. In order to prepare and respond to these challenges the Civil Contingencies Act 2004 created a national framework and structure to ensure effective information sharing, collaboration, and cooperation across a range of organizations that could be called upon to respond to a civil emergency, whether it be manmade or natural.

The Act identified two groups of responder: **Category 1** responders, who have a statutory obligation to plan and cooperate, such as the blue light services and local authorities; and **Category 2** responders, such as the utilities and transport companies, who would have a key role to play in supporting Category 1 responders.

The focal point for this coordination is the **Local Resilience Forums** (LRFs) which are generally aligned with police force areas. LRFs are multi-agency groups made up of both Category 1 and 2 responders.

The LRF is required to publish a **Community Risk Register** (CRR) which outlines the risks that are identified and planned for in that LRF area. This is a public document and open to inspection online with the respective LRF website or in public libraries. Every police officer should know the primary hazards in their area and what plans exist to deal with such events and be able to refer to them. For example, are there any chemical sites or flood risk areas? A brief list in the rear of the pocket notebook or a card insert is useful for this purpose.

All LRFs are supported at a regional level by **Regional Resilience Forums** (RRF), which sit within Regional Government Offices. They are there to support the LRFs and provide wide-scale coordination and act as the interface with central government. They have no statutory authority to direct resources, unless in times of a 'State of Emergency'. The Chief Police Officer within an LRF area retains overall authority to coordinate the emergency response to any civil emergency in that area.

30.2 Emergency Response Phase

The response to a civil emergency is usually separated into two phases. Phase 1 is the emergency phase in which the police are responsible for the coordination of activity, and Phase 2 is the recovery and return to normality. This is usually led by the local authority within whose area the incident had taken place. Emergencies can be fast onset or 'slow burn'. The key to effective emergency response is being able to recognize when a 'major incident' is at hand.

30.3 **Major Incident**

The Civil Contingencies Act 2004 created a broad definition of a civil emergency. However, the term 'major incident' is still widely recognized and used by all organizations to define, what is for them, a major incident. A major incident for one organization may not be considered such for another. The principle of the 'combined response' ensures that where one organization declares a major incident' all other emergency response organizations will offer assistance and be stood down as appropriate. It is important that one emergency response organization does not stand another organization down until they have assessed the situation and decided themselves that their services are not required.

A major incident is a situation for an organization where special arrangements have to be implemented to deal with it, above normal routine activity. For a Category 1 responder they must also ensure that they have robust **Business Continuity Plans** in place to continue to deliver their normal service. They may have to draw upon extra resources or external support to assist them to manage. The situation may involve large numbers of people or serious damage to property. It is better to declare a major incident than wait and have to play catch up, or not have sufficient essential resources or skilled personnel at hand when needed.

A major incident should never be confused with an 'unusual' incident. A major incident is about the consequences or impact of an incident, and not about the cause. Nor is it necessarily the same thing as a critical incident—see Chapter 31 below.

Declaring a major incident is important as it will activate plans and mobilize resources. Who will declare a major incident? Many organizations advocate that their first responders should be responsible for this. However, that is not always appropriate because they are too busy dealing with a fast-moving and often chaotic scene. Sometimes it is obvious that a major incident is at hand, but that is not always the case. It is suggested that by default all major incident declarations be confirmed at management level through control or communications centres where managers have a better overview and are able to make dynamic assessments relating to resource availability but relying on the first responders to inform and contribute to that decision.

30.4 **Primary Key Emergency Roles**

30.4.1 The Police

The police are responsible for the overall coordination of the emergency response phase. The police are not in command of any other service but their own, however, they can direct other agencies in some circumstances that involve terrorism. The police must be proactive and visible at any scene to ensure effective coordination starts immediately. They must ensure that other services can operate effectively by facilitating access and egress to and from a scene by managing traffic, establishing cordons, managing rendezvous points, and designating marshalling areas. The police will also facilitate control centres at Operational (Bronze), Tactical (Silver), and Strategic (Gold) levels as the incident demands (see later). This is part of their coordination function.

The police are also responsible for:

- coordinating evacuation;
- assisting with and warning the public;
- protecting property;
- collating and disseminating casualty information by obtaining information from all those directly involved in an incident, and comparing information from those reporting families or friends missing to identify those involved. This is done through a 'Casualty Bureau';
- identifying the deceased on behalf of the coroner;
- establishing the facts and pursuing or assisting in the prosecution of offenders where offences have been committed.

These are roles likely to be undertaken by frontline staff and for which staff may undergo specialist training. Identification of deceased persons in a major incident increasingly is the work of specially trained staff, some of whom are abstracted from frontline duties on an as-needed basis for this purpose.

30.4.2 The Fire and Rescue Services

The fire and rescue services are primarily responsible for:

- extinguishing fires;
- effecting rescues;
- carrying out mass decontamination.

30.4.3 The Ambulance Services

The ambulance services are primarily responsible for:

- rendering immediate medical support and treatment;
- coordinating the resources of the wider NHS;
- decontaminating casualties (assisted by the fire and rescue services when numbers are large);
- lead in the setting up of survivor reception centres for those who have no or minor injuries following an incident but do not need to go to hospital.

30.4.4 The Local Authority

The local authority is primarily responsible for:

- providing temporary accommodation, rest centres, for those displaced by an emergency and recording their names;
- coordinating and mobilizing welfare support and provisions;
- assisting in survivor reception centres;
- setting up friends and relatives centres to provide information and reunite families with survivors;

- assisting in humanitarian assistance centres to provide information and longer-term support for both survivors and families;
- establishing and equipping emergency mortuaries for dealing with large numbers of fatalities.

30.4.5 The Maritime and Coastguard Agency

The Maritime and Coastguard Agency are primarily responsible for:

- coordinating rescue off-shore;
- determining disembarkation points on shore for survivors in liaison with the police.

30.5 Scene Management

Upon arrival at the scene of an incident, the police must quickly assess the likely nature and impact of the incident.

The first police officer must *survey*, *assess*, and *report* to their control or communication centre. The officer must NOT put himself or herself in danger or get involved in rescue if it compromises their role. A simple but important point to remember in avoiding toxic smoke or chemicals, which is often overlooked by response officers, is that the direction the wind is coming from should be given (eg an easterly wind comes from the east) and that you should try to keep upwind of the scene. Police officers should not be required to wear any 'personal protective equipment' (PPE) unless they have been trained in its correct use.

In terms of health and safety generally, the fire and rescue service will advise on all issues affecting personal safety, in particular within an inner cordon.

The officer should wear high visibility clothing and report to their control or communications centre using the mnemonic CHALETS:

Mnemonic

Casualties—number, nature of injuries, and if contaminated

Hazards—describe them

Access—safe routes

Location—be precise

Emergency services—already there or needed

Type of incident—chemical, explosion, train, plane, CBRN (chemical, biological, radiological, or nuclear)

Safety—do not take unnecessary risks

Police officers must prevent and avoid unnecessary disruption of a scene. This is to preserve evidence but clearly not at the expense of assisting casualties.

The officer should maintain radio contact at all times but remembering the possibility of unexploded improvised explosive devices (IED), which can be triggered by radio signals. Do not use a radio or mobile phone within 200 metres of the device or 400 metres if a vehicle-borne device.

The officer, as part of their coordination role, MUST seek out and liaise with other emergency service 'Incident Officers' at the scene. Together they must agree their operational priorities quickly, and the police must ensure that the other emergency services have the best possible access and egress given the circumstances. If the police officer has an 'Incident Officer' jacket, they should wear it—the other services will be looking for it.

The police officer should seek out or identify:

1. **A Forward Control Point** (FCP) (later to become 'Incident Control Post' (ICP)) where emergency services liaise on site. The officer should inform Control of its location.

2. **A Rendezvous Point** (RVP)—the officer should nominate this and inform Control.

3. **A Marshalling Area**—intended for resources and vehicles to assemble. The officer should inform Control of its location.

All three points should be managed by a police officer o
support officer and the location of these facilities shoul
be confirmed with the fire and rescue service for safety rea
sons. All responding agencies and organizations acting ii
support should report to the RVP or Marshalling Area to b
sent or taken forward to the FCP/ICP. They should not g
directly to the FCP/ICP. This will cause congestion, confu
sion, and compromise safety.

Cordons are put in place for very good reasons. They ar
usually maintained by the police and the fire and rescu
service. They are very resource-intensive to maintain thei
integrity, and have to be 'line of sight', meaning each office
on the cordon can see another officer on the same cordon
Usually there are two cordons, an inner and outer cordon
In addition, the term hot zone, warm zone, and cold zone
may be used to manage a scene involving contamination
but essentially these zones are cordoned areas. Each cordo
has ideally one 'access control' to ensure only authorizec
people can gain access. Security is maintained by the police
and the inner cordon safety management is left to the fir
and rescue service unless it is a terrorist-related incident ir
which case the police will take primacy.

30.6 CBRN—Chemical, Biological, Radiological, Nuclear

These terms are now common place in emergency man
agement and have very different impacts if used. It is no
intended here to give a definitive explanation of thei
effects on humans or the environment, but they have som
characteristics that a police officer should be aware of
Essentially, the objective in a CBRN response is to deal witr
contamination effects resulting from chemical, suspectec
biological, or radiological substances. It is worth consider
ing the effects these substances have in the initial stages o
exposure.

Chemical substances will have an immediate effect as people inhale the toxic substance or it is deposited on the skin. The emergency services use the Step 1–2–3 system of approach in these circumstances.

STEP 1–2–3

This system was developed to assist emergency responders approach a scene safely by making them alert to potential chemical attack situations.

Step 1: if one casualty down—normal procedure.

Step 2: if two casualties down—approach with caution.

Step 3: if three or more casualties down, without obvious cause—do not approach, possible chemical attack.

Biological and radiological exposure will be far less dramatic, with the harmful effects emerging within a matter of hours or indeed days. A nuclear explosive device will create catastrophic devastation instantly. This is opposed to a radiological device, which is intended to spread radioactive material around by means of conventional explosive. Both the fire and rescue service and ambulance service have radiation detection devices to alert staff if that is the case.

A point to note is that this decontamination procedure now extends also to the accidental or negligent spillage or discharge of these substances and not just terrorism. The focus of the response concentrates on the effective and speedy decontamination of those exposed. In particular the new roles of the ambulance service as the primary decontamination agency supported by the fire and rescue service to deal with mass decontamination. All blue light services are now trained and equipped to deal with such incidents and have been provided with specialist equipment to do so. The key concern in these situations is keeping the public calm and reassuring them to remain where they are at the location to undergo decontamination and so prevent the spread of the toxic substance.

A schematic representation of an incident scene is shown in Figure 30.1.

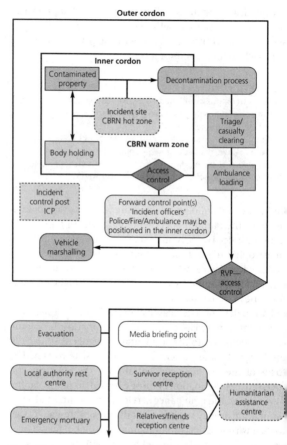

Figure 30.1

30.7 **Gold, Silver, and Bronze (GSB)**

This is a flexible approach to incident management, which is not rank-orientated but based upon function. The Bronze function is operational—actually doing the job; the Silver function is tactical—deciding how the job should be done; and the Gold function is strategic—deciding what has to be done. It is characteristic of a spontaneous incident that the operational response is the first and it builds—from the bottom up, implementing management layers as required. Therefore, the GSB system should only be implemented as required and the incident managed at the lowest possible level. Implementing a complex management structure for a simple incident will only confuse and blur accountability.

The first police officer arriving at a scene will be the **Incident Officer**. They will be responsible for carrying out the initial duties of the police. As more experienced officers arrive at the scene and there is ongoing assessment, that role may pass from one officer to another. At some point, due to the nature and scale of the incident and usually on declaration of 'major incident', a management decision will be made to separate the management functions. This will initially entail the Incident Officer assuming the role of Silver Commander and directing operational activity through a series of nominated Bronze Commanders for distinct functions, such as cordon control, traffic management, and so on. If the incident, due to the very serious nature of the circumstances, requires a separate strategic management level, a Gold Commander will be appointed, and the Silver Commander will implement their instructions and directions.

30.7.1 **Control Centres**

In terms of supporting both Silver and Gold Commanders, the police will decide if there is a need to open a Silver Control or Gold Control. These will be multi-agency facilities usually sited at police premises where the police will coordinate the response. Both control centres will need to be administered by a dedicated Silver and Gold Coordinator respectively to allow the commanders to focus on command issues and not be distracted with administration and information management within these centres. It must be remembered that a Forward Control Point can and will change into an Incident Control Post. The ICP is an on-scene management facility. However, an ICP must not be confused with a control centre, which will need considerable space, accommodation, and administration to support a multi-agency effort. A stand-alone ICP vehicle may not be able to support such a function.

The location of the Silver Commander is vital for the successful coordination of the emergency response. In most cases with an identifiable scene, the best location for the Silver Commander will be at the scene where they can discharge their role most effectively. A Silver Control will be attended by liaison officers from the respective organizations and agencies, not their Commanders. However, the opposite is true of Gold Controls, which must be attended by senior level strategic managers and commanders. They have to be in a position to take high-level decisions on issues of policy, expenditure, and strategy.

30.8 **Evacuation**

A task often requiring significant police involvement is evacuation. The police are responsible for the coordination of evacuation and the local authority will provide temporary accommodation and transport if required. Evacuation is usually sanctioned by a strategic decision in a slow-moving incident or dynamically, in many cases by the first officers on a scene.

Managing evacuation spontaneously consists primarily of directing the public in an orderly fashion away from any danger. Reassurance combined with firm, calm, and clear instructions will induce a degree of structure to an otherwise chaotic situation.

The police have no general powers to force people to evacuate apart from section 33 of the Terrorism Act 2000 in which the police can create cordons and require people to leave the area. There are also powers under section 85 of the Public Health Act 2004 to evacuate to prevent the spread of disease. However, it is accepted that effective communication and cooperation will effect evacuation efficiently.

30.9 **Media**

The media have a key public safety role to play in terms of disseminating warnings and information to the public. Every police force will have emergency media personnel and special arrangements in place to mobilize and assist in coordinating the media response following a major incident. Forward Media Briefing (FMB) points will be established near the scene to allow the media to report the incident. (See Chapter 17 for further guidance on dealing with the media.)

30.10 **Conclusion**

The purpose of this introduction to civil contingencies has been to equip frontline staff and first responders with a contextual understanding of civil contingency policing.

Chapter 31

Critical Incidents

It is recognized that high profile or large-scale incidents are, or have the potential to become, critical incidents. In addition smaller scale and internal incidents can also develop into critical incidents if they are not managed correctly, or, due to their unique circumstances, have a disproportionate impact upon the community. Critical incidents can occur post-incident following the response or investigation of an incident, or the community or media perception of the police response.

Critical incident policing is not just concerned with dealing with an incident from an operational response or investigative perspective; it is also concerned with taking pro-active steps to prevent critical incidents developing, and restoring public confidence and police–community relations post-incident.

31.1 **Offence**

A critical incident, in and of itself, is not a criminal offence. However, events giving rise to a critical incident often involve serious criminality, and there may be resulting criminality as a consequence of the incident becoming critical.

> **KEY POINTS**
>
> - Early recognition of a spontaneous critical incident.
> - Recognition of an on-going incident that may become a critical incident.
> - Article 2 of the Human Rights Act, the protection of life.
> - Article 8 of the Human Rights Act, the right to respect for privacy and family life.
> - First responders to advise supervisors of indicators of increased community tension.

31.2 **Meaning**

The concept of critical incidents was developed following the tragic murder of Stephen Lawrence and the subsequent Macpherson Inquiry (1999). The definition of a critical incident is:

> **Definition**
>
> Any incident where the effectiveness of police response is likely to have a significant impact on the confidence of the victim, their family, and/or the community.

It is clear from the above definition that critical incidents will encompass a wide range of incident types for which Standard Operating Procedures will apply. Critical incident management will not replace these procedures but enhance and provide additional quality assurance of the police response. Critical incident management will also identify if action is required to recover the quality of the police response in relation to public confidence.

31.3 **Definitions**

- 'Effectiveness' is a measure of the professionalism, competence, and integrity evident in the police response to an incident.
- 'Significant impact' defines significant as being particular to each incident but critically relates to the impact that the incident has upon the individual victim, their family, and/or communities.
- 'Confidence' refers to the long-term confidence invested in policing by victims, their family, and the community as the result of police action in attending to, and dealing with the incident.

31.4 **Illustrative Examples of Critical Incidents**

Although some of the reading below pre-dates the definition of a critical incident that evolved out of the Macpherson Inquiry, the pre-1993 case studies would today be considered to be critical incidents.

- Laming, Rt Hon The Lord (2003), *The Victoria Climbié Inquiry*, TSO, London
- Macpherson, W (1999), *The Stephen Lawrence Inquiry*, TSO, London
- Scarman, Rt Hon The Lord (1981), *The Brixton Disorders 10–12 April 1981*, HMSO Cmnd 8427, London
- Taylor, P, Lord Justice (1990), *Inquiry into the Hillsborough Stadium Disaster: Final Report*, HMSO, London
- Her Majesty's Inspectorate of Probation (2006), *An Independent Review of a Further Serious Offence Case: Anthony Rice*, HMSO, London

31.5 **Practical Considerations**

31.5.1 Strategic Consideration

- Critical incidents are managed through a three-rank command structure in which the hierarchical layers are labelled Gold, Silver, and Bronze. This structure allows the response to the incident to be scaled up or down according to the changing circumstances. The Gold Command is undertaken by the role of an Assistant Chief Constable and is responsible for overall strategic leadership and direction of the incident. The Silver Commander is normally a rank of Superintendent, while the rank of Bronze Commander is undertaken by the Duty Inspector.

- Within 24 hours of a confirmed critical incident the Gold Commander will convene a **Gold Group**. The Gold Group comprises senior police officers with specialist skills, representation from the Police Authority, and Independent Advisory Groups from the community. The purpose of a Gold Group is to support the Gold Commander, apart from the Police Authority Member who is there primarily as an observer. The Gold Group consider how the victim, family, and witnesses are supported and reassured, while restoring confidence in the community. In addressing the needs of the victims, the family, the community, and the investigation, the Gold Group also:

  - challenge assumptions and mindsets;
  - ensure that the needs of the victim, their family, and the community are being reviewed and addressed;
  - provide access to expert advice;
  - review the progress of the investigation;
  - develop a media strategy;
  - ensure accountability and transparency is maintained
  - review resources allocated to policing the critical incident;
  - provides independent and community perspectives;

- builds trust and confidence between the police, victim, their family, and the community.

- Critical incidents are classified as tier 1, 2, and 3. Tier 1 represent incidents that occur within and its impact is confined within a Basic Command Unite (BCU). Tier 2 incidents are those that impact upon more than one BCU and will also include series of linked incidents that have occurred in more than one BCU. In Tier 1 and 2 there is limited potential for the actions and risks of the incident to spread beyond the areas identified. Tier 3 is concerned with incidents that impact across one force area or several forces, or has a national dimension, and where there is a significant threat to public confidence and reputation of the police services involved.

31.5.2 Tactical Considerations

These tactical considerations must be read in conjunction with force policy.

- The Duty Inspector for the BCU will attend the scene of any actual or potential critical incident within one hour of it being reported. The Inspector will undertake an initial assessment of the incident to ascertain whether or not it is critical and update the Control Room Inspector.
- Where an incident is being identified as a critical incident, it should be managed in line with the relevant policies and procedures and use the Golden Hour principle set out in the Association of Chief Police Officers (ACPO) 2005 Practice Advice on Core Investigative Doctrine.
- The response and key tactical options to deal with the critical incident will be determined by the unique circumstances of the incident itself. However, primacy must be given to the victim, their family, the community, and the investigation process.
- The 'on-call 'Detective Inspector should be contacted as soon as possible and should attend the scene to oversee the initial stages of the investigation.

- Other initial responses to the critical incident will depend upon the nature of the specific incident.
- Securing positive lines of communication with the victim and their family or representatives is a priority within the investigative process. The services of specially trained family liaison officers are often used and these appointed family liaison roles have an important task in developing and maintaining positive relationships with victims and their family.
- Involving and obtaining the support of the community at the early stages of a critical incident will lessen the impact that a critical incident may have and provide a conduit between the community and the police. To assess police confidence on the community or different groups within the community, a Community Impact Assessment is undertaken by Community and Race Relation Officers. A Community Impact Assessment will review and consider, as part of the investigation:

  - the enhancement of investigative effectiveness;
  - protection of vulnerable individuals and groups;
  - the promotion of community confidence;
  - the development of community intelligence;
  - an understanding that all concerns of the community in relation to the incident are being dealt with;
  - provision of transparency of police response and actions.

31.6 Examples of Events from which Critical Incidents could be Generated

- Firearms incidents
- Suspicious deaths and deaths following police contact
- High risk missing persons

- Serious hate crime
- Racist incidents
- Terrorist incidents
- Serious public disorder
- Civil disasters and emergencies
- Vehicle pursuits
- Serious assault
- An incident that has been subjected to heightened media attention, such as paedophile activity or homophobic attacks.

Further Reading

The ACPO National Community Tension Team (NCTT), which leads on the 'Prevent' element of the Government's CONTEST counter-terrorism strategy, collates and disseminates intelligence concerning community tension and cohesion with particular reference to critical incidents arising from terrorism and fundamentalism issues. The NCTT website is at <http://www.acpo.police.uk/NCTT/>, accessed 20 January 2009.

Chapter 32

Public Order

Frontline staff potentially will be involved in public order policing across its entire spectrum, from patrolling to preserve a prevailing peaceful order, to being members of specialist public order policing units (subject to levels of individual training). Frontline staff will also be best positioned to identify when the normal state of society appears to be deteriorating towards an environment of disorder. Significant public disturbances are not usually wholly spontaneous. There is often a preceding period of increasing community tension. Alternatively, disorder can be associated with pre-planned events such as public protests or sporting fixtures. This chapter explains the framework of public order policing as a contextual introduction for frontline officers.

32.1 What is Meant by the Term 'Public Order'?

There is no accepted all-encompassing definition of public order; however, the following definitions give a clear sense of what is meant by a public order event or incident.

Public order is the normal state of society. This differs from place to place. The normal state of society in a market town is different from the normal state of society in a city centre. This also differs from time to time. The normal state of society in a city centre at 0600 hours is different to 1800 hours.

A firearms incident or a serious road traffic collision could disrupt the normal state of society in a given locality, but that would not make it a public order event or incident. More is needed.

The HMIC report 'Closing the Gap' (2005) by Deni O'Connor CBE QPM for the purpose of benchmarking forces used the following definition of Public Order:

> Events or incidents that are policed at force or regional level, to facilitate lawful actions and activity so as to ensure public safety and the maintenance of peace.

The Association of Chief Police Officers (ACPO) Manual of Guidance on Keeping the Peace reinforces Deni O' Connor's definition by stating that it will:

> provide direction and information to assist commanders, planners and advisors to prepare and manage events where there is a risk of public safety or a potential for disorder.

It develops this further, however, by going on to state that it:

> relates to the management of events and incidents ranging from routine operational policing through to large scale disorder.

From the above definitions it must be concluded that a public order event or incident involves a risk of disruption to the normal state of society involving a risk to public safety or potential for disorder, and ranging in size from disorder at routine policing level to disorder or a risk to public safety at regional level.

32.2 **What is the Scope of Public Order?**

Public order policing is not just about riotous situations. There is a wide range of events and incidents that fall within the spectrum of public order.

The ACPO Guide to Keeping the Peace states that:

> The scope of public order policing may be determined by the category, size, impact and frequency of any given event or incident.

The category refers to the type of incident. Size can range from a small fight involving a couple of persons to a huge event involving hundreds of thousands of people, such as the Notting Hill Carnival. Impact refers to the impact on all persons, communities, or organizations that may be affected. This may not just include the persons involved and the local community. It may extend to the business community, the media, politics, police reputation, the wider community, and the Government.

32.3 **Types of Public Order**

The ACPO Guide to Keeping the Peace categorizes public order into four broad areas:

- spontaneous
- single issue
- lawful event
- unlawful event.

32.3.1 **Spontaneous**

A spontaneous incident or event is one where the police have had no notification or had no indication that the incident or event would take place. As a consequence they will have been unable to plan for the incident or event.

An example of a spontaneous incident is urban disorder.

32.3.2 **Single Issue Protest**

A single issue protest is where protestors demonstrate their opposition to some specific issue. This may take the form of a peaceful protest or it may be violent. It may involve large numbers, raising the issue of disruption. It may be urban or rural. It may involve an assembly and/or a march. It may involve some form of direct action.

Examples of single issue protest are:

- direct action
- industrial
- environmental.

32.3.3 **Lawful Event**

A lawful event is one which is lawful to hold and which will have been notified to the appropriate authorities, depending on the event, and appropriate approval and or licence obtained.

Some examples of a lawful event include:

- sporting event
- musical event
- conference.

32.3.4 **Unlawful Event**

An unlawful event is one which has not been notified to the appropriate authorities and appropriate approval and licensing has not been obtained.

An example of an unlawful event includes:

- raves.

32.4 **Public Order Resources**

When a force is faced with an incident or event for which it has insufficient resources then a request has to be made for assistance from other forces. To facilitate this, the Police National Information and Co-ordination Centre has a National Mobilisation Plan. This states that:

> A key component of the police national mobilisation plan is that resources from different forces can work together during a mobilisation event.

To enable forces to work together there has to be a commonality in standards, tactics, and training of public order trained officers and specialist resources as set out in the ACPO Guide to Standards Tactics and Training. Below is a list of resources required in line with the ACPO guide. See also section 32.5 below.

32.4.1 **Level 3 Trained Officers**

These are defined by the ACPO Guide to Standards, Tactics and Training as:

> Officers with an awareness of public order issues and trained in **foot cordon** tactics for dealing with non-violent protest in traditional uniform.

32.4.2 **Police Support Units (PSUs)—Level 2 Trained**

One Police Support Unit (PSU) Commander, three serial supervisors, 18 constables, 3 drivers, equipped and trained to level 2 (**Common Minimum Standard**).

32.4.3 **Police Support Units (PSUs)—Level 1 Trained**

One PSU Commander, three serial supervisors, 18 constables, 3 drivers, equipped and trained to level 1(**Common Minimum Standard** and additional tactics dependent on force needs).

32.4.4 **Operational Support Medics**

The requirement for operational support medics, as first aid support, on an event or operation is determined by the risk assessment. They operate in pairs in order to protect one another and to evacuate a casualty away from the scene if necessary and are usually assigned to a PSU. They should be level 2 public order trained and trained in their role as medics.

32.4.5 **Evidence Gathering Teams**

An Evidence Gathering Team (EGT) is a team of usually two or three officers whose main role is to gather camera footage as evidence for a post-disorder investigation. They can:

- gather footage of offences and identify offenders for a post-event enquiry;
- gather footage of potential offenders for intelligence purposes;
- gather footage to justify police actions;
- calm a crowd by their presence (though it can incite them!).

Evidence Gatherers must be level 2 public order trained and Evidence Gatherer Trained.

They may be controlled by an **Intelligence Cell**, a **Bronze Commander**, or a PSU Commander.

32.4.6 **Forward Intelligence Teams**

Forward Intelligence Teams (FITs) are specially trained officers, who deploy in uniform in basic units of two or three,
to gather intelligence and information which is then passed
to the control room or Intelligence Cell. Their presence may
also have the effect of disrupting unlawful activities.

During outbreaks of disorder, they are expected to withdraw and be replaced with officers specially trained and
equipped to deal with disorder.

Ideally they are controlled by the Intelligence Cell and
have their own radio channel.

32.4.7 **Spotters**

Used extensively at football matches, spotters are officers who have a thorough knowledge of the **risk** element
associated with their affinitive club. Their role is to gather
information and intelligence to assist in the deployment of
resources. They have a key role in identifying offenders in
any post-disorder investigation.

Ideally they are controlled by the Intelligence Cell and
have their own radio channel.

32.4.8 **Dogs**

Deployed in pairs, dogs are good for supporting cordons,
escorting marches or groups, protecting key locations, and
for dispersal of a crowd. They need support when dispersing a crowd to consolidate the gains that they make, and
when making arrests, as the handler will have difficulty in
controlling a dog and a prisoner.

32.4.9 **Mounted Police**

Mounted police are good for gathering information on
crowd dynamics due to the height of the rider; as a show of
strength when supporting cordons; for escorting marches

or groups; and assisting with the dispersal of a crowd. They need support when dispersing a crowd to consolidate the gains that they make, and if they make an arrest.

32.4.10 Attenuated Energy Projectiles (AEPs— Formerly Baton Gunners)

The ACPO Guide to Keeping the Peace states that the objectives of AEPs are:

> To reduce the threat posed by specific individuals in order to protect life, prevent serious injury, or prevent substantial and serious damage to property (in circumstances likely to lead to loss of life/serious injury) during serious public disorder.

32.4.11 Logistics

Resources that have been deployed may need the support of a logistics officer whose role may simply be to provide officers with refreshment or anything else that they may need.

Depending on the size of the operation and the number of logistics officers, it is likely that they will be controlled directly by the Silver Control.

32.4.12 Prisoner Transport

In order that police personnel carriers are not taken away from their serials in order to transport prisoners, a prisoner transport vehicle may be available. Depending on the size of the operation, it is likely that such a resource will be controlled directly by the Silver Control.

32.5 Levels of Public Order Training

There are three levels of training for public order trained officers: level 3, level 2, and level 1.

32.5.1 Level 3

Level 3 trained officers are trained in **foot cordons**.

It is unlikely that Level 3 trained officers will be issued with any personal protective equipment.

Their level of training and protective equipment dictates that they can only be deployed where the threat level is relatively low.

32.5.2 Level 2

Level 2 trained officers are trained in the **Common Minimum Standard Tactics** (see section 32.8 below).

They will be issued with public order personal protective equipment, the nature of which varies between forces.

Their level of training and protective equipment allows them to be deployed to any type of public order incident.

32.5.3 Level 1

Level 1 trained officers are trained in the **Common Minimum Standard Tactics**, though more frequently than Level 2 trained officers, and additionally in other tactics depending on their Force's particular needs.

It is likely that the Level 1 trained officers form part of a team which both work and train together and are recognized as a highly effective public order resource.

32.5.4 Dress Codes

There are three nationally recognized public order dress codes: Code 1, Code 2, and Code 3. The amount of personal protective equipment and the types of personal protective equipment differs between forces.

Code 1

Full public order personal protective equipment including a shield (generally, long or intermediate for containment or buildings; round or short for dispersal).

Code 2

Personal protective equipment with normal street headgear and fluorescent jacket, if required, and with immediate access to NATO helmet and shield.

Code 3

Normal street uniform with personal protective equipment readily available.

32.5.5 Epaulet Colour Codes for Roles

To enable officers with specific roles to be easily identifiable, the guidelines from the ACPO Guide to Standards, Tactics and Training standardize this nationally in the event of officers working with other forces—see Table 32.1.

Table 32.1

Grey	Silver Commander
Yellow	Bronze Commander
Red	PSU Commander
White	Serial Supervisor
Royal Blue	Public Order Tactical Advisor
Orange	Evidence Gatherer
Green	Medic
Light Blue	AEPs

32.5.6 Helmet Markings

The ACPO Guide to Standards, Tactics and Training states that:

> A standardised layout for helmet markings is necessary for the ease of identification of officers engaged on **mutual aid**.

The recommendations are:

Front: Mutual aid force call sign and collar number

Rear: Mutual aid force call sign, divisional letter, rank for sergeants and above, and collar number.

32.6 **Command Structure**

The effectiveness of an operation can be attributed to its command structure. An understanding of the command structure for an operation and where a person fits into this structure will enable them to understand their role in relation to others. It will enable them to communicate with the correct people and ensure that they are in the right place at the right time.

There are three natural levels of command: strategic, tactical, and operational.

Strategic	Strategy can be summarized as the overall intention. In simple terms 'what' is to be achieved. The commander at this level is the 'Gold Commander'.
Tactical	Tactics are the methods used to achieve the strategy. In simple terms 'how' the strategy will be achieved. The commander at this level is the 'Silver Commander'.
Operational	The operational level is where the tactics are carried out. In simple terms the 'action'. A commander at this level is a 'Bronze Commander'.

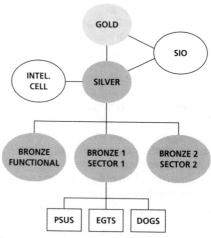

Figure 32.1

32.6.1 The Role and Responsibilities of Gold

A Gold Commander operates at force level. For large incidents or events they may have a 'Gold Control' from where they manage the event or incident together with a 'Gold Support' team to assist them. Though they have a number of responsibilities, their main ones are to:

- have overall command;
- set the strategy;
- supply resources.

In reality, Gold Control will only open for incidents which will have a major impact on the force and in most cases, having set the strategy the Gold Commander merely ensures that they are available to the Silver Commander if required.

32.6.2 The Role and Responsibilities of Silver

A Silver Commander generally operates at divisional level. They have a control room known as 'Silver Control' which is usually within the nearest police station with suitable facilities and a team of support staff, known as 'Silver Support' who assist them to run it.. Though they have a number of responsibilities their main ones are to:

- set the tactical plan to achieve Gold's strategy;
- ensure the tactical plan is carried out.

32.6.3 The Role and Responsibilities of Bronze

Depending on the size of the operation, there is likely to be more than one Bronze Commander. Each is given an area of responsibility which is either geographical or functional. They are assisted by Bronze Support, a team which may consist of a staff officer, a driver if in a vehicle, a tactical advisor, and a logist.

Geographical Bronze

A geographical Bronze Commander is given responsibility for a specific geographical area known as a 'sector'. They will be responsible for carrying out the tactical plan within that sector and are given resources by the Silver Commander to achieve this.

If resources move on to another sector they should inform the appropriate Bronzes so that one Bronze knows that they have given up resources and another knows that they have gained resources. Should the new sector be operating on a different radio channel then the resources must change to the appropriate channel. See Figure 32.2 for an example of sectorization.

Figure 32.2: An Example of Sectorisation

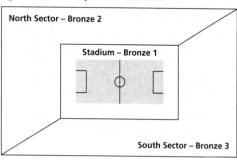

Functional Bronze

A functional bronze commander is given the responsibility for a specific function. An example of a functional Bronze Commander is where when policing a march, the responsibility for the marchers is given to a Bronze Commander, and this may cut across geographical sectors. They are responsible for carrying out the tactical plan in relation to the march and are given resources by the Silver Commander to achieve this.

There are other functional roles which are given the designation of 'Bronze' that, unless a very big incident or event, are unlikely to be fully trained Bronze Commanders but have a 'Bronze' function. Common examples are:

- Traffic Bronze
- Intelligence Bronze
- Dog Bronze.

32.6.4 Senior Investigating Officer

It is likely that at some point a Senior Investigating Officer (SIO) will be appointed for a post-disorder investigation in the event of serious disorder or potentially serious disorder. Depending on the size and nature of the disorder, this may not be a trained SIO but may be a detective constable who has been given the designation of SIO.

The SIO should be available to Gold to assist in the setting of the strategy if required. They should be available to Silver to assist both in the planning and during the event if required.

They should be able to assist the Silver Commander with information on the use of legislation and arrest policy and manage prisoner handling. They may also wish to give some direction as to what they expect from any evidence gathering teams.

32.6.5 Intelligence Cell

The role of the Intelligence Cell is one of providing the Silver Commander with up to the minute information and intelligence updates. They may have covert human intelligence sources (CHIS) providing them with up to date intelligence which they can pass on to Silver as appropriate. They may take on the role of contacting other forces or other agencies on behalf of Silver. They may have control of any spotters, evidence gatherers, or forward intelligence teams who may update them with information. They may have information passed to them from the officers on the ground, who have engaged with the participants.

32.6.6 Communications

The command structure is only as good as its communications system. Accepted best practice is for every operation to have a command channel and an operational channel or channels.

The Command Channel

This enables the Silver Commander and the Bronze Commanders to communicate with one another uninterrupted and without being overheard.

The Operational Channel

This enables the Bronze Commanders to command and control their resources. The number of operational channels open depends on the size and nature of the operation. A large amount of resources means a large amount of traffic which reduces the ability to communicate.

32.6.7 Issues

Self-deployment

This is where resources attend an incident without being sent by their Bronze Commander. This is sometimes done from a desire to get involved, sometimes accidentally by not taking a safe route and stumbling across a disorder. The implications are that the Bronze Commander loses track of their resources.

Staying in Role

It is important that resources stay within their role. An evidence gatherer making an arrest may lose several post-disorder arrests' worth of footage.

If a PSU Commander deploys individual PCs they are bypassing the serial supervisor who then loses track of their resources.

Call Signs

All commanders must know the correct call signs of their resources and all resources must know their correct call signs and the correct call signs of their commanders. If this is not the case then commanders are unable to respond to events because they are unable to contact the appropriate resources who can sit through a whole operation unused. It is likely that all resources will be listed on the Operational Order with their correct call sign. Any changes must be communicated to everyone who needs to know.

32.7 **Mutual Aid and the Police National Mobilization Plan**

All police forces could potentially require assistance from other forces or be required to provide assistance to other forces.

If a force has insufficient resources and specialists to manage and resolve the event then in the first instance they are likely to look to local mutual aid agreements with neighbouring forces. If resources or specialists are required beyond the **local mutual aid agreement** (where neighbouring forces have a local agreement to provide mutual aid) then **mobilization event** protocols are activated (where a request is made to the PNICC for additional resources nationally). The force, through their Chief Officer Team or Duty Gold Commander must contact the **Police National Information and Co-ordination Centre** (PNICC) who will deliver the additional resources.

32.8 **Common Minimum Standards**

When a force is faced with an incident or event for which it has insufficient resources then a request has to be made for assistance from other forces. To facilitate this the PNICC has a National Mobilisation Plan. This states that:

A key component of the police national mobilisation plan is that resources from different forces can work together during a mobilisation event.

To facilitate this there has to be a commonality in standards tactics and training of public order trained officers and specialist resources as set out in the ACPO Guide to Standards Tactics and Training. Below are the tactics which comprise the national common minimum standard as set out in the ACPO guide.

32.8.1 Level 3

Static cordons	A line of officers used across a given expanse, to either prevent, or restrict, the movement of persons.
Marching cordons	A line of officers used to escort a large group of persons from one place to another. Sometimes referred to as a 'bubble'.
Wedge	A wedge or 'V' formation of officers which can be forced into a crowd to reach a given point within.

32.8.2 Level 2

Level 3 tactics plus:

Free running shield line	Free running shield line—a line of officers with shields.
	Attack from the rear—dealing with an attack from the rear.
	Tactical withdrawal—a withdrawal to gain some advantage.
Junctions	Wheeling—turning a corner whilst maintaining the shield line.
	Three-sided box—the taking of a crossroads with shield lines.
	T junction—The taking of a 'T' junction with shields.
	Left and right junction—the taking of a left or right hand junction with shields.
Mixed shield dispersal	The alternate use of short shields to gain ground and longer shields to consolidate the gains.

Deployment from vehicles	The deployment of officers from vehicles with shields as a tactic.
Dealing with injured officer	How to protect an injured officer when deployed with shields.
Enclosed space tactics	How to enter a building and search a corridor with shields.
Climbing stairways	How to climb stairways with shields.
Violent person— room entry	How to deal with a violent person in a room.
Petrol reception	How to deal with a petrol bomb.

32.9 **Shield Tactics**

32.9.1 **Frontal Assault**

The police advance head on towards the crowd with the intention of dispersing them.

Considerations

The crowd must have an exit route. The compression of a large crowd could cause crushing and the crowd may be forced to stand their ground and fight.

The focus of the crowd will be on the officers facing them who, if under heavy missile attack run a high risk of injuries.

32.9.2 **Flanking Movement**

The police engage the crowd both head on and from one of their sides with the intention of dispersing them.

Considerations

The crowd must have an exit route. The compression of a large crowd could cause crushing and the crowd may be forced to stand their ground and fight.

The focus of the crowd will be split.

The police resources must be coordinated.

32.9.3 Pincer Movement

The police engage the crowd head on and from two sides with the intention of dispersing them in a specific direction.

Considerations

The crowd must have an exit route. The compression of a large crowd could cause crushing and the crowd may be forced to stand their ground and fight.

The focus of the crowd will be split.

The police resources must be coordinated.

32.9.4 Attack Against Their Rear

The police engage the crowd both head on and from their rear with the intention of disorienting and dispersing them.

Considerations

The crowd must have an exit route. The compression of a large crowd could cause crushing and the crowd may be forced to stand their ground and fight.

The focus of the crowd will be split and the crowd disoriented.

The police resources must be coordinated.

32.9.5 Tactical Withdrawal

Police withdraw seemingly as a sign of weakness to entice a hostile crowd to follow, thereby leading them away from their established position or drawing them into a position which is advantageous to the police.

32.9.6 **Diversion**

Something done to distract the attention of the crowd from the main police tactic.

32.9.7 **Feint**

A mock assault to distract attention from the main police tactic.

32.10 **Conflict Management Model**

The Conflict Management Model is designed to assist with the resolution of conflict. It is used in relation to public order, firearms, and officer safety. While the structure of the basic model remains the same (see Figure 32.3) there are variations between them. The ACPO Guide to Keeping the Peace outlines the Conflict Management Model in relation to public order.

Figure 32.3

Information/Intel	To establish the nature of the problem.
Threat Assessment	To evaluate the threat posed by the problem. This goes beyond the threat of disorder and disruption and could include such threats as:
	- the threat to commerce
	- the threat to the police reputation
	- the political threat, etc.
Powers and Policy	To establish what legal powers there are to deal with the problem, and what local, force, or national guidelines are.
Tactical Options	To establish what the options are for action.
Action	Effecting the Tactical Options.

32.10.1 The Potential Consequences of not using the Conflict Management Model

The temptation in any disorder situation when given information or intelligence is to react, ie to shortcut the Conflict Management Model by going straight to action.

By missing out 'threat assessment' there is no evaluation of the size and nature of the threat. This could result in an overreaction by the police, or worse, that officers are put at risk because the incident is under-resourced.

Under-resourcing will also mean that to respond effectively, fewer resources must respond using a higher level of force.

By missing 'powers and policy' the police run the risk of litigation by doing something that they are not empowered to do.

By missing 'tactical options' the police may not respond in the most appropriate way.

32.10.2 How can the Conflict Management Model be Used?

The Conflict Management Model will assist an officer to achieve:

- an appropriate and lawful response;
- appropriate resourcing;
- justification for police action when completing a pocket note book or log.

32.11 Basic Advice for Operating in a Public Order Environment

It is easy in a public order situation or potential public order situation for officers to put themselves at risk. Below is some basic advice for minimizing risk to officers.

KEY POINTS

- In situations of potential public order officers may choose to operate in pairs to look out for each other.
- Should a pair go to deal with something, the rest of the serial or PSU may choose to maintain line of sight so that if anyone encounters difficulties they can get help.
- If a pair of officers enter a premises such as a public house, consideration should be given to having a pair of officers on the door maintaining line of sight with the rest of the serial or PSU in the event of the first officers encountering difficulties. This may be particularly relevant for football spotters searching for risk supporters.
- If arresting a person who is resisting in a public order situation, consider allowing a minimum number of officers to assist with the arrest. Those not involved must place themselves between the arrested person and the rest of the crowd. This is firstly

because too many officers trying to arrest a person get in each other's way, and secondly to prevent the rest of the crowd from intervening.

- If restraining a person, consider the moderated ground pin as an alternative to the ground pin. By applying the ground pin with the prisoner in a public order situation an officer is vulnerable to assault. With the moderated ground pin the officer is on their feet, less vulnerable, and able to react.
- If working with police dogs, be aware of their presence. Do not rush in front of a police dog because they will not discriminate between a police officer and an offender. If there is a need to speak to a handler, approach from the side and get their attention before moving closer.
- If protected officers are deployed wearing NATO helmets then the threat level deems that protection necessary. If an officer is unprotected then they probably should not be there.

32.12 **First at the Scene**

If first at the scene of a public order incident an officer should consider the mnemonic SAD CHALET which is applied to major incidents. Dependant on the size and nature of the incident, they should consider using what is relevant.

It is easy to be impulsive and to try to deal with smaller incidents of disorder; however, the Control Room must know the location and type of incident in order that they know where to send resources and how many, in the event that the officer cannot manage.

Mnemonic—SAD CHALET	
Survey	= Survey the scene from a distance having regard to your personal safety.
Assess	= Assess the incident.
Disseminate	= Disseminate the information below to your control room.

Casualties	= Approximate number and type of casualties.
Hazards	= Present and potential.
Access	= Best routes and Rendezvous Point (RVP).
Location	= Exact location.
Emergency Services	= Emergency services required.
Type of Incident	= Size and nature.

32.12.1 Survey

By surveying the scene from a distance in so far as possible the officer can get an overview and a true picture of the disorder in order that accurate information can be gleaned.

32.12.2 Assess

An assessment can be made of how large the disorder is, what the risk is to the participants, the public, other resources attending the officer at the scene.

32.12.3 Disseminate

All relevant information is passed on to the Control Room in order that appropriate further resources can be dispatched. What further resources are needed must be stated.

32.12.4 Casualties

There are likely to be casualties at a disorder; however, it is unlikely that the ambulance service will attend a major disorder as most ambulance services have guidelines dictating how close they should get to disorder.

32.12.5 Hazards

Common hazards at a major disorder are such things as cars overturned and set alight, missiles, petrol bombs, lighting extinguished, barricades.

32.12.6 Access

To avoid further resources driving into an ambush or driving into danger, give the Control Room a safe route or safe direction of approach—ideally an RVP where further resources attending can be met and briefed before deploying.

32.12.7 Location

The Control Room needs to know where to dispatch further resources.

32.12.8 Emergency Services

What other emergency services are required? Major disorder often involves fires.

32.12.9 Type of Incident

In order that the response is appropriate the Control Room needs to know the type of incident. The response to a fight outside a nightclub is likely to be different to major urban disorder or a direct action protest.

32.12.10 Request other Resources

If an officer can deal with the situation then they should. They should not attempt the impossible. While the public often believe police officers to be superhuman they are not. If they put themselves in too much risk then who is going to rescue them? If they cannot deal then they must gather evidence, maintaining an overview if possible until sufficient resources arrive. An explanation must be given to the public to account for police apparent inactivity. This has to be balanced against the duty of a police officer and the risk to the public or to any individual. Police do a risky job and while they try to minimize risk they cannot always eliminate it.

At this stage the first officer at the scene is the person with the most information. When resources arrive they must brief appropriate personnel either taking charge and directing resources or passing to an appropriate person or supervisor.

32.13 **Responses to Threat**

32.13.1 **Tactical Options**

The ACPO Manual of Guidance on Keeping the Peace lists a number of tactical options available, mainly though not exclusively to a Bronze Commander. These are:

- normal policing;
- community mediators—the engaging with key individuals or groups within the community;
- directed response—the tasking of resources based on intelligence;
- Forward Intelligence Teams (FITs)—specially trained teams to overtly gather intelligence;
- Evidence Gathering Teams (EGTs)—specially trained teams to overtly gather evidence on footage;
- barriers—to assist with managing and controlling crowd movement;
- air support—to provide an overview;
- protected officers—officers with public order personal protective equipment;
- Tactical Support Group/Task Force (TSG)—highly trained public order resource;
- Police Support Units (PSU)—1 PSU Commander, 3 serial supervisors, 18 constables, 3 drivers, with protected personnel carriers properly equipped and trained (can include 2 operational support medics);
- cordons and intercepts—officers deployed to manage the movement of pedestrians and vehicles;

- obstacle/protestor removal—to remove anything or anyone designed to delay or obstruct;
- artificial lighting—to illuminate a specific area;
- stand off/regroup to withdraw safely when under threat;
- shield tactics—the coordinated deployment of officers with shields;
- batons—the use of batons as a group tactic;
- arrest teams—teams specially trained to make arrests;
- mounted police;
- police dogs;
- vehicle tactics—the specific use of vehicles as a tactic;
- screening smoke—used to conceal police tactics;
- water cannon—to keep crowds at a distance and disperse them;
- Attenuating Energy Projectile (AEP)—to reduce the threat posed by specific individuals in certain circumstances;
- CS agents—to disperse groups during incidents of large scale disorder (this does not refer to the CS spray that individual officers carry);
- firearms—for lethal threat.

32.14 How an Officer May Encounter a Public Order Incident and What Should be Done

This section highlights offences common to all situations of public disorder. It then lists types of disorder, covering a brief description, tactics of participants, and police response where appropriate, likely tactical options, and further legislation.

32.14.1 Offences Common to all Disorder

There are certain offences that are likely to be committed wherever there is disorder, ranging from a small street fight to a football match or a protest.

- Public Order Act 1986, section 2 (Violent Disorder);
- Public Order Act 1986, section 3 (Affray);
- Public Order Act 1986, section 4 (Fear or Provocation of Violence);
- Public Order Act 1986, section 4A (Intentional harassment, alarm, or distress);
- Public Order Act 1986, section 5 (Threatening/abusive words/behaviour);
- Breach of the Peace (*R v Howell* (1981) 3 All ER 383 CA).

32.14.2 Powers Common to all Disorder

Likewise there are certain police powers that are available wherever there is or is likely to be disorder.

- Criminal Law Act 1967, section 3 (Lawful use of force);
- Police and Criminal Evidence Act 1984, section 117 (Lawful use of force);
- Common Law (Lawful use of force);
- Criminal Justice and Public Order Act 1994, section 60 (Power to stop and search in a locality);
- Criminal Justice and Public Order Act 1994, section 60aa (Powers to require removal of disguises);
- Breach of the Peace (*Moss and others v McClachlan* (1985) 149 JP 167 QBD).

32.14.3 Disorderly Behaviour

Patrol and response officers are likely to routinely encounter disorderly behaviour, particularly on a Friday and Saturday night. It may be sufficient to deal with the offenders for anti-social behaviour; however, there may be a need, and an expectation from the public, that the offenders are removed.

Legislation

- Police Reform Act 2002, section 50 (Persons acting in an anti-social manner);
- Criminal Justice Act 1967, section 91(1) (Drunk and disorderly).

32.14.4 Small Street Fight

If attending a small street fight an officer should apply the mnemonic SAD CHALET before rushing to get involved. They should consider the offences outlined in the summary of offences common to all disorder. When sufficient resources arrive and the disorder has stopped, they should consider the potential for the disorder to resume, isolate the factions, and make arrests as appropriate; the need to obtain an authorization under section 60 of the Criminal Justice and Public Order Act 1994 to search them for weapons; the need to remove one or both factions from the scene to prevent further disorder. This can be justified to prevent a Breach of the Peace. Reasonable force can be used to achieve this and ultimately arrests can be made to prevent a Breach of the Peace. A balance often has to be struck, however, between the need to make an arrest with the fact that arrests diminish the number of officers left at the scene. If available, consideration should be given to the use of an Evidence Gathering Team to record footage both to justify police actions and to gather information on and identify persons involved which may assist with any post-disorder enquiry.

Likely Tactical Options

- normal policing;
- directed response;
- EGTs;
- police dogs.

32.14.5 Urban Disorder

Incidents of urban disorder have often been an expression of social unrest. Where there is social unrest and tension within a locality, there is a danger that even a very minor incident can be the trigger that sets off major urban disorder.

Offender Tactics

Common tactics used by offenders during incidents of urban disorder are to set fire to something, either a building or a car, in order to entice the emergency services to attend. When they do attend they are ambushed and attacked with missiles and petrol bombs. Another ploy has been to attack electricity sub-stations, causing the area to be in darkness to further hamper the emergency services. Barricades are often constructed to prevent police access.

Police Action

It is vital that officers are aware of the dangers of becoming isolated during these situations. Until the appropriate resources arrive, there may be no one to assist them if they get into difficulties.

If the threat is one of heavy missile attack or petrol bombs then only protected officers are equipped and trained to be in the vicinity and if not then the officers must be withdrawn.

It is likely that normal policing will be suspended. If there are sufficient police resources the offenders will be dispersed. If not then it is likely that the strategy will be to contain the disorder to prevent it spreading and growing until enough resources arrive to disperse the offenders. There is likely to be a post-disorder investigation.

Likely Tactical Options

- EGTs;
- Air support;

- protected officers;
- Tactical Support Group;
- PSUs;
- cordons and intercepts;
- obstacle removal;
- artificial lighting;
- stand-off regroup;
- shield tactics;
- batons;
- vehicle tactics;
- AEPs;
- firearms.

Further Legislation

- Public Order Act 1984, section 1 (Riot).

32.14.6 Protest

Protest has many forms including such events as major political demonstrations in a city centre; animal liberationists at a farm, or laboratory, or fur outlet; local residents at a mobile phone mast, to give but a few examples.

Major political demonstrations consist of a majority of law-abiding citizens but are likely to attract a minority of extremists who are prepared to cause damage and to attack police lines.

Protestor Tactics

The more extreme and organized protest groups have numerous tactics including such things as tripods and lock-ons. A tripod, made from long scaffold poles, is erected on a road and then someone will climb up and harness themselves to the top. This serves the purpose of stopping traffic, is a focus for the crowd, and a platform from which to gather information and to direct resources.

A lock-on is where a person locks themselves onto something, such as a vehicle, so that it cannot be used. They may lock themselves together in a human chain, putting their arms in pipes so that the police cannot unlock them without cutting through the pipe. By lying in the highway they can succeed in closing a highway.

It is likely to take some considerable time to move a tripod and particularly a good lock-on.

A common tactic of organized protest groups is to test the legality of police action. They have a good knowledge of relevant legislation and police powers and deploy their own evidence gatherers. They actively seek the opportunity to complain about police action. They will actively seek to be arrested, prove it to be an unlawful arrest, and claim compensation which is returned to their campaign funds.

Certain protest groups, who may be protesting against an organization such as those involved with animal research, use the tactic of not only protesting outside the premises, but also outside the homes of employees, and will even target other organizations or persons who have any dealings with the main target organization.

Police Response

The police must adopt an impartial position, neither siding with the protestors or the persons, organizations, or institutions that they are protesting about. The police role is to uphold the law.

For a march or an assembly, even as small as two persons, conditions can be set by police under sections 12 and 14 of the Public Order Act 1984 respectively.

If tripods or lock-ons have been used, as soon as a police officer engages with a person on a tripod or a person who is locked-on, they assume some responsibility for their safety. It will require a specially trained team to deal with them.

Officers should try to avoid making arrests for Breach of the Peace if possible—it has often been possible for protestors to get compensation for unlawful arrest and unlawful detention. If making an arrest, an officer should get this filmed by an Evidence Gathering Team. Some specimens of wording to be used upon arrest are available.

Likely Tactical Options

- FIT;
- EGT;
- barriers;
- protected officers;
- TSG;
- PSUs;
- cordons and intercepts;
- obstacle/protestor removal;
- shield tactics;
- batons;
- arrest teams;
- mounted police;
- police dogs;
- vehicle tactics.

Legislation

- Criminal Justice & Public Order Act 1994, Section 68 (Aggravated Trespass);
- Criminal Justice and Public Order Act 1994, Section 69 (Power to remove persons participating in aggravated trespass);
- Highways Act 1980, section 137 (Wilful Obstruction of the Highway);
- Public Order Act 1984, section 12 (Imposing Conditions on Public Processions);
- Public Order Act 1984, section 14 (Imposing Conditions on Public Assembly);
- Criminal Justice and Public Order Act 1994, section 42 (Harassment in the vicinity of a dwelling);
- Serious Organised Crime and Police Act 2005, section 145 (Interference with contractual relationships so as to harm animal research organizations);
- Serious Organised Crime and Police Act 2005, section 146 (Intimidation of persons connected with animal research organizations).

32.14.7 **Industrial**

Industrial disputes usually involve public disorder when persons blockade the entrance to premises in order to stop persons or vehicles entering the premises to halt the activity of the organization.

The police must adopt an impartial position, neither siding with the protestors or the persons, organizations, or institutions that they are protesting about. The police role is to uphold the law.

Likely Tactical Options

- normal policing;
- EGTs;
- barriers;
- protected officers;
- TSGs;
- PSUs;
- cordons and intercepts;
- shield tactics;
- batons;
- arrest teams;
- mounted police;
- police dogs;
- vehicle tactics.

Legislation

- Trade Union and Labour Relations (Consolidation) Act 1992, section 241 (Intimidation by annoyance or violence to prevent lawful activity).

32.14.8 **Football**

There are two groups of persons who are likely to engage in disorder. Most football clubs have a group associated with them who actively seek to engage in pre-arranged acts of violence with equivalent groups associated with other clubs. These are referred to by the UK Football Policing Unit as 'risk'. The other group of persons who are likely to engage in disorder are genuine football supporters, not normally 'risk', who become passionate and emotional and are liable to engage in acts of spontaneous disorder. A local derby will often result in this behaviour.

'Risk' Tactics

Common tactics used by 'risk' supporters is to communicate with their opposition and arrange a time and place for the disorder. This is sometimes well away from the stadium.

They will avoid police detection by arriving on an indirect route. If using rail travel they may get off a few stops early. They may charter a coach on some pretext other than football, so that intelligence may not pick them up from the coach companies.

They will send 'runners' to make contact with the opposition in order to pre-arrange the disorder and will often leave the stadium early.

If unable to engage with their opposition, they will often 'trash' a public house known to be used by them.

Police Action

While risk supporters are generally more interested in fighting with each other than fighting the police, there are times when they are prepared to fight with the police. It is important for officers not to get isolated. Concourses under the stand can be dangerous.

If safe to do so, officers should engage with the risk supporters. They will often freely give useful information about their numbers and their movements which can be passed to the intelligence cell.

Should there be a need to remove someone from the stand it must be borne in mind that seating areas can be dangerous, particularly if the whole crowd in a particular area is hostile. Officers should consider waiting until the offender goes for refreshment, or consider filming the offender and doing a post-disorder arrest. If there is no choice then officers should ensure that there are sufficient resources present to deal with the incident and any further potential for disorder.

The most effective strategy against football offenders is to prevent them attending with the use of banning orders. EGTs can be a very effective resource to achieve this.

The ACPO Guide to Public Safety states that the core policing responsibilities at a public event are: the prevention and detection of crime; preventing or stopping breaches of the peace; traffic regulation within the legal powers provided by statute; and activation of contingency plans where there is an immediate threat to life. If policing inside a stadium, police officers must stick to these core responsibilities. Police officers are not stewards, and other responsibilities rest with the organizer.

Likely Tactical Options

- EGTs;
- protected officers;
- TSG;
- PSUs;
- cordons and intercepts;
- shield tactics;
- batons;
- arrest teams;
- mounted police;
- police dogs;
- vehicle tactics.

Legislation

- Football (Offences) Act 1991, section 2 (Throwing objects);
- Football (Offences) Act 1991, section 3 (Racial chants);
- Football (Offences) Act 1991, section 4 (Entering the playing area);

- Sporting Events (Control of Alcohol) Act 1991, section 1 (Alcohol on supporters' vehicle);
- Sporting Events (Control of Alcohol) Act 1991, section 2 (Drunk at a designated sporting event);
- Sporting Events (Control of Alcohol) Act 1991, section 2A (Possessing article or substance).

32.14.9 Raves

> **Definition**
>
> A Rave is a gathering on land in the open air of 20 or more people, whether they are trespassers or not, or if not in the open air, of 20 or more people who must be trespassers, which is not licensed by an entertainment licence at which amplified music is played at night, with or without intermissions, and by reason of its loudness and duration and the time at which is played it is likely to cause serious distress to the inhabitants of the locality, and includes such a gathering which continues during intermissions in the music and, where the gathering extends over several days, throughout the period during which amplified music is played at night (with or without intermissions).
>
> Criminal Justice and Public Order Act 1994, section 63

Tactics of Organizers

In order to avoid detection the organizers of a rave will advertise a network of telephone numbers to be used to direct rave-goers near to the venue before the final destination is given. The police therefore have no idea where the rave will take place until it may be too late to prevent it.

Police Response—Pre-Rave

The police strategy is likely to be to disrupt rather than displace the event.

It is likely that the early vehicles on the site will be those of the organizers. Officers first at the scene must apply the SAD

CHALET mnemonic. If there are sufficient police resources, section 64 of the Criminal Justice and Public Order Act gives the power to enter the land to see if a rave is taking place, and section 63 gives the power to direct the persons preparing for or waiting for the rave to leave the land and to remove any vehicles or property they have with them. If there are insufficient resources to deal, the police must gather intelligence, gather evidence for post-event investigation, explain the reason for inactivity to complainants, and maintain a police presence on the periphery if safe to do so.

The strategy at this stage is likely to be to contain those people already in attendance and to turn back people travelling towards or arriving at the rave location and prevent its escalation.

Police Response—During Rave

Once there are sufficient persons attending the rave it will prove very resource-intensive to halt it. Dealing with an established rave may overwhelm local police resources and this, combined with the fact that if the rave could be successfully closed it may let loose hundreds of persons under the influence of drugs into the locality, the police strategy is likely to be to contain it and to prevent other persons from attending.

An incursion by police into a rave can be dangerous, and if police resources do make an incursion then they must do so with sufficient numbers.

In order to close a rave, or at the end of the rave, the police strategy is likely to be to seize the sound systems and generators. Without the sound there is no rave. It is doubtful that any one will claim ownership through fear of prosecution possibly for public nuisance under common law or other offences.

Likely Tactical Options

- normal policing;
- directed response;
- FIT;

- EGT;
- air support;
- protected officers;
- TSG;
- PSUs;
- cordons and intercepts.

Legislation

- Criminal Justice and Public Order Act 1994, section 63(2) (Power to direct persons to leave);
- Criminal Justice and Public Order Act 1994, section 64 (Power to enter land to see if a rave is taking place and seize vehicles and equipment);
- Criminal Justice and Public Order Act 1994, section 65(4) (Direction not to proceed to rave);
- Proceeds of Crime Act 2002, section 294 (Cash seizure).

Chapter 33

Strategic Roads Policing

33.1 **Introduction**

Policing the roads so that people can go about their daily life safely and without being harmed or intimidated is a fundamental role of policing. For some time forces have been moving away from a traditional traffic response, and in 2005 a joint strategy agreed between the Association of Chief Police Officers (ACPO), the Department for Transport (DfT), and the Home Office, set roads policing in the context of a wider policing role. It is important for frontline staff outside roads policing to be aware of this specialist policing arena.

The purpose of the roads policing strategy was to establish the issues which are of continuing priority, and to identify the principles which should underpin operational practice and the development of policy. The strategy, which built upon the Government's road safety strategy 'Tomorrow's Roads—Safer for Everyone' from 2000, identified five key areas which would be the focus for roads policing:

- denying criminals the use of the roads by enforcing the law;
- reducing road casualties;
- tackling the threat of terrorism;
- reducing anti-social use of the roads;
- enhancing public confidence and reassurance by patrolling roads.

Although the structure and resource deployment varies considerably from force to force, the key elements of roads policing remain the same. A healthy level of coordination between forces, across the regions and nationally through a number of ACPO committees, ensures best practice is shared and activity is coordinated on a number of national campaigns. UK police forces are also active members of TISPOL, a European-wide roads policing organization that coordinates enforcement and education campaigns throughout Europe.

For the purpose of providing an explanation of the key elements of roads policing I will address policing practice under four headings:

- Road Death Investigation
- Casualty Reduction
- Policing the Strategic Road Network
- Denying Criminals the Use of the Roads.

33.2 **Road Death Investigation**

KEY POINT

Despite the reduction in road casualties over the last decade, 3,000 people die on the UK's roads each year and ten times that number are seriously injured. Each death and life-changing injury is a human tragedy from which families never truly recover. While the cost in human terms is all but impossible to quantify, the cost in financial terms has been the subject of significant consideration; some studies have placed the cost of a fatal collision at £1.5 million.

The standards and practices of road death investigation are set nationally by a document entitled the Road Death Investigation Manual. The document was originally based closely on the Murder Investigation Manual, and has been developed and improved through the experience and the sharing of best practice. The loss of a loved one in a road collision is no less traumatic than the loss of someone through any other form of unlawful killing, and the same exhaustive standards of investigation and rigorous supervision must be applied. Whether the final report is presented to a Crown Court in a criminal case or to the Coroner's Court in an inquest, the investigation reflects a search for the truth to identify how a person came to die and the person or persons responsible for that death.

33.2.1 Inquest-only Cases

In cases where the individual who has died is identified as being the person responsible for the collision, the investigation culminates in a file prepared for the Coroner's Court. The evidence will be presented to the coroner and in the presence of the family and other interested parties to enable the coroner to determine the cause of the individual's death.

33.2.2 Criminal Cases

In criminal investigations where a surviving person is suspected of being responsible for the death in a road collision, the investigation team will collate evidence to present to the Crown Prosecution Service (CPS) so that they might consider which criminal offence, if any, a person is to be charged with. The key offences are:

- causing death by dangerous driving;
- causing death by careless driving;
- causing death whilst uninsured or disqualified;
- causing death whilst under the influence of alcohol or drugs.

Causing Death by Careless Driving, Unlicensed, Disqualified, or Uninsured

Sections 20 and 21 of the Road Safety Act 2006 (effective from 18 August 2008) introduced two new offences of causing death by driving into the Road Traffic Act 1988:

- causing death by careless, or inconsiderate, driving (section 2B);
- causing the death of another person by driving a motor vehicle on a road whilst at the time of driving he/she is committing an offence of either driving otherwise than in accordance with a licence, whilst disqualified or when uninsured or unsecured against third party risks (section 3ZB).

When considering the section 3ZB offence, Parliament took the view that causing a death by driving in these circumstances required *no fault* on the part of the offending driver because the offender should not have been driving their vehicle on the road, the simple act of driving it when they should not have been doing so would be sufficient 'cause' to constitute the offence.

33.2.3 Corporate Manslaughter

The Corporate Manslaughter and Corporate Homicide Act implemented on 6 April 2008 created a new offence of Corporate Manslaughter:

- An organization to which this section applies is guilty of an offence if the way in which its activities are managed or organized:
  - causes a person's death, and
  - amounts to a gross breach of a relevant duty of care owed by the organization to the deceased.

Although the new offence was developed primarily to deal with incidents in the workplace and such tragedies as train crashes, the reality is that many road collisions could fall within the definition. Around a third of fatal crashes involve somebody driving in the course of their work. So in cases where the organization's response to an identified risk amounted to a gross breach of its duty of care and that became a contributory factor in a death (it no longer needs to be the primary cause) the organization may be liable.

At this time we have yet to see any cases to develop our understanding of the impact of the new offence, although incidents where matters of training, vehicle condition, or bad practice, such as driver schedules, all have the potential to be addressed by the new offence.

33.2.4 The Road Death Investigation Team

Whilst road collisions involving a fatality or serious injury may range from single vehicle to a mass pile-up, the structure of the investigation team follows a nationally accepted structure. The key roles are:

- Senior Investigating Officer (SIO)
- Investigating Officer
- Family Liaison Officer
- Forensic Collision Investigator
- Exhibits Officer.

In addition, a number of other specialists may also be involved in the investigation, particularly if the vehicles involved or the circumstances of the collision require specialist technical or scientific skills and experience. Organizations such as the Vehicle Operators Standards Agency (VOSA) and the Transport Road Laboratory (TRL) are regularly involved in complicated or high-profile collision investigations.

In serious injury collisions, where an individual suffers a life-changing injury, the standard of investigation should also comply with that set for road death investigation. In addition to the police's primary role of ensuring justice is delivered, the implications for a financial settlement through insurance companies and the ongoing care of somebody with consequently lifelong needs will undoubtedly be the subject of much scrutiny.

The careful investigation of collisions involving death and serious injury provides a vital source of information and knowledge which can be an important contribution to future casualty reduction initiatives.

33.3 **Casualty Reduction**

Some would say that the most important responsibility for roads policing is the reduction in the number of people killed and seriously injured in the UK. The Casualty Reduction Strategy of each force is built upon three main elements of activity:

- enforcement
- education
- engineering.

33.3.1 Enforcement

Enforcement as part of a Casualty Reduction Strategy focuses upon those offences which are most often the contributory factors in collisions causing death and serious injury on our roads. Those factors are:

- dangerous or careless driving;
- speed;
- seat belts;
- mobile phones;
- drugs/alcohol;
- vehicle defects.

Dangerous and Careless Driving

The enforcement of offences of dangerous and careless driving is an important strand of our efforts to reduce road casualties. Those who would drive dangerously or inconsiderately have a greater risk profile and are much more likely to be involved in a future fatal crash. Two-thirds of those involved in fatal collisions have either been involved in a less serious collision or in a moving traffic offence, such as speeding, before. Offences of dangerous and careless driving most often come to notice when officers are dealing with collisions. The practice of officers allowing drivers to exchange names and addresses and sort the collision out with their insurance companies represents a missed opportunity to deal with the driver at fault and divert them into education or training that would reduce their future risk.

Excess Speed

Excessive and inappropriate speed is a cause or aggravating factor in almost all collisions that result in serious injury or death. The damage and injury involved in a crash is multiplied dramatically with additional speed. There are many people who would be alive or not suffering life-changing injuries if the vehicle that collided with them had been driving at the speed limit. The responses of drivers when questioned and from the reckless behaviour of tailgating make it clear that many drivers do not know the stopping distance for their vehicle at the speed they are driving (see Table 33.1).

Table 33.1

Speed	Stopping Distance
30 mph	23 metres
40 mph	37 metres
50 mph	53 metres
60 mph	73 metres
70 mph	96 metres

Seat Belts

Despite seat belts being compulsory since the majority of drivers in the UK started to drive, there remains a significant proportion of drivers and passengers who do not regularly wear their seat belt. Worryingly, young men as drivers and young people as passengers are some of the worst at taking this simple but vital precaution. Research would suggest that close to 500 people a year that die in road collisions would have been saved had they worn their seat belt.

4 Protective Services

Mobile Phones

Despite the offence being made endorsable, a significant number of people still use their mobile phone for calls or texting whilst driving on our roads. A person's ability to concentrate on the task of driving is significantly impaired when focusing on a phone call or a text message, so much so, that they are four times more likely to be involved in a crash, and the impairment is that equivalent to someone driving whilst over the legal limit for alcohol.

Drinking and Driving

The offences of drunk in charge of a motor vehicle and driving whilst over the prescribed limit have for many years been seen as serious offences in the eyes of the law, and yet each year hundreds of people die as a direct result of drinking and driving in the UK. There are signs of an increase in the number of people prepared to drink and drive, particularly amongst young people, and this has perhaps been fuelled by complacency among police forces whose testing levels do not reflect the size of the problem in the driving population.

To tackle this most significant threat it is vital that police officers use the powers to breath-test drivers whenever that possibility occurs, particularly all those drivers involved in collisions. It is clear that the risk of being caught is a significant deterrent to those who would otherwise drink and drive, a good reason in itself for those who would encourage the Government to grant random testing powers to the police in the UK.

The UK will soon be the only country in Europe to retain the legal limit of 80 mg of alcohol in 100 ml of blood, while other countries now have a lower level, typically 50 mg of alcohol in 100 ml of blood.

Drug Driving

In the absence of roadside testing technology, no accurate data exists to identify the number of people driving on the UK's roads whilst under the influence of, and impaired by, drugs, either prescribed medicines or illegal substances. The only reliable evidence comes from post-mortems which showed in 2006 that one in every five drivers who die whilst in charge of a motor vehicle are found to have illegal drugs in their system.

While the efforts continue to design, test, and approve roadside screening devices for drugs, there is a strong voice of opinion calling for driving with any illegal drug in one's system to be an offence; we are currently faced with a situation that to walk down the street with a controlled drug in one's pockets, no matter how small an amount, is an offence, whilst to drive down the road with that same drug in your body is not in itself an offence. At this time police must rely on Fitness Impairment Testing (FIT) to have grounds for arrest before testing at the police station, and the evidence of a medical practitioner is required.

Vehicle Defects

There are a large range of offences which deal with the construction and use of vehicles and vehicle parts on our roads. Such matters as lighting, tyres, brakes, and other equipment are all important to ensure that a motor vehicle can be used safely on the road. These things are important for cars and particularly important for large goods vehicles and public service vehicles (PSVs), where, because of their size and the number of people PSVs carry, the risks of multiple injury or death are even more significant.

Document Offences

To drive a motor vehicle on the road, individuals must be licensed and vehicles tested to ensure that they do not pose a threat to other road users. Examination of documentation plays an important part in ensuring the safety of road users and that those who have been disqualified from driving are brought to justice when they continue to do so. Document offences are also of significant importance when it comes to denying criminals the use of the road, as you will see later in this chapter.

33.3.2 Education

A significant amount of research has been undertaken to identify those who are most vulnerable on our roads and also those whose risks can be effectively addressed by improving their awareness and knowledge through education. The DfT have invested significantly in their 'Think!' campaign which is targeted at key groups throughout the year.

Diversion schemes play an important part in the Casualty Reduction Strategies of police forces, where drivers detected committing offences are offered an educational alternative to a fine or the endorsement of penalty points on their driving licence. Nationally, the Driver Improvement Scheme as an alternative to prosecution for careless driving has been in place for some time, and was joined in 2008 by the adoption of a national standard course for speed awareness for those detected by police officers or cameras at the lower ranges of speed violation (see Table 33.2).

Table 33.2

Speed limit	Diversion range
30 mph	35–39 mph
40 mph	46–50 mph
50 mph	57–61 mph
60 mph	68–72 mph
70 mph	79–83 mph

In addition, some forces, together with academic institutions and other service providers, have developed education courses for offences such as the use of mobile phones and not wearing seat belts. Specific courses aimed at vulnerable groups irrespective of the offence committed have also been developed for motorcyclists and young drivers under the age of 25. The RiDE programme, for motorcyclists, was originally piloted by 11 forces across England and Wales in 2008.

Safer Roads Partnerships

Police forces together with local highways authorities, the courts, and the CPS are members locally of the Safer Roads Partnerships. Originally the partnerships dealt only with camera enforcement of speeding offences and were financed through a system of hypothecation. Since the changes in the funding arrangements in 2007 these partnerships, funded by a supplement to the Local Transport Plan, are able to engage in a wide range of road safety initiatives.

Partnerships also act as a conduit to a not-for-profit organization called Road Safety Services (RSS). This organization can be of great assistance to local police forces when faced with very technical defences to offences committed by those who can afford to engage the best barristers in an effort to undermine police enforcement technology.

A wide range of road safety initiatives, many aimed at children and young people, involving partners such as the Fire Brigade and road safety organizations, are evidence of the commitment of all those engaged in this arena to reduce the number of people killed and injured on our roads.

Vulnerable Groups

Experience and research has focused the energy of the police and other partners on a number of particularly vulnerable groups of motorists. These groups may change over time; of particular concern at this time are young drivers and motorcyclists.

Young Drivers

Drivers under the age of 25 make up just one in every 15 motorists on our roads, and complete significantly less mileage than older drivers, and yet they make up nearly a third of those killed on our roads and a quarter of those charged with death by dangerous driving. In a range of driving behaviours and attitudes, this group are identified as a growing problem. Given also their influence on their peers that will follow them as drivers in the years to come, this is a particularly worrying trend.

Academic research has shown that brain development is not complete in humans until around 25 years of age and that the last element to mature, the frontal lobes, is the part that deals with the executive functions such as planning, risk awareness, and the ability to foresee the consequences of one's actions. Whilst this is a valuable product of human development when it comes to sending young men to the front line in times of war, it is a significant disadvantage when it comes to driving.

Motorcyclists

Motorcycles account for just 1 per cent of the vehicle miles driven in the UK and yet they make up 20 per cent of the deaths. Motorcyclists are particularly vulnerable, and although many of them are some of the most competent drivers on our roads, their propensity to drive at the very edge of their ability places them at significant risk.

A large number of motorcycle collisions involve only a single vehicle. A common profile for those that perish is a 40-something male who is a new or returning biker. Such profiled information is very important in ensuring education and awareness campaigns can be specifically targeted at those most at risk.

Engineering

Engineering solutions to deliver casualty reduction are primarily the responsibility of the Highways Agency and the local highways authorities; that said the police, generally through specialist Traffic Management staff, are consulted on new and changed road developments and also examine the scene of all fatal collisions to ensure any engineering contributory factors are addressed.

33.4 Policing the Strategic Road Network

The integrity of the motorways and the arterial routes, and the safety of those using them, are a vital element of strategic roads policing. The environment of motorways and other key trunk roads is such that the policing response to incidents and events must be led by specially trained and competent police officers. In casualty terms, motorways are some of the safest roads in the UK, but when things go wrong there is the potential for catastrophic consequences, and the cost to the UK of congestion on the core network is measured in billions of pounds per annum. Whilst the motorways and trunk roads of the UK represent just 4 per cent of the overall length of roads, they experience 36 per cent of all the vehicle kilometres travelled each year and as such, are a key element of the UK's economic infrastructure.

This special environment, the types of incidents and events that occur on it, and the range of agencies involved is reflected in the practice advice document published by the National Police Improvement Agency (NPIA) in 2007 entitled The Policing of Roads. This comprehensive document is a very useful source of detailed information relating to the subjects I will cover more generally in this part of the chapter. The generic role of police officers in everything they do is to protect life and property, to preserve order, to prevent the commission of offences, to bring offenders to justice, and to perform any duty or responsibility that arises from any common or statute law. All of the activities that the police, together with the other partners, undertake on the strategic road network are aimed at fulfilling this role.

33.4.1 Incident Management

It is vital that the police work with other agencies and partners to deal effectively with incidents and events on

the strategic road network. However, overall primac
of the scene of incidents on the network remains th
responsibility of the police, particularly to coordinat
the emergency response of the other emergency service
The Civil Contingencies Act 2004, intended to enhance th
resilience of the UK to major disruptive incidents, sets ou
the roles and responsibilities of those services that respon
to the full range of emergencies, from local major incident
through to catastrophic events. Given the specialist ski
and capability of all those involved in such incidents, it i
particularly important that the services and agencies wor
together in a coordinated and effective manner.

The nature of incidents on the strategic road networ
dictates that specific training and practices are adopte
to ensure the safety of those involved and those wh
respond. The key mnemonic, ACE CARD, used to guid
those responding to incidents on the motorway, is feature
heavily in specialist training.

Mnemonic

A = Approach—Consider the most appropriate approach

C = Caution—Caution signs (police emergency or Matrix signs)

E = Examine—Examine the scene

C = Casualties

A = Ambulance, fire and rescue, and other partnership agencies

R = Remove the obstructions

D = Detailed investigation

This systematic process for assessing and dealing with th
incident is critical to the safety of those already involved
those responding, and those approaching the scene a
high speed on the motorway. Officers should resist rush
ing straight to the scene and becoming involved withou
implementing necessary safety measures, and this is wh
approach and caution signs are important elements to b
addressed before officers engage in their responsibilitie
at the incident. Trained officers and other responders ar
given clear guidance on the placement of signs and vehicle

o protect the scene appropriately. An examination of the topping distance of vehicles (see Table 33.3) makes officers appreciate how far back such safety measures as cones need to be placed.

Table 33.3

Speed	Stopping distance
60 mph	73 metres
70 mph	96 metres
80 mph	123 metres
90 mph	153 metres
100 mph	186 metres

186 metres represents 47 car lengths. These figures are based on a reaction time of 0.68 seconds and this is generally accepted as being too quick; for the average driver it is generally between 1 and 2 seconds. The figures are also based on dry road surfaces in good condition, and assume that the vehicle's braking system is in a good, well-maintained condition. The distance will significantly increase on a damp/wet surface or where the road surface is poor. The figures are for motorcars. Commercial vehicles (transit vans, HGVs, or PSVs) will be considerably greater.

Having taken care of the safety of the environment, the next step is to examine the scene and make an effective report to the police control room for the benefit of all agencies attending. The report is best given following pneumonic SAD CHALETS, which is explained below. In accordance with the policing priorities, the first task is to identify and assess all the casualties involved, and this in turn will help to identify the need for ambulances, fire and rescue, and other partnership agencies.

To enable other agencies and specialist resources to attend it will be necessary to remove obstructions, and in due course the removal of vehicles and other debris will be required for the reinstatement of normal road use. However, it is vital that officers are aware of their responsibility for the preservation of evidence and scene management, and that nothing is done that would thwart that responsibility for securing evidence. Vehicles and other items should not be moved without the express permission of the Senior Investigating Officer (SIO) or the responsible person from the relevant investigatory body. All incidents that involve death or injury are the subject of detailed investigation, and the integrity of the evidential scene is the responsibility of the police.

Given the economic impact and disruption of closing the motorway, it is not surprising that such instances often bring into sharp focus the competing expectations of some of the agencies involved. Whilst the police must be conscious of the impact of the incident, the integrity of evidence is paramount and cannot be regained once it is lost. Vehicles travelling through a crime scene have been known to disperse and carry away the evidence from incidents and a requirement to travel half way across the country to recover a body part is not a pleasant task.

Sad Chalets

This nationally adopted mnemonic identifies the responsibility of the first officer on the scene and gives a checklist of those things that are important to report for the benefit of a coordinated response.

Mnemonic

S = Survey

A = Assess

D = Disseminate

C = Casualties (the numbers of injured, uninjured and dead)

H = Hazard (those present and potential to all at scene at in the vicinity)

A = Access (the best routes for the emergency services to attend and to leave the scene)

L = Location (exact, using common language description)

E = Emergency (services and other agencies required)

T = Type of incident (description that accurately reflects the situation and response required)

S = Safety (all aspects of Health and Safety and risk assessment must be considered by all staff working at or close to the scene)

NB: Reassessment of all these things will be required at regular intervals to ensure the response is effective and remains so.

33.4.2 Health and Safety

The strategic road network is a hazardous environment and those who work there must be given specialist training to do so safely. The most obvious risk is the speed of other vehicles, and people engaged in responding to incidents on the network must be conspicuous and alert at all times. Other risks, such as exposure to harsh weather conditions, high levels of stress from dealing with traumatic incidents, the presence of hazardous materials, and the issues of manual handling are all matters that must be addressed through training, resourcing, and care of staff. Given the responsibility to the police for the overall coordination of incidents on the strategic road network, the safety of all those engaged is an issue for the police service.

33.4.3 Enhance Public Confidence and Reassurance by Patrolling Roads

This long-standing policing role is a key element in national Roads Policing strategy. Given the number of people who travel on our strategic road network, it is important that the visibility of police officers and other emergency responders is maintained to provide public reassurance. The speed at which incidents can develop and escalate demand that the police are able to respond very quickly in this environment and it is clear that the visibility of roads policing on the network is an important factor in maintaining the law abiding behaviour of those who use the road system.

33.4.4 Tackling the Threat of Terrorism

The importance of the strategic road network and its vulnerability is not lost on terrorists, and consequently the network has been the subject of terrorist attacks and threats intended to cause major devastation or disruption to the everyday life of the citizens of the UK. The road network is also used to facilitate or enable such attacks, and service areas have been used as meeting points for those engaged in terrorist activity. The Government's counter-terrorist strategy (CONTEST) has four main strands:

- Prevent
- Pursue
- Protect
- Prepare.

The purpose of policing patrols on the strategic road network is therefore to provide security and be the eyes and ears that can thwart terrorist attacks on this part of our critical national infrastructure. The presence of roads policing vehicles can act as a visible deterrent or lead to the detection of terrorist planning, or undertaking, terrorist activity. Throughout the world, vehicle-borne devices have been used to deliver large scale attacks, and, as such, the alert roads policing officer is in a position to make a significant intervention when such a vehicle is travelling on the network.

33.4.5 Traffic Management

The police have a number of responsibilities, some statutory, in relation to the management of traffic on the highways within a force area. The local highways authority is required by law to consult the Chief Constable regarding road developments, and the police also engage with the highways authority on such matters as road closures and planned events on the highway. It is also usual practice for the traffic management specialist within the force to review any safety issues relating to the design or condition of the highway following any fatal or serious injury collision.

3.4.6 Road Events

Many significant events take place on our strategic road network and in our urban environment. The presence of large numbers of people during sporting events such as cycle races and marathons on the road network presents both a risk to those involved and significant disruption to other members of the public. Before such events take place, the police, often in the form of a traffic management specialist, are engaged to ensure the safety and success of the event. Other major public events create significant pressures upon the capacity of the road network traffic management plan; for such events it is vital to manage the impact upon other road users.

3.4.7 Vehicle Escorts

A variety of vehicle loads travel around the strategic road network that require specialist provision. Generally speaking, the police are engaged much less now in escorting sensitive or abnormal loads. However, legislation exists that requires hauliers to notify the movement of certain abnormal loads before moving them by the road network. This enables police forces and the highways authority concerned to set conditions upon the movement and, if appropriate, require an escort for all or part of the route.

3.4.8 Special Escort Group (SEG)

The capability of police motorcycles and the skill of their riders is particularly valuable in escorting a whole range of vehicle movements on the network. From the escort of those people requiring protection, or where the need to facilitate free passage is vital, police motorcyclists are an invaluable resource. The escorting of Category A prisoners and other armed escorts are conducted by police officers, and the make-up of that escort, between roads policing officers and other specialist staff, varies between different police forces.

33.4.9 Spontaneous Protest Activity

Where protesters seek to use the high profile nature of incidents on the strategic road network, specialist trained road
policing officers will engage with the Highways Agency and
other specialist police officers to ensure the safety of the
response in this particular environment. Once again, the
role of the roads policing officer will be to facilitate their
colleagues to do their job in an environment where the
roads policing officers are experienced and trained.

It is important that in the event of any protest on the
network that the Highways Agency or, if it is a local road,
the highways authority, is made aware so that the impact
and disruption can be mitigated and the response coordinated. Guidelines issued by ACPO in 2004 on vehicle
demonstrations on the strategic road network are a very
helpful guide in detailing the tactical options available to
officers engaged in such incidents. As well as dealing with
the consequences of any such protests, it is important that
evidence of offences and the identity of the offenders is
secured. As such, video-equipped vehicles used by roads
policing officers and Air Support are a valuable source of
evidence gathering.

33.4.10 Goods Vehicles

The presence of large goods vehicles on the strategic road
network poses a number of key issues for roads policing officers to address. Because of their size and sometimes because
of the goods they carry, heavy goods vehicles (HGVs) are
a significant threat to the safety of other road users and,
when involved in a collision, demand specialist resources
to ensure a safe and effective response.

33.4.11 Goods Vehicle Offences

Offences in relation to driver training, driver's hours,
the regulations around the carriage of goods, and the

roadworthiness of vehicles are all important matters that must be addressed to ensure the safety of other road users. Because goods vehicles travel across countries and continents, the role of the national roads policing intelligence unit is vital in ensuring that roads policing officers are able to focus upon those presenting the greatest risk to roads.

33.4.12 Carriage of Dangerous Goods

Hazardous material is routinely carried on goods vehicles across the strategic road network without incident, but the threat is such that all roads policing officers should receive training to enable them to identify the dangers involved and their initial response before the arrival of the fire and rescue service at any such incident. The maintenance of effective and appropriate cordon distances is essential for the safety of responders and the wider public alike.

33.4.13 Public Service Vehicles

Whilst the involvement of buses and coaches in collisions on the road network is relatively rare, the involvement of so many passengers invariably makes such a collision a major incident. It is the attention to such things as driver training and licensing, driver hours, and vehicle safety on PSVs that is vital as a preventative measure to avert such catastrophes. A raft of legislation exists to prescribe the safety practices of operators of PSVs, and the enforcement of such legislation and standards is something that roads policing officers must maintain.

33.4.14 Highways Agency and Highways Agency Traffic Officers

Following joint working between ACPO and the Highways Agency in 2002, it was agreed that there was scope for a greater operational involvement for the Agency on its network. The corporate goals for the Highways Agency are safer roads, reliable journeys, and informed travellers, and these fit well with the priorities of the police force. The Traffic Management Act 2004 details powers for the Highways Agency Traffic Officers (HATOs) which relate to the control and direction of traffic and the placement of signs on the motorway; they also have the same exemption and powers as constables under the motorway regulations. The Traffic Officers are appropriately trained and they may be used in maintaining or improving the movement of traffic, preventing or reducing congestion, avoiding danger to persons from traffic, or the risk of any such danger arising, and the prevention of damage to anything on or near the road. Their core responsibilities are to manage congestion, ensure rapid and safe removal of obstructions, and to assist vulnerable road users.

The Traffic Officers who are controlled by the Regional Control Centres are able to take over some routine demand previously placed upon roads policing officers and consequently free up police resources to address other policing priorities. Typically such incidents are the removal of debris from the carriageways, dealing with broken down or abandoned vehicles, and dealing with minor incidents on the network which do not require police powers. The police will maintain primacy for incidents involving injury or death, criminality, threats to public order and safety, allegations of criminality or threats to public order and safety, and significant coordination of emergency responders. Section 4 of the 2004 Act clarified the legal relationship between the police and the HATOs and states that:

- A Traffic Officer (HATO) shall, when carrying out his or her duties, comply with any direction of a constable.
- Subject to that, a Traffic Officer (HATO) designated by an authorized person shall, when carrying out his or her duties, comply with any direction of the appropriate national authority.

The presence of HATOs on the motorway network has added to the visibility of authority and consequently the reassurance to the public in the safety of the road network. In 2007 the Highways Agency launched its vehicle recovery project which covers two complementary strategic areas:

- securing the statutory powers to allow the Highways Agency to remove vehicles and their loads from the network;
- the delivery of a contractual means of recovering vehicles and their loads from the network.

Giving Traffic Officers the ability to deal with abandoned, broken down, and damaged vehicles from the road network will allow the Highways Agency to improve safety and cut incident-related congestion whilst freeing up police officers from this task. The roll-out of the scheme began in early 2009 and is expected to be complete by autumn 2009.

33.4.15 Vehicle and Operator Services Agency

The Vehicle and Operator Services Agency (VOSA) was formed on 1 April 2003 following the merger of the Vehicle Inspectorate and the Traffic Area Network Division of the Department for Transport. VOSA provides a range of licensing, testing, and enforcement services with the aim of improving the roadworthiness standards of vehicles, ensuring compliance of operators and drivers with road traffic legislation, and supporting the independent traffic commissioners.

VOSA conduct routine and targeted checks on systems designed to check compliance with other road traffic legislation (eg drivers' hours and load weight). They also undertake specialist inspections on vehicles transporting dangerous goods, perishable foodstuffs, and goods seals for customs purposes, and they do this at the roadside and at the operators' premises. VOSA also undertake technical investigations into potential manufacturing or design defects, highlighting safety concerns, and monitoring safety recalls. They also support police by examining vehicles involved in fatal collisions to identify contributory defects, particularly goods vehicles and PSVs. VOSA were given the power to stop vehicles under the provisions of the Police Reform Act 2002, and are given the authority to stop vehicles on the road by individual Chief Constables.

33.4.16 Vehicle Recovery

The police have a range of powers that enable them to recover vehicles that are parked illegally, abandoned, broken down, and which are causing danger or obstruction to other road users. In addition, they have separate powers to seize vehicles that are used unlawfully. The most significant powers come under the Removal and Disposal of Vehicles Regulations 1986, which also allow the police to store and dispose of vehicles that have been or appear to have been abandoned and consequently removed. Through a variety of arrangements local police forces use recovery operators to undertake vehicle recovery.

The management of recovery operations is governed by the British Standards Institution 2006 Safe Working of Vehicle Breakdown and Recovery Operators (known as PAS43). PAS43 aims to increase safety and promote best practice guidance by setting out the requirements for the management of breakdown and recovery operators. It details procedures for attending vehicle breakdowns, the recovery of vehicles at the roadside, the recovery vehicle and equipment type, maintenance and safety markings, the training and practices of vehicle breakdown and recovery technicians, the use of personal protective equipment, the maintenance of recovery operators' premises, and the implementation and maintenance of standard operating procedures.

When dealing with an incident, a police officer in charge should consult with the vehicle recovery operator at an early stage so that an assessment may be made of the appropriate resources required for the recovery. The key issues are:

* hazards relevant to the operation;
* full details of the vehicles and any loads;
* the condition of vehicles including damage;
* the location of the vehicles and any load;
* any special requirements for recovery, eg forensic preservation.

Forensic preservation would include, in the case of a vehicle involved in a collision:

* the wheels not to be turned;
* the vehicle to be forensically wrapped at the scene;
* the vehicle to be recovered and stored in an appropriately secure and forensically neutral environment prior to examination.

The charges for recovery and storage of vehicles are set out in regulations enacted on 1 October 2008. The charges are now taken from a matrix which takes into account the size, condition, and position of the vehicle.

33.4.17 Local Highways Authority

The local highways authorities have a number of important responsibilities in relation to the local roads. They are:

* the management and maintenance of the local highway authority network;
* network and traffic management;
* event planning;
* supporting the policing incident management;
* managing emergency local diversions on agreed routes;
* providing that information to the media;
* education and training and publicity in relation to road safety.

33.5 Denying Criminals the Use of the Roads

Offenders use the road network daily as part of their crimi nal activity; whether they are thieves and burglars, drug dealers or fraudsters, or part of an organized crime network Proactive intelligence-led roads policing has a very signifi cant role in tackling crime by denying criminals the use of our roads. Research and experience has demonstrated that those who commit motoring offences, particularly document offences, are also likely to be involved in othe forms of criminal activity such as theft, burglary, drug deal ing, fraud, and organized crime. It is therefore no surprise that the detection of serious criminality and the subse quent arrest of the offenders has often come about because an officer with a good nose stopped a vehicle that looked worth a check.

33.5.1 National Intelligence Model

Roads Policing Units are fully engaged with the Nationa Intelligence Model (NIM) to ensure that enforcemen resources are targeted at the times, places, and people where they can make the most impact upon the identified prob lems and priorities of local and national crime. In additior to the force's own roads policing intelligence network and its engagement with intelligence colleagues at Basic Com mand Unit (BCU) and force level, the nature of road crime demands a regional and national structure.

The ACPO National Roads Policing Intelligence Forum brings together the regional leads and colleagues from a range of other agencies and services to ensure an effec tive flow of information across the UK and Europe to iden tify and target those that use the road network for crimina purposes. The strategic road network is the lifeblood of organized criminals and terrorists to traffic people, finance and illicit goods. By sharing and gathering intelligence with such bodies as the intelligence services, Customs and Excise, immigration, and our European policing colleagues, we can be an effective and robust response to the threat of international crime.

National Intelligence Model: Levels and Tactics

By engagement with this intelligence network and by taking part in regional, national, and Europe-wide targeted operations, roads policing officers are able to make a contribution at all three levels of NIM. Intelligence- and experience-led policing enables roads policing officers to disrupt and deter criminals operating at all levels of criminal activity. At the very local level, priority criminals are usually well known and most are vulnerable when they are travelling on the road system. Appropriately targeted enforcement may detect the more serious offences, but in any case, detecting motoring offences, even if they are seen to be less serious, are a valuable disruption tactic, whilst offences like driving whilst disqualified and no insurance are often an excellent means of restricting the criminal's freedom.

33.5.2 Automatic Number Plate Recognition

Automatic Number Plate Recognition (ANPR) technology automatically reads number plates and then checks to see if that number plate is known on a range of databases. It can highlight immediately if a vehicle has been reported stolen, used in crime, or used by someone who is wanted or disqualified. The system can be mounted to police vehicles, used in portable systems, or linked to street-mounted camera systems, and has become a valuable aid in the fight against crime and the protection of the community from criminals who use the road network. The system is used in three different ways: direct intervention tactics by operational officers who can intercept vehicles highlighted by ANPR as a result of any of the database markers; as a means of gathering intelligence about the movement of criminals which can then be subject to proactive operations; and as an investigative tool, looking for offenders and witnesses after a serious crime or terrorist attack.

Police forces have enthusiastically embraced ANPR technology and it has already been responsible for thousands of arrests and the recovery of millions of pounds worth of stolen vehicles and other stolen property.

33.5.3 Vehicle Seizures

The police have a number of powers to seize motor vehicles and, in addition to dealing with the primary offences giving rise to the use of the power, the seizure of a criminal's motor vehicle is an excellent disruptive tactic.

33.5.4 Section 165 of the Road Traffic Act 1988

Sections 164 and 165 of the Road Traffic Act 1988 (Retention and Disposal of Seized Motor Vehicles) Regulations 2005 gave the police the power to seize motor vehicles when the driver is not believed to hold a valid driving licence or if it is believed that the vehicle is being driven without insurance. This power, combined with the insurance database provided by the Motor Insurers' Bureau, has been a significant boon, as the link between those who drive without insurance and commit more serious acquisitive crime has been well evidenced. The power accompanied by the £200 ticket and six penalty points is a proportionate response to those who are more likely to be involved in collisions, more likely to fail to stop, and, consequently, pose a significant risk to the community at large.

33.5.5 Other Seizure Powers

The police have a number of other powers in relation to the anti-social use of vehicles, the illegal dumping of waste, collective trespass, and the Proceeds of Crime Act which

lso allow them to seize vehicles in addition to the usual
owers to seize evidence. The Transport Act 2000 gave the
olice and the DVLA the powers to seize untaxed vehicles;
IM Revenue and Customs have the powers to seize vehi-
les suspected of being used to evade excise by smuggling;
nd the Police Reform Act gave VOSA, when accredited by
Chief Constables, the power to stop and prohibit vehicles
n certain circumstances.

33.5.6 Databases

A range of databases exist that support roads policing officers in tackling crime and criminals on the road network.
Access to police databases, the databases held by other key
agencies, and vehicle-specific intelligence all assist roads
policing officers. Such databases, available to officers at the
roadside, include:

- Police National Computer
- local force criminal intelligence database
- ANPR 'hot lists'
- prisoner photographs
- fingerprint identification
- Driver and Vehicle Licensing
- motor insurance database.

33.5.7 Road Checks

Section 163 of the Road Traffic Act 1988 states that a person driving a mechanically propelled vehicle on a road
must stop the vehicle on being required to do so by a constable in uniform or a Traffic Officer. This fundamental
power forms the basic tactical option for police officers to
address criminal activity on the road network. The use of
this power enables officers to take part in local, regional,
and national campaigns on a whole range of criminal and
road safety initiatives. Police have other powers under

the Police and Criminal Evidence Act 1984 to search for witnesses or offenders for indictable offences, under the Criminal Justice and Public Order Act 1994 to prevent anticipated violence, and under the Terrorism Act 2000. The proportionate use of all these powers provide road policing officers with the tools to deliver the Roads Policing Strategy.

33.5.8 Driver and Vehicle Licensing Agency

The Driver and Vehicle Licensing Agency (DVLA) and police forces are increasingly being involved together in investigations relating to driving licence fraud. The possession of driving documents is of significant assistance to those illegally in this country or those carrying out organized crime. The detection of fraudulently obtained driving licences has regularly been the starting point into an investigation that has uncovered widespread organized crime, money laundering, illegal immigration, and identity fraud worth millions of pounds, whilst the link to terrorism from such activities represents both a significant threat and investigative opportunity.

33.5.9 Pursuits

Inevitably those who commit crime will not always comply with the officers' instructions to stop, and in doing so will create circumstances where officers must make a judgement whether to engage in a pursuit or, in the interests of safety, to let the offender go. Along with response driving, police pursuits are one of the most dangerous activities conducted in delivering a policing service to the public. Significant effort has been made by all police forces to manage this risk by ensuring officers are appropriately trained and that pursuits are properly managed. In 2008 ACPO issued its latest guidelines on the conduct of police pursuits.

3.5.10 **Neighbourhood Policing**

The commitment of the government and police forces to Neighbourhood Policing and the genuine engagement of local communities have unsurprisingly identified anti-social use of motor vehicles, as being a key priority for local people as they seek to identify local issues that impact upon the quality of their lives. The identification of speeding or other anti-social behaviour has encouraged police forces to engage specialist roads policing expertise to ensure that the delivery of these local priorities is proportionate, effective, and coordinated.

3.5.11 **Neighbourhood Action Groups**

Local groups, called Neighbourhood Action Groups (NAGs) have identified for themselves those matters they require the police service to take action upon. The experience of most forces is that speeding and anti-social use of motor vehicles are regularly at the top of local priorities. Police forces working together with local highways authorities, often under the banner of the Safer Roads Partnership, have enabled a toolbox approach to be available in which local people have the opportunity be part of the solution as well as identifying the problem. Initiatives such as Community Speed Watch, awareness campaigns, and warning signs have all been engaged, along with more traditional forms of police enforcement.

3.5.12 **Anti-social Use of Motor Vehicles**

Section 59 of the Police Reform Act 2002 was introduced to assist the police in tackling the growing problem of motor vehicles being used in an anti-social manner. Police officers, provided prior warning has been given that continued use will lead to seizure, may seize motor vehicles which are being driven inconsiderately or carelessly on the road or in a public place (contrary to section 3 of the Road Traffic A[c] 1988), or without lawful authority off road or on any roa[d] which is a footpath, bridleway, or restricted byway (co[n] trary to section 34 of the Road Traffic Act 1988) and in suc[h] a manner as to cause, or is likely to cause, alarm, distress, [or] annoyance to members of the public. This power can be [of] significant assistance in tackling such local problems.

Chapter 34

Protecting the Public and Vulnerable Persons

34.1 Introduction

There is nothing more important than protecting the public. Public protection means protecting the most vulnerable in society; identifying and managing the most dangerous places; and identifying and dealing with the most dangerous people. Serious violence (homicide, serious and other wounding, sexual offences) costs the UK approximately £21 billion per year of which £3.3 billion falls on Criminal Justice agencies (Dodd et al, 2003/04). Kemshall (2003) clarified that public protection depends upon:

- defensible decisions;
- rigorous risk assessments;
- the delivery of risk management plans which match the identified public protection need; and
- the evaluation of performance to improve delivery.

To date, however, the police service has adopted a piecemeal approach to managing risk within this context. The 2006 HMIC Base Line Assessment for protecting vulnerable people revealed that only three forces secured a 'good' grading. In order to meet future Public Service Agreement (PSA) targets, police performance, and hence tactical responses, on risk management are likely to be just as important as the tactical approach to volume crime reduction. In order to reduce violence there will be a need to integrate risk management into the National Intelligence Model (NIM), patrol, and investigative practices.

The Association of Chief Police Officers (ACPO) is leading on this through the Public Protection and Violence Portfolio and the key areas identified are:

- the prevention of serious violence;
- the protection of vulnerable people;
- tackling dangerous offenders/people;
- managing risky places.

The emerging ACPO Violence Strategy has six interdependent strands—see Figure 34.1.

Figure 34.1

34.2 **Duty of Positive Action**

The Human Rights Act 1998 places police officers under a positive obligation to take reasonable action, within their powers, to safeguard the following rights of victims of crime: right to life (Article 2, ECHR); right not to be subjected to torture or to inhuman or degrading treatment (Article 3, ECHR); and right to private and family life (Article 8, ECHR).

The requirement for *positive action* in public protection cases incurs obligations at every stage of the police response.

These obligations extend from initial deployment to the response of the first officer on the scene, through the whole process of investigation and the protection and care of victims. Action taken at all stages of the police response should ensure the protection of victims while allowing the criminal justice system to hold the offender to account. An effective and proactive investigation should be completed in all cases where a public protection or serious violence offence is reported.

Partnership working to protect the public is recognition that the police cannot do it alone. Success depends on working effectively at every level of the police service, not just specialist units, as well as with our partners at local, national, and international level. Partner agencies must work together to manage known violent offenders/people, as well as those most at risk of involvement in serious violence either as perpetrators or victims, in order to prevent violence from occurring in the first place or escalating in seriousness. Crucial to this is information sharing across the local agencies about known and at-risk offenders/people and victims.

34.3 **Intelligence**

It is of increasing importance that analysts and police identify and target the most dangerous offenders/people and vulnerable victims within a NIM-compliant structure. There are clear links across offending behaviours in terms of child abuse, sexual violence, domestic violence, stalking and harassment, dangerous people/offenders, and missing persons and the wider issues of public protection. This effective use of intelligence across a range of offending will allow for proactive targeting of perpetrators using an evidence-based approach. It is crucial to manage the volume across public protection and identify and deal with the 'critical few'.

A common misconception is that a significant proportion of sexual offences are committed by strangers when, in fact, research suggests that the majority of such offences are perpetrated by someone known to the victim, such as a partner, family member, or acquaintance. Another misconception is that offenders generally 'specialize' in particular types of offence such as sexual offences, violent offences, or property offences. In reality there is a considerable overlap between types of offences committed. It is crucial these links are made through intelligence and analysis across the field of public protection to adopt the lessons learnt from the Bichard Inquiry (2004), which highlighted an inability to identify the offender's pattern of behaviour over time, as well as failures in the gathering and use of intelligence and sharing information.

34.4 **Missing Persons**

The ACPO (2005b) Definition of a Missing Person is:

Anyone whose whereabouts is unknown whatever the circumstances of disappearance. They will be considered missing until located and their well-being or otherwise established.

There will be circumstances where a person is missing but police involvement may not be required, ie, tracing a long-lost relative. Appropriate action may be a referral to another agency that may provide assistance.

Police forces deal with hundreds of thousands of cases every year, and the majority of persons reported missing return soon after their disappearance without suffering any harm. A small number, however, are the subject of serious crime including murder, abduction, domestic violence, honour-based violence (HBV) and forced marriage, child protection related offices, sexual exploitation, and trafficking.

KEY POINT

It should always be remembered, therefore, that the initial missing person report could be the start of a major crime enquiry.
If in doubt treat as a Murder!

The *priorities* of a police service when dealing with missing people are:

- to ensure that every report of a missing person is risk assessed so that missing people who may be vulnerable or represent a high risk are immediately identified;
- to investigate reports of missing persons;
- to have clear policies in place which describe organizational roles and responses to reports of missing persons;
- to adopt a pro-active multi-agency approach in dealing with missing persons;
- to support the needs of the family, those close to the missing person, and the community;
- to ensure the staff are adequately trained to investigate missing persons cases;
- to preserve evidence where a crime has been committed.

34.4.1 Initial Response

The majority of cases that come to police notice will start with a phone call to a control room, and all police systems will be able to allocate the call according to their protocols.

This is, however, a key area, and the first point of risk identification and assessment. There are many factors that must be considered:

- vulnerability due to age or other factors;
- suspected to be a victim of crime in progress, ie abduction;
- information as to likely harm or suicide attempt;
- weather conditions, especially if a child or elderly person;
- essential medication or medical attention;
- physical illness, disability, or mental health problems;

- subject to violence, domestic violence, homophobic and/or racist incident, HBV or forced marriage issue, o bullying etc;
- previously disappeared and suffered harm;
- behaviour out of character.

The key role is to investigate, record, and initially assess th risk and assign resources. The initial risk assessment wil involve a judgement based on the information gathered, a either 'low', 'medium', or 'high'. If it hasn't been possibl to gather sufficient information at this stage the risk mus be recorded as 'high'.

34.4.2 Actions on Arrival at the Scene

Whilst an initial assessment will have been done, it is ver important to remember that this would often have bee limited to an interaction over the phone and often with very distraught informant. The key role of the officer is t investigate and accurately record and re-assess the risk.

Checklist—actions on arrival at scene

- Have the details gathered so far been accurate?
- Gather sufficient information about the missing person to enable an effective and thorough investigation to be conducted.
- Notify a supervisor immediately in high risk cases; in cases of 'medium' risk without undue delay; and in all other cases before the end of duty.
- Conduct a search of the premises and its environs.
- Make immediate local enquiries in order to locate the missing person.
- Record on appropriate force systems and circulate on the Police National Computer (PNC).
- Consider obtaining/securing any physical evidence such as DNA sample, fingerprints, photographs.
- Identify the person who is the point of contact for the police and assess the level of support required for the family.
- Inform this person of your contact details and the details of the person handed over to, including a reference number.

34.4.3 Persons Missing from a Mental Health Setting or Under the Mental Health Act

Police may deal with people who escape from custody or absent themselves without leave from a mental health setting. There are many variations and powers available under the Mental Health Act. These can be located through the Police Legal Database which should be referred to before using the power.

Some guidance is available in the Codes of Practice under the Mental Health Act which states:

> the police should be asked to assist in returning a patient to hospital only if necessary. If the patient's location is known, the role of police should wherever possible be only to assist a suitably qualified and experienced mental health professional in returning the patient to hospital. It should not usually be necessary to involve police unless there are suggestions that violence may be used by the person or entry to the premises is required under s17 Police and Criminal Evidence Act 1984.

Clearly this will involve a risk assessment which must be carried out by a police supervisor. This task would be much easier if all previous incidents have been properly recorded on police indices. This demonstrates very clearly the importance of fully documenting previous police actions.

34.4.4 Supervised Community Treatment Orders

The revised Mental Health Act introduced a new patient treatment option. Effectively this permits certain detained patients to be discharged from hospital for long-term treatment in the community, effectively allowing them to live at home. Conditions set out by the patient's responsible clinician will be attached upon release. Patients eligible for a supervised community treatment order are those detained under section 3 of the Mental Health Act or patients detained under a hospital order following criminal proceedings, where no restriction order has been made. In practice this means patients who pose less risk to the community. They may, however, still be subject to the Multi-agency Public Protection Panel (MAPP) review.

When a patient breaks the conditions or if other concerns come to light, the doctor or responsible clinician overseeing the person's care may recall the patient to hospital for further assessment or treatment. Once the recall notice has been served (either by hand or by post) the power of arrest is triggered and the patient is liable to be taken into custody and returned in the same way as a patient who is absent without leave.

These supervised treatment orders (STOs) only became available from 3 November 2008. It is therefore not easy to predict the likely impact on police and how many people may be subject to these requirements.

Even if every person were recalled once per year this would result in less than three recalls per month. The key for police is once again good communication and information sharing. Check your local force protocols.

34.4.5 Young Persons Missing from a Care Home or a Care Setting—Child Abduction by Parents

It is a criminal offence under the Child Abduction Act 1984 for a person connected with a child under 16 years of age to take or send a child out of the UK without the appropriate consent. It is also an offence under the Act for a person not connected with the child, without lawful authority or reasonable excuse, to take or detain a child under the age of 16, or to remove or keep that child from lawful control. A complaint relating to parental abduction may be reported directly to police or through a solicitor. Guidance should be sought from a supervising officer in all cases. For further information see *Child Abduction—A Practical Guide for Police Officers*, National Ports Authority.

34.5 **Child Abuse**

Child abuse is a complex area of policing and there have been many high profile reviews and failings identified. Lord Laming said in his Victoria Climbié Enquiry report of 2003 (Laming, 2003):

> Children should enjoy the same protection from the law and the same level of service from the police, as adults. 'Child protection policing' is no more or less than the investigation of crime. To treat it otherwise or to remove it from mainstream policing in either philosophy or operational practice is to do a grave disservice to the victims of such crime.

Lord Laming is currently conducting a review on the latest death of a child 'Baby P' in London.

34.5.1 **Definitions: Child Abuse**

A child—is defined by section 105 of the Children Act 1989 as any person under the age of 18 years.

Abuse and neglect—Someone may abuse or neglect a child by inflicting harm or by failing to act to prevent harm. Children may be abused in a family or in an institutional or community setting. This can be by those known to them or, more rarely, by a stranger.

Physical abuse—Physical abuse may involve hitting, shaking, throwing, poisoning, burning or scalding, drowning, suffocating, or otherwise causing physical harm to a child. Physical harm may also be caused when a parent or carer fabricates or induces illness, or deliberately causes ill health to a child in their care.

Emotional abuse—is the persistent emotional ill-treatment of a child which causes severe and persistent adverse effects on the child's emotional development. It may involve conveying to a child that they are worthless or unloved, inadequate, or valued only so far as they meet the needs of another person. It may, as in some cases of domestic violence, involve causing children to feel frightened or in danger, and includes the exploitation or corruption of children. It may feature age or developmentally inappropriate expectations being imposed on children.

Sexual abuse—involves forcing or enticing a child or young person to take part in sexual activities whether or not the child is aware of what is happening. It may involve physical contact including penetrative or non-penetrative acts. It may include non-contact activities, such as involving children in looking at child abuse, or involving them in the production of such images, watching sexual activities, or encouraging children to behave in sexually inappropriate ways.

Neglect—is a persistent failure to meet a child's basic physical and/or psychological needs, likely to result in the serious impairment of the child's health or development.

KEY POINT

Myths, stereotypes, assumptions about particular cultures, and fears of being accused of racism should not divert officers from noting and acting upon signs of neglect or ill-treatment. No cultural or religious heritage takes precedence over standards of child care embodied in law (ACPO, 2005d).

In 2003, the Government published a Green Paper called 'Every Child Matters' (ECM). This was published alongside the formal response to the report into the death of Victoria Climbié. 'Every Child Matters: Change for Children' is a new approach to the well-being of children and young people from birth to age 19.

The Government's aim is for every child, whatever their background or their circumstances, to have the support they need to:

- Be healthy;
- Stay safe;
- Enjoy and achieve;
- Make a positive contribution;
- Achieve economic well-being.

All officers will have or shortly will be receiving training on these five 'ECM' outcomes and how their force will be sharing this information. These five key outcomes need to become part of every officer's vocabulary.

This means that the organizations involved with providing services to children, including hospitals, schools, police, and voluntary groups, will be teaming up in new ways, sharing information, and working together to protect children and young people from harm and help them achieve what they want in life.

34.5.2 First Response

Child abuse can come to police attention in many different ways, including speaking to a victim or a witness to an incident, from other agencies, or even anonymously. Occasionally there will be emergency calls to report a violent incident in progress or children left alone at home.

It is crucial that a full and thorough investigation is carried out. The correct recording of all details, especially other family members, extended family members, and others who have access to the child or children concerned is of paramount importance. It is the information you gather that will be researched and passed on to Children's Services and other appropriate agencies.

The welfare of the child is paramount throughout. Officers will need to make decisions about their welfare—this should be done by listening to the child, what they do say and what they do not say, how they look, and how they behave.

An accurate record of the conversation and content needs to be made, detailing the timing, setting, and people present. Conversations will need to be appropriate to their age and understanding, and conducted in such a way as to minimize distress and maximize the likelihood they will provide accurate information. Officers should avoid leading and suggestive questions.

In all cases of doubt the matter must be referred to a supervisor.

34.5.3 Police Protection

Is it appropriate to take the child into police protection?

Section 46 of the Children Act 1989 provides an emergency power to police officers to protect a child believed to be at risk of significant harm. This section empowers an officer to remove a child to suitable accommodation or prevent the removal of a child from a safe place. When these powers are exercised the child is considered to be in police protection. Police protection does not give parental responsibility and, for example, does not give police the ability to consent on behalf of the child to a medical examination. No child may be kept in police protection for more than 72 hours.

Frontline staff considering using this power, wherever possible, should consult a supervising officer beforehand.

34.5.4 Potential Linked Investigations

There are many associated crimes and issues linked to child abuse including:

- domestic violence;
- missing persons investigations;
- sexual offences;
- HBV;
- forced marriage;
- trafficking;
- female genital mutilation;
- stalking and harassment;
- homicide;
- prostitution;
- managing sexual and violent offenders.

A police officer must always consider when investigating any crime or incident 'Is a child involved? Are they at risk? Every Child Matters Outcomes, do they apply?'

34.5.5 Information Sharing—Duty to Cooperate

Information sharing is one of the constant themes across public protection and should now be well established. Many forces have dedicated Child Abuse Investigation Units (CAIU) and public protection desks whose job it is to assess risk and share police information with partner agencies.

If the initial investigation was thorough the job of assessing risk is made easier. Frontline staff must familiarize themselves with their force protocols regarding 'ECM'. The Children Act 2004 bought in new guidance on the 'duty to cooperate.'

It provides the legal underpinning for the transformation of children's services as set out in the 'Every Child Matters: Change for Children' programme. Section 10 of the Act provides the statutory basis for Children's Trusts (the duty to cooperate).

Revised Children's Trust guidance on the 'duty to cooperate' was published on 18 November 2008. The 'relevant partners' currently under the 'duty to cooperate' are: district councils, the police, the probation board, the youth offending team, the Strategic Health Authority and Primary Care Trusts, Connexions partnerships, and the Learning and Skills Council.

The relevant partners are placed under a 'duty to cooperate in the making of arrangements to improve well-being' and have a power to pool budgets and share other resources.

34.5.6 Partnership Working

Children can only be safeguarded properly if the key agencies work effectively together. Local Safeguarding Children Boards (LSCBs) are designed to help ensure that this happens. They put the former area child protection committees (ACPCs) on a statutory footing.

The core membership of LSCBs is set out in the Children Act 2004, and includes local authorities, health bodies, the police, and others. The objective of LSCBs is to coordinate and to ensure the effectiveness of their member agencies in safeguarding and promoting the welfare of children.

Partnership working will become a lot easier when the next part of the information-sharing protocols come in this year (2009) using a secure computer-based system called 'ContactPoint'.

ContactPoint will be the quick way for a practitioner to find out who else is working with the same child or young person across the country, making it easier to deliver more coordinated support. It will be a basic online directory, available to authorized staff who need it to do their jobs. It is a key part of the ECM programme to improve outcomes for children.

There is a lot of change planned and therefore it is important that all police officers are kept updated. It is in your interests to read force policy, Intranet articles, and local force press releases. There is also a dedicated and regularly updated government website <http://www.everychildmatters.gov.uk>.

34.6 **Vulnerable Adult Abuse**

Vulnerable adult abuse (VAA) was previously known as 'Elder Abuse' but this did not encapsulate the wide-ranging nature of such abuses. Clearly the elderly are vulnerable as are some other adults. A Code of Practice was drawn up to deal with such issues in partnership with other agencies. This was published by the Department of Health and called 'No Secrets' (Department of Health and Home Office 2000). The guidance stated that the coordination should be locally developed and delivered under section 7 of the Local Authority Act 1970. This guidance does not carry the same status as statute law. However, local authorities are assessed on how well they are complying with it as part of regular statutory inspections.

34.6.1 Definitions

Vulnerable Adult

> A vulnerable adult is a person aged 18 years or over who is or may be at risk of abuse by reason of mental or other disability, age or illness and who is or may be unable to take care of themselves, or unable to protect themselves against significant harm.[1]

Within the definition, disability could be defined as 'Physical or mental impairment which has a substantial and long-term adverse effect on an individual's ability to carry out their day to day activities'.[2]

Mental disorder is an umbrella term for all other terms such as mental impairment and mental illness. This in turn can include learning difficulties.

Officers are expected to use their professional judgement. If they believe someone is experiencing some form of mental disorder, a disability, or appears unable to take care of themselves, they should be treated as a vulnerable adult. They must take into account people's sensitivities around these issues and treat everyone according to their individual needs.

Abuse is a violation of an individual's human and civil rights by any other person or persons—a single or repeated act or lack of appropriate action occurring within any relationship where there is an expectation of trust (which can include a relative, carer, or service provider) which causes harm or distress to a vulnerable adult.[3]

34.6.2 Types of Abuse

There are generally five recognized types of abuse:

---

[1] No Secrets—Dept of Health, 20 March 2000, <http://www.dh.gov.uk/en/Publicationsandstatistics/Publications/PublicationsPolicyAndGuidance/DH_4008486>, accessed 20 June 2009.
[2] Disability Discrimination Act 1995.
[3] MPS policy 2009 (forthcoming).

1 Physical—hitting, slapping, burning, pushing, restraining, or giving too much medication or the wrong medication.
2 Psychological—the illegal or unauthorized use of a person's property, money, pension book, or other valuables.
3 Sexual—forcing a person to take part in any sexual activity without their consent—this can occur in any relationship.
4 Neglect—where a person is deprived of food, heat, clothing or comfort, or essential medication.
5 Emotional—conveying to the person that they are worthless or unloved, inadequate, or valued only so far as they meet the needs of another person.

A person may suffer from only one form of abuse, or several types of abuse at the same time. This does not cover acts of abuse or violence from strangers, nor does it cover the targeting of older people on 'pension day' or burglary artifice type offences. It is necessary for there to be some sort of relationship (ordinarily familial or care provider) and some expectation of trust between the victim and suspect.

34.6.3 The Role of Police and the Initial Investigating Officer

A lot of crime against vulnerable adults currently goes unreported and the true extent of the problem is not known. The Action on Elder Abuse Helpline took 9,000 calls in 2008. It is quite clear a pro-active approach needs to be taken and the barriers to reporting tackled.

The help-line number is 0808 808 8141.
The website is <http://www.elderabuse.org.uk/Main pages/Helpline.htm>, accessed 20 February 2009.

Checklist—the Initial Investigation

- Elder abuse for investigators encountering a frail or elderly person. They do indeed bruise easily but what is the explanation for the bruising? If they are unable to communicate, have the right questions been asked of the agency involved and most importantly have the concerns been logged on the force intelligence database?
- Does the force have an information-sharing protocol with the appropriate Adult Services, Health Partnerships, or other local authority department? Frontline staff must know what it is. As mentioned earlier, the local authorities are assessed on the process but if police do not share the intelligence how can they act in partnership?
- Has all the relevant evidence been seized?
- Have other witnesses been identified, especially written logs of treatment, etc? Is it possible to gather further evidence from specialist interviewers in Achieving Best Evidence (ABE). Don't assume that just because you cannot communicate they cannot be a competent witness. With the initial investigation comes partnership working. Consideration must be given to what notes have already been gathered by other agencies involved and whether the appropriate information-sharing protocols can be used.

Case Study[4]—Vulnerable Adult Homicide

In August 2007, Darren Stewart, 29 and his 17-year-old girlfriend were convicted of the murder of Steven Hoskins, a vulnerable man with an exceptionally low IQ. A third defendant was convicted of his manslaughter. Steven was burned with cigarettes, made to swallow a lethal dose of paracetamol, and forced off a viaduct in St Austell, Cornwall, where he fell to his death.

Adult Social Care had placed Steven in a bed-sit in April 2005. Within five months he cancelled the two hours a week of help he was given, and this was never investigated or followed up by the local authority. Things began to go

---

[4] Devon and Cornwall Serious Case Review 2009.

wrong when Stewart and his girlfriend moved in and the abuse began. He died on 6 July 2006.

A serious case review highlighted the failure of agencies to share information about Steven and said that better inter-agency working and communication would have spared him the abuse he suffered. This, and an internal manage-ment review, noted more than 40 missed opportunities by many agencies to protect Steven.

34.7 **Investigating Serious Sexual Offences**

It is important to join up public protection and include seri-ous sexual offences (SSOs). There is no common definition of what constitutes a SSO but it could include:

- rape;
- sexual assault by penetration;
- sexual assault where the assault is particularly serious or features of the offence are aggravated;
- causing a person to engage in sexual activity without consent;
- any other offence of a sexual nature deemed especially serious by the investigating officer (IO);
- an attempt to commit any of the above offences.

The *priorities* of the police service in responding to SSOs are to:

- ensure an effective investigation of SSOs;
- all victims who make allegations of SSOs should be treat-ed with dignity and respect;
- take effective action against offenders so that they can be held accountable through the criminal justice system;
- increase confidence in the criminal justice system and encourage more victims to report SSOs to the police;

use existing national systems to record information and intelligence that will assist in the identification of linked SSOs;

• adopt a pro-active multi-agency approach in the development of services to victims.

The initial response to a report of a SSO is a fundamental part of the investigation. The preservation of physical evidence is a priority and the details should be recorded accurately to provide evidence of early complaint.

Those taking initial reports from victims should remember that this requires the victim to provide intimate details of a traumatic experience. Establishing trust is essential to encourage the victim to provide full details of the offence and the surrounding circumstances of the offence at the later stage of interview.

The officer to whom the incident is reported should then assume the role of IO until the incident is allocated to a Specially Trained Officer (STO) and an IO is appointed.

Your Role

Before attending to a report:

obtain the initial disclosure from the victim/caller verbatim, eg, from the 999 call;

take an early evidence kit (EEK) with you;

• ensure that you can contact an on-duty IO or STO for real-time advice.

Checklist—Requesting Information when Taking an Initial Report of a SSO

Officers and report takers should obtain and record the following information:

• The location and identity of the person making the report.
• The exact (where possible) location and time of the incident.
• Whether they are the victim, third party, or witness, and the capacity in which they are making the report.
• Nature of the incident.

- Location and identity of the victim (if known).
- Location and identity of the suspect (if known).
- Whether medical assistance is required and the severity of any injuries.
- A first description of the suspect.
- Location of any other parties (witnesses, supporters) and their contact details.
- Whether any weapons have been used in the commission of the offence.
- Whether any person appears to be drunk or has taken drugs.
- If the suspect is known to the victim, whether there is a history of violence or sexual offences.
- Whether steps have been taken to preserve evidence.
- Whether there are any special needs considerations, for example, disability, language and whether an interpreter is required.
- Details of the demeanour of the victim or reporter.
- A first account of what the reporter says has occurred (verbatim or recorded for transcription).
- Preferred contact point if not at the scene.
- If the reporter wishes to remain anonymous, the reasons for this.

34.7.1 Potentially Associated Investigations and Antecedents

Connections can be made between serious sexual offending and other types of offences. SSOs may become apparent as part of investigations into other incidents or complaints. Some sex offenders offend against multiple types of victim, such as adults, children or partners, and strangers. Consider the following.

Domestic Abuse

There are proven links between those who rape in the home (domestic) and outside the home (stranger) (Richards,

2004). Many rapists 'practise' at home. Men who sexually and physically assault their partners are known to be
particularly dangerous. Sexual assault of a partner is a risk
factor for the homicide of the victim. Officers should also
consider whether these offences have been witnessed, for
example, by children. Refer to ACPO (2008) Guidance on
Investigating Domestic Violence.

Child Abuse

Evidence of, or convictions for, rape of a child or sexual
activity with a child (formerly unlawful sexual intercourse)
present a significant risk that the offender will go on to
commit serious sexual offences. This is particularly the case
where the former offence is with a child of the age of 13 years
or under. Cruelty to children also presents a significant risk
of a future conviction for a SSO. Domestic violence is also
associated with child sexual abuse. Refer to ACPO (2005d)
Guidance on Investigating Child Abuse and Safeguarding
Children and ACPO (2008) Guidance on Investigating
Domestic Violence.

Forced Marriage, Honour-Based Violence, and Rape

A forced marriage is where one or both of the spouses do
not consent to the marriage or consent is extracted under
duress. Forced marriage is an abuse of human rights and
a form of domestic abuse and child abuse. Where there is
forced marriage there is likely to be rape and repeated rape.
An arranged marriage to which both parties freely consent
is not the same thing as a forced marriage.)

Some societies punish the victims of rape, as well as the
perpetrators. They may hold the belief that being raped
'dishonours' the victim, and in some cases, the victim's
family and community. This can lead to the victim being
murdered or committing suicide due to the social shame
and stigma attached to being a rape victim.

Burglary, Theft, and Handling Stolen Goods

There is a strong association between serious sex offending
and previous convictions for burglary, theft, and handling

stolen goods. Some stranger rapists are reported to spend a considerable amount of time prowling in local neighbourhoods, and because of this they may be known to the police in that capacity.

Homicide, Abduction, and Kidnap

Previous convictions for kidnapping are a risk factor for subsequent serious sexual offending. There are also obvious links between sexually motivated homicides and other sexual offending. Officers should note that attempted rapes and other sexual offences may be linked to homicides or attempted homicides, and some stranger serial SSOs include several attempts at selecting and abducting a victim. Refer to ACPO (2000a) Murder Investigation Manual.

Prostitution, Sexual Exploitation, and Trafficking

There is a high risk of people involved in prostitution being exploited and becoming victims of SSOs. Children are particularly vulnerable to commercial sexual exploitation and should be seen as the victims of such offending, rather than offenders. In any investigation uncovering the sexual exploitation of a child, a notification should be made to the CAIU and every effort made to secure evidence to support a prosecution for offences linked to abusing children. Refer to ACPO (2005d) Guidance on Investigating Child Abuse and Safeguarding Children.

Adult and child victims of trafficking for the purposes of commercial sexual exploitation may not cooperate with law enforcement agencies for fear of reprisals. Trafficking is also associated with abduction, and care should be taken to protect victims from further harm. Refer to ACPO (2005e) Practice Advice on the Use of Immigration Powers Against Crime.

Robbery

There are links between previous convictions for robbery or assault with intent to rob and a subsequent conviction for a SSO.

Violence

Sex offenders often exhibit other forms of violent behaviour, and about half of such offenders may have previous convictions or intelligence for violence.

34.7.2 Actions on Arrival at the Scene

The first officers to attend the scene should focus on ensuring the safety of the victim and witnesses, and preserving all available evidence.

Checklist—Actions on Arrival at the Scene

On arrival at the scene officers should:

- re-assess victim and officer safety, including immediate risk;
- make an immediate assessment of the need for first aid or other medical assistance such as an ambulance;
- confirm the identity of the suspect (if known) and, if they are no longer at the scene, circulate a full description of them via the radio system;
- establish who is or was at the scene;
- establish the parameters of the scene(s);
- make accurate records of everything said by the suspect (if present), victim, and any witnesses, including children;
- record the demeanour of the victim, suspect (if present), and any other witnesses, including children;
- report findings to the IO;
- make sure the victim is safe, taking them to a place of safety, eg the home of a relative or a refuge, where necessary;
- obtain an overview of what has occurred.

Protecting the Crime Scene

- Identify, secure, and protect all scenes, including the victim, location(s), and the suspect (if known/present).
- Consider any possible access/exit routes used by victim and suspect, victim release sites, hiding places, vehicles used etc.

- Avoid cross-contamination of evidence; if the suspect or a further scene is identified, a different officer should be deployed to deal with this.

Arresting the Suspect

- Often victims know and identify the suspect.
- Different officers should be deployed to the victim and the suspect to prevent cross-contamination of evidence, particularly in recently committed offences.
- Obtain as much information as possible about the suspect in order to locate them as soon as possible.

Building the Investigation Log

You should start an investigation log. It will be progressed by the STO and the IO and is a record of:

- initial account of the victim and witnesses;
- offender details and/or description;
- sketch plan of scene;
- action you have taken;
- use of EEK and other measures taken to protect the scene;
- witnesses and details of witnesses of early complaint;
- list of exhibits.

Providing a Single Point of Contact

You should remain as the first point of contact until an STO and an Independent Sexual Violence Advisor (ISVA) (or similar support service) is appointed to the case. The STO will then become the police single point of contact for the victim and witnesses.

Preserving Forensic Evidence

- Victims may provide only brief or incomplete information about offence(s), presenting difficulties for giving advice about preserving evidence and for deciding which parts of the EEK to use.

- Try to establish basic information about the offence(s) without asking leading questions.
- Give an estimate of how long they might have to wait for a forensic medical examination and provide advice about how to preserve evidence prior to it taking place (refer to ACPO (2009) Briefing Note on first Response to Rape).

Notification to Specialist Teams/Departments

Ensure that the correct departments have been informed by command and control of any report of rape. This will usually mean informing the duty officer and/or a specialist investigator, according to your local arrangements. The IO will appoint an STO to the case and should also make a referral to an ISVA (or similar local equivalent service).

Crime Recording

A victim-centred approach to crime recording should be adopted when recording rape. Delays in crime recording, beyond the initial investigation, should be an exception rather than the rule.

34.7.3 Sexual Assault Referral Centres (SARCs)

A SARC is defined by the Home Office as:

'A dedicated facility to provide immediate and on going victim care within the context of a partnership arrangement between police, health and the voluntary sector.'

<http://www.crimereduction.homeoffice.gov.uk/sexual/sexual028e.doc>

SARCs provide a dedicated, forensically secure facility which is integrated with hospital services. They should be accessible for 24 hours a day, seven days a week, with availability for victims within four hours by appointment.

34.8 **Domestic Abuse**

> The ACPO (2008) definition of domestic abuse (DA) is:
>
> 'any incident of threatening behaviour, violence or abuse (psychological, physical, sexual, financial or emotional) between adults, aged 18 and over, who are or have been intimate partners or family members, regardless of gender and sexuality' (Family members are defined as mother, father, son, daughter, brother, sister and grandparents, whether directly related, in-laws or step-family)'.

The *priorities* of the police service in responding to DA are to:

- protect the lives of both adults and children who are at risk as a result of DA;
- investigate all reports of DA;
- facilitate effective action against offenders so that they can be held accountable through the criminal justice system;
- adopt a pro-active multi-agency approach in preventing and reducing DA.

34.8.1 **General Reporting**

A common feature in most DA cases is repeat victimization. This is usually defined as more than one incident reported to the police in a given period, for example, 12 months. Positive action policies should be applied in all cases of domestic abuse to reduce repeat victimization and protect victims. First-hand reporting from a victim or witness is the most common way that the police are informed about DA. The majority of DA incidents are reported via calls to the police, visits to the police station, or through contact with operational officers. Some referrals could come from another agency. All reports of DA should be recorded in compliance with ACPO (2002) National Crime Recording Standards.

The receipt of a report of DA is the beginning of the investigation. Officers and police staff should establish as much detail as possible to ensure an effective investigation.

34.8.2 Potentially Linked Investigations

The links between an investigation into another offence and associated offences of DA might not always be obvious. These potentially linked enquiries should identify DA as a line of enquiry, particularly when investigating the following types of offending:

* child abuse;
* stalking and harassment;
* homicide;
* HBV;
* missing persons investigations;
* prostitution;
* sexual offences;
* managing sexual and violent offenders;
* vulnerable adult abuse.

34.8.3 Effective Evidence Gathering in DA Cases

Figure 34.2 shows a range of evidence that can be collected by officers that can assist in supporting a prosecution. By placing your suspect at the centre of your investigation, you can build a case, which does not solely rely upon the willingness of the victim to give evidence.

Effective investigation and evidence gathering is critical. The use of 999 calls, photographs taken at the scene, the gathering of medical evidence immediately, together with an interview of the defendant under caution would all provide valuable evidence, which could enable the prosecution to proceed even where the victim subsequently wishes to withdraw. The subsequent presentation of these cases, ideally within Specialist Domestic Violence Courts (SDVC), will

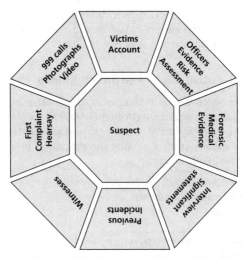

Evidence Gathering in Domestic Violence Cases

Figure 34.2

lead to lower levels of attrition at court and consequently higher numbers of offenders being brought to justice.

Checklist—Actions on Arrival at the Scene

To ensure the safety of victims and children and to preserve evidence, officers should:

- reassess victim and officer safety, including immediate risk, particularly in respect of access to or use of weapons;
- make an immediate assessment of the need for first aid or other medical assistance such as an ambulance (this should include the needs of the victim, any children, any other persons, and the suspect);
- separate parties, including any children;
- confirm the identity of the suspect (if they are no longer at the scene immediately circulate a full description);
- establish who is or was at the scene, including any children;
- request appropriate checks on the suspect and household (including warrants, bail conditions, civil orders and child

protection register, ViSOR, INI, firearms licence, or intelligence reports linking suspect and household members to weapons) if not already done;

- make accurate records of everything said by the suspect, victim, and any witnesses, including children;
- record the demeanour of the suspect, victim, and any other witnesses, including children;
- consider taking photographs and/or using a video camera to record evidence;
- report findings to the IO (if different from the first response officer);
- secure the safety of victims in their home—if this is not possible, consideration should be given to taking them to another place of safety, eg the home of a relative or a refuge (this should be done according to local arrangements for housing and refuge provision);
- obtain an overview of what has occurred, taking into account the established risk factors associated with DA.

34.8.4 Risk Identification, Assessment, and Management

It is essential that risks are identified and documented. The risk management plan should be reviewed at all stages of the investigation, including on release from custody, through to any court appearances.

In all cases investigators should:

- document a clear and effective risk identification, assessment, and management plan. Decisions need to be clearly recorded and auditable;
- use an ACPO-approved identification/assessment model such as the Domestic Abuse, Stalking and Harassment and Honour Based Violence (DASH, 2009) Risk Model;
- refer it on for action;
- put an appropriate intervention plan into place;
- ensure that information relating to the suspect is included in any risk management processes.

In HBV cases, officers should consider that:

- reporting HBV might increase risk and imminence of harm to the victim, and might act as a barrier to them seeking further help;
- other family members, such as siblings, might also be subject to HBV;
- threats might extend beyond the immediate family to the wider community;
- family members might seek to locate and pressurize the victim;
- family members might seek to remove or abduct the victim;
- threats might extend to other family members or the partner of the victim;
- attempts might be made to leave the country with the victim;
- there might be other patterns of offending which are not linked to HBV;
- there might be a history of abuse/HBV with other partners or family members.

Some form of *positive action* must *always* be taken. In managing any risks identified the mnemonic **RARA** may assist officers in making defensible decisions.

Mnemonic	
Remove the risk	= By arresting the suspect and obtaining a remand in custody.
Avoid the risk	= By re-housing victim/significant witnesses or placement in refuge/shelter in location unknown to suspect.
Reduce the risk	= By joint intervention/victim safety planning, target hardening, enforcing breaches of bail conditions, use of protective legislation, and referring high risk cases to Multi-Agency Risk Assessment Conference (MARAC).
Accept the risk:	= By continued reference to the Risk Assessment Model, continual multi-agency intervention,

planning, support and consent of the victim, and offender targeting within Pro-active Assessment and Tasking pro forma (PATP), or Risk Management Panel format (MARAC or Multi-agency Public Protection Panel (MAPPP)).

34.8.5 The Role of Neighbourhood Policing Teams

Neighbourhood Policing Teams (NPTs) (see Chapter 21 above) should be kept informed about details of DA offenders and identified high risk cases in their particular geographic area. They should work with the DA coordinator to assist with information gathering and enforcement issues, as appropriate to their role profiles. This is particularly important when NPTs can assist in the risk management of individual offenders (eg through the enforcement of civil orders or by conducting unannounced curfew checks). Team members can be key sources of information provided by, or obtained from, the community.

This information can assist in the continual risk identification process and longer term risk management processes. NPTs can also use community information to identify DA offenders and those who present a current and significant risk to others. They can be tasked to provide a regular visible presence in close proximity to the victim's address and in some circumstances pay welfare visits to the victim, provided that consent is given. Officers may also be tasked in relation to the offending behavior of the perpetrator. Where necessary, these teams should have access to relevant information which enables them to contribute to the MARAC action plan. Refer to ACPO (2006c) Practice Advice on Professionalising the Business of Neighbourhood Policing.

34.8.6 Independent Domestic Violence Advisers

An Independent Domestic Violence Adviser (IDVA) gives practical advice and support to high risk victims to help them make decisions about their future and also help them access a range of services they need.

34.8.7 Making Referrals to Multi-Agency Risk Assessment Conference

MARAC is a single meeting, attended by representatives from all agencies that have a role in a particular case, to combine up to date risk information with an assessment of the victim's needs. MARAC aims to share information to increase the safety, health, and well-being of victims and others.

The MARAC process establishes whether the offender poses a significant risk to any particular individual or to the general community. A key product from the MARAC process is the construction and implementation of a multi-agency risk management plan. The risk management plan should provide professional support to all those at risk, reducing risk of harm and repeat victimization. Refer to Co-ordinated Action Against Domestic Abuse (CAADA) (2007) Multi-Agency Risk Assessment Conferences—Implementation Guide.

34.9 Mental Health

Mental health issues are an area of policing that many find difficult and challenging. Often we are influenced by the media and sensationalist reporting. The facts are that serious violence by persons suffering mental illness are rare. An effective investigation and accurate recording of incidents by initial responders is crucial. It is important that the risks are identified and shared with appropriate partner agencies

34.9.1 Definitions

Section 1(2) of the Mental Health Act 1983 states 'mental disorder' means any disorder or disability of the mind; and mentally disordered' shall be construed accordingly.

> **Mental Health Act 1983, section 136—Mental Illness in a Public Place**
>
> If a constable finds in a place to which the public have access a person who appears to him to be suffering from a mental disorder and to be in immediate need of care or control, the constable may, if he thinks necessary to do so in the interests of that person or for the protection of other persons, remove that person to a place of safety within the meaning of the act.

Using this power is a matter of individual judgement; a person simply acting in a different way from what might be considered 'normal' does not necessarily mean they should be removed to a place of safety.

Some of the behaviours that might accompany mental illness are listed below, but on their own may not justify police action and are listed for guidance only:[5]

- the person is engaging in irrational conversation or behaviour;
- they are talking about seeing things or hearing voices which you cannot hear;
- they are putting themselves in danger, for example walking into the path of moving traffic or on railway lines;
- they are engaged in threatening behaviour towards others for no apparent/obvious reason;
- they have asked for help with their mental condition;
- they are threatening or engaged in self-harm;
- they are threatening or attempting suicide;
- the person is removing clothing for no apparent reason;
- the person is confused or agitated or unresponsive to others;

---

[5] MPS Standard Operating Procedure 3 Nov 2008.

• there is an immediate risk of harm through perhaps assaults on others or self harm.

Whilst a lot of these incidents demand immediate action, first responders can, if time permits, get further information from the control room and police intelligence checks. Consider:

• What is the degree of threat to themselves and/or others?
• Based upon their current behaviour and what is known about them, what is likely to happen if the person is not detained?

Police action that follows will depend on the arrangements that have been agreed and published in each force area. The person must be taken to a place of safety. However, it is accepted that the use of a police station should be as a last resort only. All staff must be aware of their force policy.

In all cases:

• document a clear and effective risk identification, assessment, and management plan. Decisions need to be clearly recorded and auditable;
• by far the most likely person for a mentally ill individual to harm is themselves. Gather intelligence to prevent such harm in the same way as if they were a potential victim of another person. Preventing harm to anyone is a clear policing purpose;
• advice should be sought from a supervisor;
• refer to force policy;
• find out who your Police Mental Health Liaison Officer is.

Most forces now have Public Protection Desks, Missing Person Units, or Vulnerable Person Units, and it is vital that the incident is now shared appropriately with partner agencies including Adult Social Services, Health Partners, and mental health practitioners.

Mental Health Act 1983, Section 135(1)—Mental Illness in Private Premises and Warrants

There are generally three ways in which police will be involved in using section 135:

- *Pre-planned*—where an Approved Mental Health Professional (AMHP, previously known as an approved social worker or ASW) contacts police in advance requesting help for a mental health assessment they are planning with regards to a person at home.
- *Spontaneous and notified to police by a caller* etc—where, for instance, a neighbour or relative calls police because they are concerned about a person's unusual behaviour in their own home. This can also happen where police are in attendance at a person's address for another reason, but it becomes apparent that the person is having a mental health crisis.
- *Spontaneous and notified to police by health professionals*—normally where a member of the community health team visits a person at home and finds them in crisis and calls police due to the level of risk.

Sections 2 or 3 of the Mental Health Act allow for the medical and healthcare professionals to complete papers, effectively permitting someone to be detained in a psychiatric hospital. Such powers can be used in any place, and health and social care professionals frequently attend home addresses to assess the mental condition of someone believed to be going into crisis. Where the criteria are met the person is detained using sections 2 or 3 and conveyed to hospital. This often takes place without any police involvement.

Since section 2 and 3 do not permit any power to enter private premises, obvious difficulties arise where entry is refused. Where this is anticipated in advance a warrant can be obtained granting a police officer access and allowing an assessment by health and social care professional in order to detain if required.

Pre-planned assessments provide time to arrange staff availability, apply for a warrant, and plan tactically what will take place. Spontaneous incidents by their very nature are difficult to deal with because a warrant will not be available and powers of entry and detention are restricted.

34.10 Multi-Agency Public Protection Arrangements

Multi-agency Public Protection Arrangements (MAPPA) is the process through which the police, probation, and prison services, known as the Responsible Authority (RA), work together with other agencies to manage the risks posed by violent and sexual offenders living in the community in order to protect the public. Other agencies under section 325(3) of the Criminal Justice Act 2003 have a 'duty to cooperate' with the RA. They are:

- local authority social care services;
- Primary Care Trusts, other NHS Trusts, and Strategic Health Authorities;
- Jobcentre Plus;
- Youth Offending Teams (YOTs);
- Registered Social Landlords which accommodate MAPPA offenders;
- local housing authorities;
- local education authorities; and
- electronic monitoring providers.

34.10.1 Who is Managed through MAPPA?

Three categories of violent and sexual offenders:

Registered Sexual Offenders

Registered Sexual Offenders (RSOs) are required to notify the police of their name, address, and other personal details

nder the terms of the Sexual Offences Act 2003. The length
f time an offender is required to register with police can be
ny period between 12 months and life depending on the
ge of the offender, the age of the victim, and the nature of
he offence and sentence they receive.

iolent Offenders

iolent offenders are those who have been sentenced to 12
nonths or more in custody or to detention in hospital and
vho are now living in the community subject to probation
upervision. This category also includes a small number
f people who have been disqualified from working with
hildren.

Ither Dangerous Offenders

his covers those who have committed a sexual or violent
ffence in the past and who are considered to pose a risk of
erious harm to the public.

4.10.2 How does MAPPA Work?

Il MAPPA offenders are assessed to establish the level of
isk of harm they pose to the public. Risk management
lans are then worked out for each offender to manage
hose risks. MAPPA allows agencies to assess and manage
ffenders on a multi-agency basis by working together,
haring information, and meeting, as necessary, to ensure
nat effective plans are put in place. There are three levels
f MAPPA management. They are mainly based upon the
evel of multi-agency cooperation required, but higher risk
ases tend to be managed at the higher levels. Offenders can
nove up and down the levels.

evel 1

Ordinary agency management for offenders who can be
nanaged by one or two agencies (ie police and/or proba-
ion). It will involve sharing information about the offend-
rs with other agencies, if necessary and appropriate.

Level 2

Active multi-agency management is for offenders where the ongoing involvement of several agencies is needed to manage the offender. Once at Level 2, there will be regular Multi-agency Public Protection (MAPP) meetings about the offender.

Level 3

Same arrangements as Level 2, but cases for Level 3 tend to be more demanding on resources and require involvement of senior people from the agencies, who can authorize the use of extra resources.

It is important for MAPPA to have good links with other forums: Local Safeguarding Children Boards (LSCBs); the Care Programme Approach, and Domestic Abuse Multi-agency Risk Assessment Conferences (MARACs) to ensure that identified risks are being effectively managed and that there is no duplication of effort.

34.10.3 Information Sharing

The structure of MAPPA provides a framework which supports and enables lawful, necessary, proportionate, secure, and accountable information sharing.

Section 325 of the Criminal Justice Act 2003 and section 115 of the Crime and Disorder Act 1998 provide a legal basis for data sharing, whilst the Data Protection Act 1998 puts controls on the data sharing so, together, they facilitate responsible information sharing between agencies for legitimate purposes. The legislation was established to regulate, rather than prevent, the sharing of information.

34.10.4 ViSOR

ViSOR is a database designed to hold details of all MAPPA offenders. All cases within ViSOR are known as 'nominals'

4.10.5 **Young Offenders**

Youth Offending Teams (YOTs) are responsible for the supervision of all young offenders (those aged under 18 years) on community sentences and following release from a custodial sentence. The number of young offenders meeting the MAPPA eligibility criteria will be relatively small.

4.10.6 **Potentially Dangerous Persons**

ACPO (2007)—Guidance on Protecting the Public: Managing Sexual and Violent Offenders defines a Potentially Dangerous Person (PDP) as follows:

> A Potentially Dangerous Person is a person who has not been convicted of, or cautioned for, any offence placing them in one of the three MAPPA Categories, but whose behaviour gives reasonable grounds for believing that there is a present likelihood of them committing an offence or offences that will cause serious harm'

ViSOR has the capacity to include information on PDPs. Inclusion into this group has to be authorized by a superintendent.

4.10.7 **The Role of Neighbourhood Policing Teams**

The role of Neighbourhood Policing Teams (NPTs) are the golden thread running through much of the work which is about understanding and knowing local risk and vulnerabilities and managing community knowledge and suspicions. Policing any community should reassure the public by providing visibility, accessibility, and familiarity to the community and the offenders being managed. During times of tension, it is particularly important that a high visibility approach is maintained by local and recognizable officers who are familiar with the community and its issues.

All policing activity should be in partnership with key representatives from that community so that all information and intelligence can be gathered, and rumours controlled and contained. NPTs should be kept informed about details of MAPPA offenders and PDPs.

Checklist—Tasked Information

Any individual or group tasked to provide public protection information about a particular offender or PDP should be familiar with the following information about them:

- Identity and address (including place of work).
- Appearance (where possible using a photograph).
- Nature of their offences or suspected offences.
- Nature and identities of associates.
- Nature of the danger of serious harm which they pose (ie physical violence and sexual offences) and any particular individuals or groups who are at risk.
- Any changes in behaviour or appearance.
- Any mental health issues.
- Any substance misuse issues.
- Any particular relevant risk factor or other information from the risk assessment or risk management process.
- Any restrictions or requirements in relation to civil orders, bail, or licence conditions.
- Any particular factors affecting staff safety (ie the offender's or PDP's access to firearms or other weapons).

This is particularly important when NPTs are assisting with risk management of particular offenders (ie through enforcement of civil orders or by conducting unannounced curfew checks). Team members can be key sources of public protection information provided by or obtained from the community. This information can assist in the identification of PDPs and the assessment and management of risk of offenders and PDPs. NPTs can also use community information to identify any potential threat to reveal the identity or location of a particular offender.

The management of community knowledge and suspicions about sexual and violent offenders will require contributions by the Public Protection Units (PPUs), NPTs, and, where appropriate, public order specialists.

4.10.8 Community Knowledge about an Offender's Identity

Some offenders live in a community where their offending background is common knowledge. However, the reaction to the offender can vary over time. This can depend on significant media focus relating to sexual offenders, for example, and if a serious offence has been committed in the area. Information about the identity or location of an offender can reach the public domain unexpectedly. In all cases, any developments should be notified to the PPU and be included as part of the risk management plan relating to the offender. Consideration should also be given to a media strategy and the possible need for a Community Impact Assessment (CIA).

4.10.9 Community Impact Assessments

All police forces should have contingency plans for any likely community impact situation that may arise. NPTs are key to these arrangements. The management of the risk posed by the offender and any threat from vigilante groups can be complex and requires a rapid response by agencies, particularly police. A CIA is a systematic way of determining the effect of a policy or action on all groups in the community, and they are primarily the responsibility of NPTs with support from the PPU. For further information see ACPO (2006a) Murder Investigation Manual.

Where there are unfounded community suspicions about the identity of an individual (ie misidentification of an individual as a sexual offender) a strategy meeting should be organized from the relevant NPT, PPU, and any other relevant agencies or police departments. In some cases, the meeting may include the targeted individual. In all cases, any public protection information acquired by team members should be dealt with according to ACPO (2006b) Guidance on the Management of Police Information.

Further Reading

ACPO (2002), National Crime Recording Standards
— (2005a), Guidance on the National Intelligence Model available at <http://www.acpo.police.uk/asp/policies/Data/nim2005.pdf>
— (2005b), The Management Recording and Investigation of Missing Persons
— (2005c), Practice Advice on Stalking and Harassment
— (2005d), Guidance on Investigating Child Abuse and Safeguarding Children
— (2005e), Practice Advice on the Use of Immigration Powers Against Crime
— (2006a), Murder Investigation Manual
— (2006b), Guidance on the Management of Police Information
— (2006c), Practice Advice on Professionalising the Business of Neighbourhood Policing
— (2007), Tactical Menu of Intervention Options for Honour Based Violence Victims and Offenders
— (2007), Guidance on Protecting the Public: Managing Sexual and Violent Offenders
— (2008) Guidance on Investigating Domestic Abuse,
— (forthcoming) Guidance on Investigating Child Abuse and Safeguarding Children, second edition
Bichard, Sir Michael (2004) *The Bichard Inquiry Report*, TSO Norwich available at <http://www.bichardinquiry.org.uk/10663/report.pdf>
Co-ordinated Action Against Domestic Abuse (CAADA) (2007) Multi-Agency Risk Assessment Conferences–Implementation Guide
Clarke, RV and Eck, J (2003), *Becoming a problem solving crime analyst in 55 small steps*, UCL Jill Dando Institute London

ASH (2009) Domestic Abuse, Stalking and Harassment and Honour Based Violence Risk Model accepted by ACPO Council on 26 March 2009 for roll out across the UK. The old version of the model is cited in Richards, L, Letchford, S, and Stratton, S (2008) *Policing Domestic Violence*, Oxford University Press, Oxford

Department of Health and Home Office (2000) 'No Secrets', 20 March, Crown Copyright

DfES (2004) 'Every Child Matters—Change for children' Crown Copyright at <http://www.everychildmatters. gov.uk>

Dodd, T, Nicholas, S, Povery, D and Walker, A (2003/2004) Home Office Statistical Bulletin Crime in England and Wales

HM Government (2000) 'Working Together to Safeguard Children and Safeguarding Children Involved in Prostitution: Supplementary Guidance to Working Together' TSO, London

– (2006), *What To Do If You're Worried A Child Is Being Abused*

– (2006), *Information sharing: Practitioners' Guide*

Home Office Research Study 285 (2004), *Sexual Assault Referral Centres: Developing Good Practice and Maximising Potential*

Home Office (2002), *Achieving Best Evidence Guidance*

– (2004), *Safety and Justice: Sharing Personal Information in the Context of Domestic Violence—An Overview*

– (2007), *Saving Lives. Reducing Harm. Protecting the Public: An action plan for tackling violence* 2008-11.HM Government, available at <http://www.homeoffice.gov.uk/ documents/violent-crime-action-plan-08/violent-crime-action-plan-180208>

Kemshall, H (2003) *Understanding Risk in Criminal Justice* Open University Press, Buckingham

Laming, Lord (2003) *The Victoria Climbie Inquiry*, CM 5730, TSO, London

Mental Health Today at <http://www.mental-health-today. com>

National Ports Office (2009) *Child Abduction—A Practical Guide for Police Officers*

Richards, L (2004), 'Getting Away with it: a profile of the domestic violence sexual and serious offenders', Metropolitan Police Service, London, available at <http://www.met.police.uk/csu/index.htm>

Richards, L, Letchford, S, and Stratton, S (2008), *Policing Domestic Violence*, Oxford University Press, Oxford

Stanko, EA, Kielinger, V, Paterson, S, Richards, L, Crisp, D, and Marsland, L (2003) 'Grounded Crime Prevention: Responding to and Understanding Hate Crime' in H Kury and J Obergell-Fuchs (eds), *Crime Prevention—New approaches*, Weiser Rings, Germany: 123–53

Index

Index

Index

Index

Index

Index

Index

Index

Index

Index

Index

Index

Index